MATHEMATICAL ECONOMICS TEXTS

8

DISTRIBUTED LAGS

PROBLEMS OF ESTIMATION AND FORMULATION

MATHEMATICAL ECONOMICS TEXTS

Students of mathematical economics and econometrics have two unnecessary difficulties. One is that much of what they have to read is spread over the journals, often written in different notations. The second is that the theoretical and the empirical writings often make little reference to each other, and the student is left to relate them.

The main object of this series is to overcome these difficulties. Most of the books are concerned with specific topics in economic theory, but they relate the theory to relevant empirical work. Others deal with the necessary mathematical apparatus of economic theory and econometrics. They are designed for third-year undergraduates and postgraduate students.

The editors are drawn from both sides of the Atlantic and are people who are known both for their contribution to economics and for the emphasis they place on clear exposition.

Titles in the series

Other titles are in preparation

DISTRIBUTED LAGS

PROBLEMS OF ESTIMATION AND FORMULATION

PHOEBUS J. DHRYMES

University of Pennsylvania

HOLDEN-DAY, INC.

SAN FRANCISCO

OLIVER & BOYD

EDINBURGH

658.4
D 535

ISBN: 0-8162-2285-1 (Holden-Day, Inc.)
ISBN: 0-05-002465-5 (Oliver & Boyd)
Library of Congress Catalog Card No. 70-124689

First Published 1971

Copublished by
HOLDEN-DAY, INC.
500 Sansome Street
San Francisco, California
and OLIVER & BOYD
Tweeddale Court
Edinburgh, Scotland
A Division of Longman Group Limited

Printed in the United States of America

234567890 LM 798765432

PREFACE

This book deals primarily with problems of estimation in the context of distributed lag models of various orders of complexity and only peripherally with the theoretical bases in the formulation of such models. It is addressed both to the graduate student of econometrics and the specialist. The discussion of most topics begins at a rather elementary level and progresses ultimately to the current state of the literature. Thus, certain portions may be easily utilized in courses of econometrics, particularly when they have been preceded by the standard introductory course which deals extensively with the general linear model.

No attempt has been made to render this book self-contained. The reader will find that a good grounding in the elementary aspects of mathematical statistics and the general linear model will be indispensable prerequisites. Familiarity with one of the standard advanced textbooks on econometric theory will render the material accessible in its totality.

Chapters 1 though 3 are introductory in nature and deal with basic concepts and certain conceptual problems involved in the formulation of distributed lag models. Chapters 4 through 7 deal with the many variants of the geometric lag model. Chapters 8 and 9 deal, respectively, with the polynomial and general rational lag models. Chapter 10 introduces spectral techniques in the estimation of such models and gives a brief overview of the relevant aspects of the theory of covariance stationary processes. Chapter 11 deals with (a nonexhaustive list of) unsolved research problems that arise in the empirical implementation of such models. Finally, the Appendix gives the results of some limited Monte Carlo experiments.

By and large, each chapter is written in such a way that certain sections are accessible to the graduate student who has not advanced beyond the general linear model. Other sections, however, such as those dealing with the asymptotic properties of various estimators, demand a great deal more. Although the chief estimation problem encountered in such models is, essentially, nonlinearity in the parameters, this is not the approach taken in the book. Rather, each problem is tackled separately, exploiting the specific features it embodies. I felt that, at this stage, an attempt to find a unified treatment for all problems posed by distributed lag models would lead to unnecessarily ponderous solutions, thus inhibiting the grasp of what is fundamentally involved in each problem.

I have made a conscious attempt to examine rather rigorously the asymptotic properties of the estimators developed in the course of the discussion. Since I viewed this aspect in large part as a pedagogical exercise, there is, occasionally, a tendency for the presentation to be somewhat repetitious. On the other hand, I hope by this to help, however minutely, in dispelling the aura of murkiness that envelops such topics in our literature.

In the course of the presentation, I have avoided detailed references of attribution, although I have tried to mention at least the originators of various basic contributions. This is meant in no way to ignore the contributions of others. It is merely an attempt to preserve maximal continuity and unity of presentation. An extensive list of references is given in the Bibliography.

The book contains numerous exercises but does not include extensive discussion of empirical applications. Such, however, may be found in great profusion in the professional journals.

Finally, it is a pleasure for me to acknowledge my indebtedness to those who have contributed directly or indirectly in this writing of this book. Their numbers are entirely too great to mention individually. I would, however, like to thank particularly Marc Nerlove, who read the manuscript in its entirety and provided a lengthy and incisive set of comments, and Robert M. Solow, who first kindled my interest in this subject a decade ago. Takeshi Amemiya, Jan Kmenta, and Bridger M. Mitchell read parts of the manuscript and gave me the benefit of their comments.

Work on this book began during my tenure of a Ford Foundation Faculty Research Fellowship, at the Institute for Mathematical Studies in the Social Sciences, Stanford University. Parts of the book incorporate results that appeared first in the Discussion Paper series of the University of Pennsylvania, the outcome of research supported by the National Science Foundation. The last stages in the preparation of the book were completed during my visit at the University of California, Los Angeles. To all these institutions I am very grateful.

Los Angeles   Phoebus J. Dhrymes
July 1971

CONTENTS

MATHEMATICAL ECONOMICS TEXTS

8

DISTRIBUTED LAGS

PROBLEMS OF ESTIMATION AND FORMULATION

Chapter 1

FORMULATION OF THE LAG
DISTRIBUTION PROBLEM

The origin of distributed lag analysis lies in the following type of hypothesis: Suppose, in the context of an economic system, a variable exerts a determining influence on another, not instantaneously, but over an extended, perhaps infinite, period of time. If this structure persists, then the magnitude of a given variable, say y, at time t depends not only on the determining variable, say x, at time t *but also* on the values assumed by x in some or perhaps all previous time periods.

Of course, y may depend on more than one variable, and not all determining variables need have their impact on y distributed over several time periods.

This conceptual scheme has found numerous applications in empirical work. To mention a few, the response of agricultural supply to price has been studied in this framework by Nerlove [118] and many others. Similarly, the response of capital investment to various aspects of the economic environment has been studied by, among others, Koyck [92] and more recently by Jorgenson [81]. The response of several economic variables to economic policy variations has been studied and reported in a special volume of the Commission on Money and Credit [17].

Typically, the formulation of the problem at the level of generality indicated above has been posed in an ad hoc fashion, although several special schemes may, and have been, derived from more elementary considerations.

1.1 Preliminaries

The general distributed lag model can be stated as

$$y_t = \sum_{i=0}^{\infty} w_i^* x_{t-i} + u_t \tag{1.1}$$

1

where the w_i^* are unknown constants not all of which are zero, x_t is an exogenous variable, and u_t is a random variable *independent of* x_t, having mean zero and constant variance. The last three assumptions are the classical ones in the context of the general linear model.

Now, the formulation in (1.1) is, of course, a particular case of the general linear model, its distinguishing feature being that *it contains an infinite number of parameters.* Thus, as it stands, (1.1) represents a non-operational formulation and a nonfeasible estimation scheme.

Before we attempt to properly formulate the problem, let us establish some terminology:

DEFINITION 1.1.   The model in (1.1) is said to represent the *general infinite distributed lag,* and is commonly referred to as the *general (infinite) distributed lag model.*

REMARK 1.1.   Quite frequently, the economics of the problem is such that the assumption,

$$w_i^* w_j^* \geq 0 , \quad \text{all } i, j \tag{1.2}$$

is warranted. This means that all the w_i^* are of the same sign. If (1.2) is valid, then with no loss of generality we may suppose

$$w_i^* \geq 0 , \quad i = 0, 1, 2, \ldots \tag{1.3}$$

Now suppose the variable x_t assumes the time path

$$x_t = x , \quad \text{all } t \tag{1.4}$$

where x is nonzero and finite. We would clearly wish the conditional mean of y_t, given x_t as in (1.4), to be *finite.* This implies

$$\sum_{i=0}^{\infty} w_i^* = \omega \tag{1.5}$$

for *finite* ω.

If we define

$$w_i = \frac{w_i^*}{\omega} , \quad i = 0, 1, 2, \ldots \tag{1.6}$$

then in view of (1.3), (1.5) and (1.6), we have

$$\sum_{i=0}^{\infty} w_i = 1 , \quad 0 \leq w_i \leq 1 , \quad i = 0, 1, 2, \ldots \tag{1.7}$$

DEFINITION 1.2.   The coefficients $w_i^*, i = 0, 1, 2, \ldots$ are said to be the *lag coefficients* of the model, and the *sequence*

$$w^* = \{w_i^*: \quad i = 0, 1, 2, \ldots\} \tag{1.8}$$

is said to be its *lag structure*.

DEFINITION 1.3. If (1.3) and (1.5) are valid, then the w_i, $i = 0, 1, 2, \ldots$ are said to be the *normalized lag coefficients*, and the sequence,

$$w = \left\{w_i: \quad i = 0, 1, 2, \ldots, \quad \sum_{i=0}^{\infty} w_i = 1\right\} \tag{1.9}$$

is said to be the *normalized lag structure* of the model in (1.1).

If the model admits of a normalized lag structure, we may write

$$y_t = \omega \sum_{i=0}^{\infty} w_i x_{t-i} + u_t \tag{1.10}$$

the w_i being now nonnegative and summing to unity.

EXAMPLE 1.1. In his well-known work [44], Friedman introduces the *permanent* income hypothesis in seeking to explain the relation between consumption and income. Permanent income is then taken to be, in the most common version of this school of thought, an infinite lag structure in observed income. Thus, if y^* is *permanent* and y *observed* income, then we have the relation

$$y_t^* = \sum_{i=0}^{\infty} \lambda^{*i} y_{t-i} \tag{1.11}$$

where $\lambda^* \in (0, 1)$. Observe, however, that if (1.11) is the specification, then *permanent is always higher than observed income*. Moreover,

$$\sum_{i=0}^{\infty} \lambda^{*i} = \frac{1}{1 - \lambda^*} > 1 \tag{1.12}$$

and thus (1.11) does not represent a true average. For this reason, we customarily write the following in lieu of (1.11),

$$y_t^* = \alpha \sum_{i=0}^{\infty} \lambda^i y_{t-1}, \quad \alpha = 1 - \lambda, \quad \lambda \in (0, 1) \tag{1.13}$$

The reader may now verify that (1.13) represents *an average* and that the lag structure $\{\alpha\lambda^i: \ i = 0, 1, 2, \ldots\}$ of (1.13) is a *normalized one*.

1.2 The Lag Structure as a Set of Probabilities

We have seen in the preceding section that in its perfect generality the infinite distributed lag model represents a nonfeasible estimation scheme.

On the other hand, we have also seen that in certain cases the formulation is such as to lead naturally to the *normalized lag structure*. In this section we shall exploit the formal similarity between normalized lag structures and the mass function of *discrete random variables*. Indeed, most of the early formulations of the distributed lag problem relied heavily on this similarity.

Thus, consider again the model,

$$y_t = \sum_{i=0}^{\infty} w_i^* x_{t-i} + u_t \qquad (1.14)$$

If we have in addition,

$$w_i^* \geq 0, \quad \sum_{i=0}^{\infty} w_i^* = \omega < \infty \qquad (1.15)$$

then we can rewrite (1.14) as

$$y_t = \omega \sum_{i=0}^{\infty} w_i x_{t-i} + u_t \qquad (1.16)$$

where

$$w_i = \frac{w_i^*}{\omega}, \quad i = 0, 1, 2, \ldots \qquad (1.17)$$

One consequence of the second condition of (1.15) is that

$$\lim_{i \to \infty} w_i^* = 0 \qquad (1.18)$$

which is eminently reasonable. We would clearly expect the influence of x on y to decline as time passes, so that the present behavior of the dependent variable y is not materially affected by the behavior of the determining variable x in the indefinite past. Notice further that the coefficients w_i obey

$$w_i \in [0, 1], \quad \sum_{i=0}^{\infty} w_i = 1 \qquad (1.19)$$

Given (1.19), we see that we can define a discrete random variable, say z, such that

$$\Pr\{z = i\} = w_i, \quad i = 0, 1, 2, \ldots \qquad (1.20)$$

In this fashion, the *normalized lag structure* is seen to be simply a *set of probabilities*. This aspect of lag distributions has motivated an attempt, in early research on the topic, to represent *normalized lag structures by commonly occurring mass functions containing one (or more, commonly two) parameters*. This is particularly convenient, since in many empirical situations we are typically interested, inter alia, in the average lag by which the determining variable x affects the dependent one y, or in the extent to which this effect is *concentrated* in a few periods or *diffused* over an extended period. Such questions have a natural answer in terms of the mean and variance of a mass function. Thus, interpreting the normalized lag structure as a set of probabilities has a number of convenient and attractive features, and for this reason we shall further pursue the analogy. To this effect, we have

DEFINITION 1.4. Let $a = \{a_i: i = 0, 1, 2, \ldots\}$ be a sequence of real numbers. If

$$A(t) = \sum_{i=0}^{\infty} a_i t^i \tag{1.21}$$

converges over some interval $|t| < t_0$, then $A(\cdot)$ is called the *generating function* of the sequence a.

REMARK 1.2. If the a_i constitute a *normalized lag structure*, then the sum of the $a_i, i = 0, 1, 2, \ldots$ is finite—indeed, it is unity—and it can be shown that $A(\cdot)$ of (1.21) converges *uniformly* for $|t| \leq 1$. In particular, $A(\cdot)$ is then *continuous at the origin*.

DEFINITION 1.5. Let $b = \{b_i: i = 0, 1, 2, \ldots, b_i \geq 0, \sum_{i=0}^{\infty} b_i = 1\}$ be a normalized lag structure; then

$$B(t) = \sum_{i=0}^{\infty} b_i t^i \tag{1.22}$$

is its *lag generating function*.

PROPOSITION 1.1. The lag generating function of a normalized lag structure has the following properties:

    (i) It is uniformly convergent for $t \in [-1, 1]$
    (ii) It is continuous there, indeed uniformly continuous

Proof. To show uniform convergence, we proceed as follows: Let

$$B_N(t) = \sum_{i=0}^{N} b_i t^i \tag{1.23}$$

We must then show that for *any* $t \in [-1, 1]$, there exists an N^* (independent of t) such that for all $N > N^*$,

$$|B(t) - B_N(t)| < \varepsilon \tag{1.24}$$

for any preassigned $\varepsilon > 0$.

But we observe

$$B(t) - B_N(t) = \sum_{i=N+1}^{\infty} b_i t^i \tag{1.25}$$

Thus,

$$|B(t) - B_N(t)| \leq \sum_{i=N+1}^{\infty} |b_i| \tag{1.26}$$

for *any* $t \in [-1, 1]$. Since we are dealing with a normalized lag structure, there exists an N^* such that for any preassigned $\varepsilon > 0$,

$$\sum_{i=N^*+1}^{\infty} |b_i| < \varepsilon \tag{1.27}$$

For given ε, let such an N^* be chosen. Thus, from (1.26) and (1.27), we conclude that, for all $N > N^*$,

$$|B(t) - B_N(t)| < \varepsilon \tag{1.28}$$

independently of t, which shows uniform convergence.

Uniform continuity is similarly established; details are left as an exercise for the reader.

REMARK 1.3. In view of the similarities between the normalized lag structure and a set of probabilities, it is clear that the quantity in (1.22) can be interpreted also as a *probability generating function*. We recall that if $p = \{p_i : i = 0, 1, 2, \ldots, p_i \geq 0, \sum_{i=0}^{\infty} p_i = 1\}$ is a set of probabilities corresponding to the (discrete) random variable z, then

$$P(t) = \sum_{i=0}^{\infty} p_i t^i \tag{1.29}$$

is said to be the *probability generating function corresponding to z*.

Recall further that if z is such that

$$\Pr\{z = i\} = p_i, \quad i = 0, 1, 2, \ldots \tag{1.30}$$

then $P(\cdot)$ of (1.29) is also the *moment generating function* of z.

REMARK 1.4. It is not always true that probability generating functions and moment generating functions coincide. Thus, consider the random variable x, having the following probability structure:

$$\begin{aligned} \Pr\{x = 2i + 1\} &= p_i \\ \Pr\{x = 2i\} &= 0 \end{aligned} \quad i = 0, 1, 2, \ldots \tag{1.31}$$

This is similar to the variable z of (1.30), except that x has z's probability structure over the *odd* positive integers and has zero mass over the even (nonnegative) integers. The probability generating function of x is

$$P_x(t) = \sum_{i=0}^{\infty} p_i t^i \qquad (1.32)$$

Its moment generating function (MGF) is

$$M_x(t) = E(t^x) = \sum_{i=0}^{\infty} p_i t^{2i+1} = t P_x(t^2) \qquad (1.33)$$

and the two functions are quite different.

Returning now to the lag generating function of the normalized lag structure

$$b = \left\{ b_i : i = 0, 1, 2, \ldots, \quad b_i \geq 0, \quad \sum_{i=0}^{\infty} b_i = 1 \right\} \qquad (1.34)$$

we observe that its lag generating function,

$$B(t) = \sum_{i=0}^{\infty} b_i t^i \qquad (1.35)$$

can be interpreted as the MGF of a discrete random variable, say z, having the probability structure

$$\Pr\{z = i\} = b_i, \quad i = 0, 1, 2, \ldots \qquad (1.36)$$

Thus, the lag structure can be given a summary characterization in terms of selected moments of the variable z. In this connection, we have

PROPOSITION 1.2. Let $p = \{p_i, i = 0, 1, 2, \ldots\}$ be the ordinates of the discrete random variable x such that

$$\Pr\{x = i\} = p_i \qquad (1.37)$$

Let

$$P(t) = \sum_{i=0}^{\infty} p_i t^i \qquad (1.38)$$

be its associated MGF. Then,

$$E[x(x-1)\cdots(x-k)] = \frac{d^{(k+1)}}{dt^{k+1}} P(t)\big|_{t=1} \qquad (1.39)$$

Proof. Differentiating $P(\cdot)$ $k + 1$ times and evaluating at $t = 1$, we find

$$P^{(k+1)}(1) = \sum_{i=k+1}^{\infty} [i(i-1)(i-2)\cdots(i-k)]p_i \tag{1.40}$$

$$= E[x(x-1)(x-2)\cdots(x-k)] \qquad \text{Q.E.D.}$$

COROLLARY 1.1.

$$E(x) = P'(1) \tag{1.41}$$

Proof. In (1.40), take $k = 0$, and notice

$$P'(1) = \sum_{i=1}^{\infty} ip_i = E(x) \tag{1.42}$$

COROLLARY 1.2.

$$\text{Var}(x) = P''(1) + P'(1) - [P'(1)]^2 \tag{1.43}$$

Proof. For any random variable z,

$$\text{Var}(z) = E(z^2) - [E(z)]^2 \tag{1.44}$$

In (1.40), putting $k = 1$, we find

$$P''(1) = \sum_{i=2}^{\infty} i(i-1)p_i = E[x(x-1)] = E(x^2) - E(x)$$

$$= E(x^2) - P'(1) \tag{1.45}$$

The conclusion then follows immediately from (1.42) and (1.44)

REMARK 1.5. Since the normalized lag structure constitutes a set of probabilities, the preceding discussion implies that the lag generating function,

$$B(t) = \sum_{i=0}^{\infty} b_i t^i \tag{1.46}$$

associated with the normalized lag structure

$$b = \left\{ b_i : i = 0, 1, 2, \ldots, \quad b_i \geq 0, \quad \sum_{i=0}^{\infty} b_i = 1 \right\} \tag{1.47}$$

can be interpreted as both the probability and moment generating function of a random variable, say z, whose probability structure is

$$\Pr\{z = i\} = b_i, \quad i = 0, 1, 2, \ldots \tag{1.48}$$

In this fashion, we recall that[1]

---

[1] If $f(\cdot)$ is a function of the (real) variable x, the reader should recall that $f^{(k)}(x_0)$ indicates kth order derivative of $f(\cdot)$ evaluated at the point $x = x_0$.

$$b_k = \frac{B^{(k)}(0)}{k!} \tag{1.49}$$

so that the lag generating function uniquely characterizes the normalized lag structure, and vice versa.

Moreover, the *mean lag* associated with the lag structure may be defined as

$$m(b) = B'(1) = \sum_{i=1}^{\infty} i b_i \tag{1.50}$$

Similarly, the variability of the structure may be defined as

$$V(b) = B''(1) + B'(1) - [B'(1)]^2 \tag{1.51}$$

We formalize the last two relations by

DEFINITION 1.6. Let

$$b = \left\{ b_i : i = 0, 1, 2, \ldots, \quad b_i \geq 0, \quad \sum_{i=0}^{\infty} b_i = 1 \right\} \tag{1.52}$$

be a normalized lag structure, and let

$$B(t) = \sum_{i=0}^{\infty} b_i t^i, \quad t \in [-1, 1] \tag{1.53}$$

be its generating function. Then the mean lag of the structure in (1.52) is defined by

$$m(b) = B'(1) \tag{1.54}$$

and the variability of the structure is defined by

$$V(b) = B''(1) + B'(1) - [B'(1)]^2 \tag{1.55}$$

EXAMPLE 1.2. Consider the particular distributed lag model,

$$y_t = \alpha \sum_{i=0}^{\infty} \lambda^i x_{t-i} + u_t \tag{1.56}$$

The lag structure of the model is given by

$$\lambda = \{\lambda_i : \lambda_i = \lambda^i, \quad i = 0, 1, 2, \ldots\} \tag{1.57}$$

We impose the condition $\lambda \in (0, 1)$ and observe that the structure is *not* normalized, since

$$\sum_{i=0}^{\infty} \lambda^i = \frac{1}{1 - \lambda} \neq 1 \tag{1.58}$$

To normalize it we may, if we wish, redefine the constant α by

$$\alpha^* = \frac{\alpha}{1 - \lambda} \tag{1.59}$$

We may then take

$$b_i = (1 - \lambda)\lambda^i, \quad i = 0, 1, 2, \ldots \tag{1.60}$$

The lag generating function of this normalized structure is thus

$$\Lambda(t) = (1 - \lambda) \sum_{i=0}^{\infty} \lambda^i t^i = \frac{1 - \lambda}{1 - \lambda t} \tag{1.61}$$

The mean lag is

$$m(\lambda) = \Lambda'(1) = \frac{\lambda}{1 - \lambda} \tag{1.62}$$

The variability of the structure is

$$V(\lambda) = \Lambda''(1) + \Lambda'(1) - [\Lambda'(1)]^2 = \frac{\lambda}{(1 - \lambda)^2} \tag{1.63}$$

It is easily verified that both the mean and variability of the lag structure are increasing functions of λ. The mean lag, here $m(\lambda)$, gives information on the mean length of time it takes for a change in the determining variable x to be transmitted to the dependent variable y. The variability quantity, here $V(\lambda)$, gives information on the extent to which such effects are concentrated or diffused.

Thus, consider the following time path for x:

$$x_t = \bar{x}, \quad t = 0, -1, -2, \ldots, \quad x_t = \bar{x} + 1, \quad t = 1, 2, \ldots \tag{1.64}$$

In view of our model, the conditional mean of y_t, $\bar{y}_t$ is given by

$$\begin{aligned}
\bar{y}_t &= \alpha \sum_{i=0}^{t-1} \lambda^i x_{t-i} + \alpha \sum_{i=t}^{\infty} \lambda^i x_{t-i} = \alpha(\bar{x} + 1) \frac{1 - \lambda^t}{1 - \lambda} + \alpha\bar{x} \frac{\lambda^t}{1 - \lambda} \\
&= \frac{\alpha(\bar{x} + 1)}{1 - \lambda} - \alpha \frac{\lambda^t}{1 - \lambda}
\end{aligned} \tag{1.65}$$

The first term in the last member of (1.65) represents the long-run value of the conditional mean of y. How quickly this value is approached clearly depends on the magnitude of λ.

REMARK 1.6. We recall that if x is a random variable with geometric mass function, then it obeys

$$\Pr\{x = i\} = pq^{i-1}, \quad i = 1, 2, \ldots, \quad p + q = 1 \tag{1.66}$$

Partly for this reason, the lag structure considered in the preceding example is termed the *geometric lag structure*. Indeed, several lag structures employed in econometrics are motivated by the mass function of some discrete random variable.

EXAMPLE 1.3. The lag structure considered above has the property that its associated lag coefficients form a *monotone decreasing sequence*. In particular, the *maximal impact of the determining on the dependent variable is registered instantaneously*. Thereafter, its magnitude declines geometrically to zero.

In many economic situations, this lag structure may be inappropriate. Thus, if we are considering the impact of a change in the tax rate in a macroeconomic context, it is more reasonable to suppose that the lag coefficients in the appropriate lag structure are first small, then increase to a peak, and thereafter decline. In this connection, Solow [137] suggested the use of the Pascal distribution.

More precisely, if the general model is

$$y_t = \alpha \sum_{i=0}^{\infty} w_i x_{t-i} + u_t, \quad w_i \geq 0, \quad \sum_{i=0}^{\infty} w_i = 1 \qquad (1.67)$$

then the Pascal structure results when we take

$$w_i = (1 - \lambda)^r \binom{r + i - 1}{i} \lambda^i,$$

$$\lambda \in (0, 1), \quad r \in (0, \infty), \quad i = 0, 1, 2, \ldots \qquad (1.68)$$

The mass function whose ordinates are exhibited in (1.68) is more commonly referred to as the *negative binomial*. The term becomes quite appropriate through the following considerations. Consider the function

$$f(s) = (1 + s)^{-r}, \quad r \geq 0 \qquad (1.69)$$

This is obviously a binomial expression with *negative* exponent. What is the relevance of this in terms of our discussion? If we expand $f(\cdot)$ of (1.69) by Taylor's series (about $s = 0$), we find

$$f(s) = \sum_{k=0}^{\infty} \frac{(-r)_k}{k!} s^k \qquad (1.70)$$

where the symbol $(-r)_k$ is defined by

$$(-r)_k = (-r)(-r - 1)(-r - 2) \cdots (-r - k + 1)$$

$$= (-1)^k \prod_{i=0}^{k-1} (r + i) \qquad (1.71)$$

If n is a positive integer, then the symbol $(n)_k$ is defined by

$$(n)_k = n(n - 1)(n - 2)\cdots(n - k + 1) \tag{1.72}$$

Thus, we see that the binomial coefficient in (1.68) can be written as

$$\binom{r + i - 1}{i} = \frac{(r + i - 1)_i}{i!} = (-1)^i \frac{(-r)_i}{i!} \tag{1.73}$$

Taking the lag generating function of the coefficients in (1.68), we thus determine

$$
\begin{aligned}
B(t) &= (1 - \lambda)^r \sum_{i=0}^{\infty} \binom{r + i - 1}{i} (\lambda t)^i \\
&= (1 - \lambda)^r \sum_{i=0}^{\infty} \frac{(-r)_i}{i!} (-\lambda t)^i \\
&= \left(\frac{1 - \lambda}{1 - \lambda t}\right)^r
\end{aligned} \tag{1.74}
$$

Although we have just given an argument for integer r, the same result will hold for noninteger r. However, we would then have to introduce the notion of the gamma function. Comparing with (1.61), we see that the example here is a simple generalization of the normalized geometric lag structure. If r is an integer, then the negative binomial has an interpretation as a series of r geometric distributions applied successively.

We notice that the mean lag is given by

$$B'(1) = \frac{\lambda r}{1 - \lambda} \tag{1.75}$$

The variability of the structure is

$$B''(1) + B'(1) - [B'(1)]^2 = \frac{\lambda r}{(1 - \lambda)^2} \tag{1.76}$$

The mean and variability results are quite analogous to those obtained in the case of the normalized geometric lag structure. Indeed, bearing in mind the analogy between mass functions and normalized lag structures, we see that if r is an integer, the mean and variability of the negative binomial structure are simply r times the corresponding quantities of the geometric lag. Thus, the negative binomial random variable has an interpretation as a *sum* of r mutually independent geometric variables with common parameter λ. This strengthens the interpretation of the negative binomial lag structure as the result of r geometric lags applied successively.

From (1.75) and (1.76), we easily see that the mean lag and variability of the structure are increasing functions of both r and λ.

Finally, let us verify that the lag coefficients of the negative binomial structure first increase and then decline. To this effect, consider the ratio w_{i+1}/w_i, where the w_i are given by (1.68). We have

$$\frac{w_{i+1}}{w_i} = \lambda \frac{(r+i)_{i+1}}{(r+i-1)_i} \frac{i!}{(i+1)!} = \frac{\lambda(r+i)}{i+1} \qquad (1.77)$$

Thus, $w_{i+1}/w_i > 1$, if

$$i < \frac{\lambda r - 1}{1 - \lambda} \qquad (1.78)$$

and $w_{i+1}/w_i < 1$, if

$$i > \frac{\lambda r - 1}{1 - \lambda} \qquad (1.79)$$

It is clear that given λ, the larger r is, the larger the index i for which the maximal value of the lag coefficients is attained. Thus, for given λ, the peak of the distribution is moved to the right as r increases. If $r > 1$, the same situation prevails with respect to λ, provided $\lambda r > 1$. However, if $r < 1$, the fraction $(\lambda r - 1)/(1 - \lambda)$ is always negative and hence *the lag coefficients are monotone decreasing.*

1.3 The z-Transform

In the previous section we introduced the concept of the lag generating function (LGF) and indicated some of its potentially useful properties. In particular, we noted that in the case of a normalized lag structure the LGF can be interpreted as the MGF of a certain random variable. Just as the MGF has uses that are slightly more limited than those of the corresponding characteristic function, so the LGF is slightly more restrictive than the corresponding z-transform.[2]

DEFINITION 1.7. Let

$$b = \{b_j : j = 0, 1, 2, \dots\} \qquad (1.80)$$

---

[2] We discuss the z-transform at this juncture because of its affinity with the lag generating function. We shall not employ it extensively except in Chapter 10, when we examine various applications of spectral analytic techniques to the problems of estimating lag structures. Thus the reader may, with little loss of continuity, omit this section.

be a normalized lag structure. Its z-transform is defined by

$$B(z) = \sum_{j=0}^{\infty} b_j\, z^j \tag{1.81}$$

z being a complex indeterminate.

REMARK 1.7. In engineering literature the z-transform is usually defined as $\sum_{j=0}^{\infty} b_j\, z^{-j}$. This is typographically inconvenient, and hence we shall consistently use the definition in (1.81).

For an extensive discussion of the properties of this transform, the reader may refer to the recent book by Jury [86].

REMARK 1.8. Generally, if $\alpha_j, j = 0, \pm 1, \pm 2, \ldots$ is a sequence its z-transform is defined by

$$A(z) = \sum_{j=-\infty}^{\infty} \alpha_j z^i \tag{1.82}$$

provided the right member converges for $|z| < M < \infty$.

Of course, (1.81) represents the special case in which $b_j = 0$ for $j = -1, -2, \ldots$.

The reader who is familiar with the theory of functions of a complex variable will recognize (1.81) as a discrete Laplace transform and (1.82) as the Laurent expansion of a function $A(\cdot)$, which is analytic for $|z| \leq M(1 - \delta)$, $\delta > 0$, except possibly at the origin.

If the series in (1.82) converges for $|z| < M$, then M is said to be its *radius of convergence*, and the circle defined in the complex plane by

$$|z| = M \tag{1.83}$$

is said to be its *circle* of convergence.

An important property of complex power series is contained in the following proposition, which is given without proof.

PROPOSITION 1.3. Let

$$A(z) = \sum_{j=0}^{\infty} a_j z^j \tag{1.84}$$

and suppose it converges inside a circle of radius M.

Then

(i) For $|z| < M$, $A(\cdot)$ is an analytic function; i.e. its derivative exists in some ε-neighborhood of every point z_0 such that $|z_0| < M$

(ii) The series may be differentiated term by term and converges to the derivative of $A(\cdot)$ within its circle of convergence; the same is true for higher derivatives

(iii) The series converges uniformly for $|z| \leq M(1 - \delta), \delta > 0$

The criteria of convergence for complex power series are essentially similar to those for real power series.

The relation between a sequence and its z-transform is unique, and by now there are extensive tables of z-transform pairs. Again the interested reader is referred to Jury [86], especially pages 278ff.

Finally, we give an example illustrating the convenience of this apparatus.

EXAMPLE 1.4. Suppose $\{\varepsilon_\tau : \tau = 0, \pm 1, \pm 2, \ldots\}$ is a sequence of mutually independent, identically distributed random variables with mean zero and variance σ^2. Define

$$u_t = \sum_{j=0}^{\infty} b_j \varepsilon_{t-j} \qquad (1.85)$$

where the b_j have the property that

$$\sum_{j=0}^{\infty} |b_j| < \infty \qquad (1.86)$$

The *auto-covariance kernel* of the $\{u_t : t = 1, 2, \ldots\}$ is defined by

$$K(\tau) = E(u_t u_{t-\tau}) = \sum_{j'} \sum_{j} b_j b_{j'} E(\varepsilon_{t-j} \varepsilon_{t-\tau-j'})$$

$$= \sigma^2 \sum_{j=0}^{\infty} b_{j+\tau} b_j \qquad (1.87)$$

It is clear that $K(\tau) = K(-\tau)$.

The spectral density of the $\{u_t : t = 1, 2, \ldots\}$ may be defined by

$$f(\theta) = \frac{1}{2\pi} \sum_{\tau=-\infty}^{\infty} K(\tau) e^{-i\tau\theta}, \quad \theta \in (-\pi, \pi) \qquad (1.88)$$

provided the series in the right member converges.

It would be convenient if we had a way in which the auto-covariance kernel, the lag structure and the spectral densities of the u_t and ε_τ were connected. Felicitously, this is provided by z-transform methods. Thus, the z-transform of the auto-covariance kernel is given by

$$K(z) = \sum_{\tau=-\infty}^{\infty} K(\tau) z^\tau = \sigma^2 \sum_{\tau=-\infty}^{\infty} \sum_{j=0}^{\infty} b_j z^{-j} b_{j+\tau} z^{j+\tau}$$

$$= \sigma^2 B(z) B(z^{-1}) \qquad (1.89)$$

Since

$$\sum_{\tau=-\infty}^{\infty} |K(\tau)| \leq \sum_{\tau} \sum_{j} |b_j| |b_{j+\tau}| \leq \left(\sum_{j=0}^{\infty} |b_j| \right)^2 < \infty \qquad (1.90)$$

we see that $K(z)$ converges for $z = e^{i\theta}$. But then

$$K(e^{i\theta}) = 2\pi f(\theta) \qquad (1.91)$$

and we see that the spectral density in question is a simple function of the z-transform of the lag structure evaluated at a certain point.

Thus we have a simple way of connecting the z-transform of the auto-covariance kernel, the lag structure and the spectral density of the u process. While such considerations appear to be opaque at this juncture, they will become more transparent in Chapter 8 and subsequent discussions.

Exercises and Questions

1. In Definition 1.3, why do we insist that Equations (1.2) and (1.5) be valid? (Hint: Consider the sequences $w_i^* = (-1)^i$ and $w_i^* = 1/i$, $i = 1, 2, \ldots$. Do these sequences occasion any problems?)

2. Show that the function $B(\cdot)$ of Proposition 1.1 is uniformly continuous.

3. Let $\{b_j : j = 0, 1, 2, \ldots\}$ be a normalized lag structure and let $B(z)$ be its z-transform. Show how the mean lag may be obtained from $B(z)$.

Chapter 2

THE ALGEBRA OF LAG OPERATORS

2.1 Generalities

Our discussion of the theory and estimation of distributed lags will be greatly facilitated if we introduce the notion of the *lag operator*. First, however, we recall from elementary algebra the following:

DEFINITION 2.1. A vector space V consists of a field of scalars F and a collection of objects V, called *vectors*, together with two operations, *vector addition* and *scalar multiplication*, such that for any $c \in F$, v_1, v_2 $\in V$, $cv_1 + v_2 \in V$. Moreover, for any v_1, v_2, $v_3 \in V$, vector addition obeys the following rules:

(i) $v_1 + v_2 = v_2 + v_1$
(ii) $v_1 + (v_2 + v_3) = (v_1 + v_2) + v_3$
(iii) There exists an element $0 \in V$ such that for all

$$v \in V, v + 0 = v$$

(iv) For each $v \in V$ there exists a unique element, $-v \in V$, such that $v + (-v) = 0$.

Furthermore, for any c_1, $c_2 \in F$ and v_1, $v_2 \in V$, scalar multiplication obeys:

(v) $c_1 v_1 = v_1 c_1$
(vi) $c_1(v_1 + v_2) = c_1 v_1 + c_1 v_2$
(vii) $(c_1 + c_2)v_1 = c_1 v_1 + c_2 v$
(viii) $(c_1 c_2)v_1 = c_1(c_2 v_1)$

These are the usual commutative, associative and distributive properties of vector addition and scalar multiplication.

DEFINITION 2.2. A transformation T from the vector space V *to* the vector space W is a function that to each element, $v \in V$, associates a *unique*

17

element, $w \in W$, such that

$$w = T(v) \qquad\qquad (2.1)$$

DEFINITION 2.3. A transformation T from V to W is said to be *linear* if, for $c \in F$, v_1, $v_2 \in V$, it satisfies

$$T[cv_1 + v_2] = cT(v_1) + T(v_2) \qquad\qquad (2.2)$$

where F is the field of scalars of V.

REMARK 2.1. Clearly, the definition above implies that the (scalar) field of V is at least a subfield of that of W.

DEFINITION 2.4. If T is a linear transformation from V *into* V, then T is said to be a *linear operator*.

EXAMPLE 2.1. Consider the set of all 2×2 real matrices, and take this to be the collection of objects, V. Let F be the field of real numbers. Under the usual rules for operating with matrices, the reader can easily verify that this set, together with matrix addition and scalar multiplication, constitutes a vector space.

REMARK 2.2. It is easily seen that the vector space above contains a zero element. Moreover, in the context of the example we can define the operation of multiplication between two (or more) elements of the vector space. This leads us to another useful concept.

DEFINITION 2.5. Let F be a field of scalars. A *linear algebra* $\mathscr{A}$, with identity over the field F is a vector space $\mathscr{A}$ (over F) with an additional operation, vector multiplication, which to each pair α_1, $\alpha_2 \in \mathscr{A}$ associates a vector $(\alpha_1 \cdot \alpha_2) \in \mathscr{A}$, called the product of α_1, α_2 such that for α_1, α_2, $\alpha_3 \in \mathscr{A}$ and $c \in F$,

(i) $(\alpha_1 \cdot \alpha_2) \cdot \alpha_3 = \alpha_1 \cdot (\alpha_2 \cdot \alpha_3)$

(ii) $\alpha_1 \cdot (\alpha_2 + \alpha_3) = (\alpha_1 \cdot \alpha_2) + (\alpha_1 \cdot \alpha_3)$, $(\alpha_1 + \alpha_2) \cdot \alpha_3 = (\alpha_1 \cdot \alpha_3)$
$+ (\alpha_2 \cdot \alpha_3)$

(iii) $c(\alpha_1 \cdot \alpha_2) = (c\alpha_1) \cdot \alpha_2 = \alpha_1 \cdot (c\alpha_2)$

Moreover, there exists an element $I \in \mathscr{A}$, the identity element, such that

(iv) $I\alpha_1 = \alpha_1 I = \alpha_1$

EXAMPLE 2.2. The vector space of Example 2.1 is easily shown to constitute a linear algebra with identity. Thus, we note that it contains a zero element, namely, the matrix

$$0 = \begin{bmatrix} 0 & 0 \\ 0 & 0 \end{bmatrix} \tag{2.3}$$

and an identity element, namely,

$$I = \begin{bmatrix} 1 & 0 \\ 0 & 1 \end{bmatrix} \tag{2.4}$$

Moreover, it is easily verified that the properties (i), (ii), (iii) of Definition 2.5 hold. A more detailed exposition of these concepts may be found in [74].

2.2 The Lag Operator L and Its Algebra

Let X be the set of all functions $x: N \to R$, where N is the set $0, \pm 1, \pm 2, \pm 3, \ldots$ and R is the one dimensional Euclidean space; thus, if $x \in X$, $x(t)$ is a real-valued function defined on the integers. It is clear that X forms a vector space over the field of real numbers, R. On this space, define the transformation L by

$$Lx(t) = x(t - 1), \quad x \in X \tag{2.5}$$

Now let $c \in R$, $x_1, x_2 \in X$ and define

$$w(t) = cx_1(t) + x_2(t) \tag{2.6}$$

It is obvious that $w \in X$. By the definition in (2.5) we have

$$Lw(t) = w(t - 1) = cx_1(t - 1) + x_2(t - 1) = cLx_1(t) + Lx_2(t) \tag{2.7}$$

Since $w^*(t) = w(t - 1) \in X$, we see that L is a linear transformation from X to X, and thus by Definition 2.4 is a *linear operator*. We are thus led to

DEFINITION 2.6. The operator L in (2.5) is said to be the *lag operator*.

If we define $x^*(t) = x(t - 1)$, then applying L to x^*, we have

$$Lx^*(t) = x^*(t - 1) = x(t - 2) \tag{2.8}$$

Since $x^*(t) = Lx(t - 1)$, substituting in (2.8) we find

$$Lx^*(t) = LLx(t) = x(t - 2) \tag{2.9}$$

This leads to a *natural definition of powers of the operator L in terms of* *iteration.* For example, L^k is to mean that the operator L is applied successively k times, More precisely,

$$L^k x(t) = x(t - k), \quad x \in X \tag{2.10}$$

Finally, the above easily implies the *law of exponents*:

$$L^{k+s} = L^k L^s = L^s L^k, \quad s, k > 0 \tag{2.11}$$

It is natural to define the zero-th power of L by

$$L^0 x(t) = x(t), \quad x \in X \tag{2.12}$$

Since it is obvious that L^0 has the property of the identity element in the context of our discussion, we shall denote L^0 by I. The latter symbol is *not to be confused with the identity matrix*. It simply means the operator which, when applied to any element of X, yields precisely that element.

Thus, we have defined the symbols $L^k, k = 0, 1, 2, \ldots$. It should be clear to the reader that all such are linear operators.

For completeness, we ought to define the zero operator which carries every $x \in X$ into the zero function. Thus, the zero operator, $\mathbf{0}$, may be defined by

$$\mathbf{0} x(t) = 0, \quad x \in X \tag{2.13}$$

Having defined these operators, let us consider the set of all linear combinations of elements of the set

$$\mathscr{L} = \{I, L, L^2, L^3, \ldots\} \tag{2.14}$$

It may be shown that this will constitute an algebra $[R^\infty]$ under appropriate conditions. However, this scheme is too large for our purposes, and, indeed, it introduces several extraneous mathematical problems which complicate the exposition without materially adding to the substance of the problem under consideration. For this reason, we shall confine ourselves to considering the set of *all finite linear combinations* of elements of $\mathscr{L}$ over the field of real numbers. Let us denote this set by $R[L]$. Thus, if $T_1 \in R(L)$, then it is of the form

$$T_1 = \sum_{j=0}^{n} c_{1j} L^j \tag{2.15}$$

What is the mathematical structure of the set of objects $R[L]$? Recalling the Definition 2.1, we easily see that $R[L]$ is a vector space, the vectors being polynomials in the lag operator L. Thus, if $T_1, T_2 \in R[L]$, consider

$$T = cT_1 + T_2, \quad T_1 = \sum_{j=0}^{n_1} c_{1j} L^j, \quad T_2 = \sum_{j=0}^{n_2} c_{2j} L^j \tag{2.16}$$

To determine whether $T \in R[L]$, we need to define the operations of vector addition and scalar multiplication on $R[L]$ over the field of real numbers. What would be more natural than to define vector addition by

$$T_1 + T_2 = \sum_{j=0}^{n_1} c_{1j} L^j + \sum_{j=0}^{n_2} c_{2j} L^j = \sum_{j=0}^{n_1} (c_{1j} + c_{2j}) L^j + \sum_{j=n_1+1}^{n_2} c_{2j} L^j$$

(2.17)

where we have implicitly assumed $n_1 \leq n_2$?

Similarly, scalar multiplication may be defined by

$$cT_1 = \sum_{j=0}^{n_1} cc_{1j} L^j, \quad c \in R$$

(2.18)

Given the definitions in (2.17) and (2.18), it is clear that

$$T \in R[L]$$

(2.19)

The reader may verify quite easily that properties (i) through (viii) of Definition 2.1 hold in the case of $R[L]$ thus verifying that the latter is indeed a vector space over R.

Now take an element $T \in R[L]$. Then T is of the form

$$T = \sum_{j=0}^{n} c_j L^j, \quad c_j \in R$$

(2.20)

What meaning does the preceding discussion attach to $Tx(t), x \in X$? From (2.5), (2.7) and (2.10), we conclude that

$$c_j L^j x(t) = c_j x(t - j)$$

(2.21)

Thus, summing over j, we find

$$\sum_{j=0}^{n} c_j L^j x(t) = \sum_{j=0}^{n} c_j x(t - j)$$

(2.22)

which will serve as a definition of the symbol $Tx(t)$. We further note that $w \in X$, where

$$w(t) = \sum_{j=0}^{n} c_j x(t - j)$$

(2.23)

so that T is a transformation from X into X.

Consider now the case where T is as given in (2.16). Thus,

$$\begin{aligned}
c_j &= cc_{1j} + c_{2j}, \quad j = 0, 1, \ldots, n_1 \\
&= c_{2j}, \quad\quad\quad j = n_1 + 1, \ldots, n_2
\end{aligned}$$

(2.24)

From (2.21), we see that

$$
\begin{aligned}
Tx(t) &= \sum_{j=0}^{n_1} [cc_{1j}x(t-j) + c_{2j}x(t-j)] + \sum_{j=n_1+1}^{n_2} c_{2j}x(t-j) \\
&= c \sum_{j=0}^{n_1} c_{1j}x(t-j) + \sum_{j=0}^{n_2} c_{2j}x(t-j) \\
&= c\left(\sum_{j=0}^{n_1} c_{1j}L^j \right)x(t) + \left(\sum_{j=0}^{n_2} c_{2j}L^j \right)x(t) = cT_1x(t) + T_2x(t)
\end{aligned}
$$

$$(2.25)$$

which shows that indeed, $T \in R[L]$. It also shows that T is a homomorphism of X into X. We are now led to

DEFINITION 2.7. The quantity,

$$
T = \sum_{j=0}^{n} c_j L^j \tag{2.26}
$$

as defined in the preceding discussion, is said to be a *polynomial operator* of degree n.

More is actually true of $R[L]$, beyond the fact that it forms a vector space over R. This is suggested by the law of exponents, as given in (2.11). To round out this aspect, let us ask what meaning can be given to multiplication of two polynomial operators. It will be quite natural to define the latter by

$$
T^* = T_1 \cdot T_2 = \sum_{j=0}^{n_1} \sum_{i=0}^{n_2} c_{1j}c_{2i} L^i L^j = \sum_{r=0}^{n_1+n_2} c_r^* L^r \tag{2.27}
$$

where

$$
c_r^* = \sum_{j=0}^{\min(r,n_1)} c_{1j}c_{2r-j}, \quad r = 0, 1, 2, \ldots, n_1 + n_2 \tag{2.28}
$$

It is quickly verified, in view of (2.27) and (2.28) that vector (operator) multiplication obeys the conditions given in (i), (ii), and (iii) of Definition 2.5. We thus conclude that $R[L]$ is a linear algebra with identity over the field of real numbers R.

Now let V be the set of all functions, f, from R into R, of the form

$$
f(t) = \sum_{j=0}^{n} c_i t^i, \quad c_i \in R, \quad n \text{ nonnegative integer} \tag{2.29}
$$

The reader is doubtless familiar with the fact that under the usual definition of addition and multiplication of real polynomials, the set V will form an algebra; one then knows precisely how to add, subtract, multiply, divide or find roots of such polynomials.

Denote the algebra of *polynomial functions* described above by $R[t]$. We shall show that the two algebras, $R[L]$ and $R[t]$ are *isomorphic*. This means that the two structures are the same, except that they bear different labels. In particular, this would mean that whatever operations one might wish to perform on an element of $R[L]$, one may first perform on the corresponding element of $R[t]$ and then translate the result back to $R[L]$. To this effect, we have

DEFINITION 2.8. Let F be a field, and let $\mathscr{A}$, $\mathscr{A}'$ be linear algebras with identity over F. The two algebras are said to be isomorphic if there exists a one-to-one mapping ϕ of $\mathscr{A}$ onto[3] $\mathscr{A}'$ such that for any a_1, $a_2 \in \mathscr{A}$ and $c_1, c_2 \in F$, the following are true:

$$\phi(c_1 a_1 + c_2 a_2) = c_1 \phi(a_1) + c_2 \phi(a_2) \qquad (2.30)$$
$$\phi(a_1 a_2) = \phi(a_1)\phi(a_2)$$

The mapping ϕ is said to be an *isomorphism* of $\mathscr{A}$ onto $\mathscr{A}'$.

Now consider the mapping ϕ from $R[L]$ to $R[t]$, which takes the polynomial operator,

$$T = \sum_{j=0}^{n} c_j L^j \qquad (2.31)$$

into the polynomial function,

$$f(t) = \sum_{j=0}^{n} c_j t^j = \phi(T) \qquad (2.32)$$

Is this an isomorphism? First, by definition it is *onto*, since if $f(t)$ is any polynomial belonging to $R[t]$, we can find the corresponding polynomial operator in $R[L]$ simply by substituting L and its powers for t and its powers in $f(t)$.

Now let T_1, T_2 be as in (2.16), and let $c_1, c_2 \in R$; consider

$$T = c_1 T_1 + c_2 T_2 = \sum_{j=0}^{n_1} (c_1 c_{1j} + c_2 c_{2j}) L^j + c_2 \sum_{j=n_1+1}^{n_2} c_{2j} L^j \qquad (2.33)$$

---

[3] A mapping or transformation ϕ of $\mathscr{A}$ *onto* $\mathscr{A}'$ is one whose range is *all* of $\mathscr{A}'$; i.e. for *every* element of $\mathscr{A}'$, say a', there exists an element a of $\mathscr{A}$ such that $a' = \phi(a)$.

Under ϕ, T is transformed to

$$\phi(T) = \sum_{j=0}^{n_1} (c_1 c_{1j} + c_2 c_{2j}) t^j + c_2 \sum_{j=n_1+1}^{n_2} c_{2j} t^j$$
$$= c_1 \sum_{j=0}^{n_1} c_{1j} t^j + c_2 \sum_{i=0}^{n_2} c_{2i} t^i = c_1 \phi(T_1) + c_2 \phi(T_2)$$

$$(2.34)$$

The reader may trivially verify that

$$\phi(T_1 T_2) = \phi(T_1)\phi(T_2) \tag{2.35}$$

It remains now to show that ϕ is one-to-one. Since it is linear, however, it will suffice to show that

$$\phi(T) = 0 \tag{2.36}$$

implies that T is the zero operator.

Now by definition,

$$\phi(T) = \sum_{j=0}^{n} c_j t^j = f(t), \quad T = \sum_{j=0}^{n} c_j L^j \tag{2.37}$$

We leave it as an exercise for the reader to determine that (2.36) implies $c_j = 0, j = 0, 1, 2, \ldots, n$. We have therefore proved the useful

PROPOSITION 2.1. The algebra of polynomial operators $R[L]$ is isomorphic to the algebra of polynomial functions $R[t]$, both over the field of real numbers R.

REMARK 2.3. The practical value of this proposition is that it sets up an equivalence between a lag operator and what we had termed earlier the *lag generating function*. We could, if we wished, push this equivalence further to cover power series. However, this would be cumbersome mathematically, without materially clarifying the issues involved. Thus, although we shall use this equivalence in subsequent work, we shall not trouble to demonstrate it here.

We may point out at this juncture that the theorems applying to convergence of real power series apply to the *existence* and *meaningfulness* of power series operators like $\sum_{i=0}^{\infty} w_i L^i$, which we encountered earlier.

We shall now illustrate by means of a few examples the use to which we can put the apparatus developed above.

EXAMPLE 2.3. Consider again the general distributed lag model:

$$y_t = \sum_{i=0}^{\infty} w_i x_{t-i} + u_t \tag{2.38}$$

The reader should observe that the notation x_{t-i}, customary in the econometric literature, is used interchangeably with the notation $x(t-i)$ employed earlier. Noticing that

$$x_{t-i} \equiv L^i x_t \tag{2.39}$$

and substituting in (2.36), we find

$$y_t = W(L)x_t + u_t, \quad W(L) = \sum_{i=0}^{\infty} w_i L^i \tag{2.40}$$

To determine whether the operator $W(L)$ is meaningful, we need to examine the conditions under which the corresponding power series, $W(t) = \sum_{i=0}^{\infty} w_i t^i$, converges. This will entail some constraints on the lag coefficients, $w_i: i = 0, 1, 2, \ldots$. The radius of convergence of this power series must at least contain $t = 1$.

EXAMPLE 2.4. Consider the special case where the coefficients w_i, above, are given by

$$w_i = \alpha \lambda^i \tag{2.41}$$

The operator $W(L)$ of (2.40) now becomes

$$W(L) = \alpha \sum_{i=0}^{\infty} \lambda^i L^i \tag{2.42}$$

What meaning is to be ascribed to this? Well, in view of Proposition 2.1, assuming that it applies not only to the algebra $R[L]$ but also in the present case, we proceed as follows: For $t \in R$, we have that

$$W(t) = \alpha \sum_{i=0}^{\infty} (\lambda t)^i = \frac{\alpha}{1 - \lambda t} \tag{2.43}$$

is valid, provided

$$|\lambda t| < 1 \tag{2.44}$$

Since we wish this representation to be valid for $t = 1$, we conclude from (2.44) that the restriction on λ is

$$\lambda \in (-1, 1) \tag{2.45}$$

For such λ, replacing in (2.43) t and its powers by L and its powers, we find

$$W(L) = \frac{\alpha I}{I - \lambda L} \tag{2.46}$$

This is an interesting development, in that it leads naturally to the notion of the *inverse* to a given lag operator, T. Such inverses need not always exist. It is clear that if we put

$$T = \frac{I}{I - \lambda L} \tag{2.47}$$

then

$$(I - \lambda L)T = I \tag{2.48}$$

To verify the validity of (2.48), let x be any element of X. Then it must be true that

$$(I - \lambda L)\left[\frac{I}{I - \lambda L} x(t)\right] = x(t) \tag{2.49}$$

In terms of the equivalence derived earlier, we know that

$$(I - \lambda L) \cdot \frac{I}{I - \lambda L}$$

corresponds to $(1 - \lambda t)(1/1 - \lambda t)$. But for λ as in (2.45) and $|t| \leq 1$, this last quantity clearly yields unity which, therefore, proves (2.48).

A further convenience of the operator representation is seen as follows: If $W(L)$ is as in (2.46), then the model in (2.40) may be written as

$$y_t = \frac{\alpha I}{I - \lambda L} x_t + u_t \tag{2.50}$$

Applying now $I - \lambda L$ to both sides we obtain, in view of (2.49),

$$y_t = \lambda y_{t-1} + \alpha x_t + u_t - \lambda u_{t-1} \tag{2.51}$$

which is a simpler form and rather easier to work with.

EXAMPLE 2.5. Suppose we are given the model

$$y_t = \frac{A(L)}{B(L)} x_t + u_t \tag{2.52}$$

where

$$A(L) = \sum_{i=0}^{n} a_i L^i, \quad B(L) = \sum_{j=0}^{m} b_j L^j, \quad a_i, b_j \in R, \quad n \leq m \tag{2.53}$$

What interpretation can we give to the quantity $A(L)/B(L)$? In view of Proposition 2.1, we may answer this question by considering the elements of $R[t]$ corresponding to $A(L)$ and $B(L)$. Thus, we may rephrase the question as: What meaning is to be attached to $A(t)/B(t)$? In the context of the algebra of polynomials, $A(t)$ is not divisible by $B(t)$, since the latter is of degree at least as large as that of the former. On the other hand, it is known that if we extend our discussion so that t lies in the field of complex numbers C, then the equation

$$B(t) = 0 \qquad (2.54)$$

has exactly m roots in C, provided $b_m \neq 0$. Moreover, if the latter holds, then

$$B^*(t) = 0 \qquad (2.55)$$

has exactly the same roots as (2.54), where

$$B^*(t) = \sum_{j=0}^{m} b_j^* t^j, \quad b_j^* = \frac{b_j}{b_m}, \quad j = 0, 1, 2, \dots, m \qquad (2.56)$$

Now $B^*(t)$ is a *monic* polynomial, i.e., it has unity as the coefficient of the highest power. Thus, let τ_i, $i = 1, 2, \dots, m$ be the roots of (2.55); then, as is well known, we have the representation,

$$B^*(t) = \prod_{i=1}^{m} (t - \tau_i) = \left[\prod_{i=1}^{m} (-\tau_i) \right] \prod_{i=1}^{m} \left(1 - \frac{t}{\tau_i} \right) \qquad (2.57)$$

Furthermore [146, p. 63],

$$\prod_{i=1}^{m} (-\tau_i) = (-1)^m \prod_{i=1}^{m} \tau_i = b_0^* = \frac{b_0}{b_m} \qquad (2.58)$$

Thus,

$$B(t) = b_m B^*(t) = b_0 \prod_{i=1}^{m} \left(1 - \frac{t}{\tau_i} \right) \qquad (2.59)$$

and the question of the meaning of $A(t)/B(t)$ reduces to the question of whether any meaning can be ascribed to $1/B(t)$. But

$$\frac{1}{B(t)} = \frac{1}{b_0} \prod_{i=1}^{m} \left(\frac{1}{1 - t/\tau_i} \right) \qquad (2.60)$$

Suppose now it is given that

$$\lambda_i = \frac{1}{\tau_i}, \quad |\lambda_i| < 1 \quad (\text{or} \quad |\tau_i| > 1), \quad \text{all } i \qquad (2.61)$$

Then it is clear that each term of the form $1/1 - \lambda_i t$ has a power series expansion, and moreover, that this power series converges for $|t| \leq 1$. Hence, (2.60) can be given the representation

$$\frac{1}{B(t)} = \frac{1}{b_0} \prod_{i=1}^{m} \left[\sum_{k=0}^{\infty} (\lambda_i t)^k \right] = \sum_{j=0}^{\infty} r_j t^j \qquad (2.62)$$

It is clear that the product (of m power series) in (2.62) converges [6, p. 376]. Thus, provided the condition in (2.61) holds, $1/B(t)$ has a well-defined meaning. Furthermore,

$$\frac{A(t)}{B(t)} = \left(\sum_{i=0}^{n} a_i t^i \right) \left(\sum_{j=0}^{\infty} r_j t^j \right) = \sum_{s=0}^{\infty} w_s t^s \qquad (2.63)$$

has well-defined meaning, where

$$\begin{aligned}
w_s &= \sum_{i=0}^{s} a_i r_{s-i}, \quad s = 0, 1, 2, \ldots, n \\
&= \sum_{i=0}^{n} a_i r_{s-i}, \quad s = n+1, n+2, \ldots
\end{aligned} \qquad (2.64)$$

Now that we have given meaning to the quantity $A(t)/B(t)$ as a convergent power series, we can reinterpret the coefficient w_s in terms of the basic parameters of the polynomials $A(\cdot)$, $B(\cdot)$.

Thus, write formally,

$$\frac{A(t)}{B(t)} = \sum_{s=0}^{\infty} w_s t^s \qquad (2.65)$$

and observe that multiplying through by $B(t)$, we obtain

$$A(t) = \sum_{j=0}^{m} \sum_{s=0}^{\infty} w_s b_j t^{s+j} = \sum_{r=0}^{\infty} \left(\sum_{j=0}^{\min(r,m)} w_{r-j} b_j \right) t^r \qquad (2.66)$$

Since coefficients of like powers of t must agree in both members of (2.66), we conclude

$$\begin{aligned}
a_i &= \sum_{j=0}^{i} w_{i-j} b_j, \quad i = 0, 1, 2, \ldots, n \\
0 &= \sum_{j=0}^{\min(i,m)} w_{i-j} b_j, \quad i = n+1, n+2, \ldots
\end{aligned} \qquad (2.67)$$

We observe that (2.67) is a *recursive system of equations* so that, given the a_i and b_j, one can compute quite simply as many coefficients w_s as one *wishes; thus, one sees quite clearly that the latter depend solely on the* $m + n + 2$ *parameters* a_i, b_j.

Finally, returning to the question of the interpretation of the model in (2.52), we see that we may write

$$y_t = \sum_{s=0}^{\infty} w_s x_{t-s} + u_t \qquad (2.68)$$

so that we are dealing with an infinite lag structure generated by a finite set of parameters, $m + n + 2$ to be exact.

REMARK 2.4. The model in (2.52) is referred to as the *general rational* model, and its associated lag structure is referred to as the *general rational lag structure*.

It may appear to the reader that certain restrictions had to be placed on the parameters b_j, $j = 0, 1, 2, \ldots, m$, which might make this particular form less attractive than otherwise. However, as we shall see later on, these restrictions do not represent conditions beyond what is customary for dynamic economic systems. In fact, as we shall show subsequently, all we have done is simply to insure that the difference equation generating the model is *stable*, and this is certainly in accord with the traditions of economic theory.

Exercises and Questions

1. In Example 2.1, verify that the set of all 2×2 real matrices constitutes a vector space.
2. Suppose that $\sum_{j=0}^{n} c_j t^j = 0$ for $t \in [0, 1]$. Show that this implies $c_j = 0$, $j = 0, 1, 2, \ldots, n$.
3. In Example 2.3, why must the radius of convergence of $\sum_{i=0}^{\infty} w_i t^i$ include $t = 1$?

   Hint: Consider the sequence

   $$x_t = 0 \qquad t = -1, -2, \ldots$$
   $$= 1 \qquad t = 0, 1, 2, \ldots$$

4. Obtain the z-transform of the sequence

   $$\{w_i: \ i = 0, 1, 2, \ldots\} \quad \text{when} \quad w_i = (1 - \lambda)^r \binom{r + i - 1}{i} \lambda^i$$

Chapter 3

FINITE AND INFINITE LAG STRUCTURES: APPROXIMATION

3.1 Finite Structures

In previous discussion, we considered the general distributed lag model:

$$y_t = \sum_{i=0}^{\infty} w_i x_{t-i} + u_t \tag{3.1}$$

and pointed out that such a model represents a nonfeasible estimation scheme since, without imposing further restrictions, it contains an infinite number of parameters. As a matter of research strategy, one might hypothesize that

$$w_{n+j} \equiv 0 , \quad j = 0, 1, 2, \ldots \tag{3.2}$$

In many instances, this may be justified on the basis of institutional grounds. Thus, if y_t represents expenditure on highway construction and x_t represents appropriation for that purpose, both at time t, it might be that the enabling legislation requires the funds appropriated to be expended within n time periods, else the authority lapses. In such a case we would expect that, in addition to (3.2), the following conditions would hold:

$$w_i \geq 0, \quad \sum_{i=0}^{n} w_i \leq 1 \tag{3.3}$$

This example actually represents an extreme case, in which there exists firm a priori knowledge regarding the maximal length of the lag. In many cases, this may not be so and the investigator may resort to the specification in (3.2) as a "reasonable working hypothesis." Alternatively, while firm a priori knowledge exists that the maximal lag *is* finite, the exact value of n may not be known. Whatever the motivation, the specification in (3.1) and (3.2) is perfectly plausible. We then have

DEFINITION 3.1. The lag structure exhibited in (3.1) is referred to as the *general infinite lag structure*; that exhibited in (3.1) and (3.2) is termed the *general finite lag structure of order n.*

Of course, it should be apparent to the reader that the general infinite lag structure cannot be taken seriously as a working hypothesis. It is an abstraction and represents a convenient starting point for further investigation.

3.2 The General Polynomial Lag

Suppose it is considered appropriate in a given econometric context to specify the model,

$$y_t = \sum_{i=0}^{n} w_i x_{t-i} + u_t \qquad (3.4)$$

for known n. We observe that if T observations are available and $T > n$, then in principle the application of ordinary least squares techniques will yield best linear unbiased estimators of the lag coefficients, under the standard assumptions on the error term and the explanatory variables. However, economic data are typically highly autocorrelated, and a regression in which the explanatory variables are $x_t, x_{t-1}, \ldots, x_{t-n}$ is unlikely to yield satisfactory results. This essentially has been the primary motivation for introducing certain simplifying schemes.

Here we shall not be concerned with the estimation procedure for such model, nor with the propriety of the specification. These will be dealt with in later sections. Our main concern at this point is rather expository and taxonomic.

The first suggestion along the lines of simplification considered in this section appears to have been put forth by Irving Fisher [42], who proposed that the lag coefficients in (3.4) be approximated by a linearly declining scheme; thus,

$$\begin{aligned} w_i &= \alpha_0(n + 1 - i), \quad i = 0, 1, 2, \ldots, n \\ &= 0, \qquad\qquad\qquad \text{otherwise} \end{aligned} \qquad (3.5)$$

Under the specification above, the model reduces to

$$y_t = \alpha_0 \sum_{i=0}^{n} (n + 1 - i) x_{t-i} + u_t \qquad (3.6)$$

We see, therefore, that what the Fisher scheme accomplishes is to reduce the $(n + 1)$ parameter problem as exhibited in (3.4) to a one parameter problem. In particular, since n is known, if we define

$$z_t = \sum_{i=0}^{n} (n + 1 - i)x_{t-i}, \quad t = n + 1, n + 2, \ldots, T \qquad (3.7)$$

we see that if we give up n observations, the model in (3.4) reduces to the simple univariate regression:

$$y_t = \alpha_0 z_t + u_t, \quad t = n + 1, n + 2, \ldots, T \qquad (3.8)$$

Clearly, the estimation problem posed by (3.8) is well known and its solution has been completely determined.

Notice that the Fisherian scheme involves the assumption that the lag coefficients are the *ordinates of a first degree polynomial* at the points $i = 0, 1, 2, \ldots, n$. If one insists that the lag structure be normalized, then we must have

$$\alpha_0 = \frac{2}{(n + 1)(n + 2)} \qquad (3.9)$$

so that the lag coefficients are entirely predetermined. Indeed, this seems to have been Fisher's intention; occasionally, in empirical applications similar schemes are employed in order to define the expectations concerning factor or product prices or output pertinent to the decision-making process of a given economic unit. At any rate, if we insist on a particularly simple process generating the lag coefficients as above, the scheme in (3.3) is unduly restrictive. Clearly, the obvious generalization,

$$\begin{aligned} w_i &= \alpha + \beta i, \quad i = 0, 1, 2, \ldots, n \\ &= 0 \qquad \text{otherwise} \end{aligned} \qquad (3.10)$$

preserves simplicity and at the same time introduces some flexibility. Thus, observe that the assumption in (3.10) states that the lag coefficients are the ordinates of a first degree polynomial at the points $i = 0, 1, 2, \ldots, n$, and the ordinates of the zero function elsewhere. The polynomial, however, contains two parameters. We further see that

$$\sum_{i=0}^{n} w_i x_{t-i} = \alpha \sum_{i=0}^{n} x_{t-i} + \beta \sum_{i=0}^{n} i x_{t-i} \qquad (3.11)$$

Defining

$$z_{t1} = \sum_{i=0}^{n} x_{t-i}, \quad z_{t2} = \sum_{i=0}^{n} i x_{t-i} \qquad (3.12)$$

we conclude that the assumption in (3.10) leads to the estimation scheme,

$$y_t = \alpha z_{t1} + \beta z_{t2} + u_t \,, \quad t = n + 1, n + 2, \ldots, T \quad (3.13)$$

In the Fisherian scheme, we were led to the synthetic variable z_t as defined in (3.7). A simple calculation will show that

$$z_t = (n + 1)z_{t1} - z_{t2} \quad (3.14)$$

Thus, if we have reason to believe that the lag structure is generated by a first degree polynomial, the Fisherian scheme leads to the following restrictions in terms of (3.13):

$$\alpha = \alpha_0(n + 1) \,, \quad \beta = -\alpha_0 \quad (3.15)$$

and this appears to be an unduly restrictive simplification of an already oversimplified lag hypothesis.

Of course, there is no reason why we must confine ourselves to this simple linear scheme. Generalizing Fisher's approach, we may hypothesize that in the general infinite lag structure, the following conditions obtain:

$$\begin{aligned} w_\tau &= P(\tau) \,, \quad \tau = 0, 1, 2, \ldots n \\ &= 0 \,, \quad \text{otherwise} \end{aligned} \quad (3.16)$$

where

$$P(t) = \sum_{i=0}^{k} \beta_i t^i \,, \quad k < n \quad (3.17)$$

Thus, what we are asserting is that the *lag structure is generated by the ordinates of the polynomial in* (3.17) *at the points* $\tau = 0, 1, 2, \ldots, n$, and by the ordinates of the *zero function elsewhere*. Presumably, one would expect in this specification that $k < n$; this is so since a polynomial of degree k contains $k + 1$ parameters. There seems little point in restricting the *general finite lag structure of order n* as in (3.16) and (3.17), and within this restriction encompassing as many (or more) parameters as in the unrestricted form. This introduces

DEFINITION 3.2. The lag structure as restricted by (3.16) and (3.17) is referred to as the (*finite*) *polynomial lag structure of order n and degree k*. The model

$$y_t = \sum_{i=0}^{n} w_i x_{t-i} + u_t \quad (3.18)$$

in conjunction with (3.16) and (3.17) is referred to as the (*finite*) *polynomial lag model of order n and degree k*.

If in (3.18) we substitute the hypothesized lag structure, we find

$$\sum_{\tau=0}^{n} w_{\tau}x_{t-\tau} = \sum_{\tau=0}^{n}\left(\sum_{i=0}^{k}\beta_{i}\tau^{i}\right)x_{t-\tau} = \sum_{i=0}^{k}\beta_{i}\left(\sum_{\tau=0}^{n}\tau^{i}x_{t-\tau}\right) \quad (3.19)$$

Defining

$$z_{ti} = \sum_{\tau=0}^{n}\tau^{i}x_{t-\tau} \quad (3.20)$$

we thus rewrite (3.18) as

$$y_{i} = \sum_{i=0}^{k}\beta_{i}z_{ti} + u_{t} \quad (3.21)$$

Notice that the variables z_{ti} can be computed directly from the data if observations on $x_{t}, t = 1, 2, \ldots, T$ are available. From the nature of the model, n observations are "lost" so that, in fact, the z_{ti} can only be computed for $t = n + 1, n + 2, \ldots, T$.

Now suppose we are dealing with the polynomial lag structure of order n and degree k, and suppose it is desired to convert it to a normalized one. This, of course, may not always be possible once unrestricted estimates for the parameters $\beta_{i}, i = 0, 1, 2, \ldots, k$ have been obtained. A *sufficient* but not a necessary condition for this purpose is that the estimates of the β_{i} be nonnegative. If that is so, then obtaining the normalized lag structure entails a reparameterization such that the lag coefficients add up to unity. This may be done rather easily through the following simple device:

$$\omega = \sum_{\tau=0}^{n} P(\tau) = \sum_{i=0}^{k}\beta_{i}V_{i}(n) \quad (3.22)$$

where

$$V_{i}(n) = \sum_{\tau=0}^{n}\tau^{i} \quad (3.23)$$

It is interesting that these quantities can be computed recursively as[4]

$$V_{i-1}(n) = \frac{(n+1)^{i}}{i} - \frac{1}{i}\sum_{s=0}^{i-2}\binom{i}{s}V_{s}(n) \quad (3.24)$$

---

[4] This relationship is established as follows:

$$(\tau + 1)^{i} = \sum_{k=0}^{i}\binom{i}{k}\tau^{k}$$

Summing over τ, we find

It is obvious, of course, that

$$V_0(n) = n + 1 \tag{3.25}$$

The reader may verify from (3.24) the familiar formula for the sum of the first n integers, the sum of the *squares* of the first n integers, and so on.

Now define

$$w_\tau^* = \frac{P(\tau)}{\omega}, \quad \tau = 0, 1, 2, \ldots, n$$
$$= 0, \quad \text{otherwise} \tag{3.26}$$

and observe that $\{w_\tau^* : \tau = 0, 1, \ldots\}$ constitutes a normalized lag structure provided $w_\tau^* \geq 0$.

The expression in (3.24) is particularly useful when one desires to obtain a normalized lag structure but one is in doubt as to the degree of the generating polynomial. In computing ω, and hence w_τ^*, from (3.22), we observe that the quantities $V_i(n)$ do not in any way depend on the degree of the generating polynomial.

With the polynomial lag structure, the advantages of normalization are rather marginal; ω can, of course, be interpreted as the long-run effect of the determining on the conditional mean of the dependent variable. Thus, if x_t follows the time path,

$$x_t = \bar{x}, \quad t = 0, -1, -2, \ldots$$
$$= \bar{x} + 1, \quad t = 1, 2, \ldots \tag{3.27}$$

then we observe that the conditional mean $\bar{y}$ of the dependent variable at time $t = 0$ is

$$\bar{y}_0 = \omega \bar{x} \tag{3.28}$$

On the other hand, in the long run, i.e., after the lapse of n periods we have

$$\bar{y}_{t+n} = \omega(\bar{x} + 1) = \bar{y}_0 + \omega, \quad t = 1, 2, \ldots \tag{3.29}$$

$$\sum_{\tau=0}^{n} (\tau + 1)^i = \sum_{k=0}^{i} \binom{i}{k} V_k(n)$$

We observe that the left member above yields

$$\sum_{\tau=0}^{n} (\tau + 1)^i = V_i(n) + (n + 1)^i = \sum_{k=0}^{i} \binom{i}{k} V_k(n)$$

Canceling $V_i(n)$ from both sides and rearranging, we obtain (3.24).

The interpretation of the lag coefficients becomes a bit more intuitively appealing under normalization. Thus, w_0^* is the fraction of the (unit) long-run effect on the conditional mean registered instantaneously; $w_0^* + w_1^*$ is the cumulative fraction of the long-run effect registered after the lapse of one period; and so on.

The notions of mean lag and variability that we described in an earlier section do not have particular appeal in the present case, although they can certainly be computed. To this effect, consider the lag generating function corresponding to the *normalized* polynomial structure of order n and degree k. We have

$$B(t) = \sum_{\tau=0}^{n} w_\tau^* t^\tau = \frac{1}{\omega} \sum_{i=0}^{k} \beta_i \sum_{\tau=0}^{n} \tau^i t^\tau \qquad (3.30)$$

and

$$B'(t) = \frac{1}{\omega} \sum_{i=0}^{k} \beta_i \sum_{\tau=0}^{n} \tau^{i+1} t^{\tau-1} \qquad (3.31)$$

Thus, the mean lag is given by

$$B'(1) = \frac{1}{\omega} \sum_{\tau=0}^{k} \beta_i \sum_{\tau=0}^{n} \tau^{i+1} = \frac{\displaystyle\sum_{i=0}^{k} \beta_i V_{i+1}(n)}{\displaystyle\sum_{i=0}^{k} \beta_i V_i(n)} \qquad (3.32)$$

In addition,

$$B''(t) = \frac{1}{\omega} \sum_{i=0}^{k} \beta_i \sum_{\tau=0}^{n} (\tau - 1)\tau^{i+1} t^{\tau-2} \qquad (3.33)$$

and thus the lag variability is computed as

$$B''(1) + B'(1) - [B'(1)]^2 = \frac{\displaystyle\sum_{i=0}^{k} \beta_i V_{i+2}(n)}{\displaystyle\sum_{i=0}^{k} \beta_i V_i(n)} - \left[\frac{\displaystyle\sum_{i=0}^{k} \beta_i V_{i+1}(n)}{\displaystyle\sum_{i=0}^{k} \beta_i V_i(n)}\right]^2 \qquad (3.34)$$

As we observed earlier, the quantities $V_k(n)$ do not depend on the degree of the polynomial assumed to generate the lag structure. Thus, the mean lag and lag variability can be computed directly once the estimates for the parameters β_i have been obtained.

Summarizing the development in this section, we have introduced the *general finite lag of order n* as

$$y_t = \sum_{i=0}^{\infty} w_i x_{t-i} + u_t \tag{3.35}$$

subject to the condition,

$$w_i = 0, \quad i = n + 1, n + 2, \ldots \tag{3.36}$$

We have also introduced the finite polynomial lag model of order n and degree k by the conditions (3.35) and (3.36), subject to the additional constraint that

$$w_\tau = \sum_{i=0}^{k} \beta_i \tau^i, \quad \tau = 0, 1, 2, \ldots, n \tag{3.37}$$

If the lag structure corresponding to this model can be *normalized* (a sufficient condition for this is that $\beta_i \geq 0$, $i = 0, 1, 2, \ldots, k$), then the mean lag can be computed as $\sum_{i=0}^{k} \beta_i V_{i+1}(n) / \sum_{i=0}^{k} \beta_i V_i(n)$, while the variability of the lag structure can be obtained as

$$\frac{\sum_{i=0}^{k} \beta_i V_{i+2}(n)}{\sum_{i=0}^{k} \beta_i V_i(n)} - \left[\frac{\sum_{i=0}^{k} \beta_i V_{i+1}(n)}{\sum_{i=0}^{k} \beta_i V_i(n)} \right]^2$$

If some of the β_i are negative, then the lag structure may not admit of normalization, in which case the intuitive content of the mean lag and lag variability concepts is severely impaired.

If the finite lag structure does not admit of normalization, this means that some of the w_τ are negative. In many instances, this may be an inadmissible property, given the economics of the problem.

3.3 Lagrangian Interpolation

In the discussion of the previous section, the form of the polynomial has been left unspecified beyond the *specification of its degree*. Occasionally, it may be useful to constrain the polynomial to have certain properties in the region $[0, n]$. In particular, we may have a priori knowledge concerning the shape of the lag structure. A particularly simple way of making use of this a priori knowledge is to specify one or more of its roots. We shall elucidate this consideration by means of some examples.

EXAMPLE 3.1. Consider again the Fisherian scheme. In its general form it states that the lag coefficients are generated by the ordinates of the polynomial,

$$P(\tau) = \beta_0 + \beta_1\tau, \quad \tau = 0, 1, 2, \ldots, n \qquad (3.38)$$

and by the ordinates of the zero function elsewhere. Suppose we specify that

$$P(n + 1) = \beta_0 + \beta_1(n + 1) = 0 \qquad (3.39)$$

This implies that

$$\beta_1 = -\frac{\beta_0}{n + 1} \qquad (3.40)$$

and thus the polynomial can be expressed as

$$P(\tau) = \beta_0\left(1 - \frac{\tau}{n + 1}\right) \qquad (3.41)$$

If the lag coefficients are to be nonnegative, then we must have $\beta_0 > 0$, and thus the restriction (3.39) implies a monotone declining lag structure.

On the other hand, suppose we specify

$$P(-n) = \beta_0 - \beta_1 n = 0 \qquad (3.42)$$

This implies that

$$\beta_1 = \frac{\beta_0}{n} \qquad (3.43)$$

Again, nonnegativity of lag coefficients requires that $\beta_0 > 0$. The polynomial is now of the form

$$P(\tau) = \beta_0\left(1 + \frac{\tau}{n}\right) \qquad (3.44)$$

and, thus, we are dealing with a monotone increasing lag structure. The reader should observe that with a linear function, we can only obtain a monotone behavior for the lag coefficients. No other shape is permitted. *He should also observe that although the polynomial in* (3.38) *can certainly be evaluated at points outside* [0, n], *its behavior in the complement of* [0, n] *is quite irrelevent from the point of view of the lag structure under consideration. Thus, he should not look upon the conditions* (3.39) *or* (3.42) *as being imposed by the basic specification* (3.36). The latter specifies, in the context of the model in (3.35), that the conditions (3.36) are to hold. However, *nothing in the specification requires that the polynomial* $P(\tau)$ *of* (3.38) *describe the lag coefficients outside the region* [0, n]. If the conditions (3.39) or (3.42) are to be imposed, this must be done because one has valid a priori information that they are true. The reader should note carefully that the nature of the a priori information embodied in these two conditions concerns the *shape of the lag structure.*

The point made in the preceding example may be amplified below.

EXAMPLE 3.2. Consider again the finite lag model of order n, and suppose the nonzero lag coefficients are generated by the second degree polynomial,

$$P(\tau) = \beta_0 + \beta_1\tau + \beta_2\tau^2, \quad \tau = 0, 1, 2, \ldots, n \qquad (3.45)$$

and suppose, in addition, we specify that its roots are located at $t = \alpha$ and $t = \beta$. Thus,

$$\begin{aligned} P(\alpha) &= \beta_0 + \beta_1\alpha + \beta_2\alpha^2 = 0 \\ P(\beta) &= \beta_0 + \beta_1\beta + \beta_2\beta^2 = 0 \end{aligned} \qquad (3.46)$$

The two equations imply,

$$\beta_0 = \beta_2\alpha\beta, \quad \beta_1 = -\beta_2(\alpha + \beta) \qquad (3.47)$$

The polynomial may thus be expressed as

$$P(\tau) = \beta_2[\alpha\beta - (\alpha + \beta)\tau + \tau^2] \qquad (3.48)$$

Now suppose we take $\alpha = -1$, $\beta = n + 1$.[5] The polynomial then becomes

$$P(\tau) = -\beta_2[n + 1 + n\tau - \tau^2] \qquad (3.49)$$

If the lag is to be normalizable, then we must have $\beta_2 < 0$. When this is so, the ordinates of the polynomial increase from $\tau = 0$ to $\tau = [n/2]$,[6] and thereafter decline. Thus, the implied lag structure has a *humped shape*; i.e., the lag coefficients first increase up to $w_{[n/2]}$ and thereafter decline.

Now consider the alternative specification $\alpha = -(n + 1), \beta = (n + 1)$. The polynomial becomes

$$P(\tau) = -\beta_2[(n + 1)^2 - \tau^2] \qquad (3.50)$$

Since in the range $[0, n]$ the quantity in square brackets is positive, normalizability of the lag structure again requires that $\beta_2 < 0$. In this

---

[5] This, for example, is the scheme followed by Almon [1] in her study of the lag between appropriation and expenditure. This was the first study to utilize the Lagrangian interpolation version of the polynomial lag structure.

[6] $[n/2]$ indicates the largest integer equal to or less than $n/2$.

case, however, we see that we are dealing with a monotone decreasing lag structure, since

$$\frac{P(\tau + 1)}{P(\tau)} = \frac{(n + 1)^2 - (\tau + 1)^2}{(n + 1)^2 - \tau^2} < 1, \quad \tau = 0, 1, 2, \ldots, n - 1$$

$$(3.51)$$

Finally, consider the root specification,

$$\alpha = -1, \quad \beta = 2n + 1 \tag{3.52}$$

The form of the polynomial now becomes

$$P(\tau) = -\beta_2[2n + 1 + 2n\tau - \tau^2] \tag{3.53}$$

Again, normalizability requires that $\beta_2 < 0$; it is then easily verified that the polynomial as exhibited in (3.53) implies a *monotone increasing* lag structure, since

$$\frac{P(\tau + 1)}{P(\tau)} = \frac{4n + 2(n - 1)\tau - \tau^2}{2n + 1 + 2n\tau - \tau^2} > 1, \quad \tau = 0, 1, 2, \ldots, n - 1$$

$$(3.54)$$

The import of the preceding example is to stress that, in the context of the (finite) polynomial lag structure, specification of some of the roots of the underlying polynomial has nothing to do with the ancillary conditions in (3.33) but rather with the shape of the lag structure. Hence, such conditions should not be imposed except in the face of valid a priori knowledge; certainly they should not be imposed gratuitously.

A particularly simple way of incorporating such a priori knowledge in the specification of the structure is through the use of *Lagrange interpolation polynomials*. To fix ideas, let us introduce

DEFINITION 3.3.   Let $f(\cdot)$ be an arbitrary function. Let x_i, $i = 0, 1, 2, \ldots, n$ be points in its domain of definition, and suppose

$$y_i = f(x_i), \quad i = 0, 1, 2, \ldots, n \tag{3.55}$$

Then

$$P(x) = \sum_{j=0}^{n} y_j s_j(x) \tag{3.56}$$

is called the *Lagrange interpolation polynomial of degree n* [associated with the function $f(\cdot)$], where

$$s_j(x) = \frac{\prod\limits_{i \neq j} (x - x_i)}{\prod\limits_{i \neq j} (x_j - x_i)}, \quad j = 0, 1, 2, \ldots, n \qquad (3.57)$$

REMARK 3.1. Notice that by construction,

$$s_j(x_i) = \delta_{ij} \qquad (3.58)$$

where δ_{ij} is the Kronecker delta, i.e., it is unity for $i = j$, and zero otherwise. It is then a consequence of (3.58) that

$$P(x_j) = y_j = f(x_j), \quad j = 0, 1, 2, \ldots, n \qquad (3.59)$$

so that the Lagrange interpolation polynomial of $f(\cdot)$ coincides with the function at the points x_i, $i = 0, 1, 2, \ldots, n$.

Now suppose we are dealing with the polynomial lag structure of order n and degree k. Suppose further that we wish to incorporate in our specification the requirement that the polynomial assume specific values, say b_r, at the distinct points t_r, $r = 0, 1, 2, \ldots, m$. How can this be accomplished? If the polynomial is

$$P(t) = \sum_{i=0}^{k} \beta_i t^i \qquad (3.60)$$

then what we require is that

$$b_r = \sum_{i=0}^{k} \beta_i t_r^i, \quad r = 0, 1, 2, \ldots, m \qquad (3.61)$$

We note first that if $m > k$, we cannot, in general, be certain that the specification can be observed. This is so, since a polynomial of degree k is uniquely determined by $k + 1$ points, say $[t_r, P(t_r)]$, $r = 0, 1, 2, \ldots, k$. Thus, in general, we should have $m \leq k$. Even if this last requirement is met, however, it is not clear how the restrictions are to be incorporated in the specification. We shall now show that there exists a simple reparameterization of the polynomial in (3.60) which easily admits of the desired restrictions. To this effect, let τ_j, $j = 0, 1, 2, \ldots, k$ be *any* $k + 1$ distinct points in the domain of definition of the polynomial. Let

$$P(\tau_j) = p_j, \quad j = 0, 1, 2, \ldots, k \qquad (3.62)$$

and define the *interpolation* polynomials

$$s_j(\tau) = \frac{\prod_{i \neq j} (\tau - \tau_i)}{\prod_{i \neq j} (\tau_j - \tau_i)}, \quad j = 0, 1, 2, \ldots, k \qquad (3.63)$$

to obtain

$$P^*(\tau) = \sum_{j=0}^{k} p_j s_j(\tau) \qquad (3.64)$$

We claim

$$P^*(\tau) \equiv P(\tau), \quad \text{all} \quad \tau \in D \qquad (3.65)$$

where D is the domain of definition of the polynomial $P(\cdot)$. To see this, note that $P^*(\tau)$, for given τ_i, $i = 0, 1, 2, \ldots, k$ is uniquely determined by the parameters p_j, $j = 0, 1, 2, \ldots, k$. On the other hand, the equations in (3.62) imply:

$$\begin{bmatrix} 1 & \tau_0, \tau_0^2, \ldots, \tau_0^k \\ 1 & \tau_1, \tau_1^2, \ldots, \tau_1^k \\ \vdots \\ 1 & \tau_k, \tau_k^2, \ldots, \tau_k^k \end{bmatrix} \begin{bmatrix} \beta_0 \\ \beta_1 \\ \vdots \\ \beta_k \end{bmatrix} = \begin{bmatrix} p_0 \\ p_1 \\ \vdots \\ p_k \end{bmatrix} \qquad (3.66)$$

The matrix of the system is the so-called *Vandermonde* matrix, and since the τ_i are distinct, it is nonsingular [74, ch. 4]. Hence, not only do the β_i uniquely determine the p_j but the p_j uniquely determine the β_i as well. Thus, the claim in (3.65) is proved. Indeed, as the reader may verify directly, in view of (3.62) and (3.63), coefficients of like powers of τ are identical in both members of (3.65).

Thus, given any polynomial of the form in (3.60), we can reparameterize it as in (3.64), the new parameters p_j, $j = 0, 1, 2, \ldots, k$, being well-defined functions of the basic parameters β_r, $r = 0, 1, 2, \ldots, k$, and the auxiliary points τ_i, $i = 0, 1, 2, \ldots, k$. Since the identity in (3.65) is thus respected, it is important for the reader to realize that the *ordinates of the polynomial (i.e., the values assumed by the polynomial) over its domain of definiton are unaffected by the choice of the auxiliary points τ_i; this choice affects only the transformed parameters of the problem, namely, the p_j, $j = 0, 1, 2, \ldots, k$, as is obvious from (3.66) but not the ordinates of the polynomial.*

Now if it is known a priori that

$$b_r = P(t_r), \quad r = 0, 1, 2, \ldots, m, \quad m \leq k \qquad (3.67)$$

then this a priori knowledge can be incorporated in the specification of the lag structure if we employ the alternative form of the generating polynomial given in (3.64). Thus, let $t_r \in D$, $r = 0, 1, 2, \ldots, k$, such that the first $m + 1$ points are those given in (3.67), the remaining being any other (distinct) points whatsoever. Now, using the points t_r, $r = 0, 1, 2, \ldots, k$, we can define the quantities in (3.63), and thus write the generating polynomial as

$$P^*(t) = \sum_{r=0}^{m} b_r s_r(t) + \sum_{j=1}^{k-m} p_{m+j} s_{m+j}(t) \qquad (3.68)$$

In (3.68) the first term of the right-hand member incorporates the a priori specification and contains no unknown parameters. The second term contains all the remaining (unknown) parameters of the lag structure. In particular, if (3.67) specifies $m + 1$ roots of the generating polynomial then, of course, $b_r = 0$, $r = 0, 1, 2, \ldots, m$, and the Lagrangian interpolation form exhibited in (3.68) reduces to

$$P^*(t) = \sum_{j=m+1}^{k} p_j s_j(t) \qquad (3.69)$$

It is worth pointing out that $P^*(t)$ is still a polynomial of degree k, since all the $s_j(\cdot)$ are generally polynomials of degree k, but it is one that correctly reflects the a priori restriction on the coefficients of the generating polynomial implied by (3.67) and the assertion that $b_r = 0$, $r = 0, 1, 2, \ldots, m$.

Summarizing the development in this section, we have given an alternative form for the polynomial assumed to generate the polynomial lag structure of order n and degree k. The alternative is in the form of a Lagrange interpolation polynomial. Whereas these two forms yield identical lag coefficients, the interpolation form is convenient in incorporating a priori restrictions on the generating polynomial, especially restrictions of the type that specify one or more of its roots.

The Lagrangian interpolation form is only one possible alternative, and it is given here because it has been employed extensively in the literature. Other similar representations can be given in terms of other polynomial schemes, such as those of Legendre, Chebyshev, Jacobi, Laguerre and Hermite. The interested reader may consult [22]. These schemes, however, lack the essential simplicity of the Lagrange interpolation polynomial.

3.4 Approximations

In dealing with the problem of distributed lags, it is tempting to begin with the general infinite lag model,

$$y_t = \sum_{i=0}^{\infty} w_i x_{t-i} + u_t \tag{3.70}$$

and derive all other schemes as approximations thereto. Thus, e.g., the geometric lag may be said to be derived from (3.70) through the approximation of the lag coefficients by

$$w_i = \alpha \lambda^i, \quad i = 0, 1, 2, \ldots, \quad \lambda \in (0, 1) \tag{3.71}$$

Or the general finite lag structure may be said to be derived from (3.70) through the approximation,

$$w_i = 0, \quad i = n + 1, n + 2, \ldots \tag{3.72}$$

This, however, is not a particularly fruitful approach; it facilitates neither the handling of estimation problems nor the elucidation of properties of specific lag structures. No doubt all empirically implemented lag schemes represent approximations to the true structure that has generated the data under consideration. Nevertheless, little is to be gained in terms of clarity by approximation considerations unless one has a very clear a priori perception of the general nature of the true lag structure. For this reason, our discussion here will be relatively brief.

An approximation scheme to the underlying general distributed lag structure ought to try to accomplish two objectives:

(i) To approximate the true lag coefficients closely
(ii) To do so with as few parameters as possible, while keeping the estimation scheme relatively simple

The general infinite lag structure, in the operator notation of previous sections, results from the application of the power series operator $W(L)$ to the determining variable, say x_t. The result is the conditional mean of the dependent variable, say y_t. The operator is, of course,

$$W(L) = \sum_{i=0}^{\infty} w_i L^i \tag{3.73}$$

As we have seen earlier, performing various algebraic operations on $W(L)$ is equivalent to performing the same algebraic operations on its associated lag generating function, and thereafter replacing the index variable, s (and its powers) by the lag operator, L (and its powers). Now the lag generating function associated with $W(L)$ is

$$W(s) = \sum_{i=0}^{\infty} w_i s^i \qquad (3.74)$$

s being the index variable.

Suppose we wish to approxiate $W(\cdot)$ above by a function whose first $n + 1$ derivatives (including the zero-th order derivative) coincide with it at $s = 0$. As is well known, this is simply the Taylor series expansion of $W(\cdot)$ about $s = 0$. We thus see that the approximation lag generation function is

$$\tilde{W}(s) = \sum_{i=0}^{n} w_i s^i \qquad (3.75)$$

We observe

$$\tilde{W}(0) = W(0), \quad \tilde{W}^{(r)}(0) = W^{(r)}(0), \quad r = 1, 2, \ldots, n \qquad (3.76)$$

$W^{(r)}(0)$ indicating the rth order derivative of $W(\cdot)$, evaluated at zero. It is clear that the lag structure implied by (3.75) is

$$w_{(n)} = \{w_i \colon i = 0, 1, 2, \ldots, n\} \qquad (3.77)$$

This approximation suffers from an artificiality in that it terminates the infinite lag structure at a point which is arbitrarily set by the investigator. While at face value it forces coincidence of the first $n + 1$ coefficients between the true and approximation lag structures, the approximation significantly obscures such features as the *mean lag* and *lag variability*. A somewhat more flexible scheme is provided by a rational approximation. A comprehensive review of such, and other, approximation schemes may be found in Wynne [159]. Here we shall present the original approximation given by Padè [122] in 1892. Before we do so, let us observe the following: Suppose $A(s)$, $B(s)$ are two *known* power series, with well-defined radii of convergence. What are we to mean by their *quotient*? Formally, let

$$C(s) = \sum_{i=0}^{\infty} c_i s^i = \frac{A(s)}{B(s)}, \quad A(s) = \sum_{i=0}^{\infty} a_i s^i, \quad B(s) = \sum_{j=0}^{\infty} b_j s^j \qquad (3.78)$$

The problem is to determine the c_i from the a's and b's. Again proceeding formally, we can write

$$B(s)\,C(s) = A(s) \qquad (3.79)$$

or more fully,

$$\sum_{i=0}^{\infty} a_i s^i = \sum_{i=0}^{\infty} \left(\sum_{r=0}^{i} c_r b_{i-r} \right) s^i \qquad (3.80)$$

For (3.79) to hold, we need to have equality between coefficients of like powers of s in both members. From (3.80) we see that this implies,

$$\sum_{r=0}^{i} c_r b_{i-r} = a_i , \quad i = 0, 1, 2, \ldots \qquad (3.81)$$

The first few equations of the infinite system in (3.81) are

$$a_0 = b_0 c_0 , \quad a_1 = c_0 b_1 + c_1 b_0 , \quad a_2 = c_0 b_2 + c_1 b_1 + c_2 b_0 \qquad (3.82)$$

and we see that these form a recursive system; i.e., the first equation contains only c_0, the second only c_0 and c_1, the third only c_0, c_1 and c_2, and so on. Thus, as many coefficients as we wish may be uniquely computed from (3.81).

Let us now ask the converse question. Thus, suppose the power series $C(\cdot)$ is given. Can we determine uniquely power series $A(\cdot)$, $B(\cdot)$ such that

$$C(s) = \frac{A(s)}{B(s)} ? \qquad (3.83)$$

For (3.83) to be valid, (3.81) and (3.82) must hold. However, it is obvious, especially from the latter set of equations, that the coefficients a_i and b_j cannot be uniquely determined. If, on the other hand, the b_j are given, then the a_i are trivially obtained. Similarly, if the a_i are given, then the b_j may be obtained recursively from (3.82), provided $c_0 \neq 0$. The reason for this failure is, of course, quite obvious: There are not enough conditions on the power series $A(\cdot)$, $B(\cdot)$. It is apparent that if $A(\cdot)$, $B(\cdot)$ are two series obeying (3.83), then $dA(\cdot)$, $B(\cdot)d$ will also satisfy the equation for arbitrary scalar $d \neq 0$.

Now suppose that

$$A_n(s) = \sum_{i=0}^{n} a_i s^i , \quad B_m(s) = \sum_{j=0}^{m} b_j s^j , \quad n < m \qquad (3.84)$$

Is there some sense in which an arbitrary power series can be approximated by the quotient $A_n(s)/B_m(s)$? This depends on what is meant by an "approximation." Padè [122] has solved the problem under the condition that

$$\frac{A_n(s)}{B_m(s)} - C(s) = \sum_{r=m+n+1}^{\infty} c_r^* s^r \qquad (3.85)$$

where the c_r^* are suitable constants.

Let us see precisely what this entails. First, expand formally the rational function $A_n(s)/B_m(s)$ by power series to obtain

$$\tilde{C}(s) = \sum_{i=0}^{\infty} \tilde{c}_i s^i \qquad (3.86)$$

Thus, (3.85) may be restated as

$$\tilde{C}(s) - C(s) = \sum_{i=0}^{\infty} (\tilde{c}_i - c_i)s^i = \sum_{r=m+n+1}^{\infty} c_r^* s^r \qquad (3.87)$$

Thus, the approximation criterion implies,

$$c_i = \tilde{c}_i, \quad i = 0, 1, 2, \ldots, m+n \qquad (3.88)$$

The relevance of these considerations to our discussion will become clear if we ask ourselves the following question: Given an arbitrary lag structure,

$$w = \{w_i \colon i = 0, 1, 2, \ldots\} \qquad (3.89)$$

under what conditions does there exist a pair of polynomials as in (3.84) generating the lag structure

$$\tilde{w} = \{\tilde{w}_i \colon i = 0, 1, 2, \ldots\} \qquad (3.90)$$

such that

$$\frac{A_n(s)}{B_m(s)} = \sum_{i=0}^{\infty} \tilde{w}_i s^i, \quad \tilde{w}_i = w_i, \quad i = 0, 1, 2, \ldots m + n \qquad (3.91)$$

To answer this question, we observe that if we put

$$\tilde{W}(s) = \frac{A_n(s)}{B_m(s)} \qquad (3.92)$$

we require that

$$W(s) - \tilde{W}(s) = \sum_{i=n+m+1}^{\infty} (w_i - \tilde{w}_i)s^i \qquad (3.93)$$

Multiply both sides by $B_m(s)$ to obtain

$$B_m(s)W(s) - A_n(s) = \sum_{i=n+m+1}^{\infty} w_i^* s^i \qquad (3.94)$$

where the w_i^* are suitably defined scalars. The import of (3.94) is that *the coefficients of s^i, $i = 0, 1, 2, \ldots, m + n$, in its left member vanish.* This, of course, implies that the following conditions must be satisfied:

$$\sum_{v=0}^{i} b_v w_{i-v} = a_i, \quad i = 0, 1, 2, \ldots, n \tag{3.95}$$

$$\sum_{v=0}^{\min(i,m)} b_v w_{i-v} = 0, \quad i = n + 1, n + 2, \ldots, n + m$$

We note that we are dealing with a block recursive system which admits of a unique solution if and only if the second set of equations admits of a unique solution in the b's. The latter is impossible, however, since we are dealing with a system of m equations in $m + 1$ *unknowns*. On the other hand, if the normalization, or convention,

$$b_0 = 1 \tag{3.96}$$

is imposed, then we have

$$\begin{bmatrix} w_n & , & w_{n-1} & , \ldots, w_0, & 0, & 0, \ldots, 0 \\ w_{n+1} & , & w_n & , \ldots, w_1, & w_0, & 0, \ldots, 0 \\ \vdots & & & & & \\ w_{n+m-1}, & w_{n+m-2}, & \ldots, w_{m-1}, & w_{m-2}, & \ldots, w_m \end{bmatrix} \begin{bmatrix} b_1 \\ b_2 \\ \vdots \\ b_m \end{bmatrix} = - \begin{bmatrix} w_{n+1} \\ w_{n+2} \\ \vdots \\ w_{n+m} \end{bmatrix} \tag{3.97}$$

Hence, in order to determine uniquely the b_i, $i = 1, 2, \ldots, m$, it is necessary and sufficient that

$$H_n^{(m)} = \begin{vmatrix} w_n & , & w_{n-1} & , \ldots, w_0, & 0, & 0, \ldots, 0 \\ w_{n+1} & , & w_n & , \ldots, w_1, & w_0, & 0, \ldots, 0 \\ \vdots & & & & & \\ w_{n+m-1}, & w_{n+m-2}, & \ldots, & & & w_n \end{vmatrix} \neq 0 \tag{3.98}$$

If (3.98) and (3.96) hold, then it is possible, given the power series $W(\cdot)$, to determine polynomials $A_n(\cdot)$, $B_m(\cdot)$ whose quotient appoximates the power series in the sense of (3.93).

Thus, the general infinite lag model,

$$y_t = W(L)x_t + u_t \tag{3.99}$$

may be "approximated" by the (infinite) rational lag representation,

$$y_t = \frac{A_n(L)}{B_m(L)} x_t + u_t \tag{3.100}$$

It is clear from the preceding that the approximation can be made increasingly close by increasing the degrees of the numerator and/or denominator polynomials, provided the conditions of (3.98) continue to be satisfied.

An alternative approximation rationale may be derived, using the Lagrange interpolation scheme. To this effect, let the "true" lag structure be

$$w = \{w_i : i = 0, 1, 2, \ldots\} \tag{3.101}$$

and let $Q(t)$ be *any* function such that

$$Q(t_i) = w_i, \quad i = 0, 1, 2, \ldots \tag{3.102}$$

We can certainly define the Lagrange interpolation polynomial of order k, whose ordinates coincide with $Q(\cdot)$ at the points $t_i, i = 0, 1, 2, \ldots, k$. This may be done by defining the quantities,

$$s_j(t) = \frac{\prod_{i \neq j} (t - t_i)}{\prod_{i \neq j} (t_j - t_i)}, \quad j = 0, 1, 2, \ldots, k \tag{3.103}$$

and then obtaining the interpolation polynomial as

$$P(t) = \sum_{j=0}^{k} w_j s_j(t) \tag{3.104}$$

We observe that

$$P(t_i) = w_i, \quad i = 0, 1, 2, \ldots, k \tag{3.105}$$

For convenience only, let us suppose that the points t_i are given by

$$t_i = i, \quad i = 0, 1, 2, \ldots, k \tag{3.106}$$

Then it is clear that the interpolation polynomial may be used to generate an approximating lag structure by defining

$$P(\tau) = \tilde{w}_\tau, \quad \tau = 0, 1, 2, \ldots, n \tag{3.107}$$

In principle, we can generate by this device an infinite lag structure. However, since $P(\cdot)$ is a polynomial of degree k, the approximating lag coefficients w_τ of (3.107) will be dominated by the coefficient of t^k in the polynomial when τ becomes large. This may lead to violation of certain a priori restrictions that the economics of the problem may impose on the lag structure. In particular, we shall have

$$\lim_{\tau \to \infty} \tilde{w}_\tau \neq 0 \tag{3.108}$$

and this is generally unacceptable, as we pointed out in Section 1.1.

Thus, this approximation scheme is best confined to situations in which the finiteness of the lag structure is reasonably well grounded in the nature of the problem under investigation. In such a case, one is assured that the neglected tail of the lag structure is of negligible proportions.

Now, what is the relation of the lag operator implied by this approximating scheme and the operator $W(L)$ of (3.73)? To this effect, consider the approximating lag generating function. The relevant lag coefficients are given by (3.107), and using t as the index variable, we find

$$\tilde{W}(t) = \sum_{\tau=0}^{n} \tilde{w}_\tau t^\tau = \sum_{\tau=0}^{n} \sum_{i=0}^{k} w_i s_i(\tau) t^\tau$$

$$= \sum_{\tau=0}^{k} w_\tau t^\tau + \sum_{\tau=k+1}^{n} \left(\sum_{i=0}^{k} w_i s_i(\tau) \right) t^\tau \qquad (3.109)$$

We see, therefore, that in this approximating scheme the first $k + 1$ lag coefficients of the true structure are reproduced, the next $n - k$ are expressed as linear combinations of the first $k + 1$ lag coefficients, and the remaining w_i, $i = n + 1, n + 2, \ldots$ are assumed to be zero.

Another approximation scheme that combines features of the previous two has been recently proposed by Jorgenson [82]. The rationale is as follows: If

$$w = \{w_i : i = 0, 1, 2, \ldots\} \qquad (3.110)$$

is the given lag structure, let $W(t)$ be *any continuous function defined on* $(0, 1]$ *such that*

$$W(e^{-k}) = w_k, \quad k = 0, 1, 2, \ldots \qquad (3.111)$$

We observe that (3.111) implies

$$W(0) = w_\infty \qquad (3.112)$$

and thus, if the requirements of Section 1.1 are to be met, it is necessary that

$$W(0) = 0 \qquad (3.113)$$

Now it is known from elementary analysis that any continuous function on a closed bounded set can be *uniformly* approximated by a polynomial. Hence, for $t \in [\delta, 1]$ we can uniformly approximate $W(t)$ by

$$\tilde{W}(t) = \sum_{i=1}^{m} \tilde{w}_i t^i \qquad (3.114)$$

This has the following precise meaning: Given $\varepsilon > 0$, there exists a polynomial of degree m such that

$$| W(t) - \tilde{W}(t)| < \varepsilon, \quad \text{for all} \quad t \in [\delta, 1] \tag{3.115}$$

If we now evaluate $\tilde{W}(\cdot)$ at the points $t_k = e^{-k}$, $k = 0, 1, 2, \ldots$, we will thereby generate the approximating lag structure. Thus, we obtain

$$\tilde{W}(e^{-k}) = \sum_{i=1}^{m} \tilde{w}_i e^{-ki} = w_{km}, \quad k = 0, 1, 2, \ldots \tag{3.116}$$

where

$$w_{(m)} = \{w_{km}: k = 0, 1, 2, \ldots\} \tag{3.117}$$

is the approximating lag structure. The rationale of the approximation indicates that

$$|w_k - w_{km}| < \varepsilon, \quad k = 0, 1, 2, \ldots \tag{3.118}$$

In contrast to the previous scheme, we do not obtain coincidence between any subset of lag coefficients in the "true" and approximating structure, except by accident. On the other hand, and also in contrast to the preceding, in this scheme *all* lag coefficients are approximated *equally* well by the w_{km}; the second subscript is included to indicate that the approximating polynomial is of degree m.

Furthermore, we see that the approximating scheme respects the condition in (3.113) since it is represented by a homogeneous polynomial. Thus, we see that

$$\tilde{w}_{\infty, m} = 0 \tag{3.119}$$

Now, what sort of lag operator is implied by this scheme? To answer this, let us obtain the generating function of the approximation. We have

$$\tilde{W}(s) = \sum_{k=0}^{\infty} \tilde{w}_{km} s^k = \sum_{i=1}^{m} \tilde{w}_i \sum_{k=0}^{\infty} (se^{-i})^k = \sum_{i=1}^{m} \left(\frac{\tilde{w}_i e^i}{e^i - s} \right) \tag{3.120}$$

Now define

$$D(s) = \prod_{i=1}^{m} (e^i - s) \tag{3.121}$$

and notice that $D(\cdot)$ is a polynomial of degree m; further,

$$N(s) = \sum_{i-1}^{m} \tilde{w}_i e^i \prod_{j \neq i} (e^j - s) \tag{3.122}$$

Notice that $N(\cdot)$ is a polynomial of degree $m - 1$ at most. Thus, we may write

$$\tilde{W}(s) = \frac{N(s)}{D(s)} \tag{3.123}$$

It is thus interesting that Jorgenson's uniform approximation scheme leads to a rational distributed lag. However, this is a somewhat special scheme. The perceptive reader should have noted that the denominator polynomial does not contain any unknown parameters. Indeed, the coefficient of s^r therein is simply $(-1)^r$ times the sum of all products of terms like e^i taken $(m - r)$ at a time. Thus, the m unknown parameters are concentrated in the numerator polynomial.

In addition, the approximation criterion is an unnecessarily stringent one, since it requires that all lag coefficients be uniformly approximated. This is purchased at the cost of relying on the Weierstrass approximation theorem [156, p. 355]. The latter, however, depends on a Fourier series approximation of a periodic function and a Taylor approximation of the sinusoids involved. In this case, we define $W(t)$ by suitable extension, on $(-\pi, \pi)$, and then extend it as a periodic function outside that interval by suitable definition. We approximate this function by a (finite) Fourier series and subsequently approximate each sinusoid in the series by a polynomial, using Taylor's theorem. *It is clear that in order to achieve a high degree of correspondence between $W(t)$ and its approximation, we should require a high order polynomial. Conversely, if we use only a low order polynomial, then we have little assurance that the parameters of the approximating lag structure exhibit any affinity to the parameters of the "true" structure.*

Finally, with respect to all such rationalizations, the following should be borne in mind. One might well speak of approximations that "reproduce" part of the underlying "true" lag structure. This is valid in a *mathematical* sense; thus, for example, given the lag structure $w = \{w_i : i = 0, 1, 2, \ldots\}$ there exists a finite scheme containing, say, the parameters $w_i : i = 0, 1, 2, \ldots, n$; or there exists a polynomial scheme containing the parameters $w_i : i = 0, 1, 2, \ldots, k$; or there exists an infinite rational approximation whose lag coefficients agree with the w_i for $i = 0, 1, 2, \ldots, m + n$.

However, when the parameters of the approximating scheme are estimated we must bear in mind that if the general infinite lag structure is true, then by using the approximating structure we are committing a misspecification error of generally unknown proportions. Moreover, as we mentioned earlier such approximation schemes are likely to affect the mean lag and other summary characteristics of the lag distribution. An examination of these aspects of approximation lies outside the scope of this book. The interested reader, however, might refer to the illuminating papers of Sims [133, 134] which deal with precisely these problems.

Chapter 4

GEOMETRIC LAG STRUCTURE I

4.1 Generalities

In previous discussion, the geometric lag structure was presented in an ad hoc fashion, either as a simplification of a normalized lag structure or as an approximation to a perfectly general infinite lag structure. In this section we shall motivate and derive it from more basic economic considerations.

The model we wish to examine here is

$$y_t = \alpha \sum_{i=0}^{\infty} \lambda^i x_{t-i} + u_t, \quad t = 1, 2, \ldots, T \tag{4.1}$$

In the relation above, we specify

$$\lambda \in (0, 1), \quad u \sim N(0, \sigma^2 I), \quad u = (u_1, u_2, \ldots, u_T)' \tag{4.2}$$

and that the determining variable, x_t, is independent of the error term $u_{t'}$ for all t, t'.

The normality assumption in (4.2) is not entirely essential for much of the discussion; it is included only for convenience of presentation at this stage. One can introduce other determining variables in (4.1) without materially complicating the model, provided that such variables are not subject to a distributed lag. We shall consider such extension below.

What problems are presented by the estimation of parameters in (4.1)? We first observe that we are dealing with a *nonlinear* model. In particular, λ enters the system in a highly nonlinear fashion. Second, it would appear that we are dealing with a model containing an infinite number of determining variables. This, however, is more apparent than real. Thus, notice that if we employ the lag operator notation developed in Section 2.2, then we can write

$$y_t = \frac{\alpha I}{I - \lambda L} x_t + u_t \tag{4.3}$$

where obviously

$$\frac{I}{I - \lambda L} = \sum_{i=0}^{\infty} \lambda^i L^i \tag{4.4}$$

This shows that we are dealing with a particularly simple form of *rational distributed lag*, and one that is normalizable as well! (Thus, take $\alpha = \alpha^*/(1 - \lambda)$). It is clear that ordinary least squares (OLS) cannot be employed directly in estimating the parameters of (4.3), due to the strongly nonlinear manner in which λ enters the model. On the other hand, applying to both sides the operator inverse to $I/(I - \lambda L)$, i.e. the operator $I - \lambda L$, we find

$$y_t = \lambda y_{t-1} + \alpha x_t + v_t \tag{4.5}$$

where

$$v_t = u_t - \lambda u_{t-1} \tag{4.6}$$

Now the parameters λ and α occur linearly. Unfortunately, however, (4.5) does not generally constitute a model to which application of least squares methods yields estimators possessing desirable properties, e.g. consistency.

Whether this is so or not depends on the stochastic structure of the random variable, u_t.

Since the error term in (4.1) obeys the classical assumptions,

$$E(u) = 0, \quad \text{Cov}(u) = \sigma^2 I, \quad u = (u_1, u_2, \ldots, u_T)' \tag{4.7}$$

then it is clear that in the form (4.5) we must have

$$
\begin{aligned}
E(v_t) &= 0 \\
E(v_t v_{t'}) &= -\lambda \sigma^2 & \text{if} \quad t = t' - 1 \\
&= (1 + \lambda^2)\sigma^2 & \text{if} \quad t = t' \\
&= -\lambda \sigma^2 & \text{if} \quad t = t' + 1 \\
&= 0 & \text{otherwise}
\end{aligned}
\tag{4.8}
$$

Note also that the variance of v_1 may be simply σ^2, depending on what we assume about the *initial conditions* y_0, x_0, u_0, but this is only a minor matter. Whatever may be assumed about initial conditions, it is clear from (4.8) that the error term in (4.5) exhibits (first order) serial correlation and, since y_{t-1}, an explanatory variable in (4.5), is a function of u_{t-1}, it follows that y_{t-1} is *correlated with* v_t. Thus, OLS estimators of the parameters of (4.5) will be inconsistent. *The only instance where this is not so occurs when the error term in (4.1) obeys the standard first-order Markov scheme with parameter λ.*

This means that

$$u_t = \frac{\gamma I}{I - \lambda L} \varepsilon_t \qquad (4.9)$$

where

$$E(\varepsilon) = 0, \qquad \text{Cov}(\varepsilon) = \sigma^2 I, \qquad \varepsilon = (\varepsilon_1, \varepsilon_2, \ldots, \varepsilon_T)' \qquad (4.10)$$

Hence, the reduction given in (4.5) implies that

$$v_t = \gamma \varepsilon_t \qquad (4.11)$$

If we expand the lag operator in (4.9), we find

$$u_t = \gamma \sum_{i=0}^{\infty} \lambda^i \varepsilon_{t-i} \qquad (4.12)$$

Thus, from (4.1) we see that y_{t-1} depends only on

$$\varepsilon_{t-1-i}, \quad i = 0, 1, 2, \ldots$$

and hence y_{t-1} is independent of v_t. *Thus, in these circumstances OLS estimators of the parameters of* (4.5) *are consistent.*

Excepting this special case, estimation of the geometric distributed lag model does not readily yield to standard procedures; yet this model has gained wide acceptance and its implementation in various aspects of econometric work has been extensive.

Thus, before we consider alternative estimation schemes we might well ask: How could a model that presents substantial problems of estimation have gained such wide currency? The answer is simply that at least its nonstochastic part has fundamental economic interpretation and can, in fact, be derived from more primitive assumptions regarding the behavior of economic units. It is, of course, quite true that it is desirable to deal with models to which the application of simple estimation techniques yields estimators with the standard properties of consistency, efficiency and the like, in the manner we are accustomed to in the context of the general linear model. On the other hand, we should bear in mind that it is the economic theoretic content of a model and the behavior characteristics it seeks to typify that are of crucial significance, and thus we should not turn to a theoretically deficient model simply because the estimation problems it presents can be easily tackled. An indication of the considerations above is provided by the flexible accelerator theory of investment.

Roughly speaking, this theory states that investment is proportional to the difference between actual and desired capital. Thus, let

$$K_t - K_{t-1} = \gamma[K_t^* - K_{t-1}] \qquad (4.13)$$

where K, K^* are, respectively, actual and desired capital. If we also assume that desired capital is strictly proportional to (expected) output, as in the fixed coefficients model, we can write

$$K_t^* = \alpha Q_t \tag{4.14}$$

where Q is output. Now, substituting (4.14) into (4.13), we find

$$K_t = (1 - \gamma)K_{t-1} + \alpha\gamma Q_t \tag{4.15}$$

But this is identical with the nonstochastic part of (4.5). The above is, of course, a rather fanciful example, since it is unlikely that one would wish to perform a regression of the form (4.15). Nonetheless, it gives an indication of the early origins of the distributed lag hypothesis in the simple geometric form.

There are, however, much more plausible circumstances under which an econometric model with geometric distributed lag might arise.

4.2 Motivation: The Adaptive Expectations Hypothesis

In this and subsequent sections we shall examine a number of basic economic hypotheses that generate the geometric distributed lag model.

Suppose we are dealing with an agricultural supply function. It may be reasonable to put

$$y_t = \alpha x_t^* + u_t \tag{4.16}$$

where y_t is quantity, x_t^* is *expected price*, and u_t is a random variable reflecting the exigencies of weather, soil conditions and the like.

This being so, we may plausibly assume that

$$E(u_t) = 0 , \quad E(u_t u_{t'}) = \delta_{tt'}\sigma^2 \tag{4.17}$$

The problem with (4.16) is that x_t^* is not an observable quantity. A very reasonable hypothesis about the manner in which expectations are generated is the so-called *adaptive expectations* hypothesis originally suggested by Cagan [18] in a different context.

Thus, we put

$$x_t^* - x_{t-1}^* = \gamma[x_{t-1} - x_{t-1}^*] , \quad \gamma \in (0, 1) \tag{4.18}$$

which means that decision makers revise their expectations linearly, according to their most recent experience with the accuracy of their predictions. Quite clearly, the equation (4.18) must be *nonstochastic* in x_t^*. Rewriting it in operator notation, we have

$$(I - \beta L)x_t^* = \gamma L x_t , \quad \beta = 1 - \gamma \tag{4.19}$$

and solving we find

$$x_{t+1}^* = (1 - \beta) \sum_{i=0}^{\infty} \beta^i x_{t-i} = \frac{(1 - \beta)I}{I - \beta L} x_t \qquad (4.20)$$

Inserting (4.20) in (4.16), we have

$$y_t = \alpha(1 - \beta) \sum_{i=0}^{\infty} \beta^i x_{t-i-1} + u_t \qquad (4.21)$$

which is the geometric distributed lag model.

With the hypotheses of this simple agricultural scheme, there is no statistical difficulty in estimating the parameters β and α of (4.21), since price is determined in a commodity market by the condition that supply equal demand. Since supply (y_t) is given by (4.16) and since the error term in the demand equation is presumably independent of the u_t, it follows that x_{t-i} cannot be correlated with u_t for $i = 0, 1, 2, \ldots$.

Thus, we have here a reasonable and well-grounded scheme from which the geometric lag distribution model is derived.

It is interesting that many formulations based on the permanent income hypothesis suggested by Friedman [44] lead to the geometric distributed lag.

Although Friedman has suggested an integral (Laplace transform) definition of permanent income, much of the ensuing empirical work uses a discrete definition. Thus, if x_t is measured income, one is likely to encounter a definition for permanent income, x_t^*, given by

$$x_t^* = \frac{(1 - \lambda)I}{I - \lambda L} x_t, \quad \lambda \in (0, 1) \qquad (4.22)$$

Whether (4.22) represents an ad hoc definition of the concept, or whether it is generated by an expectational pattern of the type discussed in this section, need not concern us at this juncture.

4.3 The Partial Adjustment Hypothesis

The scheme generating the geometric lag model of the previous section easily supports, or requires, the assumption that the error terms of (4.21) are intertemporally independent. As we have seen earlier, this implies that if the model is reduced by the application of the operator $(I - \beta L)$ to both sides, the resulting form does not admit of consistent estimators for its parameters by the application of ordinary least squares (OLS). In this section we shall discuss a motivation for the geometric lag model which will admit of such estimators. The rationale for this motivation originated with Nerlove [116, 118].

Thus, suppose that the desired or *optimal* quantity for an economic variable y_t^* is given by

$$y_t^* = \alpha x_t + u_t \tag{4.23}$$

where the u_t are assumed to obey, minimally,

$$E(u_t) = 0 , \quad E(u_t u_{t'}) = \delta_{tt'} \sigma^2 \tag{4.24}$$

$\delta_{tt'}$ being the Kronecker delta, The determining variable, x_t, is taken to be independent of u_t. However, the desired magnitude of the variable is not necessarily observed. The economic unit to which y_t^* refers may not always be able or willing to make the transition to the desired level instantaneously; thus, if y_t^* is desired labor employment in a given industry, this optimal level may not be attained instantaneously because of costs (of hiring or firing workers) generally associated with a rapidly changing work force. Thus, the observable magnitudes of the variable may reflect a *partial adjustment* of the economic unit from current to optimal levels. A particularly simple way of formulating this partial adjustment is as follows:

$$y_t - y_{t-1} = \gamma[y_t^* - y_{t-1}] , \quad \gamma \in (0, 1) \tag{4.25}$$

This states that *the change in the observable magnitude of the variable is proportional to the gap between its optimal and current levels.*

If we now substitute from (4.23) in (4.25) we find,

$$y_t = (1 - \gamma)y_{t-1} + \alpha\gamma x_t + \gamma u_t \tag{4.26}$$

It is clear that if u_t obeys (4.24), then γu_t is uncorrelated with y_{t-1}, and thus *application of OLS to* (4.26) *will yield consistent estimators of its parameters.*

Since (4.26) represents an alternative form of the geometric distributed lag model it would appear that we have pulled a rabbit out of a hat. A little examination, however, will show where the rabbit came from.

To this effect, solve the difference equation in (4.26) to obtain

$$y_t = \frac{\alpha\gamma I}{I - \beta L} x_t + \frac{\gamma I}{I - \beta L} u_t , \quad \beta = 1 - \gamma \tag{4.27}$$

Hence, we see that the *partial adjustment* hypothesis produces a geometric distributed lag model, but one in which the error term *is subject*

to the same geometric distributed lag as the determining (explanatory)
variable! If we put

$$v_t = \frac{\gamma I}{I - \beta L} u_t \tag{4.28}$$

then after some manipulation we find

$$v_t = \beta v_{t-1} + \gamma u_t \tag{4.29}$$

But this is, of course, a first order autoregressive process with parameter β. As we remarked in Section 4.1, this is the only instance in
which the parameters of the geometric distributed lag model can be
consistently estimated by ordinary least squares.

Although it would appear that the *partial adjustment* hypothesis solves
the estimation problem, its rationale may be questioned, in that it entails
a situation in which a desired quantity is taken to be a random variable.
If so, it is not obvious that the decision maker would, should, or could
act in accordance with (4.25) unless his choice, y_t, is randomized. However, this difficulty is more apparent than real. Thus, consider the
alternative formulation:

$$y_t^* = \alpha x_t \tag{4.30}$$

so that the optimal quantity is now a nonstochastic variable; at least, it
is so conditionally on x. The adjustment process may be specified as
being linear up to a stochastic component. Thus,

$$y_t - y_{t-1} = \gamma[y_t^* - y_{t-1}] + \varepsilon_t, \quad \gamma \in (0, 1) \tag{4.31}$$

where the ε_t have the properties given in (4.24).

The reader may readily verify that (4.30) and (4.31) imply

$$y_t = \frac{\alpha \gamma I}{I - \beta L} x_t + \frac{I}{I - \beta L} \varepsilon_t \tag{4.32}$$

Since the variance of the error term is not specified numerically, the
model in (4.32) is not distinguishable from that in (4.27).

4.4 Autocorrelated Error Terms and Geometric Distributed Lags

The perceptive reader would have noticed from the preceding that there
is some important connection between the form of the geometric distributed lag model and the question of the presence or absence of serial
correlation in the relevant error terms. Indeed, in this section we shall

explore the connection between the ordinary regression model with auto-correlated errors and the geometric lag models generated by the hypotheses of the preceding sections.

Thus, consider the simple model:

$$y_t = \alpha x_t + u_t \qquad (4.33)$$

where x_t is independent of u_t. The latter obeys

$$u_t = \rho u_{t-1} + \varepsilon_t, \quad |\rho| < 1 \qquad (4.34)$$

and moreover,

$$E(\varepsilon_t) = 0, \quad E(\varepsilon_t \varepsilon_{t'}) = \delta_{tt'} \sigma^2 \qquad (4.35)$$

Using the lag operator L, we may rewrite (4.34) as

$$u_t = \frac{I}{I - \rho L} \varepsilon_t \qquad (4.36)$$

and substituting in (4.33), we find

$$y_t = \alpha x_t + \frac{I}{I - \rho L} \varepsilon_t \qquad (4.37)$$

Upon reducing the rational operator, however, we obtain

$$y_t = \rho y_{t-1} + \alpha x_t - \alpha \rho x_{t-1} + \varepsilon_t \qquad (4.38)$$

where the error terms of this relation obey the classical conditions as exhibited in (4.35).

Comparing (4.38) with the form of the geometric lag model resulting from the hypothesis of partial adjustment, we find an exceedingly close resemblance. Indeed, if in the latter optimal y is given by

$$y_t^* = \alpha_1 x_t + \alpha_2 x_{t-1} + u_t \qquad (4.39)$$

then the analog of (4.26) will be

$$y_t = \beta y_{t-1} + \alpha_1 \gamma x_t + \alpha_2 \gamma x_{t-1} + \gamma u_t, \quad \beta = 1 - \gamma \qquad (4.40)$$

The difference between (4.38) and (4.40) is that the latter contains three parameters, $\gamma, \alpha_1, \alpha_2$, while the former contains only two, α, ρ. Both are nonlinear models. Thus, the coefficients of the explanatory variables in (4.38) are subject to the restriction that the product of the coefficients of y_{t-1} and x_t equals the negative of the coefficient of x_{t-1}. No such restriction holds with respect to the parameters of (4.40).

We shall deal with the estimation problems in later sections. For the moment, our aim is merely to point out the statistical similarities and/or differences between these two models which have widely differing economic implications.

In this connection, we should remark that the geometric lag model as generated by the adaptive expectations hypothesis, when reduced, yields

$$y_t = \lambda y_{t-1} + \alpha x_t + u_t - \lambda u_{t-1} \qquad (4.41)$$

Since the error terms, u_t, are mutually uncorrelated, the composite error term in (4.41) will be serially correlated, and this feature sets it apart from the reduced autocorrelated errors model considered in this section. Of course, if we make highly artificial assumptions regarding the error terms of the latter model, we may well obtain coincidence. Thus, suppose that in the model (4.33) we assume that its error term obeys *not* (4.34) but rather,

$$u_t = \frac{I - \lambda L}{I - \rho L} \varepsilon_t \qquad (4.42)$$

Then, reducing the model in (4.33) yields

$$y_t = \rho y_{t-1} + \alpha x_t - \alpha \rho x_{t-1} + (\varepsilon_t - \lambda \varepsilon_{t-1}) \qquad (4.43)$$

and the error term of (4.43) exhibits the same probability structure as that in (4.41). However, (4.42) is a highly artificial specification and one not commonly encountered in econometric work.

4.5 The Dynamic Demand Model

It is well established in the theory of consumer behavior that the demand on the part of an individual for a given commodity is a function of all relative prices and the consumer's real income. If relative prices are suppressed or held constant, then the demand function may be expressed solely as a function of income. This is referred to as the individual's *Engel curve*. If the function is specified to be *linear*, and if the coefficient of income is common to all individuals, then by aggregation we obtain that the market (aggregate) demand for a given commodity is a function of aggregate income.

A slight modification of this yields the dynamic demand model employed extensively in the empirical work of Houthakker and Taylor [76], among others.

Precisely, the dynamic demand model may be formulated as follows: Let

$$y_t = \alpha_0 + \alpha_1 x_t + \alpha_2 s_t + u_t \qquad (4.44)$$

where y_t is the market demand for the commodity in question, x_t is aggregate income,[7] and u_t is the error term, with suitable properties to be specified later.

The variable s_t is meant to indicate a *habit persistence* phenomenon, viz., that one's consumption now is in part determined by one's exposure to the particular commodity or commodities in the past. One might interpret s_t as the "psychological stock" of the commodity "possessed" by the individual(s). Such a stock is added to by current consumption but is also depleted by habit dissipation as time passes. One formulates this by the condition

$$s_t - s_{t-1} = \beta_0 s_{t-1} + \beta_1 y_t \qquad (4.45)$$

so that the change in the stock is made up of the dissipation component $\beta_0 s_{t-1}$, which is proportional to the magnitude of the stock and the accretion component, which is proportional to current consumption. One would normally expect that $\beta_0 < 0$ and $\beta_1 = 1$. At any rate, the difference equation expresses the *unobservable quantity* s_t in terms of the *observable forcing function* y_t. For empirical implementation, (4.44) must be expressed solely in terms of observable quantities—excepting the error term. To this effect, substitute (4.44) in (4.45) and rearrange terms to obtain

$$s_t - \left(\frac{1 + \beta_0}{1 - \alpha_2 \beta_1} \right) s_{t-1} = \frac{\alpha_0 \beta_1}{1 - \alpha_2 \beta_1} + \frac{\alpha_1 \beta_1}{1 - \alpha_2 \beta_1} x_t + \frac{\beta_1}{1 - \alpha_2 \beta_1} u_t \qquad (4.46)$$

Let

$$\beta = \frac{1 + \beta_0}{1 - \alpha_2 \beta_1}, \quad \alpha_0^* = \frac{\alpha_0 \beta_1}{1 - \alpha_2 \beta_1},$$

$$\alpha_1^* = \frac{\alpha_1 \beta_1}{1 - \alpha_2 \beta_1}, \quad \bar{\alpha}_2^* = \frac{\beta_1}{1 - \alpha_2 \beta_1} \qquad (4.47)$$

and employ the lag operator L to obtain the solution of (4.46) as

$$s_t = \frac{\alpha_0^*}{1 - \beta} + \frac{\alpha_1^* I}{I - \beta L} x_t + \frac{\bar{\alpha}_2^* I}{I - \beta L} u_t \qquad (4.48)$$

---

[7] Occasionally in such formulations, one also includes a relative price variable, usually specified as the quotient of the price index for the commodity (or group of commodities) in question to the price index of all consumption commodities—the "implicit price deflator" of consumption in the accounting framework of the Department of Commerce. We need not be concerned with such details for the purposes of our discussion.

Substitute (4.48) in (4.44) and thus deduce

$$y_t = \frac{\alpha_0(1 - \beta) + \alpha_2\alpha_0^*}{1 - \beta}$$
$$+ \frac{(\alpha_1 + \alpha_1^*\alpha_2)I - \alpha_1\beta L}{I - \beta L} x_t + \frac{(1 + \alpha_2\bar{\alpha}_2^*)I - \beta L}{I - \beta L} u_t \qquad (4.49)$$

If we now reduce the model by applying to both sides the operator $I - \beta L$ and note the relations in (4.47), we find

$$y_t = -\frac{\alpha_0\beta_0}{1 - \beta_1\alpha_2} + \frac{\alpha_1}{1 - \beta_1\alpha_2} x_t$$
$$- \alpha_1\beta x_{t-1} + \beta y_{t-1} + \frac{1}{1 - \beta_1\alpha_2} u_t - \beta u_{t-1} \qquad (4.50)$$

The form (4.50) is, of course, the empirically relevant one, since the basic equations (4.44) and (4.45) contain the unobservable s_t and are thus empirically nonoperational. From (4.50), we note that the parameters β_1 and α_2 appear only in the form $\beta_1\alpha_2$, and thus there is no prospect of identifying them separately. This may perhaps be construed as adding to the desirability of specifying in (4.45) that $\beta_1 = 1$.

Whether or not this convention is made, the preceding discussion implies certain restrictions on the parameters of the model. First we must have

$$\beta_1\alpha_2 \neq 1 \qquad (4.51)$$

If not, then the difference equation in (4.46) reduces to

$$s_{t-1} = -\frac{\alpha_0\beta_1}{1 + \beta_0} - \frac{\alpha_1\beta_1}{1 + \beta_0} x_t - \frac{\beta_1}{1 + \beta_0} u_t \qquad (4.52)$$

Hence, upon substitution in (4.44), we find

$$y_t = \frac{\alpha_0\beta_0}{1 + \beta_0} + \alpha_1 x_t - \frac{\alpha_1}{1 - \beta_0} x_{t+1} - \frac{1}{1 + \beta_0} u_{t+1} + u_t \qquad (4.53)$$

which is clearly a nonrealizable relation, since the behavior of y_t depends on the future behavior of the determining variable at time $t + 1$.

If (4.51) is thus respected, then, as was also apparent from (4.46), we must have

$$|\beta| < 1 \qquad (4.54)$$

which implies

$$|1 + \beta_0| < |1 - \alpha_2\beta_1| \qquad (4.55)$$

While the intuitive content of (4.51) is somewhat ambiguous, the condition (4.55) has a very clear-cut interpretation. It simply states that the rate of dissipation of the psychological stock must not be less than the rate at which it is added to, through the stock's own feedback, i.e. its influence on the demand for the given commodity.

The differences and similarities of (4.50) to the form resulting through reduction of the adaptive expectations and autoregressive errors models are too obvious to require comment at this stage.

4.6 Estimation of the Autocorrelated Errors Model

As we have seen earlier, there exists a fairly close connection between the geometric lag model and the general linear model whose errors, u_t, are subject to the first order autoregressive scheme:

$$u_t = \rho u_{t-1} + \varepsilon_t \qquad (4.56)$$

In (4.56), we have

$$E(\varepsilon_t) = 0 \,, \quad \mathrm{Cov}(\varepsilon_t, \varepsilon_{t'}) = \delta_{tt'}\sigma^2 \,, \quad \text{all } t, t' \,, \quad |\rho| < 1 \qquad (4.57)$$

In dealing with the estimation problems induced by the geometric distributed lag, it will be pedagogically convenient if we begin with the autocorrelated errors model. To this effect, suppose

$$y_t = \sum_{i=0}^{k} \beta_i x_{ti} + u_t \qquad (4.58)$$

where the x_{ti}, $i = 1, 2, \ldots, k$, are explanatory variables uncorrelated or independent of u_t, and the latter is the error term obeying the conditions in (4.56) and (4.57). Finally, by convention,

$$x_{t0} = 1 \,, \quad \text{all } t \qquad (4.59)$$

so that x_{t0} is the fictitious variable *unity* corresponding to the constant term of the equation, β_0.

If we are to estimate efficiently the parameters of (4.58), we must determine the properties of the error term u_t. By virtue of the third condition in (4.57), the difference equation in (4.56) can be solved by use of the lag operator L to yield,

$$u_t = \frac{I}{I - \rho L}\, \varepsilon_t = \sum_{i=0}^{\infty} \rho^i \varepsilon_{t-i} \qquad (4.60)$$

We thus easily establish

$$E(u_t) = 0 \,, \quad \text{all } t \qquad (4.61)$$

Next, observe that

$$\text{Cov}(u_t, u_{t+\tau}) = E(u_t u_{t+\tau}) = E\left\{ \sum_{i=0}^{\infty} \sum_{j=0}^{\infty} \rho^{i+j} \varepsilon_{t-i} \varepsilon_{t+\tau-j} \right\} \tag{4.62}$$

But

$$E[\varepsilon_{t-i} \varepsilon_{t+\tau-j}] = \delta_{t-i, t+\tau-j} \sigma^2 \tag{4.63}$$

Thus, in (4.62), upon taking expectations, the contribution of all terms is null *except* for the case

$$t - i = t + \tau - j \tag{4.64}$$

which implies that the nonnull terms correspond to

$$j = \tau + i \tag{4.65}$$

Hence, if $\tau \geq 0$, we find that

$$\text{Cov}(u_t, u_{t+\tau}) = \sigma^2 \rho^\tau \sum_{i=0}^{\infty} \rho^{2i} = \frac{\sigma^2 \rho^\tau}{1 - \rho^2} \tag{4.66}$$

If $\tau < 0$, then since $j = 0, 1, 2, \ldots$ the condition (4.65) implies that the summation on i will have range $i = -\tau, -\tau + 1, -\tau + 2, \ldots$. Thus we have

$$\text{Cov}(u_t, u_{t+\tau}) = \sigma^2 \sum_{i=-\tau}^{\infty} \rho^{\tau+2i} \tag{4.67}$$

Putting in the summation above

$$r = i + \tau \tag{4.68}$$

we find that

$$\sigma^2 \sum_{i=-\tau}^{\infty} \rho^{\tau+2i} = \sigma^2 \sum_{r=0}^{\infty} \rho^{\tau+2(r-\tau)} = \frac{\sigma^2 \rho^{-\tau}}{1 - \rho^2} \tag{4.69}$$

Hence, we conclude that for *any* τ,

$$\text{Cov}(u_t, u_{t+\tau}) = \frac{\sigma^2 \rho^{|\tau|}}{1 - \rho^2} \tag{4.70}$$

The preceding discussion has established

LEMMA 4.1. Let

$$y_t = \sum_{i=0}^{k} \beta_i x_{ti} + u_t, \quad t = 1, 2, \ldots, T \tag{4.71}$$

be a sample of size T on the model as specified in (4.56), (4.57), (4.58) and in the pertinent discussion. If

$$u = (u_1, u_2, \ldots, u_T)' \tag{4.72}$$

then

$$E(u) = 0 , \quad \text{Cov}(u) = \frac{\sigma^2}{1 - \rho^2} \begin{bmatrix} 1 & \rho & \cdots & \rho^{T-1} \\ \rho & 1 & \rho & \rho^{T-2} \\ \rho^{T-1} & \cdots & & 1 \end{bmatrix} = \sigma^2 V \quad (4.73)$$

We also have

LEMMA 4.2. If V is as defined implicitly in (4.73), then

$$V^{-1} = \begin{bmatrix} 1 & -\rho & 0 & \cdots & & & 0 \\ -\rho & 1+\rho^2 & -\rho & \cdots & & & 0 \\ 0 & -\rho & 1+\rho^2 & -\rho & & \cdot & 0 \\ \vdots & & & & & & \vdots \\ \vdots & & & & -\rho & 1+\rho^2 & -\rho \\ 0 & \cdots & & & 0 & -\rho & 1 \end{bmatrix} \quad (4.74)$$

Proof. The reader may verify this directly by pre- and post-multiplication, thus obtaining

$$VV^{-1} = V^{-1}V = I \quad (4.75)$$

I being the identity matrix of order T.

COROLLARY 4.1. The determinant of V is $1/(1 - \rho^2)$.

Proof. We shall show that

$$|V^{-1}| = 1 - \rho^2 \quad (4.76)$$

which will establish the corollary. Now if in (4.74) we multiply the first row by ρ and add it to the second, the value of the determinant is unaltered. Thus we have

$$|V^{-1}| = \begin{vmatrix} 1 & -\rho & 0 & \cdots & & & & 0 \\ 0 & 1 & -\rho & \cdots & & & & 0 \\ 0 & -\rho & 1+\rho^2 & -\rho & & & & 0 \\ 0 & 0 & -\rho & 1+\rho^2 & -\rho & & & 0 \\ \vdots & & & \ddots & & & & \vdots \\ 0 & & & & -\rho & 1+\rho^2 & -\rho \\ 0 & \cdot & & & 0 & & -\rho & 1 \end{vmatrix} \quad (4.77)$$

If by V_T^{-1} we denote a T-order matrix of the form of V^{-1} in (4.74), then expanding the determinant in (4.77) by the elements of the first column, we conclude that

$$|V_T^{-1}| = |V_{T-1}^{-1}| \quad \text{for all } T \geq 4 \tag{4.78}$$

But evaluating $|V_3^{-1}|$, we conclude

$$|V_3^{-1}| = 1 - \rho^2 \quad \text{Q.E.D.} \tag{4.79}$$

We next ask: For what values of ρ is V^{-1} (and hence V) a positive definite matrix? This is a pertinent query, since $\sigma^2 V$ is a covariance matrix. The answer is provided by

LEMMA 4.3. V is positive definite for $|\rho| < 1$.

Proof. We shall show equivalently that V^{-1} is positive definite for $|\rho| < 1$. To this effect, let α be an arbitrary T-element (real) vector. Then

$$\alpha' V^{-1} \alpha = \alpha_1^2 (1 - \rho^2) + \sum_{i=2}^{T} (\alpha_i - \rho \alpha_{i-1})^2,$$

$$\alpha = (\alpha_1, \alpha_2, \ldots, \alpha_T)' \tag{4.80}$$

As the reader may easily verify, (4.80) is positive for arbitrary but non-null vector α if and only if $|\rho| < 1$.   Q.E.D.

A further useful result is provided by

LEMMA 4.4. The matrix V^{-1} may be decomposed as

$$V^{-1} = M' M \tag{4.81}$$

where

$$M = \begin{bmatrix} \sqrt{1 - \rho^2} & 0 & \cdot & \cdot & \cdot & \cdot & \cdot & 0 \\ -\rho & 1 & 0 & \cdot & \cdot & \cdot & 0 \\ 0 & -\rho & 1 & \cdot & \cdot & \cdot & 0 \\ \vdots & & & & & & \vdots \\ 0 & \cdot & \cdot & \cdot & \cdot & 0 & -\rho & 1 \end{bmatrix} \tag{4.82}$$

Proof. The reader may verify this directly by carrying out the indicated multiplication.

REMARK 4.1. The decomposition above is, of course, nonunique. Thus, if A is *any* orthogonal matrix, then

$$M^* = AM \tag{4.83}$$

will also decompose V^{-1}, since

$$M^{*\prime}M^{*} = M'A'AM = M'M = V^{-1} \qquad (4.84)$$

However, (4.81) represents *a* decomposition, and a very useful one, as we shall see below.

Now let

$$x_{\cdot i} = (x_{1i}, x_{2i}, \ldots, x_{Ti})', \quad X = (x_{\cdot 0}, x_{\cdot 1}, \ldots, x_{\cdot k})$$
$$\beta = (\beta_0, \beta_1, \ldots, \beta_k)' \qquad (4.85)$$

and write the sample compactly as

$$y = X\beta + u \qquad (4.86)$$

As is well known, the efficient estimator of β is obtained[8] by minimizing

$$S = (y - X\beta)'V^{-1}(y - X\beta) \qquad (4.87)$$

Using the decomposition in (4.81), we have

$$S = (y^* - X^*\beta)'(y^* - X^*\beta) \qquad (4.88)$$

where

$$y^* = My, \quad X^* = MX \qquad (4.89)$$

It is clear that if M were known, then the efficient estimator of β could be obtained as

$$\hat{\beta} = (X^{*\prime}X^*)^{-1}X^{*\prime}y^* = (X'V^{-1}X)^{-1}X'V^{-1}y \qquad (4.90)$$

This is, of course, the *Aitken* estimator of β, and it depends on ρ. For this reason, a more appropriate notation in (4.90) might be $\hat{\beta}(\rho)$.

Alternatively, if ρ is not known, then (4.90) represents *partial minimization* of S with respect to β. Substituting in (4.88), we have

$$S(\rho) = y^{*\prime}[I - X^*(X^{*\prime}X^*)^{-1}X^{*\prime}]y^* \qquad (4.91)$$

which is now to be minimized with respect to ρ. When this is done, we obtain simultaneously the least squares estimator for both ρ and β, the latter as given in (4.90). Unfortunately, however, the expression in (4.91) is highly nonlinear in ρ; this precludes a direct approach by obtaining the solution of $\partial S(\rho)/\partial\rho = 0$. On the other hand, we observe that $S(\rho)$ *is simply the sum of the squared residuals in the regression of y^* on X^*.* Thus, in view of the restrictions in the permissible range of ρ, the fol-

---

[8] Occasionally such estimators are called *minimum chi square estimators.*

lowing procedure suggests itself: Divide the interval $(-1, 1)$ by the points ρ_i, $i = 0, 1, 2, \ldots, n$. For each ρ_i, compute $S(\rho_i)$ from (4.91). This amounts to tracing the graph of that function by numerical methods. Select now the ρ corresponding to the (global) minimum of the function; let this be $\hat{\rho}$.

The estimation of the parameters is now immediately determined from (4.90) and (4.91) as $\hat{\beta}(\hat{\rho})$, $\hat{\rho}$, $\hat{\sigma}^2(\hat{\rho})$, where, of course,

$$\hat{\sigma}^2(\hat{\rho}) = \frac{S(\hat{\rho})}{T} \tag{4.92}$$

Perhaps the essence of this approach will be better understood if we place it in the context of maximum likelihood estimation. Thus, suppose that in addition to (4.57) we assume that the ε_t are jointly normal. This is easily shown to imply that the distribution of u in (4.72) is given by

$$u \sim N(0, \sigma^2 V) \tag{4.93}$$

The (log) likelihood function of the observations is given by[9]

$$L(\beta, \rho, \sigma^2; y, X) = -\frac{T}{2} \ln(2\pi) - \frac{1}{2} \ln|\sigma^2 V|$$
$$- \frac{1}{2\sigma^2} (y - X\beta)' V^{-1}(y - X\beta) \tag{4.94}$$

In view of Corollary 4.1 and Lemma 4.4, we can rewrite (4.94) as

$$L(\beta, \sigma^2, \rho; y, X) = -\frac{T}{2} \ln(2\pi) - \frac{T}{2} \ln \sigma^2 + \frac{1}{2} \ln(1 - \rho^2)$$
$$- \frac{1}{2\sigma^2} (y^* - X^*\beta)'(y^* - X^*\beta) \tag{4.95}$$

where

$$y^* = My, \quad X^* = MX \tag{4.96}$$

Now maximize (4.95) *partially* with respect to β and σ^2 to obtain the estimators,

$$\hat{\beta}(\rho) = (X^{*\prime} X^*)^{-1} X^{*\prime} y^* = (X' V^{-1} X)^{-1} X' V^{-1} y \tag{4.97}$$

$$\hat{\sigma}^2(\rho) = \frac{1}{T} [y^* - X^*\hat{\beta}(\rho)]' [y^* - X^*\hat{\beta}(\rho)] \tag{4.98}$$

---

[9] The notation $x \sim N(\mu, \Sigma)$ will always mean the following: The vector x has the multivariate normal distribution with mean vector μ and covariance matrix Σ.

Substitute in (4.95) to determine the *concentrated* likelihood function as

$$L^*(\rho; y, X) = -\frac{T}{2}\{\ln(2\pi) + 1\} + \frac{1}{2}\ln(1 - \rho^2) - \frac{T}{2}\ln\sigma^2(\rho)$$

$$= -\frac{T}{2}\{\ln(2\pi) + 1\} - \frac{T}{2}\ln\frac{\sigma^2(\rho)}{(1 - \rho^2)^{1/T}} \tag{4.99}$$

Thus, globally maximizing the (log) likelihood function is equivalent to *globally minimizing* $\sigma^2(\rho)/(1 - \rho^2)^{1/T}$. To determine this global minimum, we proceed exactly as before: Divide the admissible[10] range of ρ, $(-1, 1)$, by the points ρ_i, $i = 0, 1, 2, \ldots, n$. For each ρ_i evaluate the criterion $\hat\sigma^2(\rho_i)/(1 - \rho_i^2)^{1/T}$ and choose as the estimator of ρ, say $\hat\rho$, that value for which

$$\frac{\hat\sigma^2(\hat\rho)}{(1 - \hat\rho^2)^{1/T}} \leq \frac{\hat\sigma^2(\rho_i)}{(1 - \rho_i^2)^{1/T}}, \quad \text{all } i$$

The estimators for β and σ^2 are then determined from (4.97) and (4.98) as $\hat\beta(\hat\rho)$, $\hat\sigma^2(\hat\rho)$, respectively. It is interesting that the criterion here is slightly different from that considered earlier. Here we are not minimizing $\hat\sigma^2(\rho)$, but rather

$$\frac{\hat\sigma^2(\rho)}{(1 - \rho^2)^{1/T}}$$

Asymptotically, however, the two procedures are equivalent since for *any* $\rho \in (-1, 1)$,

$$\lim_{T\to\infty} (1 - \rho^2)^{1/T} = 1 \tag{4.100}$$

The reader should note that for any finite (small) sample, the minimum chi square and maximum likelihood estimates will differ numerically; however, their asymptotic properties are exactly the same. We shall rigorously establish below the properties of the second estimator.[11] Before we do so, it is necessary to establish certain rudimentary aspects of central limit theorems for *dependent* random variables.

4.7 A Central Limit Theorem for *m*-Dependent Random Variables

DEFINITION 4.1. Let $\{X_n: n = 1, 2, \ldots\}$ be a sequence of random variables such that *every subsequence* $\{X_{n_j}: j = 1, 2, \ldots\}$ consists of mutually independent random variables, where for some integer, $m > 0$, $n_j + m$

---

[10] Strictly speaking, we always operate with a compact (closed bounded) subset of $(-1, 1)$, say, $[-0.999, 0.999]$.

[11] The proof given in Dhrymes [27] is not sufficiently rigorous, although it is suggestive and gives the correct results. The proof, however, is in many ways deficient.

$< n_{j+1}$; then $\{X_n: n = 1, 2, \ldots\}$ is said to be a sequence of m-dependent random variables.

REMARK 4.2. The definition simply states that if we pick from $\{X_n: n = 1, 2, \ldots\}$ a subsequence whose members are at least m terms apart, then the resultant subsequence consists of mutually independent random variables.

EXAMPLE 4.1. Consider the simple model

$$y_t = \frac{\alpha I}{I - \lambda L} x_t + \varepsilon_t, \quad t = 1, 2, \ldots, T \tag{4.101}$$

where the $\{\varepsilon_t: t = 1, 2, \ldots, T\}$ form a sequence of mutually independent identically distributed random variables. Reduce the model to obtain

$$y_t = \lambda y_{t-1} + \alpha x_t + u_t, \quad u_t = \varepsilon_t - \lambda \varepsilon_{t-1}, \quad t = 2, \ldots, T \tag{4.102}$$

We observe that $\{u_t: t = 2, \ldots, T\}$ is not a sequence of mutually independent random variables.

On the other hand, consider the subsequence corresponding, say, to even subscripts $(u_2, u_4, u_6, \ldots, u_{T/2})$, assuming that T is even. It is easily verified that this subsequence consists of mutually independent random variables. Thus, the sequence $\{u_t: t = 2, 3, \ldots\}$ is a sequence of m-dependent variables with $m = 1$.

Obviously, the case $m = 0$ corresponds to a sequence of mutually independent random variables.

We shall now establish a central limit theorem for m-dependent variables, which will play an important role in the asymptotic distribution theory of various estimators to be considered below. Before we do so, however, we recall a basic central limit theorem due to Liapounov and an extension thereof due to Bernstein. Thus, we have

THEOREM 4.1 (LIAPOUNOV). Let $\{X_t: t = 1, 2, \ldots\}$ be a sequence of mutually independent random variables such that their first three absolute moments exist. Let

$$\rho_t^3 = E|X_t - E(X_t)|^3, \quad \rho^3 = \sum_{t=1}^{T} \rho_t^3 \tag{4.103}$$

$$\sigma_t^2 = E[X_t - E(X_t)]^2, \quad \sigma^2 = \sum_{t=1}^{T} \sigma_t^2 \tag{4.104}$$

If

$$\lim_{T \to \infty} \frac{\rho}{\sigma} = 0 \tag{4.105}$$

then the asymptotic distribution of $\sum_{t=1}^{T} [X_t - E(X_t)]/\sigma$ is $N(0, 1)$.

Proof. See Cramér [24, p. 215].

Its extension, due to Bernstein, shows that the central limit theorem above remains valid even if the sequence we consider consists of certain functions of *different subsequences* in a manner to be made clear below.

THEOREM 4.2 (BERNSTEIN). If, for each T, X_{T_i}: $i = 1, 2, \ldots, h(T)$ is a set of independent random variables having, for simplicity, mean zero, and if

$$\lim_{T \to \infty} h(T) = \infty , \quad \lim_{T \to \infty} h^{-3/2}(T)\rho_T^3 = 0$$

$$\lim_{T \to \infty} \frac{\sum\limits_{i=1}^{h(T)} E(X_{T_i})^2}{h(T)} = \sigma^2 > 0 \tag{4.106}$$

where

$$\rho_{T_i}^3 = E|X_{T_i}|^3 , \quad \rho_T^3 = \sum_{i=1}^{h} \rho_{T_i}^3 \tag{4.107}$$

then the asymptotic distribution of

$$\frac{\sum\limits_{i=1}^{h} X_{T_i}}{h^{1/2}}$$

is $N(0, \sigma^2)$.

Proof. See Bernstein [12].

With these results at our disposal, we may now prove a central limit theorem for dependent variables.

THEOREM 4.3 (HOEFFDING AND ROBBINS). Let $\{X_t: t = 1, 2, \ldots\}$ be a sequence of m-dependent variables having—for simplicity—mean zero, and obeying

$$E|X_t|^3 < K^3 , \quad \text{all } t \tag{4.108}$$

for some constant K.[12] Then the asymptotic distribution of

$$\frac{\sum\limits_{t=1}^{T} X_t}{T^{1/2}}$$

---

[12] The reader should recall that if the kth absolute moment exists, then so does the k'th, for $k' < k$. Thus, (4.108) implies that the X_t have finite second order moments.

is $N(0, \sigma^2)$, where

$$\sigma^2 = \lim_{n \to \infty} \frac{1}{n} \sum_{r=1}^{n} A_{i+r} \tag{4.109}$$

and

$$A_i = 2 \sum_{j=0}^{m-1} \text{Cov}[X_{i+j}, X_{i+m}] + \text{Var}[X_{i+m}] \tag{4.110}$$

it being assumed that the right member of (4.109) converges uniformly with respect to i.

Proof. Let ν be a constant, $0 < \nu < 1/4$, and let $k = [T^\nu]$, $h = [T/k]$; then we can always write[13]

$$T = hk + r, \quad 0 < r < k \tag{4.111}$$

The strategy of the proof is to break up the sum

$$S_T = \sum_{i=1}^{T} X_i \tag{4.112}$$

into two parts, say

$$S_T = S_T' + S_T'' \tag{4.113}$$

and to show that S_T'' is negligible relative to S_T'. Thus, S_T will behave essentially like S_T' the point of it all being that S_T' can be expressed as the sum of independent (sums of) random variables to which Theorem 4.2 will be applicable. To this effect, define

$$Y_i = \sum_{j=1}^{k-m} X_{(i-1)k+j}, \quad i = 1, 2, \ldots, h \tag{4.114}$$

$$Z_i = \sum_{j=1}^{m} X_{ik-m+j}, \quad i = 1, 2, \ldots, h-1$$

$$= \sum_{j=1}^{m+r} X_{hk-m+j}, \quad i = h \tag{4.115}$$

We then observe that

$$S_T = S_T' + S_T'', \quad S_T' = \sum_{i=1}^{h} Y_i, \quad S_T'' = \sum_{i=1}^{h} Z_i \tag{4.116}$$

We must now investigate the properties of these subsidiary sums. Observe

---

[13] The notation $[x]$ means the largest integer equal to or less than x; thus, $[6.15]$ is 6, $[5/12]$ is zero, and so on.

that in (4.114) we require $k > m$, which will obviously be so if T is large enough; when this is so, the Y_i are mutually independent. What can we say about their variance? We observe that for $s > m$, we have

$$E\left(\sum_{j=1}^{s} X_{i+j}\right)^2 = E\left(\sum_{j=1}^{s-1} X_{i+j}\right)^2 + 2\sum_{j=1}^{s-1} E(X_{i+j}X_{i+s}) + E(X_{i+s}^2)$$

$$= E\left(\sum_{j=1}^{s-1} X_{i+j}\right)^2 + A_{i+s-m} \qquad (4.117)$$

The second equality follows from the fact that X_i and X_{i+r} are *independent* for $r > m$.

Applying the same procedure to $E(\sum_{j=1}^{s-1} X_{i+j})^2$ repeatedly, we conclude

$$E\left(\sum_{j=1}^{s} X_{i+j}\right)^2 = E\left(\sum_{j=1}^{m} X_{i+j}\right)^2 + \sum_{r=1}^{s-m} A_{i+r} \qquad (4.118)$$

By virtue of the boundedness of the third (absolute) moment, we have

$$E|X_i|^3 = E\{|X_i|^2\}^{3/2} \geq \{E|X_i|^2\}^{3/2} \qquad (4.119)$$

the last inequality holding in view of the convexity of the function $x^{3/2}$ (see, for example, Dhrymes [32]). Thus, we obtain

$$E[X_i]^2 \leq \{E|X_i|^3\}^{2/3} \leq K^2 \qquad (4.120)$$

and further,

$$E|X_iX_j| \leq K^2 \qquad (4.121)$$

It follows, then, that

$$E\left(\sum_{j=1}^{m} X_{i+j}\right)^2 \leq m^2K^2 \qquad (4.122)$$

Hence, from (4.114), (4.118) and (4.122) we conclude

$$\left| E(Y_i^2) - \sum_{s=1}^{k-2m} A_{(i-1)k+s} \right| \leq m^2K^2 \qquad (4.123)$$

Since

$$\text{Var}(S_T') = \sum_{i=1}^{h} \text{Var}(Y_i^2) \qquad (4.124)$$

we need to establish a bound for this sum. Now

$$\left| \sum_{i=1}^{h} \left[E(Y_i^2) - \sum_{s=1}^{k-2m} A_{(i-1)k+s} \right] \right| \leq \sum_{i=1}^{h} \left| E(Y_i^2) - \sum_{s=1}^{k-2m} A_{(i-1)k+s} \right| \leq hm^2K^2$$

$$(4.125)$$

Multiplying both sides of the inequality by $1/hk$, we have

$$\left| \frac{1}{h} \sum_{i=1}^{h} E[k^{-1/2} Y_i]^2 - \frac{k-2m}{hk} \sum_{i=1}^{h} \frac{1}{k-2m} \sum_{s=1}^{k-2m} A_{(i-1)k+s} \right| \leq \frac{m^2 K^2}{k}$$

(4.126)

Noting that as $h \to \infty$, $k \to \infty$, the last member vanishes, and further that $hk/T \to 1$, we conclude that

$$\lim_{T \to \infty} \frac{\text{Var}(S_T')}{T} = \lim_{k \to \infty} \frac{1}{k-2m} \sum_{s=1}^{k-2m} A_{(i-1)k+s} = \sigma^2$$

(4.127)

which is by hypothesis positive—nonnegative if we do not wish to rule out degenerate distributions.

Next we consider the third absolute moment of the $Y_i/k^{1/2}$. Incidentally, the variables $Y_i/k^{1/2}$ are weighted sums of certain subsequences, as we remarked prior to the statement of Bernstein's theorem (Theorem 4.2). But

$$E|k^{-1/2} Y_i|^3 \leq k^{-3/2} \sum_{j'',j',j=1}^{k-m} E|X_{(i-1)k+j} X_{(i-1)k+j'} X_{(i-1)k+j''}|$$

$$\leq k^{-3/2} (k-m)^3 K^3$$

(4.128)

Thus, the quantities corresponding to $\rho_{T_i}^3$ of (4.107) are bounded; in fact, we have

$$E|k^{-1/2} Y_i|^3 = \rho_{k(T)i}^3 \leq k^{-3/2} (k-m)^3 K^3$$

$$\rho_T^3 = \sum_{i=1}^{h} \rho_{k(T)i}^3 \leq hk^{-3/2} (k-m)^3 K^3$$

(4.129)

Now

$$h^{-3/2} \rho_T^3 \leq h^{-1/2} k^{-3/2} (k-m)^3 K^3$$

(4.130)

What is the order of magnitude of the right member of (4.130)? In the beginning of the argument, we chose $k = [T^\nu]$, $h = [T/k]$, $0 < \nu < \frac{1}{4}$. Thus, $h^{-1/2} k^{-3/2} (k-m)^3$ is of the order of magnitude:

$$T^{-(1/2)(1-\nu)} T^{-(3/2)\nu} T^{3\nu} = T^{2\nu-1/2} = T^{-\alpha}$$

(4.131)

where

$$\alpha = \frac{1}{2} - 2\nu > 0$$

(4.132)

Thus,

$$\lim_{T \to \infty} h^{-3/2} \rho_T^3 = 0$$

(4.133)

and by Bernstein's theorem, asymptotically,

$$\frac{S'_T}{T^{1/2}} \sim N(0, \sigma^2) \tag{4.134}$$

Incidentally, notice that

$$\frac{S'_T}{T^{1/2}} = \left(\frac{hk}{T}\right)^{1/2} \frac{1}{h^{1/2}} \sum_{i=1}^{h} (k^{-1/2} Y_i) \tag{4.135}$$

and

$$\lim_{T \to \infty} \left(\frac{hk}{T}\right)^{1/2} = 1 \tag{4.136}$$

To complete the proof we need to show that the quantity $S''_T / T^{1/2}$ converges in probability to zero and thus may be neglected. Since $E(S''_T) = 0$, it will be sufficient to show that

$$\lim_{T \to \infty} E\left(\frac{S''^2_T}{T}\right) = 0 \tag{4.137}$$

Now,

$$S''_T = \sum_{i=1}^{h} Z_i \tag{4.138}$$

and by construction, the Z_i are mutually independent; thus,

$$\text{Var}(S''_T) = \sum_{i=1}^{h} \text{Var}(Z_i) \tag{4.139}$$

Now,

$$\text{Var}(Z_i) = E\left(\sum_{j=1}^{m} \sum_{j'=1}^{m} X_{ik-m+j'} X_{ik-m+j}\right), \quad i = 1, 2, \ldots, h - 1$$

$$= E\left(\sum_{j=1}^{m+r} \sum_{j'=1}^{m+r} X_{ih-m+j'} X_{ih-m+j}\right), \quad i = h \tag{4.140}$$

In view of (4.121), we thus conclude that

$$\text{Var}(Z_i) \leq m^2 K^2, \qquad i = 1, 2, \ldots, h - 1$$
$$\leq (m + r)^2 K^2, \quad i = h \tag{4.141}$$

Hence,

$$\text{Var}\left(\frac{S''_T}{T^{1/2}}\right) \leq \frac{h}{T} [m^2 + (m + r)^2] K^2 \tag{4.142}$$

and obviously,

$$\lim_{T \to \infty} \text{Var}\left(\frac{S''_T}{T^{1/2}}\right) = 0 \tag{4.143}$$

which thus completes the proof.

4.8 Asymptotic Distribution of the Maximum Likelihood (ML) Estimators in the Autoregressive Errors Model

Let us now return to the maximum likelihood estimators of Section 4.6 and investigate their asymptotic distribution. For this purpose, it will be convenient to introduce the notation,

$$\gamma = \begin{pmatrix} \sigma^2 \\ \rho \\ \beta \end{pmatrix} \qquad (4.144)$$

and observe that, in fact, our estimators are solutions of the equation

$$\frac{\partial L}{\partial \gamma} = 0 \qquad (4.145)$$

Now expand the likelihood function in (4.94) about the true parameter vector, γ_0, to obtain[14]

$$\frac{\partial L}{\partial \gamma} (\gamma_0) = -\frac{\partial^2 L}{\partial \gamma \partial \gamma} (\gamma_0)(\hat{\gamma} - \gamma_0) + \text{third order term} \qquad (4.146)$$

The notation $(\partial L/\partial \gamma)(\gamma_0)$ means the gradient of the likelihood function evaluated at the point γ_0. In what follows we shall write, for simplicity, $\partial L/\partial \gamma$ or $\partial^2 L/\partial \gamma \partial \gamma$, thus suppressing the argument γ_0, which is always to be understood unless we indicate otherwise.

Now observe that

$$\frac{\partial L}{\partial \sigma^2} = -\frac{1}{2} \frac{T}{\sigma^2} + \frac{1}{2\sigma^4} u' V^{-1} u \qquad (4.147)$$

$$\frac{\partial L}{\partial \rho} = -\frac{\rho}{1-\rho^2} + \frac{1}{\sigma^2} \left[\sum_{i=2}^{T} (u_i - \rho u_{i-1})u_{i-1} + \rho u_1^2 \right] \qquad (4.148)$$

$$\frac{\partial L}{\partial \beta} = \frac{1}{\sigma^2} X' V^{-1} u \qquad (4.149)$$

Since V^{-1} has the decomposition in (4.81), and since

$$Mu = \varepsilon \sim N(0, \sigma^2 I) \qquad (4.150)$$

---

[14] The third order term will be suppressed in the argument to follow, since it can easily be shown that it converges in probability to zero in the context of the present discussion.

we see that we can write

$$\frac{\partial L}{\partial \sigma^2} = -\frac{T}{2}\frac{1}{\sigma^2} + \frac{1}{2\sigma^4}\,\varepsilon'\varepsilon \tag{4.151}$$

$$\frac{\partial L}{\partial \beta} = \frac{1}{\sigma^2}\,X'M'\varepsilon \tag{4.152}$$

Now we also have

$$u_t = \sum_{\tau=0}^{\infty} \rho^\tau \varepsilon_{t-\tau} = \sum_{\tau=0}^{N-2} \rho^\tau \varepsilon_{t-\tau} + \rho^{N-1} \sum_{\tau=0}^{\infty} \rho^\tau \varepsilon_{t-N+1-\tau}$$

$$= u_t{}^N + \rho^{N-1}u_{t-N+1} \tag{4.153}$$

Since u_{t-N+1} has mean zero and variance $\sigma^2/(1-\rho^2)$, it follows that $\rho^{N-1}u_{t-N+1}$ can be made arbitrarily small in probability by choosing N large enough. This is so since, by Chebyshev's inequality, for any $\delta > 0$,

$$\Pr\{|\rho^{N-1}u_{t-N+1}| > \delta\} < \frac{\mathrm{Var}(\rho^{N-1}u_{t-N-1})}{\delta^2} = \frac{\rho^{2(N-1)}\sigma^2}{(1-\rho^2)\delta^2} \tag{4.154}$$

and it is clear that this probability can be made arbitrarily small by proper choice of N. Let a suitable N be chosen, and notice that

$$\frac{\partial L}{\partial \rho} = \rho\left[\frac{u_1^2}{\sigma^2} - \frac{1}{1-\rho^2}\right] + \sum_{i=2}^{T} \varepsilon_i u_{i-1}^N + \rho^{N-1}\sum_{i=2}^{T} \varepsilon_i u_{i-N} \tag{4.155}$$

Now we may write:

$$\frac{\partial L}{\partial \gamma} = \sum_{t=1}^{T} w_{\cdot t} + \begin{bmatrix} 0 \\ \rho^{N-1}\sum_{i=2}^{T}\varepsilon_i u_{i-N+1} \\ 0 \end{bmatrix} \tag{4.156}$$

where

$$w_{\cdot 1} = \frac{1}{\sigma^2}\begin{bmatrix} \frac{1}{2}\left\{\left(\frac{\varepsilon_1}{\sigma}\right)^2 - 1\right\} \\ \rho\sigma^2\left(\frac{u_1^2}{\sigma^2} - \frac{1}{1-\rho^2}\right) \\ z_{\cdot 1}\varepsilon_1 \end{bmatrix}, \quad w_{\cdot t} = \frac{1}{\sigma^2}\begin{bmatrix} \frac{1}{2}\left\{\left(\frac{\varepsilon_t}{\sigma}\right)^2 - 1\right\} \\ \varepsilon_t u_{t-1}^N \\ z_{\cdot t}\varepsilon_t \end{bmatrix} \tag{4.157}$$

$$t = 2, 3, \ldots, T$$

and $z_{\cdot t}$ is the tth column of $X'M'$.

It is clear that the asymptotic distribution of $\partial L/\partial \gamma$ is that of $\sum_{t=1}^{T} w_{\cdot t}$. Thus, the second term in the right member of (5.156) will be neglected.

What have we gained by this manipulation? Simply that the vectors $w_{\cdot t}$ are N-dependent. Neglecting $w_{\cdot 1}$, which is somewhat atypical, we see that, by construction, $w_{\cdot t}$ and $w_{\cdot t+N}$ are *independent*. The reader will observe that $w_{\cdot t}$ contains the random variables $\varepsilon_t, \varepsilon_{t-1}, \varepsilon_{t-2}, \ldots, \varepsilon_{t-N+1}$, while $w_{\cdot t+N}$ contains the variables $\varepsilon_{t+N}, \varepsilon_{t+N-1}, \ldots, \varepsilon_{t+1}$; since, by assumption, the ε's are mutually independent, the conclusion is obvious. We may neglect $w_{\cdot 1}$, since we shall be interested, for the moment, in the asymptotic distribution of $(1/T^{1/2}) \sum_{t=1}^{T} w_{\cdot t}$. This can be written as

$$\frac{1}{T^{1/2}} \sum_{t=1}^{T} w_{\cdot t} = \frac{w_{\cdot 1}}{T^{1/2}} + \frac{1}{T^{1/2}} \sum_{t=2}^{T} w_{\cdot t} \qquad (4.158)$$

and it is clear that

$$\underset{T \to \infty}{\text{plim}} \frac{w_{\cdot 1}}{T^{1/2}} = 0 \qquad (4.159)$$

This is so since $E(w_{\cdot 1}/T^{1/2}) = 0$,

$$\text{Cov}\left(\frac{w_{\cdot 1}}{T^{1/2}}\right) = \frac{1}{T} \frac{1}{\sigma^4} \begin{bmatrix} \dfrac{1}{2} & \dfrac{2\sigma^4}{1-\rho^2} & 0 \\[2ex] \dfrac{2\sigma^4}{1-\rho^2} & \dfrac{2\sigma^4}{(1-\rho^2)^2} & 0 \\[2ex] 0 & 0 & \sigma^2 z_{\cdot 1} z_{\cdot 1}' \end{bmatrix} \qquad (4.160)$$

and the elements of the matrix are finite (and fixed). Thus, as $T \to \infty$, the covariance matrix vanishes, and $w_{\cdot 1}/T^{1/2}$ converges in probability to the null vector. Regarding the explanatory variables of the model, we may impose certain boundedness conditions. Thus, for $C < 0$, suppose

$$|x_{tj}| < C, \quad \lim_{T \to \infty} \sum_{t=1}^{T} x_{tj}^2 = \infty$$

$$\lim_{T \to \infty} \frac{1}{T} \sum_{t=1}^{T} x_{tj}^2 = q_j > 0, \quad j = 1, 2, \ldots, k \qquad (4.161)$$

This will be adequate for most economic data; it will obviously *not* be adequate if the relation to be estimated contains a time trend. Subsequently the assumption in (4.161) will be relaxed so that the case of time trends will be covered as well.

Our problem now is equivalent to determining the asymptotic distribution of $(1/\sqrt{T})(\partial L/\partial \gamma)$. This is because

$$\frac{1}{\sqrt{T}} \frac{\partial L}{\partial \gamma} = -\frac{1}{T} \frac{\partial^2 L}{\partial \gamma \partial \gamma} \sqrt{T} (\hat{\gamma} - \gamma_0) \qquad (4.162)$$

and $\mathrm{plim}_{T \to \infty}(1/T)(\partial^2 L/\partial \gamma \partial \gamma)$ may be shown to exist as a well-defined matrix of constants.

We may further reduce the problem to a special case of Theorem 4.3 by considering the asymptotic distribution of $\alpha^{*\prime}$ $(\partial L/\partial \gamma)$, α^* being a $(k + 3)$ element vector of constants. The reader will recall, Dhrymes [32], that if $\{X_t : t = 1, 2, \ldots\}$ is a sequence of *vector* random variables, then it converges in distribution if the sequence of *scalar* random variables $\{\lambda' X_t : t = 1, 2, \ldots\}$ converges in distribution for every real (conformable) vector of constants λ. To this effect, define

$$\alpha^{*\prime} w_{\cdot t} = s_t, \quad t = 1, 2, \ldots \qquad (4.163)$$

where, of course,

$$\sigma^2 s_t = \frac{1}{2} \alpha_1 \left[\left(\frac{\varepsilon_t}{\sigma} \right)^2 - 1 \right] + \alpha_2 u_{t-1}^N \varepsilon_t + \alpha' z_{\cdot t} \varepsilon_t, \quad t = 2, 3, \ldots$$

$$= s_{t1} + s_{t2} + s_{t3} \qquad (4.164)$$

In order to invoke Theorem 4.3, we need to verify that the two conditions (4.108) and (4.109) hold in the present case. Consider (4.108) first. We have

$$\{E|\sigma^2 s_t|^3\}^{1/3} \leq \{E|s_{t1}|^3\}^{1/3} + \{E|s_{t2}|^3\}^{1/3} + \{E|s_{t3}|^3\}^{1/3} \qquad (4.165)$$

Now,

$$E|s_{t1}|^3 \leq |\alpha_1|^3 \frac{1}{8} E \left\{ \left| \frac{\varepsilon_t}{\sigma} \right|^6 + 3 \left(\frac{\varepsilon_t}{\sigma} \right)^4 + 3 \left(\frac{\varepsilon_t}{\sigma} \right)^2 + 1 \right\}$$

$$= \frac{28}{8} |\alpha_1|^3 \qquad (4.166)$$

$$E|s_{t2}|^3 = |\alpha_2|^3 E\{|u_{t-1}^N|^3 |\varepsilon_t|^3\}$$

$$\leq |\alpha_2|^3 \{E|u_{t-1}^N|^6\}^{1/2} \{E|\varepsilon_t|^6\}^{1/2}$$

$$\leq |\alpha_2|^3 \left[\frac{15\sigma^6}{(1-\rho^2)^3} \right]^{1/2} (15\sigma^6)^{1/2} = |\alpha_2|^3 \frac{15\sigma^6}{(1-\rho^2)^{3/2}} \qquad (4.167)$$

$$E|s_{t3}|^3 = |\alpha' z_{\cdot t}|^3 15\sigma^6 \qquad (4.168)$$

Thus,

$$\{E|\sigma^2 s_t|^2\}^{1/3} \leq \left(\frac{28}{8} \right)^{1/3} |\alpha_1| + |\alpha_2| \frac{(15)^{1/3}\sigma^2}{(1-\rho^2)^{1/2}}$$

$$+ |\alpha' z_{\cdot t}| (15)^{1/3}\sigma^2 \qquad (4.169)$$

Since the elements $x_{t,j}$ are uniformly bounded, we see that

$$E|s_t|^3 < K^3 \tag{4.170}$$

for some constant K, thus satisfying condition (4.108). We must next obtain an expression for the quantity A_i of (4.110) and verify that the condition (4.109) also holds. The expression analogous to A_i in the present case is

$$A_i = 2 \sum_{j=0}^{N-1} \mathrm{Cov}(s_{i+j}, s_{i+N}) + \mathrm{Var}(s_{i+N}) \tag{4.171}$$

We note that for any $t \neq 1$, we have

$$
\begin{aligned}
\mathrm{Var}(s_t) &= \frac{1}{\sigma^4} \left\{ \frac{1}{4} E\left[\left(\frac{\varepsilon_t}{\sigma}\right)^4 - 2\left(\frac{\varepsilon_t}{\sigma}\right)^2 + 1 \right] \right. \\
&\quad \left. + E[(u_{t-1}^N)^2 \varepsilon_t^2] + \alpha' z_{.t} z_{.t}' \alpha E(\varepsilon_t^2) \right\} \\
&= \frac{1}{\sigma^4} \left[\frac{3 - 2 + 1}{4} + \sigma^4 \sum_{\tau=0}^{N-2} \rho^{2\tau} + \alpha' z_{.t} z_{.t}' \alpha \sigma^2 \right] \tag{4.172}
\end{aligned}
$$

This is so since the cross moments $E(s_{t,i} s_{t,j})$ vanish for all $t, i \neq j$, $i, j = 1, 2, 3$.

Next, let us consider, for $j < N$,

$$
\begin{aligned}
\mathrm{Cov}(s_{t+j}, s_{t+N}) = E[&s_{t+j,1} s_{t+N,1} + s_{t+j,2} s_{t+N,1} \\
&+ s_{t+j,3} s_{t+N,1} + s_{t+j,1} s_{t+N,2} \\
&+ s_{t+j,2} s_{t+N,2} + s_{t+j,3} s_{t+N,2} \\
&+ s_{t+j,1} s_{t+N,3} + s_{t+j,2} s_{t+N,3} \\
&+ s_{t+j,3} s_{t+N,3}] \tag{4.173}
\end{aligned}
$$

It turns out that all these cross moments vanish. This is quite obvious by inspection, except perhaps for the case,

$$
\begin{aligned}
E(s_{t+j,2} s_{t+N,2}) &= E\left(\varepsilon_{t+j} \varepsilon_{t+N} \sum_{\tau=0}^{N-2} \rho^\tau \varepsilon_{t+j-1-\tau} \sum_{\tau'=0}^{N-2} \rho^{\tau'} \varepsilon_{t+N-1-\tau'} \right) \\
&= \sum_{\tau=0}^{N-2} \sum_{\tau'=0}^{N-2} \rho^{\tau+\tau'} E(\varepsilon_{t+j} \varepsilon_{t+j-1-\tau} \varepsilon_{t+N} \varepsilon_{t+N-1-\tau'}) \tag{4.174}
\end{aligned}
$$

For the expectation not to vanish, we must have either pairwise coincidence of subscripts or coincidence of all subscripts, since the ε's are mutually independent variables with mean zero. But notice that it is not possible to have pairwise coincidence of subscripts. Thus, e.g., suppose we have $t + j = t + N - 1 - \tau'$ and $t + j - 1 - \tau = t + N$. Since $j < N$, it is impossible for the second equality to hold, so that even if the first equality holds, the expectation of the term in the last member of (4.174) will vanish. Thus we conclude that

$$A_i = \frac{1}{\sigma^4} \left[\frac{1}{2} \alpha_1^2 + \alpha_2^2 \sigma^4 \sum_{\tau=0}^{N-2} \rho^{2\tau} + \alpha' z_{\cdot i+N} z'_{\cdot i+N} \alpha \sigma^2 \right] \qquad (4.175)$$

If we assume that

$$\lim_{T \to \infty} \frac{X' V^{-1} X}{T} = R \qquad (4.176)$$

exists as a well-defined nonsingular matrix then it is clear that

$$\lim_{n \to \infty} \frac{1}{n} \sum_{i=1}^{\infty} A_i = A \qquad (4.177)$$

exists as a positive quantity. Thus, the conditions of Theorem 4.3 are satisfied, and we conclude that $(1/\sqrt{T})(\alpha^{*\prime})(\partial L/\partial \gamma)$ is asymptotically

$$N\left(0, \frac{1}{\sigma^4} \left[\frac{1}{2} \alpha_1^2 + \alpha_2^2 \sigma^4 \sum_{\tau=0}^{N-2} \rho^{2\tau} + \alpha' \lim_{T \to \infty} \frac{X' V^{-1} X}{T} \alpha \sigma^2 \right]\right)$$

Since this holds for every real vector α^*, we conclude that asymptotically[15]

$$\frac{1}{\sqrt{T}} \frac{\partial L}{\partial \gamma} \sim N(0, \Omega) \qquad (4.178)$$

where

$$\Omega = \frac{1}{\sigma^4} \begin{bmatrix} \dfrac{1}{2} & 0 & 0 \\[2mm] 0 & \sigma^4 \displaystyle\sum_{\tau=0}^{N-2} \rho^{2\tau} & 0 \\[2mm] 0 & 0 & \sigma^2 \displaystyle\lim_{T \to \infty} \dfrac{X' V^{-1} X}{T} \end{bmatrix} \qquad (4.179)$$

Now, in order to determine the asymptotic distribution of $\sqrt{T}\,(\hat{\gamma} - \gamma_0)$, we need first determine $\operatorname{plim}_{T \to \infty}(1/T)\,(\partial^2 L/\partial \gamma \partial \gamma.)$ But

$$\frac{\partial^2 L}{\partial \sigma^2 \partial \sigma^2} = \frac{T}{2} \frac{1}{\sigma^4} - \frac{1}{\sigma^6} u' V^{-1} u$$

$$\frac{\partial^2 L}{\partial \sigma^2 \partial \rho} = \frac{1}{2\sigma^4} u' \frac{\partial V^{-1}}{\partial \rho} u \qquad (4.180)$$

---

[15] To this effect, see Dhrymes [32].

$$\frac{\partial^2 L}{\partial \sigma^2 \partial \beta} = -\frac{1}{\sigma^4} X' V^{-1} u$$

$$\frac{\partial^2 L}{\partial \rho \partial \rho} = -\frac{(1 - \rho^2) + 2\rho^2}{(1 - \rho^2)^2} - \frac{1}{\sigma^2} \sum_{i=2}^{T} u_{i-1}^2 + \frac{u_1^2}{\sigma^2}$$

$$\frac{\partial^2 L}{\partial \rho \partial \beta} = \frac{1}{\sigma^2} \frac{X' \partial V^{-1}}{\partial \rho} u \qquad (4.181)$$

$$\frac{\partial^2 L}{\partial \beta \partial \beta} = -\frac{1}{\sigma^2} X' V^{-1} X \qquad (4.182)$$

It is clear that

$$\underset{T \to \infty}{\text{plim}} \frac{1}{T} \frac{\partial^2 L}{\partial \sigma^2 \partial \sigma^2} = \frac{1}{2\sigma^4} - \frac{1}{\sigma^4} = -\frac{1}{2\sigma^4} \qquad (4.183)$$

$$\underset{T \to \infty}{\text{plim}} \frac{1}{T} \frac{\partial^2 L}{\partial \rho \partial \rho} = -\frac{1}{1 - \rho^2} \qquad (4.184)$$

$$\underset{T \to \infty}{\text{plim}} \frac{1}{T} \frac{\partial^2 L}{\partial \beta \partial \beta} = -\lim_{T \to \infty} \left[\sigma^2 \frac{X' V^{-1} X}{T} \right] \qquad (4.185)$$

while all cross derivatives have zero probability limit. Notice that, except for the approximation $1/(1 - \rho^2) \approx \sum_{\tau=0}^{N-2} \rho^{2\tau}$,

$$\underset{T \to \infty}{\text{plim}} \frac{1}{T} \frac{\partial^2 L}{\partial \gamma \partial \gamma} = -\Omega^{-1} \qquad (4.186)$$

and thus conclude that asymptotically,

$$\sqrt{T} (\hat{\gamma} - \gamma_0) \sim N(0, \Omega^{-1}) \qquad (4.187)$$

We have therefore proved the following:

THEOREM 4.4. Consider the model

$$y = X\beta + u \qquad (4.188)$$

where y is $T \times 1$, X is $T \times (k + 1)$, β is $(k + 1) \times 1$, and u is a random vector whose elements obey

$$u_t = \rho u_{t-1} + \varepsilon_t \quad |\rho| < 1, \quad t = 1, 2, \ldots, T \qquad (4.189)$$

and

$$\varepsilon \sim N(0, \sigma^2 I), \quad \varepsilon = (\varepsilon_1, \varepsilon_2, \ldots, \varepsilon_T)' \qquad (4.190)$$

Suppose further that the elements of X obey the conditions in (4.161) and that for all admissible ρ,

$$\lim_{T \to \infty} \frac{X' V^{-1} X}{T} = R \qquad (4.191)$$

exists as a (nonstochastic) nonsingular matrix,[16] where V is the covariance matrix of u/σ. Then the joint maximum likelihood estimator of the vector

$$\gamma = \begin{pmatrix} \sigma^2 \\ \rho \\ \beta \end{pmatrix} \tag{4.192}$$

say $\hat{\gamma}$, has the asymptotic distribution

$$\sqrt{T}(\hat{\gamma} - \gamma_0) \sim N(0, \Omega^{-1}) \tag{4.193}$$

where Ω is defined by (4.179) and γ_0 is the true parameter vector.

As we remarked earlier, the assumptions on the explanatory variables rule out time trends. The following development, however, will permit such to be among the explanatory variables. To this effect, replace the the boundedness assumptions of Equation (4.161) by

$$\lim_{T \to \infty} \sum_{t=1}^{T} x_{tj}^2 = \infty, \quad \lim_{T \to \infty} \frac{\max_{t \le T} x_{tj}^2}{d_{jT}^2} = 0$$

$$j = 0, 1, 2, \ldots, k \tag{4.194}$$

$$\lim_{T \to \infty} \frac{\sum_{t=\tau+1}^{T} x_{ti} x_{t-\tau,i}}{d_{jT} d_{iT}} = r_{ii}(\tau) \quad \tau = 0, 1$$

where

$$d_{jT}^2 = \sum_{t=1}^{T} x_{tj}^2 \tag{4.195}$$

Notice that the conditions in (4.194) are satisfied for any linear or polynomial time trend; in particular, the last condition asserts that the cross autocorrelations (in the limit) exist and are finite for all variables up to the first order. Now, we shall consider the asymptotic distribution of the sequence,

$$G_T \frac{\partial L}{\partial \gamma} = \sum_{t=1}^{T} G_T w_{\cdot t} \tag{4.196}$$

where

$$G_T = \begin{bmatrix} \dfrac{1}{\sqrt{T}} & 0 & 0 \\ 0 & \dfrac{1}{\sqrt{T}} & 0 \\ 0 & 0 & D_T^{-1} \end{bmatrix}, \quad D_T = \text{diag}(d_{0T}, d_{1T}, \ldots, d_{kT}) \tag{4.197}$$

---

[16] Incidentally, note that this is implied by the condition that $\lim_{T \to \infty}(X'X/T)$ exists as a positive definite matrix.

Except for $t = 1$, the constituent random vectors of the sum in (4.196) are of the form

$$w^*_{.t} = G_T w_{.t} = \frac{1}{\sigma^2} \begin{bmatrix} \frac{1}{\sqrt{T}} \frac{1}{2}\left[\left(\frac{\varepsilon_t}{\sigma}\right)^2 - 1\right] \\ \frac{1}{\sqrt{T}} \varepsilon_t u^N_{t-1} \\ D_T^{-1} z_{.t} \varepsilon_t \end{bmatrix} \quad (4.198)$$

and following the same line of attack as previously, we shall consider instead the scalar variables,

$$s^*_t = \frac{1}{\sigma^2}\left\{ \frac{1}{2}\frac{\alpha_1}{\sqrt{T}}\left[\left(\frac{\varepsilon_t}{\sigma}\right)^2 - 1\right] + \frac{\alpha_2}{\sqrt{T}} \varepsilon_t u^N_{t-1} + \alpha' D_T^{-1} z_{.t} \varepsilon_t \right\} \quad (4.199)$$

In order to apply Theorem 4.3, we need first to verify that the third absolute moment of s^*_t is uniformly bounded.

Employing the results of (4.165) through (4.169), we conclude that

$$\sigma^2\{E|s^*_t|^3\}^{1/3} \leqq \frac{|\alpha_1|}{\sqrt{T}}\left(\frac{28}{8}\right)^{1/3} + \frac{|\alpha_2|}{\sqrt{T}}(15)^{1/3}\frac{\sigma^2}{(1 - \rho^2)^{1/2}}$$

$$+ |\alpha' D_T^{-1} z_{.t}|(15)^{1/3}\sigma^2 \quad (4.200)$$

Since

$$|\alpha' D_T^{-1} z_{.t}| = \left| \sum_{i=0}^{k} \alpha_{3+i} \frac{z_{ti}}{d_{it}} \right| \leqq \sum_{i=0}^{k} |\alpha_{3+i}| \max_{t \leqq T} \frac{|z_{ti}|}{d_{iT}} \quad (4.201)$$

we see that

$$\lim_{T \to \infty} |\alpha' D_T^{-1} z_{.t}| = 0 \quad (4.202)$$

in virtue of the assumptions in (4.194). Incidentally, notice that for $i = 0, 1, 2, \ldots, k$,

$$z_{ti} = x_{ti} - \rho x_{t-1,i}, \quad t = 2, \ldots, T$$
$$= \sqrt{1 - \rho^2}\, x_{1i}, \quad t = 1 \quad (4.203)$$

Thus, the third absolute moment of s^*_t is certainly bounded. Next, we must verify that the analog of condition (4.109) also holds. In this case, we have

$$A_i = \text{Var}[s^*_{.i+N}]$$

$$= \frac{1}{\sigma^4}\left[\frac{\alpha_1^2}{4T} + \frac{\alpha_2^2}{T}\sigma^4 \sum_{\tau=0}^{N-2} \rho^{2\tau} + \sigma^2 \alpha' D_T^{-1} z_{.i+N} z'_{.t+N} D_T^{-1}\alpha\right] \quad (4.204)$$

and we need to show that the limit

$$\lim_{T \to \infty} \sum_{i=1}^{T-N} A_i = \frac{1}{\sigma^4} \left[\frac{1}{4} \alpha_1^2 \frac{T-N}{T} + \alpha_2^2 \sigma^4 \sum_{\tau=2}^{N-2} \rho^{2\tau} \left(\frac{T-N}{T} \right) \right.$$

$$\left. + \sigma^2 \alpha' D_T^{-1} \left(\sum_{i=1}^{T-N} z_{\cdot i+N} z'_{\cdot i+N} \right) D_T^{-1} \alpha \right] \qquad (4.205)$$

exists. It is clear that the limit of the first two terms in the bracketed expression is well defined; we need only establish the same with respect to the third term. To this effect, let

$$d_{T-N,i}^2 = \sum_{t=N+1}^{T} x_{ti}^2 \qquad (4.206)$$

and observe that since

$$d_{Ti}^2 = \sum_{\tau=1}^{N} x_{ti}^2 + d_{T-N,i}^2 \qquad (4.207)$$

then in virtue of the assumptions in (4.194), we have

$$\lim_{T \to \infty} \frac{d_{T-N,i}^2}{d_{Ti}^2} = 1 \qquad (4.208)$$

Now, write

$$D_T^{-1} \left[\sum_{\tau=1}^{T-N} z_{\cdot i+N} z'_{\cdot i+N} \right] D_T^{-1}$$

$$= D_T^{-1} D_{T-N} \left[D_{T-N}^{-1} \left(\sum_{i=1}^{T-N} z_{\cdot i+N} z'_{\cdot i+N} \right) D_{T-N}^{-1} \right] D_{T-N} D_T^{-1} \qquad (4.209)$$

where

$$D_{T-N} = \text{diag}(d_{T-N,0}, d_{T-N,1}, \ldots, d_{T-N,k}) \qquad (4.210)$$

If we denote

$$R^* = \lim_{T \to \infty} D_T^{-1} X' V^{-1} X D_T^{-1} \qquad (4.211)$$

then the preceding discussion implies,

$$\lim_{T \to \infty} \text{Var} \left[\sum_{t=1}^{T} s_t^* \right]$$

$$= \frac{1}{\sigma^4} \left[\frac{1}{2} \alpha_1^2 + \alpha_2^2 \sigma^4 \sum_{\tau=0}^{N-2} \rho^{2\tau} + \sigma^2 \alpha' R^* \alpha \right] = A^* \qquad (4.212)$$

which leads to the conclusion that, asymptotically,

$$\sum_{t=1}^{T} s_t^* \sim N(0, A^*) \qquad (4.213)$$

Since this result holds for every real vector α^*, we further conclude that, asymptotically,

$$G_T \frac{\partial L}{\partial \gamma} \sim N(0, \Omega^*) \qquad (4.214)$$

where

$$\Omega^* = \frac{1}{\sigma^4} \begin{bmatrix} \frac{1}{2} & 0 & 0 \\ 0 & \sigma^4 \sum_{\tau=0}^{N-1} \rho^{2\tau} & 0 \\ 0 & 0 & \sigma^2 R^* \end{bmatrix} \qquad (4.215)$$

To establish now the asymptotic distribution of

$$\begin{bmatrix} \sqrt{T} & 0 & 0 \\ 0 & \sqrt{T} & 0 \\ 0 & 0 & D_T \end{bmatrix} (\hat{\gamma} - \gamma_0)$$

we note that the argument leading to (4.186) implies that

$$\plim_{T \to \infty} \begin{bmatrix} \frac{1}{\sqrt{T}} & 0 & 0 \\ 0 & \frac{1}{\sqrt{T}} & 0 \\ 0 & 0 & D_T^{-1} \end{bmatrix} \frac{\partial^2 L}{\partial \gamma \partial \gamma} \begin{bmatrix} \frac{1}{\sqrt{T}} & 0 & 0 \\ 0 & \frac{1}{\sqrt{T}} & 0 \\ 0 & 0 & D_T^{-1} \end{bmatrix}$$

$$= -\frac{1}{\sigma^4} \begin{bmatrix} \frac{1}{2} & 0 & 0 \\ 0 & \frac{\sigma^4}{1 - \rho^2} & 0 \\ 0 & 0 & \sigma^2 R^* \end{bmatrix} \qquad (4.216)$$

It follows, therefore, that, asymptotically,

$$\begin{bmatrix} \sqrt{T} & 0 & 0 \\ 0 & \sqrt{T} & 0 \\ 0 & 0 & D_T \end{bmatrix} (\hat{\gamma} - \gamma_0) \sim N(0, \Omega^{*-1}) \qquad (4.217)$$

where Ω^* was defined in (4.215).

Actually, there is a slight discrepancy between the second diagonal element of the last member of (4.216) and the corresponding element of Ω^*, but this can be made arbitrarily small by taking N large enough. It will be simpler to use the former. We have therefore proved the following:

THEOREM 4.5. Let the conditions of Theorem 4.4 hold but replace the assumptions on the explanatory variables by those in (4.194) and (4.195). Let $\hat{\gamma}$ be the joint maximum likelihood estimator of the parameters as derived in Section 5.6. Then, asymptotically,

$$\begin{bmatrix} \sqrt{T} & 0 & 0 \\ 0 & \sqrt{T} & 0 \\ 0 & 0 & D_T \end{bmatrix} (\hat{\gamma} - \gamma_0) \sim N(0, \Omega^{*-1}) \qquad (4.218)$$

REMARK 4.3. In the case of bounded explanatory variables we have established that the marginal asymptotic distribution of the maximum likelihood estimator, $\hat{\beta}$, is

$$\sqrt{T}(\hat{\beta} - \beta) \sim N(0, \sigma^2 R^{-1}) \qquad (4.219)$$

while in the case where the conditions (4.194) hold, we have established that, asymptotically,

$$D_T(\hat{\beta} - \beta) \sim N(0, \sigma^2 R^{*-1}) \qquad (4.220)$$

where, of course,

$$R = \lim_{T \to \infty} \left[\frac{X' V^{-1} X}{T} \right], \quad R^* = \lim_{T \to \infty} [D_T^{-1} X' V^{-1} X D_T^{-1}] \qquad (4.221)$$

and both limits are asserted to exist as (nonstochastic) nonsingular matrices. Notice that this is similar to the result obtained when the parameter ρ *is known*; when this is so, then in the context of the stochastic specifications of Theorem 4.4 the distribution of the maximum likelihood estimator of β, say $\tilde{\beta}$, for *every sample* size is

$$\tilde{\beta} \sim N[\beta, \sigma^2 (X' V^{-1} X)^{-1}] \qquad (4.222)$$

Thus, the penalty we pay for not knowing ρ—and using instead its maximum likelihood estimator in constructing the estimators for the coefficient vector β—is that the distribution result above can be established *only* asymptotically. Asymptotically, however, it makes no difference from the point of view of the properties of the estimator of β, whether ρ is known or estimated concurrently. The reader should bear in mind that this is not a general result. In subsequent discussion, we shall show that this is not so, e.g. when there are lagged dependent amongst the explanatory variables.

REMARK 4.4. It is possible to generalize the results of the preceding two theorems by relaxing the normality assumption for the error terms of the system.

Let us see exactly what this entails. The assumptions on the exogenous variables are still valid, except that now we only assert, in (4.189), that the sequence $\{\varepsilon_t : t = 0, \pm 1, \pm 2, \ldots\}$ is one of mutually independent identically distributed (*i.i.d.*) random variables. As the argument unfolds, we shall see what further conditions are required of this sequence in order for the conclusions of the theorems to hold.

The estimator whose asymptotic properties we shall now investigate is that given in Equations (4.87) through (4.92).

We observe that this estimator, say $(\tilde{\beta}', \tilde{\rho})$, obeys

$$\frac{\partial S}{\partial \beta} = 0$$

$$\frac{\partial S}{\partial \rho} = 0 \tag{4.223}$$

Letting $\delta = (\beta', \rho)'$, we see that if we expand $\partial S/\partial \delta$ by Taylor's series about δ_0—the true parameter vector—we have

$$\frac{\partial S}{\partial \delta}(\tilde{\delta}) = \frac{\partial S}{\partial \delta}(\delta_0) + \frac{\partial^2 S}{\partial \delta \partial \delta}(\delta_0)(\tilde{\delta} - \delta_0) + \text{third order terms} \tag{4.224}$$

$\tilde{\delta}$ being the estimator under consideration.

As before, the third order term may be shown to vanish in probability. Thus, our problem is reduced to that of finding the conditions under which $(1/\sqrt{T})(\partial S/\partial \delta)(\delta_0)$ has an asymptotic distribution. But we observe that

$$\frac{\partial S}{\partial \delta} = -2 \begin{pmatrix} X'V^{-1}u \\ \rho u_1^2 + \sum_{t=2}^{T} (u_t - \rho u_{t-1})u_{t-1} \end{pmatrix} \tag{4.225}$$

If we make use of the decomposition $V^{-1} = M'M$, as in (4.81), we see that we can write

$$\frac{\partial S}{\partial \delta} = -2 \begin{pmatrix} \sqrt{1 - \rho^2}\, x_{\cdot 1}^* u_1 \\ \rho u_1^2 \end{pmatrix} - 2 \sum_{t=2}^{T} \begin{pmatrix} x_{\cdot t}^* \\ u_{t-1} \end{pmatrix} \varepsilon_t \tag{4.226}$$

where $x_{\cdot t}^*$ is the tth column of $X'M'$. If the u_t have bounded *fourth absolute moment*, then clearly,

$$\plim_{T \to \infty} \frac{1}{\sqrt{T}} \left(\frac{\sqrt{1 - \rho^2} \; x_{\cdot1}^* u_1}{\rho u_1^2} \right) = 0 \qquad (4.227)$$

so that the first term may be neglected.

Writing

$$u_t = \sum_{i=0}^{\infty} \rho^i \varepsilon_{t-i}$$

$$= \sum_{i=0}^{N-2} \rho^i \varepsilon_{t-1} + \rho^{N-1} \sum_{i=0}^{\infty} \rho^\tau \varepsilon_{t-N+1-\tau} = u_t^N + \rho^{N-1} u_{t-N+1} \qquad (4.228)$$

we see that if the u_t have finite variance, the truncation argument made with respect to Equation (4.153) is still valid. But if the ε_t have finite variance, so do the u_t. Thus, (4.226) can be simplified further to

$$\frac{\partial S}{\partial \delta} = -2 \left(\frac{\sqrt{1 - \rho^2} \; x_{\cdot1}^* u_1}{\rho u_1^2} \right) - 2\rho^{N-1} \sum_{t=2}^{T} \binom{0}{u_{t-N+1}} \varepsilon_t - 2 \sum_{t=2}^{T} \binom{x_{\cdot t}^*}{u_{t-1}^N} \varepsilon_t$$

$$(4.226)$$

The asymptotic distribution of $(1/\sqrt{T})(\partial S/\partial \delta)$ is thus determined solely by the last term. This is exactly the subvector of $w_{\cdot t}$ in (4.157), obtained by deleting its first element.

The argument as presented earlier in this section requires the boundedness of the sixth absolute moment of u_{t-1}^N; but if the sixth absolute moment of the ε sequence is bounded, the condition is satisfied, so that Theorems 4.2 and 4.3 may be applied to the last term in (4.229). Thus, the asymptotic distribution of this estimator is exactly that given in Theorems 4.4 or 4.5 depending on the assumptions we make on the explanatory variables $\{x_{ti}: i = 0, 1, \ldots, k; t = 1, 2 \ldots\}$. Consequently, dropping the normality assumption on the ε process requires that we assume *finiteness of the sixth absolute moment*. Of course, this is necessitated only by the step involved in (4.167). It is conceivable that a different approach would place less stringent requirements on the ε process.

REMARK 4.5. It is natural to ask whether the estimators derived above are efficient in some sense. To answer this, we confine ourselves to the parameter β and recall Remark 4.3. Now if ρ were known, then the estimator

$$\tilde{\beta} = (X' V^{-1} X)^{-1} X' V^{-1} y \qquad (4.230)$$

is best linear unbiased, where in V^{-1} we have inserted the "true" value of ρ. Since the asymptotic distribution of $\tilde{\beta}$ in (4.230) is exactly that of the $\hat{\beta}$ in (4.219), the latter is asymptotically efficient in the same sense that $\tilde{\beta}$ of (4.230) is.

REMARK 4.6. In the discussion leading to Theorem 4.4, it was implicitly assumed that the estimator $\hat{\gamma}$ is consistent. Observing that

$$\hat{\beta} = (X'\hat{V}^{-1}X)^{-1}X'\hat{V}^{-1}y \tag{4.231}$$

we see that consistency of $\hat{\rho}$ implies the consistency of β. The consistency of $\hat{\rho}$ was proved by a rather cumbersome argument in Hildreth and Lu [72].

An alternative approach to this estimate is given by Cochrane and Orcutt [21]. Their procedure is as follows: Estimate β by OLS and compute the residuals

$$\tilde{u} = y - X\tilde{\beta} \tag{4.232}$$

From the $\tilde{u}_t$, estimate ρ as

$$\tilde{\rho}^{(0)} = \frac{\sum_{t=2}^{T} \tilde{u}_t \tilde{u}_{t-1}}{\sum_{t=2}^{T} \tilde{u}_{t-1}^2} \tag{4.233}$$

Subject the data to the transformation $y_t - \tilde{\rho}^{(0)}y_{t-1}$, $x_{ti} - \tilde{\rho}^{(0)}x_{t-1i}$ and estimate β again. Compute the residuals and reestimate ρ. Continue until convergence is obtained.

The convergence properties of this procedure were investigated by Sargan [132].

In what follows we shall give an alternative proof of consistency and further justify the truncation in (4.146). We shall actually prove that the assumptions made in connection with the model under consideration support the conclusion that the search estimator $\hat{\rho}_T$, converges to ρ_0 *with probability one*. For an explanation of this term see Dhrymes [32, ch. 3]. Convergence with probability one implies convergence in probability. We say that a sequence $\{\xi_n\}$ converges to ξ with probability one if

$$\Pr\{\lim_{n \to \infty} \xi_n = \xi\} = 1$$

Thus, sequences of random variables which converge (to a constant) with probability one may be treated as ordinary sequences of real numbers.

Returning now to the problem under consideration, we recall that the estimator $\hat{\rho}_T$ is determined by the condition

$$L_T(\hat{\rho}_T; y, X) \geq L_T(\rho; y, X) \tag{4.235}$$

for all admissible ρ. We shall assume that this is the set $[-1 + \delta_1, 1 - \delta_1]$, where $\delta_1 > 0$, but small. As observed in footnote 10, in practice we would be searching, say, over the set $[-0.999, 0.999]$ so that the restrictive implications of the assertion that ρ lies in a closed subset of $(-1, 1)$ are inconsequential.

In the above we define $L_T(\rho; y, X)$ by

$$L_T(\rho; y, X) = -\frac{1}{2}[\ln(2\pi) + 1] + \frac{1}{2T}\ln(1 - \rho^2) - \frac{1}{2}\ln S_T(\rho; y; X)$$

$$(4.236)$$

$$S_T(\rho; y, x) = \tilde{\sigma}^2(\rho) = \frac{1}{T}y'Ay$$

$$A = V^{-1} - V^{-1}X(X'V^{-1}X)^{-1}X'V^{-1} \qquad (4.237)$$

It will suffice to show that the estimator defined by

$$S_T(\hat{\rho}_T; y, X) \leq S_T(\rho; y, X) \quad \text{for all} \quad \rho \in [-1 + \delta_1, 1 - \delta_1] \quad (4.238)$$

converges to ρ_0 with probability one.

We first observe that for any admissible ρ we have

$$S_T(\rho; y, X) = \frac{1}{T}u'[V^{-1} - V^-X(X'V^{-11}X)^{-1}X'V^{-1}]u \qquad (4.239)$$

The plan of the argument is as follows: we shall show that $S_T(\rho; y, X)$ converges to its limit, say $S(\rho)$, with probability one uniformly in ρ.

We shall then argue that the sequence of estimators defined by (4.238) has a subsequence converging to, say, ρ_*. We shall then show that $\rho_* = \rho_0$, thus completing the proof.

Now to show convergence with probability one uniformly in ρ, it will be sufficient, in the context of (4.239), to show that $(1/T)(X'V^{-1}X)$, $(1/T)(u'V^{-1}X)$, $(1/T)(u'V^{-1}u)$, converge to their limits uniformly in ρ and, where the occasion requires it, with probability one.

But, if $x_{t.}$ is the tth row of X we have

$$\frac{1}{T}X'V^{-1}X$$

$$= \frac{1}{T}\left[\sum_{t=1}^{T}x'_{t.}x_{t.} - \rho\sum_{t=2}^{T}x'_{t-1.}x_{t.} - \rho\sum_{t=2}^{T}x'_{t.}x_{t-1.} + \rho^2\sum_{t=2}^{T-1}x'_{t.}x_{t.}\right] \quad (4.240)$$

and the uniform convergence (in ρ) of the limit above is assured by the fact that

$$\lim_{T\to\infty}\frac{1}{T}X'X, \qquad \lim_{T\to\infty}\frac{X'_{-1}X}{T}$$

are well-defined matrices with finite elements.

Next we observe that

$$\frac{1}{T} u' V^{-1} X$$

$$= \frac{1}{T} \left[\sum_{t=1}^{T} u_t x_t. - \rho \sum_{t=2}^{T} u_{t-1} x_t. - \rho \sum_{t=2}^{T} u_t x_{t-1}. + \rho^2 \sum_{t=2}^{T} u_t x_t. \right] \quad (4.241)$$

and moreover that x_t. is a $(k + 1)$ element vector of bounded non-stochastic explanatory variables. Let K be a constant such that $|x_{ti}| < K$, all t, i.

It will suffice to show, in (4.241), that the ith element of the (row) vector $(1/T)(\sum_{t=1}^{T} u_t x_t.)$ converges to zero with probability one. A similar argument will show convergence to zero with probability one for the other three terms as well. Uniformity (in ρ) is obvious from the representation in the right member. We, thus, consider the ith element of the vector,

$$\frac{1}{T} \sum_{t=1}^{T} u_t x_{ti} = \frac{u_0}{T} \left(\sum_{t=1}^{T} \rho_0^t x_{ti} \right) + \frac{1}{T} \sum_{t=1}^{T} \left(\sum_{j=0}^{t-1} \rho_0^j \varepsilon_{t-j} \right) x_{ti} \quad (4.242)$$

In the above we have used the relation

$$u_t = \rho_0^t u_0 + \sum_{j=0}^{t-1} \rho_0^j \varepsilon_{t-j}$$

and employed the symbol ρ_0 to stress the fact that the u-process is defined in terms of the true parameter. In (4.241) the quantity $(1/T)$ $(u' V^{-1} X)$ is viewed as a function of ρ—which enters only through V^{-1}—and our objective is to show that it converges to zero *uniformly in* ρ.

The first term in the right member of (4.242) obeys

$$\left| \frac{u_0}{T} \sum_{t=1}^{T} \rho_0^t x_{ti} \right| \leq \left| \frac{u_0}{T} \right| \frac{K}{\delta_1}$$

and, since u_0 is a finite-valued random variable, quite obviously u_0/T converges to zero with probability one. The second term may be written as

$$\frac{1}{T} \sum_{t=1}^{T} \left(\sum_{j=0}^{t-1} \rho_0^j \varepsilon_{t-j} \right) x_{ti} = \sum_{j=0}^{T-1} \rho_0^j W_{T,j} \quad (4.243)$$

where

$$W_{T,j} = \frac{1}{T} \sum_{t=j+1}^{T} x_{ti} \varepsilon_{t-j}.$$

Since

$$\left| \sum_{j=0}^{T-1} \rho_0{}^j W_{T,j} \right| \leq \sum_j |\rho_0|^j \sup_j | W_{T,j} | < \frac{1}{\delta_1} \sup_j | W_{T,j} |$$

we shall accomplish our objective if we show that

$$\sup_j | W_{T,i} | \to 0$$

with probability one. In fact, this will prove more than we need since it will also show that convergence to zero is *uniform* in ρ_0.

In Remark 4.4 we noted that dropping the normality assumption on the ε-process required us to assert that its sixth moment was bounded. It is interesting that this will suffice in the present context as well. To show that $\sup_j | W_{T,j} |$ converges to zero with T it will be sufficient to show that[17]

$$\sum_{T=1}^{\infty} \sum_{j=0}^{T-1} E(W_{T,j}^6) < \infty \qquad (4.244)$$

But

$$E(W_{T,j}^6) < K_1 \frac{(T-j)^3}{T^6}$$

where K_1 is a constant not depending on x_{ti}, j, ρ_0, or T. Thus

$$\sum_{T=1}^{\infty} \sum_{j=0}^{T-1} E(W_{T,j}^6) < K_1 \sum_{T=1}^{\infty} \frac{1}{T^2} < \infty$$

and consequently we are able to establish that

$$\frac{1}{T} u'V^{-1}X \to 0$$

with probability one uniformly in ρ.

Finally, we must show that

$$\frac{1}{T} u'V^{-1}u$$

converges to its limit with probability one uniformly in ρ. We note that

$$\frac{1}{T} u'V^{-1}u = \frac{1}{T} \left[\sum_{t=1}^{T} u_t^2 - 2\rho \sum_{t=2}^{T} u_t u_{t-1} + \rho^2 \sum_{t=2}^{T-1} u_t^2 \right]$$

---

[17] A discussion of material that bears on the argument employed below may be found in [16, p. 41] in connection with the Borel-Cantelli lemma.

and that it is sufficient to show that $(1/T)(\sum u_t^2)$, $(1/T)(\sum u_t u_{t-1})$ converge to their limits with probability one. But $\{u_t: t = 0, \pm 1, \pm 2, \ldots\}$ is a strictly stationary process[18] and thus so are $\{u_t^2\}$ and $\{u_t u_{t-1}\}$. Moreover

$$E(u_0^2) = \frac{\sigma_0^2}{1 - \rho_0^2} < \infty, \qquad E|u_0 u_{-1}| < \infty \qquad (4.245)$$

Consequently, from Corollary 2 [47, p. 129], $(1/T)(\sum u_t^2)$, $(1/T)(\sum u_t u_{t-1})$ converge to their respective limits, say ζ_0, ζ_1, with probability one. Convergence with probability one, however, implies convergence in probability. Since

$$\operatorname*{plim}_{T \to \infty} \frac{1}{T} \sum_{t=1}^{T} u_t^2 = \frac{\sigma_0^2}{1 - \rho_0^2}, \qquad \operatorname*{plim}_{T \to \infty} \frac{1}{T} \sum_{t=2}^{T} u_t u_{t-1} = \frac{\sigma_0^2 \rho_0}{1 - \rho_0^2}$$

we have identified these limits and we thus conclude that with probability one uniformly in ρ

$$\frac{1}{T} u' V^{-1} u \to \sigma_0^2 + \frac{\sigma_0^2 (\rho - \rho_0)^2}{1 - \rho^2}$$

The preceding discussion has shown that $S_T(\rho; y, x)$ converges to its limit, say $S(\rho)$, with probability one uniformly in ρ and moreover

$$S(\rho) = \sigma_0^2 + \frac{\sigma_0^2 (\rho - \rho_0)^2}{1 - \rho_0^2} \qquad (4.246)$$

We observe that for any admissible ρ

$$S(\rho_0) \leq S(\rho) \qquad (4.247)$$

The above has also shown that $L_T(\rho; y, x)$ converges to its limit, say $L(\rho)$, with probability one, uniformly in ρ and moreover that

$$L(\rho) = -\frac{1}{2}[\ln(2\pi) + 1] - \frac{1}{2} \ln\left[\sigma_0^2 + \sigma_0^2 \frac{(\rho - \rho_0)^2}{1 - \rho_0^2}\right] \qquad (4.248)$$

Consider now the sequence of estimates $\{\hat{\rho}_T\}$ defined by (4.238). The sequence constitutes a bounded infinite set; thus it has at least one limit point, say ρ_*, and there exists a subsequence $\{\hat{\rho}_{T_i}\}$ which converges to ρ_*.

For such a subsequence we have

$$S_{T_i}(\hat{\rho}_{T_i}; y, x) \leq S_{T_i}(\rho; y, x)$$

---

[18] For an explanation of the meaning of this term, see [32, ch. 9].

and because $S_T(\rho; y, x)$ converges to $S(\rho)$ with probability one uniformly in ρ, we conclude

$$S(\rho_*) \leq S(\rho)$$

In particular, the above holds for $\rho = \rho_0$. In view of (4.247) we conclude

$$\sigma_0^2 + \frac{\sigma_0^2(\rho_* - \rho_0)^2}{1 - \rho_0^2} = \sigma_0^2 \qquad (4.249)$$

which immediately implies

$$\rho_* = \rho_0$$

Since ρ_* is *any* limit point we conclude that

$$\hat{\rho}_T \to \rho_0$$

with probability one. Hence, also in probablility. An entirely similar argument will show that the estimator defined by (4.235) converges to ρ_0 with probability one. Indeed, what we have established is that estimators obtained from (4.235) and (4.238) have the same limiting behavior.

REMARK 4.7. It is worth pointing out that convergence of $S_T(\rho; y, X)$ to $S(\rho)$ *with probability one uniformly in ρ* is indispensable for the argument given in Remark 4.6. It is *not* enough to show that $\mathrm{plim}_{T \to \infty} S_T(\rho; y, X) = S(\rho)$, since the fact that

$$S_T(\hat{\rho}_T; y, X) \leq S_T(\rho; y, X)$$

does not necessarily imply that

$$S(\rho_*) = \underset{i \to \infty}{\mathrm{plim}}\, S_{T_i}(\hat{\rho}_{T_i}; y, X) \leq \underset{i \to \infty}{\mathrm{plim}}\, S_{T_i}(\rho; y, X) = s(\rho)$$

REMARK 4.8. In order to obtain the asymptotic normality of the estimator in Section 4.8 it is necessary to assume that ρ_0, the true parameter, is an interior point of $[-1 + \delta_1, 1 - \delta_1]$. Otherwise, the Taylor series expansion given in (4.146) would not be valid.

Exercises and Questions

1. Obtain $\partial^3 L / \partial \beta_i \partial \beta \partial \beta$ for $i = 0, 1, 2, \ldots, k$, and verify that they are null matrices.
2. Obtain $(1/T)(\partial^3 L / \partial \rho \partial \beta \partial \beta)$, and verify that its probability limit is finite.

3. Obtain $(1/T)(\partial^3 L/\partial\sigma^2\partial\beta\partial\beta)$, and show that its probability limit is finite.

4. Obtain $(1/T)(\partial^3 L/\partial\rho^2\partial\beta)$, and verify that its probability limit is finite.

5. Obtain $(1/T)(\partial^3 L/\partial\rho^3)$, and verify that its limit is null.

6. Show that $\hat{\sigma}^2$ of (4.92) is a consistent estimator of σ^2.

7. Show that if $\hat{\rho}$ is a consistent estimator of ρ_0 and ρ^* lies between $\hat{\rho}$ and ρ_0, then, provided the last limit exists,

$$\operatorname*{plim}_{T\to\infty} \frac{X'V^{*-1}X}{T} = \operatorname*{plim}_{T\to\infty} \frac{X'V_0^{-1}X}{T}$$

where V^* is defined with ρ^* replacing ρ_0.

8. Show that the maximum likelihood and minimum chi square estimators in the model of Sections 4.6 and 4.8 have the same limiting distribution. (Hint: Show that asymptotically they satisfy the same conditions.)

9. Suppose that the matrix X consists of a single vector, a bona fide explanatory variable x_t, find conditions on the x process so that $\operatorname{plim}_{T\to\infty} x'V^{-1}x/T$ exists as a finite nonzero quantity.

10. In establishing the asymptotic distribution of the estimator $\hat{\gamma}$ in Section 4.8, we have resorted to the expansion [Equation (4.146)],

$$\frac{\partial L}{\partial\gamma}(\hat{\gamma}_0) = \frac{\partial L}{\partial\gamma}(\gamma_0) + \frac{\partial^2 L}{\partial\gamma\partial\gamma}(\gamma_0)(\hat{\gamma} - \gamma_0) + \text{third order terms}$$

Consider instead the following expansion, by the mean value theorem:

$$\frac{\partial L}{\partial\gamma}(\hat{\gamma}) = \frac{\partial L}{\partial\gamma}(\gamma_0) + \frac{\partial^2 L}{\partial\gamma\partial\gamma}(\gamma^*)(\hat{\gamma} - \gamma_0)$$

where γ^* lies between $\hat{\gamma}$ and γ_0. Establish the asymptotic distribution of $\sqrt{T}(\hat{\gamma} - \gamma_0)$, based on the last expansion. What are the similarities and differences in the two approaches?

Chapter 5

GEOMETRIC LAG STRUCTURE II

5.1 Maximum Likelihood Methods and Mutually Independent Errors

We shall now consider the problems posed by the estimation of parameters in the model

$$y_t = \frac{\alpha I}{I - \lambda L} x_t + u_t, \qquad t = 1, 2, \ldots, T \qquad (5.1)$$

where x_t is an explanatory variable independent of the error process, and the latter obeys

$$u \sim N(0, \sigma^2 I), \qquad u = (u_1, u_2, \ldots, u_T)' \qquad (5.2)$$

The difficulty with the model in (5.1) is the strongly nonlinear way in which λ enters the specification. A subsidiary problem is that it is impossible, at least superficially, to compute the quantity $[I/(I - \lambda L)]x_t$ on the basis of the T observations at hand, even if λ were known. To handle this problem, we first observe that

$$\frac{I}{I - \lambda L} x_t = \sum_{i=0}^{\infty} \lambda^i x_{t-i} = \sum_{i=0}^{t-1} \lambda^i x_{t-i} + \lambda^t \sum_{i=0}^{\infty} \lambda^i x_{-i} \qquad (5.3)$$

But in (5.3) the first term of the last member is obtainable from the observations *if* λ is known. On the other hand,

$$a_0 = \sum_{i=0}^{\infty} \lambda^i x_{-i} \qquad (5.4)$$

does *not* depend at all on the sample observations and is merely a summary characterization of the history of the explanatory variable prior to the sampling period. We notice that

$$\alpha a_0 = y_0 - u_0 = \alpha_0 \qquad (5.5)$$

and we term α_0 the *truncation remainder*. Notice that insofar as the

98

model under consideration is concerned, α_0 is one of the *parameters* to be estimated. Thus, rewrite (5.1) as

$$y_t = \alpha_0 \lambda^t + \alpha \sum_{i=0}^{t-1} \lambda^i x_{t-i} + u_t, \quad t = 1, 2, \ldots, T \quad (5.6)$$

It should be clear to the reader that, as the sample size (T) becomes large, the influence of the term $\alpha_0 \lambda^t$—which reflects the initial conditions of the process—diminishes in importance. We shall have occasion to make this statement more precise at a later stage.

At any rate, operating with the form in (5.6), we obtain the log likelihood function of the observations as

$$L(\alpha_0, \alpha, \lambda, \sigma^2; y, x) = -\frac{T}{2} \ln(2\pi) - \frac{T}{2} \ln \sigma^2 - \frac{1}{2\sigma^2} (y - Xa)'(y - Xa)$$

$$(5.7)$$

where

$$X = (x_{\cdot 0}^*, x_{\cdot 1}^*), \quad x_{\cdot 0}^* = (\lambda, \lambda^2, \ldots, \lambda^T)', \quad x_{\cdot 1}^* = (x_1^*, x_2^*, \ldots, x_T^*)' \quad (5.8)$$

$$x_t^* = \sum_{i=0}^{t-1} \lambda^i x_{t-i}, \quad a = \binom{\alpha_0}{\alpha} \quad (5.9)$$

It is clear that, for given λ, the matrix X is easily computed from the observations; in fact, we have the simple recursive scheme,

$$x_1^* = x_1, \quad x_t^* = \lambda x_{t-1}^* + x_t, \quad t = 2, 3, \ldots, T \quad (5.10)$$

provided we take, for example, $x_0^* = 0$.

Maximizing (5.7) partially with respect to a and σ^2, we obtain

$$\hat{a}(\lambda) = (X'X)^{-1}X'y, \quad \hat{\sigma}^2(\lambda) = \frac{(y - X\hat{a})'(y - X\hat{a})}{T} \quad (5.11)$$

Inserting these expressions in (5.7), we obtain the *concentrated* likelihood function,

$$L(\lambda; y, x) = -\frac{T}{2}[\ln(2\pi) + 1] - \frac{T}{2} \ln \hat{\sigma}^2(\lambda) \quad (5.12)$$

and it is clear that the global maximum of the likelihood function corresponds to the global minimum of $\hat{\sigma}^2(\lambda)$ with respect to λ.

If nothing further were known about λ, it would be extremely difficult to determine even a relative minimum of $\hat{\sigma}^2(\lambda)$, let alone the *global* minimum, since from (5.11), we see that we are dealing with a strongly nonlinear function of λ. Fortunately, the conditions of the problem are such that we require $\lambda \in (0, 1)$. From a purely mathematical point of view, the weaker requirement, $\lambda \in (-1, 1)$, will also do. However, when $\lambda \in (-1, 0)$ the lag coefficients will regularly oscillate in sign, a phenomenon to which we would be hard put to give a reasonable economic justification. At any rate, since $\lambda \in (0, 1)$, we can proceed exactly as we did in connection with the autoregressive errors model. Thus, partition the admissible[17] range of λ by the points λ_i, $i = 1, 2, \ldots, n$.

For each λ_i, compute the elements of the matrix X and then the estimators $\hat{a}(\lambda)$ and $\hat{\sigma}^2(\lambda)$ of (5.11). Choose the estimator of λ, say $\hat{\lambda}$, by the condition

$$\hat{\sigma}^2(\hat{\lambda}) = \min_i \hat{\sigma}^2(\lambda_i) \tag{5.13}$$

The estimators of a and σ^2 are then obtained as

$$\hat{a} = \hat{a}(\hat{\lambda}), \quad \hat{\sigma}^2 = \hat{\sigma}^2(\hat{\lambda}) \tag{5.14}$$

The triplet $(\hat{a}, \hat{\lambda}, \hat{\sigma}^2)$ globally maximizes (5.7), and is thus the ML estimator of the corresponding parameters. Before we attempt to determine the asymptotic distribution of the estimators let us look a bit more closely at the additional parameter we have introduced above, namely, α_0. It is evident from (5.6) that the "variable" to which it attaches, λ^t, assumes values approaching zero as the sample size increases; thus, its relative contribution to the estimation process becomes smaller as the sample size increases. To see this more clearly, write the maximizing equations as:

$$\frac{\partial L}{\partial \alpha_0} = \frac{1}{\sigma^2} \sum_{t=1}^{T} \lambda^t (y_t - \alpha_0 \lambda^t - \alpha x_t^*) = 0$$

$$\frac{\partial L}{\partial \alpha} = \frac{1}{\sigma^2} \left[\sum_{t=1}^{T} (y_t - \alpha x_t^*) x_t^* - \alpha_0 \sum_{t=1}^{T} \lambda^t x_t^* \right] = 0 \tag{5.15}$$

$$\frac{\partial L}{\partial \lambda} = \frac{1}{\sigma^2} \left[\alpha \sum_{t=1}^{T} (y_t - \alpha x_t^*) \frac{\partial x_t^*}{\partial \lambda} + \alpha_0 \sum_{t=1}^{T} (y_t - \alpha x_t^*)(t\lambda^{t-1}) \right.$$

$$\left. - a_0^2 \sum_{t=1}^{T} t\lambda^{2t-1} - \alpha_0 \alpha \sum_{t=1}^{T} \lambda^t \frac{\partial x_t^*}{\partial \lambda} \right] = 0$$

If we assume, as is eminently reasonable, that $\lim_{T \to \infty} \sum_{t=1}^{T} \lambda^t x_t^*$ is *finite* for all admissible λ, then

$$\operatorname*{plim}_{T \to \infty} \frac{1}{\sqrt{T}} \frac{\partial L}{\partial \alpha_0} = 0 \tag{5.16}$$

---

[17] In practice, of course, we operate with a compact subset, e.g., [0.001, 0.999].

Moreover, for large T, we may write, approximately,

$$\frac{1}{\sqrt{T}}\frac{\partial L}{\partial \alpha} = \frac{1}{\sigma^2}\frac{1}{\sqrt{T}}\sum_{t=1}^{T}(y_t - \alpha x_t^*)x_t^* = 0$$

$$\frac{1}{\sqrt{T}}\frac{\partial L}{\partial \lambda} = \frac{1}{\sigma^2}\frac{1}{\sqrt{T}}\sum_{t=1}^{T}(y_t - \alpha x_t^*)\frac{\partial x_t^*}{\partial \lambda} = 0$$

(5.17)

Thus, the preceding procedure yields, for large T, estimators close to those obtained by solving (5.17). Indeed, taking into account the truncation remainder is only useful for small or moderate samples.[18] Hence, in deriving the asymptotic distribution of

$$\begin{pmatrix} \hat{\alpha} \\ \hat{\lambda} \end{pmatrix}$$

we shall operate with the equations in (5.17). In fact, the following alternative procedure, which we shall call the *prefiltering procedure*, has been suggested by Steiglitz and McBride [138]: Let

$$S = \sum_{t=1}^{T}\left(y_t - \frac{\alpha I}{I - \lambda L}x_t\right)^2$$

(5.18)

and minimize S with respect to α and λ to obtain

$$\frac{\partial S}{\partial \alpha} = -2\sum_{t=1}^{T}\left[\left(y_t - \frac{\alpha I}{I - \lambda L}x_t\right)\frac{I}{I - \lambda L}x_t\right] = 0$$

$$\frac{\partial S}{\partial \lambda} = 2\sum_{t=1}^{T}\left[\left(y_t - \frac{\alpha I}{I - \lambda L}x_t\right)\frac{I}{(I - \lambda L)^2}x_{t-1}\right] = 0$$

(5.19)

If we define

$$y_t^* = \frac{I}{I - \lambda L}y_t, \quad x_t^* = \frac{I}{I - \lambda L}x_t, \quad x_t^{**} = \frac{I}{I - \lambda L}x_t^* \quad (5.20)$$

---

[18] This aspect is borne out by the Monte Carlo study of Morrison [110]. Actually, it is not possible to obtain a consistent estimator of α_0, as claimed in Dhrymes [30]. This claim is erroneous. Formally, it is a consequence of the fact that

$$\lim_{T \to \infty}\sum_{t=1}^{T}\lambda^{2t} < \infty .$$

Intuitively, one observes that if the system generating the data is stable, then as T becomes larger and larger, the position of the system depends less and less on initial conditions. Hence, we cannot shed additional light on α_0 by increasing the length of the series. This remark will also explain the considerable instability of the estimator of α_0 as reported by Morrison [110].

we can rewrite (5.19) as

$$\alpha \sum_{t=2}^{T} x_t^{*2} + \lambda \sum_{t=2}^{T} y_{t-1}^* x_t^* = \sum_{t=2}^{T} y_t^* x_t^* \qquad (5.21)$$

$$\alpha \sum_{t=2}^{T} x_t^* x_{t-1}^{**} + \lambda \sum_{t=2}^{T} y_{t-1}^* x_{t-1}^{**} = \sum_{t=2}^{T} y_t^* x_{t-1}^{**}$$

It is then suggested that we compute

$$y_t^* = \lambda y_{t-1}^* + y_t, \quad x_t^* = \lambda x_{t-1}^* + x_t, \quad x_t^{**} = \lambda x_{t-1}^{**} + x_t^* \quad (5.22)$$

where we take, as a matter of convention and convenience,

$$y_0^* = x_0^* = x_0^{**} = 0 \qquad (5.23)$$

If the convention in (5.23), is accepted, note that although the definition of the quantity x_t^* in (5.20) *differs* from that in (5.9), in fact the convention makes them identical. Thus, the first order conditions in (5.19), together with the convention in (5.23), are *equivalent* to those in (5.17). Steiglitz and McBride [139] recommend that we begin with a trial value of λ and then compute the quantities in (5.22). When this is done, Equations (5.21) yield estimators for α, λ. We can use this estimator of λ to recompute the quantities in (5.22) and repeat the procedure until convergence is obtained. If convergence is rapid, it is obvious that considerable time and expense will be saved. It is not clear, however, that this procedure necessarily converges. Notice that if convergence is obtained, then the equations in (5.21) are equivalent to those in (5.19), and thus we obtain a solution of the former. If the error terms of the model are as in (5.2), i.e. normal, then this procedure will not necessarily yield the ML estimator we obtained earlier by the *search procedure*. This is so because we are not assured that the solution to (5.19) determined by the prefiltering procedure will correspond to the *global minimum* of S, which is what is required for coincidence with the ML estimator. On the other hand if we start the procedure with a consistent estimator of λ, then (provided the procedure converges) we shall find a consistent root of the equations in (5.19).

One can then verify that this is exactly the ML estimator of α and λ, where we neglect the truncation remainder α_0. Let us reiterate that the point of using the truncation remainder is to insure that initial conditions are taken into account when the sample size is small. Asymptotically, i.e., for large samples, we may as well operate with (5.17), since the impact of initial conditions declines with sample size. When we operate with (5.17), and when the prefiltering procedure is *properly carried out and converges*, the latter is equivalent to the search procedure outlined above. Thus, when we obtain the asymptotic distribution of the ML estimators, the result should then be understood to apply to the estimators obtained by the prefiltering procedure properly executed.

To determine the asymptotic distribution of the ML estimators, we observe that since the error terms of the model are mutually independent, identically distributed random variables, the basic theorem of ML estimation (see Dhrymes [32]) implies that, asymptotically,

$$\sqrt{T}\left[\begin{pmatrix}\hat{\alpha}\\\hat{\lambda}\\\hat{\sigma}^2\end{pmatrix}-\begin{pmatrix}\alpha\\\lambda\\\sigma^2\end{pmatrix}\right]\sim N(0,C_M) \qquad (5.24)$$

where

$$C_M^{-1}=-\lim_{T\to\infty}\frac{1}{T}E\left[\frac{\partial^2 L}{\partial\begin{pmatrix}\alpha\\\lambda\\\sigma^2\end{pmatrix}\partial(\alpha,\lambda,\sigma^2)}\right] \qquad (5.25)$$

In this particular case, we may easily verify that

$$C_M^{-1}=\lim_{T\to\infty}\frac{1}{\sigma^2}\frac{1}{T}\begin{bmatrix}\sum_{t=1}^{T}x_t^{*2} & \alpha\sum_{t=1}^{T}\left[x_t^*\frac{\partial x_t^*}{\partial\lambda}\right] & 0\\ \alpha\sum_{t=1}^{T}\left[x_t^*\frac{\partial x_t^*}{\partial\lambda}\right] & \alpha^2\sum_{t=1}^{T}\left(\frac{\partial x_t^*}{\partial\lambda}\right)^2 & 0\\ 0 & 0 & \dfrac{T}{2\sigma^2}\end{bmatrix} \qquad (5.26)$$

In (5.26), we should bear in mind that x_t^* is defined by

$$x_t^*=\frac{I}{I-\lambda L}x_t=\sum_{i=0}^{\infty}\lambda^i x_{t-i} \qquad (5.27)$$

and *not* by (5.9). It should, of course, be obvious that the contribution of the truncation remainder in the elements of the matrix in (5.26) will vanish as we let $T\to\infty$; thus, for large samples, it is irrelevant which of the two expressions for x_t^* we use in obtaining consistent estimators for C_M. Naturally, only the one in (5.9) is computationally feasible. The reader should note that a consistent estimator for C_M can be obtained by substituting therein the consistent[19] estimators of α, λ and σ^2.

Before we formalize the results above, it is convenient to obtain a slightly different expression for the submatrix of C_M corresponding to the covariance matrix of the asymptotic distribution of $\hat{\alpha}$ and $\hat{\lambda}$.

To this effect, define the matrix

$$
D = \begin{bmatrix}
1 & 0 & 0 & \cdot & \cdot & \cdot & \cdot \\
\lambda & 1 & 0 & \cdot & \cdot & \cdot & \cdot \\
\lambda^2 & \lambda & 1 & \cdot & \cdot & \cdot & \cdot \\
\cdot & \cdot & \lambda & \cdot & \cdot & \cdot & \cdot \\
\cdot & \cdot & \cdot & \cdot & \cdot & \cdot & \cdot \\
\lambda^{T-1} & \lambda^{T-2} & \lambda^{T-3} & \cdot & \cdot & \cdot & 1
\end{bmatrix}
\tag{5.28}
$$

and notice that

$$
x^* - Dx = a_0 \begin{bmatrix} \lambda \\ \lambda^2 \\ \cdot \\ \vdots \\ \lambda^T \end{bmatrix}
\tag{5.29}
$$

where

$$
x = \begin{bmatrix} x_1 \\ x_2 \\ \vdots \\ x_T \end{bmatrix}, \quad x^* = \begin{bmatrix} x_1^* \\ x_2^* \\ \vdots \\ x_T^* \end{bmatrix}
\tag{5.30}
$$

x_t^* is as defined in (5.27) and a_0 is as defined in (5.4). We next note that we have

$$
\frac{\partial x_t^*}{\partial \lambda} = \sum_{i=0}^{\infty} i\lambda^{i-1} x_{t-i} = \sum_{i=0}^{t-1} i\lambda^{i-1} x_{t-i} + a_0 t\lambda^{t-1} + \lambda^t \left(\sum_{s=0}^{\infty} s\lambda^{s-1} x_{-s} \right)
\tag{5.31}
$$

and that the tth element of Dx_{-1}^*, where

$$
x_{-1}^* = (x_0^*, x_1^*, \ldots, x_{T-1}^*)'
\tag{5.32}
$$

---

[19] It should be noted that we have not explicitly shown the consistency of the ML estimators. Referring to a basic theorem by Wald [148], as extended by Wolfowitz [158], the reader should be able to conclude that the root of the ML equations corresponding to the global maximum is indeed a consistent estimator for the parameters α, λ, σ^2. Alternatively, one may use the results of Jennrich [79].

is given by $\sum_{i=0}^{t-1} \lambda^{t-1-i} x_i^*$. Writing this out in detail, we find

$$\lambda^{t-1}(x_0 + \lambda\, x_{-1} + \lambda^2\ \ x_{-2} + \lambda^3\ \ x_{-3} + \cdots)$$
$$\lambda^{t-2}(x_1 + \lambda\, x_0 + \lambda^2 x_{-1} + \lambda^3\ \ x_{-2} + \lambda^4\ \ x_{-3} + \cdots)$$
$$\lambda^{t-3}(x_2 + \lambda x_1 + \lambda^2 x_0 + \lambda^3 x_{-1} + \lambda^4\ \ x_{-2} + \lambda^5\ \ x_{-3} + \cdots)$$
$$\vdots$$
$$(x_{t-1} + \lambda x_{t-2} + \lambda^2 x_{t-3} \cdots + \lambda^{t-1} x_0 + \lambda^t x_{-1} + \lambda^{t+1} x_{-2} + \lambda^{t+2} x_{-3} + \cdots)$$

Adding up the terms, we see that the contribution of the terms x_{-i}, $i = 0, 1, 2, \ldots$ amounts to $a_0 t \lambda^{t-1}$. The remaining terms contribute

$$\sum_{i=1}^{t-1} (t-i)\lambda^{t-1-i} x_i = \sum_{j=1}^{t-1} j\lambda^{j-1} x_{t-j} \tag{5.33}$$

where in the second member of (5.33), we have made the change of index $j = t - i$.

Hence, the difference between the tth elements of $\partial x^*/\partial \lambda$ and Dx_{-1}^* is given by

$$\sum_{i=0}^{t-1} i\,\lambda^{i-1} x_{t-i} + a_0 t \lambda^{t-1} + \lambda^t \left(\sum_{s=0}^{\infty} {}_{s}\lambda^{s-1} x_{-s} \right) - \sum_{j=0}^{t-1} j\lambda^{j-1} x_{t-j}$$
$$= a_0 t \lambda^{t-1} + a_0^* \lambda^t \tag{5.34}$$

where, of course,

$$a_0^* = \sum_{s=0}^{\infty} s\lambda^{s-1} x_{-s}$$

We shall now show that

$$\frac{1}{T} \sum_{t=1}^{T} x_t^{*2} \approx \frac{x'D'Dx}{T},$$

$$\frac{1}{T} \sum_{t=1}^{T} \left[x_t^* \frac{\partial x_t^*}{\partial \lambda} \right] \approx \frac{x'D'Dx_{-1}^*}{T} \tag{5.35}$$

$$\frac{1}{T} \sum_{t=1}^{T} \left(\frac{\partial x_t^*}{\partial \lambda} \right)^2 \approx \frac{x_{-1}^{*\prime}D'Dx_{-1}^*}{T}$$

But from (5.29), we see that

$$\frac{1}{T} x^{*\prime} x^* = \frac{1}{T} \left[x'D'Dx + 2a_0 x'D'(\lambda, \lambda^2, \ldots, \lambda^T)' + a_0^2 \sum_{i=1}^{T} \lambda^{2i} \right] \tag{5.36}$$

It is then clear from (5.36) that as $T \to \infty$, all terms in the right member will vanish save the first. Further,

$$\frac{1}{T} x^{*\prime} \frac{\partial x^*}{\partial \lambda} = \frac{1}{T} \left[x' D' D' x^*_{-1} + 2x' D' \right.$$
$$\times (a_0 + a_0^* \lambda, \, 2a_0 \lambda + a_0^* \lambda^2, \dots, Ta_0 \lambda^{T-1} + a_0^* \lambda^T)'$$
$$\left. + \left(a_0^2 \lambda \sum_{t=1}^{T} t \lambda^{2(t-1)} + a_0 a_0^* \sum_{t=1}^{T} \lambda^{2t} \right) \right] \tag{5.37}$$

and again all terms in the right member save one will vanish. Finally, using the same technique, the reader should verify that

$$\frac{1}{T} \left(\frac{\partial x^*}{\partial \lambda} \right)' \left(\frac{\partial x^*}{\partial \lambda} \right) \approx \frac{1}{T} x^{*\prime}_{-1} D' D x^*_{-1} \tag{5.38}$$

Thus we conclude that, asymptotically,

$$\sqrt{T} \left[\begin{pmatrix} \hat{\alpha} \\ \hat{\lambda} \end{pmatrix} - \begin{pmatrix} \alpha \\ \lambda \end{pmatrix} \right] \sim N(0, C_M) \tag{5.39}$$

where now,

$$C_M^{-1} = \frac{1}{\sigma^2} \lim_{T \to \infty} \frac{1}{T} \begin{bmatrix} x' D' D x & \alpha x' D' D x^*_{-1} \\ \alpha x^{*\prime}_{-1} D' D x & \alpha^2 x^{*\prime}_{-1} D' D x^*_{-1} \end{bmatrix}$$
$$= \frac{1}{\sigma^2} \lim_{T \to \infty} \frac{1}{T} \left[\begin{pmatrix} x' \\ \alpha x^{*\prime}_{-1} \end{pmatrix} D' D (x, \, \alpha x^*_{-1}) \right] \tag{5.40}$$

The preceding discussion has established:

THEOREM 5.1. Consider the model,

$$y_t = \frac{\alpha I}{I - \lambda L} x_t + u_t, \quad t = 1, 2, \dots, T \tag{5.41}$$

and suppose that x_t is nonstochastic such that $\lim_{T \to \infty} (\sum_{t=1}^{T} x_t^2)/T$ exists, and is nonnull; suppose further that

$$u \sim N(0, \sigma^2 I), \quad u = (u_1, u_2, \dots, u_T)' \tag{5.42}$$

Then the maximum likelihood estimator of the parameters α and λ obtained by the search procedure has the asymptotic distribution,

$$\sqrt{T} \left[\begin{pmatrix} \hat{\alpha} \\ \hat{\lambda} \end{pmatrix} - \begin{pmatrix} \alpha \\ \lambda \end{pmatrix} \right] \sim N(0, C_M) \tag{5.43}$$

provided C_M as defined in (5.40) exists as a well-defined (nonsingular) matrix.

Moreover, the estimator of σ^2 is asymptotically independent of $\hat{\alpha}, \hat{\lambda}$ and is distributed as

$$\sqrt{T}(\hat{\sigma}^2 - \sigma^2) \sim N(0, 2\sigma^4) \qquad (5.44)$$

The estimators obtained by the search and prefiltering procedures are asymptotically equivalent, provided the latter begins with an initial consistent estimator of λ and converges.

REMARK 5.1. As in the discussion of Section 4.8, the assumption of finiteness of $\lim_{T \to \infty} \sum_{t=1}^{T} x_t^2 / T$ may be replaced by the assumptions in (4.194) and (4.195). If we define

$$d_T^2 = \sum_{t=1}^{T} x_t^2 \qquad (5.45)$$

the result in (5.43) will still hold, provided we replace therein $\sqrt{T}$ by d_T. It would be superfluous to repeat the argument here.

REMARK 5.2. The reader may easily verify, using the techniques involved in the discussion following (5.28), that we may write

$$x_{-1}^* = Dx_{-1} + a_0 \begin{bmatrix} 1 \\ \lambda \\ \lambda^2 \\ \vdots \\ \lambda^{T-1} \end{bmatrix}, \quad x_{-1} = (0, x_1, x_2, \ldots, x_{T-1})' \qquad (5.46)$$

Thus,

$$\frac{1}{T} x_{-1}^{*'} D'Dx \approx \frac{1}{T} x_{-1}' D'^2 Dx, \quad \frac{1}{T} x_{-1}^{*'} D'Dx_{-1}^* \approx \frac{1}{T} x_{-1}' D'^2 D^2 x_{-1}$$

$$(5.47)$$

so that, in fact, a consistent estimator of the covariance matrix C_M can be easily obtained from the data simply by substituting therein the consistent estimators $\hat{\alpha}, \hat{\lambda}, \hat{\sigma}^2$. The reader should also note that the relations in (5.47) become exact as $T \to \infty$.

We shall now consider a simple generalization of the model under discussion by introducing additional explanatory variables, none of which, however, are subject to an infinite distributed lag. Thus consider

$$y_t = \frac{\alpha_1 I}{I - \lambda L} x_{t1} + \sum_{i=2}^{m} \alpha_i x_{ti} + u_t, \qquad t = 1, 2, \ldots, T$$

$$(5.48)$$

Defining

$$\alpha_0 = \alpha_1 \sum_{i=0}^{\infty} \lambda^i x_{-i,1}, \quad x_{t1}^* = \sum_{i=0}^{t-1} \lambda^i x_{t-i,1} \qquad (5.49)$$

we can rewrite the model as

$$y_t = \alpha_0 \lambda^t + \alpha_1 x_{t1}^* + \sum_{t=2}^{m} \alpha_i x_{ti} + u_t \qquad (5.50)$$

It is clear that under the same assumptions on the error term, proceeding in the same manner as above, we shall obtain the ML estimators of σ^2, λ, α_i, $i = 0, 1, 2, \ldots, m$ by the search procedure. As before, the use of initial conditions, i.e., the truncation remainder is important only for moderate samples; its significance to the estimation procedure vanishes as the sample size tends to infinity.

Let

$$x_{\cdot i} = (x_{1i}, x_{2i}, \ldots, x_{Ti})', \quad i = 2, 3, \ldots, m$$
$$x_{\cdot 1}^* = (x_{11}^*, x_{21}^*, \ldots, x_{T1}^*)'$$

$$(5.51)$$

where x_{ti}^* is as defined in (5.49).

Let

$$x_{\cdot 0} = (\lambda, \lambda^2, \ldots, \lambda^T)', \quad \alpha = (\alpha_1, \alpha_2, \ldots, \alpha_m)', \quad \alpha^{*\prime} = (\alpha_0, \alpha')$$
$$X = (x_{\cdot 1}^*, x_{\cdot 2}, \ldots, x_{\cdot m}), \quad X^* = (x_{\cdot 0}, X)$$

$$(5.52)$$

Then for small samples, the search procedure is carried out by dividing the range of λ by points λ_i, $i = 1, 2, \ldots, n$ and for each λ_i, computing the matrix X^*. One then obtains

$$\hat{\alpha}^*(\lambda_i) = (X^{*\prime} X^*)^{-1} X^{*\prime} y, \quad \hat{\sigma}^2(\lambda_i) = \frac{1}{T} y'[I - X^*(X^{*\prime} X^*)^{-1} X^{*\prime}] y$$

$$(5.53)$$

The ML estimators are $\hat{\alpha}^*(\hat{\lambda})$, $\hat{\sigma}^2(\hat{\lambda})$, $\hat{\lambda}$, where $\hat{\lambda}$ is determined by the condition,

$$\hat{\sigma}^2(\hat{\lambda}) = \min_i \hat{\sigma}^2(\lambda_i) \qquad (5.54)$$

Thus, it is easily established that, asymptotically,

$$\sqrt{T}\left[\begin{pmatrix}\hat{\alpha}\\\hat{\lambda}\end{pmatrix} - \begin{pmatrix}\alpha\\\lambda\end{pmatrix}\right] \sim N(0, C_M) \tag{5.55}$$

where in this case,

$$C_M^{-1} = \frac{1}{\sigma^2}\lim_{T\to\infty}\frac{1}{T}\begin{bmatrix} X'X & \alpha_1 X'\dfrac{\partial x_{\cdot1}^*}{\partial\lambda} \\[2ex] \alpha_1\left(\dfrac{\partial x_{\cdot1}^*}{\partial\lambda}\right)'X & \alpha_1^2\left(\dfrac{\partial x_{\cdot1}^*}{\partial\lambda}\right)'\left(\dfrac{\partial x_{\cdot1}^*}{\partial\lambda}\right) \end{bmatrix} \tag{5.56}$$

In the above we have, of course,

$$\hat{\alpha} = \hat{\alpha}(\hat{\lambda}) \tag{5.57}$$

As before, $\hat{\sigma}^2[= \hat{\sigma}^2(\hat{\lambda})]$ is asymptotically independent of $\hat{\alpha}, \hat{\lambda}$ and is distributed as

$$\sqrt{T}\,(\hat{\sigma}^2 - \sigma^2) \sim N(0, 2\sigma^4) \tag{5.58}$$

Again, if one does not wish to impose the condition that $\lim_{T\to\infty} X'X/T$ exists as a nonsingular matrix—this being the case if time trends are among the explanatory variables—one may impose the less restrictive condition in (4.194), (4.195), and consider instead the asymptotic distribution of

$$D_T\left[\begin{pmatrix}\hat{\alpha}\\\hat{\lambda}\end{pmatrix} - \begin{pmatrix}\alpha\\\lambda\end{pmatrix}\right]$$

where

$$D_T = \text{diag}\,(d_{1T}, d_{2T}, \ldots, d_{mT}, d_{1T}) \tag{5.59}$$

and

$$d_{Ti}^2 = \sum_{t=1}^{T} x_{ti}^2 \tag{5.60}$$

5.2 Estimation of the Geometric Lag Model; Alternative Methods

In this section we shall take up two relatively simple estimation methods. One consists of a straightforward instrumental variables approach proposed by Liviatan [96]; the other is a curious mixture of Aitken and ordinary least squares methods (OLS), applied to the reduced version of the model. This was suggested originally by Koyck [92] and later elaborated upon by Klein [88].

We shall only examine the simple model,

$$y_t = \frac{\alpha I}{I - \lambda L} x_t + u_t, \quad t = 1, 2, \ldots, T \tag{5.61}$$

leaving the details of the extension to the case of additional explanatory variables to the reader.

The instrumental variables (IV) approach is as follows: First reduce the model to obtain

$$y_t = \alpha x_t + \lambda y_{t-1} + w_t, \quad w_t = u_t - \lambda u_{t-1}, \quad t = 2, 3, \ldots, T \tag{5.62}$$

Notice that if we operate with the version in (5.62), we thereby lose one observation. The simplest choice of instruments for estimation is x_t, x_{t-1}. Thus, the instrumental variables equations to be solved are:

$$\alpha \sum_{t=2}^{T} x_t^2 + \lambda \sum_{t=2}^{T} x_t y_{t-1} = \sum_{t=2}^{T} x_t y_t$$

$$\alpha \sum_{t=2}^{T} x_{t-1} x_t + \lambda \sum_{t=2}^{T} x_{t-1} y_{t-1} = \sum_{t=2}^{T} x_{t-1} y_t \tag{5.63}$$

Solving, and substituting from (5.62), we obtain

$$\begin{pmatrix} \tilde{\alpha} \\ \tilde{\lambda} \end{pmatrix} = \begin{pmatrix} \alpha \\ \lambda \end{pmatrix} + \begin{bmatrix} \sum x_t^2 & \sum x_t y_{t-1} \\ \sum x_{t-1} x_t & \sum x_{t-1} y_{t-1} \end{bmatrix}^{-1} \begin{bmatrix} \sum x_t w_t \\ \sum x_{t-1} w_t \end{bmatrix} \tag{5.64}$$

If we assume that the explanatory variable is nonrandom and that the probability limit of T times the matrix in the right member of (5.64) is finite and nonstochastic, then it is trivial to show that such estimates are consistent. This is so since

$$\operatorname*{plim}_{T \to \infty} \frac{1}{T} \sum_{t=i+1}^{T} x_{t-i} w_t = 0, \quad i = 0, 1 \tag{5.65}$$

We shall next assume that either

$$u \sim N(0, \sigma^2 I), \quad u = (u_1, u_2, \ldots, u_T)' \tag{5.66}$$

or the u_t are independent identically distributed variables with finite variance σ^2 and finite third (absolute) moment. This is necessary in order to establish the asymptotic distribution of the estimators. In what follows, the assumption in (5.66) is not needed. We shall operate with the alternative, and weaker, assumption. Thus,

$$\sqrt{T}\left[\begin{pmatrix} \tilde{\alpha} \\ \tilde{\lambda} \end{pmatrix} - \begin{pmatrix} \alpha \\ \lambda \end{pmatrix}\right] = \left\{\frac{1}{T}\left[\begin{matrix} \sum x_t^2 & \sum x_t y_{t-1} \\ \sum x_{t-1} x_t & \sum x_{t-1} y_{t-1} \end{matrix}\right]\right\}^{-1}$$

$$\times \frac{1}{\sqrt{T}} \sum_{t=2}^{T} \begin{pmatrix} x_t \\ x_{t-1} \end{pmatrix} w_t \qquad (5.67)$$

It is then apparent that we need only establish the asymptotic distribution of the vector in the right member of (5.67). But since $w_t = u_t - \lambda u_{t-1}$ and the u_t are mutually independent identically distributed, it follows that $\{w_t : t = 2, 3, \ldots\}$ is a sequence of m-dependent variables with $m = 1$; moreover, the conditions of Theorem 4.3 are satisfied in the present case. We shall not carry out a detailed verification of this fact. We did so at considerable length in Section 4.8, and it would be redundant to repeat the steps here.

To proceed with our task: Consider the scalar sequence,

$$s_t = (a_1 x_t + a_2 x_{t-1}) w_t \qquad (5.68)$$

We need to determine that the quantity

$$R_i = 2 \sum_{i=1}^{m-1} \text{Cov}\,(s_{i+1}, s_{i+m}) + \text{Var}(s_{i+m}) \qquad (5.69)$$

obeys

$$\lim_{n \to \infty} \frac{1}{n} \sum_{i=1}^{n} R_{i+r} = R < \infty \qquad (5.70)$$

uniformly in r.

In the present case, $m = 1$ and (5.70) in fact holds, since

$$R_i = 2(a_1 x_i + a_2 x_{i-1})(a_1 x_{i+1} + a_2 x_i) E(w_i w_{i+1}) + (a_1 x_{i+1} + a_2 x_i)^2 E(w_{i+1}^2)$$

$$= \sigma^2 (1 + \lambda^2)(a_1, a_2)$$

$$\times \begin{bmatrix} x_{i+1}^2 - \dfrac{2\lambda}{1 + \lambda^2} x_i x_{i+1} & \begin{matrix} x_i x_{i+1} - \dfrac{\lambda}{1 + \lambda^2} \\ \times (x_i^2 + x_{i+1} x_{i-1}) \end{matrix} \\ \begin{matrix} x_i x_{i+1} - \dfrac{\lambda}{1 + \lambda^2} \\ \times (x_i^2 + x_{i+1} x_{i-1}) \end{matrix} & x_i^2 - \dfrac{1 + \lambda^2}{2\lambda} x_i x_{i+1} \end{bmatrix} \begin{bmatrix} a_1 \\ a_2 \end{bmatrix}$$

$$(5.71)$$

It follows that, asymptotically,

$$\frac{1}{\sqrt{T}} \sum_{t=2}^{T} \binom{x_t}{x_{t-1}} w_t \sim N(0, \sigma^2 B_t) \tag{5.72}$$

where

$$B_t = (1 + \lambda^2) \lim_{T \to \infty} \frac{1}{T}$$

$$\times \begin{bmatrix} x'x - \dfrac{2\lambda}{1 + \lambda^2} x'x_{-1} & x'x_{-1} - \dfrac{\lambda}{1 + \lambda^2} (x'x + x'x_{-2}) \\ x'x_{-1} - \dfrac{\lambda}{1 + \lambda^2} (x'x + x'x_{-2}) & x'x - \dfrac{2\lambda}{1 + \lambda^2} x'x_{-1} \end{bmatrix}$$

$$\tag{5.73}$$

and

$$x = (x_2, x_3, \ldots, x_T)', \quad x_{-1} = (x_1, x_2, \ldots, x_{T-1})$$
$$x_{-2} = (0, x_1, x_2, \ldots, x_{T-2})' \tag{5.74}$$

To complete our task, we need to determine the probability limit of the matrix in (5.67). We first observe that

$$\sum_{t=2}^{T} x_t y_{t-1} = \sum_{t=2}^{T} x_t (\alpha x_{t-1}^* + u_{t-1}) \tag{5.75}$$

since

$$y_{t-1} = \frac{\alpha I}{I - \lambda L} x_{t-1} + u_{t-1} = \alpha x_{t-1}^* + u_{t-1} \tag{5.76}$$

But it is clear that

$$\operatorname*{plim}_{T \to \infty} \frac{1}{T} \sum_{t=2}^{T} x_t u_{t-1} = 0 \tag{5.77}$$

Thus, we conclude that

$$\operatorname*{plim}_{T \to \infty} \frac{1}{T} \sum_{t=2}^{T} x_t y_{t-1} = \alpha \lim_{T \to \infty} \frac{1}{T} \sum_{t=2}^{T} x_t x_{t-1}^* \tag{5.78}$$

As in the previous section, we observe that

$$\lim_{T \to \infty} \frac{1}{T} \sum_{t=2}^{T} x_t x_{t-1}^* = \lim_{T \to \infty} \frac{1}{T} x'Dx_{-1} \tag{5.79}$$

where D is as defined in (5.30), except that its dimension is $T - 1$ (instead of T, reflecting the fact that we now use only $T - 1$ observations); x and x_{-1} are as defined in (5.74).

Thus,

$$\text{plim}_{T \to \infty} \frac{1}{T} \begin{bmatrix} \sum x_t^2 & \sum x_t y_{t-1} \\ \sum x_t x_{t-1} & \sum x_{t-1} y_{t-1} \end{bmatrix} = \lim_{T \to \infty} \frac{1}{T} \begin{bmatrix} x'x & \alpha x' D x_{-1} \\ x' x_{-1} & \alpha x'_{-1} D x_{-1} \end{bmatrix} = A_I$$

(5.80)

It follows that, asymptotically,

$$\sqrt{T} \left[\begin{pmatrix} \tilde{\alpha} \\ \tilde{\lambda} \end{pmatrix} - \begin{pmatrix} \alpha \\ \lambda \end{pmatrix} \right] \sim N(0, C_I)$$

(5.81)

where

$$C_I = \sigma^2 A_I^{-1} B_I A_I'^{-1}$$

(5.82)

Turning now to the estimator proposed by Koyck, we observe, as a matter of historical interest, that the original formulation was as follows. Reducing the model, we have

$$y_t = \lambda y_{t-1} + \alpha x_t + (u_t - \lambda u_{t-1})$$

(5.83)

Koyck's initial suggestion was to obtain the OLS estimator of the parameters α, λ from (5.83) and then solve the equations

$$\alpha \sum_{t=2}^{T} x_t^2 + \lambda \sum_{t=2}^{T} x_t y_{t-1} = \sum_{t=2}^{T} x_t y_t$$

$$\alpha \sum_{t=2}^{T} x_t y_{t-1} + \lambda \sum_{t=2}^{T} y_{t-1}^2 = \sum_{t=2}^{T} y_t y_{t-1} + \frac{\lambda \tilde{w}' \tilde{w}}{1 + \lambda \tilde{\lambda}}$$

(5.84)

for the final estimators of α and λ. In (5.84), $\tilde{w}' \tilde{w}$ is the sum of squares of the OLS residuals from (5.83) and $\tilde{\lambda}$ is the OLS estimator of λ. It is entirely proper to wonder whether such estimators are consistent, since $\tilde{w}' \tilde{w}$, $\tilde{\lambda}$ are not consistent estimators of the corresponding quantities. Actually, the substitutions made in (5.84) are entirely superfluous; given the substitutions, we have a quadratic in the parameters to be estimated—particularly λ. If no substitutions are made, we still have to solve a quadratic. We shall therefore derive this estimator in a slightly different way. To this effect, observe that the covariance matrix of the error terms in (5.83) is given by

$$\text{Cov}(w) = \sigma^2 \begin{bmatrix} 1+\lambda^2 & -\lambda & 0 & \cdot & \cdot & 0 \\ -\lambda & 1+\lambda^2 & -\lambda & 0 & \cdot & 0 \\ 0 & -\lambda & \vdots & \cdot & \cdot & \vdots \\ \vdots & & 0 & \cdot & & 0 \\ \vdots & & \vdots & \cdot & & -\lambda \\ 0 & 0 & 0 & & -\lambda & 1+\lambda^2 \end{bmatrix} = \sigma^2 \Phi$$

$$(5.85)$$

where

$$w = (w_2, w_3, \ldots, w_T)', \quad w_t = u_t - \lambda u_{t-1}, \quad t = 2, 3, \ldots, T$$

$$(5.86)$$

Thus, the minimum chi square estimator of the parameters in (5.83) is obtained by minimizing

$$Q = (y - \alpha x - \lambda y_{-1})' \Phi^{-1}(y - \alpha x - \lambda y_{-1}) \qquad (5.87)$$

with respect to α and λ, where

$$y = (y_2, y_3, \ldots, y_T)', \quad y_{-1} = (y_1, y_2, \ldots, y_{T-1})'$$
$$x = (x_2, x_3, \ldots, x_T)' \qquad (5.88)$$

Since the inverse is difficult to obtain, and since the w_t are 1-dependent variables, if we *neglect* dependence,[20] then the covariance matrix in (5.85) will take the form

$$\text{Cov}(w) \approx \sigma^2(1 + \lambda^2)I \qquad (5.89)$$

Using this form in (5.87), we obtain the alternative minimand,

$$Q = \frac{1}{1 + \lambda^2} (y - \alpha x - \lambda y_{-1})'(y - \alpha x - \lambda y_{-1}) \qquad (5.90)$$

Minimizing with respect to α and λ, we have

$$\frac{\partial Q}{\partial \alpha} = -\frac{2}{1 + \lambda^2} (y - \alpha x - \lambda y_{-1})' x = 0$$

$$\frac{\partial Q}{\partial \lambda} = -\frac{2}{1 + \lambda^2} (y - \alpha x - \lambda y_{-1})' y_{-1} \qquad (5.91)$$

$$- \frac{2\lambda}{(1 + \lambda^2)^2} (y - \alpha x - \lambda y_{-1})'(y - \alpha x - \lambda y_{-1}) = 0$$

---

[20] If one examines the appendix of Klein [88], one notices the implicit disregard of the dependence of successive error terms. The rationale of Klein's procedure, however, is somewhat different from the one presented here.

But the system in (5.91) is equivalent to

$$\alpha x'x + \lambda x'y_{-1} = x'y$$

$$\alpha y'_{-1}x + \lambda y'_{-1}y_{-1} = y'_{-1}y + \frac{\lambda}{1 + \lambda^2}\,w'w \qquad (5.92)$$

A comparison of (5.92) with (5.84) shows an exact coincidence if in (5.84) we do *not* substitute for $w'w$ and λ their OLS estimators. Thus, in what follows we shall examine the Koyck-Klein estimator from the point of view of (5.92). As we develop the argument, the reader will notice that the substitutions in (5.84) do not, in fact, result in any simplifications. While it might appear that (5.84) is quadratic in λ and (5.92) is cubic in λ, it will turn out that (5.92) is only *quadratic*. It should also be apparent to the reader that the cancellation of the factor $1/(1 + \lambda^2)$ in the transition from (5.91) to (5.92) is innocuous, since λ is a real parameter. Thus, $1 + \lambda^2 > 0$ for all admissible values of λ.

A further remark is also useful in connection with the above, which we shall henceforth term the Koyck-Klein estimator. The minimum chi square estimator is obtained by minimizing (5.87). The OLS estimator is obtained by minimizing $(y - \alpha x - \lambda y_{-1})'(y - \alpha x - \lambda y_{-1})$, which is equivalent to committing the error of considering that

$$\mathrm{Cov}(w) = \sigma^2 I \qquad (5.93)$$

is true. The Koyck-Klein estimator is, thus, a cross between Aitken and OLS; it recognizes that the variance of w_t depends on λ, but it fails to recognize the (stochastic) dependence of the error terms

$$\{w_t: t = 2, 3, \ldots, T\}\,.$$

With these preliminaries aside, let us determine the nature of the estimator as obtained from (5.92). First, we simplify the second equation to obtain

$$\alpha y'_{-1}x + \lambda y'_{-1}y_{-1} + \alpha\lambda^2 y'_{-1}x + \lambda^3 y'_{-1}y_{-1} - \lambda^2 y'_{-1}y - \lambda y'y + 2\alpha\lambda x'y$$
$$+ 2\lambda^2 y'y_{-1} - 2\alpha\lambda^2 x'y_{-1} - \alpha^2\lambda x'x - \lambda^3 y'_{-1}y_{-1} = y'_{-1}y$$

$$(5.94)$$

After cancellation and collection of terms, we have

$$\alpha y'_{-1}x + \lambda[y'_{-1}y_{-1} - y'y] + 2\alpha\lambda x'y + \lambda^2 y'_{-1}y - \alpha\lambda^2 x'y_{-1} - \alpha^2\lambda x'x = y'_{-1}y$$

$$(5.95)$$

The first equation in (5.92) yields

$$\alpha = \frac{x'y - \lambda x'y_{-1}}{x'x} \qquad (5.96)$$

Substituting in (5.95), we have

$$\frac{(x'y)(x'y_{-1})}{x'x} - \lambda\frac{(x'y_{-1})^2}{x'x} + \lambda[y'_{-1}y_{-1} - y'y] + 2\lambda\frac{(x'y)^2}{x'x}$$

$$- 2\lambda^2\frac{(x'y)(x'y_{-1})}{x'x} + \lambda^2 y'_{-1}y - \lambda^2\frac{(x'y)(x'y_{-1})}{x'x}$$

$$+ \lambda^3\frac{(x'y_{-1})^2}{x'x} - \lambda\frac{(x'y)^2}{x'x} + 2\lambda^2\frac{(x'y)(x'y_{-1})}{x'x} \qquad (5.97)$$

$$- \lambda^3\frac{(x'y_{-1})^2}{x'x} = y'_{-1}y$$

But this is equivalent to the quadratic,

$$\lambda^2[(x'x)(y'_{-1}y) - (x'y_{-1})(x'y)]$$
$$+ \lambda[(y'_{-1}y_{-1} - y'y)x'x + (x'y)^2 - (x'y_{-1})^2]$$
$$- [(x'x)(y'_{-1}y) - (x'y_{-1})(x'y)] = 0$$

$$(5.98)$$

The estimator of λ is taken to be the smallest root of (5.98), say $\tilde{\lambda}$. The estimator of α is then taken to be

$$\tilde{\alpha} = \frac{x'y - \tilde{\lambda}x'y_{-1}}{x'x} \qquad (5.99)$$

This bears out our earlier contention that even if we make the simplifications suggested in (5.84), we shall gain nothing in terms of computational ease, since we should still have to solve[21] a quadratic in λ.

We shall now show that the solution of (5.98) in conjunction with (5.99) yields consistent estimators for α and λ. We shall then determine their asymptotic distribution. To this effect, rewrite (5.98) in the standard form,

$$\lambda^2 + b\lambda - 1 = 0 \qquad (5.100)$$

where, of course

$$b = \frac{(y'_{-1}y_{-1} - y'y)x'x + (x'y)^2 - (x'y_{-1})^2}{(x'x)(y'_{-1}y) - (x'y_{-1})(x'y)} \qquad (5.101)$$

---

[21] Although Klein [88] appears to suggest that Equations (5.84) yield the same estimators as (5.92), or, equivalently, (5.96) and (5.97), this is rather surprising. In general, $\tilde{w}'\tilde{w}$ and $\tilde{\lambda}$ in (5.84) are *inconsistent* estimators of the corresponding quantities.

The solutions are given by the formula

$$\tilde{\lambda} = \frac{-b \pm \sqrt{b^2 + 4}}{2} \tag{5.102}$$

It follows that

$$\operatorname*{plim}_{T \to \infty} \tilde{\lambda} = \frac{-\operatorname{plim} b \pm \sqrt{\operatorname{plim} b^2 + 4}}{2} \tag{5.103}$$

gives the probability limit of the two roots. Thus, we need only evaluate $\operatorname{plim}_{T \to \infty} b$ in order to evaluate the consistency properties of $\tilde{\lambda}$. Incidentally, this will also indicate which of the roots of (5.98) we should select as the estimator of λ. It should be obvious that

$$\operatorname*{plim}_{T \to \infty} b = \operatorname*{plim}_{T \to \infty} \left[\frac{(x'y)^2 - (x'y_{-1})^2}{(x'x)(y'_{-1}y) - (x'y_{-1})(x'y)} \right] \tag{5.104}$$

This is so, since

$$y'_{-1}y_{-1} - y'y = y_1^2 - y_T^2 \tag{5.105}$$

and this difference vanishes upon division by T as $T \to \infty$. Now to evaluate the probability limit in (5.104), we require some additional assumptions on the explanatory variable x_t. In addition to the fact that it is independent of the error terms of the equation, we shall assume that the sequence $\{x_t : t = 0, \pm 1, \pm 2, \ldots\}$ obeys the following conditions.

The quantities[22]

$$c_\tau = \lim_{T \to \infty} \frac{1}{T} \sum_{t=1}^{T} x_t x_{t-\tau} \tag{5.106}$$

exist (and are finite), at least one nonnull, and they satisfy

$$c_\tau = c_{-\tau} \quad \text{all} \quad \tau \tag{5.107}$$

If x_t is a random variable, then c_τ is to be defined by

$$c_\tau = \operatorname*{plim}_{T \to \infty} \frac{1}{T} \sum_{t=1}^{T} x_t x_{t-\tau} \tag{5.108}$$

In either case, c_τ will be assumed to exist and satisfy the condition in (5.107).

---

[22] If the sequence of explanatory variables is assumed to be stochastic, conditions analogous to those in (5.106) and (5.107) will define a *covariance stationary stochastic process*—a term to be defined in Chapter 8.

Now consider the quantity,

$$\operatorname*{plim}_{T\to\infty} \frac{1}{T} x'y = \alpha \operatorname*{plim}_{T\to\infty} \frac{1}{T} \sum_{i=0}^{\infty} \lambda^i \sum_{t=2}^{T} x_t x_{t-i} + \operatorname*{plim}_{T\to\infty} \frac{1}{T} \sum_{t=2}^{T} x_t u_t$$

(5.109)

Since x_t, u_t are mutually independent, the second term in the right member of (5.109) vanishes. Putting

$$\sigma_0 = \sum_{i=0}^{\infty} \lambda^i c_i$$

(5.110)

we conclude that

$$\operatorname*{plim}_{T\to\infty} \frac{1}{T} x'y = \alpha \sigma_0$$

(5.111)

We next observe that

$$x'y_{-1} = \alpha \sum_{i=0}^{\infty} \lambda^i \sum_{t=2}^{T} x_t x_{t-1-i} + \sum_{t=2}^{T} x_t u_{t-1}$$

(5.112)

Thus,

$$\operatorname*{plim}_{T\to\infty} \frac{1}{T} x'y_{-1} = \alpha \sum_{i=0}^{\infty} \lambda^i c_{i+1} = \frac{\alpha}{\lambda} \sum_{i=0}^{\infty} \lambda^{i+1} c_{i+1} = \frac{\alpha}{\lambda} [\sigma_0 - c_0]$$

(5.113)

Of course,

$$\lim_{T\to\infty} \frac{1}{T} x'x = c_0$$

(5.114)

by definition.

Finally, to evaluate $y'_{-1}y$, introduce the convenient notation,

$$\bar{y}_t = \frac{\alpha I}{I - \lambda L} x_t$$

(5.115)

Thus,

$$y_t = \bar{y}_t + u_t$$

(5.116)

and

$$y'_{-1}y = \sum_{t=2}^{T} \bar{y}_t \bar{y}_{t-1} + \sum_{t=2}^{T} \bar{y}_t u_{t-1} + \sum_{t=2}^{T} \bar{y}_{t-1} u_t + \sum_{t=2}^{T} u_t u_{t-1}$$

(5.117)

Since the x_t and u_t are mutually independent, and since the covariance between u_t and u_{t-1} is zero, we conclude that

$$\operatorname*{plim}_{T \to \infty} \frac{1}{T} y'_{-1} y = \lim_{T \to \infty} \frac{1}{T} \bar{y}'_{-1} \bar{y} \tag{5.118}$$

To evaluate this, we note that

$$\bar{y} = \alpha x + \lambda \bar{y}_{-1}, \quad \bar{y}'_{-1} \bar{y} = \alpha x' \bar{y}_{-1} + \lambda \bar{y}'_{-1} \bar{y}_{-1} \tag{5.119}$$

Thus, we need only evaluate $\bar{y}' \bar{y}$. But

$$\frac{1}{T} \bar{y}' \bar{y} = \alpha^2 \sum_{i=0}^{\infty} \sum_{j=0}^{\infty} \lambda^i \lambda^j \frac{1}{T} \left[\sum_{t=1}^{T} x_{t-i} x_{t-j} \right] \tag{5.120}$$

Hence,

$$\lim_{T \to \infty} \frac{1}{T} \bar{y}' \bar{y} = \alpha^2 \sum_{i=0}^{\infty} \sum_{j=0}^{\infty} \lambda^i \lambda^j c_{i-j} \tag{5.121}$$

The double sum is obtained as follows: For each i, evaluate the sum over j and then add all the partial sums. Thus,

$$i = 0 \qquad \sum_{j=0}^{\infty} \lambda^j c_j = \sigma_0$$

$$i = 1 \qquad \sum_{j=0}^{\infty} \lambda^{1+j} c_{1-j} = \lambda c_1 + \lambda^2 \sigma_0$$

$$i = 2 \qquad \sum_{j=0}^{\infty} \lambda^{2+j} c_{2-j} = \lambda^2 c_2 + \lambda^3 c_1 + \lambda^4 \sigma_0$$

$$i = 3 \qquad \sum_{j=0}^{\infty} \lambda^{3+j} c_{3-j} = \lambda^3 c_3 + \lambda^4 c_2 + \lambda^5 c_1 + \lambda^6 \sigma_0$$

$$\vdots$$

Adding up all the terms containing σ_0, we find

$$\sigma_0 \sum_{i=0}^{\infty} \lambda^{2i} = \frac{\sigma_0}{1 - \lambda^2}$$

adding up all the terms containing c_j, we find

$$\frac{\lambda^j c_j}{1 - \lambda^2}, \quad j = 1, 2, \ldots$$

Thus,

$$\lim_{T \to \infty} \frac{1}{T} \bar{y}'\bar{y} = \alpha^2 \left[\frac{\sigma_0}{1 - \lambda^2} + \frac{1}{1 - \lambda^2} \sum_{j=1}^{\infty} \lambda^j c_j \right]$$

$$= \frac{\alpha^2}{1 - \lambda^2} [2\sigma_0 - c_0] \tag{5.122}$$

But it is obvious that

$$\lim_{T \to \infty} \frac{1}{T} \bar{y}'_{-1}\bar{y}_{-1} = \lim_{T \to \infty} \frac{1}{T} \bar{y}'\bar{y} \tag{5.123}$$

and (5.119) implies that

$$\lim_{T \to \infty} \frac{1}{T} \bar{y}'_{-1}\bar{y} = \alpha \lim_{T \to \infty} \frac{1}{T} x'\bar{y}_{-1} + \lambda \lim_{T \to \infty} \frac{1}{T} \bar{y}'_{-1}\bar{y}_{-1}$$

$$= \frac{\alpha^2}{\lambda} [\sigma_0 - c_0] + \frac{\lambda\alpha^2}{1 - \lambda^2} [2\sigma_0 - c_0] \tag{5.124}$$

$$= \frac{\alpha^2}{\lambda(1 - \lambda^2)} [\sigma_0 - c_0 + \lambda^2\sigma_0]$$

Thus,

$$\operatorname*{plim}_{T \to \infty} b = \frac{(\alpha^2/\lambda^2)[\lambda^2\sigma_0 - \sigma_0{}^2 - c_0{}^2 + 2c_0\sigma_0]}{[\alpha^2/\lambda(1 - \lambda^2)][\lambda^2\sigma_0{}^2 - \sigma_0{}^2 - c_0{}^2 + 2c_0\sigma_0]} = \frac{1 - \lambda^2}{\lambda} \tag{5.125}$$

Consequently

$$\operatorname*{plim}_{T \to \infty} \tilde{\lambda} = \frac{-(1 - \lambda^2)/\lambda \pm \sqrt{(1 - \lambda^2)^2/\lambda^2 + 4}}{2}$$

$$= \frac{-(1 - \lambda^2) \pm (1 + \lambda^2)}{2\lambda} \tag{5.126}$$

This yields

$$\operatorname*{plim}_{T \to \infty} \tilde{\lambda} = \lambda \quad \text{or} \quad \operatorname*{plim}_{T \to \infty} \tilde{\lambda} = -\frac{1}{\lambda} \tag{5.127}$$

Since $|\lambda| < 1$, it follows that if in (5.98) we select the smallest root in absolute value, we shall obtain thereby a consistent estimator of λ.

From (5.99), we then note that

$$\operatorname*{plim}_{T \to \infty} \tilde{\alpha} = \frac{\alpha\sigma_0 - \alpha[\sigma_0 - c_0]}{c_0} = \alpha \tag{5.128}$$

which shows that $\tilde{\alpha}$ is a consistent estimator of α as well.

REMARK 5.3. In this complicated scheme, the question will naturally arise as to whether at least one of the roots of (5.98) is less than one in absolute value. We see that

$$\tilde{\lambda} = \frac{-b \pm \sqrt{b^2 + 4}}{2} \tag{5.129}$$

Consider now the conditions under which the root corresponding to the positive square root is less than one in absolute value. We must have

$$-2 + b < \sqrt{b^2 + 4} < 2 + b \tag{5.130}$$

and we see that this is always satisfied if $b > 0$. This is so because in that case, the right inequality is always satisfied; if $b \leq 2$, the left inequality is also satisfied. If $b > 2$, then $-2 + b > 0$; squaring both sides of the (left) inequality in (5.130) we see

$$b^2 - 4b + 4 < b^2 + 4 \tag{5.131}$$

which is obviously satisfied. Thus, if $b > 0$, the root

$$\tilde{\lambda}^+ = \frac{-b + \sqrt{b^2 + 4}}{2} \tag{5.132}$$

is less than unity in absolute value.

Consider next the root

$$\tilde{\lambda}^- = \frac{-b - \sqrt{b^2 + 4}}{2} \tag{5.133}$$

For this to be less than unity in absolute value we must have

$$-2 + b < -\sqrt{b^2 + 4} < 2 + b \tag{5.134}$$

If $b < 0$, then the left inequality is always satisfied, since

$$\sqrt{b^2 + 4} < |b| + 2$$

unless $b = 0$, which we exclude from consideration. If $|b| \leq 2$, the right inequality is also satisfied. Thus, we need only concern ourselves with the case $|b| > 2$. In that case, we must have

$$-\sqrt{b^2 + 4} < -|b| + 2 = -(|b| - 2) \tag{5.135}$$

Squaring both sides (and reversing the sense of the inequality), we have

$$b^2 + 4 > b^2 - 4|b| + 4 \tag{5.136}$$

which is, of course, satisfied.

Thus we have shown that

$$|\tilde{\lambda}^{+}| < 1 \quad \text{if} \quad b > 0$$
$$|\tilde{\lambda}^{-}| < 1 \quad \text{if} \quad b < 0 \tag{5.137}$$

If we consider the proper specification to be $\lambda \in (0, 1)$, then, in addition to the above, we must verify that at least one of the two roots is positive and less than one. The reader may derive, as an exercise, the conditions (if any) under which this will hold.

Let us now deal with the asymptotic distribution of the Koyck-Klein estimator. As we have seen earlier, this is obtained as a solution to the equations in (5.91). Let

$$\gamma = \begin{pmatrix} \alpha \\ \lambda \end{pmatrix} \tag{5.138}$$

and use a Taylor series expansion with remainder to obtain

$$\frac{\partial Q}{\partial \gamma}(\tilde{\gamma}) = \frac{\partial Q}{\partial \gamma}(\gamma_0) + \frac{\partial^2 Q}{\partial \gamma \partial \gamma}(\gamma_0)(\tilde{\gamma} - \gamma_0) + \text{third order terms}$$

$$\tag{5.139}$$

where γ_0 is the true parameter vector and $\tilde{\gamma}$ is the Koyck-Klein estimator. The third order terms involve the derivatives

$$\frac{\partial^3 Q}{\partial \alpha^3} = 0, \quad \frac{\partial^3 Q}{\partial \alpha^2 \partial \lambda} = -\frac{4\lambda}{(1 + \lambda^2)} x'x$$

and so on; they are evaluated at a point γ^* such that

$$|\gamma^* - \gamma_0| < |\tilde{\gamma} - \gamma_0| \tag{5.140}$$

Since we have shown that $\tilde{\gamma}$ converges to γ_0 in probability, then obviously so does γ^*. In the context of the argument to follow, the third order terms can be shown to vanish in probability so that we shall neglect them *ab initio*.

By definition, the estimator $\tilde{\gamma}$ obeys $(\partial Q/\partial \gamma)(\tilde{\gamma}) = 0$. Thus, we can rewrite (5.139) as

$$\frac{\partial Q}{\partial \gamma}(\gamma_0) = -\frac{\partial^2 Q}{\partial \gamma \partial \gamma}(\gamma_0)[\tilde{\gamma} - \gamma_0] \tag{5.141}$$

The argument will proceed as follows: First, we shall determine the asymptotic distribution of $(1/\sqrt{T})(\partial Q/\partial \gamma)(\gamma_0)$; having done so, we shall derive, rather easily, the asymptotic distribution of the Koyck-Klein estimator.

Now, dropping the argument γ_0, we have

$$\frac{\partial Q}{\partial \gamma} = -\frac{2}{1 + \lambda^2} \sum_{t=2}^{T} \left(\alpha x_{t-1}^* + u_{t-1} + \frac{\lambda}{1 + \lambda^2} w_t \right) w_t \quad (5.142)$$

where the term $\alpha x_{t-1}^* + u_{t-1}$ resuts from writing

$$y_{t-1} = \frac{\alpha I}{I - \lambda L} x_{t-1} + u_{t-1} = \alpha x_{t-1}^* + u_{t-1} \quad (5.143)$$

We also observe that

$$
\begin{aligned}
u_{t-1} + \frac{\lambda}{1 + \lambda^2} w_t &= \frac{1}{1 + \lambda^2} [(1 + \lambda^2) u_{t-1} + \lambda u_t - \lambda^2 u_{t-1}] \\
&= \frac{1}{1 + \lambda^2} [\lambda u_t + u_{t-1}]
\end{aligned}
\quad (5.144)
$$

Thus, we are called upon to determine the asymptotic distribution of

$$\frac{1}{\sqrt{T}} \frac{\partial Q}{\partial \gamma} = -\frac{2}{1 + \lambda^2} \frac{1}{T} \sum_{t=2}^{T} \left[\alpha x_{t-1}^* + \frac{1}{1 + \lambda^2} (\lambda u_t + u_{t-1}) \right] w_t$$

$$(5.145)$$

We note that the vectors in the right member of (5.145) are m-dependent with $m = 1$. As before, we convert the problem to one involving scalar m-dependent variables by considering instead

$$s_t = \left[a_1 x_t + a_2 \alpha x_{t-1}^* + a_2 \frac{1}{1 + \lambda^2} (\lambda u_t + u_{t-1}) \right] w_t \quad (5.146)$$

Invoking Theorem 4.3, we see that we need to determine the quantities,

$$R_i = 2 \sum_{j=0}^{m-1} \text{Cov}(s_{i+j}, s_{i+m}) + \text{Var}(s_{i+m}) \quad (5.147)$$

In the present case, $m = 1$, so that

$$R_i = 2(a_1x_i + a_2\alpha x^*_{i-1})(a_1x_{i+1} + a_2\alpha x^*_i)E[w_iw_{i+1}] + 2(a_1x_i + a_2\alpha x^*_{i-1})$$

$$\times \frac{a_2}{1 + \lambda^2} E[(\lambda u_{i+1} + u_i)w_iw_{i+1}] + 2(a_1x_{i+1} + a_2\alpha x^*_i)\frac{a_2}{1 + \lambda^2}$$

$$\times E[(\lambda u_i + u_{i-1})w_iw_{i+1}] + \frac{2a_2^2}{(1 + \lambda^2)^2} E[(\lambda u_i + u_{i-1})$$

$$\times (\lambda u_{i+1} + u_i)w_iw_{i+1}] + (a_1x_{i+1} + a_2\alpha x^*_i)^2 E(w^2_{i+1})$$

$$+ 2(a_1x_{i+1} + a_2\alpha x^*_i)\frac{a_2}{1 + \lambda^2} E[(\lambda u_{i+1} + u_i)w^2_{i+1}]$$

$$+ \frac{a_2^2}{(1 + \lambda^2)^2} E[(\lambda^2 u^2_{i+1} + 2\lambda u_{i+1}u_i + u_i^2)w^2_{i+1}] \tag{5.148}$$

We note that

$$w_iw_{i+1} = u_iu_{i+1} - \lambda u_i^2 - \lambda u_{i+1}u_{i-1} + \lambda^2 u_iu_{i-1} \tag{5.149}$$

It follows, therefore, that

$$R_i = -2\lambda\sigma^2[(a_1x_i + a_2\alpha x^*_{i-1})(a_1x_{i+1} + a_2\alpha x^*_i)]$$

$$- 2a_2\frac{\lambda\rho_3}{1 + \lambda^2}(a_1x_i + a_2\alpha x^*_{i-1}) - 2a_2\frac{\lambda^2\rho_3}{1 + \lambda^2}(a_1x_{i+1} + a_2\alpha x^*_i)$$

$$+ 2a_2^2\frac{\lambda^2}{(1 + \lambda^2)^2}\sigma^4 - 2a_2^2\frac{\lambda^2}{(1 + \lambda^2)^2}\rho_4 - 2a_2^2\frac{\lambda^2}{(1 + \lambda^2)^2}\sigma^4$$

$$+ 2a_2^2\frac{\lambda^2}{(1 + \lambda^2)^2}\sigma^4 + \sigma^2(1 + \lambda)^2(a_1x_{i+1} + a_2\alpha x^*_i)^2$$

$$+ 2a_2(a_1x_{i+1} + a_2\alpha x^*_i)\frac{(\lambda + \lambda^2)}{1 + \lambda^2}\rho_3 + \frac{a_2^2}{(1 + \lambda^2)^2}$$

$$\times [\lambda^2\rho_4 + (1 - 4\lambda^2 + \lambda^4)\sigma^4 + \lambda^2\rho_4] \tag{5.150}$$

where

$$\rho_3 = E(u_i^3), \quad \rho_4 = E(u_i^4) \quad \text{all } i \tag{5.151}$$

We see from (5.150) that if R_i is to be defined, at least the third and fourth order moments of the random variable must exist.

Collecting terms, we find that

$$R_i = a_1^2[\sigma^2(1 + \lambda^2)x^2_{i+1} - 2\lambda\sigma^2x_ix_{i+1}]$$

$$+ 2a_1a_2[\sigma^2(1 + \lambda^2)\alpha x_{i+1}x^*_i - \lambda\sigma^2(\alpha x_ix^*_i + \alpha x_{i+1}x^*_{i-1}]$$

$$+ a_2^2\left[\sigma^2(1 + \lambda^2)\alpha^2x^{*2}_i - 2\lambda\sigma^2\alpha^2x^*_ix^*_{i-1} + \left(\frac{1 - \lambda^2}{1 + \lambda^2}\right)^2\sigma^4\right]$$

$$+ 2a_2\frac{\lambda\rho_3}{1 + \lambda^2}[a_1(x_{i+1} - x_i) + a_2\alpha(x^*_i - x^*_{i-1})] \tag{5.152}$$

Thus, upon summing and taking limits, the term containing ρ_3 will vanish [the terms containing ρ_4 in (5.150) have canceled in the transition to (5.152)]. Asserting that the variable x_t is nonstochastic, and obeys the conditions in (5.106) and (5.107) we observe that

$$\lim_{n\to\infty}\frac{1}{n}\sum_{i=1}^{n}R_{i+r} = a_1^2\lim_{n\to\infty}\frac{1}{n}\sum_{i=1}^{n}[\sigma^2(1+\lambda^2)x_{i+1+r}^2 - 2\lambda\sigma^2 x_{i+t}x_{i+r-1}]$$

$$+ 2a_1a_2\lim_{n\to\infty}\frac{1}{n}\sum_{i=1}^{n}[\sigma^2(1+\lambda^2)\alpha x_{i+r+1}x_{i+r}^*$$

$$- \lambda\sigma^2\alpha(x_{i+r}x_{i+r}^* + x_{i+r+1}x_{i+r-1}^*)]$$

$$+ a_2\lim_{n\to\infty}\frac{1}{n}\sum_{i=1}^{n}\left[\sigma^2(1+\lambda^2)\alpha^2 x_{i+r}^{*2} - 2\lambda\sigma^2\alpha^2 x_{i+r}^* x_{i+r-1}^*\right.$$

$$\left.+ \frac{1-\lambda^2}{1+\lambda^2}\sigma^4\right] \tag{5.153}$$

which clearly converges uniformly in r.

It follows, therefore,[23] that, asymptotically,

$$\frac{1}{\sqrt{T}}\frac{\partial Q}{\partial\gamma} \sim N\left[0, \frac{4\sigma^2}{(1+\lambda^2)^2}B_K\right] \tag{5.154}$$

where

$$B_K = \lim_{T\to\infty}\frac{1}{T}$$

$$\times\begin{bmatrix} (1+\lambda^2)x'x - 2\lambda x'x_{-1} & (1+\lambda)\alpha x'x_{-1}^* \\ & \quad - \lambda\alpha(x'x^* + x'x_{-2}^*) \\ (1+\lambda)\alpha x'x_{-1}^* & (1+\lambda^2)\alpha^2 x^{*\prime}x^* \\ \quad - \lambda\alpha(x'x^* + x'x_{-2}^*) & \quad - 2\lambda\alpha^2 x^{*\prime}x_{-1}^* + T\left(\frac{1-\lambda^2}{1+\lambda^2}\right)^2\sigma^2 \end{bmatrix}$$

$$\tag{5.155}$$

We next observe that

$$\frac{1}{\sqrt{T}}\frac{\partial Q}{\partial\gamma} = -\frac{1}{T}\frac{\partial^2 Q}{\partial\gamma\partial\gamma}\sqrt{T}\,(\tilde{\gamma} - \gamma_0) \tag{5.156}$$

---

[23] Actually, for the validity of this assertion, we require uniformly bounded third order absolute moments for s_t. For this to be so, the sixth order moments of u_t must exist and the explanatory variable, x_t, must obey certain conditions similar to those in (4.194) and (4.195), or it must be uniformly bounded.

Thus, the asymptotic distribution of the estimator will be determined if we establish the probability limit of the matrix $(1/T)(\partial^2 Q/\partial\gamma\partial\gamma)$. But

$$\frac{\partial^2 Q}{\partial\alpha\partial\alpha} = \frac{2}{1+\lambda^2}\, x'x$$

$$\frac{\partial^2 Q}{\partial\alpha\partial\lambda} = \frac{2}{1+\lambda^2}\, x'y_{-1} + \frac{4\lambda}{(1+\lambda^2)^2}\, x'w$$

$$\operatorname*{plim}_{T\to\infty} \frac{1}{T}\frac{\partial^2 Q}{\partial\alpha\partial\lambda} = \frac{2\alpha}{1+\lambda^2}\lim_{T\to\infty}\frac{1}{T}\, x'x^*_{-1}$$

$$\frac{\partial^2 Q}{\partial\lambda\partial\lambda} = \frac{2}{1+\lambda^2}\, y'_{-1}y_{-1} + \frac{4\lambda}{(1+\lambda^2)^2}\, y'_{-1}w$$

$$+\; \frac{4\lambda}{(1+\lambda^2)^2}\, y'_{-1}w - \frac{2-6\lambda^2}{(1+\lambda^2)^3}\, w'w$$

$$\operatorname*{plim}_{T\to\infty} \frac{1}{T}\frac{\partial^2 Q}{\partial\lambda\partial\lambda} = \frac{2}{1+\lambda^2}\,\sigma^2 + 2\lim_{T\to\infty}\frac{\alpha^2}{1+\lambda^2}\frac{1}{T}\, x^{*\prime}x^*$$

$$-\; \frac{8\lambda^2}{(1+\lambda^2)^2}\,\sigma^2 - \frac{2-6\lambda^2}{(1+\lambda^2)^2}\,\sigma^2$$

$$=\lim_{T\to\infty}\frac{2\alpha^2}{1+\lambda^2}\frac{1}{T}\, x^{*\prime}x^*$$

(5.157)

Thus,

$$\operatorname*{plim}_{T\to\infty} \frac{1}{T}\frac{\partial^2 Q}{\partial\gamma\partial\gamma} = \frac{2}{1+\lambda^2}\lim_{T\to\infty}\frac{1}{T}\begin{bmatrix} x'x & \alpha x'x^*_{-1} \\ \alpha x^{*\prime}_{-1}x & \alpha^2 x^{*\prime}x^* \end{bmatrix} = \frac{2}{1+\lambda^2}A_K$$

(5.158)

It follows, therefore that, asymptotically,

$$\sqrt{T}\,(\tilde{\gamma} - \gamma_0) \sim N(0, C_K)$$

(5.159)

where

$$C_K = \sigma^2 A_K^{-1} B_K A_K^{\prime -1}$$

(5.160)

5.3 Relative Efficiency of Alternative Estimators

In the preceding two sections, we established the following results relative to the model:

$$y_t = \frac{\alpha I}{I - \lambda L}\, x_t + u_t\,, \quad t = 1, 2, \ldots, T$$

(5.161)

where

$$u = (u_1, u_2, \ldots, u_T)'\,, \quad u \sim N(0, \sigma^2 I)$$

(5.162)

The asymptotic distribution of the ML estimator is $N(0, C_M)$ and

$$C_M = \sigma^2 \lim_{T \to \infty} T[(x, \bar{y}_{-1})'D'D(x, \bar{y}_{-1})]^{-1} \qquad (5.163)$$

where

$$x = (x_1, x_2, \ldots, x_T)', \qquad \bar{y}_{-1} = \alpha(x_0^*, x_1^*, x_2^*, \ldots, x_{T-1}^*)'$$
$$\bar{y} = \alpha(x_1^*, x_2^*, \ldots, x_T^*)', \qquad x_{-1} = (x_0, x_1, x_2, \ldots, x_{T-1})' \qquad (5.164)$$

The asymptotic distribution of the instrumental variables estimator is $N(0, C_I)$ and

$$C_I = \sigma^2 A_I^{-1} B_I A_I'^{-1} \qquad (5.165)$$

where

$$A_I = \lim_{T \to \infty} \frac{1}{T} \begin{bmatrix} x'x & x'\bar{y}_{-1} \\ x'_{-1}x & x'_{-1}\bar{y}_{-1} \end{bmatrix}$$

$$B_I = \lim_{T \to \infty} \frac{1}{T} \begin{bmatrix} (1 + \lambda^2)x'x - 2\lambda x'x_{-1} & (1 + \lambda^2)x'x_{-1} \\ & \qquad - \lambda(x'x + x'x_{-2}) \\ (1 + \lambda^2)x'x_{-1} & (1 + \lambda^2)x'x - 2\lambda x'x_{-1} \\ \qquad - \lambda(x'x + x'x_{-2}) & \end{bmatrix}$$

$$(5.166)$$

Finally, the asymptotic distribution of the Koyck-Klein estimator is $N(0, C_K)$, and

$$C_K = \sigma^2 A_K^{-1} B_K A_K'^{-1} \qquad (5.167)$$

where

$$A_K = \lim_{T \to \infty} \frac{1}{T} \begin{bmatrix} x'x & x'_{-1}\bar{y}_{-1} \\ \bar{y}'_{-1}x & \bar{y}'_{-1}\bar{y}_{-1} \end{bmatrix}$$

$$B_K = \lim_{T \to \infty} \frac{1}{T} \begin{bmatrix} (1 + \lambda^2)x'x - 2\lambda x'x_{-1} & (1 + \lambda^2)x'\bar{y}_{-1} \\ & \qquad - \lambda(x'\bar{y} + x'\bar{y}_{-2}) \\ (1 + \lambda^2)x'\bar{y}_{-1} & (1 + \lambda^2)(\bar{y}'\bar{y} - 2\lambda\bar{y}'\bar{y}_{-1}) \\ \qquad - \lambda(x'\bar{y} + x'\bar{y}_{-2}) & \qquad + T\left(\frac{1 - \lambda^2}{1 + \lambda^2}\right)^2\sigma^2 \end{bmatrix}$$

$$(5.168)$$

The criterion for ranking alternative estimators is that of relative efficiency, a term to be elucidated below.

DEFINITION 5.1. Let $\tilde{\theta}^1$, $\tilde{\theta}^2$ be two estimators of a parameter (vector) θ, and suppose both to be unbiased. Then $\tilde{\theta}^1$ is said to be efficient relative to $\tilde{\theta}^2$ if $\Sigma^2 - \Sigma^1$ is a positive semidefinite matrix, $\Sigma^i, i = 1, 2$ being the covariance matrices of $\tilde{\theta}^i, i = 1, 2$, respectively.

DEFINITION 5.2. Let $\tilde{\theta}^i, i = 1, 2$ be two estimators of a parameter (vector) θ, and suppose $\sqrt{T}(\tilde{\theta}^i - \theta)$ converges uniformly (in the admissible space of parameter values) to an $N(0, \Sigma^i)$ variable, $i = 1, 2$. Then $\tilde{\theta}^1$ is said to be asymptotically efficient relative to $\tilde{\theta}^2$ if and only if $\Sigma^2 - \Sigma^1$ is positive semidefinite.

In subsequent discussion, we shall rely primarily on the second definition; we shall have little occasion to use the first.

In dealing with the relative asymptotic efficiency of the three estimators, it is well to review the somewhat confusing symbolism we have employed; this confusion is inherent in the fact that the instrumental variables (IV) and Koyck-Klein estimators operate with the "reduced" model which "loses" one observation. Thus, in these two models we define

$$x = (x_2, x_3, \ldots, x_T)', \qquad x_{-1} = (x_1, x_2, \ldots, x_{T-1})',$$
$$\bar{y}_{-1} = \alpha(x_1^*, x_2^*, \ldots, x_{T-1}^*)', \quad \bar{y}_{-2} = \alpha(0, x_1^*, x_2^*, \ldots, x_{T-2}^*)'$$

$$(5.169)$$

However, there exists a very close connection between the quadratic forms involved in the IV, Koyck-Klein and ML estimators. To see this, recall that

$$D = \begin{bmatrix} 1 & 0 & 0 & 0 & \cdots & 0 \\ \lambda & 1 & 0 & 0 & \cdots & 0 \\ \lambda^2 & \lambda & 1 & 0 & \cdots & 0 \\ \lambda^3 & \lambda^2 & \lambda & 1 & \cdots & 0 \\ \vdots & \vdots & \vdots & \cdot & \ddots & \vdots \\ \lambda^{T-1} & \lambda^{T-2} & \cdot & \cdot & \cdots & \lambda & 1 \end{bmatrix}$$

$$D^{-1} = \begin{bmatrix} 1 & 0 & 0 & 0 & \cdot & \cdot & 0 \\ -\lambda & 1 & 0 & 0 & \cdot & \cdot & 0 \\ 0 & -\lambda & 1 & 0 & \cdot & \cdot & 0 \\ 0 & 0 & \cdot & \cdot & \cdot & \cdot & 0 \\ \cdot & \cdot & \cdot & \cdot & \cdot & \cdot & 0 \\ \cdot & \cdot & \cdot & \cdot & -\lambda & 1 & 0 \\ 0 & \cdot & \cdot & \cdot & 0 & -\lambda & 1 \end{bmatrix} \qquad (5.170)$$

both being $T \times T$ matrices.

For $x, \bar{y}, \bar{y}_{-1}$ as in (5.164), we have

$$x'D^{-1}D'^{-1}x = x_1^2 + (1 + \lambda^2) \sum_{t=2}^{T} x_t^2 - 2\lambda \sum_{t=2}^{T} x_t x_{t-1}$$

$$x'D^{-1}D'^{-1}\bar{y}_{-1} = x_1 \bar{y}_0 + (1 + \lambda^2) \sum_{t=2}^{T} x_t \bar{y}_{t-1} - \lambda \sum_{t=2}^{T} x_t \bar{y}_t - \lambda \sum_{t=2}^{T} x_t \bar{y}_{-2}$$

$$\tag{5.171}$$

and so on.

But the right members of (5.171) differ only insignificantly from corresponding expressions in (5.166) and (5.168) when the vectors $x, x_{-1}, \bar{y}_{-1}$, etc., are defined according to (5.169). We conclude, therefore, that

$$B_I = \lim_{T \to \infty} \frac{1}{T} (x, x_{-1})' D^{-1} D'^{-1} (x, x_{-1}) \tag{5.172}$$

$$B_K = \lim_{T \to \infty} \frac{1}{T} (x, \bar{y}_{-1})' D^{-1} D'^{-1} (x, \bar{y}_{-1}) \tag{5.173}$$

where the vectors $x, x_{-1}, \bar{y}, \bar{y}_{-1}$, *etc., are now defined according to* (5.164). The reader should further convince himself that similar meaning can be given to the vectors $x, x_{-1}, \bar{y}_{-1}$ appearing in A_I and A_K.

To simplify the notation, let

$$\Sigma = D^{-1} D'^{-1} \tag{5.174}$$

and write the various covariance matrices in the *common notation,*

$$C_M = \sigma^2 \lim_{T \to \infty} T[(x, \bar{y}_{-1})' \Sigma^{-1}(x, \bar{y}_{-1})]^{-1} \tag{5.175}$$

$$C_K = \sigma^2 \lim_{T \to \infty} T\{[(x, \bar{y}_{-1})'(x, \bar{y}_{-1})]^{-1}(x, \bar{y}_{-1})' \Sigma (x, \bar{y}_{-1})[(x, \bar{y}_{-1})'(x, \bar{y}_{-1})]^{-1}\}$$

$$+ \sigma^2 A_K^{-1} \begin{bmatrix} 0 & 0 \\ 0 & \left(\dfrac{1 - \lambda^2}{1 + \lambda^2}\right)^2 \sigma^2 \end{bmatrix} A_K^{-1} \tag{5.176}$$

$$C_I = \sigma^2 \lim_{T \to \infty} T\{[(x, x_{-1})'(x, \bar{y}_{-1})]^{-1}(x, x_{-1})' \Sigma (x, x_{-1})[(x, \bar{y}_{-1})'(x, x_{-1})]^{-1}\}$$

$$\tag{5.177}$$

where now all vectors $x, x_{-1}, \bar{y}_{-1}$, etc., have the meaning given them in (5.164).

We may now prove

THEOREM 5.2. Let

$$y_t = \frac{\alpha I}{I - \lambda L} x_t + u_t, \quad t = 1, 2, \ldots, T \tag{5.178}$$

where

$$u \sim N(0, \sigma^2 I), \quad u = (u, u_2, \ldots, u_T)', \quad \lambda \in (0, 1) \quad (5.179)$$

and x_t is independent of the error term u_t (and obeys certain boundedness conditions).

Let C_M, C_I, C_K be the covariance matrices, respectively, of the asymptotic distributions of the ML, IV and Koyck-Klein estimators. Then the ML is asymptotically efficient relative to the IV and Koyck-Klein estimators.

Proof. In the notation of (5.175) through (5.177), we must prove that $C_I - C_M$, $C_K - C_M$ are positive semidefinite matrices.

It will facilitate matters to introduce the notation,

$$P = (x, \bar{y}_{-1}), \quad S = (x, x_{-1}) \quad (5.180)$$

Thus,

$$C_M = \sigma^2 \lim_{T \to \infty} T(P'\Sigma^{-1}P)^{-1} \quad (5.181)$$

$$C_K = \sigma^2 \left\{ \lim_{T \to \infty} T[(P'P)^{-1}P'\Sigma P(P'P)^{-1}] + A_K^{-1} \begin{bmatrix} 0 & 0 \\ 0 & \left(\dfrac{1 - \lambda^2}{1 + \lambda^2}\right)^2 \sigma^2 \end{bmatrix} A_K^{-1} \right\}$$

$$(5.182)$$

$$C_I = \sigma^2 \lim_{T \to \infty} T[(S'P)^{-1}S'\Sigma S(P'S)^{-1}] \quad (5.183)$$

Further, define H_K by

$$(P'P)^{-1}P' = (P'\Sigma^{-1}P)^- P'\Sigma^{-1} + H_K \quad (5.184)$$

and observe that it satisfies

$$H_K P = 0 \quad (5.185)$$

Similarly, define H_I by

$$(S'P)^{-1}S' = (P'\Sigma^{-1}P)^{-1} P'\Sigma^{-1} + H_I \quad (5.186)$$

and note that

$$H_I P = 0 \quad (5.187)$$

Now,

$$(P'P)^{-1} P'\Sigma = (P'\Sigma^{-1}P)^{-1} P' + H_K\Sigma \quad (5.188)$$

Postmultiply (5.188) by the transpose of the matrices in (5.184) to obtain—in virtue of (5.185),

$$(P'P)^{-1} P'\Sigma P(P'P)^{-1} = (P'\Sigma^{-1}P)^{-1} + H_K\Sigma H_K' \quad (5.189)$$

and observe that $H_K \Sigma H_K'$ is at least positive semidefinite. From (5.186), obtain

$$(S'P)^{-1} S'\Sigma = (P'\Sigma^{-1}P)^{-1} P' + H_I \Sigma \qquad (5.190)$$

and postmultiply by the transpose of the matrices in (5.186) to deduce

$$(S'P)^{-1} S'\Sigma S(P'S)^{-1} = (P'\Sigma^{-1}P)^{-1} + H_I \Sigma H_I' \qquad (5.191)$$

The matrix $H_I \Sigma H_I'$ is at least positive semidefinite. It follows that

$$C_K - C_M = \sigma^2 \left\{ \lim_{T \to \infty} T(H_K \Sigma H_K') + A_K^{-1} \begin{bmatrix} 0 & 0 \\ 0 & \left(\dfrac{1 - \lambda^2}{1 + \lambda^2} \right)^2 \sigma^2 \end{bmatrix} A_K^{-1} \right\}$$

$$(5.192)$$

$$C_I - C_M = \sigma^2 \lim_{T \to \infty} T(H_I \Sigma H_I') \qquad (5.193)$$

which demonstrates the asymptotic efficiency of the ML relative to the Koyck-Klein and IV estimators.[24]   Q.E.D.

It is now natural to ask whether we can prove a similar result with respect to the IV and Koyck-Klein estimators.

Unfortunately this is not so, and the two estimators connot be ranked unambiguously according to the relative efficiency criterion. In fact, we shall produce below a case in which the difference of the covariance matrices of their asymptotic distribution is indefinite, i.e., it is neither positive nor negative semidefinite.

To handle this problem, it will be convenient to revert to the case where the explanatory variable is such that conditions (5.106) and (5.107) are satisfied. Making use of the results of Section 5.2, we have the following representation:

$$A_I = \begin{bmatrix} c_0 & \dfrac{\alpha}{\lambda}(\sigma_0 - c_0) \\ c_1 & \alpha\sigma_0 \end{bmatrix}$$

$$B_I = \begin{bmatrix} (1 + \lambda^2)c_0 - 2\lambda c_1 & (1 + \lambda^2)c_1 - \lambda(c_0 + c_2) \\ (1 + \lambda^2)c_1 - \lambda(c_0 + c_2) & (1 + \lambda^2)c_0 - 2\lambda c_1 \end{bmatrix} \qquad (5.194)$$

---

[24] The reader should convince himself that

$$\lim_{T \to \infty} T(H_I \Sigma H_I') \quad \text{and} \quad \lim_{T \to \infty} T(H_K \Sigma H_K')$$

are well defined quantities.

$$A_K = \begin{bmatrix} c_0 & \dfrac{\alpha}{\lambda}(\sigma_0 - c_0) \\ \dfrac{\alpha}{\lambda}(\sigma_0 - c_0) & \dfrac{\alpha^2}{1 - \lambda^2}(2\sigma_0 - c_0) \end{bmatrix}$$

$$B_K = \begin{bmatrix} (1 + \lambda^2)c_0 - 2\lambda c_1 & (1 + \lambda^2)\dfrac{\alpha}{\lambda}(\sigma_0 - c_0) - \lambda \\ & \quad \times \left\{ \alpha\sigma_0 + \dfrac{\alpha}{\lambda^2}(\sigma_0 - c_0 - \lambda c_1) \right\} \\ (1 + \lambda^2)\dfrac{\alpha}{\lambda}(\sigma_0 - c_0) & \dfrac{1 + \lambda^2}{1 - \lambda^2}\alpha^2(2\sigma_0 - c_0) \\ \quad - \lambda \left\{ \alpha\sigma_0 + \dfrac{\alpha}{\lambda} \right. & \quad - \dfrac{2\alpha^2}{1 - \lambda^2}(\sigma_0 - c_0 + \lambda^2\sigma_0) \\ \left. \quad \times (\sigma_0 - c_0 - \lambda c_1) \right\} & \quad + \left(\dfrac{1 - \lambda^2}{1 + \lambda^2} \right)^2\sigma^2 \end{bmatrix}$$

$$(5.195)$$

The elements of B_K can be simplified considerably; in fact, the matrix reduces to

$$B_K = \begin{bmatrix} (1 + \lambda^2)c_0 - 2\lambda c_1 & \alpha(c_1 - \lambda c_0) \\ \alpha(c_1 - \lambda c_0) & \alpha^2 c_0 + \left(\dfrac{1 - \lambda^2}{1 + \lambda^2} \right)^2\sigma^2 \end{bmatrix} \quad (5.196)$$

Thus, we obtain

$$C_I = \sigma^2 \begin{bmatrix} c_0 & \dfrac{\alpha}{\lambda}(\sigma_0 - c_0) \\ c_1 & \alpha\sigma_0 \end{bmatrix}^{-1}$$

$$\times \begin{bmatrix} (1 + \lambda^2)c_0 - 2\lambda c_1 & (1 + \lambda^2)c_1 - \lambda(c_0 + c_2) \\ (1 + \lambda^2)c_1 - \lambda(c_0 + c_2) & (1 + \lambda^2)c_0 - 2\lambda c_1 \end{bmatrix} \quad (5.197)$$

$$\times \begin{bmatrix} c_0 & c_1 \\ \dfrac{\alpha}{\lambda}(\sigma_0 - c_0) & \alpha\sigma_0 \end{bmatrix}^{-1}$$

$$C_K = \sigma^2 \begin{bmatrix} c_0 & \dfrac{\alpha}{\lambda}(\sigma_0 - c_0) \\ \dfrac{\alpha}{\lambda}(\sigma_0 - c_0) & \dfrac{\alpha^2}{1 - \lambda^2}(2\sigma_0 - c_0) \end{bmatrix}^{-1}$$

$$\times \begin{bmatrix} (1 + \lambda^2)c_0 - 2\lambda c_1 & \alpha(c_1 - \lambda c_0) \\ \alpha(c_1 - \lambda c_0) & \alpha^2 c_0 + \left(\dfrac{1 - \lambda^2}{1 + \lambda^2} \right)^2\sigma^2 \end{bmatrix} \quad (5.198)$$

$$\times \begin{bmatrix} c_0 & \dfrac{\alpha}{\lambda}(\sigma_0 - c_0) \\[2ex] \dfrac{\alpha}{\lambda}(\sigma_0 - c_0) & \dfrac{\alpha^2}{1 - \lambda^2}(2\sigma_0 - c_0) \end{bmatrix}^{-1}$$

The expressions above are quite useful, in that they permit a choice between the two estimators when the parameters $\alpha, \lambda, \sigma_0, c_0, c_1, c_2, \sigma^2$ have been specified.

To demonstrate our claim that, in general, no ranking is possible in terms of our criterion of relative efficiency, it is sufficient to produce only one instance where this is the case. For this purpose, consider the the case

$$c_i = 0, \qquad i \neq 0 \tag{5.199}$$

This is the case of nonautocorrelated explanatory variables. Now the following simplification occurs.

$$\sigma_0 = c_0, \qquad c_1 = c_2 = 0 \tag{5.200}$$

The covariance matrices reduce to

$$C_I = \sigma^2 \begin{bmatrix} c_0 & 0 \\ 0 & \alpha c_0 \end{bmatrix}^{-1} \begin{bmatrix} (1 + \lambda^2)c_0 & -\lambda c_0 \\ -\lambda c_0 & (1 + \lambda^2)c_0 \end{bmatrix} \begin{bmatrix} c_0 & 0 \\ 0 & \alpha \sigma_0 \end{bmatrix}^{-1}$$

$$= \frac{\sigma^2}{c_0} \begin{bmatrix} 1 + \lambda^2 & -\dfrac{\lambda}{\alpha} \\[2ex] -\dfrac{\lambda}{\alpha} & \dfrac{1 + \lambda^2}{\alpha^2} \end{bmatrix} \tag{5.201}$$

$$C_K = \sigma^2 \begin{bmatrix} c_0 & 0 \\ 0 & \dfrac{\alpha^2}{1 - \lambda^2} c_9 \end{bmatrix}^{-1} \begin{bmatrix} (1 + \lambda^2)c_0 & -\alpha \lambda c_0 \\ -\alpha \lambda c_0 & \alpha^2 c_0 + \left(\dfrac{1 - \lambda^2}{1 + \lambda^2}\right)^2 \sigma^2 \end{bmatrix}$$

$$\times \begin{bmatrix} c_0 & 0 \\ 0 & \dfrac{\alpha^2 c_0}{1 - \lambda^2} \end{bmatrix}^{-1} \tag{5.202}$$

$$= \frac{\sigma^2}{c_0} \begin{bmatrix} (1 + \lambda^2) & -\dfrac{\lambda(1 - \lambda^2)}{\alpha} \\[3ex] -\dfrac{\alpha}{\lambda(1 - \lambda^2)} & \dfrac{(1 - \lambda^2)^2}{\alpha^2} + \dfrac{(1 - \lambda^2)^4}{(1 + \lambda^2)^2} \dfrac{\sigma^2}{\alpha^4 c_0} \end{bmatrix}$$

and we obtain

$$C_I - C_K = \begin{bmatrix} 0 & -\dfrac{\lambda^3}{\alpha} \\[2ex] -\dfrac{\lambda^3}{\alpha} & \dfrac{\lambda^2(3 - \lambda^2)}{\alpha^2} - \dfrac{(1 - \lambda^2)^4}{(1 + \lambda^2)^2}\dfrac{\sigma^2}{\alpha^4 c_0} \end{bmatrix} \tag{5.203}$$

Since the determinant of this matrix is negative, it follows that its characteristic roots are of opposite signs; hence, the matrix is indefinite.

This is, of course, quite sufficient to establish a claim; but it may be useful to consider the problem of ranking of the two estimators when the explanatory variable is autoregressive—a characteristic very common in economic data. Thus, working with the simplest case, suppose that

$$c_i = \mu^i c_0, \quad i = 1, 2, \ldots \quad |\mu| < 1 \tag{5.204}$$

In virtue of the assumption[25] above, we determine

$$A_I = \begin{bmatrix} c_0 & \dfrac{\alpha\mu c_0}{1 - \lambda\mu} \\[2ex] \mu c_0 & \dfrac{\alpha c_0}{1 - \lambda\mu} \end{bmatrix} \tag{5.205}$$

$$B_I = \begin{bmatrix} (1 - 2\lambda\mu + \lambda^2)c_0 & (1 - \lambda\mu)(\mu - \lambda)c_0 \\ (1 - \lambda\mu)(\mu - \lambda)c_0 & (1 - 2\lambda\mu + \lambda^2)c_0 \end{bmatrix}$$

$$A_K = \begin{bmatrix} c_0 & \dfrac{\alpha\mu c_0}{1 - \lambda\mu} \\[2ex] \dfrac{\alpha\mu c_0}{1 - \lambda\mu} & \dfrac{\alpha^2(1 + \lambda\mu)c_0}{(1 - \lambda^2)(1 - \lambda\mu)} \end{bmatrix} \tag{5.206}$$

$$B_K = \begin{bmatrix} (1 - 2\lambda\mu + \lambda^2)c_0 & \alpha(\mu - \lambda)c_0 \\[2ex] \alpha(\mu - \lambda)c_0 & \alpha^2 c_0 + \left(\dfrac{1 - \lambda^2}{1 + \lambda^2}\right)^2\sigma^2 \end{bmatrix}$$

By the same sequence of operations leading to (5.201) and (5.202), we conclude that

$$C_I = \frac{\sigma^2}{c_0(1 - \mu^2)}$$

$$\times \begin{bmatrix} 1 + \lambda^2 & -\dfrac{\mu(1 - \lambda\mu)^2 + \lambda(1 - \lambda^2\mu^2)}{\alpha} \\[2ex] -\dfrac{\mu(1 - \lambda\mu)^2 + \lambda(1 - \lambda^2\mu^2)}{\alpha} & \dfrac{(1 + \lambda^2)(1 - \lambda\mu)^2}{\alpha^2} \end{bmatrix}$$

$$\tag{5.207}$$

---

[25] The reader should note that this assumption means that $\{x_t: t = 1, 2, \ldots\}$ is a first order autoregressive process with parameter μ.

$$C_K = C_{K_1} + C_{K_2} \tag{5.208}$$

where

$$C_{K_1} = \frac{\sigma^2}{c_0(1 - \mu^2)}$$

$$\times \begin{bmatrix} (1 - \lambda\mu)^2(1 + 2\lambda\mu + \lambda^2) & -\dfrac{(1 - \lambda\mu)^2(1 - \lambda^2)(\mu + \lambda)}{\alpha} \\[2mm] -\dfrac{(1 - \lambda\mu)^2(1 - \lambda^2)(\mu + \lambda)}{\alpha} & \dfrac{(1 - \lambda^2)(1 - \lambda\mu)^2}{\alpha^2} \end{bmatrix}$$

$$\tag{5.209}$$

$$C_{K_2} = \frac{\sigma^2}{c_0(1 - \mu)}$$

$$\times \begin{bmatrix} \dfrac{\mu^2\sigma^2(1 - \lambda\mu)^2(1 - \lambda^2)^4}{\alpha^2 c_0(1 - \mu^2)(1 + \lambda^2)^2} & -\dfrac{\mu\sigma^2(1 - \lambda\mu)^3(1 - \lambda^2)^4}{\alpha^3 c_0(1 - \mu^2)(1 + \lambda^2)^2} \\[3mm] -\dfrac{\mu\sigma^2(1 - \lambda\mu)^3(1 - \lambda^2)^4}{\alpha^3 c_0(1 - \mu^2)(1 + \lambda^2)^2} & \dfrac{\sigma^2(1 - \lambda\mu)^4(1 - \lambda^2)^4}{\alpha^4 c_0(1 - \mu^2)(1 + \lambda^2)^2} \end{bmatrix}$$

$$\tag{5.210}$$

This representation is quite enlightening in that it suggests an instrumental variables interpretation of the Koyck-Klein estimator in the context of asymptotic distribution theory. Notice that C_{K_2} results solely from the term $[(1 - \lambda^2)/(1 + \lambda^2)]^2\sigma^2$ in B_K, and is thus easily shown to be a positive semidefinite matrix.

On the other hand, it is easily shown that if the instrumental variables $x_t, \bar{y}_{t-1}$ were used in estimating the parameters of

$$y_t = \alpha x_t + \lambda y_{t-1} + u_t - \lambda u_{t-1} \tag{5.211}$$

then the resulting estimators would have an asymptotic distribution which is normal with covariance matrix C_{K_1}. This may lead us to conclude that if we generally make the decomposition in (5.208), then $C_I - C_{K_1}$ is positive semidefinite; unfortunately, this is not entirely correct. The intuitive notion which gives rise to this conjecture is that $\bar{y}_{t-1}$ is more correlated with y_{t-1} than is x_{t-1}. Generally, this intuition is justified in terms of the intimate connection of the covariance matrix of such estimators and the vector correlation between instruments and the explanatory variables they replace (see Dhrymes, [32, ch. 6]). In fact, the latter is proportional to the generalized variance of such estimators. This, however, holds when the error terms of the problem constitute *a random sample, i.e., are mutually independent identically distributed.* In the present case, this is *not* so; the errors here exhibit *negative serial correlation*, as is obvious from (5.211) and the fact that we assume $\lambda \in (0, 1)$.

To see that $C_I - C_{K_1}$ cannot, in general, be positive semidefinite, consider the first element of that matrix. It is given by

$$f(\mu) = \frac{\sigma^2}{c_0(1 - \mu^2)} [2\lambda^3\mu(1 - \mu^2) + \lambda^2\mu^2(1 - \lambda^2) + 2\lambda^2\mu^2] \quad (5.212)$$

We easily verify that

$$f(0) = 0 \quad f'(0) > 0 \quad (5.213)$$

Thus, $f(\mu) < 0$ for μ negative and near zero. The reader may further verify that

$$f\left(-\frac{\lambda}{3}\right) = \frac{\sigma^2}{c_0[1 - (\lambda^2/9)]}\left[-\frac{1}{3}\lambda^4 - \frac{1}{27}\lambda^6\right] < 0 \quad (5.214)$$

But if the first element of $C_I - C_{K_1}$ is negative, the matrix cannot be positive semidefinite. On the other hand, the reader may verify that if $\mu \in (0, 1)$, then $C_I - C_{K_1}$ is positive semidefinite.

Nevertheless, the argument above does not make transparent the connection between the IV and the Koyck-Klein estimators, since it did not take into account the C_{K_2} component of the latter's asymptotic covariance matrix.

To make this clear and thus elucidate the reason for our inability to rank such estimators generally, we shall give the Koyck-Klein an instrumental variables interpretation, although not one that is computationally feasible.

Return to (5.211) and consider the instruments

$$x_t, \bar{y}_{t-1} + \frac{1 - \lambda^2}{(1 + \lambda^2)^{3/2}} u_{t-1-r}$$

where r may be any one of $\pm 2, \pm 3, \pm 4, \ldots$. For simplicity, take $r = 2$. This instrumental set is uncorrelated with the error term at time t and the resulting estimator is easily shown to be consistent. The resulting instrumental variables estimator obeys

$$\sqrt{T}\left[\begin{pmatrix} \tilde{\alpha} \\ \tilde{\lambda} \end{pmatrix} - \begin{pmatrix} \alpha \\ \lambda \end{pmatrix}\right] = \begin{bmatrix} \dfrac{x'x}{T} & \dfrac{x'\bar{y}_{-1}}{T} + s_1 \\ \dfrac{y'_{-1}x}{T} & \dfrac{y'_{-1}\bar{y}_{-1}}{T} + s_2 \end{bmatrix}^{-1}$$

$$\times \frac{1}{\sqrt{T}} \sum_{t=2}^{T} \begin{bmatrix} x_t \\ \bar{y}_{t-1} + \dfrac{1 - \lambda^2}{(1 + \lambda^2)^{3/2}} u_{t-3} \end{bmatrix} w_t$$

$$(5.215)$$

where

$$w_t = u_t - \lambda u_{t-1}$$

$$s_1 = \frac{1 - \lambda^2}{(1 + \lambda^2)^{3/2}} \frac{1}{T} \sum x_t u_{t-3}, \qquad (5.216)$$

$$s_2 = \frac{1 - \lambda^2}{(1 + \lambda^2)^{3/2}} \frac{1}{T} \sum y_{t-1} u_{t-3}$$

It is easily verified that

$$\plim_{T \to \infty} s_2 = \plim_{T \to \infty} s_1 = 0 \qquad (5.217)$$

and hence the matrix in the right member of (5.215) converges in probability to A_K as defined, e.g., in (5.168).

The vectors in the right member of (5.215) constitute a set of 3-dependent variables; applying Theorem 4.3, the reader can readily verify that their sum converges to a $N(0, B_K)$ variable, B_K being as defined in (5.168).

But then

$$\sqrt{T} \left[\begin{pmatrix} \tilde{\alpha} \\ \tilde{\lambda} \end{pmatrix} - \begin{pmatrix} \alpha \\ \lambda \end{pmatrix} \right]$$

has the same asymptotic distribution as the Koyck-Klein estimator, and in this sense, the two estimators are equivalent.

Now it is clear why ranking of the Koyck-Klein and the IV estimator is not generally possible. Both use the instrument x_t; the former, in addition, utilizes $\bar{y}_{t-1}$ as an instrument which, one may think, is superior to x_{t-1}, *but it contaminates it with the irrelevant component,*

$$\frac{1 - \lambda^2}{(1 + \lambda^2)^{3/2}} u_{t-1\pm r}, \quad r = 2, 3, \ldots.$$

The extent to which the procedure is rendered inferior to that of the usual IV estimator depends, of course, on the variance parameter σ^2.

The preceding informal discussion has established:

THEOREM 5.3. Assume the conditions of Theorem 5.2, with the exception of normality of the error terms of the model. Then:

(i) It is not possible, generally, to rank the IV and Koyck-Klein estimators according to the criterion in Definition 5.2.[26]

---

[26] The term "generally" in this statement means: for all admissible parameter values and exogenous variable characteristics, i.e. for all admissible α, λ and sequences $\{x_t: t = 1, 2, \ldots\}$.

(ii) The Koyck-Klein can be interpreted as an instrumental variables estimator, using as instruments x_t and *any* one of

$$\bar{y}_{t-1} + \frac{1 - \lambda^2}{(1 + \lambda^2)^{3/2}} u_{t-1\pm r}, \quad r = 2, 3, \ldots$$

The sense of this interpretation is that both estimators have the same asymptotic distribution.

Exercises and Questions

1. Establish the asymptotic distribution of the ML estimator of $(\alpha, \lambda, \sigma^2)'$.

   Hint: Use Wald's result [148], as extended by Wolfowitz [158], or that of Jennrich [79] to show consistency. Then make a Taylor series expansion of the first order conditions, and apply the appropriate central limit theorem. Alternatively, consider the prefiltering procedure which begins with an initial consistent estimator of α and λ.

2. In Equation (5.36), obtain an explicit expression for

$$\frac{1}{T} (\lambda, \lambda^2, \ldots, \lambda^T) Dx$$

   Under what conditions on the explanatory variable, x_t, will the expression above converge to zero as $T \to \infty$?

   Hint: Suppose the x_t are uniformly bounded or that they are random with mean μ.

3. In Equation (5.37), obtain an explicit expression for all terms except $(1/T)x'D'D'x^*_{-1}$, and find conditions on the sequence

$$\{x_t : t = 1, 2, \ldots\}$$

   such that the limit of such terms vanishes as $T \to \infty$.

4. In Equation (5.56), what assumption on the

$$\{x_{ti} : i = 1, 2, \ldots, m, \quad t = 1, 2, \ldots\}$$

   is necessary in order to insure that the matrix C_M^{-1} is nonsingular?
   Hint: Consider $X^* = [X, \alpha_1(\partial x^*_{.1}/\partial \lambda)]$.

5. In Equation (5.80), what assumption on the explanatory sequence $\{x_t : t = 1, 2, \ldots\}$ will insure that A_t is a nonsingular matrix?

6. Find conditions under which Equation (5.100) has a root which is positive and less than unity, assuming that the true parameter λ is positive.

7. Construct an alternative proof of the asymptotic distribution of the Koyck-Klein estimator, based on the following expansion [corresponding to Equation (5.139)]:

$$\frac{\partial Q}{\partial \gamma} (\tilde{\gamma}) = \frac{\partial Q}{\partial \gamma} (\gamma_0) + \frac{\partial^2 Q}{\partial \gamma \partial \gamma} (\gamma^*)(\tilde{\gamma} - \gamma_0)$$

where γ^* lies between γ_0, $\tilde{\gamma}$, i.e. $|\gamma^* - \gamma_0| < |\tilde{\gamma} - \gamma_0|$. How would such argument differ from that given in the text?

8. In deriving the asymptotic distribution of the Koyck-Klein estimator, suppose that the quantities c_τ of Equation (5.106) obey

$$c_\tau = c_0 \mu^\tau$$

where $|\mu| < 1$. Express the matrices A_K and B_K in terms of the parameters σ^2, α, λ, c_0 and μ, and find conditions under which they are nonsingular.

9. Deduce the conditions under which the quantities $\lim_{T \to \infty} T(H_I \Sigma H'_I)$ and $\lim_{T \to \infty} T(H_K \Sigma H'_K)$ occurring in the proof of Theorem 5.2 are well defined.

10. Find conditions under which the Koyck-Klein is asymptotically efficient relative to the IV estimator. When, if ever, is the opposite true?

Chapter 6

GEOMETRIC LAG STRUCTURE III

6.1 Geometric Distributed Lag with Autocorrelated Errors: Maximum Likelihood Estimators

In Sections 5.2 and 5.3, we examined the simplest form of the geometric lag model and derived a number of estimators for its parameters. One of the assumptions under which estimation was carried out was that the observations on the error terms of the model constituted a set of mutually independent identically distributed (*i.i.d.*) random variables. In many econometric investigations, there is reason to doubt the validity of this assumption. Thus, in this section we shall examine the estimation of the model

$$y_t = \frac{\alpha I}{I - \lambda L} x_t + u_t \tag{6.1}$$

subject to the conditions

$$u_t = \rho u_{t-1} + \varepsilon_t, \quad |\rho| < 1 \tag{6.2}$$

and

$$\varepsilon \sim N(0, \sigma^2 I) \quad \varepsilon = (\varepsilon_1, \varepsilon_2, \ldots, \varepsilon_T)' \tag{6.3}$$

The probability characteristics of the error vector in (6.1) have been studied in Section 4.6, and will not be recounted here. We shall draw liberally on the results of that section, as well as on these of Sections 4.7 and 4.8. Indeed, much of the development here has been anticipated by previous sections.

We first note that the log likelihood function is given by

$$
\begin{aligned}
L(\alpha, \lambda, , \rho, \sigma^2; y, x) = &-\frac{T}{2} \ln 2\pi - \frac{T}{2} \ln \sigma^2 + \frac{1}{2} \ln(1 - \rho^2) \\
&- \frac{1}{2\sigma^2} \left(y - \frac{\alpha I}{I - \lambda L} x \right)' V^{-1} \left(y - \frac{\alpha I}{I - \lambda L} x \right)
\end{aligned}
\tag{6.4}
$$

As in Section 5.1 we observe that

$$\frac{I}{I - \lambda L}x_t = a_0\lambda^t + \sum_{i=0}^{t-1} \lambda^i x_{t-i} = \lambda^t \sum_{i=0}^{\infty} \lambda^i x_{-i} + \sum_{i=0}^{t-1} \lambda^i x_{t-i} = a_0\lambda^t + x_t^*$$

(6.5)

As in Section 4.6, we define the matrix

$$M = \begin{bmatrix} \sqrt{1 - \rho^2} & 0 & & & \\ -\rho & 1 & & 0 & \\ 0 & -\rho & 1 & \cdot & 0 \\ \cdot & \cdot & \cdot & \cdot & \cdot \\ \cdot & \cdot & \cdot & \cdot & \cdot \\ 0 & \cdot & 0 & -\rho & 1 \end{bmatrix}, \qquad V^{-1} = M'M \quad (6.6)$$

We then observe that for given λ *and* ρ, the ML estimator of α_0, α and σ^2 is obtained as the solution to

$$\frac{\partial L}{\partial \alpha_0} = \frac{1}{\sigma^2}(y - \alpha_0\lambda - \alpha x^*)' V^{-1}\lambda = 0$$

$$\frac{\partial L}{\partial \alpha} = \frac{1}{\sigma^2}(y - \alpha_0\lambda - \alpha x^*)' V^{-1}x^* = 0 \qquad (6.7)$$

$$\frac{\partial L}{\partial \sigma^2} = -\frac{T}{2}\frac{1}{\sigma^2} + \frac{1}{2\sigma^4}\left(y - \frac{\alpha I}{I - \lambda L}x\right)' V^{-1}\left(y - \frac{\alpha I}{I - \lambda L}\right) = 0$$

where

$$\alpha_0 = a_0\alpha, \quad x^* = (x_1^*, x_2^*, \dots, x_T^*)', \quad \lambda = (\lambda, \lambda^2, \lambda^3 \dots, \lambda^T)' \quad (6.8)$$

so that

$$\begin{bmatrix} \hat{\alpha}_0(\lambda, \rho) \\ \hat{\alpha}(\lambda, \rho) \end{bmatrix} = [(\lambda, x^*)' V^{-1}(\lambda, x^*)]^{-1}(\lambda, x^*)' V^{-1}y$$

$$= [(M\lambda, Mx^*)'(M\lambda, Mx^*)]^{-1}(M\lambda, Mx^*)' My \qquad (6.9)$$

and the estimator in (6.9) is seen to be the Aitken estimator for α_0, α conditional on λ and ρ. Substituting (6.9) in the last equation of (6.7), we find that

$$\hat{\sigma}^2(\lambda, \rho) = \frac{1}{T}(My)'\{I - (M\lambda, Mx^*)$$

$$\times [(M\lambda, Mx^*)'(M\lambda, Mx^*)]^{-1}(M\lambda, Mx^*)'\}(My) \qquad (6.10)$$

Inserting (6.9) and (6.10) in (6.4), we obtain the concentrated likelihood function, expressed now *solely* in terms of λ and ρ. Thus,

$$L(\lambda, \rho; y, x) = -\frac{T}{2}[\ln(2\pi) + 1] - \frac{T}{2}\ln\left[\frac{\hat{\sigma}^2(\lambda, \rho)}{(1 - \rho^2)^{1/T}}\right] \quad (6.11)$$

and the ML estimators are obtained by finding the pair, say $\hat{\lambda}$, $\hat{\rho}$, that *minimizes* the quantity

$$\frac{\hat{\sigma}^2(\lambda, \rho)}{(1 - \rho^2)^{1/T}}$$

Thus, the estimating procedure may be summarized as follows:

(i) Divide the admissible[27] range of the parameters λ and ρ by the points $\lambda_i : i = i, 2, \ldots, n_1, \rho_j : j = 1, 2, \ldots, n_2$.

(ii) For each pair (λ_i, ρ_j), determine the vectors λ, x^* and the matrix M.

(iii) Obtain the Aitken estimators for α_0 and α, as in (6.9); obtain also the estimator for σ^2, as in (6.9).

(iv) As the estimator of λ and ρ, select the pair $(\hat{\lambda}, \hat{\rho})$ for which

$$\frac{\hat{\sigma}^2(\hat{\lambda}, \hat{\rho})}{(1 - \hat{\rho}^2)^{1/T}} \leq \frac{\sigma^2(\lambda_i, \rho_j)}{(1 - \rho_j^2)^{1/T}} \quad \text{all } i, j \quad (6.12)$$

The ML estimators for α_0, α and σ^2 are then determined from (6.9) and (6.10) as $\hat{\alpha}_0(\hat{\lambda}, \hat{\rho}), \hat{\alpha}(\hat{\lambda}, \hat{\rho}), \hat{\sigma}^2(\hat{\lambda}, \hat{\rho})$.

It is clear that the procedure above provides an estimator for the parameters $\alpha_0, \alpha, \lambda, \rho, \sigma^2$ which corresponds to the *global* maximum of the likelihood function, and that this estimator is a root, i.e. a solution, of the system

$$\frac{\partial L}{\partial \beta} = 0 \quad (6.13)$$

where $\beta = (\alpha_0, \alpha, \lambda, \rho, \sigma^2)'$, provided $\hat{\lambda}$ and $\hat{\rho}$ do not occur at end points.

Arguments similar to those of the preceding sections will also show that the parameter α_0 becomes inconsequential as the sample size increases. Thus, in dealing with the asymptotic properties of these estimators, we may dispense with α_0. Consequently, we shall conduct the remainder of the discussion as if the estimators are obtained as a

---

[27] As pointed out earlier, in practice, we would operate with, say, [0.001, 0.999], [−0.999, 0.999] as the ranges for λ and ρ, respectively.

solution to the system

$$\frac{\partial L}{\partial \gamma} = 0, \qquad \gamma = (\alpha, \lambda, \rho, \sigma^2)' \tag{6.14}$$

the solution, $\hat{\gamma}$, chosen so that

$$L(\hat{\gamma}; y, x) \geq L(\gamma; y, x) \tag{6.15}$$

for all γ in the admissible parameter space.

We shall now establish the asymptotic properties of this estimator. We have

LEMMA 6.1. If $\theta = (\lambda, \rho)'$ is restricted to lie in a compact subset Θ of $(0, 1) \times (-1, 1)$, say $[\delta_1, 1 - \delta_1] \times [-1 + \delta_2, 1 - \delta_2]$, $\delta_1, \delta_2 > 0$ but small, and the x-sequence obeys the bound $|x_t| < K$, for all t, then the estimator $\hat{\gamma}$ of the parameters of the model in (6.1) through (6.3) is consistent—in fact it converges to the true parameter with probability one.

Proof. The proof of this lemma will be somewhat informal and will follow the general line of argument given in Remark 4.6. To develop the proof fully would require a number of mathematical results which lie outside the scope of this book.

Let

$$L_T(\theta; y, x) = -\frac{1}{2}[\ln(2\pi) + 1] + \frac{1}{2T}\ln(1 - \rho^2) - \frac{1}{2}\ln S_T(\theta; y, x) \tag{6.16}$$

where

$$S_T(\theta; y, x) = \hat{\sigma}^2(\theta) = \frac{1}{T}y'Ay,$$

$$A = V^{-1} - V^{-1}x^*(x^{*'}V^{-1}x^*)^{-1}x^{*'}V^{-1} \tag{6.17}$$

As we observed earlier, we shall neglect initial conditions and define the tth element of x^* by

$$\sum_{i=0}^{t-1} \lambda^i x_{t-i}$$

Since in this context the distinction between true parameters and elements of the set Θ of admissible parameters, is crucial we shall always use a zero subscript to indicate true parameters. Thus, e.g., $\theta_0 = (\lambda_0, \rho_0)'$ will indicate true paraments, and similarly with σ_0^2 and α_0.

The structure of the proof is as follows: First, we shall show that

$S_T(\theta; y, x)$ converges to its limit, say, $S(\theta)$ with probability one uniformly in θ, and argue that this also implies that $L_T(\theta; y, x)$ converges to its limit, say $L(\theta)$, with probability one uniformly in θ. Second, we shall argue that the sequence of estimates defined by

$$S_T(\hat{\theta}_T; y, x) \leq S_T(\theta; y, x), \qquad \text{for all } \theta \in \Theta$$

has at least one limit point, say θ_*, that there exists a subsequence $\{\hat{\theta}_{T_i}\}$ which converges to θ_* and that $\theta_* = \theta_0$. This, in conjunction with an identifiability condition will establish that $\hat{\theta}_T \to \theta_0$ with probability one. Since $\hat{\alpha}$ is a continuous function of $\hat{\theta}_T$ the preceding will also establish that $\hat{\alpha} \to \alpha_0$ (the true parameter) with probability one. Moreover, since $S_T(\theta; y, x)$ is bounded away from zero the estimator obtained by the condition

$$L_T(\hat{\theta}_T; y, x) \geq L_T(\theta; y, x), \qquad \text{for all } \theta \in \Theta$$

will have similar properties.

We observe that

$$S_T(\theta; y, x) = \frac{1}{T} u'Au + \frac{2}{T} \alpha_0 u'Ax_0^* + \frac{1}{T} \alpha_0^2 x_0^{*\prime} Ax_0^*$$

It will suffice to show that each of the three terms in the right member of the equation above converges to its limit uniformly in θ, and, when the occasion requires it, with probability one. Noting that

$$\frac{1}{T} u'Au = \frac{1}{T} [u'V^{-1}u - u'V^{-1}x^*(x^{*\prime}V^{-1}x^*)^{-1}x^{*\prime}V^{-1}u]$$

we see that we need be concerned only with the behavior of $(1/T)u'V^{-1}x^*$. Recall that $(1/T)u'V^{-1}u$ was shown to converge to its limit with probability one uniformly in θ in the discussion of Remark 4.6 and note that we shall assume

$$\lim_{T \to \infty} \frac{1}{T} x^{*\prime}V^{-1}x^* > 0$$

and that $x^{*\prime}V^{-1}x^*/T$ is bounded away from zero. Such conditions can be shown to follow from certain restrictions on the x-sequence.

Now

$$\frac{1}{T} u'V^{-1}x^* = \frac{1}{T} \left[\sum_{t=1}^{T} x_t^* u_t - \rho \sum_{t=2}^{T} x_t^* u_{-1} - \rho \sum_{t=2}^{T} x_{t-1}^* u_t + \rho^2 \sum_{t=2}^{T-1} x_t^* u_t \right]$$

and it will be sufficient to show that $(1/T) \sum x_t^* u_t$ converges to zero uniformly in λ. An entirely similar argument will show the same for the other terms. Uniformity of convergence with respect to ρ is quite apparent from the representation above. We note that $u_t = \rho_0{}' u_0 + \sum_{i=0}^{t-1} \rho_0{}^i \varepsilon_{t-i}$ and thus

$$\frac{1}{T} \sum_{t=1}^{T} x_t^* u_t = \frac{u_0}{T} \sum_{t=1}^{T} \rho_0{}' x_t^* + \frac{1}{T} \sum_{t=1}^{T} \left(\sum_{i=0}^{t=1} \rho_0{}^i \varepsilon_{t-i} \right) x_t^*$$

Moreover

$$\left| \frac{u_0}{T} \sum_{t=1}^{T} \rho_0{}' x_t^* \right| \le \left| \frac{u_0}{T} \right| \frac{K}{\delta_1 \delta_2}$$

where K is the bound of the sequence of explanatory variables. Since u_0 is a finite valued random variable it follows that $(u_0/T) \sum_{t=1}^{T} \rho_0{}' x_1^* \to 0$ with probability one uniformly in λ (and ρ_0). Turning to the second term we have that

$$\frac{1}{T} \sum_{t=1}^{T} \left(\sum_{i=0}^{t-1} \rho_0{}^i \varepsilon_{t-i} \right) \left(\sum_{j=0}^{t-1} \lambda^j x_{t-j} \right) = \sum_{i=1}^{T-1} \sum_{j=0}^{T-1} \rho_0{}^i \lambda^j \frac{1}{T} \sum_{t=\max(i,j)+1} \varepsilon_{t-i} x_{t-j}$$

Let

$$W_{T,i,j} = \frac{1}{T} \sum_{t} \varepsilon_{t-i} x_{t-j}$$

and observe

$$\left| \frac{1}{T} \sum_{t=1}^{T} \left(\sum_{i=0}^{t-1} \rho_0{}^i \varepsilon_{t-i} \right) \left(\sum_{j=0}^{t-1} \lambda^j x_{t-j} \right) \right| \le \sum_{i=0}^{T-1} \sum_{j=0}^{T-1} |\rho_0|{}^i \lambda^j \sup_{i,j} |W_{T,i,j}|$$

$$< \frac{1}{\delta_1 \delta_2} \sup_{i,j} |W_{T,i,j}|$$

Consequently to show convergence with probability one uniformly in λ (and ρ_0) it will be sufficient to show that

$$\sup_{i,j} |W_{T,i,j}| \to 0$$

with probability one.

If the ε-sequence has bounded eighth order moment—in the present context since normality is assumed eighth order moments are indeed bounded—we have, using Chebyshev's inequality [47, p. 103], for any $r > 0$

$$\Pr\{ |W_{T,i,j}| > r \} \le \frac{E(W_{T,i,j}^8)}{r^8} < \frac{K_1}{r^8} \frac{1}{T^4} \tag{6.18}$$

where K_1 is a constant not depending on i, j, T or x_t. To show that $\sup_{i,j} |W_{T,i,j}| \to 0$ with probability one it is thus sufficient, by the Borel-Cantelli lemma [16, p. 41], to verify that

$$\sum_{T=1}^{\infty} \sum_{i=0}^{T-1} \sum_{j=0}^{T-1} E(W^8_{T,i,j}) < \infty$$

But this is obvious from the representation in (6.18). Consequently, we have established that

$$\frac{1}{T} u' A x^* \to 0$$

with probability one uniformly in θ.

We must now show the uniform convergence (in θ) of

$$\frac{1}{T} x_0^{*\prime} A x_0^* = \frac{1}{T} x_0^{*\prime} V^{-1} x_0^* - \frac{1}{T} x_0^{*\prime} V^{-1} x^* (x^{*\prime} V^{-1} x^*)^{-1} x^{*\prime} V^{-1} x_0^* \quad (6.19)$$

Notice that (6.19) does not contain random variables. That the first term in the right member of (6.19) converges uniformly in ρ (it does *not* contain λ; it only contains λ_0) is quite obvious. Consequently, we need only deal with the second term. We shall not do this in any detail; instead we shall determine the conditions under which $(1/T) \sum_{t=1}^{T} x_t^{*2}$ converges to its limit uniformly in λ. A similar argument will easily cover the other terms as well. For notational convenience put

$$g_t(\lambda) = x_t^* = \sum_{i=0}^{\infty} \lambda^i x_{t-i} \qquad (\text{or } \sum_{i=0}^{t-1} \lambda^i x_{t-i}, \text{ it is immaterial})$$

and note that $|g_t(\lambda)| < K/\delta_1$ for all t.

Moreover,

$$|g_t(\lambda_2) - g_t(\lambda_1)| < |\lambda_2 - \lambda_1| K_2 \quad (6.20)$$

where K_2 is a constant not depending on λ, t or x_t. What (6.20) shows is that $\{g_t\}$ is a sequence of continuous (bounded) functions (of λ) which are also equicontinuous, i.e., given any $\varphi_1 > 0$ there exists $\varphi_2 > 0$ such that for *all* g_t, $|\lambda_2 - \lambda_1| < \varphi_2$ implies $|g_t(\lambda_2) - g_t(\lambda_1)| < \varphi_1$.

Moreover since

$$|g_t^2(\lambda_2) - g_t^2(\lambda_1)| = |g_t(\lambda_2) + g_t(\lambda_1)| |g_t(\lambda_2) - g_t(\lambda_1)|$$

the same may be said of the sequence $\{g_t^2\}$. Let

$$f_{t,T}(\lambda) = \frac{1}{T} g_t^2(\lambda), \qquad f_T(\lambda) = \sum_{t=1}^{T} f_{t,T}(\lambda)$$

By the arguments above, $\{f_T\}$ is a sequence of bounded equicontinuous functions, as well. For given λ,

$$f_T(\lambda) = \frac{1}{T} \sum_{t=1}^{T} \sum_{i=0}^{t-1} \sum_{j=0}^{t-1} \lambda^{i+j} x_{t-i} x_{t-j}$$

and the limit of this will exist if we assert that

$$\lim_{T \to \infty} \frac{1}{T} \sum_{t=1}^{T} x_{t-\tau} x_t = c_\tau \tag{6.21}$$

exist as finite quantities.

Given (6.21), $\{f_T\}$ converges pointwise and thus by the Arzelà theorem, [90, p. 54], $\{f_T\}$ converges uniformly in λ.

The preceding discussion has established that $S_T(\theta; y, x)$ converges to its limit, say $S(\theta)$, with probability one uniformly in θ and moreover

$$S(\theta) = \lim_{T \to \infty} \frac{1}{T} x_0^{*\prime} A x_0^* + \sigma_0^2 + \frac{\sigma_0^2 (\rho_0 - \rho_0)^2}{1 - \rho_0^2}$$

Similarly, that $L_T(\theta; y, x)$ converges to its limit, say $L(\theta)$, with probability one and that

$$L(\theta) = -\frac{1}{2} [\ln(2\pi) + 1] - \frac{1}{2} \ln S(\theta)$$

It is obvious that for any admissible θ,

$$L(\theta_0) \geq L(\theta)$$

Now, consider the estimators defined by

$$L_T(\hat{\theta}_T; y, x) \geq L_T(\theta; y, x), \qquad \text{for all admissible } \theta$$

The sequence $\{\hat{\theta}_T\}$, being an infinite bounded set, has at least one limit point, say θ_*, and there exists a subsequence $\{\hat{\theta}_{T_i}\}$ converging to θ_*. Because $L_T(\theta; y, x)$ converges to its limit with probability one uniformly in θ we have

$$L_{T_i}(\hat{\theta}_{T_i}; y, x) \geq L_{T_i}(\theta; y, x)$$

and thus

$$L(\theta_*) \geq L(\theta)$$

In particular this holds for $\theta = \theta_0$ and consequently we conclude

$$L(\theta_*) = L(\theta_0)$$

which states

$$\lim_{T \to \infty} \frac{1}{T} x_0^{*\prime} A x_0^* + \frac{\sigma_0^2 (\rho_* - \rho_0)^2}{1 - \rho_0^2} = 0 \qquad (6.22)$$

But this immediately implies $\rho_* = \rho_0$. To conclude the argument we must show that

$$\lim_{T \to \infty} \frac{1}{T} x_0^{*\prime} A_0^* x_0^* = 0 \qquad (6.23)$$

implies $\lambda_* = \lambda_0$.

It will be combersome to do so here. Instead we give it as a problem at the end of the chapter for certain types of x-sequences. It is clear, however, that it is necessary for (6.23) to imply $\lambda_* = \lambda_0$, otherwise the model will not be identified, since we could then, have $L(\theta_*) = L(\theta_0)$ and $\theta_* \neq \theta_0$. In turn, this imposes certain conditions on admissible x-sequences.

Now, *assuming* that (6.23) implies $\lambda_* = \lambda_0$, we see that $\{\hat{\theta}_T\}$ converges to θ_0 with probability one, since θ_* is any limit point.

Recalling that $\hat{\sigma}^2(\hat{\theta}_T) = S_T(\hat{\theta}_T; y, x)$ and noting that $\hat{\alpha}(\hat{\theta}_T)$ is a continuous function (of $\hat{\theta}_T$) we thus conclude

$$\Pr\{\lim_{T \to \infty} \hat{\gamma} = \gamma_0\} = 1 \qquad (6.24)$$

which shows that the estimator $\hat{\gamma}$ of the parameters of the model γ_0 converges to the latter with probability one—hence in probability.

Nothing of any substance will change if we introduce additional variables in the model, none of which is subject to an infinite lag structure.

In further discussions we shall assume that θ_0 is an *interior* point of Θ.

Let us now determine the asymptotic distribution of the ML estimator in a somewhat more general context than before. Thus we shall consider the model

$$y_t = \frac{\alpha_1 I}{I - \lambda L} x_{t1} + \sum_{i=2}^{n} \alpha_i x_{ti} + u_t, \qquad t = 1, 2, \ldots, T \quad (6.25)$$

The following conditions are assumed to hold

$$u_t = \rho u_{t-1} + \varepsilon_t, \qquad |\rho| < 1 - \delta, \qquad \delta > 0$$
$$\varepsilon \sim N(0, \sigma^2 I), \qquad \varepsilon = (\varepsilon_1, \varepsilon_2, \ldots, \varepsilon_T)' \qquad (6.26)$$

$$\lim_{T \to \infty} d_{Ti}^2 = \infty, \qquad d_{Ti}^2 = \sum_{t=1}^{T} x_{ti}^2 \tag{6.27}$$

$$\lim_{T \to \infty} \frac{\max_{t \leq T} x_{ti}^2}{d_{Ti}^2} = 0$$

The reader may easily verify that the introduction of additional explanatory variables does not present any problems from the point of view of the estimation procedure outlined above. The reader should also check that the consistency property is preserved as well.

Let

$$\gamma = (\alpha_1, \alpha_2, \ldots, \alpha_n, \lambda, \rho, \sigma^2)' \tag{6.28}$$

and observe that the log likelihood function is

$$L(\gamma; y, x) = -\frac{T}{2} \ln(2\pi) + \frac{1}{2} \ln(1 - \rho^2) - \frac{T}{2} \ln \sigma^2$$
$$- \frac{1}{2\sigma^2} (y - X\alpha)' V^{-1} (y - X\alpha) \tag{6.29}$$

where

$$X = (x_{\cdot 1}^*, x_{\cdot 2}, \ldots, x_{\cdot n})$$
$$x_{\cdot i} = (x_{1i}, x_{2i}, \ldots, x_{Ti})' \quad i = 2, 3, \ldots, n$$
$$x_{\cdot 1}^* = (x_{11}^*, x_{21}^*, \ldots, x_{T1}^*)' \tag{6.30}$$
$$x_{t1}^* = \frac{I}{I - \lambda L} x_{t1}, \quad \alpha = (\alpha_1, \alpha_2, \ldots, \alpha_n)'$$

Expanding $\partial L / \partial \gamma$ by Taylor series about $\gamma = \gamma_0$, the true parameter point, we obtain

$$\frac{\partial L}{\partial \gamma}(\gamma) = \frac{\partial L}{\partial \gamma}(\gamma_0) + \frac{\partial^2 L}{\partial \gamma \partial \gamma}(\gamma^*)[\gamma - \gamma_0] \tag{6.31}$$

where γ^* is a point such that $|\gamma^* - \gamma_0| < |\gamma - \gamma_0|$. In particular, (6.32) holds with respect to the ML estimator, $\hat{\gamma}$, so that we may operate with

$$\frac{\partial L}{\partial \gamma}(\gamma_0) = -\frac{\partial^2 L}{\partial \gamma \partial \gamma}(\gamma^*)(\hat{\gamma} - \gamma_0) \tag{6.32}$$

since $\hat{\gamma}$ is such that $(\partial L / \partial \gamma)(\hat{\gamma}) = 0$. We observe that since γ^* lies between $\hat{\gamma}$ and γ_0, and $\hat{\gamma}$ is consistent for γ_0, it follows that γ^* converges to γ_0 in probability. Moreover, we easily conclude that

$$\operatorname*{plim}_{T\to\infty} \frac{1}{T} \frac{\partial^2 L}{\partial\gamma\partial\gamma}(\gamma^*) = \operatorname*{plim}_{T\to\infty} \frac{1}{T} \frac{\partial^2 L}{\partial\gamma\partial\gamma}(\gamma_0) \tag{6.33}$$

Thus, we may operate instead with the relation

$$\frac{\partial L}{\partial\gamma}(\gamma_0) = - \frac{\partial^2 L}{\partial\gamma\partial\gamma}(\gamma_0)(\hat{\gamma} - \gamma_0) \tag{6.34}$$

As before, we first establish the asymptotic distribution of $D_T^{-1}(\partial L/\partial\gamma)$, we determine $\operatorname{plim}_{T\to\infty}(1/T)(\partial^2 L/\partial\gamma\partial\gamma)$, and thus deduce the asymptotic distribution of $G_T[\hat{\gamma} - \gamma_0]$, where

$$D_T = \operatorname{diag}(d_{T1}, d_{T2}, \ldots, d_{Tn}, d_{T1}), \quad G_T = \begin{bmatrix} D_T & 0 & 0 \\ 0 & \sqrt{T} & 0 \\ 0 & & \sqrt{T} \end{bmatrix} \tag{6.35}$$

From (6.29), we have

$$\frac{\partial L}{\partial\gamma} = \frac{1}{\sigma^2} \begin{bmatrix} X' V^{-1}(y - X\alpha) \\ \alpha_1\left(\dfrac{\partial x_{.1}^*}{\partial\lambda}\right)' V^{-1}(y - X\alpha) \\ -\dfrac{\sigma^2\rho}{1 - \rho^2} + \dfrac{1}{2} u' \dfrac{\partial V^{-1}}{\partial\rho} u \\ -\dfrac{T}{2} + \dfrac{1}{2\sigma^2} u' V^{-1} u \end{bmatrix} \tag{6.36}$$

Using the decomposition of V^{-1} in (6.6), one obtains

$$X' V^{-1}(y - X\alpha) = X' M'\varepsilon, \quad \alpha_1\left[\frac{\partial x_{.1}^*}{\partial\lambda}\right]' V^{-1}(y - X\alpha) = \alpha_1\left(\frac{\partial x_{.1}^*}{\partial\lambda}\right)' M'\varepsilon \tag{6.37}$$

where, of course,

$$\varepsilon = Mu, \qquad \varepsilon \sim N(0, \sigma^2 I) \tag{6.38}$$

Since M does not contain λ, we can write

$$\left(\frac{\partial x_{.1}^*}{\partial\lambda}\right)' M' = \left[\frac{\partial}{\partial\lambda}(Mx_{.1}^*)\right]' \tag{6.39}$$

For notational convenience, put

$$Mx_{.i} = z_{.i}, \quad i = 2, \ldots, n, \quad Mx_{.1}^* = z_{.1}, \quad Z = (z_{.1}, z_{.2}, \ldots, z_{.n})$$
$$\frac{\partial z_{.1}}{\partial\lambda} = z_{.1}^*, \quad z_{t.} = (z_{t1}, z_{t2}, \ldots, z_{tn}), \qquad t = 1, 2, \ldots, T \tag{6.40}$$

Next, recall from Section 4.8 that

$$\frac{1}{2} u' \frac{\partial V^{-1}}{\partial \rho} u = \rho u_1^2 + \sum_{t=2}^{T} u_{t-1} \varepsilon_t \qquad (6.41)$$

Again recalling the results of that section, we can write

$$u_t = \sum_{\tau=0}^{N-2} \rho^\tau \varepsilon_{t-\tau} + \rho^{N-1} \sum_{\tau=0}^{\infty} \rho^\tau \varepsilon_{t-N+1-\tau} = u_t^N + \rho^{N-1} u_{t-N+1} \qquad (6.42)$$

and we can choose N so large that the term $\rho^{N-1} u_{t-N+1}$ is smaller in absolute value that any small preassigned quantity with probability arbitrarily close to unity.

Thus, we can write

$$\frac{\partial L}{\partial \gamma} = \frac{1}{\sigma^2} \begin{bmatrix} z_{1\cdot}' \varepsilon_1 \\ \alpha_1 z_{11}^* \varepsilon_1 \\ \rho u_1 - \dfrac{\rho \sigma^2}{1-\rho^2} \\ \dfrac{1}{2}\left\{\left(\dfrac{\varepsilon_1}{\sigma}\right)^2 - 1\right\} \end{bmatrix}$$

$$+ \frac{1}{\sigma^2} \sum_{t=2}^{T} \begin{bmatrix} z_{t\cdot}' \varepsilon_t \\ \alpha_1 z_{t1}^* \varepsilon_t \\ u_{t-1}^N \varepsilon_t \\ \dfrac{1}{2}\left\{\left(\dfrac{\varepsilon_t}{\sigma}\right)^2 - 1\right\} \end{bmatrix} + \frac{1}{2} \rho^{N-1} \sum_{t=2}^{\infty} \begin{bmatrix} 0 \\ 0 \\ u_{t-N} \varepsilon_t \\ 0 \end{bmatrix} \qquad (6.43)$$

Upon multiplication on the left by G_T^{-1}, the first term in the right member is seen to converge to zero in probability as $T \to \infty$; we may also neglect the third term. Hence, the asymptotic distribution of $\partial L / \partial \gamma$ is, essentially, determined by the middle term.

Let

$$s_t = a^{*'} w_{\cdot t}, \quad w_{\cdot t} = \frac{1}{\sigma^2} G_T^{-1} \begin{bmatrix} z_{t\cdot}' \varepsilon_t \\ \alpha_1 z_{t1}^* \varepsilon_t \\ u_{t-1}^N \varepsilon_t \\ \dfrac{1}{2}\left\{\left(\dfrac{\varepsilon_t}{\sigma}\right)^2 - 1\right\} \end{bmatrix}, \quad t = 2, \ldots, T \qquad (6.44)$$

where a^* is an arbitrary $n + 3$ element real vector. By construction, $\{s_t: t = 2, 3, \ldots\}$ forms a sequence of N-dependent variables having mean zero. Repeating the arguments after Equation (4.199) we see that the third absolute moment of the elements of the sequence are bounded. Thus, to invoke Theorem 4.3 we need only show that the second moment conditions hold.

Let

$$A_i = 2 \sum_{j=0}^{N-1} \mathrm{Cov}(s_{i+j}, s_{i+N}) + \mathrm{Var}(s_{i+N}) \tag{6.45}$$

Repeating the steps following Equation (4.171), with some minor modifications due to the different normalization we now employ, we conclude that all covariance terms vanish, and we obtain

$$A_i = \mathrm{Var}(s_{i+N}) = \frac{1}{\sigma^4} \left\{ a' D_T^{-1} \begin{bmatrix} z_{t\cdot}' z_{t\cdot} & \alpha_1 z_{t\cdot}' z_{t1}^* \\ \alpha_1 z_{t1}^* z_{t\cdot} & \alpha_1^2 z_{t1}^{*2} \end{bmatrix} D_T^{-1} a\sigma^2 \right. $$

$$\left. + a_{n+2}^2 \sigma^4 \sum_{t=0}^{N-2} \rho^{2\tau} + \frac{1}{2} a_{n+3}^2 \right\} \tag{6.46}$$

a being the subvector of a^*, consisting of its first $n + 1$ element. We therefore conclude that, asymptotically,

$$G_T^{-1} \frac{\partial L}{\partial \gamma}(\gamma_0) \sim N[0, \Phi] \tag{6.47}$$

where

$$\Phi = \frac{1}{\sigma^4} \begin{bmatrix} \Sigma & 0 & 0 \\ 0 & \sigma^4 \sum_{\tau=0}^{N-2} \rho^{2\tau} & 0 \\ 0 & 0 & \frac{1}{2} \end{bmatrix}$$

$$\Sigma = \sigma^2 \lim_{T \to \infty} \left\{ D_T^{-1} \begin{bmatrix} X' V^{-1} X & \alpha_1 X' V^{-1} \left(\dfrac{\partial x_{\cdot 1}^*}{\partial \lambda}\right) \\ \alpha_1 \left(\dfrac{\partial x_{\cdot 1}^*}{\partial \lambda}\right)' V^{-1} X & \alpha_1^2 \left(\dfrac{\partial x_{\cdot 1}^*}{\partial \lambda}\right)' V^{-1} \left(\dfrac{\partial x_{\cdot 1}^*}{\partial \lambda}\right) \end{bmatrix} D_T^{-1} \right\}^{28} \tag{6.48}$$

The reader may further verify that

---

[28] The reader should note that the typical element of $X' V^{-1} X$—except in the first row and column—consists of $\sum_t (x_{ti} - \rho x_{t-1 i})(x_{tj} - \rho x_{t-1 j})$, and thus upon division by the quantities $d_{Ti} d_{Tj}$ is essentially a linear combination of first order auto- and cross autocorrelations.

$$\underset{T \to \infty}{\text{plim}} \; G_T^{-1} \frac{\partial^2 L}{\partial \gamma \partial \gamma} (\gamma_0) G_T^{-1} = -\frac{1}{\sigma^2} \begin{bmatrix} \Sigma & 0 & 0 \\ 0 & \dfrac{\sigma^2}{1-\rho^2} & 0 \\ 0 & 0 & \dfrac{1}{2\sigma^2} \end{bmatrix} \quad (6.49)$$

Thus we conclude that, asymptotically,

$$G_T(\hat{\gamma} - \gamma_0) \sim N[0, \Omega^{-1}] \quad (6.50)$$

where

$$\Omega = \begin{bmatrix} \Sigma & 0 & 0 \\ 0 & \left[(1-\rho^2)^2 \displaystyle\sum_{\tau=0}^{N-2} \rho^{2\tau} \right]^{-1} & 0 \\ 0 & 0 & \dfrac{1}{2\sigma^4} \end{bmatrix} \approx \begin{bmatrix} \Sigma & 0 & 0 \\ 0 & \dfrac{1}{1-\rho^2} & 0 \\ 0 & 0 & \dfrac{1}{2\sigma^4} \end{bmatrix} \quad (6.51)$$

The approximation in the last member of (6.51) is quite accurate, since $N - 2$ will, generally, be large enough, so that

$$\left[(1-\rho^2)^2 \left(\sum_{\tau=0}^{N-2} \rho^{2\tau} \right) \right]^{-1} \approx \frac{1}{1-\rho^2} \quad (6.52)$$

The discussion above has established

THEOREM 6.1. Consider the model in (6.25) in conjunction with the conditions stated in (6.26) and (6.27). Then the maximum likelihood estimator of the parameter vector, $\hat{\gamma}$, obeying

$$L(\hat{\gamma}; y, x) \geq L(\gamma; y, x) \quad (6.53)$$

is consistent for all admissible γ and is distributed asymptotically as

$$G_T(\hat{\gamma} - \gamma) \sim N[0, \Omega^{-1}] \quad (6.54)$$

where

$$G_T = \text{diag}(d_{T1}, d_{T2}, \ldots, d_{Tn}, d_{T1}, \sqrt{T}, \sqrt{T})$$

$$\Omega = \begin{bmatrix} \Sigma & 0 & 0 \\ 0 & \dfrac{1}{1-\rho^2} & 0 \\ 0 & 0 & \dfrac{1}{2\sigma^4} \end{bmatrix} \quad (6.55)$$

and

$$\Sigma = \sigma^2 \lim_{T \to \infty} \left\{ D_T^{-1} \begin{bmatrix} X'V^{-1}X & \alpha_1 X'V^{-1}\dfrac{\partial x_{\cdot 1}^*}{\partial \lambda} \\[2mm] \alpha_1 \dfrac{\partial x_{\cdot 1}^*}{\partial \lambda} V^{-1}X & \alpha_1^2 \dfrac{\partial x_{\cdot 1}^*}{\partial \lambda} V^{-1} \dfrac{\partial x_{\cdot 1}^*}{\partial \lambda} \end{bmatrix} D_T^{-1} \right\} \quad (6.56)$$

$$D_T = \operatorname{diag}(d_{T1}, d_{T2}, \ldots, d_{Tn}, d_{T1})$$

REMARK 6.1. The development in this section complements the results given in Dhrymes [30]; in that paper, there are a number of inaccuracies and the asymptotic distribution of the estimators is not derived.

REMARK 6.2. Strictly speaking, we have not established, in the preceding, the asymptotic distribution of $G_T(\hat{\gamma} - \gamma_0)$ but rather that of a vector differing from it by a quantity that can be made as close to zero as desired, with probability as close to one, by proper choice of N. This is the context in which the central limit theorem for m-dependent variables has been applied and will be applied in later sections. For a discussion of such aspects the reader may refer to Mann and Wald [102].

6.2 Geometric Distributed Lag with Autocorrelated Errors: Alternative Estimators

In Section 5.3 we examined the instrumental variables (IV) and Koyck-Klein, as alternatives to the ML estimator in the context of the simple geometric lag model with mutually independent errors.

In the present context, the Koyck-Klein estimator does not merit consideration since one can easily show that it is inconsistent. Although not constituting a proof, the interpretation given it earlier as an instrumental variables estimator with instruments, say, x_t, $\bar{y}_{t-1} + [(1 - \lambda^2)/(1 + \lambda^2)^{3/2}] u_{t-3}$, is sufficient to lend credibility to this assertion.

In this section, we shall consider the standard instrumental variables estimator, as well as certain two-step procedures. For simplicity, we shall confine our attention to the case where there is only one explanatory variable.

The standard instrumental variables estimator first proposed by Livi-atan [96] in just this context is obtained as the solution to

$$\begin{aligned} \tilde{\alpha} \Sigma x_t^2 + \tilde{\lambda} \Sigma x_t y_{t-1} &= \Sigma x_t y_t \\ \tilde{\alpha} \Sigma x_t x_{t-1} + \tilde{\lambda} \Sigma x_{t-1} y_{t-1} &= \Sigma x_{t-1} y_t \end{aligned} \quad (6.57)$$

It has the representation

$$\begin{pmatrix} \tilde{\alpha} \\ \tilde{\lambda} \end{pmatrix} - \begin{pmatrix} \alpha \\ \lambda \end{pmatrix} = \begin{bmatrix} x'x & x'y_{-1} \\ x'_{-1}x & x'_{-1}y_{-1} \end{bmatrix}^{-1} \begin{bmatrix} x'w \\ x'_{-1}w \end{bmatrix} \tag{6.58}$$

Here we define

$$\begin{aligned}
x &= (x_2, x, \dots, x_T)', & x_{-1} &= (x_1, x_2, \dots, x_{T-1})' \\
y &= (y_2, y_3, \dots, y_T)', & y_{-1} &= (y_1, y_2, \dots, y_{T-1})' \\
u &= (u_2, u_3, \dots, u_T)', & u_{-1} &= (u_1, u_2, \dots, u_{T-1})' \\
w &= u - \lambda u_{-1}
\end{aligned} \tag{6.59}$$

This results from the fact that this estimator utilizes the reduced model, which thus loses one observation. The consistency of this estimator is a trivial consequence of the assumption that the errors are independent of the explanatory variable.

Assuming boundedness conditions on the explanatory variable similar to those in (6.27), we shall now consider the asymptotic distribution of

$$d_T\left[\begin{pmatrix} \tilde{\alpha} \\ \tilde{\lambda} \end{pmatrix} - \begin{pmatrix} \alpha \\ \lambda \end{pmatrix}\right] = \left\{d_T^{-2}\begin{bmatrix} x'x & x'y_{-1} \\ x'_{-1}x & x'_{-1}y_{-1} \end{bmatrix}\right\}^{-1} d_T^{-1}\begin{bmatrix} x'w \\ x'_{-1}w \end{bmatrix} \tag{6.60}$$

Since the matrix in the right member of (6.60) has a well-defined probability limit, the asymptotic distribution of the estimator is essentially determined by that of

$$d_T^{-1}\begin{bmatrix} x'w \\ x'_{-1}w \end{bmatrix}$$

where

$$d_T^2 = \sum_{t=1}^{T} x_t^2 \tag{6.61}$$

It will facilitate our task of comparing alternative estimators if we introduce the following notation:

$$w = Fu \tag{6.62}$$

where F is the $(T - 1) \times T$ matrix,

$$F = \begin{bmatrix} -\lambda & 1 & 0 & 0 & \cdot & 0 \\ 0 & -\lambda & 1 & 0 & \cdot & \cdot \\ \cdot & & & & & \cdot \\ \cdot & & & & & \cdot \\ \cdot & & & & & 0 \\ 0 & \cdot & & 0 & -\lambda & 1 \end{bmatrix} \tag{6.63}$$

and $u = (u_1, u_2, \dots, u_T)'$.

Notice that w is the error vector of the *reduced model*. It follows immediately that

$$\text{Cov}(w) = \sigma^2 FVF' = \sigma^2 \Phi \tag{6.64}$$

If $u \sim N(0, \sigma^2 V)$, then, in virtue of the independence of x_t and u_t, we conclude that for *every* T,

$$\begin{bmatrix} x'w \\ x'_{-1}w \end{bmatrix} \sim N[0, \sigma^2(x, x_{-1})'\Phi(x, x_{-1})] \tag{6.65}$$

If u is *not* normally distributed, but its elements possess (uniformly) bounded third absolute moment, then, asymptotically,

$$d_T^{-1}\begin{bmatrix} x'w \\ x'_{-1}w \end{bmatrix} \sim N\left[0, \sigma^2 \lim_{T\to\infty} d_T^{-2}(x, x_{-1})'\Phi(x, x_{-1})\right] \tag{6.66}$$

Since the matrix in the right member of (6.60) has a well-defined probability limit, we further conclude that, asymptotically,

$$d_T\left[\begin{pmatrix} \tilde{\alpha} \\ \lambda \end{pmatrix} - \begin{pmatrix} \alpha \\ \lambda \end{pmatrix}\right] \sim N(0, C_I) \tag{6.67}$$

where

$$C_I = \sigma^2 A_I^{-1} B_I A_I'^{-1} \tag{6.68}$$

and

$$A_I = \lim_{T\to\infty} d_T^{-2}\begin{bmatrix} x'x & x'\bar{y}_{-1} \\ x'_{-1}x & x'_{-1}\bar{y}_{-1} \end{bmatrix}, \quad B_I = \lim_{T\to\infty} d_T^{-2}(x, x_{-1})'\Phi(x, x_{-1})$$

$$\bar{y}_t = \alpha \sum_{i=0}^{\infty} \lambda^i x_{t-i}, \quad \bar{y}_{-1} = (\bar{y}_1, \bar{y}_2, \ldots, \bar{y}_{T-1})' \tag{6.69}$$

The marginal asymptotic distribution of the ML estimators of α and λ, as determined in the previous section, is given by

$$d_T\left[\begin{pmatrix} \hat{\alpha} \\ \hat{\gamma} \end{pmatrix} - \begin{pmatrix} \alpha \\ \lambda \end{pmatrix}\right] \sim N(0, C_M) \tag{6.70}$$

where

$$C_M = \sigma^2 \lim_{T\to\infty}\left\{d_T^{-2}\begin{bmatrix} x^{*'}V^{-1}x^* & \alpha x^{*'}V^{-1}\dfrac{\partial x^*}{\partial \lambda} \\ \alpha \dfrac{\partial x^{*'}}{\partial \lambda}V^{-1}x^* & \alpha^2 \dfrac{\partial x^{*'}}{\partial \lambda}V^{-1}\dfrac{\partial x^*}{\partial \lambda} \end{bmatrix}\right\}^{-1} \tag{6.71}$$

In the above, x^* is exactly $x_{.1}^*$ of (6.30).

It is natural, now, to ask whether the ML is asymptotically efficient relative to this IV estimator. Although in the notation of (6.69) and

(6.70) an answer to this appears to be hopeless, a slight change in the notation will make such comparison rather simple.

As we noted in Section 5.11, the meaning of the vector x in the context of IV estimation differs slightly from that in the context of ML estimation. We had also indicated there, that in the covariance matrices of the asymptotic distributions, it involves no loss of accurary to represent the vector $x^* = (x_1^*, x_2^*, \ldots, x_T^*)'$ by

$$x^* = Dx, \quad x = (x_1, x_2, \ldots, x_T)'$$

$$D = \begin{bmatrix} 1 & 0 & \cdot & & 0 \\ \lambda & 1 & & & \cdot \\ \cdot & \lambda & & & \cdot \\ \cdot & \cdot & & & \cdot \\ \cdot & \cdot & \cdot & & 0 \\ \lambda^{T-1} & \lambda^{T-2} & \lambda & & 1 \end{bmatrix} \tag{6.72}$$

Since

$$\frac{\partial x_t^*}{\partial \lambda} = \frac{I}{(I - \lambda L)^2} x_{t-1} = \frac{I}{I - \lambda L} \left(\frac{I}{I - \lambda L} x_{t-1} \right) \tag{6.73}$$

we have

$$\alpha \frac{\partial x_t^*}{\partial \lambda} = \frac{I}{I - \lambda L} \bar{y}_{t-1}, \quad \bar{y}_{t-1} = \frac{\alpha I}{I - \lambda L} x_{t-1} \tag{6.74}$$

Hence we can write, without loss of accuracy in (6.71),

$$\alpha \frac{\partial x^*}{\partial \lambda} = D \bar{y}_{-1}, \quad \bar{y}_{t-1} = (\bar{y}_0, \bar{y}_1, \ldots, \bar{y}_{T-1})' \tag{6.75}$$

But then we can obviously write

$$C_M = \sigma^2 \lim_{T \to \infty} \left\{ d_T^{-2} \begin{bmatrix} x'D'V^{-1}Dx & x'D'V^{-1}D\bar{y}_{-1} \\ \bar{y}_{-1}'D'V^{-1}Dx & \bar{y}_{-1}'D'V^{-1}D\bar{y}_{-1} \end{bmatrix}^{-1} \right\} \tag{6.76}$$

Let

$$D'V^{-1}D = \Psi \tag{6.77}$$

and note that

$$\Psi^{-1} = D^{-1}VD'^{-1}, \quad D^{-1} = \begin{bmatrix} 1 & 0 & \cdot & \cdot & 0 \\ -\lambda & 1 & \cdot & \cdot & 0 \\ 0 & -\lambda & 1 & \cdot & 0 \\ \vdots & & & & \\ 0 & & 0 & -\lambda & 1 \end{bmatrix} \tag{6.78}$$

Define the T-element vector $e = (1, 0, \ldots, 0)'$ and write, in virtue of (6.63),

$$D^{-1} = \begin{pmatrix} e' \\ F \end{pmatrix} \tag{6.79}$$

Hence,

$$D^{-1}VD'^{-1} = \begin{pmatrix} e' \\ F \end{pmatrix} V(e, F') = \begin{bmatrix} e'Ve & e'VF' \\ FVe & FVF' \end{bmatrix} = \begin{bmatrix} e'Ve & e'VF' \\ FVe & \Phi \end{bmatrix} \tag{6.80}$$

Now the vector x appearing in (6.65) is defined by $x = (x_2, x_3, \ldots, x_T)'$, $x_{-1} = (x_1, x_2, \ldots, x_{T-1})'$. For the purpose of this argument only, denote these by x^2, x^1_{-1}. Thus the vector x appearing in the ML estimator becomes

$$x = \begin{pmatrix} x_1 \\ x^2 \end{pmatrix}, \quad x_{-1} = \begin{pmatrix} x_0 \\ x^1_{-1} \end{pmatrix} \tag{6.81}$$

Using (6.80) and (6.81), we have

$$x'D^{-1}VD'^{-1}x = x_1^2 e'Ve + 2x_1 e'VF'x^2 + x^{2'}\Phi x^2 \tag{6.82}$$

But

$$x_1^2 e'Ve = \frac{x_1^2}{1 - \rho^2}, \quad x_1 e'VF'x^2 = \frac{(\rho - \lambda)x_1}{1 - \rho^2} \sum_{i=0}^{T-2} \rho^i x_{i+2} \tag{6.83}$$

and it is clear that

$$\lim_{T \to \infty} d_T^{-2}[x'D^{-1}VDx] = \lim_{T \to \infty} [d_T^{-2}x^{2'}\Phi x^2] \tag{6.84}$$

Entirely similar arguments will convince the reader that the asymptotic covariance matrix of the IV estimator can be written as

$$C_I = \sigma^2 \lim_{T \to \infty} [d_T^2(S'P)^{-1}S'\Psi^{-1}S(P'S)^{-1}] \tag{6.85}$$

where

$$S = (x, x_{-1}), \quad P = (x, \bar{y}_{-1}) \tag{6.86}$$

the vectors $x, x_{-1}, \bar{y}_{-1}$ having exactly the same meaning as in ML estimation.

In the notation of (6.86), we can rewrite (6.76) as

$$C_M = \sigma^2 \lim_{T \to \infty} [d_T^2(P'\Psi P)^{-1}] \tag{6.87}$$

Now define H_I by

$$(S'P)^{-1}S' = (P'\Psi P)^{-1}P'\Psi + H_I \tag{6.88}$$

and observe that

$$H_I P = 0 \tag{6.89}$$

Further,

$$(S'P)^{-1}S'\Psi^{-1} = (P'\Psi P)^{-1}P' + H_I\Psi^{-1} \tag{6.90}$$

Post-multiplying by the transpose of (6.88) and noting (6.89), we conclude that

$$(S'P)^{-1}S'\Psi^{-1}S(P'S)^{-1} = (P'\Psi P)^{-1} + H_I\Psi^{-1}H'_I \tag{6.91}$$

Thus,

$$C_I - C_M = \sigma^2 \lim_{T\to\infty} d_T^2 (H_I\Psi^{-1}H'_I) \tag{6.92}$$

which is a positive semidefinite matrix.

We have therefore proved:

THEOREM 6.2. Consider the model

$$y_t = \frac{\alpha I}{I - \lambda L} x_t + u_t, \quad t = 1, 2, \ldots, T \tag{6.93}$$

$$u_t = \rho u_{t-1} + \varepsilon_t, \quad |\rho| < 1 \tag{6.94}$$

where

$$\varepsilon \sim N(0, \sigma^2 I), \quad \varepsilon = (\varepsilon_1, \varepsilon_2, \ldots, \varepsilon_T)' \tag{6.95}$$

and the explanatory variable x_t is nonstochastic and obeys the boundedness conditions,

$$d_T^2 = \sum_{t=1}^T x_t^2, \quad \lim_{T\to\infty} d_T^2 = \infty, \quad \lim_{T\to\infty} \frac{\max\limits_{t\le T} x_t^2}{d_T^2} = 0 \tag{6.96}$$

Then the maximum likelihood estimator obeys, asymptotically,

$$d_T\left[\begin{pmatrix} \hat\alpha \\ \hat\lambda \end{pmatrix} - \begin{pmatrix} \alpha \\ \lambda \end{pmatrix}\right] \sim N(0, C_M) \tag{6.97}$$

The standard instrumental variables estimator obeys, asymptotically,

$$d_T\left[\begin{pmatrix} \hat\alpha \\ \hat\lambda \end{pmatrix} - \begin{pmatrix} \alpha \\ \lambda \end{pmatrix}\right] \sim N(0, C_I) \tag{6.98}$$

and the former is efficient relative to the latter in the sense that

$$C_I - C_M = \sigma^2 \lim_{T\to\infty} d_T^2 (H_I\Psi^{-1}H'_I) \tag{6.99}$$

is a positive semidefinite matrix.

In the above,

$$C_M = \sigma^2 \lim_{T \to \infty} [d_T^2 (P' \Psi P)^{-1}],$$

$$C_I = \sigma^2 \lim_{T \to \infty} [d_T^2 (S' P)^{-1} S' \Psi^{-1} S (P' S)^{-1}] \qquad (6.100)$$

and

$$S = (x, x_{-1}), \quad P = (x, \bar{y}_{-1}), \quad \Psi = D' V^{-1} D \qquad (6.101)$$

6.3 Geometric Distributed Lag with Autocorrelated Errors: Two-Step Estimators

In the preceding section we examined the IV estimator and compared it, in a relative efficiency sense, to the maximum likelihood estimator. The standard IV estimator, however, is patently inefficient in that it fails to take into account the probabilistic structure of the error term. Thus, in the case of the autoregressive errors model, it is best regarded as an initial estimator for an iterative or a two-stage procedure.

In this section we shall examine a number of two-step estimators; our purpose is to establish procedures which are somewhat simpler to execute than the ML estimator, and to point out certain limitations in the efficiency characteristics of such two-step estimators.

In an attempt to simplify the estimation problem with respect to the model

$$y_t = \frac{\alpha I}{I - \lambda L} x_t + \frac{I}{I - \rho L} \varepsilon_t \qquad (6.102)$$

one may proceed as follows.

Observe that we can write

$$\frac{\alpha I}{I - \lambda L} x_t = \alpha x_t + \lambda \bar{y}_{t-1}, \quad \bar{y}_t = \frac{\alpha I}{I - \lambda L} x_t \qquad (6.103)$$

Hence, if initial consistent estimators are available for α and λ, say the IV ones $\tilde{\alpha}$, $\tilde{\lambda}$, we can compute

$$\bar{y}_t = \tilde{\alpha} \sum_{i=0}^{t-1} \tilde{\lambda}^i x_{t-i} \qquad (6.104)$$

and thus obtain the residuals

$$\tilde{u}_t = y_t - \tilde{\alpha} x_t - \tilde{\lambda} \bar{y}_{t-1} \qquad (6.105)$$

From these we can obtain an estimator of ρ by

$$\tilde{\rho} = \frac{\sum_{t=2}^{T} \tilde{u}_t \tilde{u}_{t-1}}{\sum_{t=2}^{T} \tilde{u}_{t-1}^2} \tag{6.106}$$

This completes the first stage. In the second stage, we obtain the estimator

$$\begin{pmatrix} \tilde{\alpha} \\ \tilde{\lambda} \end{pmatrix}_* = [(x, \tilde{y}_{-1})' \tilde{V}^{-1}(x, \tilde{y}_{-1})]^{-1}(x, \tilde{y}_{-1})' \tilde{V}^{-1}y \tag{6.107}$$

This is simply the feasible Aitken estimator applied to the model[29]

$$y_t = \alpha x_t + \lambda \tilde{y}_{t-1} + u_t \tag{6.108}$$

It may be thought that since α, λ and ρ are consistently estimated, the quantity in (6.108) has the same asymptotic distribution as the estimators obtained by ML techniques. Unfortunately, this is not so. Before we proceed to this aspect, however, let us examine the properties of ρ as given in (6.106). To this effect, recall the definition of D in (6.72) and notice that, for sufficiently large T,

$$\tilde{u} = u - (\tilde{\alpha} - \alpha)x - (\tilde{\lambda}\tilde{D} - \lambda D)x, \quad \tilde{u} = (\tilde{u}_1, \tilde{u}_2, \ldots, \tilde{u}_T)' \tag{6.109}$$

If for simplicity of argument we assume that $\lim_{T \to \infty} d_T^2/T$ is finite, then we can write

$$\frac{1}{T}\tilde{u}'\tilde{u} = \frac{1}{T}u'u - 2(\tilde{\alpha} - \alpha)\frac{x'u}{T} - 2\frac{x'(\tilde{\lambda}\tilde{D} - \lambda D)u}{T}$$
$$+ (\tilde{\alpha} - \alpha)\frac{x'(\tilde{\lambda}\tilde{D} - \lambda D)'x}{T} + (\tilde{\alpha} - \alpha)\frac{x'(\tilde{\lambda}\tilde{D} - \lambda D)'x}{T} \tag{6.110}$$
$$+ \frac{x'(\tilde{\lambda}\tilde{D} - \lambda D)'(\tilde{\lambda}\tilde{D} - \lambda D)x}{T}$$

It is easily seen that, in view of the consistency of $\tilde{\alpha}$ and $\tilde{\lambda}$, the finiteness of the second moment of the explanatory variable and its inde-

---

[29] The Aitken estimator in the context of the model of (6.102), as expressed in (6.103), would have been $[(x, \tilde{y}_{-1})' V^{-1}(x, \tilde{y}_{-1})]^{-1}(x, \tilde{y}_{-1})' V^{-1}y$. Since V is generally not known, this is not a feasible estimator. The term *feasible Aitken* estimator refers to the fact that for the unknown (inverse) covariance matrix V^{-1}, we substitute its consistent estimator $\tilde{V}^{-1}$, and for $\tilde{y}_{-1}$ we substitute $\tilde{y}_{-1}$.

pendence of the error term,

$$\plim_{T\to\infty} \frac{1}{T} u'u = \plim_{T\to\infty} \frac{1}{T} \tilde{u}'\tilde{u} = \frac{\sigma^2}{1-\rho^2} \qquad (6.111)$$

But it is then apparent from (6.110) that

$$\plim_{T\to\infty} \tilde{\rho} = \frac{\plim_{T\to\infty} (1/T) \sum_{t=2}^{T} \tilde{u}_t \tilde{u}_{t-1}}{\plim_{T\to\infty} (1/T) \sum_{t=2}^{T} \tilde{u}_{t-1}^2}$$

$$= \frac{\plim_{T\to\infty} (1/T) \sum u_t u_{t-1}}{\plim_{T\to\infty} (1/T) \sum u_{t-1}^2} = \rho_0. \qquad (6.112)$$

Incidentally, (6.112) shows that, asymptotically, $\sqrt{T}\,(\tilde{\rho} - \rho_0)$ behaves like

$$\frac{1-\rho^2}{\sigma^2} \frac{1}{\sqrt{T}} \sum_{t=2}^{T} u_{t-1}\varepsilon_t$$

Now, what is the asymptotic distribution of $(\tilde{\alpha}, \tilde{\lambda})_*$? Substituting from (6.1) and (6.2) in (6.107), we have

$$\begin{pmatrix} \tilde{\alpha} \\ \tilde{\lambda} \end{pmatrix}_* = [(x, \tilde{y}_{-1})' \tilde{V}^{-1}(x, \tilde{y}_{-1})]^{-1}(x, \tilde{y}_{-1})' \tilde{V}^{-1}(x, \tilde{y}_{-1})\begin{pmatrix} \alpha \\ \lambda \end{pmatrix}$$

$$+ [(x, \tilde{y}_{-1})' \tilde{V}^{-1}(x, \tilde{y}_{-1})]^{-1}(x, \tilde{y}_{-1})' \tilde{V}^{-1}u \qquad (6.113)$$

Now, it is clearly the case that

$$\plim_{T\to\infty} \frac{\tilde{P}' \tilde{V}^{-1} \tilde{P}}{T} = \plim_{T\to\infty} \frac{\tilde{P}' V^{-1} P}{T}, \quad \tilde{P} = (x, \tilde{y}_{-1}) \qquad (6.114)$$

and P is as defined (6.86). Since

$$\plim_{T\to\infty} \frac{1}{T} (x, \tilde{y}_{-1})' \tilde{V}^{-1}u = \plim_{T\to\infty} \frac{1}{T} (x, \tilde{y}_{-1})' V^{-1}u = 0 \qquad (6.115)$$

we conclude that

$$\plim_{T\to\infty} \begin{pmatrix} \tilde{\alpha} \\ \tilde{\lambda} \end{pmatrix}_* = \begin{pmatrix} \alpha \\ \lambda \end{pmatrix} \qquad (6.116)$$

so that this estimator is consistent.

However, the asymptotic distribution of

$$\sqrt{T}\left[\begin{pmatrix} \tilde{\alpha} \\ \tilde{\lambda} \end{pmatrix}_* - \begin{pmatrix} \alpha \\ \lambda \end{pmatrix}\right]$$

is not that of $(\tilde{P}'\tilde{V}^{-1}\tilde{P}/T)^{-1}(\tilde{P}'\tilde{V}^{-1}u/\sqrt{T})$. This is so because it is apparent from (6.113) that

$$(\tilde{P}'\tilde{V}^{-1}\tilde{P})^{-1}\,\tilde{P}'\tilde{V}^{-1}P \neq I \tag{6.117}$$

and herein lies the essential difference between this estimator and the one obtained when $\bar{y}_t$ is known. Of course, this is a rather moot point, since this will generally be impossible. At any rate, we shall presently see that the cost of using $\tilde{y}_{t-1}$ instead of $\bar{y}_{t-1}$ will be that the asymptotic distribution of the estimator will depend on terms due to the relation in (6.117).

Let us now be more precise. We have

$$\sqrt{T}\left[\begin{pmatrix}\tilde{\alpha}\\\tilde{\lambda}\end{pmatrix}_* - \begin{pmatrix}\alpha\\\lambda\end{pmatrix}\right] = \sqrt{T}\left[\left(\frac{\tilde{P}'\tilde{V}^{-1}\tilde{P}}{T}\right)^{-1}\frac{\tilde{P}'\tilde{V}^{-1}P}{T} - I\right]\begin{bmatrix}\alpha\\\lambda\end{bmatrix} \\ + \left(\frac{\tilde{P}'\tilde{V}^{-1}\tilde{P}}{T}\right)^{-1}\frac{\tilde{P}\tilde{V}^{-1}u}{\sqrt{T}} \tag{6.118}$$

and the problem is to appraise the asymptotic behavior of the first term of the right member of (6.118).

We can obviously expand by Taylor series to obtain

$$\tilde{P} = P + \frac{\partial P}{\partial\alpha}(\tilde{\alpha} - \alpha_0) + \frac{\partial P}{\partial\lambda}(\tilde{\lambda} - \lambda_0) + \text{second order terms}^{30} \tag{6.119}$$

where

$$\frac{\partial}{\partial\alpha}P = (0,\, x_{-1}^*),\quad \frac{\partial}{\partial\lambda}P = \left(0,\, \alpha\frac{\partial x_{-1}^*}{\partial\lambda}\right),\quad x_{-1}^* = Dx_{-1} \tag{6.120}$$

Thus,

$$\tilde{P}'\tilde{V}^{-1}P = \tilde{P}'\tilde{V}^{-1}\tilde{P} - \left[\tilde{P}'\tilde{V}^{-1}\frac{\partial P}{\partial\alpha}\right](\tilde{\alpha} - \alpha_0) - \left[\tilde{P}'\tilde{V}^{-1}\frac{\partial P}{\partial\alpha}\right](\tilde{\lambda} - \lambda_0)$$

$$+ \text{ contributions of second order terms} \tag{6.121}$$

---

[30] This expansion may appear to be invalid since as $T \to \infty$, $\tilde{P}$ becomes infinite dimensional. However, this difficulty is more apparent than real. In fact, we can expand $\tilde{P}'\tilde{V}^{-1}\tilde{P}$, which is always finite dimensional, and obtain exactly the same results. We choose the present approach because of its essential simplicity and because its meaning is immediately transparent to the reader.

These remarks will apply to subsequent expansions and we shall not repeat them.

It follows that

$$\sqrt{T}\left[\left(\frac{\tilde{P}'\tilde{V}^{-1}\tilde{P}}{T}\right)^{-1}\frac{\tilde{P}'\tilde{V}^{-1}P}{T} - I\right] = -\left(\frac{\tilde{P}'\tilde{V}^{-1}\tilde{P}}{T}\right)^{-1}$$

$$\times\left[\frac{1}{T}\left(\tilde{P}'\tilde{V}^{-1}\frac{\partial P}{\partial\alpha}\right)\sqrt{T}\,(\tilde{\alpha} - \alpha_0) + \frac{1}{T}\left(\tilde{P}'\tilde{V}^{-1}\frac{\partial P}{\partial\lambda}\right)\sqrt{T}\,(\tilde{\lambda} - \lambda_0)\right]$$

+ contributions of second order terms   (6.122)

Since

$$\operatorname*{plim}_{T\to\infty}\frac{1}{T}\tilde{P}'\tilde{V}^{-1}\frac{\partial P}{\partial\alpha} = \lim_{T\to\infty}\frac{1}{T}\begin{bmatrix} 0 & x'V^{-1}x^*_{-1} \\ 0 & \bar{y}_{-1}V^{-1}x^*_{-1} \end{bmatrix} = Q_1 \qquad (6.123)$$

is a matrix with nonstochastic elements, as is

$$\operatorname*{plim}_{T\to\infty}\frac{1}{T}\tilde{P}'\tilde{V}^{-1}\frac{\partial P}{\partial\lambda} = \lim_{T\to\infty}\frac{1}{T}\begin{bmatrix} 0 & \alpha x'V^{-1}\dfrac{\partial x^*_{-1}}{\partial\lambda} \\ 0 & \alpha \bar{y}'_{-1}V^{-1}\dfrac{\partial x^*_{-1}}{\partial\lambda} \end{bmatrix} = Q_2 \quad (6.124)$$

we conclude that, asymptotically, the behavior of the first term in the right member of (6.118) is that of

$$-\left[\operatorname*{plim}_{T\to\infty}\left(\frac{\tilde{P}'\tilde{V}^{-1}\tilde{P}}{T}\right)^{-1}\right][Q_1\sqrt{T}\,(\tilde{\alpha} - \alpha_0) + Q_2\sqrt{T}\,(\tilde{\lambda} - \lambda_0)]\begin{bmatrix} \alpha \\ \lambda \end{bmatrix}$$

Define the matrix,

$$Q = \left[Q_1\begin{pmatrix} \alpha \\ \lambda \end{pmatrix}, \quad Q_2\begin{pmatrix} \alpha \\ \lambda \end{pmatrix}\right] \qquad (6.125)$$

and recall that the IV estimators $\tilde{\alpha}$, $\tilde{\lambda}$, used above have the asymptotic behavior

$$\sqrt{T}\begin{pmatrix} \tilde{\alpha} - \alpha \\ \tilde{\lambda} - \lambda \end{pmatrix} \sim \left(\frac{S'P}{T}\right)^{-1}\frac{S'D^{-1}u}{\sqrt{T}}, \quad u = (u_1, u_2, \ldots, u_T)' \quad (6.126)$$

Since the asymptotic behavior of $\tilde{P}'\tilde{V}^{-1}u/\sqrt{T}$ is that of $P'V^{-1}u/\sqrt{T}$, we have that, asymptotically,

$$\sqrt{T}\left[\begin{pmatrix} \tilde{\alpha} \\ \tilde{\lambda} \end{pmatrix}_* - \begin{pmatrix} \alpha \\ \lambda \end{pmatrix}\right]$$

$$\sim \left[\operatorname*{plim}_{T\to\infty}\left(\frac{\tilde{P}'\tilde{V}^{-1}\tilde{P}}{T}\right)^{-1}\right]\frac{1}{\sqrt{T}}\left[P'V^{-1} - Q\left(\frac{S'P}{T}\right)^{-1}S'D^{-1}\right]u \quad (6.127)$$

Let

$$A = \plim_{T \to \infty} \left(\frac{\bar{P}' V^{-1} \bar{P}}{T} \right)^{-1}, \quad B = \plim_{T \to \infty} \left(\frac{S' P}{T} \right)^{-1}$$

$$G = \plim_{T \to \infty} \frac{P' D'^{-1} S}{T}, \quad \Psi^{-1} = D^{-1} V D'^{-1} \tag{6.128}$$

It follows quite easily from (6.127) that the asymptotic distribution of $(\tilde{\alpha}, \tilde{\lambda})_*$ is given by

$$\sqrt{T} \left[\begin{pmatrix} \tilde{\alpha} \\ \tilde{\lambda} \end{pmatrix}_* - \begin{pmatrix} \alpha \\ \lambda \end{pmatrix} \right] \sim N(0, C_*) \tag{6.129}$$

where

$$C_* = \sigma^2 [A - AQBG'A' - AGB'Q'A'] + AQC_I Q'A' \tag{6.130}$$

C_I being the covariance matrix of the asymptotic distribution of the standard IV estimator, discussed in the preceding section. In (6.130), the component $\sigma^2 A$ is the asymptotic covariance matrix of the estimator when $\bar{y}_{t-1}$ is actually known, and corresponds to the contribution of the term $(1/\sqrt{T}) P' V^{-1} u$; the component $AQC_I Q'A'$ is due to the fact that $\bar{y}_{t-1}$ is not known but is estimated by $\tilde{y}_{t-1}$, through the use of the estimators $\tilde{\alpha}, \tilde{\lambda}$, and corresponds to the contribution of the term $(1/\sqrt{T}) Q(S'P/T)^{-1} S'D^{-1}$; finally, the component $-\sigma^2 [AQBG'A' + AGB'Q'A]$ corresponds to the cross covariance of the two terms.

It would be an interesting problem for further research to deduce the efficiency of the estimator above relative to the ML and IV estimators; evidently, it should be asymptotically inferior to the former.

One thing, however, is quite clear from the preceding discussion. *The estimator derived above does not have the same asymptotic distribution as the ML estimator; nor is it the case that it has the same asymptotic distribution as the one obtained when $\bar{y}_{t-1}$ is known, in which case α and λ can be obtained from a feasible Aitken estimator in the context of*

$$y_t = \alpha x_t + \lambda \bar{y}_{t-1} + u_t \tag{6.131}$$

In the balance of this section, we shall deal with the simplified two-step estimators proposed, respectively, by Gupta [59] and Dhrymes [30]. The two-step procedure suggested by Gupta is as follows: Noting the probability structure of the error term in the Equation (6.131), apply the operator $(I - \rho L)$ to both sides to obtain

$$y_t = \alpha x_t + \lambda \bar{y}_{t-1} + \rho[y_{t-1} - \alpha x_{t-1} - \lambda \bar{y}_{t-2}] + \varepsilon_t \tag{6.132}$$

If initial consistent estimators, e.g., the IV ones, are available for α and λ, we can compute the quantities

$$\bar{y}_t = \tilde{\alpha} \sum_{i=0}^{t-1} \tilde{\lambda}^i x_{t-i}, \quad \tilde{u}_t = \bar{y}_t - \tilde{\alpha} x_t - \tilde{\lambda} \bar{y}_{t-1} \qquad (6.133)$$

and thus obtain parameter estimates by ordinary least squares (OLS) after substitution of the quantities $\bar{y}_{t-1}, \tilde{u}_{t-1}$ for $\bar{y}_{t-1}, u_{t-1}$ in (6.132). Precisely, the estimator is

$$\begin{pmatrix} \tilde{\alpha} \\ \tilde{\lambda} \\ \tilde{\rho} \end{pmatrix}_G = (\tilde{Z}'\tilde{Z})^{-1}\tilde{Z}'y \qquad (6.134)$$

where, of course,

$$\tilde{Z} = (x, \bar{y}_{-1}, \tilde{u}_{-1}), \qquad \bar{y}_{-1} = (\bar{y}_1, \bar{y}_2, \ldots, \bar{y}_{T-1})' \\ \tilde{u}_{-1} = (\tilde{u}_1, \tilde{u}_2, \ldots, \tilde{u}_{T-1})' \qquad (6.135)$$

If we denote

$$Z = (x, \bar{y}_{-1}, u_{-1}) \qquad (6.136)$$

and make the appropriate substitutions in (6.134), we find that

$$\begin{pmatrix} \tilde{\alpha} \\ \tilde{\lambda} \\ \tilde{\rho} \end{pmatrix}_G - \begin{pmatrix} \alpha \\ \lambda \\ \rho \end{pmatrix} = \left[\left(\frac{\tilde{Z}'\tilde{Z}}{T} \right)^{-1} \frac{\tilde{Z}'Z}{T} - I \right] \begin{bmatrix} \alpha \\ \lambda \\ \rho \end{bmatrix} + \left(\frac{\tilde{Z}'\tilde{Z}}{T} \right)^{-1} \frac{\tilde{Z}'\epsilon}{T} \quad (6.137)$$

Since it is easily verified that

$$\operatorname*{plim}_{T \to \infty} \frac{\tilde{Z}'\tilde{Z}}{T} = \operatorname*{plim}_{T \to \infty} \frac{\tilde{Z}'Z}{T}, \quad \operatorname*{plim}_{T \to \infty} \frac{\tilde{Z}'\epsilon}{T} = 0 \qquad (6.138)$$

consistency is immediate.

The asymptotic distribution of this estimator is obtained by exactly the same techniques we employed earlier. Thus, our first task is to ascertain the contribution made by

$$\sqrt{T} \left[\left(\frac{\tilde{Z}'\tilde{Z}}{T} \right)^{-1} \frac{\tilde{Z}'Z}{T} - I \right] \begin{bmatrix} \alpha \\ \lambda \\ \rho \end{bmatrix}$$

to the asymptotic distribution. To this effect, observe that

$$\tilde{Z} = Z + \left(\frac{\partial}{\partial \alpha} Z \right)(\tilde{\alpha} - \alpha_0) + \left(\frac{\partial}{\partial \lambda} Z \right)(\tilde{\lambda} - \lambda_0) + \text{second order terms}$$

$$(6.139)$$

Thus,

$$\frac{\breve{Z}'Z}{T} = \frac{\breve{Z}'\breve{Z}}{T} - \left(\breve{Z}'\frac{\partial}{\partial\alpha}Z\right)(\tilde{\alpha} - \alpha_0) - \left(\breve{Z}'\frac{\partial}{\partial\lambda}Z\right)(\tilde{\lambda} - \lambda_0)$$

$$+ \text{ second order terms.} \tag{6.140}$$

Hence,

$$\left(\frac{\breve{Z}'\breve{Z}}{T}\right)^{-1}\frac{\breve{Z}'Z}{T} - I = -\left(\frac{\breve{Z}'\breve{Z}}{T}\right)^{-1}\frac{1}{T}\left[\left(\breve{Z}'\frac{\partial}{\partial\alpha}Z\right)(\tilde{\alpha} - \alpha_0)\right.$$

$$\left. + \left(\breve{Z}'\frac{\partial}{\partial\lambda}Z\right)(\tilde{\lambda} - \lambda_0) + \text{ second order terms}\right] \tag{6.141}$$

Since

$$\frac{\partial}{\partial\alpha}Z = (0, x_{-1}^*, -x_{-1} - \lambda x_{-2}^*)$$

$$\frac{\partial}{\partial\lambda}Z = \left(0, \alpha\frac{\partial x_{-1}^*}{\partial\lambda}, -\bar{y}_{-2} - \lambda\alpha\frac{\partial x_{-2}^*}{\partial\lambda}\right) \tag{6.142}$$

and since $\sqrt{T}(\tilde{\alpha} - \alpha_0)$, $\sqrt{T}(\tilde{\lambda} - \lambda_0)$ have a well-defined asymptotic distribution, we conclude that the contribution of the second order terms vanishes and that $\sqrt{T}$ times the left member of (6.141) behaves like

$$\sqrt{T}\left[\left(\frac{\breve{Z}'\breve{Z}}{T}\right)^{-1}\frac{\breve{Z}'Z}{T} - I\right] \sim -\operatorname*{plim}_{T\to\infty}\left(\frac{\breve{Z}'\breve{Z}}{T}\right)^{-1}\left[\operatorname*{plim}_{T\to\infty}\frac{1}{T}\left(\breve{Z}'\frac{\partial}{\partial\alpha}Z\right)\right.$$

$$\times \sqrt{T}(\tilde{\alpha} - \alpha_0) + \operatorname*{plim}_{T\to\infty}\frac{1}{T}\left(\breve{Z}'\frac{\partial}{\partial\lambda}Z\right)\sqrt{T}(\tilde{\lambda} - \lambda_0)\right] \tag{6.143}$$

But we note that

$$\operatorname*{plim}_{T\to\infty}\left(\frac{\breve{Z}'\breve{Z}}{T}\right)^{-1} = \lim_{T\to\infty}\begin{bmatrix}\left(\frac{P'P}{T}\right)^{-1} & 0 \\ 0 & 0\end{bmatrix} + \begin{bmatrix}0 & 0 \\ 0 & \dfrac{1-\rho^2}{\sigma^2}\end{bmatrix} \tag{6.144}$$

where, of course,

$$P = (x, \bar{y}_{-1}) \tag{6.145}$$

In addition,

$$\operatorname*{plim}_{T\to\infty}\frac{1}{T}\left(\breve{Z}'\frac{\partial}{\partial\alpha}Z\right) = \lim_{T\to\infty}\frac{1}{T}\begin{bmatrix}0 & x'x_{-1}^* & -x'x_{-1} - \lambda x'x_{-2}^* \\ 0 & \bar{y}_{-1}'x_{-1}^* & -\bar{y}_{-1}'x_{-1} - \lambda\bar{y}_{-1}'x_{-2}^* \\ 0 & 0 & 0\end{bmatrix}$$

$$\tag{6.146}$$

Similarly,

$$\operatorname*{plim}_{T\to\infty}\frac{1}{T}\left(\tilde{Z}'\frac{\partial}{\partial\lambda}Z\right)=\lim_{T\to\infty}\frac{1}{T}\begin{bmatrix}0 & x'\dfrac{\partial\bar{y}_{-1}}{\partial\lambda} & -x'\bar{y}_{-2}-\lambda x'\dfrac{\partial\bar{y}_{-2}}{\partial\lambda}\\[2mm] 0 & \bar{y}'_{-1}\dfrac{\partial\bar{y}_{-1}}{\partial\lambda} & -\bar{y}'_{-1}\bar{y}_{-2}-\lambda\bar{y}'_{-1}\dfrac{\partial\bar{y}_{-2}}{\partial\lambda}\\[2mm] 0 & 0 & 0\end{bmatrix}$$

(6.147)

Thus, asymptotically,

$$\sqrt{T}\left[\left(\frac{\tilde{Z}'\tilde{Z}}{T}\right)^{-1}\frac{\tilde{Z}'Z}{T}-I\right]\begin{bmatrix}\alpha\\\lambda\\\rho\end{bmatrix}\sim\begin{bmatrix}-\left(\dfrac{P'P}{T}\right)^{-1}Q^*\sqrt{T}\begin{pmatrix}\tilde{\alpha}-\alpha_0\\\tilde{\lambda}-\lambda_0\end{pmatrix}\\[4mm] 0\end{bmatrix}$$

(6.148)

where

$$Q^*=\lim_{T\to\infty}\frac{1}{T}\begin{bmatrix}\lambda x'x^*_{-1}-\rho x'x_{-1}-\lambda\rho x'x^*_{-1}\\[3mm] \lambda\bar{y}'_{-1}x^*_{-1}-\rho\bar{y}'_{-1}x_{-1}-\lambda\rho\bar{y}'_{-1}x_{-2}\end{bmatrix}$$
$$\begin{bmatrix}\lambda x'\dfrac{\partial\bar{y}_{-1}}{\partial\lambda}-\rho x'\bar{y}_{-2}-\lambda\rho x'\dfrac{\partial\bar{y}_{-2}}{\partial\lambda}\\[3mm] \lambda\bar{y}'_{-1}\dfrac{\partial\bar{y}_{-1}}{\partial\lambda}-\rho\bar{y}'_{-1}\bar{y}_{-2}-\lambda\rho\bar{y}'_{-1}\dfrac{\partial\bar{y}_{-2}}{\partial\lambda}\end{bmatrix}$$

(6.149)

and therefore,

$$\sqrt{T}\left[\begin{pmatrix}\tilde{\alpha}\\\tilde{\lambda}\\\tilde{\rho}\end{pmatrix}_G-\begin{pmatrix}\alpha\\\lambda\\\rho\end{pmatrix}\right]\sim\frac{1}{\sqrt{T}}\begin{bmatrix}\left(\dfrac{P'P}{T}\right)^{-1}\left[P'-Q^*\left(\dfrac{S'P}{T}\right)^{-1}S'D^{-1}M^{-1}\right]\varepsilon\\[4mm] \dfrac{1-\rho^2}{\sigma^2}u'_{-1}\varepsilon\end{bmatrix}$$

(6.150)

This follows from the fact that

$$\sqrt{T}\begin{pmatrix}\tilde{\alpha}-\alpha_0\\\tilde{\lambda}-\lambda_0\end{pmatrix}=\frac{1}{\sqrt{T}}\left(\frac{S'P}{T}\right)^{-1}S'(u-\lambda u_{-1})\sim\left(\frac{S'P}{T}\right)^{-1}\frac{S'D^{-1}u}{\sqrt{T}}$$
$$\varepsilon=Mu$$

(6.151)

and the asymptotic behavior of $\tilde{Z}'\varepsilon/\sqrt{T}$ is given by

$$\frac{\tilde{Z}'\varepsilon}{\sqrt{T}}\sim\frac{1}{\sqrt{T}}\begin{bmatrix}P'\varepsilon\\u'_{-1}\varepsilon\end{bmatrix}$$

(6.152)

But the asymptotic distribution of the quantity in the right member of (6.150) is easily established by the techniques developed in Section 4.8. As in that discussion, we can write

$$u_{t-1} = u_{t-1}^N + \rho^{N-1}u_{t-N}, \quad u_{t-1}^N = \sum_{\tau=0}^{N-2} \rho^{\tau}\varepsilon_{t-1-\tau} \quad (6.153)$$

If N is chosen sufficiently large, $\rho^{N-1}u_{t-N}$ can be made arbitrarily small, and thus we need only deal with

$$\frac{1}{\sqrt{T}}\begin{bmatrix} \left(\dfrac{P'P}{T}\right)^{-1}\left[P' - Q^*\left(\dfrac{S'P}{T}\right)^{-1}S'D^{-1}M^{-1}\right]\varepsilon \\[2ex] \dfrac{1-\rho^2}{\sigma^2}u_{-1}^N\varepsilon \end{bmatrix}$$

If $r_{.t}$ is the tth column of the matrix multiplying ε above, we may write

$$\frac{1}{\sqrt{T}}\begin{bmatrix} \left(\dfrac{P'P}{T}\right)^{-1}\left[P' - Q^*\left(\dfrac{S'P}{T}\right)^{-1}S'D^{-1}M^{-1}\right]\varepsilon \\[2ex] \dfrac{1-\rho^2}{\sigma^2}u_{-1}^N\varepsilon \end{bmatrix}$$

$$= \frac{1}{\sqrt{T}}\sum_{t=2}^{T}\begin{bmatrix} r_{.t} \\[1ex] \dfrac{1-\rho^2}{\sigma^2}u_{t-1}^N \end{bmatrix}\varepsilon_t \quad (6.154)$$

But this is seen to be the sum of N-dependent (vector) random variables. Defining

$$s_t = \left(a'r_{.t} + a^*\left(\frac{1-\rho^2}{\sigma^2}\right)u_{t-1}^N\right)\varepsilon_t \quad (6.155)$$

and noting that

$$\mathrm{Cov}(s_{i+j}, s_{i+N}) = 0, \quad j = 0, 1, 2, \ldots, N-1 \quad (6.156)$$

$$\mathrm{Var}(s_t) = \sigma^2(a', a^*)\begin{bmatrix} r_{.t}r_{.t}' & 0 \\[1ex] 0 & \dfrac{1}{\sigma^2}\left(\dfrac{1-\rho^2}{\sigma^2}\right)^2\sigma^4\sum_{\tau=0}^{N-2}\rho^{2\tau} \end{bmatrix}\begin{pmatrix} a \\ a^* \end{pmatrix}$$

$$\approx \sigma^2(a', a^*)\begin{bmatrix} r_{.t}r_{.t}' & 0 \\[1ex] 0 & \dfrac{1-\rho^2}{\sigma^2} \end{bmatrix}\begin{pmatrix} a \\ a^* \end{pmatrix} \quad (6.157)$$

we conclude, in view of Theorem 4.3, that asymptotically, $(\tilde{\alpha}, \tilde{\lambda})_G$ is independent of $\tilde{\rho}$; moreover, its marginal (asymptotic) distribution is

$$\sqrt{T}\left[\begin{pmatrix}\tilde{\alpha}\\\tilde{\lambda}\end{pmatrix}_G - \begin{pmatrix}\alpha\\\lambda\end{pmatrix}\right] \sim N(0, C_G) \tag{6.158}$$

where

$$C_G = \sigma^2[A^* - A^*Q^*BG^{*\prime}A^* - A^*G^*B'Q^{*\prime}A^*] + A^*Q^*C_iQ^{*\prime}A^* \tag{6.159}$$

and

$$A^* = \lim_{T\to\infty}\left(\frac{P'P}{T}\right)^{-1}, \quad G^* = \lim_{T\to\infty}\frac{P'M'^{-1}D'^{-1}S}{T} \tag{6.160}$$

The estimator $(\tilde{\alpha}, \tilde{\lambda})_G$ is thus seen to be quite similar to $(\tilde{\alpha}, \tilde{\lambda})_*$ in its asymptotic distribution aspects; since $A^* - A$ is an indefinite matrix for $\rho \neq 0$, $\rho \in (-1, 1)$, one may surmise that it is impossible to rank the two estimators in terms of relative asymptotic efficiency, although upon closer examination the two may turn out to have same asymptotic distribution. Certainly, this is a fit topic for further research.

The two-step estimator proposed by Dhrymes [30] is as follows: Reducing the model, we have

$$y_t = \alpha x_t + \lambda y_{t-1} + w_t, \quad w_t = u_t - \lambda u_{t-1}, \quad t = 2, 3, \ldots, T \tag{6.161}$$

Noting that

$$\text{Cov}(w) = \sigma^2\Phi, \quad w = (w_2, w_3, \ldots, w_T)' \tag{6.162}$$

we can obtain the feasible Aitken estimator as

$$\begin{pmatrix}\tilde{\alpha}\\\tilde{\lambda}\end{pmatrix}_D = [(x, y_{-1})'\tilde{\Phi}^{-1}(x, y_{-1})]^{-1}(x, y_{-1})'\tilde{\Phi}^{-1}y \tag{6.163}$$

This is feasible since Φ depends only on the parameters λ, ρ which can be estimated as follows: By instrumental variables techniques, obtain $\tilde{\alpha}$, $\tilde{\lambda}$ and then compute

$$\tilde{u}_t = y_t - \tilde{\alpha}x_t - \tilde{\lambda}\tilde{y}_{t-1}, \quad \tilde{y}_t = \tilde{\alpha}\sum_{i=0}^{t-1}\tilde{\lambda}^i x_{t-i} \tag{6.164}$$

From these residuals, we estimate

$$\tilde{\rho} = \frac{\sum \tilde{u}_t\tilde{u}_{t-1}}{\sum \tilde{u}_{t-1}^2} \tag{6.165}$$

much as we did in connection with $(\tilde{\alpha}, \tilde{\lambda})_*$.

Recalling the discussion following Equation (6.80), we see that $(\tilde{\alpha}, \tilde{\lambda})'_D$ is identical, in the limit, with the estimator

$$\begin{pmatrix} \tilde{\alpha} \\ \tilde{\lambda} \end{pmatrix}_D = [(x, y_{-1})'\tilde{\Psi}(x, y_{-1})]^{-1}[(x, y_{-1})'\tilde{\Psi}y] \qquad (6.166)$$

where now x, y_{-1} are vectors with T elements—instead of $T - 1$—and

$$\tilde{\Psi} = \tilde{D}'\tilde{V}^{-1}\tilde{D} \qquad (6.167)$$

It will be considerably more convenient to deal with the expression in (6.166).

We shall first show that this estimator is consistent. Now,

$$\begin{pmatrix} \tilde{\alpha} \\ \tilde{\lambda} \end{pmatrix}_D - \begin{pmatrix} \alpha \\ \lambda \end{pmatrix} = \left[\frac{1}{T}(x, y_{-1})'\tilde{\Psi}(x, y_{-1})\right]^{-1}\frac{1}{T}(x, y_{-1})'\tilde{\Psi}w \qquad (6.168)$$

and since the probability limit of the matrix in the right member of (6.168) is well-defined, we need only be concerned with

$$\plim_{T\to\infty}\frac{1}{T}(x, y_{-1})'\tilde{\Psi}w = \plim_{T\to\infty}\frac{1}{T}(x, \bar{y}_{-1})'\tilde{\Psi}w + \plim_{T\to\infty}\frac{1}{T}\begin{pmatrix} 0 \\ u'_{-1}\tilde{\Psi}w \end{pmatrix}$$

$$(6.169)$$

This follows because we can write

$$y_t = \bar{y}_t + u_t, \qquad \bar{y}_t = \alpha\sum_{i=0}^{\infty}\lambda^i x_{t-i} \qquad (6.170)$$

But the first term in the right member of (6.169) vanishes. Now, expand $\tilde{\Psi}$ by Taylor series about λ_0, ρ_0—the true parameter values—to obtain

$$\tilde{\Psi} = \Psi + \left[\frac{\partial}{\partial\lambda}\Psi\right](\tilde{\lambda} - \lambda_0) + \left[\frac{\partial}{\partial\rho}\right](\tilde{\rho} - \rho_0) + \text{second order terms}$$

$$(6.171)$$

Ψ and all derivatives being evaluated at λ_0, ρ_0.

Since it was established earlier that $\sqrt{T}(\tilde{\lambda} - \lambda_0)$, $\sqrt{T}(\tilde{\rho} - \rho_0)$ have well-defined asymptotic distributions, we see that

$$\plim_{T\to\infty}\frac{1}{T}u'_{-1}\left[\frac{\partial}{\partial\lambda}\Psi\right]w(\tilde{\lambda} - \lambda_0) = \plim_{T\to\infty}\frac{1}{T^{3/2}}u'_{-1}\left[\frac{\partial}{\partial\lambda}\Psi\right]w\sqrt{T}(\tilde{\lambda} - \lambda_0) = 0$$

$$(6.172)$$

Similarly, all other terms vanish beyond the first, so that we have

$$\operatorname*{plim}_{T \to \infty} \frac{1}{T} u'_{-1} \tilde{\Psi} w = \operatorname*{plim}_{T \to \infty} \frac{1}{T} u'_{-1} \Psi w \tag{6.173}$$

But

$$u'_{-1} \Psi w = \varepsilon'_{-1} M'^{-1} D' V^{-1} D D^{-1} u = \varepsilon'_{-1} M'^{-1} D' M' \varepsilon \tag{6.174}$$

where, of course,

$$\varepsilon = Mu \tag{6.175}$$

is a vector containing mutually independent identically distributed elements.

The matrix $M'^{-1} D' M'$ is *upper triangular*; thus, we conclude that

$$\operatorname*{plim}_{T \to \infty} \frac{1}{T} u'_{-1} \tilde{\Psi} w = 0 \tag{6.176}$$

which establishes the consistency of $(\tilde{\alpha}, \tilde{\lambda})_D$.

We next observe that

$$\operatorname*{plim}_{T \to \infty} \frac{1}{T} (x, y_{-1})' \tilde{\Psi} (x, y_{-1}) = \operatorname*{plim}_{T \to \infty} \frac{1}{T} P' \Psi P + \operatorname*{plim}_{T \to \infty} \frac{1}{T} \begin{bmatrix} 0 & 0 \\ 0 & u'_{-1} \Psi u_{-1} \end{bmatrix} \tag{6.177}$$

But

$$\operatorname*{plim}_{T \to \infty} \frac{1}{T} u'_{-1} \Psi u_{-1} = \operatorname*{plim}_{T \to \infty} \frac{1}{T} u'_{-1} D' V^{-1} D u_{-1} \tag{6.178}$$

Observe that the tth element of $D u_{-1}$ is simply

$$u_t^* = \sum_{i=0}^{t-1} \lambda^i u_{t-1-i}, \quad u^* = (u_1^*, u_2^*, \dots, u_T^*)' \tag{6.179}$$

Thus,

$$\frac{1}{T} u^{*\prime} V^{-1} u^* = \frac{1}{T} u_1^{*2} (1 - \rho^2) + \frac{1}{T} \sum_{t=2}^{T} (u_t^* - \rho u_{t-1}^*)^2 \tag{6.180}$$

Evidently,

$$\operatorname*{plim}_{T \to \infty} \frac{1}{T} u_1^{*2} (1 - \rho^2) = 0 \tag{6.181}$$

so that the probability limit of the left member of (6.180) is determined solely by the second term in the right member of that equation.

We observe that

$$u_t^* - \rho u_{t-1}^* = \sum_{j=0}^{t-1} \lambda^j u_{t-j} - \rho \sum_{i=0}^{t-2} \lambda^i u_{t-1-i}$$

$$= \lambda^{t-1} u_1 + \sum_{i=0}^{t-2} \lambda^i (u_{t-i} - \rho y_{t-1-i})$$

$$= \lambda^{t-1} u_1 + \sum_{i=0}^{t-2} \lambda^i \varepsilon_{t-i} \qquad (6.182)$$

Consequently,

$$\sum_{t=2}^{T} (u_t^* - \rho u_{t-1}^*)^2 = \sum_{t=2}^{T} [\varepsilon_t^* + \lambda^{t-1}(u_1 - \varepsilon_1^*)]^2$$

$$= \sum_{t=2}^{T} \varepsilon_t^{*2} + 2(u_1 - \varepsilon_1^*) \sum_{t=2}^{T} \lambda^{t-1} \varepsilon_t^*$$

$$+ (u_1 \varepsilon_1^*)^2 \sum_{t=2}^{T} \lambda^{2(t-1)} \qquad (6.183)$$

where

$$\varepsilon_t^* = \sum_{i=0}^{\infty} \lambda^i \varepsilon_{t-i} \qquad (6.184)$$

Since for all t,

$$E(\varepsilon_t^*) = 0 \qquad (6.185)$$

$$\mathrm{Var}(\varepsilon_t^*) = \frac{\sigma^2}{1 - \lambda^2} \qquad (6.186)$$

we immediately conclude that

$$\plim_{T \to \infty} \frac{1}{T} \sum_{t=2}^{\infty} \varepsilon_t^{*2} = \frac{\sigma^2}{1 - \lambda^2} \qquad (6.187)$$

We further observe that

$$\plim_{T \to \infty} \frac{1}{T} (u_1 - \varepsilon_1^*)^2 \sum_{t=2}^{T} \lambda^{2(t-1)} = 0 \qquad (6.188)$$

$$\plim_{T \to \infty} \frac{1}{T} (u_1 - \varepsilon_1^*) \sum_{t=2}^{T} \lambda^{t-1} \varepsilon_t^* = 0 \qquad (6.189)$$

We have therefore established that

$$\plim_{T \to \infty} \frac{1}{T} u_{-1}^{*\prime} V^{-1} u_{-1}^* = \frac{\sigma^2}{1 - \lambda^2} \qquad (6.190)$$

and hence that

$$\operatorname*{plim}_{T \to \infty} \frac{1}{T} u'_{-1} \Psi u_{-1} = \frac{\sigma^2}{1 - \lambda^2} \tag{6.191}$$

But this immediately implies

$$\operatorname*{plim}_{T \to \infty} \frac{1}{T} (x, y_{-1})' \Psi (x, y_{-1}) = \lim_{T \to \infty} \frac{1}{T} \begin{bmatrix} x' \Psi x & x' \Psi \bar{y}_{-1} \\ \bar{y}'_{-1} \Psi x & \bar{y}'_{-1} \Psi \bar{y}_{-1} + \dfrac{T\sigma^2}{1 - \lambda^2} \end{bmatrix} \tag{6.192}$$

Hence, the asymptotic distribution of the estimator hinges on the behavior of $(1/\sqrt{T})(x, y_{-1})' \Psi w$.

We may write

$$\frac{1}{\sqrt{T}} (x, y_{-1})' \tilde{\Psi} w = \frac{1}{\sqrt{T}} (x, \bar{y}_{-1})' \tilde{\Psi} w + \frac{1}{\sqrt{T}} (0, u_{-1})' \tilde{\Psi} w \tag{6.193}$$

It should be apparent by now that the asymptotic behavior of $(1/\sqrt{T}) \times (x, \bar{y}_{-1})' \tilde{\Psi} w$ is exactly that of $(1/\sqrt{T})(x, \bar{y}_{-1})' \Psi w$.

From (6.193), we see that we must also determine the behavior of $(1/\sqrt{T})(u'_{-1} \tilde{\Psi} w)$. Using the expansion in (6.171), we find that

$$\begin{aligned}
\frac{1}{\sqrt{T}} u'_{-1} \tilde{\Psi} w &= \frac{1}{\sqrt{T}} u'_{-1} \Psi w + \left[\frac{1}{T} u'_{-1} \left(\frac{\partial \Psi}{\partial \lambda} \right) w \right] \sqrt{T} (\tilde{\lambda} - \lambda_0) \\
&\quad + \left[\frac{1}{T} u'_{-1} \frac{\partial \Psi}{\partial \rho} w \right] \sqrt{T} (\tilde{\rho} - \rho_0)
\end{aligned} \tag{6.194}$$

The contribution of all second order terms is easily seen to vanish in probability; thus, we neglect them *ab initio*. Since $\sqrt{T}(\tilde{\lambda} - \lambda_0)$, $\sqrt{T}(\tilde{\rho} - \rho_0)$ have a well-defined asymptotic distribution, we need to determine $\operatorname{plim}_{T \to \infty} (1/T) u'_{-1} (\partial \Psi / \partial \lambda) w$, $\operatorname{plim}_{T \to \infty} (1/T) u'_{-1} (\partial \Psi / \partial \rho) w$.

Now,

$$\frac{\partial \Psi}{\partial \lambda} = \left(\frac{d}{d\lambda} D' \right) V^{-1} D + D' V^{-1} \left(\frac{d}{d\lambda} D \right) \tag{6.195}$$

and

$$\begin{aligned}
\frac{1}{T} u'_{-1} \left(\frac{d}{d\lambda} D' \right) V^{-1} D w &= \frac{1}{T} u'_{-1} \left(\frac{d}{d\lambda} D' \right) V^{-1} u \\
&= \frac{1}{T} \varepsilon'_{-1} M'^{-1} \left(\frac{d}{d\lambda} D' \right) M' \varepsilon
\end{aligned} \tag{6.196}$$

Since $M'^{-1}[(d/d\lambda)\,D']\,M'$ is an *upper triangular* matrix and the elements of ε are mutually independent, the probability limit of this expression is easily seen to vanish. In addition

$$\frac{1}{T}u'_{-1}D'\,V^{-1}\left(\frac{d}{d\lambda}D\right)w = \frac{1}{T}u'_{-1}D'\,V^{-1}\left(\frac{d}{d\lambda}D\right)D^{-1}u \qquad (6.197)$$

and we note that

$$\left(\frac{d}{d\lambda}D\right)D^{-1} = \begin{bmatrix} 0 & 0 & 0 & 0 & 0 \\ 1 & 0 & \cdot & \cdot & 0 \\ 2\lambda & 1 & \cdot & \cdot & \cdot \\ 3\lambda^2 & 2\lambda & \cdot & \cdot & \cdot \\ \cdot & \cdot & \cdot & \cdot & \cdot \\ \cdot & \cdot & \cdot & \cdot & \cdot \\ (T-1)\lambda^{T-2} & (T-2)\lambda^{T-3} & 2\lambda & 1 & 0 \end{bmatrix}$$

$$\times \begin{bmatrix} 1 & 0 & 0 & 0 & 0 & 0 \\ -\lambda & 1 & \cdot & \cdot & \cdot & \cdot \\ 0 & \cdot & \cdot & \cdot & \cdot & \cdot \\ \cdot & \cdot & \cdot & \cdot & \cdot & \cdot \\ \cdot & \cdot & \cdot & \cdot & \cdot & \cdot \\ 0 & \cdot & \cdot & 0 & -\lambda & 1 \end{bmatrix} = \begin{bmatrix} 0 & \cdot & \cdot & \cdot & 0 \\ 1 & 0 & \cdot & \cdot & \cdot \\ \lambda & \cdot & \cdot & \cdot & \cdot \\ \lambda^2 & \cdot & \cdot & \cdot & \cdot \\ \cdot & & & & \\ \cdot & & & & \\ \lambda^{T-1} & \cdot & \lambda & 1 & 0 \end{bmatrix} = DH \quad (6.198)$$

where

$$H = \begin{bmatrix} 0 & \cdot & \cdot & \cdot & \cdot & \cdot & \cdot & 0 \\ 1 & 0 & \cdot & \cdot & \cdot & \cdot & \cdot & 0 \\ 0 & 1 & 0 & \cdot & \cdot & \cdot & \cdot & \cdot \\ \cdot & \cdot & \cdot & \cdot & \cdot & \cdot & \cdot & \cdot \\ \cdot & \cdot & \cdot & \cdot & \cdot & \cdot & \cdot & \cdot \\ \cdot & \cdot & \cdot & \cdot & \cdot & \cdot & \cdot & \cdot \\ 0 & \cdot & \cdot & \cdot & \cdot & 0 & 1 & 0 \end{bmatrix} \qquad (6.199)$$

Thus,

$$\frac{1}{T}u'_{-1}D'\,V^{-1}\left(\frac{d}{d\lambda}D\right)D^{-1}u = \frac{1}{T}u'_{-1}D'\,V^{-1}D\,Hu \qquad (6.200)$$

But

$$Hu = \begin{bmatrix} 0 \\ u_1 \\ u_2 \\ \vdots \\ u_{T-1} \end{bmatrix} \tag{6.201}$$

which differs from u_{-1} *only in the first element*; from (6.191), we thus conclude that

$$\plim_{T \to \infty} \frac{1}{T} u'_{-1} \left(\frac{\partial}{\partial \lambda} \Psi \right) w = \frac{\sigma^2}{1 - \lambda^2} \tag{6.202}$$

Next,

$$\frac{\partial}{\partial \rho} \Psi = D' \begin{bmatrix} 0 & -1 & & & & 0 \\ -1 & 2\rho & -1 & & & 0 \\ 0 & & & & & \\ \cdot & & & & & \\ \cdot & & & & & \\ \cdot & & & & 2\rho & -1 \\ 0 & & & 0 & -1 & 0 \end{bmatrix} D \tag{6.203}$$

and

$$\frac{1}{T} u'_{-1} D' \begin{bmatrix} -u_2 \\ -u_1 + 2\rho u_2 - u_3 \\ \vdots \\ -u_{T-2} + 2\rho u_{T-1} - u_T \\ - u_{T-1} \end{bmatrix} = \frac{1}{T} \left[-u_0 u_2 \right.$$

$$+ \sum_{t=2}^{T-1} \left\{ \sum_{i=0}^{t-1} \lambda^i u_{t-1+i}(-u_{t-1} + 2\rho u_t - u_{t+1}) \right\} - u_{T-1} \sum_{i=0}^{T-1} \lambda^i u_{T-1-i} \right] \tag{6.204}$$

Thus,

$$\plim_{T \to \infty} \frac{1}{T} u'_{-1} \frac{\partial \Psi}{\partial \rho} w = \frac{\sigma^2}{1 - \rho^2} \left[-\frac{1}{1 - \lambda\rho} + \frac{\rho^2}{1 - \lambda\rho} \right] = -\frac{\sigma^2}{1 - \lambda\rho} \tag{6.205}$$

Therefore, the estimator behaves, asymptotically, as

$$
\sqrt{T}\left[\begin{pmatrix}\tilde{\alpha}\\\tilde{\lambda}\end{pmatrix}_D - \begin{pmatrix}\alpha\\\lambda\end{pmatrix}\right] \sim \operatorname*{plim}_{T\to\infty}\left[\frac{1}{T}(x,y_{-1})'\Psi(x,y_{-1})\right]^{-1}\left[\frac{1}{\sqrt{T}}\begin{pmatrix}x'\\\bar{y}'_{-1}\end{pmatrix}\Psi w\right.
$$

$$
\left. + \begin{pmatrix}0\\\dfrac{1}{\sqrt{T}}u'_{-1}\Psi w + \dfrac{\sigma^2}{1-\lambda^2}\sqrt{T}\,(\tilde{\lambda}-\lambda_0) - \dfrac{\sigma^2}{1-\lambda\rho}\sqrt{T}\,(\tilde{\rho}-\rho_0)\end{pmatrix}\right]
$$

$$\tag{6.206}$$

As it stands, this expression does not easily lend itself to easy determination of its distribution; fortunately, however, further simplifications are possible. As noted in the discussion following Equation (6.112), the asymptotic behavior of $\sqrt{T}\,(\tilde{\rho}-\rho_0)$ is given by

$$
\sqrt{T}\,(\tilde{\rho}-\rho_0) \sim \frac{1-\rho^2}{\sigma^2}\frac{1}{\sqrt{T}}\sum_t u_{t-1}\varepsilon_t \tag{6.207}
$$

Similarly, the expression involving $\sqrt{T}\,(\tilde{\lambda}-\lambda_0)$ can be simplified as follows:

$$
\sqrt{T}\,(\tilde{\lambda}-\lambda_0) = \sqrt{T}\left[\frac{(x'x)x'_{-1} - (x'x)x'}{(x'x)(x'_{-1}\bar{y}_{-1}) - (x'\bar{y}_{-1})(x'_{-1}x)}\right]w \tag{6.208}
$$

Put

$$
\varphi^* = \operatorname*{plim}_{T\to\infty}\frac{1}{T^2}[(x'x)x'_{-1}y_{-1} - (x'y_{-1})x'_{-1}x]
$$

$$
\varphi^*\varphi_1 = \lim_{T\to\infty}\frac{1}{T}x'x, \quad \varphi^*\varphi_2 = \lim_{T\to\infty}\frac{x'_{-1}x}{T} \tag{6.209}
$$

and observe that, asymptotically,

$$
\sqrt{T}\,(\tilde{\lambda}-\lambda_0) \sim \frac{1}{\sqrt{T}}(\varphi_1 x'_{-1} - \varphi_2 x')w
$$

$$
= \frac{1}{\sqrt{T}}(\varphi_1 x'_{-1} - \varphi_2 x')D^{-1}M^{-1}\varepsilon \tag{6.210}
$$

since

$$
w = D^{-1}u, \quad \varepsilon = Mu \tag{6.211}
$$

Thus, using the same simplifications as in (6.211), we can write

$$
\sqrt{T}\left[\begin{pmatrix} \tilde{\alpha} \\ \tilde{\lambda} \end{pmatrix}_D - \begin{pmatrix} \alpha \\ \lambda \end{pmatrix}\right] \sim \operatorname*{plim}_{T \to \infty} \left[\frac{1}{T}(x, y_{-1})' \Psi(x, y_{-1})\right]^{-1}
$$

$$
\times \frac{1}{\sqrt{T}} \begin{bmatrix} x'D'M' \\[6pt] \bar{y}'_{-1}D'M' + u'_{-1}D'M' + \dfrac{\sigma^2 \varphi_1}{1 - \lambda^2} x'_{-1}D^{-1}M^{-1} \\[10pt] - \dfrac{\sigma^2 \varphi_2}{1 - \lambda^2} x'D^{-1}M^{-1} - \dfrac{1 - \rho^2}{1 - \lambda \rho} u'_{-1} \end{bmatrix} \varepsilon \quad (6.212)
$$

This renders the problem of determination of the asymptotic distribution quite simple except for the term $u'_{-1}D'M'$. But notice that the first element of this vector is $\sqrt{1 - \rho^2}\, u_0$, while the tth element, $t = 2, 3, \ldots, T - 1$, is given by

$$
\sum_{i=0}^{t-1} \lambda^i u_{t-1-i} - \rho \sum_{i=0}^{t-2} \lambda^i u_{t-2-i} = \sum_{i=0}^{t-2} \lambda^i (u_{t-1-i} - \rho u_{t-2-i}) \lambda^{t-1} u_0
$$
$$
= \lambda^{t-1} u_0 + \sum_{i=0}^{t-2} \lambda^i \varepsilon_{t-1-i} \quad (6.213)
$$

Now,

$$
\operatorname*{plim}_{T \to \infty} \frac{1}{\sqrt{T}} u_0 \sum_{t=2}^{T} \lambda^{t-1} \varepsilon_t = 0 \quad (6.214)
$$

and the component $\lambda^{t-1} u_0$ in (6.213) may be neglected. Thus, define the tth component $(t > 1)$ of $u'_{-1}D'M'$ as

$$
u_t^* = \sum_{i=}^{t-2} \lambda^i \varepsilon_{t-1-i} \quad (6.215)
$$

and let

$$x_t^* \qquad \text{be the } t\text{th element of} \qquad x'D'M'$$

$$y_{t-1}^* \qquad \text{be the } t\text{th element of} \qquad \bar{y}'_{-1}D'M'$$

$$r_{t1}^* \qquad \text{be the } t\text{th element of} \qquad \varphi_1 \frac{\sigma^2}{1 - \lambda^2} x'_{-1}D^{-1}M^{-1}$$

$$r_{t2}^* \qquad \text{be the } t\text{th element of} \qquad -\varphi_2 \frac{\sigma^2}{1 - \lambda^2} x'D^{-1}M^{-1}$$

The quantity whose asymptotic distribution we seek to establish is of the form

$$
\frac{1}{\sqrt{T}} \sum_{t=2}^{T} \begin{pmatrix} x_t^* \\ \bar{y}_{t-1}^* + r_{t1}^* + r_{t2}^* + u_t^* - \dfrac{1 - \rho^2}{1 - \lambda \rho} u_{t-1} \end{pmatrix} \varepsilon_t
$$

Since, for t sufficiently large, we can write

$$u_t^* = \sum_{i=0}^{N_1-2} \lambda^i \varepsilon_{t-1-i} + \lambda^{N_1-1} \sum_{i=0}^{t-N_1-1} \lambda^j \varepsilon_{t-N_1-j} \qquad (6.216)$$

N_1 may be taken sufficiently large so that the second term of the right member of (6.216) can be made arbitrarily small in probability. Hence we may confine ourselves to the first term. Further,

$$u_t = \sum_{i=0}^{N_2-2} \rho^i \varepsilon_{t-i} + \rho^{N_2-1} u_{t-N_2+1} \qquad (6.217)$$

and again, N_2 may be taken large enough so that the second term in the right member is made arbitrarily small in probability. Let

$$N = \max(N_1, N_2) \qquad (6.218)$$

and notice that

$$\frac{1}{\sqrt{T}} \sum_{t=2}^{T} \left(\begin{matrix} x_t^* \\ \bar{y}_{t-1}^* + r_{t1}^* + r_{t2}^* + u_t^* - \dfrac{1-\rho^2}{1-\lambda\rho} u_{t-1} \end{matrix} \right) \varepsilon_t$$

$$= \frac{1}{\sqrt{T}} \sum_{t=2}^{N-1} \left(\begin{matrix} x_t^* \\ y_{t-1}^* + r_{t1}^* + r_{t2}^* + u_t^* - \dfrac{1-\rho^2}{1-\lambda\rho} u_{t-1} \end{matrix} \right) \varepsilon_t$$

$$+ \frac{\sqrt{T-N}}{\sqrt{T}} \frac{1}{\sqrt{T-N}}$$

$$\times \sum_{t=N}^{T} \left(\begin{matrix} x_t^* \\ \bar{y}_{t-1}^* + r_{t1}^* + r_{t2}^* + \displaystyle\sum_{i=0}^{N-2} \lambda \varepsilon_{t-1-i}^i - \dfrac{1-\rho^2}{1-\lambda\rho} \displaystyle\sum_{i=0}^{N-2} \rho^i \varepsilon_{t-1-i} \end{matrix} \right) \varepsilon_t$$

$$+ \frac{1}{\sqrt{T}} \sum_{t=N}^{T} \left(\begin{matrix} 0 \\ \lambda^{N-1} \displaystyle\sum_{i=0}^{t-N-1} \lambda^i \varepsilon_{t-N-i} - \dfrac{1-\rho^2}{1-\lambda\rho} \rho^{N-1} \displaystyle\sum_{j=0}^{\infty} \rho^j \varepsilon_{t-N-j} \end{matrix} \right) \varepsilon_t$$

$$(6.219)$$

The first and third terms of the right member of (6.219) can be made arbitrarily small in probability and thus may be neglected. Since $\sqrt{T-N}/\sqrt{T}$ obviously converges to unity with T, we need only be concerned with the middle term. But this is entirely similar to the situation encountered in Section 4.8. Applying the same techniques employed there, we conclude that the middle term has the asymptotic distribution,

$$N(0, B_D)$$

where

$$B_D = \sigma^2 \lim_{T \to \infty} \frac{1}{T}$$

$$\times \begin{bmatrix} x'\Psi x & x'\Psi \bar{y}_{-1} + x'D'M'r \\ \bar{y}'_{-1}\Psi x + r'MDx & \bar{y}'_{-1}\Psi \bar{y}_{-1} + r'r \\ & + 2\bar{y}'_{-1}D'M'r + T\dfrac{\sigma^2(\lambda - \rho)^2}{(1 - \lambda\rho)^2(1 - \lambda^2)} \end{bmatrix}$$

$$(6.220)$$

and

$$r = \frac{\sigma^2}{1 - \lambda^2}[\varphi_1 M'^{-1}D'^{-1}x_{-1} - \varphi_2 M'^{-1}D'^{-1}x] \qquad (6.221)$$

But notice that

$$x'D'M'r = x'D'M'[M'^{-1}D'^{-1}x_{-1}\varphi_1 - M'^{-1}D'^{-1}x\varphi_2]\frac{\sigma^2}{1 - \lambda^2}$$

$$= \frac{\sigma^2}{1 - \lambda^2}[\varphi_1 x'x_{-1} - \varphi_2 x'x] \qquad (6.222)$$

Hence,

$$\lim_{T \to \infty} \frac{1}{T} x'D'M'r = \frac{\sigma^2}{1 - \lambda^2}[\varphi^*\varphi_1\varphi_2 - \varphi^*\varphi_1\varphi_2] = 0 \qquad (6.223)$$

Similarly,

$$\bar{y}'_{-1}D'M'r = \bar{y}'_{-1}D'M'[M'^{-1}D'^{-1}x_{-1}\varphi_1 - M'^{-1}D'^{-1}x\varphi_2]\frac{\sigma^2}{1 - \lambda^2}$$

$$= \frac{\sigma^2}{1 - \lambda^2}[\varphi_1 x'_{-1}\bar{y}_{-1} - \varphi_2 x'\bar{y}_{-1}] \qquad (6.224)$$

and

$$\lim_{T \to \infty} \frac{1}{T} \bar{y}'_{-1}D'M'r = \frac{\sigma^2}{1 - \lambda^2} \qquad (6.225)$$

Finally,

$$\lim_{T \to \infty} \frac{1}{T} r'r = \left(\frac{\sigma^2}{1 - \lambda^2}\right)^2 \varphi'\frac{S'\Psi^{-1}S}{T}\varphi$$

$$S = (x, x_{-1}), \quad \varphi' = (\varphi_1, -\varphi_2) \qquad (6.226)$$

Thus, B_D may be written in the more suggestive form,

$$B_D = \sigma^2 \lim_{T \to \infty} \frac{1}{T}$$

$$\times \begin{bmatrix} x'\Psi x & x'\Psi \bar{y}_{-1} \\ \bar{y}'_{-1}\Psi x & \bar{y}'_{-1}\Psi \bar{y}_{-1} + \dfrac{T\sigma^2}{1 - \lambda^2} + \dfrac{T\sigma^2}{1 - \lambda^2}\left\{\dfrac{(\lambda - \rho)^2}{(1 - \lambda\rho)^2}\right. \\ \left. + \dfrac{\sigma^2}{1 - \lambda^2}\varphi'\left(\dfrac{S'\Psi^{-1}S}{T}\right)\varphi\right\} \end{bmatrix} \quad (6.227)$$

Defining

$$A_D = \operatorname*{plim}_{T \to \infty} \frac{1}{T}(x, y_{-1})'\Psi(x, y_{-1})$$

$$= \lim_{T \to \infty} \frac{1}{T}\begin{bmatrix} x'\Psi x & x'\Psi \bar{y}_{-1} \\ \bar{y}'_{-1}\Psi x & \bar{y}'_{-1}\Psi \bar{y}_{-1} + \dfrac{T\sigma^2}{1 - \lambda^2} \end{bmatrix} \quad (6.228)$$

we see that we may write

$$B_D = \sigma^2 A_D^{-1} + \sigma^2 B_{D_1} \quad (6.229)$$

where

$$B_{D_1} = \lim_{T \to \infty}\begin{bmatrix} 0 & 0 \\ 0 & \dfrac{\sigma^2}{1 - \lambda^2}\left\{1 + \dfrac{(\lambda - \rho)^2}{(1 - \lambda\rho)^2} + \dfrac{\sigma^2}{1 - \lambda^2}\varphi'\left(\dfrac{S'\Psi^{-1}S}{T}\right)\varphi\right\} \end{bmatrix}$$

$$(6.230)$$

The argument above has therefore established that

$$\sqrt{T}\left[\begin{pmatrix} \tilde{\alpha} \\ \tilde{\lambda} \end{pmatrix}_D - \begin{pmatrix} \alpha \\ \lambda \end{pmatrix}\right] \sim N(0, C_D) \quad (6.231)$$

where

$$C_D = A_D^{-1}B_D A_D^{-1} = \sigma^2 A_D^{-1} + \sigma^2 A_D^{-1}B_{D_1}A_D^{-1} \quad (6.232)$$

REMARK 6.3. Notice, in (6.232), that the term $\sigma^2 A_D^{-1}$ corresponds to the covariance matrix of the asymptotic distribution of the estimator *when it is known that* $\lambda = \rho$. In such a case, we would estimate

$$\begin{pmatrix} \tilde{\alpha} \\ \tilde{\lambda} \end{pmatrix}_D = [(x, y_{-1})'(x, y_{-1})]^{-1}\begin{bmatrix} x'y \\ y'_{-1}y \end{bmatrix}$$

$$= \begin{pmatrix} \alpha \\ \lambda \end{pmatrix} + [(x, y_{-1})'(x, y_{-1})]^{-1}\begin{bmatrix} x'\varepsilon \\ y'_{-1}\varepsilon \end{bmatrix} \quad (6.233)$$

and the reader may verify the assertion directly, noting that in such a case Ψ becomes the identity matrix. However, if this fact is *not* known but nevertheless true, and we obtain the estimator as above, we pay a price in terms of the relative efficiency criterion. This price is reflected in the term $\sigma^2 A_D^{-1} B_{D_1} A_D^{-1}$, which does *not* vanish if $\lambda = \rho$.

REMARK 6.4. The reader should notice that the covariance matrix of the asymptotic distribution of the ML estimator can be written as

$$C_M = \sigma^2 \lim_{T \to \infty} \left\{ \frac{1}{T} \begin{bmatrix} x'\Psi x & x'\Psi \bar{y}_{-1} \\ \bar{y}'_{-1}\Psi x & \bar{y}'_{-1}\Psi \bar{y}_{-1} \end{bmatrix} \right\}^{-1} \qquad (6.234)$$

He should further observe that $C_M - \sigma^2 A_D^{-1}$ is necessarily positive semidefinite. Now this prompts us to inquire as to whether $\sigma^2 A_D^{-1}$ is the covariance matrix of the asymptotic distribution of some interesting estimator.

It turns out that if in the reduced model,

$$y_t = \alpha x + \lambda y_{t-1} + w_t, \quad t = 2, \ldots, 7 \qquad (6.235)$$

the covariance matrix of w were known—up to a multiplicative constant—then the asymptotic distribution of the *Aitken estimator*

$$\begin{pmatrix} \tilde{\alpha} \\ \tilde{\lambda} \end{pmatrix} = [(x, y_{-1})'\Psi(x, y_{-1})]^{-1}(x, y_{-1})'\Psi y$$

is

$$N(0, \sigma^2 A_D^{-1})$$

This estimator, of course, is rather contrived, since to know Ψ, one must know λ; if one knows that, however, there is no point in estimating it from (6.235).

Still, the above shows that the *asymptotic distribution of the feasible Aitken estimator does not coincide with that of the Aitken estimator when the equation contains an explanatory variable that is correlated with the error term.* This phenomenon was pointed out by Amemiya and Fuller [3] and Dhrymes [29].

REMARK 6.5. The derivation of the asymptotic distributions of the estimators $(\tilde{\alpha}, \tilde{\lambda})_*$ and $(\tilde{\alpha}, \tilde{\lambda})_G$ serves to point out another important limitation of various two-step procedures. *If in an equation to be estimated there occurs a nonobservable quantity, then an OLS or Aitken procedure that operates with the equation in which a consistent estimator has been substituted for the nonobservable quantity, will not, in general, have the same asymptotic distribution as the corresponding estimator obtained when the nonobservable quantity is actually known.*

The preceding discussion has established:

THEOREM 6.3. Consider the model,

$$y_t = \frac{\alpha I}{I - \lambda L} x_t + \frac{I}{I - \rho L} \varepsilon_t, \qquad t = 1, 2, \ldots, T \qquad (6.236)$$

where $|\rho| < 1$, the explanatory variable obeys the usual boundedness conditions, and

$$\varepsilon \sim N(0, \sigma^2 I), \qquad \varepsilon = (\varepsilon_1 \varepsilon_2, \ldots, \varepsilon_T)' \qquad (6.237)$$

Let $\tilde{\alpha}, \tilde{\lambda}$ be the usual instrumental variables estimator and obtain

$$\tilde{y}_t = \tilde{\alpha} \sum_{i=0}^{t-1} \tilde{\lambda} x_{t-i}, \quad \tilde{u}_t = y_t - \tilde{\alpha} x_t - \tilde{\lambda} \tilde{y}_{t-1}, \quad \tilde{\rho} = \frac{\sum \tilde{u}_t \tilde{u}_{t-1}}{\sum \tilde{u}_{t-1}^2} \quad (6.238)$$

Then:

(i) the asymptotic distribution of the estimator

$$\begin{pmatrix} \tilde{\alpha} \\ \tilde{\lambda} \end{pmatrix}_* = [(x, \tilde{y}_{-1})' \tilde{V}^{-1}(x, \tilde{y}_{-1})]^{-1}(x, \tilde{y}_{-1})' \tilde{V}^{-1} y \qquad (6.239)$$

is

$$N(0, C_*)$$

where

$$C_* = \sigma^2 [A - AQBG'A' - AGB'Q'A] + AQC_lQ'A \qquad (6.240)$$

(ii) the (marginal) asymptotic distribution of the first two components of

$$\begin{pmatrix} \tilde{\alpha} \\ \tilde{\lambda} \\ \tilde{\rho} \end{pmatrix}_G = (\tilde{Z}'\tilde{Z})^{-1}\tilde{Z}'y \qquad (6.241)$$

is

$$N(0, C_G)$$

where

$$C_G = \sigma^2 [A^* - A^* Q^* BG^{**'} A^{*'} - A^* G^* B'Q^{*'} A^{*'}] \\ + A^* Q^* C_l Q^{*'} A^{*'} \qquad (6.242)$$

(iii) the asymptotic distribution of

$$\begin{pmatrix} \tilde{\alpha} \\ \tilde{\lambda} \end{pmatrix}_D = [(x, y_{-1})' \tilde{\Phi}^{-1}(x, y_{-1})]^{-1}(x, y_{-1})' \tilde{\Phi}^{-1} y \qquad (6.243)$$

is

$$N(0, C_D)$$

where

$$C_D = \sigma^2 A_D^{-1} + \sigma^2 A_D^{-1} B_{D_1} A_D^{-1} \qquad (6.244)$$

In the above, $\sigma^2 V$ is the covariance matrix of the error terms of the model in (6.236) and $\tilde{V}$ is a consistent estimator of V obtained by substituting therein $\tilde{\rho}$, as in (6.238); $\sigma^2 \Phi$ is the covariance matrix of the terms

$$w_t = u_t - \lambda u_{t-1}, \quad t = 2, 3, \ldots, T \tag{6.245}$$

and $\tilde{\Phi}$ is a a consistent estimate of Φ obtained by substituting therein $\tilde{\lambda}$ and $\tilde{\rho}$, as in (6.238). In addition, C_I is the covariance matrix of the asymptotic distribution of the IV estimator $(\tilde{\alpha}, \tilde{\lambda})$ and

$$\tilde{P} = (x, \bar{y}_{-1}), \qquad P = (x, \bar{y}_{-1}),$$

$$x = (x_1, x_2, \ldots, x_T)', \qquad x_{-1} = (x_0, x_1, \ldots, x_{T-1})'$$

$$\bar{y} = (\bar{y}_1, \bar{y}_2, \ldots, \bar{y}_T)', \qquad \bar{y}_{-1} = (\bar{y}_0, \bar{y}_1, \ldots, \bar{y}_{T-1})' \tag{6.246}$$

$$\bar{y} = \frac{\alpha I}{I - \lambda L} x_t$$

$$A = \plim_{T \to \infty} \left[\frac{\tilde{P}' \tilde{V}^{-1} \tilde{P}}{T} \right]^{-1}, \quad B = \lim_{T \to \infty} \left[\frac{1}{T} S'P \right]^{-1}, \quad S = (x, x_{-1}) \tag{6.247}$$

$$G = \lim_{T \to \infty} \frac{1}{T} P'D'^{-1}S, \quad \Psi^{-1} = D^{-1}VD'^{-1} \tag{6.248}$$

$$D^{-1} = \begin{bmatrix} 1 & 0 & \cdot & \cdot & \cdot & 0 \\ -\lambda & 1 & & & & 0 \\ 0 & -\lambda & 1 & & & 0 \\ \cdot & & & & & \\ \cdot & & & & & \\ \cdot & & & & & 0 \\ 0 & & & 0 & -\lambda & 1 \end{bmatrix}$$

$$A^* = \lim_{T \to \infty} \left[\frac{1}{T} P'P \right]^{-1}, \quad G^* = \lim_{T \to \infty} \frac{1}{T} P'M'^{-1}D'^{-1}S \tag{6.249}$$

Q and Q^* are as defined in (6.125) and (6.149), respectively. Finally,

$$A_D = \plim_{T \to \infty} \frac{1}{T} (x, y_{-1})' \Psi (x, y_{-1}), \quad y_{-1} = (y_0, y_1, \ldots, y_{T-1})'$$

$$B_{D_1} = \begin{bmatrix} 0 & 0 \\ 0 & \dfrac{\sigma^2}{1 - \lambda^2} \left\{ 1 + \dfrac{(\lambda - \rho)^2}{(1 - \lambda\rho)^2} + \dfrac{\sigma^2}{1 - \lambda^2} \varphi' \lim_{T \to \infty} \left(\dfrac{S' \Psi^{-1} S}{T} \right) \varphi \right\} \end{bmatrix} \tag{6.250}$$

φ being as defined in (6.226) and (6.209).

REMARK 6.6. When deriving the probability limit in Equation (6.180) we resorted to a very cumbersome but straightforward procedure, and the result was obtained by using only elementary properties. If the reader is prepared to accept, on intuitive grounds, the approximation

$$u_t^* = \sum_{i=0}^{t-1} \lambda^i u_{t-i} \approx \frac{I}{I - \lambda L} u_t \qquad (6.251)$$

then the following simplification results. We have

$$u^{*\prime} V^{-1} u^* = (1 - \rho^2) u_1^{*2} + \sum_{t=2}^{T} [(I - \rho L) u_t^*]^2 \qquad (6.252)$$

But

$$(I - \rho L) u_t^* = \frac{I - \rho L}{I - \lambda L} u_t = \frac{I}{I - \lambda L} \varepsilon_t = \varepsilon_t^* \qquad (6.253)$$

since

$$u_t = \frac{I}{I - \rho L} \varepsilon_t \qquad (6.254)$$

Thus,

$$\operatorname*{plim}_{T \to \infty} \frac{1}{T} u^{*\prime} V^{-1} u^* = \operatorname*{plim}_{T \to \infty} \frac{1}{T} \sum_{t=2}^{T} \varepsilon_t^{*2} = \frac{\sigma^2}{1 - \lambda^2} \qquad (6.255)$$

in view of the fact that

$$\operatorname{Var}(\varepsilon_t^*) = \frac{\sigma^2}{1 - \lambda^2}, \quad \text{all} \quad t \qquad (6.257)$$

Exercises and Questions

1. In connection with Lemma 6.1, refer to Equation (6.21) and suppose the x sequence has the property that

$$\lim_{T \to \infty} \frac{1}{T} \sum_{t=1}^{T} x_{t-\tau} x_t = c_\tau$$

and $c_\tau = 0$ if $\tau \neq 0$.

   Prove that the condition in (6.23) implies $\lambda_* = \lambda_0$
2. Work out the same argument in the case where c_τ of Problem 1 obeys

$$c_\tau = \mu^{|\tau|} c_0, \qquad \tau = 0, \pm 1, \pm 2, \ldots$$

3. Suppose that $\rho_0 = 0$ in (6.22), and give a direct proof of consistency of the estimator of λ when the errors of the system are mutually

independent identically distributed, i.e. verify the consistency claim made in Footnote 19 of the previous chapter.

Hint: Use the result in Jennrich [79].

4. What are the minimal conditions on the x sequence needed to insure the validity of (6.84)?

5. Justify the representation of the covariance matrix of the IV estimator as in (6.85).

6. Verify, step by step, the assertion in (6.112).

7. Consider the relation,

$$\left(\frac{\tilde{P}' \tilde{V}^{-1} \tilde{P}}{T}\right)^{-1} \frac{\tilde{P} \tilde{V}^{-1} P}{T} - I = -\left(\frac{\tilde{P}' \tilde{V}^{-1} \tilde{P}}{T}\right)^{-1} \left[\frac{\tilde{P} \tilde{V}^{-1}(\tilde{P} - P)}{T}\right]$$

and notice that

$$\tilde{P} - P = (0, \tilde{y}_{-1} - y_{-1}), \qquad \tilde{y}_{-1} - y_{-1} = \tilde{\alpha}\tilde{D}x_{-1} - \alpha Dx_{-1} - u_{-1}$$

Consequently,

$$\tilde{\alpha}\tilde{D}x_{-1} - \alpha Dx_{-1} = (\tilde{\alpha} - \alpha)\tilde{D}x_{-1} + \alpha(\tilde{D} - D)x_{-1}$$

Moreover, the tth row of $\tilde{D} - D$ consists of

$$\tilde{\lambda}^{t-1} - \lambda^{t-1}, \tilde{\lambda}^{t-2} - \lambda^{t-2}, \ldots, \tilde{\lambda} - \lambda, 0, \ldots 0$$

and the matrix has a strictly zero main diagonal. Since

$$\tilde{\lambda}^n - \lambda^n = (\tilde{\lambda} - \lambda) \sum_{i=0}^{n-1} \tilde{\lambda}^{n-1-i}\lambda^i$$

express

$$\tilde{D} - D = (\tilde{\lambda} - \lambda)D^*$$

for an appropriate matrix D^*, and then give an alternative justification for the relation in (6.127) which does not rely on a Taylor series expansion.

8. Prove that $A^* - A$ is an indefinite matrix.

Hint: $A^* - A = \lim_{T \to \infty} [P'(I - V^{-1})P/T]$; but this is also identical with

$$\lim_{T \to \infty} \frac{1}{T} \left[P'(I - V^{-1})P + P' \begin{pmatrix} -\rho^2 & 0 & \cdots & 0 \\ & 0 & \cdots & \\ & & \cdots & 0 & 0 \\ 0 & 0 & \cdots & 0 & -\rho^2 \end{pmatrix} P \right]$$

$$= \lim_{T \to \infty} \left\{ P' \begin{bmatrix} -\rho^2 & \rho & \cdots & 0 \\ \rho & -\rho^2 & \rho & \cdot & 0 \\ \cdot & \cdot & \cdot & \cdot & \cdot \\ \cdot & \cdot & \cdots & \rho \\ 0 & \cdot & 0 & \rho & -\rho^2 \end{bmatrix} P \right\}$$

Then show that the roots of the last matrix in square brackets are

$$-\rho^2 - 2|\rho|\cos k\theta, \quad \theta = \frac{\pi}{T+1}, \quad k = 1, 2, \ldots, T$$

The result would then follow, since for every T we deal with an indefinite matrix.

9. In Equation (6.171), consider instead

$$\check{\Psi} - \Psi = \tilde{D}'\tilde{V}^{-1}\tilde{D} - D'V^{-1}D$$
$$= (\tilde{D} - D)'\tilde{V}^{-1}\tilde{D} + D'V^{-1}(\tilde{D} - D) + D'(\tilde{V}^{-1} - V^{-1})\tilde{D}$$

Use the results of Problem 7, and hence restructure the argument leading to (6.173) so that it does not depend on a Taylor series expansion.

10. In connection with the estimator in (6.107), consider the following modification:

$$\begin{pmatrix} \tilde{\alpha} \\ \tilde{\lambda} \end{pmatrix}_{**} = [(x, \tilde{y}_{-1})'\tilde{\Phi}^{-1}(x, y_{-1})]^{-1}(x, \tilde{y}_{-1})'\tilde{\Phi}^{-1}y$$

the symbols having the same meaning as in Equation (6.113) and the ensuing discussion, and Φ is as defined in Equation (6.80). Derive its asymptotic distribution and compare it with that of

$$\begin{pmatrix} \tilde{\alpha} \\ \tilde{\lambda} \end{pmatrix}_{*}$$

and the ML estimator.

Hint: Can you give an IV interpretation to the ML estimator?

Chapter 7

GEOMETRIC LAG STRUCTURE IV

7.1 Dynamic Demand Model, Three Pass Least Squares (3 *PLS*) and Alternative Estimators

Generalities. As we saw in Section 4.5, the dynamic demand model consists of the system

$$y_t = \alpha_0 + \alpha_1 x_t + \alpha_2 s_t + u_t$$
$$s_t - s_{t-1} = \beta_0 s_{t-1} + \beta_1 y_t \tag{7.1}$$

where y_t is the market demand for the commodity in question, x_t is income and s_t is the "psychological stock" of the commodity possessed by the individual(s); u_t is a random variable whose properties we shall specify presently.

We further saw that, eliminating the generally unobservable variable s_t, we find

$$y_t = -\frac{\alpha_0 \beta_0}{1 - \beta_1 \alpha_2} + \frac{\alpha_1}{1 - \beta_1 \alpha_2} x_t$$
$$- \alpha_1 \beta x_{t-1} + \beta y_{t-1} + \frac{1}{1 - \beta_1 \alpha_2} u_t - \beta u_{t-1} \tag{7.2}$$

where

$$\beta = \frac{1 + \beta_0}{1 - \beta_1 \alpha_2} \tag{7.3}$$

From (7.2) we see that β_1, α_2 enter the estimating equation only in the form $(\beta_1 \alpha_2)$ and hence cannot be identified separately. On the other hand, it is customary in such models to make the assumption $\beta_1 = 1$. This may be thought of as a convention regarding the units in which variables are measured, so that one unit of y consumption is translated into one unit of stock, s.

In empirical work involving such models—e.g., Houthakker and Taylor [76]—the parameters of the model in (7.2) are not estimated directly. Rather, one writes

$$y_t = a_0 + a_1 x_t + a_2 x_{t-1} + a_3 y_{t-1} + w_t \tag{7.4}$$

then estimates the parameters a_i, $i = 0, 1, 2, 3$ and derives from these, estimators of the *structural* parameters β_0 and α_i, $i = 0, 1, 2$.

In addition, the error term of the equation, w_t, is treated as a *first order autoregressive process*. For this to be justified in the context of the dynamic demand model, as discussed extensively in Section 4.5, we must have

$$u_t - (1 + \beta_0)u_{t-1} = \rho[u_{t-1} - (1 + \beta_0)u_{t-2}] + \varepsilon_t \tag{7.5}$$

since by definition,

$$w_t = \frac{1}{1 - \beta_1 \alpha_2} [u_t - (1 + \beta_0)u_{t-1}] \tag{7.6}$$

The factor $1/(1 - \beta_1 \alpha_2)$ may be omitted from (7.5) because its presence or absence affects only the magnitude of the variance of ε_t, which is a parameter that is left unspecified. In (7.5), the ε's are mutually independent identically distributed (*i.i.d.*) random variables with mean zero, variance σ^2 and $|\rho| < 1$.

Now, Equation (7.5) implies that the error term in the initial demand equation (7.1) is the *second order autoregressive process*,

$$u_t + \rho_1 u_{t-1} + \rho_2 u_{t-2} = \varepsilon_t \tag{7.7}$$

with

$$\rho_1 = -(1 + \beta_0 + \rho), \quad \rho_2 = \rho(1 + \beta_0)$$

If we wish the process in (7.5) to be stable, i.e. to have finite variance, the parameters ρ_1 and ρ_2 must obey

$$\rho_1 \in (-2, 2), \quad \rho_2 \in (-1, 1) \tag{7.8}$$

Since $\rho \in (-1, 1)$, the conditions above imply

$$\beta_0 \in (-2, 0) \tag{7.9}$$

This is a rather peculiar turn of events, in that what appears to be an innocuous condition on the variance of the error terms of the estimating equation (7.2) leads to a fairly strong condition on the rate of depreciation of the "psychological stock." To see that this is a strong condition indeed, consider the second equation of (7.1) for $\beta_1 = 1$. After substitution of y_t from the first equation, we find

$$s_t = \frac{\alpha_0}{1 - \alpha_2} + \frac{\alpha_1}{1 - \alpha_2} x_t + \frac{1 + \beta_0}{1 - \alpha_2} s_{t-1} + \frac{1}{1 - \alpha_2} u_t \tag{7.10}$$

For stability of this equation—which is certainly a reasonable requirement—we need only have

$$\frac{1 + \beta_0}{1 - \alpha_2} \in (-1, 1) \qquad (7.11)$$

Since, in some empirically relevant cases, we would expect

$$\alpha_2 < 0 \qquad (7.12)$$

we see that (7.9) restricts β_0 beyond what is implied by (7.11). On the other hand, if we require that

$$\alpha_2 > 0 \qquad (7.13)$$

then the restriction in (7.9) is not binding.

In most empirical discussions, the error term is not introduced in (7.1); rather, once s_t is eliminated from the system and a difference equation is obtained in the dependent variable—as in (7.2)—one attaches a random variable to the estimating equation. *The properties of the random variable are specified at that stage.* As we have seen earlier, this may entail some unintended implicit theorizing about the structural parameters of the system.

3 PLS and Alternative Estimators. In connection with the model of Equation (7.4), Taylor and Wilson [141] have proposed an estimation procedure known as *three pass least squares* (3 PLS). We shall now examine the properties of this procedure and propose alternative estimators in the context of the following slightly more general model:

$$y_t = \beta_n y_{t-1} + \sum_{i=1}^{n-1} \beta_i x_{ti} + w_t, \quad t = 2, 3, \ldots, T \qquad (7.14)$$

The error term, w_t, obeys

$$w_t = \rho w_{t-1} + \varepsilon_t \qquad (7.15)$$

the ε_t being *i.i.d.* random variables with the properties,

$$E(\varepsilon_t) = 0, \quad E(\varepsilon_t^2) = \sigma^2, \quad \text{all } t \qquad (7.16)$$

The reader should note that this model is equivalent to

$$y_t = \sum_{i=1}^{n-1} \beta_i \left(\frac{I}{I - \beta_n L} x_{ti} \right) + \frac{I}{(I - \beta_n L)(I - \rho L)} \varepsilon_t \qquad (7.17)$$

which requires that *all explanatory variables be subject to the same infinite (geometric) lag structure and that the error term be a rather special second order autoregressive process.*

The 3 *PLS* procedure entails three steps:

(i) Regress y_t on y_{t-1} and x_{ti}, $i = 1, 2, \ldots, n - 1$; at this step, it is claimed that the estimators of the β_i, say $\bar{\beta}_i$, $i = 1, 2, \ldots, n - 1$ are consistent, provided that the x_i, $i = 1, 2, \ldots, n - 1$ *are nonautocorrelated.*

(ii) Using the estimators of step (i), compute

$$\bar{y}_t = y_t - \sum_{i=1}^{n-1} \bar{\beta}_i x_{ti} \tag{7.18}$$

and regress $\bar{y}_t$ on y_{t-1}, y_{t-2} and the *residual* of the regression in step (i), lagged one period.

It is claimed that the coefficient of y_{t-1} in this regression, say $\bar{\beta}_n$, is a consistent estimator of β_n.

(iii) Using the estimators $\bar{\beta}_i$, $i = 1, 2, \ldots, n - 1$ of step (i) and $\bar{\beta}_n$ of step (ii), compute the residuals

$$\bar{w}_t = y_t - \sum_{i=1}^{n-1} \bar{\beta}_i x_{ti} - \bar{\beta}_n y_{t-1} \tag{7.19}$$

and regress y_t on x_{ti}, $i = 1, 2, \ldots, n - 1$, y_{t-1} and $\bar{w}_{t-1}$, thus obtaining consistent estimators for all parameters.

If the claims in (i), (ii) and (iii) are correct, it is clear that we have two sets of consistent estimators for the parameters β_i, $i = 1, 2, \ldots, n$.

Now, define

$$\begin{aligned}
x_{\cdot i} &= (x_{2i}, x_{3i}, \ldots, x_{Ti})', & i &= 1, 2, \ldots, n - 1 \\
y_{-1} &= (y_1, y_3, \ldots, y_{T-1})', & y &= (y_2, y_3, \ldots, y_T)' \\
\beta &= (\beta_1, \beta_2, \ldots, \beta_n)', & w &= (w_2, w_3, \ldots, w_T)' \\
X &= (x_{\cdot 1}, x_{\cdot 2}, \ldots, x_{\cdot n-1}, y_{-1})
\end{aligned} \tag{7.20}$$

and write the model compactly as

$$y = X\beta + w \tag{7.21}$$

The first stage yields

$$\bar{\beta} = (X'X)^{-1} X'y = \beta + (X'X)^{-1} X'w \tag{7.22}$$

Taking probability limits, we have

$$\operatorname*{plim}_{T \to \infty} \tilde{\beta} = \beta + \operatorname*{plim}_{T \to \infty} \left(\frac{X'X}{T} \right)^{-1} \operatorname*{plim}_{T \to \infty} \frac{X'w}{T} \qquad (7.23)$$

For stability of the difference equation in (7.14), we require that

$$|\beta_n| < 1 \qquad (7.24)$$

To evaluate the probability limits in (7.23), we need to make certain assumptions on the explanatory variables. The most elementary assumptions are that the x_{it}, $i = 1, 2, \ldots, n - 1$ are independent of the error term, that for every T, the matrix $X'X$ is nonsingular, and $\operatorname{plim}_{T \to \infty} X'X/T$ exists as a nonsingular matrix. Thus, we have

$$E(w_t x_{t'i}) = 0 \quad i = 1, 2, \ldots, n - 1, \quad \text{all } t, t' $$
$$\text{rank}(X) = n \qquad (7.25)$$

In virtue of the condition in (7.24), we obtain

$$y_t = \sum_{j=1}^{n-1} \beta_j \left(\sum_{k=0}^{\infty} \beta_n^k x_{t-k,j} \right) + \sum_{k=0}^{\infty} \beta_n^k w_{t-k} \qquad (7.26)$$

Thus,

$$\operatorname*{plim}_{T \to \infty} \frac{1}{T} \sum_{t=2}^{T} y_{t-1} w_t = \frac{\sigma^2 \rho}{(1 - \beta_n \rho)(1 - \rho^2)} \qquad (7.27)$$

Hence,

$$\operatorname*{plim}_{T \to \infty} \frac{1}{T} X'w = \left(0, \ldots, 0, \frac{\sigma^2 \rho}{(1 - \beta_n \rho)(1 - \rho^2)} \right)' \qquad (7.28)$$

Consider the partition

$$\operatorname*{plim}_{T \to \infty} \frac{1}{T} X'X = \begin{bmatrix} A & a \\ a' & \alpha \end{bmatrix} \qquad (7.29)$$

where A is $(n - 1) \times (n - 1)$, α is a scalar and a is $(n - 1) \times 1$. By the usual formula for the inverse of a partitioned matrix, we have

$$\operatorname*{plim}_{T \to \infty} \left(\frac{X'X}{T} \right)^{-1} = \begin{bmatrix} \left(A - \dfrac{aa'}{\alpha} \right)^{-1} & -\dfrac{A^{-1}a}{\alpha - a'A^{-1}a} \\ -\dfrac{a'A^{-1}}{\alpha - a'A^{-1}a} & \dfrac{1}{(\alpha - a'A^{-1}a)} \end{bmatrix} \qquad (7.30)$$

Thus, a necessary and sufficient condition for the $\tilde{\beta}_i$, $i = 1, 2, \ldots, n - 1$ to be consistent is that

$$a = 0 \qquad (7.31)$$

But a is the vector of second moments—or covariances if all observations are centered about their respective sample means—between y_{t-1} and x_{ti}, $i = 1, 2, \ldots, n - 1$.

It follows, therefore, that if the set $\{x_i: i = 1, 2, \ldots, n - 1\}$ contains (one-period) *lagged exogenous variables*, as would be the case with the dynamic demand model of Equation (7.2), *the first stage of 3 PLS cannot possibly yield consistent estimators for all of the parameters β_i, $i = 1, 2, \ldots, n - 1$, even if the x_i are nonautocorrelated.*

But if the claims of the first step are invalid, it is clear that all succeeding claims are invalid as well. Thus, 3 *PLS* cannot yield consistent estimators for the parameters of the dynamic demand model.

Let us now verify that the *absence of autocorrelation condition* imposed in step (i) is an essential one, in the sense that it is necessary for the consistency of the estimators β_i of step (i).

We have seen that consistency requires the validity of (7.31). For simplicity of argument, suppose that all variables are measured as deviations from their respective sample means, so that

$$a = (\sigma_{1n}, \sigma_{2n}, \ldots, \sigma_{n-1,n})' \tag{7.32}$$

the σ_{in} being the covariances between x_{ti} and y_{t-1}.

Now, it is easily shown that

$$\sigma_{in} = \sum_{j=1}^{n-1} \beta_j \sum_{k=0}^{\infty} \beta_n^k \sigma_{ij}(k + 1) \tag{7.33}$$

where

$$\sigma_{ij}(k) = \text{Cov}(x_{ti}, x_{t-k,j}) \tag{7.34}$$

Since the β_j are arbitrary parameters, we must have

$$\omega_{ij} = \sum_{k=0}^{\infty} \beta_n^k \sigma_{ij}(k + 1) = 0 \tag{7.35}$$

and this must hold for all $\beta_n \in (-1, 1)$.

But it is now obvious that

$$\sigma_{ij}(k + 1) = 0 \quad k = 0, 1, 2, \ldots, \quad i, j = 1, 2, \ldots, n - 1 \tag{7.36}$$

is necessary for the validity of (7.35). Hence, absence of auto- (and cross auto-) correlation is both a necessary *and* a sufficient condition on the exogenous variables—the x_i—in order for the consistency claim of step (i) to be valid.

Since most economic data exhibit substantial autocorrelation, *we conclude that this procedure* (3 *PLS*) *is not very useful in estimating the para-*

meters of the model in (7.14) *or of the dynamic demand model as exhibited in* (7.2).

To estimate the parameters of the model in (7.14) in conjuction with the assumption in (7.15), we may use the search procedure employed in Section 4.6. In the absence of normality for the error terms of the system, the procedure is as follows. In the notation of (7.21), let

$$S = (y - X\beta)' V^{-1}(y - X\beta) \tag{7.37}$$

where V is given by

$$\text{Cov}(w) = \sigma^2 V \tag{7.38}$$

Here V is of dimension $T - 1$ and is of the form given in (4.73). Since $\rho \in (-1, 1)$, divide the interval by the points ρ_j, $j = 1, 2, \ldots, m$. For given ρ_j the elements of V^{-1} are known and thus S may be minimized with respect to β. This procedure yields

$$\hat{\beta}(\rho_j) = (X' V^{-1} X)^{-1} X' V^{-1} y \tag{7.39}$$

Substituting in (7.37) we find

$$S(\rho_j) = [y - X\hat{\beta}(\rho_j)]' V^{-1}[y - X\hat{\beta}(\rho_j)] \tag{7.40}$$

The estimator of ρ, say $\hat{\rho}$, is chosen by the criterion

$$S(\hat{\rho}) = \min_j S(\rho_j) \tag{7.41}$$

The estimators of β and σ^2 are then obtained as

$$\hat{\beta} = \hat{\beta}(\hat{\rho}) , \quad \hat{\sigma}^2 = \frac{S(\hat{\rho})}{T - 1} \tag{7.42}$$

This procedure differs from that outlined in Section 4.8 only because normality is not assumed. If it were, the criterion function would have been

$$S(\rho_j)/(T - 1)(1 - \rho_j^2)^{1/(T-1)}$$

and we would have exactly the situation dealt with in Section 4.8. However, even though the estimation procedures would be identical, the *distribution characteristics* would differ. The important difference in the present context is that one of the explanatory variables, namely y_{t-1}, is correlated with the error term.

The consistency of the estimators in (7.41) and (7.42) may be established by the same techniques employed in Lemma 6.1.

Now, taking consistency as given, let us establish the asymptotic distribution of the vector estimator

$$\hat{\gamma} = \begin{pmatrix} \hat{\beta} \\ \hat{\rho} \end{pmatrix} \tag{7.43}$$

as defined in (7.41) and (7.42).

We observe, first, that this estimator obeys[31]

$$\frac{\partial S}{\partial \gamma} = 0 \tag{7.44}$$

Let γ_0 be the true parameter vector, expand $\partial S/\partial \gamma$ by Taylor's series about $\gamma = \gamma_0$, and evaluate at $\gamma = \hat{\gamma}$ to obtain,

$$\frac{\partial S}{\partial \gamma}(\hat{\gamma}) = \frac{\partial S}{\partial \gamma}(\gamma_0) + \frac{\partial^2 S}{\partial \gamma \partial \gamma}(\gamma^*)(\hat{\gamma} - \gamma_0) \tag{7.45}$$

where γ^* lies between $\hat{\gamma}$ and γ_0. Since

$$\operatorname*{plim}_{T \to \infty} \frac{1}{T} \frac{\partial^2 S}{\partial \gamma \partial \gamma}(\gamma^*) = \operatorname*{plim}_{T \to \infty} \frac{1}{T} \frac{\partial^2 S}{\partial \gamma \partial \gamma}(\gamma_0) \tag{7.46}$$

we may determine the asymptotic distribution of the estimator in (7.43) in terms of the relation

$$\frac{1}{\sqrt{T}} \frac{\partial S}{\partial \gamma}(\gamma_0) = -\frac{1}{T} \frac{\partial^2 S}{\partial \gamma \partial \gamma}(\gamma_0) \sqrt{T}(\hat{\gamma} - \gamma_0) \tag{7.47}$$

For notational simplicity, we shall drop the argument γ_0 in the discussion below.

The gradient of S may be written as

$$\frac{1}{\sqrt{T}} \frac{\partial S}{\partial \gamma} = -2 \begin{pmatrix} X' V^{-1} w \\ \rho w_2^2 + \sum\limits_{t=3}^{T} w_{t-1} \varepsilon_t \end{pmatrix} \tag{7.48}$$

---

[31] The assertion in (7.44) implies that the minimum we have located is an *interior* one. If the true parameter ρ_0 lies in the *interior* of $[-1 + \delta_1, 1 - \delta_1]$, the latter being the interval over which search is carried out, the assertion in (7.44) is quite proper. This is so since if the sample is sufficiently large then, with probability arbitrarily close to unity, we should indeed locate an interior minimum. This remark is applicable to all estimators obtained by the search procedure and not only the one we are currently considering.

To find the asymptotic distribution of this quantity, we recall that V^{-1} may be decomposed as

$$V^{-1} = M'M \tag{7.49}$$

such that

$$Mw = \varepsilon \tag{7.50}$$

and the elements of ε are *i.i.d.* random variables. We further recall from (7.26) that we can write

$$y_t = \bar{y}_t + \frac{I}{I - \beta_n L} w_t, \quad \bar{y}_t = \sum_{j=1}^{n-1} \beta_j \left(\frac{I}{I - \beta_n L} x_{tj} \right) \tag{7.51}$$

Evidently, $\bar{y}_t$ is a nonstochastic quantity if we assume that the x_{tj} are nonstochastic, which we shall do.

Let

$$\bar{y}_{-1} = (\bar{y}_1, \bar{y}_2, \ldots, \bar{y}_{T-1})' \tag{7.52}$$

and observe that we can write

$$X = (X^*, \bar{y}_{-1}) + (0, w^*_{-1}) \tag{7.53}$$

where

$$X^* = (x_{.1}, x_{.2}, \ldots, x_{.n-1}), \quad w^*_{-1} = (w^*_1, w^*_2, \ldots, w^*_{T-1})' \tag{7.54}$$

and

$$w^*_t = \frac{I}{I - \beta_n L} w_t \tag{7.55}$$

Thus we have

$$\frac{1}{\sqrt{T}} \frac{\partial S}{\partial \gamma} = -\frac{2}{\sqrt{T}} \begin{bmatrix} X^{*\prime} M' \varepsilon \\ \bar{y}'_{-1} M' \varepsilon + w^{*\prime}_{-1} M' \varepsilon \\ \rho w_2^2 + \sum_{t=1}^{T} w_{t-1} \varepsilon_t \end{bmatrix} \tag{7.56}$$

Now what is $w^{*\prime}_{-1} M'$? Its first element is $\sqrt{1 - \rho^2} w^*_1$; its rth element, $r \geq 2$, however, is

$$w^*_r - \rho w^*_{r-1} = \frac{I}{I - \beta_n L} (w_r - \rho w_{r-1}) = \frac{I}{I - \beta_n L} \varepsilon_r \tag{7.57}$$

Denote

$$u_t = \frac{I}{I - \beta_n L} \varepsilon_t \tag{7.58}$$

and observe that given any small quantities δ_1, δ_2, there exists an integer, N_1, such that

$$\Pr\{|\beta_n^{N_1-1}u_t| > \delta_1\} < \delta_2 \tag{7.59}$$

But then we can write

$$u_t = \sum_{k=0}^{\infty} \beta_n^k \varepsilon_{t-k} = \sum_{k=0}^{N_1-2} \beta_n^k \varepsilon_{t-k} + \beta_n^{N_1-1} \sum_{\tau=0}^{\infty} \beta_n^\tau \varepsilon_{t-N_1+1-\tau}$$

$$= u_t^{N_1} + \beta_n^{N_1-1} u_{t-N_1+1} \tag{7.60}$$

Similarly for w_t, there exists an integer N_2 such that $\rho^{N_2-1}w_t$ may be made arbitrarily small in probability. We can thus write

$$w_t = w_t^{N_2} + \rho^{N_2-1}w_{t-N_2+1} \tag{7.61}$$

Let

$$N = \max(N_1, N_2) \tag{7.62}$$

and observe that if we write

$$u_t = u_t^N + \beta_n^{N-1}u_{t-N+1}, \quad w_t = w_t^N + \rho^{N-1}w_{t-N+1} \tag{7.63}$$

the second components above are arbitrarily small in probability. Now the vector in (7.56) can be written as the sum of $T - 1$ vectors, each containing the observations on *all* the variables at time t, $t = 2, 3, \ldots, T$. Neglecting the first vector, namely, that corresponding to $t = 2$, we can write

$$\frac{1}{\sqrt{T}} \frac{\partial S}{\partial \gamma} = -2 \frac{1}{\sqrt{T}} \left[\sum_{t=3}^{T} \begin{pmatrix} z_{\cdot t} \\ \bar{y}_{t-1}^* + u_{t-1}^N \\ w_{t-1}^N \end{pmatrix} \varepsilon_t + \sum_{t=3}^{T} \begin{pmatrix} 0 \\ \beta_n^{N-1}u_{t-N+1} \\ \rho^{N-1}w_{t-N+1} \end{pmatrix} \varepsilon_t \right]$$

$$\tag{7.64}$$

where $z_{\cdot t}$ is the $(t - 1)$th column of X^*M' and y_{t-1}^* is the $(t - 1)$th element of $\bar{y}_{-1}'M'$. Since the second component of the right member of (7.64) can be made arbitrarily small in probability, we need concern ourselves only with the first.

If we impose on the explanatory variables conditions similar to those in Equation (7.25), and if we assume that they are uniformly bounded, we may verify that Theorem 4.3 is applicable, provided the sixth moment of the ε_t is bounded. Reducing the problem to a univariate one, let α be an arbitrary $n - 1$ element vector of constants and define

$$s_t = (\alpha'z_{\cdot t} + \alpha_n \bar{y}_{t-1} + \alpha_n u_{t-1}^N + \alpha_{n+1} w_{t-1}^N)\varepsilon_t \tag{7.65}$$

The reader may then easily verify that the sequence $\{s_t: t = 3, 4, \ldots\}$ is a sequence of N-dependent random variables having mean zero and obeying the conditions of Theorem 4.3.

Let

$$A_i = 2 \sum_{j=0}^{N-1} \text{Cov}(s_{i+j}, s_{i+N}) + \text{Var}(s_{i+N}) \tag{7.66}$$

But

$$\text{Cov}(s_{i+j}, s_{i+N}) = 0 \quad j = 0, 1, 2, \ldots, N-1 \tag{7.67}$$

while

$$\text{Var}(s_{i+N}) = \left(\alpha' z_{\cdot i+N} z'_{\cdot i+N} \alpha + \alpha_n^2 \, \bar{y}_{i+N-1}^2 + \alpha_n^2 \frac{\sigma^2}{1 - \beta_n^2} \right.$$
$$\left. + \alpha_{n+1}^2 \frac{\sigma^2}{1 - \rho^2} + 2\alpha_n \alpha_{n+1} \frac{\sigma^2}{1 - \beta_n \rho} \right) \sigma^2 \tag{7.68}$$

In the preceding equation, we have used the approximation

$$\sum_{\tau=0}^{N-1} \beta_n^{2\tau} \approx \frac{1}{1 - \beta_n^2}, \quad \sum_{\tau=0}^{N-2} \rho^{2\tau} \approx \frac{1}{1 - \rho^2},$$
$$\sum_{\tau=0}^{N-2} (\beta_n \rho)^\tau \approx \frac{1}{1 - \beta_n \rho} \tag{7.69}$$

Since

$$\lim_{k \to \infty} \frac{1}{k} \sum_{r=1}^{k} A_{i+r} = \Omega \tag{7.70}$$

converges uniformly for every i, we conclude that, asymptotically,

$$\frac{1}{\sqrt{T}} \frac{\partial S}{\partial \gamma} \sim N(0, 4\sigma^2 \Omega) \tag{7.71}$$

But what is Ω? A simple calculation yields

$$\Omega = \lim_{T \to \infty} \frac{1}{T} \begin{bmatrix} X^{*\prime} V^{-1} X^* & X^{*\prime} V^{-1} \bar{y}_{-1} & 0 \\ \bar{y}'_{-1} V^{-1} X^* & \bar{y}'_{-1} V^{-1} \bar{y}_{-1} + \dfrac{T\sigma^2}{1 - \beta_n^2} & \dfrac{T\sigma^2}{1 - \beta_n \rho} \\ 0 & \dfrac{T\sigma^2}{1 - \beta_n \rho} & \dfrac{T\sigma^2}{1 - \rho^2} \end{bmatrix} \tag{7.22}$$

we also find

$$\underset{T \to \infty}{\text{plim}} \frac{1}{T} \frac{\partial^2 S}{\partial \gamma \partial \gamma} = 2\Omega \tag{7.73}$$

Hence, we conclude that, asymptotically,

$$\sqrt{T}\,(\hat{\gamma} - \gamma_0) \sim N(0, \sigma^2\Omega^{-1}) \tag{7.74}$$

The development above was carried out on the implicit assumption that the x_{tj} were bounded. If only the conditions of Equation (6.27) are assumed, one may consider instead the asymptotic distribution of $D_T(\hat{\gamma} - \gamma_0)$. We have done so in previous sections, and it would serve no useful purpose to repeat that development here. In this case, D_T may be defined, say by

$$D_T = \text{diag}\left(d_{T1}, d_{T2}, d_{T3}, \ldots, d_{T,n-1}, \sum_{i=1}^{n-1} d_{Ti}\right) \tag{7.75}$$

where

$$d_{Ti}^2 = \sum_{t=2}^{T} x_{ti}^2, \quad d_{Ti} = \sqrt{d_{Ti}^2}, \quad i = 1, 2, \ldots, n - 1 \tag{7.76}$$

We have therefore proved:

THEOREM 7.1. Consider the model,

$$y_t = \sum_{j=1}^{n-1} \beta_j x_{tj} + \beta_n y_{t-1} + w_t, \quad t = 2, 3, 4, \ldots, T \tag{7.77}$$

and suppose that the explanatory variables, x_{tj}, obey the conditions in (7.25) and the discussion immediately preceding. Furthermore, let

$$w_t = \rho w_{t-1} + \varepsilon_t, \quad |\rho| < 1 \tag{7.78}$$

the ε_t being *i.i.d.* random variables obeying

$$E(\varepsilon_t) = 0, \quad E(\varepsilon_t^2) = \sigma^2 \tag{7.79}$$

and having bounded sixth absolute moment.

Let

$$\gamma = \begin{pmatrix} \beta \\ \rho \end{pmatrix}, \quad \beta = (\beta_1, \beta_2, \ldots, \beta_n)' \tag{7.80}$$

Then the estimator, γ, obtained by the search procedure is asymptotically distributed as

$$\sqrt{T}\,(\hat{\gamma} - \gamma_0) \sim N(0, \sigma^2\Omega^{-1}) \tag{7.81}$$

where γ_0 is the true parameter vector.

What is the *marginal* asymptotic distribution of $\hat{\beta}$? We have

COROLLARY 7.1. The marginal asymptotic distribution of $\hat{\beta}$ is given by

$$\sqrt{T}\,(\hat{\beta} - \beta_0) \sim N(0, \sigma^2\Omega^{*-1}) \tag{7.82}$$

where

$$\Omega^* = \lim_{T \to \infty} \frac{1}{T}$$

$$\times \begin{bmatrix} X^{*\prime} V^{-1} X^* & X^{*\prime} V^{-1} \bar{y}_{-1} \\ \bar{y}'_{-1} V^{-1} X^* & \bar{y}'_{-1} V^{-1} \bar{y}_{-1} + T\sigma^2 \\ & \times \left(\dfrac{1}{1 - \beta_n^2} - \dfrac{1 - \rho^2}{(1 - \beta_n \rho)^2} \right) \end{bmatrix} \qquad (7.83)$$

which may be further simplified to

$$\Omega^* = \lim_{T \to \infty} \frac{1}{T} \begin{bmatrix} X^{*\prime} V^{-1} X^* & X^{*\prime} V^{-1} \bar{y}_{-1} \\ \bar{y}'_{-1} V^{-1} X^* & \bar{y}'_{-1} V^{-1} \bar{y}_{-1} + T\sigma^2 \dfrac{(\rho - \beta_n)^2}{(1 - \beta_n^2)(1 - \beta_n \rho)^2} \end{bmatrix}$$

$$(7.84)$$

The proof of this is left as an exercise for the reader.

An interesting consequence of the corollary is that if

$$\rho = \beta_n \qquad (7.85)$$

then the *size* of the matrix Ω^{*-1} would tend to increase. This is so because the condition in (7.85) tends to reduce the last diagonal element of Ω^*.

The model in Equation (7.77) offers a singularly clear-cut demonstration of the phenomenon noted in Remark 6.4, namely, that when the equation under consideration contains an explanatory variable which is correlated with the error term, the asymptotic distribution of the *feasible* Aitken estimator does not coincide with that of the *Aitken estimator*.

The distribution given in (7.82) can be construed as that of a *feasible* Aitken estimator of the parameter vector β of the model in (7.77) when the covariance matrix, which in this case depends only on ρ, is simultaneously estimated.

If ρ is known, the Aitken estimator of the parameter β is given by

$$\tilde{\beta} = (X'V^{-1}X)^{-1}X'V^{-1}y \qquad (7.86)$$

The reader may then easily verify that, asymptotically,

$$\sqrt{T}(\tilde{\beta} - \beta_0) \sim N(0, \sigma^2 \Sigma^{-1}) \qquad (7.87)$$

where

$$\Sigma = \lim_{T \to \infty} \frac{1}{T} \begin{bmatrix} X^{*\prime} V^{-1} X^* & X^{*\prime} V^{-1} \bar{y}_{-1} \\ \bar{y}'_{-1} V^{-1} X^* & \bar{y}'_{-1} V^{-1} \bar{y}_{-1} + \dfrac{T\sigma^2}{1 - \beta_n^2} \end{bmatrix} \qquad (7.88)$$

A comparison with Ω^* shows that

$$\Sigma - \Omega^* = \begin{bmatrix} 0 & 0 \\ 0 & \dfrac{\sigma^2(1 - \rho^2)}{(1 - \beta_{n}\rho)^2} \end{bmatrix} \tag{7.89}$$

which is positive semidefinite. But this implies that

$$C = \Omega^{*-1} - \Sigma^{-1} \tag{7.90}$$

is positive semidefinite, and *we see that not knowing ρ in the present context leads to asymptotically relatively inefficient estimators, as compared with the case where ρ is known.*

REMARK 7.1. A consistent estimator of the covariance matrix Ω^{-1} in (7.72) may be obtained by substituting therein the consistent estimators $\hat\sigma^2$, $\hat\beta$, $\hat\rho$, as given in Equations (7.41) and (7.42). The reader may note the following additional simplification:

$$\lim_{T\to\infty} \frac{1}{T} \begin{bmatrix} X^{*\prime} V^{-1} X^* & X^{*\prime} V^{-1} \bar{y}_{-1} \\ \bar{y}'_{-1} V^{-1} X^* & \bar{y}'_{-1} V^{-1} \bar{y}_{-1} + \dfrac{T\sigma^2}{1 - \beta_n^{\,2}} \end{bmatrix} = \plim_{T\to\infty} \frac{1}{T}\,(X' \hat{V}^{-1} X) \tag{7.91}$$

Hence this submatrix of Ω can be estimated consistently by $(1/T)(X' \hat{V}^{-1} X)$, which is a quantity that one has already computed in the process of estimating the vector γ. Consequently, the consistent estimator of Ω^{-1} proposed here is:

$$\hat{\Omega}^{-1} = \begin{bmatrix} \dfrac{X' \hat{V}^{-1} X}{T} & a \\ a' & \dfrac{\hat\sigma^2}{1 - \hat\rho^2} \end{bmatrix}^{-1} \tag{7.92}$$

where a is an n-element vector, all of whose elements are zero save the last, which is $\hat\sigma^2/(1 - \hat\beta_{n}\hat\rho)$.

Before we leave the problem of estimating the parameters of the model in (7.14), let us consider the following two-step procedure: Suppose we obtain consistent estimators of the parameter vector β by instrumental variables. Let the IV estimator of β be $\tilde\beta$. For this to remain a simple procedure, the instruments chosen might be x_{ti}, $i = 1, 2, \ldots, n - 1$ and, say, $x_{t-1,1}$ (or some other such simple function of the x_{ti} and their lags). Now, we can certainly compute the residuals to obtain

$$\tilde{w}_t = y_t - \sum_{i=1}^{n-1} \tilde\beta_i x_{ti} - \tilde\beta_n y_{t-i}, \quad t = 2, 3, \ldots, T \tag{7.93}$$

The parameter ρ may be estimated as

$$\tilde{\rho} = \frac{\sum_{t=3}^{T} \tilde{w}_t \tilde{w}_{t-1}}{\sum_{t=3}^{T} \tilde{w}_{t-1}^2} \tag{7.94}$$

and we may thus obtain an estimator of β as

$$\tilde{\tilde{\beta}} = (X'\tilde{V}^{-1}X)^{-1}X'\tilde{V}^{-1}y \tag{7.95}$$

where, of course, $\tilde{V}$ is the consistent estimator of V resulting when, for ρ, we substitute $\tilde{\rho}$.

This is an estimation procedure which is executed somewhat more easily, and it is natural to ask whether, asymptotically, $\tilde{\tilde{\beta}}$ is as good as $\hat{\beta}(\hat{\rho})$ of (7.42). If it is, then obtaining $\hat{\beta}(\hat{\rho})$ may not be worth the extra effort.

To examine this question, let us derive the asymptotic distribution of $\tilde{\tilde{\beta}}$. We have

$$\tilde{\tilde{\beta}} - \beta = (X'\tilde{V}^{-1}X)^{-1}X'\tilde{V}^{-1}w \tag{7.96}$$

Since

$$\operatorname*{plim}_{T\to\infty} \frac{X'\tilde{V}^{-1}X}{T} = \operatorname*{plim}_{T\to\infty} \frac{X'V^{-1}X}{T} \tag{7.97}$$

is a nonstochastic matrix, we need only be concerned with the asymptotic distribution of $X'\tilde{V}^{-1}w/\sqrt{T}$. But we have

$$\frac{X'\tilde{V}^{-1}w}{\sqrt{T}} = \frac{X'V^{-1}w}{\sqrt{T}} + \frac{1}{T}\left(X'\frac{\partial V^{-1}}{\partial \rho}w\right)\sqrt{T}\,(\tilde{\rho} - \rho_0)$$

$$+ \text{ higher order terms} \tag{7.98}$$

All higher order terms can be shown to vanish in probability; hence, we shall neglect them in the discussion to follow.

The reader will recall from Equation (7.48) that we have already dealt with the asymptotic behavior of $X'V^{-1}w/\sqrt{T}$, so that the novel element here is contributed by the term $[(1/T)X'(\partial V^{-1}/\partial\rho)w]\sqrt{T}\,(\tilde{\rho} - \rho_0)$. But it is easily verified that all elements of the vector in brackets vanish (in probability), except for the last, which is given by[32]

$$\operatorname*{plim}_{T\to\infty} \frac{1}{T}\left(-\sum_{i=2}^{T-2} w_i^* w_{i+2} - \sum_{i=2}^{T-1} w_i^* w_i + 2\rho \sum_{i=2}^{T-2} w_i^* w_{i+1}\right) = -\frac{\sigma^2}{1 - \beta_n \rho}$$

$$\tag{7.99}$$

---

[32] In the discussion immediately following, we shall dispense with the zero subscript in denoting true parameters. This is necessary in order to avoid confusion with subscripts relating to *elements* of the vector β. The reader should understand, however, that in (7.99) (for example) $\sigma^2/(1 - \beta_n\rho)$ refers to the true parameters $\sigma_0^2, \beta_{n0}, \rho_0$.

How does $\sqrt{T}(\tilde{\rho} - \rho)$ behave asymptotically? We recall from Equation (7.94) that

$$\tilde{\rho} = \frac{\tilde{w}'\tilde{w}_{-1}}{\tilde{w}'_{-1}\tilde{w}_{-1}} \tag{7.100}$$

where

$$\tilde{w} = (\tilde{w}_3, \tilde{w}_4, \ldots, \tilde{w}_T)', \quad \tilde{w}_{-1} = (\tilde{w}_2, \tilde{w}_3, \ldots, \tilde{w}_{T-1})'$$

$$\tilde{w}_t = y_t - \sum_{i=1}^{n-1} \tilde{\beta}_i x_{ti} - \tilde{\beta}_n y_{t-1} \tag{7.101}$$

Thus,

$$\sqrt{T}(\tilde{\rho} - \rho) = \frac{(1/\sqrt{T})(\tilde{w} - \rho\tilde{w}_{-1})'\tilde{w}_{-1}}{\tilde{w}'_{-1}\tilde{w}_{-1}/T} \tag{7.102}$$

and since

$$\operatorname*{plim}_{T\to\infty} \frac{\tilde{w}'_{-1}\tilde{w}_{-1}}{T} = \frac{\sigma^2}{1 - \rho^2}$$

we see that we need to determine the asymptotic distribution of the numerator in (7.102). We recall from (7.93) that

$$\tilde{w} = y - X\tilde{\beta} = w - X(\tilde{\beta} - \beta),$$
$$\tilde{w}_{-1} = y_{-1} - X_{-1}\tilde{\beta} = w_{-1} - X_{-1}(\tilde{\beta} - \beta) \tag{7.103}$$

where, in order to conform with the usage in (7.101) X differs from its usual definition in that observations relating to $t = 2$ have been deleted. One obtains X_{-1} from X by reducing, in the latter, all "time" indices by one; thus, x_{ti} in X becomes $x_{t-1,i}$ in X_{-1} and so on.

In view of the relations in (7.103) we may rewrite the numerator of (7.102) as

$$\frac{1}{\sqrt{T}}\left[w - \rho w_{-1} - (X - \rho X_{-1})(\tilde{\beta} - \beta)\right]'\left[w_{-1} - X_{-1}(\tilde{\beta} - \beta)\right]$$

$$= \frac{1}{\sqrt{T}}\varepsilon'w_{-1} - \sqrt{T}(\tilde{\beta} - \beta)'\frac{(X - \rho X_{-1})'w_{-1}}{T} - \frac{\varepsilon'X_{-1}}{T}\sqrt{T}(\tilde{\beta} - \beta)$$

$$+ \sqrt{T}(\tilde{\beta} - \beta)'\frac{(X - \rho X_{-1})'X_{-1}}{T^{3/2}}\sqrt{T}(\tilde{\beta} - \beta)$$

where we have made use of the relation $w - \rho w_{-1} = \varepsilon$, the latter being a $(T - 3)$ element vector. Now $\sqrt{T}(\tilde{\beta} - \beta)$ has a well-defined asymptotic distribution and it is easily seen, in view of the assumptions of the problem, that

$$\operatorname*{plim}_{T\to\infty} \frac{\varepsilon'X_{-1}}{T} = 0, \quad \operatorname*{plim}_{T\to\infty} \frac{(X - \rho X_{-1})'X_{-1}}{T^{3/2}} = 0 \tag{7.104}$$

Moreover, we see that all elements of the vector

$$\operatorname*{plim}_{T \to \infty} \frac{(X - \rho X_{-1})' w_{-1}}{T}$$

vanish, except for the last which is given by

$$\operatorname*{plim}_{T \to \infty} \frac{1}{T} \sum_{t=3}^{T} (w^*_{t-1} - \rho w^*_{t-2}) w_{t-1} = \frac{\sigma^2(1 - \rho^2)}{(1 - \rho^2)\,(1 - \beta_n \rho)} = \frac{\sigma^2}{1 - \beta_n \rho}$$

Consequently, we find that, asymptotically,[33]

$$\sqrt{T}\,(\tilde{\rho} - \rho) \sim \frac{1 - \rho^2}{\sigma^2} \frac{1}{\sqrt{T}} w'_{-1}\varepsilon - \frac{1 - \rho^2}{1 - \beta_n \rho} \sqrt{T}\,(\tilde{\beta}_n - \beta_n) \quad (7.105)$$

From the definition of the IV estimator, we have

$$\sqrt{T}\,(\tilde{\beta} - \beta) = \left(\frac{\tilde{X}'X}{T}\right)^{-1} \frac{\tilde{X}'w}{\sqrt{T}} \quad\quad (7.106)$$

where

$$\tilde{X} = (X^*, r) \quad\quad (7.107)$$

and r is the instrument replacing y_{-1}. Thus

$$\frac{X'\tilde{V}^{-1}w}{\sqrt{T}} \sim \frac{1}{\sqrt{T}}\left[X'V^{-1}w - \begin{pmatrix} 0 \\ \vdots \\ \dfrac{1 - \rho^2}{1 - \beta_n \rho} \end{pmatrix} w'_{-1}\varepsilon + \begin{pmatrix} 0 \\ \vdots \\ \dfrac{\sigma^2(1 - \rho^2)}{(1 - \beta_n \rho)^2} \end{pmatrix} p'\tilde{X}'w \right]$$

$$(7.108)$$

p' being the *last row* of $(\tilde{X}'X/T)^{-1}$ and $\sqrt{T}\,(\tilde{\beta}_n - \beta_n) = (p'\tilde{X}'w)/\sqrt{T}$.
Asymptotically, we may thus write, in the notation of Equation (7.54),

$$\frac{X\tilde{V}^{-1}w}{\sqrt{T}} \sim \frac{1}{\sqrt{T}} \begin{bmatrix} X^{*\prime}M'\varepsilon \\[4pt] \bar{y}'_{-1}M'\varepsilon + w^{*\prime}_{-1}M'\varepsilon - \dfrac{1 - \rho^2}{1 - \beta_n \rho} w'_{-1}\varepsilon \\[8pt] + \dfrac{\sigma^2(1 - \rho^2)}{(1 - \beta_n \rho)^2} p'\tilde{X}'M^{-1}\varepsilon \end{bmatrix} \quad (7.109)$$

---

[33] In the interesting paper by Wallis [152], which first suggested this particular two-step estimator, a similar derivation is attempted; however, the second term in the right member of (7.105) is given as

$$-\frac{1 + \rho^2}{1 - \beta_n \rho} \sqrt{T}\,(\tilde{\beta}_n - \beta_n)$$

This miscalculation arises because Wallis operates in his derivation with $\sqrt{T}\,\tilde{\rho}$, whereas one ought to consider $\sqrt{T}\,(\tilde{\rho} - \rho)$ *ab initio*; the difficulty is that $\sqrt{T}\,\tilde{\rho}$ has a systematic component, $\sqrt{T}\,\rho$, which diverges to $\pm\infty$ with T.

Using exactly the same argument leading to (7.71), we conclude that, asymptotically,

$$\frac{X'\tilde{V}^{-1}w}{\sqrt{T}} \sim N(0, \sigma^2\Omega_0) \tag{7.110}$$

where

$$\Omega_0 = \operatorname*{plim}_{T\to\infty} \frac{1}{T}$$

$$\times \begin{bmatrix} X^{*\prime}V^{-1}X^* & X^{*\prime}V^{-1}\bar{y}_{-1} + X^{*\prime}M'p^* \\ \bar{y}'_{-1}V^{-1}X^* + p^{*\prime}MX^* & \bar{y}'_{-1}V^{-1}\bar{y}_{-1} \\ & + \dfrac{T\sigma^2(\rho - \beta_n)^2}{(1 - \beta_n^2)(1 - \beta_n\rho)^2} + T\varphi^* \end{bmatrix} \tag{7.111}$$

and

$$p^* = M'^{-1}\check{X}p \,,$$

$$\varphi^* = \frac{1}{T} p^{*\prime}p^* \frac{\sigma^4(1 - \rho^2)^2}{(1 - \beta_n\rho)^4} + \frac{2}{T} \frac{\sigma^2(1 - \rho^2)}{(1 - \beta_n\rho)^2} \bar{y}^{*\prime}_{-1}p^* \tag{7.112}$$

But in view of the definitions of p^* and $\bar{y}^*_{-1}(=M\bar{y}_{-1})$, we easily conclude that

$$\operatorname*{plim}_{T\to\infty} \frac{1}{T} X^{*\prime}M'p^* = 0 \,, \quad \operatorname*{plim}_{T\to\infty} \frac{1}{T} p^{*\prime}\bar{y}^*_{-1} = 1 \tag{7.113}$$

Hence, (7.111) may be simplified to

$$\Omega_0 = \lim_{T\to\infty} \frac{1}{T} \begin{bmatrix} X^{*\prime}V^{-1}X^* & X^{*\prime}V^{-1}\bar{y}_{-1} \\ \bar{y}'_{-1}V^{-1}X^* & \bar{y}'_{-1}V^{-1}\bar{y}_{-1} + \dfrac{T\sigma^2(\rho - \beta_n)^2}{(1 - \beta_n^2)(1 - \beta_n\rho)^2} + T\varphi \end{bmatrix} \tag{7.114}$$

where

$$\varphi = \frac{2\sigma^2(1 - \rho)^2}{(1 - \beta_n\rho)^2} + \frac{\sigma^4(1 - \rho^2)^2}{(1 - \beta_n\rho)^4} \operatorname*{plim}_{T\to\infty} \frac{1}{T} (p'\check{X}'V\check{X}p) \tag{7.115}$$

The reader should notice that

$$\sigma^2 s^{nn} = \sigma^2 \operatorname*{plim}_{T\to\infty} \frac{1}{T} (p'\check{X}'V\check{X}p) \tag{7.116}$$

is the *asymptotic variance of the instrumental variables estimator of β_n*, *as obtained in the first step of this two-step procedure.*

We conclude that, asymptotically,

$$\sqrt{T}(\bar{\bar{\beta}} - \beta) \sim N(0, \sigma^2\Sigma^{-1}\Omega_0\Sigma^{-1}) \tag{7.117}$$

where

$$\Sigma^{-1} = \operatorname*{plim}_{T \to \infty} \left(\frac{X'V^{-1}X}{T} \right)^{-1} \tag{7.118}$$

A natural question to ask at this stage is whether the two-step estimator is asymptotically equivalent to the estimator obtained by the search procedure. To answer this question, we first observe that we can write

$$\Omega_0 = \Sigma + \begin{pmatrix} 0 & 0 \\ 0 & \nu \end{pmatrix}, \quad \nu = \frac{\sigma^2(1 - \rho^2)}{(1 - \beta_n \rho)^2} + \frac{\sigma^4(1 - \rho^2)^2}{(1 - \beta_n \rho)^4} s^{nn} \tag{7.119}$$

Hence,

$$\Sigma^{-1}\Omega_0\Sigma^{-1} = \Sigma^{-1} + \Sigma^{-1} \begin{pmatrix} 0 & 0 \\ 0 & \nu \end{pmatrix} \Sigma^{-1} \tag{7.120}$$

and we see that the cost of not knowing ρ in the two-step procedure is given by

$$\Sigma^{-1} \begin{pmatrix} 0 & 0 \\ 0 & \nu \end{pmatrix} \Sigma^{-1}$$

On the other hand, the cost of not knowing ρ in the search procedure is $\Omega^{*-1} - \Sigma^{-1}$.

Thus, in making judgments concerning the relative asymptotic efficiency of the two-step procedure, we must compare the magnitude of the two costs. Formally, we must determine whether

$$\Sigma^{-1}\Omega_0\Sigma^{-1} - \Omega^{*-1} = (\Sigma^{-1} - \Omega^{*-1}) + \Sigma^{-1} \begin{pmatrix} 0 & 0 \\ 0 & \nu \end{pmatrix} \Sigma^{-1} \tag{7.121}$$

is a positive semidefinite matrix.

We note, however, that

$$\Sigma^{-1} - \Omega^{*-1} = -\Omega^{*-1}(\Sigma - \Omega^*)\Sigma^{-1} = -\Omega^{*-1} \begin{pmatrix} 0 & 0 \\ 0 & \mu \end{pmatrix} \Sigma^{-1} \tag{7.122}$$

where

$$\mu = \frac{\sigma^2(1 - \rho)^2}{(1 - \beta_n \rho)^2} \tag{7.123}$$

Hence,

$$\Sigma^{-1}\Omega_0\Sigma^{-1} - \Omega^{*-1} = \Sigma^{-1} \begin{pmatrix} 0 & 0 \\ 0 & \nu \end{pmatrix} \Sigma^{-1} - \Omega^{*-1} \begin{pmatrix} 0 & 0 \\ 0 & \mu \end{pmatrix} \Sigma^{-1} \tag{7.174}$$

But the matrix in the right member above is positive semidefinite if and only if

$$\begin{pmatrix} 0 & 0 \\ 0 & \nu \end{pmatrix} - \Sigma\Omega^{*-1} \begin{pmatrix} 0 & 0 \\ 0 & \mu \end{pmatrix}$$

is positive semidefinite.

Observing that

$$\Sigma = \Omega^* + \begin{bmatrix} 0 & 0 \\ 0 & \mu \end{bmatrix} \tag{7.175}$$

we conclude that

$$\Sigma\Omega^{*-1} = I + \begin{bmatrix} 0 & 0 \\ 0 & \mu \end{bmatrix} \Omega^{*-1} \tag{7.126}$$

Thus,

$$\begin{bmatrix} 0 & 0 \\ 0 & \nu \end{bmatrix} - \Sigma\Omega^{*-1} \begin{bmatrix} 0 & 0 \\ 0 & \mu \end{bmatrix}$$

$$= \begin{bmatrix} 0 & 0 \\ 0 & \nu \end{bmatrix} - \begin{bmatrix} 0 & 0 \\ 0 & \mu \end{bmatrix} - \begin{bmatrix} 0 & 0 \\ 0 & \mu \end{bmatrix} \Omega^{*-1} \begin{bmatrix} 0 & 0 \\ 0 & \mu \end{bmatrix} \tag{7.127}$$

and we see that the question of the relative asymptotic efficiency of the two-step estimator hinges on the sign of

$$\nu - \mu - \mu^2 \omega^{*nn} = \mu^2(s^{nn} - \omega^{*nn}) \tag{7.128}$$

We recall that $\sigma^2 s^{nn}$ is the asymptotic variance of $\tilde{\beta}_n$, i.e., the estimator of β_n obtained by IV, methods, while $\sigma^2 \omega^{*nn}$ is the asymptotic variance of $\hat{\beta}_n$, i.e., the estimator of β_n obtained by the search procedure.[34] It should be apparent to the reader without further argument that, indeed, $s^{nn} \geq \omega^{*nn}$, and thus,

$$\nu - \mu - \mu^2 \omega^{*nn} \geq 0 \tag{7.129}$$

thereby proving the relative efficiency of the search procedure. For the sake of completeness, however, we shall now show that

$$s^{nn} \geq \omega^{*nn} \tag{7.130}$$

First, we note that the asymptotic distribution of the IV estimator is

$$\sqrt{T} (\tilde{\beta} - \beta) \sim N(0, \sigma^2 \tilde{\Sigma}^{-1}) \tag{7.131}$$

where

$$\tilde{\Sigma}^{-1} = \plim_{T \to \infty} \frac{1}{T} \left[\left(\frac{\tilde{X}'X}{T} \right)^{-1} \tilde{X}'V\tilde{X} \left(\frac{X'\tilde{X}}{T} \right)^{-1} \right] \tag{7.132}$$

We remind the reader that

$$\tilde{X} = (X^*, r) \tag{7.133}$$

r being the instrument replacing y_{-1}.

Let

$$\bar{X} = (X^*, \bar{y}_{-1}) \tag{7.134}$$

---

[34] In this notation, ω^{*nn} is the nth diagonal element of Ω^{*-1}.

and observe that we can write

$$\tilde{\Sigma}^{-1} = \lim_{T \to \infty} \frac{1}{T} \left[\left(\frac{\tilde{X}' \overline{X}}{T} \right)^{-1} \tilde{X}' V \tilde{X} \left(\frac{\overline{X}' \tilde{X}}{T} \right)^{-1} \right] \qquad (7.135)$$

In addition, note that if we put

$$\overline{\Omega}^{*-1} = \lim_{T \to \infty} \left(\frac{\overline{X}' V^{-1} \overline{X}}{T} \right)^{-1} \qquad (7.136)$$

then $\overline{\Omega}^{*-1} - \Omega^{*-1}$ is positive semidefinite. Thus we can write

$$\tilde{\Sigma}^{-1} - \Omega^{*-1} = \tilde{\Sigma}^{-1} - \overline{\Omega}^{*-1} + \overline{\Omega}^{*-1} - \Omega^{*-1} \qquad (7.137)$$

and we see that our task will be completed if we show that $\tilde{\Sigma}^{-1} - \overline{\Omega}^{*-1}$ is positive semidefinite.

Now define a matrix C by

$$(\tilde{X}' \overline{X})^{-1} \tilde{X}' = (\overline{X}' V^{-1} \overline{X})^{-1} \overline{X}' V^{-1} + C \qquad (7.138)$$

and observe that

$$C \overline{X} = 0 \qquad (7.139)$$

Multiply Equation (7.138) on the left by

$$V \tilde{X} (\overline{X}' \tilde{X})^{-1} = \overline{X} (\overline{X}' V^{-1} \overline{X})^{-1} + V C'$$

to obtain

$$(\tilde{X}' \overline{X})^{-1} \tilde{X}' V \tilde{X} (\overline{X}' \tilde{X})^{-1} = (\overline{X}' V^{-1} \overline{X})^{-1} + C V C' \qquad (7.140)$$

Multiplying through by T and taking limits, we have

$$\tilde{\Sigma}^{-1} - \overline{\Omega}^{*-1} = \lim_{T \to \infty} T C V C' \qquad (7.141)$$

Since for every T, $C V C'$ is a positive semidefinite matrix, the claims made in Equations (7.129) and (7.130) are fully validated.

The conclusions of this section may be summarized in

THEOREM 7.2. Consider the model

$$y_t = \sum_{i=1}^{n-1} \beta_i x_{ti} + \beta_n y_{t-1} + w_t \qquad (7.142)$$

where the explanatory variables, x_{tj}, obey the conditions in (7.25) and the discussion immediately preceding.

Let

$$w_t = \rho w_{t-1} + \varepsilon_t, \qquad \rho \in (-1, 1) \qquad (7.143)$$

Let the ε's be *i.i.d.* random variables with

$$E(\varepsilon_t) = 0 , \quad E(\varepsilon_t^2) = \sigma^2 \tag{7.144}$$

and finite sixth order (absolute) moments. Then

(i) 3 *PLS* cannot yield consistent estimators of the β_i, $i = 1, 2, \ldots, n$ if among the x_{ti}, $i = 1, 2, \ldots, n - 1$, there are lagged *exogenous* variables.

(ii) The estimator $\hat{\beta}$ obtained by the search method is consistent and its (marginal) asymptotic distribution is given by

$$\sqrt{T} \, (\hat{\beta} - \beta) \sim N(0, \sigma^2 \Omega^{*-1}) \tag{7.145}$$

Ω^* being as defined in (7.84) and $\beta = (\beta_1, \beta_2, \ldots, \beta_n)'$.

(iii) The two-step estimator as given in (7.95) has the asymptotic distribution,

$$\sqrt{T} \, (\tilde{\tilde{\beta}} - \beta) \sim N(0, \sigma^2 \Sigma^{-1} \Omega_0 \Sigma^{-1}) \tag{7.146}$$

Ω_0, Σ^{-1} being as defined, respectively, in (7.114) and (7.118).

(iv) The estimator $\hat{\beta}$ obtained by the search procedure is asymptotically efficient relative to the two-step estimator $\tilde{\tilde{\beta}}$ in the sense that

$$\Sigma^{-1} \Omega_0 \Sigma^{-1} - \Omega^{*-1}$$

is positive semidefinite.

REMARK 7.2. The discussion of the aysmptotic distribution of the two-step estimator serves to emphasize again the sensitivity of feasible Aitken estimators to the method by which the covariance matrix is estimated in the first stage. If no lagged dependent variable appears among the explanatory variables, the reader may easily verify that, asymptotically, it is a matter of complete indifference which consistent estimator of ρ is used in obtaining the feasible Aitken estimator of the β_i. *In the present case, however, this is not true at all. How we estimate, initially, the parameters β_i, $i = 1, \ldots, n$, is a matter of considerable import, as seen from the definition of Ω_0 in (7.114) through (7.116).* Since, with economic data, the usual instrumental variables approach is likely to yield very poor estimators, one should be wary of two-step procedures for the type of model given in (7.142) or models exhibiting similar characteristics. Indeed, if the choice of instruments is poor, the relative efficiency of two-step estimators may be extremely small, in the sense that $|\Omega^{*-1}|/|\Sigma^{-1}\Omega_0\Sigma^{-1}|$ is quite small.

Finally, notice that the discussion following Equation (7.137) implies

COROLLARY 7.2. In the context of the model in Theorem 7.2, the minimum chi square (or ML, as the case may be) estimator of the parameter vector β, is asymptotically efficient relative to *any simple* IV estimator.

The proof of this corollary follows immediately if we note that in showing the positive semidefiniteness of $\tilde{\Sigma} - \Omega^{*-1}$, no use was made of the composition of the instrumental matrix $\tilde{X}$.

7.2 Direct Estimation of the Dynamic Demand Model

The important feature of the dynamic demand model is that it contains the unobservable variable, s_t; this variable may be eliminated in virtue of the second equation in (7.1), which describes the growth of the "psychological stock". Thus, in the presence of this variable, parameters can be estimated only from the reduced form,

$$
\begin{aligned}
y_t = & -\frac{\alpha_0 \beta_0}{1 - \alpha_2} + \frac{\alpha_1}{1 - \alpha_2} x_t - \frac{\alpha_1(1 + \beta_0)}{1 - \alpha_2} x_{t-1} \\
& + \frac{1 + \beta_0}{1 - \alpha_2} y_{t-1} + u_t - (1 + \beta_0) u_{t-1}
\end{aligned}
\tag{7.147}
$$

or certain reformulations of it.

In the preceding, we have made use of the assumption,

$$
\beta_1 = 1
\tag{7.148}
$$

and we have redefined the error term, so that what appears as u_t in (7.1) is $u_t/(1 - \alpha_1)$ in (7.147). Thus, if σ^2 is the variance of the error term in (7.1), then $\sigma^2/(1 - \alpha_2)^2$ is the variance of the error term u_t as it appears in (7.147). Since σ^2 is unspecified, this redefinition occasions no difficulty whatsoever.

It will be convenient to put, as a matter of notation,

$$
\lambda = 1 + \beta_0, \quad \alpha_0^* = \frac{\alpha_0}{1 - \alpha_2}, \quad \alpha_1^* = \frac{\alpha_1}{1 - \alpha_2}, \quad \alpha_2^* = \frac{\alpha_2}{1 - \alpha_2}
\tag{7.149}
$$

and rewrite (7.147) as

$$
y_t = \alpha_0^*(1 - \lambda) + \alpha_1^*(I - \lambda L)x_t + \frac{1}{1 - \alpha_2}\lambda L y_t + (I - \lambda L)u_t
\tag{7.150}
$$

Subtracting $\lambda L y_t$ from both sides, we find

$$
\begin{aligned}
(I - \lambda L)y_t = & \, \alpha_0^*(1 - \lambda) + \alpha_1^*(I - \lambda L)x_t \\
& + \alpha_2^* \lambda L y_t + (I - \lambda L)u_t
\end{aligned}
\tag{7.151}
$$

Canceling the operator $(I - \lambda L)$, we have

$$y_t = \alpha_0^* + \alpha_1^* x_t + \alpha_2^* \frac{\lambda L}{I - \lambda L} y_t + u_t \qquad (7.152)$$

Define

$$y_t^* = \frac{I}{I - \lambda L} y_t \qquad (7.153)$$

and observe that this may be written as

$$y_t^* = \lambda^t y_0^* + \sum_{i=0}^{t-1} \lambda^i y_{t-i} \qquad y_0^* = \sum_{i=0}^{\infty} \lambda^i y_{-i} \qquad (7.154)$$

Thus, the model may be further reduced to

$$y_t = \alpha_0^* + \alpha_1^* x_t + \alpha_2^* \lambda y_{t-1}^* + (\alpha_2^* y_0^*) \lambda^t + u_t \qquad (7.155)$$

where, for notational simplicity we have redefined y_t^* by

$$y_t^* = \sum_{i=0}^{t-1} \lambda^i y_{t-i} \qquad t > 0 \qquad (7.156)$$

which *is thus a quantity that may be computed from the sample data if λ were known.* As we pointed out in Section 6.1, the impact of the term $(\alpha_2^* y_0^*) \lambda^t$ on the estimation process declines with sample size and may thus be suppressed when operating with sufficiently large samples. For simplicity, we shall do so in the discussion to follow; the reader may supply the details, if he wishes to include such a parameter—$\alpha_2^* y_0^*$—in his estimation process.

With y_t^* an in (7.156), define

$$X = (e, x, \lambda y_{-1}^*), \quad \alpha^* = (\alpha_0^*, \alpha_1^*, \alpha_2^*)' \qquad (7.157)$$

where

$$x = (x_2, x_3, \ldots, x_T)', \quad y_{-1}^* = (y_1^*, y_2^*, \ldots, y_{T-1}^*)' \\ e = (1, 1, \ldots, 1)' \qquad (7.158)$$

and let us obtain parameter estimators by minimizing

$$Q = (y - X\alpha^*)'(y - X\alpha^*) \qquad (7.159)$$

where, of course,

$$y = (y_2, y_3, \ldots, y_T)' \qquad (7.160)$$

Solving the normal equations

$$\frac{\partial Q}{\partial \alpha^*} = 0 \qquad (7.161)$$

we obtain

$$\tilde{\alpha}^*(\lambda) = (X'X)^{-1}X'y \qquad (7.162)$$

Substituting in (7.159), we have the concentrated minimand,

$$Q = Q^*(\lambda) = y'[I - X(X'X)^{-1}X']y \qquad (7.163)$$

which is now to be minimized with respect to λ. Since $Q^*(\lambda)$ is a highly nonlinear function of λ, it is neither simple nor convenient to find the minimizing value of λ by differentiation. Thus, we resort again to the search procedure. To this effect, divide the admissible range of λ, $(-1, 1)$, by the points λ_j, $j = 1, 2, \ldots, m$, and choose the estimator of λ, say, $\hat{\lambda}$, by the condition

$$Q^*(\hat{\lambda}) = \min_j Q^*(\lambda_j) \qquad (7.164)$$

Estimators for α^* and σ^2 are obviously obtained by

$$\hat{\alpha}^* = \tilde{\alpha}^*(\hat{\lambda}), \quad \hat{\sigma}^2 = \frac{1}{T}Q^*(\hat{\lambda}) \qquad (7.165)$$

All such estimators can be shown to be consistent. But more important from the point of view of the distributional aspects of such estimators is the fact that the estimators of the basic parameters of the model, α_i, $i = 0, 1, 2$, obtained as

$$\hat{\alpha}_0 = \frac{\hat{\alpha}_0^*}{1 + \hat{\alpha}_2^*}, \quad \hat{\alpha}_1 = \frac{\hat{\alpha}_1^*}{1 + \hat{\alpha}_2^*}, \quad \hat{\alpha}_2 = \frac{\hat{\alpha}_2^*}{1 + \hat{\alpha}_2^*} \qquad (7.166)$$

are solutions of the *normal* equations,

$$\frac{\partial Q}{\partial \alpha} = 0, \quad \alpha = (\alpha_0, \alpha_1, \alpha_2)' \qquad (7.167)$$

This is so because

$$\frac{\partial Q}{\partial \alpha_0} = \frac{1}{1 - \alpha_2}\frac{\partial Q}{\partial \alpha_0^*}, \quad \frac{\partial Q}{\partial \alpha_1} = \frac{1}{1 - \alpha_2}\frac{\partial Q}{\partial \alpha_1^*}$$
$$\frac{\partial Q}{\partial \alpha_2} = \frac{\alpha_0}{(1 - \alpha_2)^2}\frac{\partial Q}{\partial \alpha_0^*} + \frac{\alpha_1}{(1 - \alpha_2)^2}\frac{\partial Q}{\partial \alpha_1^*} + \frac{1}{(1 - \alpha_2)^2}\frac{\partial Q}{\partial \alpha_2^*} \qquad (7.168)$$

and hence,

$$\frac{\partial Q}{\partial \alpha} = \begin{bmatrix} \dfrac{1}{1 - \alpha_2} & 0 & 0 \\[2ex] 0 & \dfrac{1}{1 - \alpha_2} & 0 \\[2ex] \dfrac{\alpha_0}{(1 - \alpha_2)^2} & \dfrac{\alpha_1}{(1 - \alpha_2)^2} & \dfrac{1}{(1 - \alpha_2)^2} \end{bmatrix} \frac{\partial Q}{\partial \alpha^*} \qquad (7.169)$$

Thus, because the $\hat{\alpha}_i$, $i = 0, 1, 2$ of (7.166) satisfy the condition $\partial Q/\partial \alpha^* = 0$, we conclude that they also satisfy the condition

$$\frac{\partial Q}{\partial \alpha} = 0 \qquad (7.170)$$

If the minimum in (7.164) occurs for $\hat{\lambda} \in (-1, 1)$, then the estimator

$$\hat{\gamma} = \begin{pmatrix} \hat{\alpha} \\ \hat{\lambda} \end{pmatrix} \qquad (7.171)$$

of the true parameter vector $\gamma = (\alpha', \lambda)'$ satisfies the condition

$$\frac{\partial Q}{\partial \gamma}(\hat{\gamma}) = 0 \qquad (7.172)$$

Recapitulating, our estimation procedure is as follows:

(i) Reformulate the estimating equation as in (7.155) and, for the purpose of this discussion only, neglect the term $\alpha_2^* y_0^* \lambda^t$.

(ii) Divide the admissible range of λ, $(-1, 1)$, by the points λ_j, $j = 1, 2, \ldots, m - m$ being as large as is necessary in view of the numerical accuracy desired for the estimator $\hat{\lambda}$. For example, we might take $\lambda_j - \lambda_{j-1} = 0.01$ or some other suitable interval. For each λ_j, compute the quantities $\lambda_j y_{t-1}^*$ and thus obtain the estimator in (7.162).

(iii) Substitute $\tilde{\alpha}^*(\lambda_j)$ in (7.159) to obtain the quantities $Q^*(\lambda_j)$, $j = 1, 2, \ldots, m$. Choose the estimator of λ, say $\hat{\lambda}$, by the condition $Q^*(\hat{\lambda}) = \min_j Q^*(\lambda_j)$ and substitute in (7.162) to obtain the estimators of α^* and σ^2 as in (7.165).

(iv) Finally, obtain an estimator for α as in (7.166) and notice that the estimator $\hat{\gamma} = (\hat{\alpha}', \hat{\lambda})'$ has the property

$$\frac{\partial Q}{\partial \gamma}(\hat{\gamma}) = 0$$

In order to solve the inference problem posed by this model, it is necesaary to obtain, at least, the asymptotic distribution of the estimator $\hat{\gamma}$. To this effect, expand $\partial Q/\partial \gamma$ by Taylor series about γ_0, the true parameter vector, to obtain

$$\frac{\partial Q}{\partial \gamma}(\gamma) = \frac{\partial Q}{\partial \gamma}(\gamma_0) + \frac{\partial^2 Q}{\partial \gamma \partial \gamma}(\gamma_0)[\gamma - \gamma_0] + \text{third order terms} \quad (7.173)$$

In particular, (7.173) is valid for $\gamma = \hat{\gamma}$; since in this case all third and higher order terms can be shown to vanish in probability,[35] we shall neglect them in the argument to follow.

---

[35] This claim assumes that $\hat{\gamma}$ is a consistent estimator for γ_0. While consistency is indeed a property of $\hat{\gamma}$, it is somewhat cumbersome to establish directly in the present case.

For $\gamma = \hat{\gamma}$, the expansion yields

$$\frac{1}{\sqrt{T}} \frac{\partial Q}{\partial \gamma}(\gamma_0) = -\frac{1}{T} \frac{\partial^2 Q}{\partial \gamma \partial \gamma}(\gamma_0) \sqrt{T} (\hat{\gamma} - \gamma_0) \qquad (7.174)$$

Let

$$\gamma^* = \begin{pmatrix} \alpha^* \\ \lambda \end{pmatrix}, \quad A^* = \begin{bmatrix} A & 0 \\ 0 & 1 \end{bmatrix}$$

$$A = \begin{bmatrix} \dfrac{1}{1 - \alpha_2} & 0 & 0 \\[2ex] 0 & \dfrac{1}{1 - \alpha_2} & 0 \\[2ex] \dfrac{\alpha_0}{(1 - \alpha_2)^2} & \dfrac{\alpha_1}{(1 - \alpha_2)^2} & \dfrac{\alpha_2}{(1 - \alpha_2)^2} \end{bmatrix} \qquad (7.175)$$

Since

$$\frac{\partial Q}{\partial \gamma} = A^* \frac{\partial Q}{\partial \gamma^*} \qquad (7.176)$$

we see that the asymptotic distribution $(1/\sqrt{T})(\partial Q/\partial \gamma)$ is readily obtained from that of $(1/\sqrt{T})(\partial Q/\partial \gamma^*)$. The latter is considerably easier to deal with than the former. Now,

$$\frac{\partial Q}{\partial \gamma^*} = -2 \begin{bmatrix} X' \\ \left(\dfrac{\alpha_2}{1 - \alpha_2}\right)\left(y^*_{-1} + \lambda \dfrac{\partial y^*_{-1}}{\partial \lambda}\right) \end{bmatrix} u \qquad (7.177)$$

The quantity $y^*_{-1} + \lambda(\partial y^*_{-1}/\partial \lambda)$ will occur frequently, so that a more convenient expression for it is required. Because we are dealing with asymptotic aspects of the problem, we may consider y^*_t as defined by

$$y^*_t = \frac{I}{I - \lambda L} y_t \qquad (7.178)$$

Thus,

$$\frac{\partial}{\partial \lambda} y^*_t = \frac{L}{(I - \lambda L)^2} y_t \qquad (7.179)$$

But then

$$y^*_{-1} + \lambda \frac{\partial y^*_{-1}}{\partial \lambda} = \frac{I}{I - \lambda L} y_{t-1} + \frac{\lambda L}{(I - \lambda L)^2} y_{t-1}$$

$$= \frac{I}{(I - \lambda L)^2} y_{t-1} \qquad (7.180)$$

Denote

$$y_t^{**} = \frac{I}{I - \lambda L} y_t^* \tag{7.181}$$

and thus observe that

$$y_{t-1}^* + \lambda \frac{\partial y_{t-1}^*}{\partial \lambda} = y_{t-1}^{**} \tag{7.182}$$

We may further verify that

$$y_t^* = \bar{y}_t^* + \frac{I}{I - \lambda^* L} u_t$$

$$y_t^{**} = \bar{y}_t^{**} + \frac{I}{(I - \lambda^* L)(I - \lambda L)} u_t \tag{7.183}$$

$$\lambda^* = \frac{\lambda}{1 - \alpha_2}$$

The reader may recall that

$$\lambda^* = \frac{1 + \beta_0}{1 - \alpha_2} = \beta \tag{7.184}$$

and when discussing this model in Section 7.1, we required that $|\beta| < 1$. Now the need for this assumption becomes obvious; it is required so as to insure that the final form[36] of the dependent variable exists and constitutes a covariance stationary process. Particularly, the reader should observe that if $|\beta| > 1$, then y_t^* will exhibit a variance increasing with time.

In (7.183), $\bar{y}_t^*$, $\bar{y}_t^{**}$ are the nonstochastic parts of y_t^* and y_t^{**}. They are obviously obtained by applying, respectively, the operators $I/(I - \lambda L)$, $I/(I - \lambda L)^2$ to the *exogenous variables* as they appear in the final form of the model. For example, the variable x_t appears as the term $[\alpha_1(I - \lambda L)/(1 - \alpha_2)(I - \lambda^* L)]x_t$ in the final form; hence, it will appear as $[(\alpha_1 I)/(1 - \alpha_2)(I - \lambda^* L)]x_t$ in $\bar{y}_t^*$ and as $[(\alpha_1 I)/(1 - \alpha_2)(I - \lambda L))(I - \lambda^* L)]x_t$ in $\bar{y}_t^{**}$.

With the aid of this notation, we may write (7.177) in the more suggestive form

$$\frac{\partial Q}{\partial \gamma^*} = -2 \sum_{t=2}^{T} \begin{bmatrix} 1 \\ x_t \\ \lambda y_{t-1}^* \\ \frac{\alpha_2}{(1 - \alpha_2)} y_{t-1}^{**} \end{bmatrix} u_t \tag{7.185}$$

---

[36] By "final form" we mean an equation expressing y_t solely as a function of the *exogenous variables and the error terms of the model.*

thus expressing it as the sum of $(T - 1)$ random vectors, each with mean zero.

Unfortunately, however, these vectors are not mutually independent, or even N-dependent, since they contain y_{t-1}^* and y_{t-1}^{**}; the error components of these two quantities are, respectively, first and second order autoregression processes, as is quite evident from (7.183). On the other hand, exactly this property allows us to convert the problem into one involving, essentially, N-dependent random vectors and thus apply the results of Theorem 4.3. To see how this may be accomplished, put

$$v_{t1} = \frac{I}{I - \lambda^* L} u_t, \quad v_{t2} = \frac{I}{I - \lambda L} u_t, \quad \lambda^* > \lambda \quad (7.186)$$

In the above, we recall that

$$\lambda^* = \frac{\lambda}{1 - \alpha_2} \quad (7.187)$$

and thus $\lambda^* > \lambda$ implies $\alpha_2 \in (0, 1)$. If $\alpha_2 \in (-1, 0)$, nothing will be changed except the order in which certain summations are carried out. Of course, in either case the condition $|\lambda^*| < 1$ must be obeyed.

We next observe that

$$w_t = \frac{I}{(I - \lambda^* L)(I - \lambda L)} u_t = \frac{1}{\alpha_2} v_{t1} - \frac{1 - \alpha_2}{\alpha_2} v_{t2} \quad (7.188)$$

In virtue of the fact that $|\lambda|, |\lambda^*| < 1$, for any specified (positive) small quantities δ_1, δ_2 there exists an integer N such that

$$Pr\{|w_t^N| > \delta_1\} < \delta_2, \quad Pr\{|v_{t1}^N| > \delta_1\} < \delta_2 \quad (7.189)$$

where

$$v_{t1}^N = \sum_{k=0}^{N-1} \lambda^{*k} u_{t-k}, \quad v_{t2}^N = \sum_{k=0}^{N-2} \lambda^k u_{t-k},$$

$$w_t^N = \frac{1}{\alpha_2} v_{t1}^N - \frac{1 - \alpha_2}{\alpha_2} v_{t2}^N \quad (7.190)$$

Hence, the asymptotic behavior of $\partial Q / \partial \gamma^*$ is given, essentially, by

$$\frac{\partial Q}{\partial \gamma^*} \sim -2 \sum_{t=2}^{T} \begin{bmatrix} 1 \\ x_t \\ \lambda \bar{y}_{t-1}^* + \lambda v_{t-1,1}^N \\ \dfrac{\alpha_2}{1 - \alpha_2} \bar{y}_{t-t}^{**} + \dfrac{1}{1 - \alpha_2} v_{t-1,1}^N - v_{t-1,2}^N \end{bmatrix} u_t \quad (7.191)$$

The reader may now verify that the sum above is defined *over a sequence of N-dependent random vectors.*

We therefore conclude in virtue of Theorem 4.3 that, asymptotically,

$$\frac{\partial Q}{\partial \gamma^*} \sim N(0, 4\sigma^2 \Omega) \tag{7.192}$$

where

$$\Omega = \plim_{T \to \infty} \frac{1}{T} \begin{bmatrix} X'X & \left(\dfrac{\alpha_2}{1-\alpha_2}\right)X'y_{-1}^{**} \\[2ex] \left(\dfrac{\alpha_2}{1-\alpha_2}\right)y_{-1}^{**'}X & \left(\dfrac{\alpha_2}{1-\alpha_2}\right)^2 y_{-1}^{**'}y_{-1}^{**} \end{bmatrix} \tag{7.193}$$

In (7.193), the reader should note that

$$\plim_{T \to \infty} \frac{1}{T}X'X = \lim_{T \to \infty} \frac{1}{T} \begin{bmatrix} e'e & e'x & \lambda e' \bar{y}_{-1}^* \\ x'e & x'x & \lambda x' \bar{y}_{-1}^* \\ \lambda \bar{y}_{-1}^{*'}e & \lambda \bar{y}_{-1}^{*'}x & \lambda^2 \bar{y}_{-1}^{*'}\bar{y}_{-1}^* + \dfrac{T\lambda^2\sigma^2}{1-\lambda^{*2}} \end{bmatrix} \tag{7.194}$$

$$\plim_{T \to \infty} \frac{1}{T}y_{-1}^{**'}y_{-1}^{**} = \lim_{T \to \infty} \frac{1}{T}\bar{y}_{-1}^{**'}\bar{y}_{-1}^{**} + \frac{1}{\alpha_2^2}\frac{\sigma^2}{1-\lambda^{*2}}$$

$$+ \left(\frac{1-\alpha_2}{\alpha_2}\right)^2 \frac{\sigma^2}{1-\lambda^2} - \frac{2(1-\alpha_2)}{\alpha_2^2}\frac{\sigma^2}{1-\lambda^*\lambda} \tag{7.195}$$

$$\plim_{T \to \infty} \frac{1}{T}y_{-1}^{**'}X = \lim_{T \to \infty} \left[\frac{e'\bar{y}_{-1}^{**}}{T}, \frac{x'\bar{y}_{-1}^{**}}{T}, \frac{\lambda\bar{y}_{-1}^{*'}\bar{y}_{-1}^{**}}{T} \right.$$

$$\left. + \frac{\lambda}{\alpha_2}\frac{\sigma^2}{(1-\lambda^{*2})} - \left(\frac{1-\alpha_2}{\alpha_2}\right)\frac{\lambda\sigma^2}{1-\lambda^*\lambda} \right] \tag{7.196}$$

From (7.176) we then conclude that asymptotically,

$$\frac{\partial Q}{\partial \gamma} \sim N(0, 4\sigma^2 A^*\Omega^* A^{*'}) \tag{7.197}$$

We must now evaluate the quantity

$$\plim_{T \to \infty} \frac{1}{T}\frac{\partial^2 Q}{\partial \gamma \partial \gamma}$$

It is very cumbersome, however, to do so directly. Instead, we employ the following useful device.

Notice that, in view of (7.176), we can write

$$\frac{\partial^2 Q}{\partial\gamma\partial\gamma} = A^* \frac{\partial^2 Q}{\partial\gamma^*\partial\gamma^*} A^{*\prime}$$

$$+ \left[\left(\frac{\partial}{\partial\alpha_0} A^* \right) \frac{\partial Q}{\partial\gamma^*}, \left(\frac{\partial}{\partial\alpha_1} A^* \right) \frac{\partial Q}{\partial\gamma^*}, \left(\frac{\partial}{\partial\alpha_2} A^* \right) \frac{\partial Q}{\partial\gamma^*}, \left(\frac{\partial}{\partial\lambda} A^* \right) \frac{\partial Q}{\partial\gamma^*} \right]'$$

$$\tag{7.198}$$

Upon division by T, it is easily verified that the probability limit of the matrix in square brackets vanishes. But then we conclude, immediately, that

$$\operatorname*{plim}_{T\to\infty} \frac{1}{T} \frac{\partial^2 Q}{\partial\gamma\partial\gamma} = 2A^*\Omega A^{*\prime} \tag{7.199}$$

Thus from (7.174) we see that, asymptotically,

$$\sqrt{T}\,(\hat{\gamma} - \gamma_0) \sim N[0, \sigma^2(A^*\Omega A^{*\prime})^{-1}] \tag{7.200}$$

We have therefore proved the following,

THEOREM 7.3. Consider the model,

$$y_t = \alpha_0 + \alpha_1 x_t + \alpha_2 s_t + u_t$$
$$s_t - s_{t-1} = \beta_0 s_{t-1} + y_t, \qquad t = 1, 2, \ldots, T \tag{7.201}$$

where y_t is the demand for a given commodity, x_t is some suitable exogenous variable and u_t, $t = 1, 2, \ldots, T$ is a set of *i.i.d.* random variables with the properties

$$E(u_t) = 0, \quad E(u_t^2) = \sigma^2, \qquad \text{all } t \tag{7.202}$$

and bounded sixth order absolute moment.

Let

$$\gamma = \begin{bmatrix} \alpha_0 \\ \alpha_1 \\ \alpha_2 \\ \lambda \end{bmatrix} \quad \lambda = 1 + \beta_0, \ |\lambda| < 1, \ \left| \frac{\lambda}{1 - \alpha_2} \right| < 1 \tag{7.203}$$

Then the estimator of γ, $\hat{\gamma}$, as defined in Equations (7.164), (7.165) and (7.166) has, asymptotically, the distribution,

$$\sqrt{T}\,(\hat{\gamma} - \gamma_0) \sim N[0, \sigma^2(A^*\Omega A^{*\prime})^{-1}] \tag{7.204}$$

where γ_0 is the true parameter vector, A^* is as defined in (7.175), and Ω is as defined in (7.193).

REMARK 7.3. It is clear that Ω is consistently estimated by

$$\hat{\Omega} = \frac{1}{T} \begin{bmatrix} X'X & \dfrac{\hat{\alpha}_2}{1 - \hat{\alpha}_2} X' y_{-1}^{**} \\ \left(\dfrac{\hat{\alpha}_2}{1 - \hat{\alpha}_2}\right) y_{-1}^{**'} X & \left(\dfrac{\hat{\alpha}_2}{1 - \hat{\alpha}_2}\right)^2 y_{-1}^{**'} y_{-1}^{**} \end{bmatrix} \tag{7.205}$$

it being understood, of course, that the tth element of the last column of X, i.e. λy_{-1}^*, is given by $\hat{\lambda} \sum_{i=0}^{t-2} \hat{\lambda}^i y_{t-1-i}$ and the tth element of y_{-1}^{**} is given by $\sum_{i=0}^{t-2} \hat{\lambda}^i y_{t-1-i}^*$. The quantity σ^2 may, of course, be estimated consistently by

$$\hat{\sigma}^2 = \frac{Q^*(\hat{\lambda})}{T} \tag{7.206}$$

Tests of significance on individual elements of the vector γ may thus be based, asymptotically, on the $N(0, 1)$ distribution. What this means is that the usual *t-ratio* for parameter estimators is, asymptotically, $N(0, 1)$.

REMARK 7.4. The development of this section suggests an interesting research problem. We have seen in the preceding section that often, in estimating the dynamic demand model, it had been the practice to write the estimating equation of the model considered in this section as

$$y_t = b_0 + b_1 x_{t1} + b_2 x_{t2} + b_3 y_{t-1} + \text{error} \tag{7.207}$$

and assume the error to be a first order autoregressive process. As we indicated earlier, this is an incorrect procedure if the model is as specified in (7.201) and (7.202).

On the other hand, this procedure can be viewed roughly as engaging in the following tradeoff: In the proper estimating equation, one truly has a geometric lag in the explanatory variable y_{t-1}, but its error term is a sequence of *i.i.d.* random variables. The situation in (7.207) is that one transposes the geometric lag to the error term and uses y_{t-1} as the explanatory variable. This is clearly an intriguing compromise; it would be interesting to investigate, by Monte Carlo methods, the consequences of this compromise from the point of view of the properties of the parameters α_0, α_1, α_2, β_0. Clearly, if the parameter λ is very small, both procedures should give very similar results.

Exercises and Questions

1. Prove the consistency of the two-step estimator in (7.95). Is it (asymptotically) necessary efficient relative to the initial (simple) IV estimator? Prove the consistency of the minimum chi square estimator in (7.42).

2. Give a proof of Corollary 7.1.

3. In connection with Equation (7.98) write

$$\frac{1}{\sqrt{T}} X'(\tilde{V}^{-1} - V^{-1})w$$

and without relying on a Taylor series expansion, give an expression for this vector which preserves the validity of (7.109).

Hint:

$$\tilde{V}^{-1} - V^{-1} = (\tilde{\rho} - \rho)$$

$$\times \begin{bmatrix} 0 & -1 & 0 & \cdot & \cdot & \cdot & \cdot & \cdot & 0 \\ -1 & \tilde{\rho}+\rho & -1 & \cdot & \cdot & \cdot & & \cdot \\ 0 & -1 & \tilde{\rho}+\rho & -1 & \cdot & \cdot & & \cdot \\ \cdot & \cdot & \cdot & \cdot & \cdot & \cdot & & \cdot \\ \cdot & \cdot & \cdot & \cdot & \cdot & \cdot & & \cdot \\ & & & & -1 & \tilde{\rho}+\rho & -1 \\ 0 & \cdot & & \cdot & \cdot & \cdot & 0 & -1 & 0 \end{bmatrix}$$

4. Deduce the conditions under which $\operatorname{plim}_{T\to\infty}(X'X/T)$ exists for the model of Theorem 7.1, then $\operatorname{plim}_{T\to\infty}(X'X_{-1}/T^{3/2})$ vanishes.

5. Verify the results of Equation (7.113).

Hint: Observe that

$$\operatorname*{plim}_{T\to\infty} \frac{\tilde{X}'X}{T} = \lim_{T\to\infty} \frac{\tilde{X}'\bar{X}}{T}, \quad \text{where} \quad \bar{X} = (X^*, \bar{y}_{-1})$$

6. Give an intuitive explanation why $\tilde{\Sigma}^{-1} - \bar{\Omega}^{*-1}$ is positive semidefinite.

Hint: Consider the asymptotic distribution of the IV estimator obtained when $V^{-1}\bar{X}$ is used as the matrix of instruments.

7. In connection with Remark 7.2, does it make any difference from the point of view of its substance whether the error term is a second order autoregressive process, i.e.,

$$u_t = \rho_1 u_{t-1} + \rho_2 u_{t-2} + \varepsilon_t$$

the ε's being *i.i.d.* random variables with mean zero and finite variance? Does it make any difference whether other lagged "endogenous" variables are included, e.g. y_{t-2}, y_{t-3}, etc.?

8. Verify that the probability limit of $1/T$ times the matrix in square brackets in the right member of Equation (7.198) vanishes.

Chapter 8

FINITE LAG STRUCTURES

8.1 The General Polynomial Lag Structure

Consider the economic model,

$$y_t = \sum_{\tau=0}^{\infty} w_\tau x_{t-\tau} + u_t, \quad t = 1, 2, \ldots, T \tag{8.1}$$

where it is known a priori that

$$w_\tau = 0, \quad \tau = n + 1, n + 2, \ldots \tag{8.2}$$

If, in addition, it is specified that

$$w_\tau = P(\tau), \quad \tau = 0, 1, 2, \ldots, n \tag{8.3}$$

and

$$P(t) = \sum_{i=0}^{k} \beta_i t^i \tag{8.4}$$

then we are dealing with the *polynomial lag structure of order n and degree k*. A somewhat detailed discussion of this structure was given in Section 3.2. Here we shall examine the estimation problems it poses.

In (8.1) we make the customary assumption on the exogenous variable x_t, namely, that it is either nonstochastic or, if stochastic, possesses finite second moment and is distributed independently of the error term, u_t. Regarding the latter, we may assume that $\{u_t : t = 1, 2, \ldots\}$ is a sequence of *i.i.d.* random variables with the properties

$$E(u_t) = 0, \quad E(u_t^2) = \sigma^2, \quad \text{all } t \tag{8.5}$$

and possessing finite third order absolute moment.

Now, substituting (8.2) and (8.3) in (8.1), we have

$$y_t = \sum_{\tau=0}^{n} \left(\sum_{i=0}^{k} \beta_i \tau^i \right) x_{t-\tau} + u_t = \sum_{i=0}^{k} \beta_i z_{ti} + u_t \tag{8.6}$$

where

$$z_{ti} = \sum_{\tau=0}^{n} \tau^i x_{t-\tau} \tag{8.7}$$

and the first problem is to estimate the β_i, $i = 0, 1, 2, \ldots, k$. To this effect, define

$$\begin{aligned} Z &= (z_{ti}), \quad t = n+1, n+2, \ldots, T, \quad i = 0, 1, 2, \ldots, k \\ \beta &= (\beta_0, \beta_1, \ldots, \beta_k)' \end{aligned} \tag{8.8}$$

and write the model compactly as

$$y = Z\beta + u \tag{8.9}$$

y, u being the $(T - n)$ element vectors of the dependent and random variables, respectively.

Provided

$$\text{rank } (Z) = k + 1 \tag{8.10}$$

unique estimators for the β_i can be obtained by ordinary least squares. By the Markov theorem, such estimators may be shown to be best linear unbiased. However, we are not interested in the β_i *per se*, but rather in the w_τ, $\tau = 0, 1, 2, \ldots, n$; the important question is thus whether efficient estimators can be obtained for the lag coefficients. We have the following useful result:

LEMMA 8.1. Let θ be a parameter vector of interest and suppose that $\hat{\theta}$ is an unbiased efficient estimator of it, in the sense that if θ^1 is any other unbiased estimator of θ, then

$$\Sigma = \Sigma^1 - \Sigma^0 \tag{8.11}$$

is positive semidefinite, Σ^1, Σ^0 being, respectively, the covariance matrices of θ^1 and $\hat{\theta}$.

Let A be a matrix with known nonstochastic elements. Then the unbiased efficient estimator of

$$r = A\theta \tag{8.12}$$

is given by

$$\hat{r} = A\hat{\theta} \tag{8.13}$$

Proof. In view of the properties of $\hat{\theta}$ we have

$$E(\hat{r}) = AE(\hat{\theta}) = A\theta = r \tag{8.14}$$

which shows unbiasedness.

Since A is known, estimators of r are to be derived from estimators of θ. Thus, consider any other unbiased estimator, say,

$$r^1 = A\theta^1 \tag{8.15}$$

and let Σ^1 be the covariance matrix of θ^1. Then

$$\mathrm{Cov}(r^1) - \mathrm{Cov}(\hat{r}) = A(\Sigma^1 - \Sigma^0)A' \tag{8.16}$$

is positive semidefinite.

What is the bearing of the lemma on our discussion? It is simply this. If we can show that the $w_\tau, \tau = 0, 1, 2, \ldots, n$ are related to the $\beta_i, i = 0, 1, 2, \ldots, k$, by a set of linear transformations with fixed coefficients, the applicability of the lemma will become evident. Thus, let

$$s_0 = (1, 0, \ldots, 0) \tag{8.17}$$
$$s_\tau = (\tau^0, \tau^1, \tau^2, \ldots \tau^k), \quad \tau = 1, 2, \ldots, n$$

and define the $(n + 1) \times (k + 1)$ matrix,

$$S = \begin{bmatrix} s_0 \\ s_1 \\ \vdots \\ s_n \end{bmatrix} \tag{8.18}$$

We have

$$w = S\beta, \quad w = (w_0, w_1, \ldots, w_n)' \tag{8.19}$$

Since $\hat{\beta}$ is the linear unbiased efficient estimator of β, the lemma implies that the best linear (in y) unbiased (efficient) estimator of w is simply

$$\hat{w} = S\hat{\beta} \tag{8.20}$$

where

$$\hat{\beta} = (Z'Z)^{-1}Z'y \tag{8.21}$$

The distributional aspects of these estimators are easily established. First, if the error terms of the model are jointly normal, we conclude immediately that

$$\hat{\beta} \sim N[\beta, \sigma^2(Z'Z)^{-1}] \tag{8.22}$$

Hence,

$$\hat{w} \sim N[w, \sigma^2 S(Z'Z)^{-1}S'] \tag{8.23}$$

The reader should note that the distribution of $\hat{w}$ is *degenerate*, since its covariance matrix is singular. If the u_t are not normal but the explanatory variable obeys certain boundedness conditions, then by one of the standard central limit theorems (see Dhrymes, [32, ch. 3]) we conclude that, asymptotically,

$$\sqrt{T}(\hat{\beta} - \beta) \sim N\left[0, \sigma^2 \lim_{T\to\infty} \left(\frac{Z'Z}{T}\right)^{-1}\right] \tag{8.24}$$

and

$$\sqrt{T}(\hat{w} - w) \sim N\left[0, \sigma^2 S \lim_{T\to\infty} \left(\frac{Z'Z}{T}\right)^{-1} S'\right] \tag{8.25}$$

The main conclusions of the discussion above are summarized in

THEOREM 8.1. Consider the model of (8.6) in conjunction with the conditions in (8.5), (8.10) and the requirement that $\lim_{T\to\infty} Z'Z/T$ exists as a nonsingular matrix. Then the efficient estimator of β is given by (8.21) and that of w by (8.20), where efficiency is defined according to Lemma 8.1, subject to the additional restriction that estimators be linear in y. The asymptotic distribution of the estimators $\hat{\beta}, \hat{w}$ is given by (8.24) and (8.25), respectively.

If, in addition to (8.5), it is assumed that

$$u \sim N(0, \sigma^2 I) \tag{8.26}$$

then the distribution of $\hat{\beta}$ and $\hat{w}$ for *any sample size* is given, respectively, by (8.22) and (8.23).

REMARK 8.1. Under the assumption in (8.26), the estimator of σ^2, given by

$$\hat{\sigma}^2 = \frac{1}{T - n - k - 1} u'[I - Z(Z'Z)^{-1}Z']u \tag{8.27}$$

has the distribution,

$$(T - n - k - 1)\frac{\hat{\sigma}^2}{\sigma^2} \sim \chi^2_{T-n-k-1} \tag{8.28}$$

Hence, inferences with respect to elements of $\hat{\beta}$ (or $\hat{w}$) can be based on the t-distribution with $T - n - k - 1$ degrees of freedom. In this scheme, n observations are lost because the z_{ti} can only be defined for $t = n + 1, n + 2, \ldots, T$; in addition, $k + 1$ degrees of freedom are lost because we estimate $k + 1$ parameters—the elements of the vector β.

REMARK 8.2. The reader might ask: Since in this scheme, we lose n observations anyway, why not estimate w directly from the model

$$y = Xw + u \tag{8.29}$$

where

$$X = \begin{bmatrix} x_{n+1} & x_n & \cdots & x_1 \\ x_{n+2} & x_{n+1} & \cdots & x_2 \\ \vdots & & & \vdots \\ x_T & x_{T-1} & \cdots & x_{T-n} \end{bmatrix} \tag{8.30}$$

The estimator is

$$\tilde{w} = (X'X)^{-1}X'y \tag{8.31}$$

One would argue, then, that this is certainly a consistent estimator; moreover, if the errors are jointly normal, then for every sample size

$$\tilde{w} \sim N[w, \sigma^2(X'X)^{-1}] \tag{8.32}$$

There are two points to be noted in a formal examination of the desirability of this scheme. First, in order for estimation to be carried out in the present context, we must have

$$\text{rank } (X) = n + 1 \tag{8.33}$$

On the other hand, the reader should notice that for the earlier estimation scheme we only required that

$$\text{rank } (Z) = k + 1 \tag{8.34}$$

Since

$$Z = XS \tag{8.35}$$

the condition in (8.34) only implies that

$$\text{rank } (X) \geq k + 1 \tag{8.36}$$

which is certainly a somewhat weaker requirement. Even so, this is not the major reason why one might not use the estimator in (8.31); in general, we would expect (8.33) to hold.

If, in fact, it is true that

$$w = S\beta \tag{8.37}$$

and the errors are jointly normal, then

$$\hat{w} \sim N[w, \sigma^2 S(S'X'XS)^{-1}S'] \tag{8.38}$$

while

$$\bar{w} \sim N[w, \sigma^2(X'X)^{-1}] \tag{8.39}$$

We shall now show that

$$C = (X'X)^{-1} - S(S'X'XS)^{-1}S' \tag{8.40}$$

is positive semidefinite. Consider the roots of $S(S'X'XS)^{-1}S'$ in the metric of $(X'X)^{-1}$. Thus, consider the solutions to

$$|\lambda(X'X)^{-1} - S(S'X'XS)^{-1}S'| = 0 \tag{8.41}$$

The solutions of (8.41) are exactly those of

$$|\lambda I - S(S'X'XS)^{-1}S'X'X| = 0 \tag{8.42}$$

and the nonzero solutions of this are exactly those of[37]

$$|\lambda I - (S'X'XS)^{-1}S'X'XS| = 0 \tag{8.43}$$

It follows, therefore, (see Dhrymes [32, Appendix]) that there exists a nonsingular matrix P such that

$$P'P = (X'X)^{-1}, \quad S(S'X'XS)^{-1}S' = P'\Lambda P \tag{8.44}$$

where

$$\Lambda = \text{diag} (\lambda_1, \lambda_2, \ldots, \lambda_{n+1}) \tag{8.45}$$

the λ_i being the roots of (8.41) arranged, say, by descending order of magnitude. But (8.43) implies that

$$\Lambda = \begin{bmatrix} I & 0 \\ 0 & 0 \end{bmatrix} \tag{8.46}$$

I being the identity matrix of order $k + 1$. Hence,

$$C = P'\begin{bmatrix} 0 & 0 \\ 0 & I \end{bmatrix}P \tag{8.47}$$

is obviously positive semidefinite, I being the identity matrix of order $n - k$.

This is the compelling reason why, if (8.37) is known to be true, the estimator $\bar{w}$ is inferior to $\hat{w}$, since (8.47) shows that *provided the degree of the polynomial is less than the maximal lag, $\hat{w}$ is efficient relative to $\bar{w}$.*

---

[37] This is a consequence of the fact that if A is $m \times n$, B is $n \times m$, $m \leq n$, AB is nonsingular and λ satisfies $|\lambda I - AB| = 0$, then λ also satisfies $|\lambda I - BA| = 0$. It follows that the nonzero roots of the latter are exactly the roots of the former.

REMARK 8.3. The discussion above shows quite clearly that the estimation of the polynomial lag structure is equivalent—in its standard formulation—to the problem of obtaining estimators of the parameters of the general linear model, when the parameters obey a set of linear restrictions.

Finally, we should note that as a practical matter, the data matrix X is likely to be such that $X'X$ is ill-conditioned in the sense of being *nearly* singular. Thus, computations based on $(X'X)^{-1}$ would tend to be subject to considerable roundoff errors. However, it would be a rare occurrence indeed to have $|X'X| = 0$, despite the well known fact that time series of economic data are appreciably autocorrelated.

8.2 Test of the Polynomial Lag Hypothesis

Since earlier we had seen that the estimation of the polynomial lag structure of order n and degree k is equivalent to the problem of estimating the parameters of a general linear model subject to a number of linear restrictions, we have immediately at our disposal a means of testing the null hypothesis

$$H_0: \; w = S\beta$$

as against the alternative,

$$H_1: \; w \text{ is an unconstrained vector}$$

The symbols S, β were defined in (8.18) and (8.8), respectively. The test will be applicable for any sample size provided the error vector obeys the normality assumption in (8.26).

Now, the sum of squared residuals under the null hypothesis is given by

$$Q_0 = u'[I - XS(S'X'XS)^{-1}S'X']u \tag{8.48}$$

Under the alternative hypothesis, it is given by

$$Q_1 = u'[I - X(X'X)^{-1}X']u \tag{8.49}$$

Since the matrices of the two quadratic forms above are idempotent, we conclude, in view of (8.26), that under H_0

$$\frac{Q_0}{\sigma^2} \sim \chi^2_{T-n-k-1}, \quad \frac{Q_1}{\sigma^2} \sim \chi^2_{T-2n-1} \tag{8.50}$$

Now consider the difference,

$$Q = Q_0 - Q_1 = u'[X(X'X)^{-1}X' - XS(S'X'XS)^{-1}S'X']u \tag{8.51}$$

The matrix of this quadratic form is also idempotent; hence,

$$\frac{Q}{\sigma^2} \sim \chi^2_{n-k} \qquad (8.52)$$

In order to show that Q is distributed independently of Q_1, it is sufficient to show (see Graybill [50, ch. 4]) that the matrices of these two quadratic forms are mutually orthogonal.

We first observe that

$$X(X'X)^{-1}X'XS(S'X'XS)^{-1}S'X' = XS(S'X'XS)^{-1}S'X' \qquad (8.53)'$$

which immediately implies that

$$[I - X(X'X)^{-1}X'][X(X'X)^{-1}X' - XS(S'X'XS)^{-1}S'X'] = 0 \qquad (8.54)$$

We thus conclude that under H_0,

$$\frac{Q}{Q_1} \frac{T-2n-1}{n-k} \sim F_{n-k, T-2n-1} \qquad (8.55)$$

and the null hypothesis will be rejected if this statistic exceeds a certain quantity determined by the specified level of significance.

We have therefore proved

THEOREM 8.2. Consider the model,

$$y_t = \sum_{\tau=0}^{n} w_\tau x_{t-\tau} + u_t, \quad t = 1, 2, \ldots, T \qquad (8.56)$$

Suppose that the conditions of Theorem 8.1 hold and, in addition, that

$$\text{rank}(X) = n + 1 \qquad (8.57)$$

where X is as defined in (8.30). Then a test of the hypothesis,

$$H_0 : w_\tau = P(\tau), \quad P(t) = \sum_{j=0}^{k} \beta_i t^i$$

as against the alternative,

$$H_1 : \text{ the } w_\tau, \quad \tau = 0, 1, 2, \ldots, n \quad \text{are free parameters}$$

can be based on the central F-distribution with $n - k$ and $T - 2n - 1$ degrees of freedom.

REMARK 8.4. The preceding test entails the computation of the constrained sum of squared residuals, Q_0, and the sum of squared residuals of the unconstrained regression of y on X, Q_1; the difference of the two divided by Q_1 and multiplied by an appropriate constant has the central F-distribution. We reject the hypothesis at the α level of significance if

$$\frac{Q}{Q_1} \frac{T - 2n - 1}{n - k} > F_\alpha \qquad (8.58)$$

where F_α is defined by

$$Pr\{F \geq F_\alpha\} = \alpha \qquad (8.59)$$

F being central F with $n - k$, $T - 2n - 1$ degrees of freedom. Although such tests are seldom performed by empirical investigators, it would be a good practice to carry them out routinely; in fact, it would be desirable to incorporate in the appropriate (computer) program the requirement that

$$\frac{Q}{Q_1} \frac{T - 2n - 1}{n - k}$$

be printed out.

8.3 Lagrange Interpolation

This topic has been extensively discussed in Section 3.3, particularly with regard to its relation to the polynomial scheme employed in Section 8.1.

Since the two approaches are conceptually identical, the discussion here will be brief.

If $t_i, i = 0, 1, 2, \ldots, k$ are arbitrary points in the interval $[0, n]$, we define the polynomials

$$s_i(t) = \frac{\prod_{j \neq i} (t - t_j)}{\prod_{j \neq i} (t_i - t_j)}, \quad i = 0, 1, 2, \ldots, k \qquad (8.60)$$

Notice that each $s_i(\cdot)$ is a polynomial of degree k and has the property

$$s_i(t_j) = \delta_{ij} \qquad (8.61)$$

δ_{ij} being the Kronecker delta.

The lag coefficients of the model

$$y_t = \sum_{\tau=0}^{n} w_\tau x_{t-\tau} + u_t \qquad (8.62)$$

are then assumed to obey

$$w_\tau = P^*(\tau) \qquad (8.63)$$

where

$$P^*(t) = \sum_{i=0}^{k} b_i s_i(t) \tag{8.64}$$

Define the matrix

$$S^* = \begin{bmatrix} s_0(0) & s_1(0) & \cdots & s_k(0) \\ s_0(1) & s_1(1) & \cdots & s_k(1) \\ s_0(2) & s_1(2) & \cdots & s_k(2) \\ \vdots & & & \\ s_0(n) & s_1(n) & \cdots & s_k(n) \end{bmatrix} \tag{8.65}$$

and observe that the model in (8.62) can be written compactly as

$$y = XS^*b + u, \quad b = (b_0, b_1, \ldots, b_k)' \tag{8.66}$$

X, y and u being as defined in Section 8.1.

Clearly, the best linear unbiased estimator of b is

$$\hat{b} = (Z^{*\prime}Z^*)^{-1}Z^{*\prime}y, \quad Z^* = XS^* \tag{8.67}$$

and the best linear unbiased estimator of w is

$$\hat{w} = S^*\hat{b} \tag{8.68}$$

All inference theory developed in Section 8.1 is fully applicable here and requires no repeating.

We ought, however, to ask the following question: Suppose we carry out one estimation scheme of the polynomial lag structure of order n and degree k according to the methods of Section 8.1 and another based on the Lagrange Interpolation of this section. Are the resulting estimates of the vector w numerically identical? One would suspect that the answer is yes, since, as we had shown in Section 3.3, what is different in the two cases is only the parametrization of the polynomial and this ought not to affect its ordinates. However, the relation there was an exact one and would correspond here to the fact that the *probability limits* of the estimators obtained by the techniques of Sections 8.1 and 8.3 coincide. We are now asking about the *numerical equality* of the two sets of estimates, and this is, of course, a stronger requirement.

The proof of this claim is straightforward if, in fact, the polynomial specification is correct. To see this, let

$$\hat{w}^{(1)} = S\hat{\beta} = S(S'X'XS)^{-1}S'X'y \tag{8.69}$$

$$\hat{w}^{(2)} = S^*\hat{b} = S^*(S^{*\prime}X'XS^*)^{-1}S^{*\prime}X'y \tag{8.70}$$

If the specification is, in fact, true, then

$$E[\hat{w}^{(1)}] = E[\hat{w}^{(2)}] = w \qquad (8.71)$$

Hence, taking expectations in (8.69) and (8.70) we conclude, in view of (8.71), that

$$[S(S'X'XS)^{-1}S'X'X - S^*(S^{*\prime}X'XS^*)^{-1}S^{*\prime}X'X]w = 0 \qquad (8.72)$$

Since w is arbitrary, we conclude that

$$S(S'X'XS)^{-1}S'X'X = S^*(S^{*\prime}X'XS^*)^{-1}S^{*\prime}X'X \qquad (8.73)$$

Since we assume that $X'X$ is nonsingular, we have

$$S(S'X'XS)^{-1}S' = S^*(S^{*\prime}X'XS^*)^{-1}S^{*\prime} \qquad (8.74)$$

which shows that, indeed,

$$\hat{w}^{(1)} = \hat{w}^{(2)} \qquad (8.75)$$

Finally, it is possible that the same result may be arrived at by comparing the two matrices in (8.74) element by element and showing them to be equal. This, however, is an exceedingly cumbersome operation.

Now, if the estimation schemes of Sections 8.1 and 8.3 give the same results, why should anyone use the Lagrange Interpolation approach developed in this section? There is really little reason why one should, unless there exists a priori information concerning particular values known to be assumed by the polynomial. As pointed out in Section 3.3, if it is known that the polynomial assumes the value P_0 at the point $t = \alpha$, then take, in the notation of (8.60),

$$t_0 = \alpha \qquad (8.76)$$

and verify that if $P^*(\cdot)$ is evaluated at α, it yields

$$P^*(\alpha) = b_0 = P_0 \qquad (8.77)$$

If it is further known that

$$P_0 = 0 \qquad (8.78)$$

then the information is readily incorporated in the specification by defining

$$P^*(t) = \sum_{i=1}^{k} b_i s_i(t) \qquad (8.79)$$

and herein lies the usefulness of this approach, since it would be difficult to incorporate restrictions involving the zeros[38] *of the polynomial if the alternative representation were employed.*

The popularity of this approach is due to the first use of the Lagrange Interpolation form by Almon [1], who specified, in addition, that

$$P^*(-1) = P^*(n + 1) = 0 \qquad (8.80)$$

Unless there is evidence that (8.80) is in fact true, there is no reason for imposing this restriction. Indeed, *its imposition may have the unintended effect of predetermining the shape of the lag structure.* This point was made analytically in Section 3.3. We give below an empirical demonstration of the problems involved.

EXAMPLE 8.1. The considerations above may be illustrated in connection with the investment model presented by Jorgenson [81] as part of the Brookings model.

Here we shall deal with Total Durables (Manufacturing) and following Jorgenson we shall define net investment as gross investment minus 0.0279 times capital stock lagged one period.

Since the results cited in [81] indicate that lag coefficients tend to be quite small after w_8, the following specification was used:

$$I_t - 0.0279\, K_{t-1} = \sum_{i=3}^{\infty} w_i x_{t-i} + \beta(IC)_{t-1} + u_t \qquad (8.81)$$

In the preceding equation, I_t is gross investment, K_t capital stock, IC is the Wharton capacity utilization index and x_t, in Jorgenson's notation in [81], is the variable $(P_t X_t/c_t) - (P_{t-1} X_{t-1}/c_{t-1})$ and essentially corresponds to the change in the optimal stock of capital. The lag begins with the third period, again in conformity with Jorgenson's practice. The data consist of quarterly observations between 1948 and 1962.

In the results of Table 8.1, we have assumed that

$$w_\tau = P(\tau), \quad \tau = 3, 4, \ldots, 8 \qquad (8.82)$$

$P(\cdot)$ being a *second degree* polynomial.

The lag structure was obtained under the alternative specifications that

$$P(\alpha) = P(\beta) = 0, \quad \alpha < \beta \qquad (8.83)$$

with the pair (α, β) being $(2, 9)$, $(1, 9)$, $(0, 9)$, $(-1, 9)$, $(-2, 9)$ and $(-3, 9)$.

---

[38] A zero of a polynomial $P(\cdot)$ is said to be a point, say t_0, in its domain of definition, such that $P(t_0) = 0$. The terms *zero* or *root* of a polynomial are used synonymously.

Table 8.1

Lag Coefficients in the Relation

$$I_t - 0.0279\, K_{t-1} = \sum_{i=3}^{8} w_i x_{t-i} + \beta(IC)_{t-1} + u_t$$

Total Durables
U.S. Quarterly Data 1948–1962

Period (Quarter)	Zeros at (2, 9) Lag Coeff.	Zeros at (1, 9) Lag Coeff.	Zeros at (0, 9) Lag Coeff.	Zeros at (−1, 9) Lag Coeff.	Zeros at (−2, 9) Lag Coeff.	Zeros at (−3, 9) Lag Coeff.	No Zeros Specified Lag Coeff.
1	0	0	0	0	0	0	0
2	0	0	0	0	0	0	0
3	0.0288	0.0355	0.0367	0.0364	0.0356	0.0349	−0.0459
4	0.0481	0.0444	0.0407	0.0379	0.0356	0.0339	−0.0037
5	0.0577	0.0473	0.0407	0.0364	0.0333	0.0310	0.0339
6	0.0577	0.0444	0.0367	0.0318	0.0285	0.0262	0.0667
7	0.0481	0.0355	0.0285	0.0242	0.0214	0.0194	0.0950
8	0.0288	0.0207	0.0163	0.0136	0.0119	0.0107	0.1185
9	0	0	0	0	0	0	0
$\bar{R}^2$	0.1970	0.1845	0.1779	0.1740	0.1714	0.1697	0.2635

The lag structure was also obtained *when no zeros of the polynomial were specified.* The results of the table illustrate quite dramatically the crucial role of the zero specifications in determining the shape of the lag structure. Thus, when the zeros are at $(2, 9)$, the shape is decidedly humped, while when the zeros are at $(-2, 9)$ or $(-3, 9)$, we have monotone *declining* coefficients.

Finally, the unrestricted polynomial case gives a *monotone increasing* set of lag coefficients. Hence, when using the Lagrange Interpolation form, one should be very careful in formulating it. Doubtless, humped shapes have been obtained by researchers solely because of the location of the zeros of the polynomial when it was not their intention to impose this requirement a priori. Thus, the original formulation of the Lagrangean Interpolation scheme in Almon [1] will, in general, carry certain implications about the shape of the lag structure which the investigator may not wish to employ. In that case, one ought to use the simpler formulation of Section 8.1 in which the zeros of the polynomial are left entirely unspecified.

REMARK 8.5. The fact that the explanatory power of the relations in Table 8.1 is rather low when compared with those of Jorgenson [1] would seem to suggest that the model used in the latter is rather one of the form

$$y_t = w_3 x_{t-3} + w_5 x_{t-5} + u_t \tag{8.84}$$

where the error terms, u_t, constitute *a second order autoregressive process,* so that, in fact, *we do not have a rational lag structure in the effects of the determining variable, x_t, on investment.*

This remark should be tempered by the fact that there is evidence of autocorrelation in the residuals of the relationships reported in Table 8.1, and thus the estimators given therein are inefficient, assuming that one of these specifications is correct. Clearly, not all can be correct simultaneously.

Exercises and Questions

1. In the discussion of Remark 8.2, what is the intuitive reason that the estimator $\hat{w}$ is efficient relative to $\bar{w}$?

    Hint: If we *know* something about the structure of the model we attempt to estimate, do we gain anything by explicitly incorporating this knowledge in the estimation scheme?
2. Again, in the discussion of Remark 8.2, what happens if $n = k$?

Hint: What is the rank of S in this case?

3. Why is it necessary to *assert the truth* of the condition in (8.37) in ranking $\hat{w}$ and $\bar{w}$?

4. In the discussion leading to Equation (8.75), what is the role played by the (truth of the) assertion that the polynomial specification is indeed

$$w_\tau = P(\tau), \quad w_\tau = P^*(\tau)$$

5. Consider again the model given in Equations (8.1) through (8.4) and suppose that the explanatory variable is the pure time trend

$$x_t = a_0 + a_1 t, \quad t = 1, 2, \ldots, T$$

Can you estimate the lag coefficients?

Hint: In this case what is the rank of the matrix Z as defined in Equations (8.7) and (8.8)?

Chapter 9

THE GENERAL RATIONAL LAG STRUCTURE

9.1 Motivation and Generalities

The model to be considered below is

$$y_t = \frac{A(L)}{B(L)} x_t + u_t, \quad t = 1, 2, \ldots, T \tag{9.1}$$

where

$$A(L) = \sum_{i=0}^{m} a_i L^i, \quad B(L) = \sum_{j=0}^{n} b_j L^j, \quad b_0 = 1 \tag{9.2}$$

We easily see that both the finite lag and the geometric lag models are special cases of (9.1). In the case of the former, we have

$$B(L) \equiv I \tag{9.3}$$

In the case of the latter, we have

$$A(L) = \alpha I, \quad B(L) = I - \lambda L \tag{9.4}$$

We have treated these two models separately, since their specificity renders the estimation problem considerably more tractable than would be the case with the general model in (9.1).

The reader should further bear in mind that the final form of the general (linear) structural dynamic econometric model is a set of rational lags, typically involving more than one exogenous variable. A discussion of this aspect may be found in Dhrymes [32, ch. 12].

Thus, the present model is well-motivated even beyond the approximation rationale given in Section 3.4. However, before we consider its estimation aspect, it is well to offer the following additional rationalization.

Suppose an economic variable of interest, say y_t, is generated according to

$$y_t = \beta' p_t + u_t \tag{9.5}$$

where β is a vector of unknown constants and p_t is an n-element vector of unobservable quantities determined by the process

$$p_t = A p_{t-1} + B x_t \tag{9.6}$$

We shall consider two cases of (9.6), namely, x_t, a scalar, and x_t, a k-element vector. In (9.6), x_t is an observable quantity and A, B are matrices with fixed but unknown elements.

The reader may provide his own economic interpretation for the system in (9.5) and (9.6). One possibility is to look upon (9.5) as an investment function; p_t would be the vector of desired investment in n types of capital goods and x_t a scalar (or vector) denoting relevant exogenous variables; Equation (9.6) may be deduced from an appropriate suboptimizing scheme on the part of the economic unit. It x_t is a vector of factor prices, (9.6) simply states that optimal investment in the n capital goods is a distributed lag function of past factor prices, some might say of permanent factor prices; if x_t is change in aggregate output —x_t scalar—or in the output of the components of the unit whose investment function we are considering in (9.5), then (9.6) states that desired investment is a (linear) function of permanent changes in output(s).[39]

Be that as it may, we can assume, as is eminently reasonable, that the roots of A are less than unity in absolute value; if that is so, we may solve (9.6) to obtain

$$p_t = (I - AL)^{-1} B x_t = \sum_{k=0}^{\infty} A^k B x_{t-k} \tag{9.7}$$

For simplicity, we shall assume that the roots of A are real and denote them by λ_i, $i = 1, 2, \ldots, n$. Let

$$\Lambda = \text{diag}(\lambda_1, \lambda_2, \ldots, \lambda_n) \tag{9.8}$$

---

[39] If this interpretation is followed, then the elements of the vector β may be assumed to lie in the interval $(0, 1]$ and will denote the portion of the desired investment in the ith capital good that is actually realized.

and let A be diagonalizable so that we can write[40]

$$A = P\Lambda P^{-1} \tag{9.9}$$

Thus,

$$A^k = P\Lambda^k P^{-1} \tag{9.10}$$

and so we can write

$$p_t = \sum_{k=0}^{\infty} P\Lambda^k P^{-1} B x_{t-k} \tag{9.11}$$

Substituting in (9.5), we have

$$y_t = \sum_{k=0}^{\infty} \beta' P\Lambda^k P^{-1} B x_{t-k} + u_t \tag{9.12}$$

Consider first the case where x_t is a scalar—so that B is an n-element vector—and let β_i^*, b_i^* be, respectively, the ith element of $\beta' P$ and $P^{-1}B$. Then

$$\sum_{k=0}^{\infty} \beta' P\Lambda^k P^{-1} B x_{t-k} = \sum_{i=1}^{n} \sum_{k=0}^{\infty} \beta_i^* b_i^* \lambda_i^k x_{t-k} = \sum_{i=1}^{n} \frac{(\beta_i^* b_i^*)I}{I - \lambda_i L} x_t \tag{9.13}$$

Define

$$B(L) = \prod_{i=1}^{n} (I - \lambda_i L), \quad A_i(L) = \beta_i^* b_i^* \prod_{j \neq i} (I - \lambda_j L) \tag{9.14}$$

and observe that we may write

$$y_t = \frac{A(L)}{B(L)} x_t + u_t \tag{9.15}$$

where

$$A(L) = \sum_{i=1}^{n} A_i(L) \tag{9.16}$$

---

[40] A square matrix A is diagonalizable as in (9.9) if and only if its characteristic vectors span E^n, the n-dimensional Euclidean space. A sufficient condition is that its roots be *distinct*. However, it can be shown, see Bellman [10], that given *any matrix*, A, there exists another matrix A^*, such that $\sum_{i,j} |a_{ij} - a_{ij}^*| < \varepsilon$, where ε is any preassigned (small) positive quantity, and the roots of A^* are distinct; a_{ij}, a_{ij}^* are, respectively, the (i, j) elements of A and of A^*.

Thus, we see that in the present context diagonalizability does not entail serious constraints.

is a polynomial of degree at most $n - 1$. But this is exactly the form given in (9.1).

9.2 Estimation of the Rational Lag Structure

In this section we shall take as given the model

$$y_t = \frac{A(L)}{B(L)} x_t + u_t, \quad t = 1, 2, \ldots, T \tag{9.17}$$

the symbols having the same meaning as in (9.1). In addition, we shall assume that the scalar sequence $\{x_t : t = 1, 2, \ldots\}$ is bounded and non-stochastic, and that the error terms u_t are *i.i.d.* random variables with

$$E(u_t) = 0, \quad E(u_t^2) = \sigma^2 \tag{9.18}$$

and bounded third order absolute moment.

Let us obtain estimators for the parameters of the model by minimizing

$$Q = \left[y - \frac{A(L)}{B(L)} x \right]' \left[y - \frac{A(L)}{B(L)} x \right] \tag{9.19}$$

where $x = (x_1, x_2, \ldots, x_T)', y = (y_1, y_2, \ldots, y_T)'$.

Recalling that by convention,

$$b_0 = 1 \tag{9.20}$$

define

$$a = (a_0, a_1, a_2, \ldots, a_m)', \quad b = (b_1, b_2, \ldots, b_n)' \tag{9.21}$$

Estimators are thus to be obtained by solving

$$\frac{\partial Q}{\partial \gamma} = 0 \tag{9.22}$$

where

$$\gamma = \begin{pmatrix} a \\ -b \end{pmatrix} \tag{9.23}$$

Let us see exactly what (9.22) entails. We have

$$\frac{\partial Q}{\partial a_i} = -2 \sum_t \left[y_t - \frac{A(L)}{B(L)} x_t \right] \frac{L^i}{B(L)} x_t = 0, \quad i = 0, 1, 2, \ldots, m$$

$$\frac{\partial Q}{\partial b_j} = 2 \sum_t \left[y_t - \frac{A(L)}{B(L)} x_t \right] \frac{A(L) L^j}{[B(L)]^2} x_t = 0, \quad j = 1, 2, \ldots, n \tag{9.24}$$

As a method for solving this system of (highly) nonlinear equations, the following procedure has been suggested by Steiglitz and McBride [138, 139]. Define

$$y_t^* = \frac{I}{B(L)}y_t, \quad x_t^* = \frac{I}{B(L)}x_t, \quad x_t^{**} = \frac{A(L)}{B(L)}x_t^* \qquad (9.25)$$

As pointed out at an earlier stage, if the coefficient vectors a, b are known, then the starred quantities above can be easily computed recursively as, say,

$$y_t^* = -\sum_{i=1}^{n} b_i y_{t-i}^* + y_t, \quad t = 1, 2, \ldots, T \qquad (9.26)$$

under the assumption,

$$y_{-i}^* = 0, \quad i = 0, 1, 2, \ldots, n - 1 \qquad (9.27)$$

Thus, the equations in (9.24) can be written more suggestively, as

$$\frac{\partial Q}{\partial a_i} = -2\sum_t \left[\frac{B(L)}{B(L)}y_t - \frac{A(L)}{B(L)}x_t \right]\frac{I}{B(L)}x_{t-i} = 0,$$

$$i = 0, 1, 2, \ldots, m$$

$$\frac{\partial Q}{\partial b_j} = 2\sum_t \left[\frac{B(L)}{B(L)}y_t - \frac{A(L)}{B(L)}x_t \right]\frac{A(L)}{[B(L)]^2}x_{t-j} = 0,$$

$$j = 1, 2, \ldots, n$$

(9.28)

Define now,

$$X^* = \begin{bmatrix} x_{n+1}^* & x_n^* & \cdots & x_{n+1-m}^* \\ x_{n+2}^* & x_{n+1}^* & \cdots & x_{n+2-m}^* \\ \vdots & & & \\ x_T^* & x_{T-1}^* & \cdots & x_{T-m}^* \end{bmatrix}, \quad X^{**} = \begin{bmatrix} x_n^{**} & x_{n-1}^{**} & \cdots & x_1^{**} \\ x_{n+1}^{**} & x_n^{**} & \cdots & x_2^{**} \\ \vdots & & & \\ x_{T-1}^{**} & x_{T-2}^{**} & \cdots & x_{T-n}^{**} \end{bmatrix}$$

$$Y^* = \begin{bmatrix} y_n^* & y_{n-1}^* & \cdots & y_1^* \\ y_{n+1}^* & y_n^* & \cdots & y_2^* \\ \vdots & & & \\ y_{T-1}^* & y_{T-2}^* & \cdots & y_{T-n}^* \end{bmatrix}, \quad y^* = \begin{bmatrix} y_{n+1}^* \\ y_{n+2}^* \\ \vdots \\ y_T^* \end{bmatrix} \qquad (9.29)$$

and write (9.28) as

$$\begin{bmatrix} X^{*\prime}X^* & X^{*\prime}Y^* \\ X^{**\prime}X^* & X^{**\prime}Y^* \end{bmatrix}\begin{pmatrix} a \\ -b \end{pmatrix} = \begin{bmatrix} X^{*\prime} \\ X^{**\prime} \end{bmatrix}y^* \qquad (9.30)$$

The elements of X^*, X^{**}, Y^* and y^* can easily be obtained if an initial consistent estimator for a, b is available, say, $\bar{a}^{(0)}$, $\bar{b}^{(0)}$. We can then solve (9.30) to obtain the first iterate $\bar{a}^{(1)}$, $\bar{b}^{(1)}$. Using this set of estimators, we can recompute the elements of X^*, X^{**}, Y^* and y^* and obtain from (9.30) a second iterate, say $\bar{a}^{(2)}$, $\bar{b}^{(2)}$ and so on.

We shall terminate this procedure if, at the kth iteration,

$$\max_{i,j} \left\{ |\bar{a}_i^{(k)} - \bar{a}_i^{(k-1)}|, \ |\bar{b}_j^{(k)} - \bar{b}_j^{(k-1)}| \right\} < \varepsilon \tag{9.31}$$

where ε is some preassigned (small) positive quantity. If convergence is obtained at the kth iteration, in accordance with the criterion (9.31), then we have solved the normal equations in (9.24). To see why this is so, write

$$\tilde{A}_k(L) = \sum_{i=0}^{m} \bar{a}_i^{(k)} L^i, \ \ \tilde{B}_k(L) = \sum_{j=0}^{n} \bar{b}_j^{(k)} L^j, \ \ \bar{b}_0^{(k)} \equiv 1, \ \text{all } k \tag{9.32}$$

and observe that at the kth iteration the vectors $\bar{b}^{(k)}$, $\bar{a}^{(k)}$ obey

$$\sum_t \left[\frac{\tilde{B}_k(L)}{\tilde{B}_{k-1}(L)} y_t - \frac{\tilde{A}_k(L)}{\tilde{B}_{k-1}(L)} x_t \right] \frac{I}{\tilde{B}_{k-1}(L)} x_{t-i} = 0,$$

$$i = 0, 1, 2, \ldots, m$$

$$\sum_t \left[\frac{\tilde{B}_k(L)}{\tilde{B}_{k-1}(L)} y_t - \frac{\tilde{A}_k(L)}{\tilde{B}_{k-1}(L)} x_t \right] \frac{\tilde{A}_{k-1}(L)}{[\tilde{B}_{k-1}(L)]^2} x_{t-j} = 0,$$

$$j = 1, 2, \ldots, n$$

$$\tag{9.33}$$

If conditions (9.31) are satisfied, then

$$\tilde{B}_k(L) \approx \tilde{B}_{k-1}(L), \ \ \tilde{A}_k(L) \approx \tilde{A}_{k-1}(L) \tag{9.34}$$

Hence, within the limit of accuracy entailed by the condition in (9.31), we have found a solution to the normal equations in (9.28) and thus have determined the estimator of the vectors a, b.

REMARK 9.1. Steiglitz and McBride have not actually recommended this particular estimator; their main objective was to solve the nonlinear system of equations in (9.28), and they were not especially concerned with the stochastic properties of their estimator. In particular, they recommended that we begin the iteration from an arbitrary vector, say a^0, b^0. This, however, does not guarantee that the solution to which the iteration might converge is a consistent estimator.

The experience with the convergence properties of this procedure has not been a happy one. For this reason we shall suggest an alternative estimator below.

Returning now to the estimator produced by the iterative solution of the system in (9.30), let us first establish its consistency. For this purpose we need a more convenient notation. Thus, put

$$S = (X^*, X^{**}), \quad P = (X^*, Y^*) \tag{9.35}$$

and observe that the system may be written as

$$W(\gamma)\gamma = S'y^* \tag{9.36}$$

where γ is as defined in (9.23) and

$$W = S'P \tag{9.37}$$

The iterative solution is obtained as the fixed point in the scheme

$$\tilde{\gamma}^{(k)} = [W(\tilde{\gamma}^{(k-1)})]^{-1} S'(\tilde{\gamma}^{(k-1)}) y^*(\tilde{\gamma}^{(k-1)}) \tag{9.38}$$

For simplicity of notation, in what follows we shall omit the arguments and write instead $\tilde{W}, \tilde{S}, \tilde{y}^*$. This will indicate that the elements of these quantities have been evaluated using a consistent estimator for the parameter vectors a, b.

We have

LEMMA 9.1. Consider the model in (9.17), (9.18), with the subsidiary assumptions that $\{x_t : t = 1, 2, \ldots\}$ is a suitably bounded nonstochastic sequence; that $\text{plim}_{T \to \infty} W/T$ exists as a nonstochastic nonsingular matrix; and that the roots of

$$\sum_{i=0}^{n} b_i \rho^{n-i} = 0 \tag{9.39}$$

have modulus less than unity. Then, if in the scheme (9.38), $\tilde{\gamma}^{(k-1)}$ is a consistent estimator of γ, so is $\tilde{\gamma}^{(k)}$.

Proof. Noting that

$$\text{plim}_{T \to \infty} \frac{\tilde{X}^{*'} \tilde{Y}^*}{T} = \lim_{T \to \infty} \frac{X^{*'} X^{**}}{T} \tag{9.40}$$

we conclude that the estimator in (9.38) obeys

$$\left[\lim_{T \to \infty} \frac{S'S}{T} \right] \text{plim}_{T \to} \tilde{\gamma}^{(k)} = \lim_{T \to \infty} \frac{S'x^{**}}{T} \tag{9.41}$$

where

$$x^{**} = (x^{**}_{n+1}, x^{**}_{n+2}, \ldots, x^{**}_T)' \tag{9.42}$$

This is so because

$$y^*_t = \frac{I}{B(L)} y_t = \frac{A(L)}{[B(L)]^2} x_t + \frac{I}{B(L)} u_t = x^{**}_t + \frac{I}{B(L)} u_t \tag{9.43}$$

and x_t is nonstochastic.

In (9.41), the absence of tilde over S indicates that the elements of this matrix are evaluated with respect to the true parameter vectors, a and b.

Now from (9.17) we see that the model obeys

$$y^*_t = \sum_{i=0}^{m} a_i x^*_{t-i} - \sum_{j=1}^{n} b_j y^*_{t-j} + u_t \tag{9.44}$$

Hence we can write

$$y^* = P\gamma + u^n, \quad u^n = (u_{n+1}, u_{n+2}, \ldots, u_T)' \tag{9.45}$$

Premultiplying by S', we have

$$\operatorname*{plim}_{T\to\infty} \frac{S'y^*}{T} = \left[\operatorname*{plim}_{T\to\infty}\left(\frac{S'P}{T}\right)\right]\gamma + \operatorname*{plim}_{T\to\infty} \frac{1}{T} \frac{S'u^n}{T} \tag{9.46}$$

In view of (9.40) and the nonstochastic nature of the x sequence—actually, independence of the u sequence will do as well—we have

$$\left[\lim_{T\to\infty}\left(\frac{S'S}{T}\right)\right]\gamma = \operatorname*{plim}_{T\to\infty} \frac{S'y^*}{T} \tag{9.47}$$

Comparing with (9.41) we conclude, in view of the nonsingularity of the matrix $\lim_{T\to\infty} S'S/T$, that

$$\operatorname*{plim}_{T\to\infty} \tilde{\gamma}^{(k)} = \gamma \quad \text{Q.E.D.} \tag{9.48}$$

COROLLARY 9.1. If the iteration procedure of the lemma converges in a finite number of steps, then we have found a consistent estimator of γ which is a root of the equation

$$\frac{\partial Q}{\partial \gamma} = 0 \tag{9.49}$$

Proof. Obvious from the lemma and the iteration procedure as exhibited in (9.33).

As we noted earlier, the prefiltering procedure leads to considerable difficulties with regard to convergence, if the number of parameters is at all large. For this reason, the following two-step estimator is particularly attractive.

Observe that the problem is to find a root of the equation in (9.49). What if we found a root not of (9.49) but of a suitably linearized version? Thus, suppose we expand that gradient about $\gamma = \gamma^*$ to obtain

$$\frac{\partial Q}{\partial \gamma}(\gamma) = \frac{\partial Q}{\partial \gamma}(\gamma^*) + \frac{\partial^2 Q}{\partial \gamma \partial \gamma}(\gamma^*)[\gamma - \gamma^*] + \text{third order terms} \quad (9.50)$$

and we try to find a γ such that the first two terms in the right member of (9.50) add up to the zero vector. This is equivalent to finding a root of the *linearized* version of (9.49).

Let us see what this estimator is and what properties it possesses. For the vector γ^* choose the initial instrumental variables estimator, say, $\tilde{\gamma}$.

Thus, we have to solve the system

$$\frac{\partial^2 Q}{\partial \gamma \partial \gamma}(\tilde{\gamma})[\gamma - \tilde{\gamma}] = -\frac{\partial Q}{\partial \gamma}(\tilde{\gamma}) \quad (9.51)$$

If the matrix in the left member is invertible, we have

$$\hat{\gamma} = \tilde{\gamma} - \left[\frac{\partial^2 Q}{\partial \gamma \partial \gamma}(\tilde{\gamma}) \right]^{-1} \frac{\partial Q}{\partial \gamma}(\tilde{\gamma}) \quad (9.52)$$

Since $\tilde{\gamma}$ is known, $\hat{\gamma}$ is easily computed through a single matrix inversion. Is $\hat{\gamma}$ consistent? Since $\tilde{\gamma}$ is consistent, and since for the true parameter vector,

$$\plim_{T \to \infty} \frac{1}{T} \frac{\partial Q}{\partial \gamma} = 0 \quad (9.53)$$

we see that

$$\plim_{T \to \infty} \hat{\gamma} = \gamma - \plim_{T \to \infty} \left[\frac{1}{T} \frac{\partial^2 Q}{\partial \gamma \partial \gamma}(\gamma) \right]^{-1} \plim_{T \to \infty} \left[\frac{1}{T} \frac{\partial Q}{\partial \gamma} \right] \quad (9.54)$$

Hence $\hat{\gamma}$ is consistent if the matrix $\plim_{T \to \infty} (1/T)(\partial^2 Q/\partial \gamma \partial \gamma)$ is nonsingular. But an easy computation shows that

$$\plim_{T \to \infty} \frac{1}{T} \frac{\partial^2 Q}{\partial \gamma \partial \gamma} = 2 \lim_{T \to \infty} \frac{S'S}{T} = 2\Sigma \quad (9.55)$$

It follows from (9.55) that we can just as well write the two-step estimator as

$$\hat{\gamma} = \tilde{\gamma} - \frac{1}{2}(\tilde{S}'\tilde{S})^{-1}\frac{\partial Q}{\partial \gamma}(\tilde{\gamma}) \tag{9.56}$$

Further, since

$$\frac{\partial Q}{\partial \gamma}(\tilde{\gamma}) = -2[\tilde{S}'y^* - \tilde{S}'\tilde{P}\tilde{\gamma}] \tag{9.57}$$

the estimator may, in fact, be expressed as

$$\hat{\gamma} = \tilde{\gamma} - (\tilde{S}'\tilde{S})^{-1}\tilde{S}'\tilde{P}\tilde{\gamma} + (\tilde{S}'\tilde{S})^{-1}\tilde{S}'\tilde{y}^* \tag{9.58}$$

Unquestionably the estimator in Equation (9.58) is far simpler to obtain, and the only problem is whether asymptotically it is as good as the one obtained by the prefiltering procedure.

But it is obvious from (9.52) that asymptotically,

$$\sqrt{T}(\hat{\gamma} - \gamma_0) \sim \sqrt{T}(\tilde{\gamma} - \gamma_0) - \frac{1}{2}\Sigma^{-1}\frac{1}{\sqrt{T}}\frac{\partial Q}{\partial \gamma}(\tilde{\gamma}) \tag{9.59}$$

where γ_0 is the true parameter vector.

Thus, we need to develop the asymptotic distribution of $(1/\sqrt{T})$ $(\partial Q/\partial \gamma)(\tilde{\gamma})$. Since $\tilde{\gamma}$ is a consistent estimator of γ_0, we can write

$$\frac{1}{\sqrt{T}}\frac{\partial Q}{\partial \gamma}(\tilde{\gamma}) = \frac{1}{\sqrt{T}}\frac{\partial Q}{\partial \gamma}(\gamma_0) + \frac{1}{T}\frac{\partial^2 Q}{\partial \gamma \partial \gamma}(\gamma_0)\sqrt{T}(\tilde{\gamma} - \gamma_0)$$

$$+ \text{ third order terms} \tag{9.60}$$

The third order terms may be neglected, since they vanish in probability. Thus asymptotically,

$$\Sigma^{-1}\frac{1}{\sqrt{T}}\frac{\partial Q}{\partial \gamma}(\tilde{\gamma}) \sim \Sigma^{-1}\left[\frac{1}{\sqrt{T}}\frac{\partial Q}{\partial \gamma}(\gamma_0)\right] + 2\sqrt{T}(\tilde{\gamma} - \gamma_0) \tag{9.61}$$

and (9.61) in conjunction with (9.59) implies that

$$\sqrt{T}(\hat{\gamma} - \gamma_0) \sim -\frac{1}{2}\Sigma^{-1}\frac{1}{\sqrt{T}}\frac{\partial Q}{\partial \gamma}(\gamma_0) \tag{9.62}$$

But it is rather easy to see that this is exactly the asymptotic distribution of the prefiltering (iterated) estimator outlined above when the procedure begins with an initial consistent estimator. Let the iterated estimator be denoted, for this immediate discussion only, by γ^*. Expand $\partial Q/\partial \gamma$ about the true parameter vector γ_0 to obtain

$$\frac{\partial Q}{\partial \gamma}(\gamma^*) = \frac{\partial Q}{\partial \gamma}(\gamma_0) + \frac{\partial^2 Q}{\partial \gamma \partial \gamma}(\gamma_0)(\gamma^* - \gamma_0) + \text{third order terms} \quad (9.63)$$

In virtue of the consistency of γ^*, the third order terms converge in probability to zero and thus may be neglected. The iterated estimate has the property that $(\partial Q/\partial \gamma)(\gamma^*) = 0$. Hence, asymptotically,

$$\sqrt{T}(\gamma^* - \gamma_0) \sim -\frac{1}{2}\Sigma^{-1}\frac{1}{\sqrt{T}}\frac{\partial Q}{\partial \gamma}(\gamma_0) \quad (9.64)$$

which is exactly the distribution of the simplified (linearized) estimator in (9.62).

REMARK 9.2. The simplified (linearized) estimator derived above is quite similar to the first iterate of the method of scoring; see Dhrymes [32, ch. 7] or Rao [130, ch. 4]. As in the common variant of that method, we use the expected value of $\partial^2 Q/\partial \gamma \partial \gamma$; in contrast with that variant, however, we begin with *an initial consistent estimator of the parameter in question.*

Let us now determine the asymptotic distribution of $(1/\sqrt{T})(\partial Q/\partial \gamma)(\gamma_0)$. We have

$$\frac{1}{\sqrt{T}}\frac{\partial Q}{\partial \gamma}(\gamma_0) = -2\frac{S'u^n}{\sqrt{T}} \quad (9.65)$$

Thus, (9.62) and (9.63) imply that

$$\sqrt{T}(\hat{\gamma} - \gamma_0) \sim \Sigma^{-1}\frac{S'u^n}{\sqrt{T}} \quad (9.66)$$

In view of the conditions on the error term and the explanatory variable, one of the standard central limit theorems applies, see, e.g., Dhrymes [32, ch. 3], and we conclude immediately that

$$\frac{S'u^n}{\sqrt{T}} \sim N(0, \sigma^2\Sigma) \quad (9.67)$$

Hence,

$$\sqrt{T}(\hat{\gamma} - \gamma_0) \sim N(0, \sigma^2\Sigma^{-1}) \quad (9.68)$$

In order to complete the estimation problem, we need to produce a consistent estimator of σ^2. To this effect, observe that

$$y_t = \sum_{i=0}^{m} a_i x^*_{t-i} + u_t, \quad t = m + 1, m + 2, \ldots, T \quad (9.69)$$

Since an initial consistent estimator $\tilde{\gamma}$ is available, we can take as an estimator of σ^2,

$$\tilde{\sigma}^2 = \frac{1}{T}(y^m - \tilde{X}^*_m \tilde{a})'(y^m - \tilde{X}^*_m \tilde{a}) \quad (9.70)$$

where

$$y^m = (y_{m+1}, y_{m+2}, \ldots, y_T)' \quad (9.71)$$

and $\tilde{X}^*_m$ differs from $\tilde{X}^*$ in that the first column of the former is $(\tilde{x}_{m+1}, \tilde{x}^*_{m+2}, \ldots, \tilde{x}^*_T)'$ and so on. The point here is that we need not "lose" the additional $n - m$ observations at this stage.

The reader may convince himself that $\tilde{\sigma}^2$ is a consistent estimator of σ^2 by noting that

$$y^m = X^*_m a + u^m, \quad u^m = (u_{m+1}, \ldots, u_T)' \quad (9.72)$$

Thus,

$$y^m - \tilde{X}^*_m \tilde{a} = u^m - X^*_m(\tilde{a} - a) - (\tilde{X}^*_m - X^*_m)\tilde{a} \quad (9.73)$$

and one easily establishes that

$$\operatorname*{plim}_{T\to\infty} \tilde{\sigma}^2 = \operatorname*{plim}_{T\to\infty} \frac{1}{T} u^{m\prime} u^m = \sigma^2 \quad (9.74)$$

It is, of course, just as simple and perhaps more desirable to estimate σ^2 at the second step, by using the vector $\hat{\gamma}$ instead of $\tilde{\gamma}$. This would mean recomputing X^* on the basis of $\hat{\gamma}$ and using the residuals

$$\hat{u}_t = y_t - \hat{X}^*_m \hat{a}, \quad t = m + 1, m + 2, \ldots, T \quad (9.75)$$

where $\hat{X}^*_m$ is the matrix resulting when the elements of X^* are computed on the basis of $\hat{\gamma}$ instead of the true parameter vector, and $\hat{a}$ is the appropriate subvector of $\hat{\gamma}$.

If we estimate σ^2 by

$$\hat{\sigma}^2 = \frac{1}{T} \hat{u}^{m\prime} \hat{u}^m, \quad \hat{u}^m = (\hat{u}_{m+1}, \ldots, \hat{u}_T)' \quad (9.76)$$

we incur the additional cost of computing $\hat{X}^*_m$ which is not required for any other aspect of this estimation procedure. As the reader may easily verify, $\hat{\sigma}^2$ is also a consistent estimator of σ^2.

REMARK 9.3. The discussion above, in particular the result in (9.57), shows that it is extremely convenient in (9.56) to use $\tilde{S}'\tilde{S}$ in lieu of $\partial^2 Q/\partial\gamma\partial\gamma$. Not only does this simplify the computations there, but it also yields a consistent estimator, within a factor of proportionality, of the covariance matrix of the asymptotic distribution of $\hat{\gamma}$.

We have therefore proved

THEOREM 9.1. Consider the model

$$y_t = \frac{A(L)}{B(L)}x_t + u_t \tag{9.77}$$

where $\{x_t : t = 1, 2, \ldots\}$ is a suitably bounded nonstochastic sequence such that

$$\sum_{t=1}^{T} x_t^2 \to \infty \quad \text{with} \quad T \tag{9.78}$$

and $\{u_t : t = 1, 2, \ldots\}$ is a sequence of *i.i.d.* random variables with

$$E(u_t) = 0, \quad \text{Var}(u_t) = \sigma^2 \tag{9.79}$$

and bounded third order (absolute) moment.

Suppose further that

$$A(L) = \sum_{i=0}^{m} a_i L^i, \quad B(L) = \sum_{j=0}^{n} b_j L^j, \quad b_0 = 1 \tag{9.80}$$

that the roots of

$$\sum_{j=0}^{n} b_j \rho^{n-j} = 0 \tag{9.81}$$

are less than unity in absolute value and that

$$\lim_{T \to \infty} \frac{S'S}{T} = \Sigma \tag{9.82}$$

exists as a nonsingular matrix, where S is as defined in (9.35). In addition, define P, y^*, W as in (9.35) and (9.37), and let $\tilde{S}$, $\tilde{P}$, $\tilde{y}^*$ result when in the corresponding quantities we substitute the (initial) consistent estimator $\tilde{\gamma}$ for the true parameter vector γ_0.

Then

(i) The iterated estimator, obtained as the fixed point of

$$\tilde{\gamma}^{(k)} = [W(\tilde{\gamma}^{(k-1)})]^{-1} S'(\tilde{\gamma}^{(k-1)}) y^*(\tilde{\gamma}^{(k-1)}) \tag{9.83}$$

is consistent, it being understood that $\tilde{\gamma}^{(0)} = \tilde{\gamma}$.

(ii) This estimator is asymptotically equivalent to the simplified estimator

$$\hat{\gamma} = \tilde{\gamma} - (\tilde{S}'\tilde{S})^{-1}\tilde{S}'\tilde{P}\tilde{\gamma} + (\tilde{S}'\tilde{S})^{-1}\tilde{S}'\tilde{y}^* \tag{9.84}$$

in the sense that both have the same asymptotic distribution.

(iii) The asymptotic distribution of $\hat{\gamma}$ is given by

$$\sqrt{T}(\hat{\gamma} - \gamma_0) \sim N\left(0, \sigma^2 \sum{}^{-1}\right) \tag{9.85}$$

where

$$\sum = \lim_{T \to \infty} \frac{1}{T} S'S \tag{9.86}$$

(iv) The parameters of the asymptotic distribution are consistently estimated by $\tilde{\sigma}^2(\tilde{S}'\tilde{S}/T)^{-1}$, $\tilde{\sigma}^2$ being defined as in (9.70), or alternatively by $\hat{\sigma}^2(\tilde{S}'\tilde{S}/T)^{-1}$, $\hat{\sigma}^2$ being as defined in (9.76).

REMARK 9.4. If to the model of Theorem 9.1 we add the assumption that

$$u \sim N(0, \sigma^2 I) \tag{9.87}$$

then it is clear that boundedness of the third absolute moment of the error terms is not needed as a separate condition, since it is implied by (9.87).

If (9.87) is, in fact, valid, we have the likelihood function

$$L(\gamma, \sigma^2; y, x) = -\frac{T}{2}\ln(2\pi) - \frac{T}{2}\ln\sigma^2 - \frac{1}{2\sigma^2}\sum_{t=1}^{T}\left(y_t - \frac{A(L)}{B(L)}x_t\right)^2 \tag{9.88}$$

We note that the condition

$$\frac{\partial L}{\partial \gamma} = 0 \tag{9.89}$$

yields exactly the same equations as in (9.28), and thus the problem of obtaining the ML estimator of γ is exactly the one we handled earlier. On the other hand, the condition

$$\frac{\partial L}{\partial \sigma^2} = 0 \tag{9.90}$$

implies that σ^2 should be estimated as in (9.76), rather than as in (9.70).

The linearized estimator obtained earlier is, of course, exactly a linearized maximum likelihood estimator.

REMARK 9.5. In the discussion above, as in all discussions of two-step estimators, it is suggested that we obtain an initial consistent estimator. It is almost invariably suggested that this estimator be obtained by instrumental variables techniques. When we dealt with the simple geometric model, this requirement occasioned little difficulty, since one could always suggest that the lagged exogenous variable serve as the additional instrument.

In the case of the general rational lag model, however, we have to estimate parameters from the following relation;

$$y_t = -\sum_{j=1}^{n} b_j y_{t-j} + \sum_{i=0}^{m} a_i x_{t-i} + \sum_{s=0}^{n} b_s u_{t-s}, \quad b_0 = 1 \quad (9.91)$$

While in most econometric applications the order of the polynomials is small, say at most four, still economic time series exhibit a high degree of autocorrelation; thus, it is doubtful that using as instruments, x_t, x_{t-1}, ..., x_{t-7} in (9.91), for example, would be a desirable way of obtaining the initial estimator.[41] In empirical applications it has been found useful to obtain instruments as follows: If $m + n + 1$ instruments are required, consider the set $\{x_{t-i} : i = 0, 1, 2, \ldots, 2(m + n + 1)\}$. From this set extract the first $m + n + 1$ principal components and use them as instruments. Another, and perhaps a more desirable, alternative might be to include explicitly in the set of instruments, the variables x_t, x_{t-1}, ..., x_{t-m}. The remaining instruments are then to be chosen as follows: Consider the variables $x_{t-m-j}, j = 1, 2, \ldots, 2n$, and obtain the first n principal components of this set, say $z_{ts}, s = 1, 2, \ldots, n$.

The set of instrumental variables may then be chosen as $\{(x_{t-i}, z_{ts}) : i = 0, 1, 2, \ldots, m, s = 1, 2, \ldots, n\}$. Unfortunately, there is no rigorous criterion by which to determine the maximal lag in the set of variables from which principal components are to be obtained. The recommended procedure takes as a *rule of thumb* that the maximal lag should be at least twice the number of principal components desired.

9.3 The General Rational Lag Structure with Autocorrelated Errors

Suppose we complicate the model of the previous section by introducing the assumption

$$u_t = \rho u_{t-1} + \varepsilon_t, \quad |\rho| < 1 \quad (9.92)$$

the sequence $\{\varepsilon_t : t = 1, 2, \ldots\}$ being one of *i.i.d.* random variables, with

---

[41] This, of course, implies that $m + n + 1 = 8$.

the properties

$$E(\varepsilon_t) = 0, \quad \mathrm{Var}(\varepsilon_t) = \sigma^2 \tag{9.93}$$

and bounded sixth order (absolute) moment.

How should we estimate the parameters of the rational lag in the face of (9.92)?

The discussion of this problem will be somewhat informal. We have already seen in the previous section that estimation of this model confronts us with formidable convergence difficulties, so that when the number of parameters is at all large,[42] we are, for all practical purposes, reduced to the simplified linearized estimator.

Since, at a later stage, we shall deal with very general estimation problems by spectral techniques, there seems to be little point in treating the present problem extensively. As noted before, the covariance matrix of the error process in (9.92) is given by

$$\mathrm{Cov}(u) = \sigma^2 V, \quad u = (u_1, u_2, \ldots, u_T)' \tag{9.94}$$

where

$$V = \frac{1}{1 - \rho^2} \begin{bmatrix} 1 & \rho & \rho^2 & \cdot & \cdot & \rho^{T-1} \\ \rho & 1 & \rho & \cdot & \cdot & \rho^{T-2} \\ \cdot & \cdot & \cdot & \cdot & \cdot & \cdot \\ \cdot & \cdot & \cdot & \cdot & \cdot & \cdot \\ \cdot & \cdot & \cdot & \cdot & \cdot & \cdot \\ \rho^{T-1} & \cdot & \cdot & \cdot & \cdot & 1 \end{bmatrix} \tag{9.95}$$

Moreover, we have

$$V^{-1} = \begin{bmatrix} 1 & -\rho & 0 & \cdot & \cdot & 0 \\ -\rho & 1 + \rho^2 & -\rho & 0 & \cdot & \cdot \\ 0 & -\rho & 1 + \rho^2 & -\rho & \cdot & \cdot \\ \cdot & \cdot & \cdot & \cdot & \cdot & \cdot \\ \cdot & \cdot & \cdot & \cdot & \cdot & \cdot \\ \cdot & \cdot & \cdot & -\rho & 1 + \rho^2 & -\rho \\ 0 & \cdot & \cdot & 0 & -\rho & 1 \end{bmatrix} = M'M \tag{9.96}$$

where

---

[42] The reader should note that what creates problems is not the number of parameters in the numerator polynomial, but that in the denominator polynomial.

$$M = \begin{bmatrix} \sqrt{1-\rho^2} & 0 & \cdot & \cdot & & \cdot & 0 \\ -\rho & 1 & \cdot & \cdot & & \cdot & \cdot \\ 0 & -\rho & 1 & \cdot & & \cdot & \cdot \\ \cdot & & \cdot & \cdot & & \cdot & \cdot \\ \cdot & & & \cdot & & \cdot & \cdot \\ \cdot & & & \cdot & \cdot & 1 & 0 \\ 0 & & \cdot & \cdot & 0 & -\rho & 1 \end{bmatrix} \qquad (9.97)$$

We may obtain estimators for the parameters of the model by minimizing

$$Q = \left(y - \frac{A(L)}{B(L)} x \right)' V^{-1} \left(y - \frac{A(L)}{B(L)} x \right) \qquad (9.98)$$

REMARK 9.6. Before we proceed with the solution of the estimation problem posed by this model, the following observations are in order. In the previous section we defined the quantities

$$x_t^* = \frac{I}{B(L)} x_t, \quad y_t^* = \frac{I}{B(L)} y_t \qquad (9.99)$$

and so on. We also indicated that the starred quantities may be computed recursively, as, for example,

$$x_t^* = x_t - \sum_{j=1}^{n} b_j x_{t-j}^* \qquad (9.100)$$

on the assumption that

$$x_{-i}^* = 0, \quad i = 0, 1, 2, \ldots, (n-1) \qquad (9.101)$$

When actually deriving estimators for the parameters of the model, we in effect discarded the first n observations[43] and operated instead with $y_t, x_t, t = n + 1, n + 2, \ldots, T$. Thus, recall the definition of the matrices X^*, X^{**}, Y^* in (9.29). This was done in order to lessen the impact of the assumption (9.101) on the estimation procedure, which would be substantial if the sample size is relatively small. On the other hand, if we are solely concerned with the asymptotic properties of the estimators, or if the sample is relatively large, there is no reason for discarding the first n observations.

In the following discussion we shall not follow this practice, for two reasons: First, in order to demonstrate that nothing changes whether we

---

[43] Thus we implicitly assumed that $m \leq n$.

do or do not discard observations; and second, because in the context of the present model discarding observations will make the notation unduly cumbersome.

In view of the remark above, define

$$X^* = \begin{bmatrix} x_1^* & 0 & \cdot & \cdot & \cdot & 0 \\ x_2^* & x_1^* & 0 & \cdot & \cdot & \\ x_3^* & x_2^* & x_1^* & \cdot & \cdot & \\ \cdot & \cdot & \cdot & \cdot & \cdot & \\ \cdot & \cdot & \cdot & \cdot & \cdot & 0 \\ x_{m+1}^* & \cdot & \cdot & \cdot & \cdot & x_1^* \\ x_{m+2}^* & \cdot & \cdot & \cdot & \cdot & x_2^* \\ \cdot & \cdot & \cdot & \cdot & \cdot & \\ \cdot & \cdot & \cdot & \cdot & \cdot & \\ \cdot & \cdot & \cdot & \cdot & \cdot & \\ x_T^* & x_{T-1}^* & \cdot & \cdot & \cdot & x_{T-m}^* \end{bmatrix}, \quad X^{**} = \begin{bmatrix} 0 & 0 & \cdot & \cdot & \cdot & 0 \\ x_1^{**} & 0 & \cdot & \cdot & \cdot & \\ x_2^{**} & x_1^{**} & 0 & \cdot & \cdot & \\ \cdot & \cdot & \cdot & \cdot & \cdot & \\ \cdot & \cdot & \cdot & \cdot & \cdot & 0 \\ x_{n+1}^{**} & \cdot & \cdot & \cdot & \cdot & x_1^{**} \\ x_{n+2}^{**} & \cdot & \cdot & \cdot & \cdot & x_2^{**} \\ \cdot & \cdot & \cdot & \cdot & \cdot & \\ \cdot & \cdot & \cdot & \cdot & \cdot & \\ \cdot & \cdot & \cdot & \cdot & \cdot & \\ x_{T-1}^{**} & \cdot & \cdot & \cdot & \cdot & x_{T-n}^{**} \end{bmatrix}$$

$$Y^* = \begin{bmatrix} 0 & \cdot & \cdot & \cdot & \cdot & 0 \\ y_1^* & 0 & \cdot & \cdot & \cdot & \\ y_2^* & y_1^* & 0 & \cdot & \cdot & \\ \cdot & \cdot & \cdot & \cdot & \cdot & \\ \cdot & \cdot & \cdot & \cdot & \cdot & \\ \cdot & \cdot & \cdot & \cdot & \cdot & 0 \\ y_{n+1}^* & \cdot & \cdot & \cdot & \cdot & y_1^* \\ y_{n+2}^* & \cdot & \cdot & \cdot & \cdot & y_2^* \\ \cdot & \cdot & \cdot & \cdot & \cdot & \\ \cdot & \cdot & \cdot & \cdot & \cdot & \\ y_{T-1}^* & \cdot & \cdot & \cdot & \cdot & y_{T-n}^* \end{bmatrix}, \quad S = (X^*, X^{**}), \quad P = (X^*, Y^*)$$

$$(9.102)$$

and observe that the first order conditions are given by

$$\frac{\partial Q}{\partial \gamma} = -2(S'V^{-1}y^* - S'V^{-1}P\gamma) = 0$$

$$\frac{\partial Q}{\partial \rho} = (y - X^*a)'\frac{\partial V^{-1}}{\partial \rho}(y - X^*a) = 0$$

$$(9.103)$$

where now

$$y^* = (y_1^*, y_2^*, \ldots, y_T^*)', \quad y = (y_1, y_2, \ldots, y_T)' \qquad (9.104)$$

The equations (9.103) are extremely nonlinear; however, the prefiltering method, suitably modified, will in principle yield a solution. Thus, suppose an initial consistent estimator, say $\tilde{\gamma}$, is available. Given $\tilde{\gamma}$, we can certainly compute the elements of X^* and thus obtain the residual vector

$$\tilde{u} = y - \tilde{X}^* \tilde{a} \qquad (9.105)$$

where the tilde over X^* indicates that in computing its elements $\tilde{\gamma}$ was used in lieu of γ_0—the true parameter vector.

Having obtained the residual vector, we see that the last equation of (9.103) implies that

$$-2\rho\tilde{u}_1^2 - 2 \sum_{t=2}^{T} (\tilde{u}_t - \rho\tilde{u}_{t-1})\tilde{u}_{t-1} = 0 \qquad (9.106)$$

which yields the estimator

$$\tilde{\rho} = \frac{\sum_{t=2}^{T} \tilde{u}_t \tilde{u}_{t-1}}{\sum_{t=3}^{T} \tilde{u}_{t-1}^2} \qquad (9.107)$$

This differs from the usual estimator of the autocorrelation coefficient, in that the denominator above *does not contain* $\tilde{u}_1^2$. Given $\tilde{\rho}$ we can define $\tilde{V}^{-1}$, and given $\tilde{\gamma}$ we can define $\tilde{S}$, $\tilde{P}$, $\tilde{y}^*$ by using $\tilde{\gamma}$ instead of γ_0 in computing their elements. But then we can solve the first set in (9.103) to obtain the first iterate, say $\hat{\gamma}^{(1)}$, as

$$\hat{\gamma}^{(1)} = (\tilde{S}'\tilde{V}^{-1}\tilde{S})^{-1}\tilde{S}'\tilde{V}^{-1}\tilde{y}^* \qquad (9.108)$$

Using $\hat{\gamma}^{(1)}$ we can recompute the elements of X^* and thus obtain another set of residuals from (9.105); then we can compute $\hat{\rho}^{(1)}$ from the formula in (9.107). Recomputing the elements of X^{**}, Y^*, y^* with $\hat{\gamma}^{(1)}$ and using $\hat{\rho}^{(1)}$ to obtain $\tilde{V}^{-1}$ we can, from (9.108), obtain a second iterate $\hat{\gamma}^{(2)}$, and so on until convergence is attained. By the arguments of the previous section, we can show that if at the $(k + 1)$th iteration $\hat{\gamma}^{(k)}$, $\hat{\rho}^{(k)}$ are consistent estimators of the corresponding parameters, then so are $\hat{\gamma}^{(k+1)}$, $\hat{\rho}^{(k+1)}$.

Thus, this procedure, if it converges, yields a consistent solution to the system in (9.103).

It is interesting that we can employ a linearized estimator as in the previous section; this estimator will have the same asymptotic distribu-

tion as the one obtained by solving (9.103) through the prefiltering procedure.

The linearized estimator may be obtained as follows: Put

$$\delta = \begin{pmatrix} \gamma \\ \rho \end{pmatrix} \tag{9.109}$$

and observe that the problem is to find a root of

$$\frac{\partial Q}{\partial \delta} = 0 \tag{9.110}$$

As before, expand the gradient above by Taylor series about $\delta = \delta^*$ to
obtain

$$\frac{\partial Q}{\partial \delta}(\delta) = \frac{\partial Q}{\partial \delta}(\delta^*) + \frac{\partial^2 Q}{\partial \delta \partial \delta}(\delta^*)[\delta - \delta^*] + \text{ third order term } \tag{9.111}$$

We may set as our objective the determination of a vector, say $\mathring{\delta}$, such
that if we take $\delta^* = \begin{pmatrix} \tilde{\gamma} \\ \tilde{\rho} \end{pmatrix} = \tilde{\delta}$, the first two terms of the right member
of (9.111) sum to the zero vector.

Neglecting third order terms, we thus determine that

$$\mathring{\delta} = \tilde{\delta} - \left[\frac{\partial^2 Q}{\partial \delta \partial \delta}(\tilde{\delta}) \right]^{-1} \frac{\partial Q}{\partial \delta}(\tilde{\delta}) \tag{9.112}$$

One easily verifies that

$$\operatorname*{plim}_{T \to \infty} \frac{1}{T} \frac{\partial Q}{\partial \delta}(\tilde{\delta}) = 0, \quad \operatorname*{plim}_{T \to \infty} \left[\frac{1}{T} \frac{\partial^2 Q}{\partial \delta \partial \delta}(\tilde{\delta}) \right] = 2 \begin{bmatrix} \Phi & 0 \\ 0 & \dfrac{\sigma^2}{1 - \rho^2} \end{bmatrix} \tag{9.113}$$

where

$$\Phi = \lim_{T \to \infty} \frac{S'V^{-1}S}{T} \tag{9.114}$$

Since Φ may be assumed to be nonsingular, we conclude that

$$\operatorname*{plim}_{T \to \infty} \mathring{\delta} = \operatorname*{plim}_{T \to \infty} \tilde{\delta} = \delta \tag{9.115}$$

REMARK 9.7. Equation (9.115) shows quite clearly why it is important,
in these linearized (simplified) estimators, to begin the process with a
consistent estimator. Thus, observe that the consistency of $\mathring{\delta}$ is a simple
consequence of the consistency of $\tilde{\delta}$. If the latter is not consistent, the

former will, in general, fail to be consistent. Incidentally, the reader should verify for himself that $\tilde{\rho}$ of (9.107) is a consistent estimator of ρ, given that $\tilde{\gamma}$ is an IV estimator of γ.

The development in (9.113) and (9.114) shows that we may, in fact, operate with the still simpler expressions:

$$\hat{\gamma} = \tilde{\gamma} - \frac{1}{2T}\tilde{\Phi}^{-1}\frac{\partial Q}{\partial \gamma}(\tilde{\delta})$$
$$= \tilde{\gamma} - (\tilde{S}'\tilde{V}^{-1}\tilde{S})^{-1}\tilde{S}'\tilde{V}^{-1}\tilde{\gamma} + (\tilde{S}'\tilde{V}^{-1}\tilde{S})^{-1}\tilde{S}'\tilde{V}^{-1}\tilde{y}^* \qquad (9.116)$$

$$\hat{\rho} = \tilde{\rho} - \frac{1}{2}\frac{1 - \tilde{\rho}^2}{\tilde{\sigma}^2}\frac{\partial Q}{\partial \rho}(\tilde{\delta})$$

where, of course,

$$\tilde{\Phi} = \frac{\tilde{S}'\tilde{V}^{-1}\tilde{S}}{T} \qquad (9.117)$$

We see, then, that we have a decomposable system, so that $\hat{\gamma}$ can be computed independently of $\hat{\rho}$. The reader should note further than if $\tilde{\rho}$ is computed according to (9.107), then

$$\frac{\partial Q}{\partial \rho}(\tilde{\delta}) = 0 \qquad (9.118)$$

so that

$$\hat{\rho} = \tilde{\rho} \qquad (9.119)$$

Since we are not generally interested in estimating ρ per se, the result in (9.120) need not occasion any consternation.

We shall now show that the estimator of γ in (9.116) and the one obtained by a convergent prefiltering procedure in (9.103) or, equivalently, (9.107) and (9.108), have the same asymptotic distribution.

We first obtain the asymptotic distribution of the convergent prefiltering estimator, which we denote by δ^*. We have

$$\frac{\partial Q}{\partial \delta}(\delta^*) = \frac{\partial Q}{\partial \delta}(\delta_0) + \frac{\partial^2 Q}{\partial \delta \partial \delta}(\delta_0)[\delta^* - \delta_0]$$
$$+ \text{ third order terms} \qquad (9.120)$$

where δ_0 is the true parameter vector.

The estimator has the property that

$$\frac{\partial Q}{\partial \delta}(\delta^*) = 0 \qquad (9.121)$$

Hence

$$\sqrt{T}(\hat\delta^* - \delta_0) = -\left[\frac{1}{T}\frac{\partial^2 Q}{\partial\delta\partial\delta}(\delta_0)\right]^{-1}\frac{1}{\sqrt{T}}\frac{\partial Q}{\partial\delta}(\delta_0)$$

$$+ \text{ third order terms} \qquad (9.122)$$

In view of (9.113) and the fact that all third order terms may be shown to vanish in probability, we conclude that asymptotically,

$$\sqrt{T}(\hat\delta^* - \delta_0) \sim -2\begin{bmatrix}\Phi & 0 \\ 0 & \dfrac{\sigma^2}{1-\rho_0^2}\end{bmatrix}^{-1}\frac{1}{\sqrt{T}}\frac{\partial Q}{\partial\delta}(\delta_0) \qquad (9.123)$$

Now consider the linearized estimator as given in (9.112). We have

$$\sqrt{T}(\hat\delta - \delta_0) = \sqrt{T}(\tilde\delta - \delta_0) - \left[\frac{1}{T}\frac{\partial^2 Q}{\partial\delta\partial\delta}(\tilde\delta)\right]^{-1}\frac{1}{\sqrt{T}}\frac{\partial Q}{\partial\delta}(\tilde\delta) \qquad (9.124)$$

Expand $(\partial Q/\partial\delta)(\tilde\delta)$ to obtain

$$\frac{\partial Q}{\partial\delta}(\tilde\delta) = \frac{\partial Q}{\partial\delta}(\delta_0) + \frac{\partial^2 Q}{\partial\delta\partial\delta}(\delta_0)[\tilde\delta - \delta_0] + \text{ third order terms} \qquad (9.125)$$

Since third order terms vanish in probability, we have, asymptotically,

$$\sqrt{T}(\hat\delta - \delta_0) \sim -\left\{\operatorname*{plim}_{T\to\infty}\left[\frac{1}{T}\frac{\partial^2 Q}{\partial\delta\partial\delta}(\tilde\delta)\right]^{-1}\right\}\frac{1}{\sqrt{T}}\frac{\partial Q}{\partial\delta}(\delta_0)$$

$$+ \sqrt{T}(\tilde\delta - \delta_0) - \operatorname*{plim}_{T\to\infty}\left\{\left[\frac{1}{T}\frac{\partial^2 Q}{\partial\delta\partial\delta}(\tilde\delta)\right]^{-1}\left[\frac{1}{T}\frac{\partial^2 Q}{\partial\delta\partial\delta}(\delta_0)\right]\right\}\sqrt{T}(\tilde\delta - \delta_0)$$

$$= -2\begin{bmatrix}\Phi & 0 \\ 0 & \dfrac{\sigma^2}{1-\rho^2}\end{bmatrix}^{-1}\frac{1}{\sqrt{T}}\frac{\partial Q}{\partial\delta}(\delta_0) \qquad (9.126)$$

which is exactly the expression we had in (9.123).

To determine the exact form of the asymptotic distribution, we need only be concerned with the term $(1/\sqrt{T})(\partial Q/\partial\delta)(\delta_0)$. But we have

$$\frac{1}{\sqrt{T}}\frac{\partial Q}{\partial\delta}(\delta_0) = -\frac{2}{\sqrt{T}}\begin{pmatrix}S'V^{-1}u \\ \rho u_1^2 + \displaystyle\sum_{t=2}^{T} u_{t-1}\varepsilon_t\end{pmatrix}$$

$$= -\frac{2}{\sqrt{T}}\begin{pmatrix}S'M'\varepsilon \\ \rho u_1^2 + \displaystyle\sum_{t=2}^{T} u_{t-1}\varepsilon_t\end{pmatrix} \qquad (9.127)$$

Let $z_{.t}$ be the tth column of $S'M'^{-1}$, and observe that we can write

$$\frac{1}{\sqrt{T}}\frac{\partial Q}{\partial \delta}(\delta_0) = -\frac{2}{\sqrt{T}}\binom{z_{.1}\varepsilon_1}{\rho u_1^2} - \frac{2}{\sqrt{T}}\sum_{t=2}^{T}\binom{z_{.t}}{u_{t-1}^N}\varepsilon_t$$
$$-\frac{2}{\sqrt{T}}\sum_{t=2}^{T}\binom{0}{\rho^{N-1}u_{t-N+1}}\varepsilon_t \tag{9.128}$$

where N is chosen sufficiently large so as to make the probability arbitrarily small that $\rho^{N-1}u_{t-N+1}$ exceeds, in absolute value, some specified quantity.

Hence, the asymptotic distribution of $(1/\sqrt{T})(\partial Q/\partial \delta)(\delta_0)$ is determined, essentially, by the second term in the right member of (9.128). We thus conclude that asymptotically,

$$\frac{1}{\sqrt{T}}\frac{\partial Q}{\partial \delta}(\delta_0) \sim N(0, 4\sigma^2\Omega) \tag{9.129}$$

where

$$\Omega = \begin{bmatrix} \Phi & 0 \\ 0 & \sigma^2 \sum_{i=0}^{N-2}\rho^2_i \end{bmatrix} \approx \begin{bmatrix} \Phi & 0 \\ 0 & \dfrac{\sigma^2}{1-\rho^2} \end{bmatrix} \tag{9.130}$$

But then (9.126) implies that

$$\sqrt{T}(\hat{\delta} - \delta_0) \sim N(0, \sigma^2\Omega^{-1}) \tag{9.131}$$

REMARK 9.8. The result above shows that $\hat{\rho}$ is asymptotically independent of $\hat{\gamma}$. Hence, there is no difficulty whatsoever in obtaining only $\hat{\gamma}$ at the second stage in (9.116), and thus neglecting the last equation. Actually, we must have $\hat{\rho} = \tilde{\rho}$, as pointed out earlier, because of the manner in which $\tilde{\rho}$ is computed in (9.107).

REMARK 9.9. A consistent estimator of the covariance matrix of the asymptotic distribution of $\hat{\delta}$ is given by

$$\tilde{\sigma}^2\tilde{\Omega}^{-1} = \tilde{\sigma}^2 \begin{bmatrix} \left(\dfrac{\tilde{S}'\tilde{V}^{-1}\tilde{S}}{T}\right)^{-1} & 0 \\ 0 & \dfrac{1-\tilde{\rho}^2}{\tilde{\sigma}^2} \end{bmatrix} \tag{9.132}$$

where we can estimate

$$\left(\widetilde{\frac{\sigma^2}{1-\rho^2}}\right) = \frac{\tilde{u}'\tilde{u}}{T}, \quad \tilde{\sigma}^2 = \left(\widetilde{\frac{\sigma^2}{1-\rho^2}}\right)(1-\tilde{\rho}^2) \tag{9.133}$$

$\tilde{u}$ being defined by

$$\tilde{u} = y - \bar{X}^*\tilde{a} \tag{9.134}$$

We remind the reader, that if the sample is relatively small, the end point problem will be somewhat troublesome. In particular, it could make an appreciable difference whether σ^2 is estimated according to (9.133) or from the sum of squared residuals in the regression of $\tilde{u}_t$ or $\tilde{u}_{t-1}$. In the latter case, we would have

$$T\hat{\sigma}^2 = \tilde{u}'\tilde{u} - \frac{(\tilde{u}'\tilde{u}_{-1})^2}{\tilde{u}'_{-1}\tilde{u}_{-1}}, \quad \tilde{u} = (\tilde{u}_2, \tilde{u}_3, \ldots, \tilde{u}_T)',$$
$$\tilde{u}_{-1} = (\tilde{u}_1, \tilde{u}_2, \ldots \tilde{u}_{T-1})' \tag{9.135}$$

But

$$\tilde{\rho} = \frac{\tilde{u}'\tilde{u}_{-1}}{\tilde{u}'_{-1}\tilde{u}_{-1} - \tilde{u}_1^2} \tag{9.136}$$

Thus,

$$T\tilde{\sigma}^2 = \tilde{u}'\tilde{u} - \frac{(\tilde{u}'\tilde{u})(\tilde{u}'\tilde{u}_{-1})^2}{(\tilde{u}'_{-1}\tilde{u}_{-1} - \tilde{u}_1^2)^2} \tag{9.137}$$

and we see that $\hat{\sigma}^2$ is somewhat different from $\tilde{\sigma}^2$. Unless the sample is quite small, it would seem simpler to cperate with $\tilde{\sigma}^2$.

The discussion of this section may be summarized in

THEOREM 9.2. Consider the model

$$y_t = \frac{A(L)}{B(L)}x_t + u_t, \quad t = 1, 2, \ldots, T \tag{9.138}$$

where

$$A(L) = \sum_{i=0}^{m} a_i L^i, \quad B(L) = \sum_{j=0}^{n} b_j L^j, \quad b_0 = 1 \tag{9.139}$$

and the roots of

$$\sum_{j=0}^{n} b_j \varphi^{n-j} = 0 \tag{9.140}$$

are less than unity in absolute value.

Suppose that $\{x_t : t = 1, 2, \ldots\}$ is a bounded nonstochastic sequence with $\sum_{t=1}^{T} x_t^2 \to \infty$ as $T \to \infty$, and that

$$u_t = \rho u_{t-1} + \varepsilon_t, \quad |\rho| < 1 \tag{9.141}$$

$\{\varepsilon_t : t = 1, 2, 3, \ldots\}$ being a sequence of *i.i.d.* random variables with

$$E(\varepsilon_t) = 0, \quad \text{Var}(\varepsilon_t) = \sigma^2 \tag{9.142}$$

and bounded sixth order (absolute) moment.
Let

$$a = (a_0, a_1, \ldots, a_m)', \quad b = (b_1, b_2, \ldots, b_n),$$

$$\gamma = \begin{pmatrix} a \\ -b \end{pmatrix}, \quad \delta = \begin{pmatrix} \gamma \\ \rho \end{pmatrix} \tag{9.143}$$

Then the following statements are true:

(i) The prefiltering procedure beginning with an initial (IV) consistent estimator $\tilde{\gamma}$, $\tilde{\rho}$ yields, if it converges, a consistent estimator of δ.

(ii) The linearized estimator given in (9.116) is consistent.

(iii) The estimators under (i) and (ii) have the same asymptotic distribution, which is given by

$$\sqrt{T}(\hat{\delta} - \delta_0) \sim N(0, \sigma^2 \Omega^{-1}) \tag{9.144}$$

Ω being as defined in (9.130)

(iv) $\hat{\gamma}$ and $\hat{\rho}$ are asymptotically mutually independent.

(v) The covariance parameters of the asymptotic distribution of the estimator $\hat{\delta}$, as above, are consistently estimated by $\tilde{\sigma}^2 \tilde{\Omega}^{-1}$, where $\tilde{\sigma}^2$ and $\tilde{\Omega}$ are as in (9.132) and (9.133).

REMARK 9.10. If in Theorem 9.2 we assume, in conjunction with (9.141), that

$$\varepsilon \sim N(0, \sigma^2 I), \quad \varepsilon = (\varepsilon_1, \varepsilon_2, \ldots, \varepsilon_T)' \tag{9.145}$$

then it is clear that the boundedness of the sixth absolute moment is not needed, since it is implied by (9.145). Further, nothing in the estimation procedures discussed in this section will change, except that the last equation in (9.103) will now read

$$-\frac{\rho}{1 - \rho^2} + \frac{\rho}{\sigma^2}\tilde{u}_1^2 + \frac{1}{\sigma^2} \sum_{t=2}^{T} (\tilde{u}_t - \rho\tilde{u}_{t-1})\tilde{u}_{t-1} = 0 \tag{9.146}$$

instead of the expression given in (9.106). Additionally, the maximum likelihood procedure will suggest the estimator

$$\tilde{\sigma}^2 = \frac{\tilde{u}' \tilde{V}^{-1} \tilde{u}}{T} \tag{9.147}$$

Exercises and Questions

1. Derive the lag structure implied by (9.5) and (9.6) when x_t is a vector.

2. In Equation (9.60), use the mean value theorem and write instead

$$\frac{1}{\sqrt{T}} \frac{\partial Q}{\partial \gamma}(\tilde{\gamma}) = \frac{1}{\sqrt{T}} \frac{\partial Q}{\partial \gamma}(\gamma_0) + \frac{1}{T} \frac{\partial^2 Q}{\partial \gamma \partial \gamma}(\bar{\gamma}) \sqrt{T}(\tilde{\gamma} - \gamma_0)$$

where $\bar{\gamma}$ lies between γ_0 and $\tilde{\gamma}$. Then, argue that $\bar{\gamma}$ converges in probability to γ_0 and, consequently, that $\text{plim}_{T\to\infty} \sum^{-1} (1/T)(\partial^2 Q/\partial \gamma \partial \gamma) = I$, thus justifying the conclusion in (9.62) without reference to the third order terms in (9.60).

3. Apply the procedure of Problem 2 to the expansion in (9.63).

4. Verify that $\hat{\sigma}^2$ as defined in Equation (9.76) is a consistent estimator of σ^2.

5. Reformulate Equation (9.111) and the discussion following, so that the argument does not depend on the asymptotic vanishing of the third order terms in (9.111).

6. Verify the assertions in Equation (9.113).

7. Reformulate the argument following Equation (9.120), so that it does not depend on the asymptotic vanishing of the third order term.
   Hint: Consider $(\partial^2 Q/\partial \delta \partial \delta)(\bar{\delta})$ where $\bar{\delta}$ lies between δ_0 and δ^*.

8. In Equation (9.126), why did we ignore the first vector in the right hand side? What is the expected value of that vector?
   Hint: What is the connection, if any, between this problem and Equation (9.146)?

9. In their original formulation of the prefiltering algorithm, Steiglitz and McBride have recommended that, instead of (9.36), one should solve iteratively

$$P'P\gamma = S'y^*$$

the meaning of the matrices P, S being defined in Equation (9.35). The reason given for this suggestion is that it is simpler and more economical to invert a *symmetric matrix*. Is this estimator the same as the one obtained by a converging iteration of (9.38)? If not, which is relatively more efficient? Can you give an interpretation of the Steiglitz and McBride suggestion which will make the answer to the preceding question intuitively obvious?
   Hint:

$$\text{plim}_{T\to\infty} \frac{S'P}{T} = \text{plim}_{T\to\infty} \frac{S'S}{T}$$

it being understood that all elements of such matrices are evaluated with respect to consistent estimators $\tilde{\gamma}$. If we want symmetry and we use $P'P$ in lieu of $S'P$, what can we say about $\operatorname{plim}_{T\to\infty}(P'P/T)$ in relation to $\operatorname{plim}_{T\to\infty}(S'P/T)$? What is the minimand for which the equations solved in the Steiglitz-McBride suggestion are the normal equations (first order conditions)?

Chapter 10

SPECTRAL ANALYSIS AND ESTIMATION OF DISTRIBUTED LAG MODELS

10.1 Preliminaries

The general distributed lag model

$$y_t = \sum_{\tau=0}^{\infty} w_\tau x_{t-\tau} + u_t \qquad (10.1)$$

is characterized by the lag *structure*

$$w = \{w_\tau : \tau = 0, 1, 2, \ldots\} \qquad (10.2)$$

which has the property that its *lag coefficients*, w_τ, do not depend on t, i.e., the time subscript (argument) of the dependent variable.

In previous discussion, we had sought to estimate the lag structure under varying assumptions on the error term, u_t, when the lag coefficients were assumed to be a function of a finite (small) number of parameters.

Now in the literature of communications engineering (and time series analysis), a sequence of the form (10.2) coupled with the model in (10.1) is said to be a *linear time invariant filter* and the sequence in (10.2) is said to be the *kernel* of the filter. Thus, in (10.1) the exogenous variable is *passed through a filter*, and this, together with the additive error term, yields the dependent variable.

A great deal is known about such relations in the context of spectral analysis, and thus it would be helpful if the problem of lag structure estimation were to be placed in that framework.

In addition, we have observed in previous chapters that when the number of parameters in terms of which we characterize the lag structure is even moderately large, the estimation problem becomes hopelessly complex even if the error term is assumed to obey the simplest possible condition, namely, that it is a set of *i.i.d.* random variables.

As we shall see below, in a spectral analytic context we shall be able to handle, without undue difficulties, the estimation problem with respect to a far more general model than was hitherto possible. Before we do so, however, we need a number of elementary results from the theory of spectral analysis. These are presented in the following three sections.

10.2 Elementary Aspects of Stochastic Processes

From elementary mathematical statistics, we are familiar with the notion of a *random variable*; this is a *real valued function* defined on a sample space. Thus we denote a random variable by $X(s)$, $s \in S$, where $X(\cdot)$ is the random variable and S is the sample space. As an example, consider the game of throwing two perfectly balanced dice, and recording the *sum* of the faces showing. Here the sample space consists of the the events

$$
\begin{array}{cccc}
(1, 1), & (1, 2), & (1, 3) & \cdots & (1, 6) \\
(2, 1), & (2, 2), & (2, 3) & \cdots & (2, 6) \\
\vdots \\
(6, 1), & (6, 2), & (6, 3) & \cdots & (6, 6)
\end{array}
$$

where in each pair, the first element corresponds to the face showing on the first die and the second element corresponds to the face showing on the second die. Number these pairs, in the order presented above, s_{ij}, $i, j = 1, 2, \ldots, 6$. Then the sample space is

$$
S = \{s_{ij} : i, j = 1, 2, \ldots, 6\} \tag{10.3}
$$

and the random variable is defined by

$$
X(s_{ij}) = i + j \tag{10.4}
$$

Typically, the agument (here s_{ij}) is suppressed. If we throw the dice successively, we may denote the outcome at the tth throw by x_t. This is interpreted as *an observation* on the random variable $X(\cdot)$. If we have n observations, then we can process these data and test, for example, whether or not the dice are perfectly balanced.

However, in all the above we assume that we are dealing with a *single random variable* and that we have n observations on this same random variable.

Frequently, it is necessary to change our point of view. Thus, suppose we consider the behavior of the price of a stock on the New York Stock Exchange, or an average of stock prices. We may consider this to be a random variable. However, it would be more appropriate to take the point of view that we are dealing with a *family of random variables*, so that what we observe at time t, is an observation on the random variable $X(t, \cdot)$—the presumption being that a different random variable governs the behavior of the phenomenon at different points in time. In this context, if we have n observations, say at times t_i, $i = 1, 2, \ldots, n$, then we have one observation each, on n possibly distinct random variables.

Notice that the standard scheme of elementary mathematical statistics is a special case of the preceding. With these preliminaries aside, let us now consider formally several aspects of the theory of stochastic processes. Of necessity, our discussion will be elliptical. The reader desiring greater detail may consult Parzen [125], Hannan [63], Doob [34], Jenkins and Watts [78], Grenander and Rosenblatt [52], Dhrymes [32] or Fishman [43].

DEFINITION 10.1. Let T be a set; if for every $t_1, t_2 \in T$, $t_1 + t_2 \in T$, then T is said to be a *linear set*.

DEFINITION 10.2. Let $\{X(t, \cdot) : t \in T\}$ be a family of random variables indexed by the linear (index) set T; then it is said to be a *stochastic process*, or a *time series*.

The reader has no doubt observed that one of the major problems encountered in the study of random variables deals with inferences concerning the parameters of their probability distribution—in particular, the mean and variance, or covariance matrix, as the case may be. Inferences are based on information conveyed by a sample on the random variable—usually a *random sample*. This affords us the opportunity to compute sample moments which are known to be consistent estimators of the corresponding population moments. The importat feature here is that the *sample is random*, i.e., all of the constitutent observations are *i.i.d.* random variables.

On the other hand, if we are dealing with a stochastic process $\{X(t, \cdot)$; $t \in T\}$ and we have n observations, say at t_i, $i = 1, 2, \ldots, n$, $t_i \in T$, then we have one *observation each or n random variables*. Unless these variables have something in common, little information can be deduced from this sample. In this connection, the property of covariance stationarity becomes important. Thus,

DEFINITION 10.3. Let $\{X(t, \cdot) : t \in T\}$ be a (real) stochastic process. [For simplicity of notation, denote $X(t, \cdot)$ by X_t.] Then the process is said to be *covariance stationary* if

$$K(t, s) = E\{[X_t - E(X_t)] [X_s - E(X_s)]\} \tag{10.5}$$

exists and is an even function of $t - s$, only.

REMARK 10.1. It is customary, but not necessary in terms of the definition above, to assume in addition that the mean function

$$E(X_t) = m(t) \tag{10.6}$$

is a constant independent of t. We shall adhere to this convention in subsequent discussion. The *covariance function or covariance kernel* $K(\cdot\cdot\cdot)$ is customarily written as a function of only one argument; thus, $K(\tau)$, where $\tau = t - s$. Since $K(\cdot)$ is an even function, then $K(\tau) = K(-\tau)$.

EXAMPLE 10.1. Let $\beta \sim N(0, \sigma^2)$, and consider the stochastic process

$$X_t = e^{\beta t}, \quad t \in R \tag{10.7}$$

where R is the set of all real numbers. Is this process covariance stationary? We have

$$E(X_t) = e^{-\frac{1}{2}\sigma^2 t^2} \tag{10.8}$$

Thus,

$$K(t, s) = e^{-\frac{1}{2}\sigma^2 (t+s)^2} - e^{-\frac{1}{2}\sigma^2 (t^2 + s^2)} \tag{10.9}$$

which is clearly not an even function of $t - s$ alone. Hence the process is not covariance stationary.

EXAMPLE 10.2. Consider the process,

$$X_t = A_1 \cos \lambda t + A_2 \sin \lambda t \tag{10.10}$$

where the A_i, $i = 1, 2$, are mutually independent random variables with

$$E(A_i) = \mu_i, \quad \text{Var}(A_i) = \sigma_{ii}, \quad i = 1, 2 \tag{10.11}$$

Thus,

$$\begin{aligned}
\text{Cov}(X_t, X_s) &= K(t, s) \\
&= \sigma_{11} \cos \lambda t \cos \lambda s + \sigma_{22} \sin \lambda t \sin \lambda s \tag{10.12}
\end{aligned}$$

Thus, this process is *not* covariance stationary. On the other hand, suppose $\sigma_{11} = \sigma_{22} = \sigma^2$. Then

$$K(t, s) = \sigma^2 \cos \lambda(t - s) \tag{10.13}$$

Since $\cos \theta = \cos(-\theta)$, *the process is now covariance stationary.*

REMARK 10.2. The mean function of the process above is

$$E(X_t) = \mu_1 \cos \lambda t + \mu_2 \sin \lambda t \tag{10.14}$$

This illustrates the fact that for covariance stationarity, the mean function need not be constant.

Before we proceed with the discussion of further aspects of such processes, we remind the reader of

DEFINITION 10.4. A quantity of the form $Ae^{i\lambda t}$ is said to be a *complex sinusoid* of frequency λ and amplitude $|A|$.

For the balance of this section, we shall deal exclusively with (real) covariance stationary processes which (a) have mean function identically zero and (b) are defined on the index set $N = \{0, \pm 1, \pm 2, \ldots\}$, i.e. with real discrete time series.

With every covariance stationary process X_t as above,[44] we can associate the (continuous) *complex* process $\{Z(\lambda): \lambda \in (-\pi, \pi]\}$ having the following properties

$$Z(\lambda) = \frac{1}{2}[u(\lambda) - iv(\lambda)]$$

$$u(-\lambda) = u(\lambda), \quad v(-\lambda) = -v(\lambda) \tag{10.15}$$

$$X_t = \int_{-\pi}^{\pi} e^{i\lambda t} dZ(\lambda) \tag{10.16}$$

$$E[dZ(\lambda)\overline{dZ(\lambda')}] = dF(\lambda) \quad \text{if } \lambda = \lambda'$$
$$= 0 \quad \text{if } \lambda \neq \lambda' \tag{10.17}$$

Notice that (10.15) easily implies that

$$dZ(-\lambda) = \overline{dZ(\lambda)} \tag{10.18}$$

The interpretation one places on (10.16) is as follows: It can be shown that for every covariance stationary process there exists a sequence $\{\zeta_s: s = 1, 2, \ldots\}$, of complex mutually uncorrelated random variables having mean zero, such that for any $t \in [-N_1, N_1] \subset N, N_1 > 0$ and $\varepsilon > 0$ there exists an integer m for which the following is true

$$E\left| X_t - \sum_{k=1}^{m} e^{i\lambda_k t} \zeta_k \right|^2 < \varepsilon, \quad \lambda_k \in (-\pi, \pi] \tag{10.19}$$

---

[44] In order to simplify the notation, in the following discussion we shall use X_t instead of the more cumbersome $X(t, \cdot)$.

Thus, the integral in (10.16) represents convergence in quadratic mean and has the interpretation

$$\int_{-\pi}^{\pi} e^{i\lambda t} dZ(\lambda) = \lim_{\max|\lambda_k - \lambda_{k-1}| \to 0} \sum_{k=1}^{m} e^{i\lambda_k t}\zeta_k \qquad (10.20)$$

for any $t \in N$.

DEFINITION 10.5.   The function $F(\cdot)$ defined by (10.17) is said to be the *spectral distribution function* corresponding to the stochastic process. If $F(\cdot)$ is differentiable, its derivative $f(\cdot)$ is said to be the *spectral density function*, or simply the *spectrum* of the stochastic process.

The relation between the spectral density and covariance kernel is formalized in

PROPOSITION 10.1.   Let $\{X(t, \cdot): t \in N\}$ be a covariance stationary process. Let $K(\cdot), f(\cdot)$ be respectively, its covariance kernel and specral density. Suppose the latter is a continuous function,[45] of bounded variation, on $[-\pi, \pi]$.

Then $K(\tau)$ and $f(\cdot)$ form a Fourier transform pair.

Proof.   By definition,

$$K(\tau) = E(X_{t+\tau}X_t) = E\left[\int_{-\pi}^{\pi}\int_{-\pi}^{\pi} e^{i(t+\tau)\lambda}e^{-it\lambda}dZ(\lambda)\overline{dZ(\lambda')}\right]$$

$$= \int_{-\pi}^{\pi} e^{i\tau\lambda} dF(\lambda) = \int_{-\pi}^{\pi} e^{i\tau\lambda}f(\lambda)\,d\lambda \qquad (10.21)$$

which shows that $K(\tau)$ is the τth (complex) Fourier transform of the function $f(\lambda)$.

By a basic result of Fourier analysis, we know that the Fourier series of a continuous function of bounded variation converges to that function, in the mean square sense. Hence, we conclude that

$$f(\lambda) = \frac{1}{2\pi} \sum_{\tau=-\infty}^{\infty} K(\tau)e^{-i\tau\lambda} \qquad (10.22)$$

In view of (10.21) the proposition is established.

REMARK 10.3.   Notice that (10.16) has the simpler representation,

$$X_t = \int_0^{\pi} \cos t\lambda\,du(\lambda) + \int_0^{\pi} \sin t\lambda\,dv(\lambda) \qquad (10.23)$$

---

[45] Continuity is an overly strong assumption and is not strictly required. Its assertion, however, makes the proof of the proposition quite simple.

Notice further that

$$f(-\lambda) = f(\lambda) \tag{10.24}$$

It can also be shown that in (10.15) we have the additional relation,

$$g(\lambda) = E[du(\lambda)\,du(\lambda)] = E[dv(\lambda)\,dv(\lambda)]$$
$$E[du(\lambda)\,dv(\lambda)] = 0 \tag{10.25}$$

Thus,

$$g(\lambda) = 2f(\lambda) \tag{10.26}$$

Perhaps, since the processes $u(\lambda)$ and $v(\lambda)$ are essentially defined on $(0, \pi]$ and then extended symmetrically about zero, a better way of representing (10.26) would be

$$g(\lambda) = f(\lambda) + f(-\lambda), \quad \lambda \in (0, \pi] \tag{10.27}$$

10.3 Multivariate Stochastic Processes

If $\{X_\mu(t, \cdot): \mu = 1, 2, \ldots, m; t \in N\}$ is a set of time series having mean functions identically zero, the covariance kernel between the μth and νth process is defined by

$$K_{\mu\nu}(t, s) = E[X_\mu(t)X_\nu(s)] \tag{10.28}$$

Notation in this context is somewhat more delicate than in the previous section. Observe, in (10.28), that the subscripts and arguments of the covariance kernel correspond to the order in which the variables appear after the expectation operator. Thus, for example,

$$K_{\nu\mu}(t, s) = E[X_\nu(t)X_\mu(s)] \; not \; E[X_\nu(s)X_\mu(t)] \tag{10.29}$$

To simplify notation, we shall always denote $X_\mu(t, \cdot)$ by $X_\mu(t)$, except in the context of a definition.

For multiple time series, we have

DEFINITION 10.6. The set of stochastic processes $\{X_\mu(t, \cdot): \mu = 1, 2, \ldots, m; t \in N\}$ is said to be *jointly covariance stationary* if for every $\tau \in N$,

$$E[X_\mu(t + \tau)X_\nu(t)] = K_{\nu\mu}(\tau), \quad \mu, \nu = 1, 2, \ldots, m \tag{10.30}$$

REMARK 10.4. Since by convention all stochastic processes here have mean function identically zero, putting $\mu = \nu$, above, we have the definition of stationarity given in the previous section. Thus, with each $X_\mu(t, \cdot)$ is associated a process $\{Z_\mu(\lambda): \lambda \in (-\pi, \pi]\}$ such that

$$X_\mu(t) = \int_{-\pi}^{\pi} e^{i\lambda t} dZ_\mu(\lambda), \quad \mu = 1, 2, \ldots, m \tag{10.31}$$

Now in the previous section we saw that

$$E[dZ_\mu(\lambda)\overline{dZ_\mu(\lambda)}] = dF_{\mu\mu}(\lambda) \tag{10.32}$$

and the derivative of $F_{\mu\mu}(\cdot), f_{\mu\mu}(\cdot)$, was termed the spectral density function. Similarly, in the multiple time series case we have

$$\begin{aligned} E[dZ_\mu(\lambda)\overline{dZ_\nu(\lambda')}] &= dF_{\mu\nu}(\lambda) \quad \text{if } \lambda = \lambda' \\ &= 0 \quad \text{if } \lambda \neq \lambda' \end{aligned} \tag{10.33}$$

Again, we should caution the reader that the order of appearance of the quantities after the expectation operator in (10.33) is important. Thus, for example,

$$E[dZ_\nu(\lambda)\overline{dZ_\mu(\lambda)}] = dF_{\nu\mu}(\lambda) \tag{10.34}$$

We shall generally assume that the functions $F_{\mu\nu}(\cdot)$ are differentiable and denote their derivatives by $f_{\mu\nu}(\cdot)$. As before, we shall assume the $f_{\mu\nu}(\cdot)$ to be continuous functions of bounded variation on $[-\pi, \pi]$.

DEFINITION 10.7. The function $F_{\mu\nu}(\cdot)$, $\mu \neq \nu$, is termed the *cross-spectral distribution function*, associated with the μth and νth process. The function $f_{\mu\nu}(\cdot)$, $\mu \neq \nu$, is termed the *cross-spectral density function*. Since it is a complex function, we may write

$$f_{\mu\nu}(\lambda) = c_{\mu\nu}^*(\lambda) + i q_{\mu\nu}^*(\lambda) \tag{10.35}$$

where $c_{\mu\nu}^*(\cdot)$ and $q_{\mu\nu}^*(\lambda)$ are *real functions*. The latter are termed, respectively, the *cospectrum* and *quadrature spectrum*, associated with the μth and νth processes.

What is the relation between cross spectra and covariance kernels, and what are the properties of the former? First, we note that

$$\begin{aligned} K_{\mu\nu}(\tau) &= E[X_\mu(t + \tau) X_\nu(t)] \\ &= E\left[\int_{-\pi}^{\pi} \int_{-\pi}^{\pi} e^{i(t+\tau)\lambda} e^{-it\lambda'} dZ_\mu(\lambda)\overline{dZ_\mu(\lambda')}\right] \\ &= \int_{-\pi}^{\pi} e^{i\tau\lambda} f_{\mu\nu}(\lambda) \, d\lambda \end{aligned} \tag{10.36}$$

From this, we conclude that $K_{\mu\nu}(\tau)$ is the τth (complex) Fourier coefficient of $f_{\mu\nu}(\lambda)$. Since the latter is assumed to be a continuous function of bounded variation, we have

$$f_{\mu\nu}(\lambda) = \frac{1}{2\pi} \sum_{\tau=-\infty}^{\infty} e^{-i\tau\lambda} K_{\mu\nu}(\tau) \qquad (10.37)$$

Thus, the *cross-spectral densities and covariance kernels form pairs of Fourier transforms*.

Let us now explore some of the properties of these quantities. In the previous section we saw that

$$K_{\mu\mu}(\tau) = K_{\mu\mu}(-\tau) \qquad (10.38)$$

Does this hold for the (cross) covariance kernels $K_{\mu\nu}(\cdot)$, $\mu \neq \nu$? The answer is no. Thus, observe that

$$
\begin{aligned}
K_{\mu\nu}(-\tau) &= E[X_\mu(t-\tau)X_\nu(t)] = E[X_\mu(s)X_\nu(s+\tau)] \\
&= E[X_\nu(s+\tau)X_\mu(s)] = K_{\nu\mu}(\tau) \qquad (10.39)
\end{aligned}
$$

where we have made the change of index $s = t - \tau$. Next, consider

$$
\begin{aligned}
2\pi f_{\mu\nu}(-\lambda) &= \sum_{\tau=-\infty}^{\infty} e^{i\tau\lambda} K_{\mu\nu}(\tau) = \sum_{\tau=-\infty}^{\infty} e^{-i\tau\lambda} K_{\mu\nu}(-\tau) \\
&= \sum_{\tau=-\infty}^{\infty} e^{-i\tau\lambda} K_{\nu\mu}(\tau) = 2\pi f_{\nu\mu}(\lambda) \qquad (10.40)
\end{aligned}
$$

The second equality sign is obtained by changing τ to $-\tau$. Finally,

$$
\begin{aligned}
\overline{2\pi f_{\mu\nu}(\lambda)} &= \sum_{\tau=-\infty}^{\infty} e^{i\tau\lambda} K_{\mu\nu}(\tau) \\
&= \sum_{\tau=-\infty}^{\infty} e^{-i\tau\lambda} K_{\mu\nu}(-\tau) = 2\pi f_{\nu\mu}(\lambda) \qquad (10.41)
\end{aligned}
$$

Again, the second equality follows by changing τ to $-\tau$.

Thus we conclude that

$$\overline{f_{\mu\nu}(\lambda)} = f_{\mu\nu}(-\lambda) = f_{\nu\mu}(\lambda) \qquad (10.42)$$

What does this imply for the cospectra and quadrature spectra? From (10.35), we see that

$$
\begin{aligned}
\overline{f_{\mu\nu}(\lambda)} &= c_{\mu\nu}^*(\lambda) - iq_{\mu\nu}^*(\lambda) \\
&= f_{\mu\nu}(-\lambda) = c_{\mu\nu}^*(-\lambda) + iq_{\mu\nu}^*(-\lambda) \qquad (10.43)
\end{aligned}
$$

whence we conclude that

$$c_{\mu\nu}^*(-\lambda) = c_{\mu\nu}^*(\lambda), \quad q_{\mu\nu}^*(-\lambda) = -q_{\mu\nu}^*(\lambda) \qquad (10.44)$$

The second equality in (10.42) implies

$$c_{\mu\nu}^*(\lambda) = c_{\nu\mu}^*(\lambda), \quad q_{\mu\nu}^*(\lambda) = -q_{\nu\mu}^*(\lambda) \tag{10.45}$$

Thus, the spectral matrix, F^*, obeys[46]

$$F^* = C^* + iQ^*, \quad \bar{F}^{*\prime} = F^* \tag{10.46}$$

where

$$F^* = [f_{\mu\nu}(\lambda)], \quad C^* = [c_{\mu\nu}^*(\lambda)], \quad Q^* = [q_{\mu\nu}^*(\lambda)] \tag{10.47}$$

The second equation in (10.46) indicates that F^* is a Hermitian matrix; (10.45) indicates that C^* and Q^* are, respectively, symmetric and skew symmetric.

REMARK 10.5. The development above shows that, for real covariance stationary processes, the cross-spectra and quadrature spectra need be defined only on $(0, \pi]$.

In fact, one can show that the processes $\{Z_\mu(\lambda): \lambda \in (-\pi, \pi]; \; \mu = 1, 2, \ldots, m\}$ can be written as

$$Z_\mu(\lambda) = \frac{1}{2}[u_\mu(\lambda) - iv_\mu(\lambda)] \tag{10.48}$$

such that

$$u_\mu(-\lambda) = u_\mu(\lambda), \quad v_\mu(-\lambda) = -v_\mu(-\lambda), \quad \lambda \in (0, \pi] \tag{10.49}$$

and

$$E[du_\mu(\lambda)du_\mu(\theta)] = E[dv_\mu(\lambda)dv_\mu(\theta)] = \delta_{\lambda\theta} \, dG_{\mu\mu}(\lambda) \tag{10.50}$$

$\delta_{\lambda\theta}$ being the Kronecker delta. In addition,

$$E[du_\mu(\lambda)du_\nu(\theta)] = E[dv_\mu(\lambda)dv_\nu(\theta)] = \delta_{\lambda\theta}c_{\mu\nu}(\lambda)$$
$$E[du_\mu(\lambda)dv_\nu(\theta)] = -E[dv_\mu(\lambda)du_\nu(\theta)] = \delta_{\lambda\theta}q_{\mu\nu}(\lambda) \tag{10.51}$$

Thus,

$$f_{\mu\nu}(\lambda) = c_{\mu\nu}^*(\lambda) + iq_{\mu\nu}^*(\lambda) = E[dZ_\mu(\lambda)\overline{dZ_\nu(\lambda)}]$$
$$= \frac{1}{2}[c_{\mu\nu}(\lambda) + iq_{\mu\nu}(\lambda)] = \frac{1}{2}g_{\mu\nu}(\lambda) \tag{10.52}$$

where $g_{\mu\nu}(\cdot)$ is the derivative of $G_{\mu\nu}(\cdot)$. It is then convenient to write

---

[46] The notation $\bar{F}^{*\prime}$ indicates the transpose of a matrix whose elements are the *complex conjugates* of the elements of F^*.

$$c_{\mu\nu}(\lambda) = c_{\mu\nu}^*(\lambda) + c_{\mu\nu}^*(-\lambda), \quad q_{\mu\nu}(\lambda) = q_{\lambda\nu}^*(\lambda) - q_{\mu\nu}^*(-\lambda),$$

$$g_{\mu\nu}(\lambda) = f_{\mu\nu}(\lambda) + f_{\mu\nu}(-\lambda) \tag{10.53}$$

While the double notation, e.g. $c_{\mu\nu}^*$ and $c_{\mu\nu}$ etc., may create some confusion initially, it is best introduced at this level. In the literature of time series analysis one customarily deals with complex processes, and the reader is prone to encounter the notation of Equations (10.35) through (10.47). Finally, we ought to stress again that for *real covariance stationary processes*, the spectral representation involves an integral over $(0, \pi]$, and that the elements of the spectral matrix

$$G = C + iQ, \quad G = [g_{\mu\nu}(\lambda)],$$

$$C = [c_{\mu\nu}(\lambda)], \quad Q = [q_{\mu\nu}(\lambda)] \tag{10.54}$$

need be defined only over $(0, \pi]$.

Before we conclude this section, it is useful to introduce

DEFINITION 10.8. Let $\{X(t, \cdot): t \in T\}$ be a stochastic process, and consider

$$Y_t = \sum_{\tau=0}^{\infty} \varphi_\tau X_{t-\tau} \tag{10.55}$$

The two processes (Y and X) are said to be connected by a *linear time invariant filter* with kernel $\{\varphi_\tau : \tau = 0, 1, 2, \ldots,\}; X, Y$ are said to be, respectively, the *input* and *output* processes.

REMARK 10.6. Time invariance, in the context above, means that the elements of the sequence do not depend on t. The meaning of linearity is quite obvious from (10.55).

We have

PROPOSITION 10.2. Let $\{x(t, \cdot): t \in N\}$ be a (real) covariance stationary process, and define the process $\{y(t, \cdot): t \in N\}$ by

$$y_t = \sum_{\tau=0}^{\infty} \varphi_\tau x_{t-\tau} \tag{10.56}$$

Then the y process is also covariance stationary; moreover,

$$f_{yy}(\theta) = |\Phi(\lambda)|^2 f_{xx}(\lambda), \quad f_{yx}(\lambda) = \Phi(\lambda) f_{xx}(\lambda) \tag{10.57}$$

where $f_{yy}(\cdot), f_{xx}(\cdot)$ are, respectively, the spectral densities of the y and x processes, and

$$\Phi(\lambda) = \sum_{\tau=0}^{\infty} \varphi_\tau e^{-i\tau\lambda} \tag{10.58}$$

Proof. Since the x process is covariance stationary, it has the spectral representation

$$x_t = \int_{-\pi}^{\pi} e^{it\lambda} dZ_x(\lambda) \qquad (10.59)$$

the Z process having the properties discussed at the beginning of this section. Hence we have

$$y_t = \sum_{\tau=0}^{\infty} \varphi_\tau x_{t-\tau} = \sum_{\tau=0}^{\infty} \varphi_\tau \int_{-\pi}^{\pi} e^{i(t-\tau)\lambda} dZ_x(\lambda)$$

$$= \int_{-\pi}^{\pi} e^{it\lambda} dZ_y(\lambda) \qquad (10.60)$$

where

$$dZ_y(\lambda) = \Phi(\lambda) dZ_x(\lambda) \qquad (10.61)$$

Next consider

$$E(y_{t+\tau} y_t) = E\left[\int_{-\pi}^{\pi} \int_{-\pi}^{\pi} e^{i(t+\tau)\theta} e^{-it\lambda} dZ_y(\theta) \overline{dZ_y(\lambda)} \right]$$

$$= \int_{-\pi}^{\pi} e^{i\tau\lambda} f_{yy}(\lambda) \, d\lambda \qquad (10.62)$$

where

$$E[dZ_y(\lambda) \overline{dZ_y(\lambda)}] = |\Phi(\lambda)|^2 f_{xx}(\lambda) d\lambda \qquad (10.63)$$

Thus,

$$E(y_{t+\tau} y_t) = K_{yy}(\tau), \quad K_{yy}(\tau) = K_{yy}(-\tau) \qquad (10.64)$$

Finally, the cross-spectrum of y and x is given by

$$f_{yx}(\lambda) \, d\lambda = E[dZ_y(\lambda) \overline{dZ_x(\lambda)}] = \Phi(\lambda) f_{xx}(\lambda) \, d\lambda \qquad (10.65)$$

which completes the proof of the proposition.

Before we conclude this section, it would be useful to give an indication of how z-transform methods, introduced in Chapter 1, may be applied in the problems under consideration here.[47]

Thus, let $\{x(t; \cdot): t \in N\}$ and $\{y(t; \cdot): t \in N\}$ be two processes as in Proposition 10.1. Then the y process is also covariance stationary, and its covariance kernel is given by

$$K_{yy}(\tau) = \sum_{s=0}^{\infty} \sum_{s=0}^{\infty} \varphi_s \varphi_{s'} K_{xx}(\tau + s' - s) \qquad (10.66)$$

---

[47] It would appear that the first application of z-transform methods in an econometric context is to be found in Phillips [128].

where $K_{xx}(\cdot)$ is the covariance kernel of the x process.

Taking the z-transform of both sides of (10.66), we obtain

$$K_{yy}(z) = \sum_{\tau=-\infty}^{\infty} K_{yy}(\tau)z^\tau$$

$$= \sum_{\tau=-\infty}^{\infty} \sum_{s=0}^{\infty} \sum_{s'=0}^{\infty} \varphi_s z^s \varphi_{s'} z^{-s'} K_{xx}(\tau + s' - s)z^{\tau+s'-s} \qquad (10.67)$$

Make the change in indices

$$\tau' = \tau + s' - s, \quad s' = s', \quad s = s \qquad (10.68)$$

and thus conclude

$$K_{yy}(z) = \Phi(z)\Phi(z^{-1})K_{xx}(z) \qquad (10.69)$$

Since, for $z = e^{i\theta}$

$$\frac{1}{2\pi}K_{yy}(z) = f_{yy}(\theta) \qquad (10.70)$$

we find that

$$f_{yy}(\theta) = \Phi(e^{i\theta})\Phi(e^{-i\theta})f_{xx}(\theta) = |\Phi(\theta)|^2 f_{xx}(\theta) \qquad (10.71)$$

Similarly, consider the cross-covariance kernel

$$K_{xy}(\tau) = \sum_{s=0}^{\infty} \varphi_s K_{xx}(\tau + s) \qquad (10.72)$$

Obtaining the z-transform, we find

$$K_{xy}(z) = \sum_{\tau=0}^{\infty} K_{xy}(\tau)z^\tau = \sum_{\tau=-\infty}^{\infty} \sum_{s=0}^{\infty} \varphi_s z^{-s} K_{xx}(\tau + s)z^{\tau+s}$$

$$= \Phi(z^{-1})K_{xx}(z) \qquad (10.73)$$

Since[48] for $z = e^{-i\theta}$

---

[48] In Chapter 1 we remarked that the z-transform is defined in terms of z^{-1}, so that, e.g., the z-transform of the autocovariance kernel of the x process should have been

$$K_{xx}(z) = \sum_{\tau=-\infty}^{\infty} K_{xx}(\tau)z^{-\tau}$$

The relation in (10.74) makes clear why this is convenient expression. If the z-transform in (10.73) were defined in terms of z^{-1}, then (10.74) would have been evaluated at $z = e^{i\theta}$, which would have conformed with the practice in (10.70). Actually, in (10.70), it makes no difference whether $z = e^{i\theta}$ or $z = e^{-i\theta}$ is used. We have chosen, in this book, to define the z-transform in terms of z for typographical convenience only.

$$\frac{1}{2\pi} K_{xy}(z) = f_{xy}(z) \tag{10.74}$$

we conclude that

$$f_{xy}(\theta) = \overline{\Phi}(\theta) f_{xx}(\theta) \tag{10.75}$$

REMARK 10.7. The discussion above may be construed as an alternative proof of Proposition 10.1 and is presented here in order to acquaint the reader with the usefulness of this approach. Little further use will be made in the discussion to follow.

10.4 Estimation of the Spectral Matrix

In the preceding section we saw that the cross-spectrum and (cross) covariance kernel of two jointly covariance stationary processes, $X_\mu(t, \cdot)$ and $X_\nu(t, \cdot)$, form a pair of Fourier transforms. In particular,

$$f_{\mu\nu}(\lambda) = \frac{1}{2\pi} \sum_{\tau=-\infty}^{\infty} K_{\mu\nu}(\tau) e^{-i\tau\lambda} \tag{10.76}$$

A natural estimator for the ordinates of this function is the so-called *cross-periodogram*,

$$P_{\mu\nu}^{(n)}(\lambda) = \frac{1}{2\pi n} \left[\sum_{t=1}^{n} X_\mu(t) e^{-it\lambda} \right] \left[\sum_{s=1}^{n} X_\nu(s) e^{is\lambda} \right]$$

$$= \frac{1}{2\pi} \sum_{\tau=-n}^{n} \hat{K}_{\mu\nu}(\tau) e^{-i\tau\lambda} \tag{10.77}$$

where we define

$$\hat{K}_{\mu\nu}(\tau) = \frac{1}{n} \sum_{t=1}^{n-\tau} X_\mu(t+\tau) X_\nu(t) \qquad \text{if } \tau \geq 0$$

$$= \frac{1}{n} \sum_{t=-\tau+1}^{n} X_\nu(t+\tau) X_\mu(t) \quad \text{if } \tau < 0 \tag{10.78}$$

Notice that the second definition in (10.78) is really $\hat{K}_{\nu\mu}(\tau)$. But we saw earlier that $K_{\mu\nu}(-\tau) = K_{\nu\mu}(\tau)$, and the definitions in (10.78) preserve this relation. By convention, and only in order to simplify the notation, we have put

$$\hat{K}_{\mu\nu}(-n) = \hat{K}_{\mu\nu}(n) = 0 \tag{10.79}$$

Unfortunately, however, the (cross) periodogram, while an asymptotically unbiased estimator of the (cross) spectral ordinates, is an inconsistent one.[49] Consistent estimators can be obtained by the use of so-called *spectral window generators*. If $a(\cdot)$ is such a generator, a consistent estimator is given by

$$\hat{f}_{\mu\nu}(\lambda) = \frac{1}{2\pi} \sum_{\tau=-n}^{n} a\left(\frac{\tau}{m}\right) \hat{K}_{\mu\nu}(\tau) e^{-i\tau\lambda} \tag{10.80}$$

m being the maximal lagged (cross) autocovariance employed. In most applications, one usually takes $m \approx n^{1/2}$.

A spectral window generator has the properties

$$a(0) = 1, \quad |a(\theta)| \leq 1, \quad \theta \in [-1, 1] \tag{10.81}$$

Many spectral window generators have been suggested in the literature. Unfortunately, numerous issues remain unresolved in the choice of windows and more generally in the efficient estimation of (cross) spectral ordinates. Such issues, however, are not important in connection with the estimation of distributed lag models, and we shall not discuss them here. An example of a spectral window generator is the Parzen window, which has the useful property of insuring that estimated spectral ordinates are nonnegative. This window is defined by

$$a\left(\frac{\tau}{m}\right) = 1 - 6\left(\frac{\tau}{m}\right)^2 + 6\left|\frac{\tau}{m}\right|^3 \quad \text{if } \tau = 0, \pm 1, \pm 2, \ldots, \pm\left[\frac{m}{2}\right]$$

$$= 2\left(1 - \left|\frac{\tau}{m}\right|\right)^3 \quad \text{if } \tau = \pm\left\{\left[\frac{m}{2}\right] + 1\right\}, \ldots, \pm m$$

$$= 0 \quad \text{otherwise} \tag{10.82}$$

$[m/2]$ being the largest integer equal to or less than $m/2$.

The domain of the function $a(\cdot)$ is generally $[-1, 1]$, and the reader will notice that the window in (10.82) is defined to be zero outside that interval.

REMARK 10.8. One may study the properties of a stochastic process either in terms of its spectral density or in terms of its (auto) covariance kernel. The former is commonly referred to as consideration in the *frequency domain*, the latter as consideration in the *time domain*.

---

[49] For a discussion of this aspect see Dhrymes [32, ch. 10].

10.5 Estimation of the Geometric Lag Structure

Spectral analytic techniques in the estimation of distributed lags were first introduced by Hannan [66] in connection with the model

$$y_t = \alpha \sum_{j=0}^{\infty} \lambda^j x_{t-j} + u_t \tag{10.83}$$

where

$$u_t = \sum_{j=0}^{\infty} \alpha_j \varepsilon_{t-j} \tag{10.84}$$

the ε_t, $t = 0, \pm 1, \pm 2, ..$, being a sequence of *i.i.d.* random variables with mean zero, variance one and finite third (absolute) moment.

It can be shown that, under certain rather mild restrictions, *every covariance stationary process can be represented as in* (10.84). Thus we are dealing here with a very general specification, something we were unable to do in earlier discussions when we considered the estimation problem in the time domain. Regarding the coefficients of the process in (10.84), we assume that

$$\sum_{j=0}^{\infty} j|\alpha_j| < \infty \tag{10.85}$$

an assumption whose significance and role in the problem under consideration will become apparent below.

It will simplify the exposition considerably if, at this stage, we assume that the sequence $\{x_t : t = 0, \pm 1, \pm 2, ...\}$ is a covariance stationary process with mean zero, and that it is *independent of the error process*. The assumption of zero mean is innocuous; if the x process has a constant mean simply consider the centered observations, $y_t - \bar{y}, x_t - \bar{x}, \bar{x}, \bar{y}$, being the sample means. The assumption of covariance stationarity rules out explanatory variables containing time trends and is a restrictive one. However, it is not strictly needed for this development; indeed, it will be replaced by a less restrictive one in the following section, where we shall examine the asymptotic properties of the resulting estimator. For the moment, the more general conditions on the explanatory variable will merely render the exposition more cumbersome without benefit of clarification of the problems involved.

Now, observe that the covariance kernel of the error process is

$$K_u(\tau) = E(u_{t+\tau}u_t) = \sum_{j=0}^{\infty} \alpha_{j+\tau}\alpha_j \tag{10.86}$$

If we have n observations on the model, let

$$u = (u_1, u_2, \ldots, u_n)', \quad y = (y_1, y_2, \ldots, y_n)'$$

$$r = (r_1, r_2, \ldots, r_n)', \quad r_t = \alpha \sum_{j=0}^{\infty} \lambda^i x_{t-r} \tag{10.87}$$

and observe that

$$\text{Cov}(u) = \begin{bmatrix} K_u(0) & K_u(1) & \cdots & K_u(n-1) \\ K_u(1) & K_u(0) & \cdots & K_u(n-2) \\ \vdots & \vdots & \vdots & \vdots \\ K_u(n-1) & K_u(n-2) & & K_u(0) \end{bmatrix} = K_u \tag{10.88}$$

We may obtain Aitken estimators for the parameters α and λ by minimizing

$$S = (y - r)' K_u^{-1}(y - r) \tag{10.89}$$

The reader should notice that the r and x processes are connected—as output and input respectively—by a *linear time invariant filter* with kernel $\{\alpha \lambda^i : i = 0, 1, 2, \ldots\}$.

By Proposition 10.1, the r process is covariance stationary with spectral density

$$f_{rr}(\theta) = |\Phi(\theta)|^2 f_{xx}(\theta) \tag{10.90}$$

$f_{xx}(\cdot)$ being the spectral density of the x process, and

$$\Phi(\theta) = a \sum_{j=0}^{\infty} \lambda^j e^{-ij\theta} = \frac{\alpha}{1 - '\lambda e^{-i\theta}} \tag{10.91}$$

The spectral density of the y process is given by

$$f_{yy}(\theta) = |\Phi(\theta)|^2 f_{xx}(\theta) + f_{uu}(\theta) \tag{10.92}$$

$f_{uu}(\cdot)$ being the spectral density of the error process. In fact,

$$f_{uu}(\theta) = \frac{1}{2\pi} \left| \sum_{j=0}^{\infty} \alpha_j e^{-ij\theta} \right|^2 \tag{10.93}$$

The cross-spectral density between the x and y processes is

$$f_{xy}(\theta) = \overline{\Phi}(\theta) f_{xx}(\theta) \tag{10.94}$$

since the x and u processes are mutually independent. Of course,

$$f_{yx}(\theta) = \Phi(\theta) f_{xx}(\theta) \tag{10.95}$$

We also have

$$f_{ry}(\theta) = f_{yr}(\theta) = |\Phi(\theta)|^2 f_{xx}(\theta) = \Phi(\theta) f_{xy}(\theta) \qquad (10.96)$$

Finally, there is another relation in connection with the matrix K_u which is of fundamental importance to the development of this topic. It may be shown that there exists a unitary matrix[50] V, such that $(1/2\pi)V^*K_uV$ is a diagonal matrix whose elements are certain spectral ordinates of the u process. We shall give a brief account of this below; for a fuller discussion, the reader is referred to Wahba [146].

Recalling the relation in (10.86) we observe that

$$|\tau|K_u(\tau) = |\tau| \left| \sum_{j=0}^{\infty} \alpha_{j+\tau}\,\alpha_j \right|$$

$$\leq \sum_{j=0}^{\infty} (|j+\tau|\,|\alpha_{j+\tau}|\,|\alpha_j| + j|\alpha_{j+\tau}|\,|\alpha_j|) \qquad (10.97)$$

Thus,

$$\sum_{\tau=-\infty}^{\infty} |\tau|\,|K_u(\tau)| \leq \sum_{\tau=-\infty}^{\infty} \sum_{j=0}^{\infty} |j+\tau|\,|\alpha_{j+\tau}|\,|\alpha_j| + \sum_{\tau=-\infty}^{\infty} \sum_{j=0}^{\infty} j|\alpha_{j+\tau}|\,|\alpha_j|$$

$$= 2\left(\sum_{j=0}^{\infty} j|\alpha_j|\right)\left(\sum_{j=0}^{\infty} |\alpha_j|\right) < \infty \qquad (10.98)$$

The last inequality holds in view of (10.85).

Since

$$f_{uu}(\theta) = \frac{1}{2\pi} \sum_{\tau=-\infty}^{\infty} K_u(\tau)e^{-i\tau\theta} \qquad (10.99)$$

the condition in (10.98) implies that the derivative of $f_{uu}(\cdot)$ exists and is *bounded*. We shall also make the additional, rather innocuous assumption that $f_{uu}(\cdot)$ is bounded away from zero, i.e. that

$$f_{uu}(\theta) > 0, \quad \theta \in (-\pi, \pi] \qquad (10.100)$$

For the purpose of the discussion immediately following, it would be convenient to define the spectral density over $(0, 2\pi]$ instead of $(-\pi, \pi)$. This involves no difficulty whatsoever, since from (10.99) we have

---

[50] A matrix A is said to be *unitary* if $A^* = A^{-1}$, where $A^* = \overline{A}'$, i.e. if it is the transpose of the matrix whose elements are the complex conjugates of the elements of A. If A is *real*, then the relation $A^* = A^{-1}$ indicates that A is orthogonal, and we see that a unitary matrix over the field of complex numbers is the analog of an orthogonal matrix over the field of real numbers.

$$f_{uu}(\theta + 2\pi) = \frac{1}{2\pi} \sum_{\tau=-\infty}^{\infty} K_u(\tau) e^{-i\tau(\theta+2\pi)}$$

$$= \frac{1}{2\pi} \sum_{\tau=-\infty}^{\infty} K_u(\tau) e^{-i\tau\theta} = f_{uu}(\theta) \qquad (10.101)$$

Thus $f_{uu}(\theta)$, for $\theta \in (-\pi, 0]$, yields exactly the same values as for $\theta \in (\pi, 2\pi]$.

Return now to the matrix V, define its elements by

$$v_{ts} = \frac{1}{\sqrt{n}} e^{i(2\pi/n)ts}, \quad t, s = 1, 2, \dots, n \qquad (10.102)$$

and consider the (r, α) element of the matrix $V^* K V$. It is given by

$$\frac{1}{n} \sum_{t=1}^{n} \sum_{s=1}^{n} e^{-i(2\pi/n)rt} K_u(t - s) e^{i(2\pi/n)s\alpha}$$

$$= \sum_{\tau=-n+1}^{n-1} \left(1 - \frac{|\tau|}{n}\right) K_u(\tau) e^{-i(2\pi\alpha/n)\tau}, \qquad \text{if } \alpha = r$$

$$= \frac{1}{n} \sum_{\tau=-n+1}^{n-1} K_u(\tau) e^{-i(2\pi\alpha/n)\tau} \sum_{v=0}^{n-|\tau|-1} e^{-i(2\pi/n)(n-v)(r-\alpha)}, \text{ if } \alpha \neq r \quad (10.103)$$

In the case $\alpha = r$, the right member of (10.103) converges to $2\pi f_{uu}(\theta)$, where $\theta \in (0, 2\pi]$. If $r \neq \alpha$, however, we find that

$$\sum_{v=0}^{n-|\tau|-1} \exp\left[-i\frac{2\pi}{n}(n-v)(r-\alpha)\right] = \frac{e^{-i(|\tau|+1)\varphi} - e^{-i(n+1)\varphi}}{1 - e^{-i\varphi}},$$

$$\varphi = \frac{2\pi}{n}(r - \alpha) \qquad (10.104)$$

As $n \to \infty$, this quantity converges to $-|\tau|$. Thus[51]

$$\lim_{n\to\infty} \frac{1}{n} \sum_{\tau=-n+1}^{n-1} K_u(\tau) \exp\left(-i\frac{2\pi\alpha\tau}{n}\right) \sum_{v=0}^{n-|\tau|-1} \exp\left[-i\frac{2\pi}{n}(n-v)(r-\alpha)\right]$$

$$= -\lim_{n\to\infty} \frac{1}{n} \sum_{\tau=-n+1}^{n-1} |\tau| K_u(\tau) \exp\left(-i\frac{2\pi\alpha}{n}\tau\right) = 0 \qquad (10.105)$$

---

[51] The last equality in (10.105) holds in virtue of (10.98), which in turn is valid because of (10.85). This shows the role played by the latter in the development of this topic.

Hence if n is large enough, the approximation

$$V^* K_u V \approx 2\pi \, \text{diag} \left[f_{uu}\left(\frac{2\pi}{n}\right), \, f_{uu}\left(\frac{4\pi}{n}\right), \, \ldots, f_{uu}(2\pi) \right] \qquad (10.106)$$

can be made sufficiently accurate, element by element. In fact, Wahba [146] has also shown that the sum of absolute values of the differences of all elements of the matrices in either side of (10.106) can be made arbitrarily small.[53]

Using the results of the preceding development, we see that

$$K_u^{-1} = V V^* K_u^{-1} V V^* \approx V D V^* \qquad (10.107)$$

where

$$D = \frac{1}{2\pi} \, \text{diag} \left[\frac{1}{f_{uu}(\theta_1)}, \, \ldots, \frac{1}{f_{uu}(\theta_n)} \right]$$

$$\theta_j = \frac{2\pi j}{n}, \quad j = 1, 2, \ldots, n \qquad (10.108)$$

Hence the minimand of (10.79) can be rewritten as

$$S = (y - r)' V D V^* (y - r) \qquad (10.109)$$

The αth element of the vector $V^*(y - r)$ is seen to be

$$J_n(\theta_\alpha; y) - J_n(\theta_\alpha; r) = \frac{1}{\sqrt{n}} \sum_{t=1}^n e^{-(2\pi i \alpha/n)t} y_t - \frac{1}{\sqrt{n}} \sum_{t=1}^n e^{(2\pi i \alpha/n)t} r_t \quad (10.110)$$

and S is thus the sum of n terms:

$$S = \frac{1}{2\pi} \sum_{\alpha=1}^n \left\{ \frac{|J_n(\theta_\alpha); y - J_n(\theta_\alpha; r)|^2}{f_{uu}(\theta_\alpha)} \right\} \qquad (10.111)$$

Next, observe that

$$\frac{1}{2\pi} |J_n(\theta_\alpha; y)|^2 = P_{yy}^{(n)}(\theta_\alpha) \qquad (10.112)$$

i.e. it is the periodogram of the y process; similarly,

---

[53] This is a matter of some import, since it is possible that, element by element, the differences of the two matrices may be small, while the sum of all such absolute differences diverges. Notice that we are adding n^2 elements. It is, in part, for this reason that the assumption in (10.85) is required. Otherwise, we could do with the weaker assumption $\sum_{j=0}^\infty |\alpha_j| < \infty$

$$\frac{1}{2\pi} J_n(\theta_\alpha; y)\overline{J_n(\theta_\alpha; r)} = P_{yr}^{(n)}(\theta_\alpha) \tag{10.113}$$

is the cross-periodogram of the y and r processes, and

$$\frac{1}{2\pi} |J_n(\theta_\alpha; r)|^2 = P_{rr}^{(n)}(\theta_\alpha) \tag{10.114}$$

is the periodogram of the r process.

Notice that up to this point all we have done is to rewrite the minimand using the approximation

$$V^* K_u^{-1} V \approx D \tag{10.115}$$

which will be accurate to any desired degree if n is sufficiently large.

Since $f_{uu}(\cdot)$ is boundedly differentiable, it is not unreasonable to suppose that it is approximately constant over a band of frequencies of length π/m, m large. Hence we can average the numerator over this band. However, it was shown by Bartlett [9] that such averages of (cross) periodograms converge in probability to the corresponding spectral and cross-spectral densities. To make this intuitively meaningful to the reader, suppose $m \approx n^{1/2}$; consequently over a band of length π/m there are approximately $n^{1/2}/2$ points θ_α. The average, then, has variance that vanishes as $n \to \infty$, and it is this feature that produces consistency.

Once this is noted, one should also observe that the numerator may be replaced by any (windowed) consistent estimator of the spectral and cross-spectral densities—in particular, the one induced by the Parzen window discussed in the preceding section; we recall that this window has the desirable property of always yielding nonnegative estimators of spectral density ordinates.

Since

$$\Phi(\theta) = \frac{\alpha}{1 - \lambda e^{-i\theta}} \tag{10.116}$$

we may write the minimand in the form

$$S = \frac{1}{2\pi}$$

$$\times \sum_{j=-m+1}^{m} \left[\frac{\hat{f}_{yy}(\theta_j) - 2\alpha(1 - \lambda e^{i\theta_j})^{-1} \hat{f}_{xy}(\theta_j) + \alpha^2 |1 - \lambda e^{-i\theta_j}|^{-2} \hat{f}_{xx}(\theta_j)}{f_{uu}(\theta_j)} \right] \tag{10.117}$$

In the preceding $\hat{f}_{yy}, \hat{f}_{xy}, \hat{f}_{yx}, \hat{f}_{xx}$ are consistent estimators of the corresponding spectral and cross-spectral quantities; we have also reverted to the definition of the spectrum over $(-\pi, \pi]$, The index of summation runs over $[-m + 1, m]$, since over the interval $(0, \pi]$ there are m bands of length π/m, and from each we select a point.

Finally, the points θ_j are chosen so that $\theta_{-j} = -\theta_j$, thus covering the interval $(-\pi, 0]$ as well; in particular, we take $\theta_j = \pi j/m$, $j = -m + 1, -m + 2, \ldots, m$.

In view of the definitions of the relevant quantities, we note that

$$\sum_{j=-m+1}^{m} \left[\frac{\hat{f}_{yx}(\theta_j)}{(1 - \lambda e^{i\theta_j})f_{uu}(\theta_j)} \right] = \sum_{j=-m+1}^{m} \left[\frac{\hat{f}_{xy}(\theta_j)}{(1 - \lambda e^{-i\theta_j})f_{uu}(\theta_j)} \right] \quad (10.118)$$

Hence, minimizing (10.117) with respect to α and λ, we find

$$\frac{\partial S}{\partial \alpha} = \frac{2}{2\pi}\alpha \sum_{j=-m+1}^{m} \left\{ \frac{\hat{f}_{xx}(\theta_j)}{|1 - \lambda e^{i\theta_j}|^2 f_{uu}(\theta_j)} \right\}$$

$$- \frac{2}{2\pi} \sum_{j=-m+1}^{m} \left\{ \frac{\hat{f}_{xy}(\theta_j)}{(1 - \lambda e^{-i\theta_j})f_{uu}(\theta_j)} \right\} = 0 \quad (10.119)$$

$$\frac{\partial S}{\partial \lambda} = \frac{2}{2\pi}\alpha^2 \sum_{j=-m+1}^{m} \left\{ \frac{(1 - \lambda e^{i\theta_j})e^{-i\theta_j}\hat{f}_{xx}(\theta_j)}{|1 - \lambda e^{i\theta_j}|^4 f_{uu}(\theta_j)} \right\}$$

$$- \frac{2}{2\pi}\alpha \sum_{j=-m+1}^{m} \left\{ \frac{\hat{f}_{xy}(\theta_j)e^{-i\theta_j}}{(1 - \lambda e^{-i\theta_j})^2 f_{uu}(\theta_j)} \right\} = 0 \quad (10.120)$$

Notice that if we define

$$u_t^* = (I - \lambda L)u_t \quad (10.121)$$

then the spectral density of the u^* process is given by

$$f_{**}(\theta) = |1 - \lambda e^{i\theta}|^2 f_{uu}(\theta) \quad (10.122)$$

and this is a quantity that occurs repeatedly in the normal equations above. By a slight rearrangement we may rewrite these equations as

$$\alpha \sum_{j=-m+1}^{m} \left[\frac{\hat{f}_{xx}(\theta_j)}{\hat{f}_{**}(\theta_j)} \right] + \lambda \sum_{j=-m+1}^{m} \left[\frac{\hat{f}_{xy}(\theta_j)e^{i\theta_j}}{\hat{f}_{**}(\theta_j)} \right] = \sum_{j=-m+1}^{m} \left[\frac{\hat{f}_{xy}(\theta_j)}{\hat{f}_{**}(\theta_j)} \right]$$

$$\alpha \sum_{j=-m+1}^{m} \left[\frac{\hat{f}_{xx}(\theta_j)e^{-i\theta_j}}{(1 - \lambda e^{-i\theta_j})\hat{f}_{**}(\theta_j)} \right] + \lambda \sum_{j=-m+1}^{m} \left[\frac{\hat{f}_{xy}(\theta_j)}{(1 - \lambda e^{-i\theta_j})\hat{f}_{**}(\theta_j)} \right]$$

$$= \sum_{j=-m+1}^{m} \left[\frac{\hat{f}_{xy}(\theta_j)e^{-i\theta_j}}{(1 - \lambda e^{-i\theta_j})\hat{f}_{**}(\theta_j)} \right] \quad (10.123)$$

In the equations above, $\hat{f}_{**}(\theta_j)$ represents a consistent estimator of the spectral density of the u^* process. We shall indicate later how it may be obtained. For the moment, however, observe that the second equation of (10.123) is nonlinear in λ. If a prior, consistent, estimate of λ is obtained, say $\tilde{\lambda}$, and if it is substituted in the denominators of the second equation in lieu of λ, then the system is easily soluble and one obtains the estimators $\hat{\alpha}$, $\hat{\lambda}$.

Before we deal with the properties of these estimators, let us examine the procedure somewhat more closely.

First, consider the reduced model,

$$y_t = \alpha x_t + \lambda y_{t-1} + u_t^* \qquad (10.124)$$

and use the instruments, say, x_t, x_{t-1} to obtain the IV estimators $\tilde{\alpha}$, $\tilde{\lambda}$. From the residuals

$$\tilde{u}_t^* = y_t - \tilde{\alpha} x_t - \tilde{\lambda} y_{t-1} \qquad (10.125)$$

one easily obtains a consistent estimator of the spectral density $f_{**}(\cdot)$.

Second, observe the extreme similarity between the normal equations in (10.123) and those corresponding to the prefiltering procedure, as exhibited in Equation (5.21). The only difference is that there, the error terms were assumed to be a sequence of *i.i.d.* random variables, while here they are assumed to be a general covariance stationary process.

Let us make this perfectly transparent. In what follows we shall deal with the spectral and cross-spectral quantities in (10.123), *not* with their estimators; hence we shall dispense with the carets. Now, observe that if $K_{xy}(\cdot)$ is the cross-covariance kernel of the x and y processes, we have

$$f_{xy}(\theta)e^{i\theta} = \frac{1}{2\pi} \sum_{\tau=-\infty}^{\infty} K_{xy}(\tau)e^{-i(\tau-1)\theta}$$

$$= \frac{1}{2\pi} \sum_{\tau=-\infty}^{\infty} K_{xy}(\tau+1)e^{-i\tau\theta} = f_{xy_{-1}}(\theta) \qquad (10.126)$$

i.e. it is the cross-spectrum between x_t and y_{t-1}. Similarly,

$$f_{xy}(\theta)e^{-i\theta} = \frac{1}{2\pi} \sum_{\tau=-\infty}^{\infty} K_{xy}(\tau)e^{-i(\tau+1)\theta}$$

$$= \frac{1}{2\pi} \sum_{\tau=-\infty}^{\infty} K_{xy}(\tau-1)e^{-i\tau\theta} = f_{x_{-1}y}(\theta) \qquad (10.127)$$

i.e. it is the cross-spectrum between x_{t-1} and y_t. Furthermore, if we define

$$x_t^* = \frac{I}{I - \lambda L} x_t, \quad x_t^{**} = \frac{I}{I - \lambda L} x_t^*, \quad y_t = \frac{I}{I - \lambda L} y_t \quad (10.128)$$

we find

$$f_{x^* x^*}(\theta) = |1 - \lambda e^{i\theta}|^{-2} f_{xx}(\theta)$$

$$f_{x^{**} x^*}(\theta) = (1 - \lambda e^{-i\theta})^{-1} |1 - \lambda e^{i\theta}|^{-2} f_{xx}(\theta)$$

$$f_{x^{**} y^*}(\theta) = (1 - \lambda e^{-i\theta})^{-1} |1 - \lambda e^{-i\theta}|^{-2} f_{xy}(\theta) \quad (10.129)$$

Hence (10.123) may be rewritten more suggestively as

$$\alpha \frac{1}{2m} \sum_{j=-m+1}^{m} \left[\frac{f_{x^* x^*}(\theta_j)}{f_{uu}(\theta_j)} \right] + \lambda \frac{1}{2m} \sum_{j=-m+1}^{m} \left[\frac{f_{x^* y^*}{}_{-1}(\theta)_j}{f_{uu}(\theta_j)} \right]$$

$$= \frac{1}{2m} \sum_{j=-m+1}^{m} \left[\frac{f_{x^* y^*}(\theta_j)}{f_{uu}(\theta_j)} \right] \quad (10.130)$$

$$\alpha \frac{1}{2m} \sum_{j=-m+1}^{m} \left[\frac{f_{x^{**}{}_{-1} x^*}(\theta_j)}{f_{uu}(\theta_j)} \right] + \lambda \frac{1}{2m} \sum_{j=-m+1}^{m} \left[\frac{f_{x^{**} y^*}(\theta_j)}{f_{uu}(\theta_j)} \right]$$

$$= \frac{1}{2m} \sum_{j=-m+1}^{m} \left[\frac{f_{x^{**}{}_{-1} y^*}(\theta_j)}{f_{uu}(\theta_j)} \right]$$

Now suppose the u process is one of *i.i.d.* random variables; then its spectrum is known to be

$$f_{uu}(\theta) = \frac{\sigma^2}{2\pi} \quad (10.131)$$

σ^2 being the common variance of the error terms. The equations in (10.130) now become

$$\frac{1}{2m} \left[\alpha \sum_{k=-m+1}^{m} f_{x^* x^*}(\theta_j) + \lambda \sum_{k=-m+1}^{m} f_{x^* y^*}{}_{-1}(\theta_j) \right]$$

$$= \frac{1}{2m} \sum_{j=-m+1}^{m} f_{x^* y^*}(\theta_j) \quad (10.132)$$

$$\frac{1}{2m} \left[\alpha \sum_{j=-m+1}^{m} f_{x^{**}{}_{-1} x^*}(\theta_j) + \lambda \sum_{j=-m+1}^{m} f_{x^{**} y^*}(\theta_j) \right]$$

$$= \frac{1}{2m} \sum_{j=-m+1}^{m} f_{x^{**}{}_{-1} y^*}(\theta_j)$$

If m is sufficiently large,

$$\frac{1}{2m} \sum_{j=-m+1}^{m} f_{x^*x^*}(\theta_j) \approx \int_{-\pi}^{\pi} f_{x^*x^*}(\theta)d\theta = K_{x^*x^*}(0) \qquad (10.133)$$

The approximation is valid since the first member of (10.133) is simply the Riemann sum corresponding to the integral. The last equality is valid in view of (10.36).

Hence, the relations in (10.132) essentially read

$$\alpha K_{x^*x^*}(0) + \lambda K_{x^*y_{-1}}*(0) = K_{x^*y}*(0)$$

$$\alpha K_{x_{-1}^**x^*}(0) + \lambda K_{x^**y}*(0) = K_{x_{-1}^**y}*(0) \qquad (10.134)$$

A comparison with Equation (5.21) *shows the two sets of relations to be exactly identical if* (10.134) *is interpreted in a sampling sense.*

If the error term is a general linear (covariance stationary) process, the presence of the term $f_{uu}(\cdot)$ in the denominators indicates that we are obtaining Aitken estimators. This may be seen, somewat heuristically, as follows. Since the matrix K_u of Equation (10.88) is positive definite, there exists a matrix H such that

$$K_u = H^{-1}H'^{-1} \qquad (10.135)$$

Now define a new process:

$$\bar{u}_t = \sum_{i=1}^{n} h_{tj}u_j \qquad (10.136)$$

If the ε process is assumed to be normal, then it is easy to see that

$$Hu = \varepsilon \qquad (10.137)$$

This is so since $Hu \sim N(0, I)$, which is exactly the property of the ε process.

Now we observe that the spectrum of $\bar{u}_t$ may be obtained as follows:

$$\bar{u}_t = \int_{-\pi}^{\pi} \sum_{i=1}^{n} h_{tj}e^{ij\theta} \, dZ_u(\theta) \qquad (10.138)$$

Hence,

$$f_{\bar{u}\bar{u}}(\theta) = \left| \sum_{j=1}^{n} h_{tj}e^{ij\theta} \right|^2 f_{uu}(\theta) \qquad (10.139)$$

since $f_{\bar{u}\bar{u}}(\theta) = 1/2\pi$, we conclude that

$$2\pi \left| \sum_{j=1}^{n} h_{tj}e^{ij\theta} \right|^2 = \frac{1}{f_{uu}(\theta)} \qquad (10.140)$$

Thus in (10.130) $f_{x^*x^*}(\theta)/f_{uu}(\theta)$ is the spectral density of $[I/I(-\lambda L)]\bar{x}_t$, where $\bar{x}_t = \lim_{n\to\infty} \sum_{j=1}^{n} h_{tj}x_j$, $f_{x^*y^*-1}(\theta)/f_{uu}(\theta)$ is the cross-spectral density of $[I/(I-\lambda L)]\bar{x}_t$ and $[I/(I-\lambda L)]\bar{y}_{t-1}$, $\bar{y}_t = \lim_{n\to\infty} \sum_{j=1}^{n} h_{tj}y_j$, and so on. The nonlinearity in the relations (10.123) is minimized by the fact that an estimator of $f_{**}(\cdot)$ can be obtained directly from the reduced model.

An estimator analogous to the iterative prefiltering estimator would result if, after we obtain an estimator—say $\hat{\alpha}^{(1)}$, $\hat{\lambda}^{(1)}$—from (10.123)—we recompute the residuals $\tilde{u}_t^{(1)} = y_t - \hat{\alpha}^{(1)}x_t - \hat{\lambda}^{(1)}y_{t-1}$, obtain another estimator of $f_{**}(\cdot)$, say $\hat{f}_{**}^{(1)}(\cdot)$, substitute $\hat{\lambda}^{(1)}$ and $\hat{f}_{**}^{(1)}(\cdot)$ in the denominators of (10.123) and solve again to obtain a second iterate $\hat{\alpha}^{(2)}$, $\hat{\lambda}^{(2)}$ and so on untill convergence is obtained.

Notice the wide scope afforded us by the application of spectral analysis to the problem. First, we see that we have a very close approximation to the equations defining the maximum likelihood estimator of α and λ when the error terms are normal *i.i.d.* random variables. Second instead of repeatedly computing the covariance quantities in (10.134) as we do in the prefiltering version of the maximum likelihood solution, we compute the spectral and cross-spectral densities $f_{xy}(\cdot), f_{xx}(\cdot), f_{**}(\cdot)$. This clearly entails a greater computational burden. On the other hand, if the error process is merely assumed to be covariance stationary, the problem entails too many (covariance) parameters, and it is not feasible to handle it by the usual (time domain) maximum likelihood or minimum chi square approaches. However, hardly anything more is required beyond the computations of the preceding paragraph if spectral techniques are employed. It is this feature that makes spectral analysis a very convenient and potentially useful adjunct to the solution of estimation problems that one typically encounters in econometrics.

Let us now recapitulate the development in this section: If we have the problem of estimating the parameters of

$$y_t = \alpha \sum_{\tau=0}^{\infty} \lambda^\tau x_{t-\tau} + u_t, \quad t = 1, 2, \ldots, n \qquad (10.141)$$

where $\{x_t : t = 0, \pm 1, \pm 2, \ldots\}$ is a covariance stationary process, with mean function identically zero, and

$$u_t = \sum_{j=0}^{\infty} \alpha_j \varepsilon_{t-j}, \quad \sum_{j=0}^{\infty} j|\alpha_j| < \infty \qquad (10.142)$$

If the ε's are a sequence of *i.i.d.* random variables with mean zero, variance one and finite third (absolute) moment, then:

(i) The problem of minimizing

$$S = (y - r)'K_u^{-1}(y - r) \tag{10.143}$$

where

$$r_t = \alpha \sum_{\tau=0}^{\infty} \lambda^\tau x_{t-\tau}, \qquad r = (r_1, r_2, \ldots, r_n)'$$

$$y = (y_1, y_2, \ldots, y_n)', \quad K_u = \text{Cov(u)} \tag{10.144}$$

is approximately equivalent to mimimizing

$$S =$$

$$\sum_{j=-m+1}^{m} \left[\frac{\hat{f}_{yy}(\theta_j) - 2\alpha(1 - \lambda e^{-i\theta_j})^{-1}\hat{f}_{xy}(\theta_j) + \alpha^2 |1 - \lambda e^{i\theta_j}|^{-2}\hat{f}_{xx}(\theta_j)}{f_{uu}(\theta_j)} \right]$$

$$\tag{10.145}$$

where a caret over a quantity indicates a corresponding consistent estimator; in (10.145) $\hat{f}_{yy}(\cdot), \hat{f}_{xx}(\cdot), \hat{f}_{xy}(\cdot)$ are, respectively, the (estimated) spectral densities of the y and x processes and their cross-spectral density; $f_{uu}(\cdot)$ is the spectral density of the u process. The points θ_j are defined by

$$\theta_j = \frac{\pi j}{m}, \quad j = -m+1, -m+2, \ldots, m \tag{10.146}$$

(ii) The minimizing conditions are given by (10.123) and are equivalent to the corresponding conditions when we deal with the problem in the time domain and employ the prefiltering procedure in solving the (nonlinear) normal equations of the minimum chi square problem.

(iii) The steps involved in the estimating scheme are as follows: from the reduced model $y_t = \alpha x_t + \lambda y_{t-1} + u_t^*$, obtain IV estimators, say, $\tilde{\alpha}$ and $\tilde{\lambda}$, and use these to obtain the residuals

$$\tilde{u}_t^* = y_t - \tilde{\alpha}x_t - \tilde{\lambda}y_{t-1} \tag{10.147}$$

Compute consistent estimators of the spectral and cross-spectral densities $f_{**}(\cdot), f_{xy}(\cdot), f_{xx}(\cdot)$ at the points θ_j noted in i; m is the maximal lag employed. Substitute $\tilde{\lambda}$ and $\hat{f}_{**}(\theta_j)$ for λ and $f_{**}(\theta_j)$ in the denominators of (10.123), and solve the resulting linear system to obtain estimators $\hat{\alpha}, \hat{\lambda}$ for the corresponding parameters.

If desired, this procedure may be repeated until convergence is obtained. Whether iteration is or is not warranted depends on the properties of the resulting estimators, a matter to be dealt with in the following section. To anticipate matters, no gain is obtained by iteration in terms of the *asymptotic properties* of the estimators. Whether iteration will produce estimators with more desirable "small sample" properties is an open question.

10.6 Asymptotic Properties of the Spectral Estimator

The development of the preceding section is best understood as the motivation leading to the estimators defined implicitly in Equation (10.123). Whether or not the latter are desirable estimators will depend on their properties, as we shall see in the following discussion.

In the previous section we asserted, in order to simplify the exposition, that the explanatory variable x_t constituted a covariance stationary process. This assertion is unduly strong. Here we shall operate with a weaker set of assumptions—one we had already employed in previous chapters. Thus, we require of the x process that

$$d_n^2 = \sum_{t=1}^{n} x_t^2, \quad \lim_{n \to \infty} d_n^2 = \infty, \quad \lim_{n \to \infty} \frac{\max_{t \leq n} x_t^2}{d_n^2} = 0$$

$$\rho(\tau) = \lim_{n \to \infty} \frac{\sum_{t=1}^{n-\tau} x_{t+\tau} x_t}{d_n^2}, \qquad \text{if } \tau \geq 0 \qquad (10.148)$$

$$= \lim_{n \to \infty} \frac{\sum_{t=-\tau+1}^{n} x_{t+\tau} x_t}{d_n^2}, \qquad \text{if } \tau < 0$$

The process is implicitly taken to be nonstochastic; if it is stochastic, then the lim operator is to be replaced by plim; $\rho(\tau)$ is the τ th order autocorrelation coefficient and has the property $\rho(\tau) = \rho(-\tau)$. Notice that the condition $d_n^2 \to \infty$ is necessary to induce consistency, and in this connection recall also the discussion in Section 4.9. Notice further that we *do not* assume that $\lim d_n^2/n$ is finite; hence the assumptions in (10.148) permit us to consider time trends as explanatory variables which are ruled out if we require finiteness of d_n^2/n in the limit.

Finally, the assumptions on the explanatory variable are sufficient to insure the existence of a distribution function $F(\cdot)$, defined on $[-\pi, \pi]$ and such that

$$\rho(\tau) = \int_{\pi}^{\pi} e^{i\tau\theta} dF(\theta), \qquad \tau = 0, \pm 1, \pm 2, \ldots \qquad (10.149)$$

The development of Section 10.5 is fully valid under the assumptions in (10.148); thus, we are dealing with the estimator

$$\begin{pmatrix} \hat{\alpha} \\ \hat{\lambda} \end{pmatrix} = P^{-1}q* \tag{10.150}$$

where

$$P = \frac{1}{2m} \sum_{j=-m+1}^{m} \begin{bmatrix} \dfrac{\hat{f}_{xx}(\theta_j)}{\hat{f}_{**}(\theta_j)} & \dfrac{\hat{f}_{xy}(\theta_j)e^{i\theta_j}}{\hat{f}_{**}(\theta_j)} \\[2ex] \dfrac{\hat{f}_{xx}(\theta_j)e^{-i\theta_j}}{(1 - \tilde{\lambda}e^{-i\theta_j})\hat{f}_{**}(\theta_j)} & \dfrac{\hat{f}_{xy}(\theta_j)}{(1 - \tilde{\lambda}e^{-i\theta_j})\hat{f}_{**}(\theta_j)} \end{bmatrix}$$

$$q* = \frac{1}{2m} \sum_{j=-m+1}^{m} \begin{bmatrix} \dfrac{\hat{f}_{xy}(\theta_j)}{\hat{f}_{**}(\theta_j)} \\[2ex] \dfrac{\hat{f}_{xy}(\theta_j)e^{-i\theta_j}}{(1 - \tilde{\lambda}e^{-i\theta_j})\hat{f}_{**}(\theta_j)} \end{bmatrix} \tag{10.151}$$

and $\tilde{\lambda}$ is a prior IV estimator of λ. Perhaps for clarity we ought to write $P(\hat{f}_{**}, \tilde{\lambda})$ to stress the fact that the matrix is defined in terms of the estimators of the quantities $f_{**}(.)$ and λ.

In dealing with the distributional aspects of spectral estimators, we employ exactly the same procedure as in previous chapters when we considered estimators in the time domain. Our first task is to express the estimator in (10.150) as the true parameter vector plus an error component. Then we normalize the error component by an appropriate sequence of constants and deduce the asymptotic distribution. If the latter is well-behaved, then we have also shown that the estimator is consistent, a matter that will become quite clear as the argument is developed. That is what we are about to do.

First, we notice that

$$y_t = \alpha x_t + \lambda y_{t-1} + u_t^*, \quad u_t^* = u_t - \lambda u_{t-1} \tag{10.152}$$

Thus, as a matter of notation,

$$\hat{f}_{xy} = \alpha \hat{f}_{xx} + \lambda \hat{f}_{xy_{-1}} + \hat{f}_{xu^*}$$
$$\hat{f}_{x_{-1}y} = \alpha \hat{f}_{x_{-1}x} + \lambda \hat{f}_{xy} + \hat{f}_{x_{-1}u^*} \tag{10.153}$$

This is a simple consequence of the linearity of the spectral estimator in terms of the relevant covariance kernel.

The reader should notice that

$$\hat{f}_{xu^*}(\theta) = \frac{1}{2\pi} \sum_{\tau=-n}^{n} a\left(\frac{\tau}{m}\right) \hat{K}_{xu^*}(\tau)e^{-i\tau\theta} \tag{10.154}$$

cannot be computed, since u_t^* is not an observable quantity; on the other hand, we do not need to compute it. It plays the same role as $X'u/T$ in the ordinary least squares estimator

$$\hat{\beta} = (X'X)^{-1}X'y = \beta + (X'X/T)^{-1}(X'u/T)$$

in the context of the general linear model $y = X\beta + u$, X being a matrix of order Txk.

Noting that $\hat{f}_{xy}(\theta)e^{-i\theta} \approx \hat{f}_{x_{-1}y}(\theta)$, and making the substitutions (10.153) in the vector of the right member of (10.150), we conclude

$$\frac{1}{2m} \sum_{j=-m+1}^{m} \left[\begin{array}{c} \dfrac{\hat{f}_{xy}(\theta_j)}{\hat{f}_{**}(\theta_j)} \\[2ex] \dfrac{\hat{f}_{x_{-1}y}(\theta_j)}{(1 - \tilde{\lambda}e^{-i\theta_j})\hat{f}_{**}(\theta_j)} \end{array} \right]$$

$$= P\begin{pmatrix} \alpha \\ \lambda \end{pmatrix} + \frac{1}{2m} \sum_{j=-m+1}^{m} \left[\begin{array}{c} \dfrac{\hat{f}_{xu^*}(\theta_j)}{\hat{f}_{**}(\theta_j)} \\[2ex] \dfrac{\hat{f}_{x_{-1}u^*}(\theta_j)}{(1 - \tilde{\lambda}e^{-i\theta_j})\hat{f}_{**}(\theta_j)} \end{array} \right] \qquad (10.155)$$

Hence the estimator can be written as

$$\begin{pmatrix} \hat{\alpha} \\ \hat{\lambda} \end{pmatrix} - \begin{pmatrix} \alpha \\ \lambda \end{pmatrix} \approx P^{-1}q \qquad (10.156)$$

where

$$q = \frac{1}{2m} \sum_{j=-m+1}^{m} \left[\begin{array}{c} \dfrac{\hat{f}_{xu^*}(\theta_j)}{\hat{f}_{**}(\theta_j)} \\[2ex] \dfrac{\hat{f}_{x_{-1}u^*}(\theta_j)}{(1 - \tilde{\lambda}e^{-i\theta_j})\hat{f}_{**}(\theta_j)} \end{array} \right] \qquad (10.157)$$

Again, as with P, we should write $q(\hat{f}_{**}, \tilde{\lambda})$.

Now, is the estimator as exhibited in (10.156) consistent? To answer this question, we must determine the probability limits of P and q. In this case, it will be simpler to establish the asymptotic distribution of the estimator, suitably normalized. Then consistency will follow immediately.

We thus consider the asymptotic behavior of

$$d_n\left[\begin{pmatrix} \hat{\alpha} \\ \hat{\lambda} \end{pmatrix} - \begin{pmatrix} \alpha \\ \lambda \end{pmatrix} \right] = [nd_n^{-2}P]^{-1}nd_n^{-1}q \qquad (10.158)$$

We shall now give a fairly detailed derivation of two of the elements of

$\text{plim}_{n\to\infty} nd_n^{-2}P$. The reader should then be able to supply the details for the remaining elements. First we observe that the condition imposed on the u process guarantees the representation[53]

$$[f_{**}(\theta)]^{-1} = \sum_{\tau=-\infty}^{\infty} c_\tau e^{i\tau\theta}$$

$$[f_{**}(\theta)(1 - \lambda e^{-i\theta})]^{-1} = \sum_{\tau=-\infty}^{\infty} g_\tau e^{i\tau\theta} \qquad (10.159)$$

$$[f_{**}(\theta) \,|\, 1 - \lambda e^{i\theta} \,|^2]^{-1} = \sum_{\tau=-\infty}^{\infty} h_\tau e^{i\tau\theta}$$

Second, it is clear that the probability limit is unaffected if we deal instead with $P(f_{**}, \lambda)$, thus using the true parameters $f_{**}(\theta)$, λ rather than their estimators. Now by construction,

$$\hat{f}_{xx}(\theta_j) = \frac{1}{2\pi} \sum_{\tau=-n}^{n} a\left(\frac{\tau}{m}\right) \hat{K}_{xx}(\tau) e^{-i\tau\theta} \qquad (10.160)$$

and

$$nd_n^{-2} \hat{K}_{xx}(\tau) = \frac{\sum_{t=1}^{n-\tau} x_{t+\tau} x_t}{d_n^2} \qquad (10.161)$$

where we are dealing with the case $\tau \geq 0$ only for the sake of simplicity of exposition. Hence,

$$\frac{1}{2m} \frac{n}{d_n^2} \sum_{j=-m+1}^{m} \frac{\hat{f}_{xx}(\theta_j)}{f_{**}(\theta_j)}$$

$$= \frac{1}{2\pi} \frac{1}{2m} \sum_{j=-m+1}^{m} \sum_{r=-\infty}^{\infty} c_r \sum_{\tau=-n}^{n} a\left(\frac{\tau}{m}\right) nd_n^{-2} \hat{K}_{xx}(\tau) e^{-i(\tau-r)\theta_j} \qquad (10.162)$$

Bearing in mind that $\theta_j = \pi j/m$ and summing over j, we conclude that

$$\sum_{j=-m+1}^{m} e^{-i(\tau-r)\theta_j} = \delta_{\tau r} 2m \qquad (10.163)$$

---

[53] This is the so-called *Wiener-Levy theorem*; see, for example, Zygmund [163]. The theorem states that if $f(\cdot)$ has an absolutely convergent Fourier series and if $f(\theta) \neq 0$ over its domain of definition, then $1/f(\cdot)$ has an absolutely convergent Fourier series. In the present application, we require the assumption that $f_{uu}(\cdot)$ obeys the conditions of the theorem above. The fact that $f_{**}(\cdot)$ also obeys these conditions results from the assumption that $|\lambda| < 1$. Similarly, when we deal with the general rational lag, $f_{**}(\cdot)$ is defined by $f_{**}(\theta) = |B(\theta)|^2 f_{uu}(\theta)$, where $B(\theta) = \sum_{j=0}^{k} b_j e^{-ij\theta}$. Again, if the assumptions of the Wiener-Levy theorem hold with respect to $f_{uu}(\cdot)$, they will hold with respect to $f_{**}(\cdot)$ in virtue of the stability conditions imposed on $B(\cdot)$.

where $\delta_{\tau r}$ is the Kronecker delta. Hence the right member of (10.162) is, approximately

$$\frac{1}{2\pi} \sum_{\tau=-n}^{n} c_{\tau} a\left(\frac{\tau}{m}\right) n d_n^{-2} \hat{K}_{xx}(\tau)$$

Now as $n\to\infty$, so does m. Thus, since for fixed τ $a(\tau/m)$ converges to 1 as $n\to\infty$ and moreover, $\lim_{n\to\infty} n d_n^{-2} \hat{K}_{xx}(\tau) = \rho(\tau)$, we conclude

$$\operatorname*{plim}_{n\to\infty} \frac{1}{2m} \frac{n}{d_n^2} \sum_{j=-m+1}^{m} \frac{\hat{f}_{xx}(\theta_j)}{\hat{f}_{**}(\theta_j)} = \frac{1}{2\pi} \sum_{\tau=-\infty}^{\infty} c_{\tau}\rho(\tau) \qquad (10.164)$$

In view of (10.149) and (10.150), we may thus write

$$\frac{1}{2\pi} \sum_{\tau=-\infty}^{\infty} c_{\tau}\rho(\tau) = \frac{1}{2\pi} \sum_{\tau=-\infty}^{\infty} c_{\tau} \int_{-\tau}^{\pi} e^{i\tau\theta}dF(\theta) = \frac{1}{2\pi} \int_{-\pi}^{\pi} \frac{dF(\theta)}{f_{**}(\theta)} \qquad (10.165)$$

We now consider

$$\operatorname*{plim}_{n\to\infty} \frac{1}{2m} \frac{n}{d_n^2} \sum_{j=-m+1}^{m} \frac{\hat{f}_{xy}(\theta_j)}{(1 - \tilde{\lambda}e^{-i\theta_j})(\hat{f}_{**}(\theta_j))}$$

and note that

$$y_t = \alpha \sum_{s=0}^{\infty} \lambda^s x_{t-s} + u_t \qquad (10.166)$$

Hence,

$$\hat{f}_{xy}(\theta) = \alpha \sum_{s=0}^{\infty} \lambda^s \hat{f}_{xx_{-s}}(\theta) + \hat{f}_{xu}(\theta) \approx \alpha\left(\sum_{s=0}^{\infty} \lambda^s e^{is\theta}\right)\hat{f}_{xx}(\theta) + \hat{f}_{xu}(\theta)$$

$$= \frac{\alpha\hat{f}_{xx}(\theta)}{1 - \lambda e^{i\theta}} + \hat{f}_{xu}(\theta) \qquad (10.167)$$

Since the cross-spectrum of x and u vanishes, we conclude that

$$\operatorname*{plim}_{n\to\infty} \frac{1}{2m} \frac{n}{d_n^2} \sum_{i=-m+1}^{m} \frac{\hat{f}_{xy}(\theta_j)}{(1 - \tilde{\lambda}e^{-i\theta_j})\hat{f}_{**}(\theta_j)}$$

$$= \operatorname*{plim}_{n\to\infty} \frac{1}{2m} \frac{n}{d_n^2} \sum_{j=-m+1}^{m} \frac{\alpha\hat{f}_{xx}(\theta_j)}{|1 - \lambda e^{i\theta_j}|^2 f_{**}(\theta_j)} \qquad (10.168)$$

$$= \frac{1}{2\pi} \int_{-\pi}^{\pi} \frac{\alpha}{|1 - \lambda e^{i\theta}|^2} \frac{dF(\theta)}{f_{**}(\theta)}$$

We have thus established

$$\operatorname*{plim}_{n \to \infty} n d_n^{-2} P = \frac{1}{2\pi} \left[\int_{-\pi}^{\pi} a(\theta) \bar{a}'(\theta) \frac{dF(\theta)}{f_{**}(\theta)} \right] \begin{bmatrix} 1 & 0 \\ 0 & \alpha \end{bmatrix} = \frac{1}{2\pi} \bar{P} A$$

(10.169)

where

$$a(\theta) = \begin{pmatrix} 1 \\ \dfrac{e^{-i\theta}}{1 - \lambda e^{-i\theta}} \end{pmatrix}, \quad \bar{a}'(\theta) = \left(1, \dfrac{e^{i\theta}}{1 - \lambda e^{i\theta}} \right), \quad A = \begin{bmatrix} 1 & 0 \\ 0 & \alpha \end{bmatrix}$$

(10.170)

We now turn to the problem of determining the asymptotic distribution of $n d_n^{-1} q$. As we indicated earlier,

$$n d_n^{-1} q(\hat{f}_{**}, \tilde{\lambda}) \sim n d_n^{-1} q(f_{**}, \lambda)$$

(10.171)

and so we shall deal with the vector defined in terms of $f_{**}(\theta_j)$ and $1 - \lambda e^{-i\theta_j}$, instead of $\hat{f}_{**}(\theta_j)$, $1 - \tilde{\lambda} e^{-i\theta_j}$. Following the argument employed when dealing with the probability limit of the matrix P, we have that, asymptotically,

$$n d_n^{-1} q \sim \frac{1}{2\pi} \sum_{\tau=-n}^{n} a\left(\frac{\tau}{m}\right) \begin{bmatrix} c_\tau & 0 \\ 0 & g_\tau \end{bmatrix} n d_n^{-1} \begin{pmatrix} \hat{K}_{xu*}(\tau) \\ \hat{K}_{x_{-1}u*}(\tau) \end{pmatrix}$$

(10.172)

The strategy for the (somewhat heuristic) derivation of the asymptotic distribution of $n d_n^{-1} q$ is as follows:

First, we shall show that the asymptotic distribution of

$$n d_n^{-1} \begin{pmatrix} \hat{K}_{xu*}(\tau) \\ \hat{K}_{x_{-1}u*}(\tau) \end{pmatrix}$$

is normal with mean zero and a certain covariance matrix. This involves an application of Theorems 4.2 and 4.3, theorems that are central to the development of many results in this book.

Second, we shall observe that if we truncate the sum over τ at $-n^*$ and n^*, $n^* < n$, then in (10.172) we are dealing with a finite sum of (asymptotically) normal vectors. Since $a(\tau/m)$ converges to 1 with n (and hence m) and the linear combination entails only the matrices diag (c_τ, g_τ) whose elements are nonstochastic, this finite linear combination is also normal with mean zero. At this stage, we have to derive the cross-covariance of the vectors involved in the sum.

Third, since the development above is valid for arbitrary $n^*(<n)$, we

conclude, letting n^* approach infinity, that the sum is asymtotically normal with mean zero and covariance matrix equal to the limiting form of the covariance matrix of the truncated sum.

A more straightforward and rigorous approach would be to prove a central limit theorem with respect to the sum appearing in (10.171). This, however, would be extremely cumbersome and will contribute little to the reader's understanding of the issues involved.

To simplify the exposition, at the first step we shall give the derivation only for the case $\tau \geq 0$; the reader may easily supply the details for $\tau < 0$ and verify that similar conclusions are obtained. Thus,

$$nd_n^{-1} \binom{\hat{K}_{xu^*}(\tau)}{\hat{K}_{x_{-1}u^*}(\tau)} = \frac{1}{d_n} \sum_{t=1}^{n-\tau} \binom{x_{t+\tau}}{x_{t-1+\tau}} u_t^* \qquad (10.173)$$

We observe, however, that

$$u_t^* = \sum_{j=0}^{N-1} \alpha_j^* \varepsilon_{t-j} + \sum_{j=N}^{\infty} \alpha_j^* \varepsilon_{t-j} \qquad (10.174)$$

where

$$\alpha_j^* = \alpha_j - \lambda \alpha_{j-1}, \quad \alpha_0^* = \alpha_0 \qquad (10.175)$$

In view of the condition,

$$\sum_{j=0}^{\infty} j \, |\alpha_j| < \infty \qquad (10.176)$$

for any given $\delta_1, \delta_2 > 0$ we can find an N such that

$$\Pr\left\{ |\sum_{j=N}^{\infty} \alpha_j^* \varepsilon_{t-j}| > \delta_1 \right\} < \delta_2 \qquad (10.177)$$

Hence, we may neglect the second component of (10.174) and deal instead with

$$u_t^{*N} = \sum_{j=0}^{N-1} \alpha_j^* \varepsilon_{t-j} \qquad (10.178)$$

Let b_1, b_2 be arbitrary real numbers; the above imply that to find the asymptotic distribution of the quantity in (10.173) we need be concerned only with the behavior of the sum $\sum_{t=1}^{n-\tau} \varphi(t, \tau, n) u_t^{*N}$, where

$$\varphi(t, \tau, n) = \frac{b_1 x_{t+\tau} + b_2 x_{t-1+\tau}}{d_n} \qquad (10.179)$$

But $\{\varphi(t, \tau, n)u_t^{*N}\}$ forms a sequence of N-dependent variables[54] and we further observe that

$$E\,|\varphi(t, \tau, n)u_t^{*N}|^3 = \left(\frac{\varphi(t, \tau, n)}{d_n}\right)^2 \frac{|\varphi(t, \tau, n)|}{d_n}\, E\,|u_t^{*N}|^3$$

$$\leq \left[\left(\frac{\varphi(t, \tau, n)}{d_n}\right)^2 \frac{\max\limits_{t \leq n}|\varphi(t, \tau, n)|}{d_n}\right]\left(\sum_{j=0}^{N-1}|\alpha_j^*|\right)^3 \sigma_3$$

$$\tag{10.180}$$

where σ_3 is the (finite) third absolute moment of the ε process. In view of the conditions in (10.148), the quantity in (10.180) converges to zero with n; hence, by neglecting a finite number of observations, if necessary, we can assert that the third absolute moment of the quantities $\varphi(t, \tau, n)$ $\cdot u_t^{*N}$ is *bounded*.

By Theorems 4.2 and 4.3 we know, then, that the limiting distribution is normal. Since the quantities $\varphi(t, \tau, n)u_t^{*N}$ have mean zero, we need only obtain the variance parameter. To this effect, define, according to Theorem 4.3, the quantities

$$R_t = 2\sum_{j=0}^{N-1} \text{Cov}\,[\varphi(t+j, 0, n)u_{t+j}^{*N}, \varphi(t+N, 0, n)u_{t+N}^{*N}]$$

$$+ \text{Var}\,[\varphi(t+N, 0, n)u_{t+N}^*]$$

$$= 2\sum_{j=0}^{N-1} \varphi(t+j, 0, n)\varphi(t+N, 0, n)K_{**}(N-j) \tag{10.181}$$

$$+ [\varphi(t+N, 0, n)]^2 K_{**}(0)$$

where

$$K_{**}(\tau) = E\,[u_{t+\tau}^* u_t^*] \approx E\,[u_{t+\tau}^{*N} u_t^{*N}], \quad K_{**}(\tau) = K_{**}(-\tau)$$

$$\tag{10.182}$$

Further,

$$\sum_{t=1}^{n-\tau} R_{t+\tau} = \sum_{t=1}^{n-\tau}\left[2\sum_{j=0}^{N-1} \varphi(t+j, \tau, n)\varphi(t+N, \tau, u)K_{**}(N-j)\right.$$

$$\left. + [\varphi(t+N, \tau, n)]^2 K_{**}(0)\right] \tag{10.183}$$

---

[54] To verify this, observe that u_t^{*N} contains the variables $(\varepsilon_t, \varepsilon_{t-1}, \ldots, \varepsilon_{t-N+1})$. On the other hand, u_{t+N}^{*N} contains the variables $(\varepsilon_{t+N}, \varepsilon_{t+N-1}, \ldots, \varepsilon_{t+1})$; since the ε's are mutually independent and the two sets above are disjoint, the conclusion follows immediately.

converges to a finite quantity independent of τ, as $n \to \infty$. In particular, we have

$$
\lim_{n \to \infty} \sum_{t=1}^{n-\tau} R_{t+\tau} = \sum_{j=0}^{N-1} \left\{ \lim_{n \to \infty} 2 \sum_{t=1}^{n-\tau} \left[b_1^2 \frac{x_{t+j+\tau} x_{t+N+\tau}}{d_n^2} + b_1 b_2 \frac{x_{t+j+\tau} x_{t-1+N+\tau}}{d_n^2} \right. \right.
$$

$$
\left. \left. + b_1 b_2 \frac{x_{t-1+j+\tau} x_{t+N+\tau}}{d_n^2} + b_2^2 \frac{x_{t-1+j+\tau} x_{t-1+N+\tau}}{d_n^2} \right] K_{**}(N-j) \right\}
$$

$$
+ \lim_{n \to \infty} \sum_{t=1}^{n-\tau} [\varphi(t+N, \tau, n)]^2 K_{**}(0) = 2 \sum_{j=0}^{N-1} [b_1^2 \rho(N-j)
$$

$$
+ b_1 b_2 \rho(N-j-1) + b_1 b_2 \rho(N-j+1) + b_2^2 \rho(N-j)] K_{**}(N-j)
$$

$$
+ [b_1^2 \rho(0) + b_1 b_2 \rho(-1) + b_1 b_2 \rho(1) + b_2^2 \rho(0)] K_{**}(0) \qquad (10.184)
$$

Notice that the sum over j yields, for example, $b_1^2 [\rho(N) K_{**}(N) + \rho(N-1) K_{**}(N-1) + \cdots + \rho(1) K_{**}(-1)]$; since $\rho(-\tau) = \rho(\tau)$ and $K_{**}(\tau) = K_{**}(-\tau)$, we see that the coefficient of b_1^2 in (10.184) is simply

$$
\sum_{s=-N}^{N} \rho(s) K_{**}(s)
$$

Similarly, the coefficients of the two expressions containing $b_1 b_2$ are, respectively,

$$
\sum_{s=-N}^{N} \rho(s+1) K_{**}(s), \quad \sum_{s=-N}^{N} \rho(s-1) K_{**}(s)
$$

Finally, the coefficient of b_2^2 is

$$
\sum_{s=-N}^{N} \rho(s) K_{**}(s)
$$

Hence we conclude that, asymptotically,

$$
nd_n^{-1} \begin{pmatrix} K_{xu^*}(\tau) \\ K_{x_{-1}u^*}(\tau) \end{pmatrix} \sim N(0, C_0) \qquad (10.185)
$$

where

$$
C_0 \approx \sum_{s=-\infty}^{\infty} K_{**}(s) \begin{bmatrix} \rho(s) & \rho(s+1) \\ \rho(s-1) & \rho(s) \end{bmatrix} \qquad (10.186)
$$

the approximation sign merely indicating that we have extended the sum to $-\infty$ and $+\infty$, instead of $-N$ and N.

Notice that the above result is independent of τ; hence it applies equally well to all such vectors, although the derivation will have to be modified somewhat for $\tau < 0$.

Using the same techniques, one can easily show that asymptotically, the covariance of the vectors

$$nd_n^{-1} \begin{pmatrix} \hat{K}_{xu}(\tau) \\ \hat{K}_{x_{-1}u^*}(\tau) \end{pmatrix} \quad \text{and} \quad nd_n^{-1} \begin{pmatrix} \hat{K}_{xu^*}(\tau^f) \\ \hat{K}_{x_{-1}u^*}(\tau') \end{pmatrix}$$

is given by

$$C_{\tau-\tau'} = \sum_{j=-\infty}^{\infty} K_{**}(s) \begin{bmatrix} \rho(s+\tau-\tau') & \rho(s+\tau-\tau'+1) \\ \rho(s+\tau-\tau'-1) & \rho(s+\tau-\tau') \end{bmatrix} \tag{10.187}$$

Observe that this specializes to the covariance matrix in (10.186) when $\tau = \tau'$. Moreover, as $n \to \infty$ (and hence $m \to \infty$), $a(\tau/m)$, for fixed τ, approaches unity; hence we conclude that the truncated sum in (10.172) is asymptotically normal with mean zero and covariance matrix

$$\left(\frac{1}{2\pi}\right)^2 \sum_{\tau=-n^*}^{n^*} \sum_{\tau'=-n^*}^{n^*} \begin{bmatrix} c_\tau & 0 \\ 0 & g_\tau \end{bmatrix} C_{\tau-\tau'} \begin{bmatrix} \bar{c}_{\tau'} & 0 \\ 0 & \bar{g}_{\tau'} \end{bmatrix} = \left(\frac{1}{2\pi}\right)^2 \sum_{s=-\infty}^{\infty} K_{**}(s)$$

$$\times \sum_{\tau=-n^*}^{n^*} \sum_{\tau'=-n^*}^{n} \begin{bmatrix} c_\tau \bar{c}_{\tau'} \rho(s+\tau-\tau') & c_\tau \bar{g}_{\tau'} \rho(s+\tau-\tau'+1) \\ g_\tau \bar{c}_{\tau'} \rho(s+\tau-\tau'-1) & g_\tau \bar{g}_{\tau'} \rho(s+\tau-\tau') \end{bmatrix} \tag{10.188}$$

Since

$$\rho(k) = \int_{-\pi}^{\pi} e^{ik\theta}\, dF(\theta) \tag{10.189}$$

we see that letting $n^* \to \infty$, the right member of (10.188) converges to

$$\frac{1}{2\pi} \int_{-\pi}^{\pi} \left\{ \left[\frac{1}{2\pi} \sum_{s=-\infty}^{\infty} K_{**}(s) e^{is\theta} \sum_{\tau=-\infty}^{\infty} c_\tau e^{i\tau\theta} \sum_{\tau'=-\infty}^{\infty} \bar{c}_{\tau'} e^{-i\tau',\theta} \right] \right.$$

$$\times \begin{bmatrix} 1 & \dfrac{e^{i\theta}}{1-\lambda e^{i\theta}} \\ \dfrac{e^{-i\theta}}{1-\lambda e^{-i\theta}} & \dfrac{1}{|1-\lambda e^{i\theta}|^2} \end{bmatrix} dF(\theta) \right\}$$

$$= \frac{1}{2\pi} \int_{-\pi}^{\pi} a(\theta)\bar{a}'(\theta)\, \frac{dF(\theta)}{f_{**}(\theta)} = \frac{1}{2\pi}\, \bar{P} \tag{10.190}$$

The last equality follows since

$$\frac{1}{2\pi} \sum_{s=-\infty}^{\infty} K_{**}(s)e^{is\theta} = f_{**}(\theta)$$

$$\sum_{\tau=-\infty}^{\infty} c_{\tau}e^{i\tau\theta} = \sum_{\tau=-\infty}^{\infty} \bar{c}_{\tau'}e^{-i\tau\theta} = \frac{1}{f_{**}(\theta)} \tag{10.191}$$

$$\sum_{\tau=-\infty}^{\infty} g_{\tau}e^{i\tau\theta} = [(1 - \lambda e^{-i\theta})f_{**}(\theta)]^{-1} = \frac{1}{1 - \lambda e^{-i\theta}} \sum_{\tau=-\infty}^{\infty} c_{\tau}e^{i\tau\theta}$$

$$\bar{a}'(\theta) = \left(1, \frac{e^{i\theta}}{1 - \lambda e^{i\theta}}\right)$$

Thus, we conclude

$$d_n\left[\begin{pmatrix}\hat{\alpha}\\\hat{\lambda}\end{pmatrix} - \begin{pmatrix}\alpha\\\lambda\end{pmatrix}\right] \sim N(0, C^{-1}) \tag{10.192}$$

where

$$C = \frac{1}{2\pi} A\bar{P}A \tag{10.193}$$

Defining

$$\beta(\theta) = \begin{pmatrix}1\\\dfrac{\alpha e^{-i\theta}}{1 - \lambda e^{-i\theta}}\end{pmatrix}, \quad \bar{\beta}'(\theta) = \left(1, \frac{\alpha e^{i\theta}}{1 - \lambda e^{i\theta}}\right) \tag{10.194}$$

we observe that

$$A\bar{P}A = \int_{-\pi}^{\pi} \frac{\beta(\theta)\bar{\beta}'(\theta)}{f_{**}(\theta)}\, dF(\theta) \tag{10.195}$$

Thus,

$$\hat{C} = (\hat{A}P) \tag{10.196}$$

is a consistent estimator of $\hat{C}$, where

$$\hat{A} = \begin{bmatrix}1 & 0\\0 & \hat{\alpha}\end{bmatrix} \tag{10.197}$$

provided we have shown that the estimators $\hat{\alpha}$, $\hat{\lambda}$ are consistent. But this is an obvious by product of the preceding. If

$$d_n\left[\begin{pmatrix}\hat{\alpha}\\\hat{\lambda}\end{pmatrix} - \begin{pmatrix}\alpha\\\lambda\end{pmatrix}\right]$$

converges in distribution to the random variable ξ, which is normal with zero mean and covariance matrix having fiinite elements, then

$$\operatorname*{plim}_{n \to \infty} \frac{\xi}{d_n} = 0 \tag{10.198}$$

But

$$\operatorname*{plim}_{n \to \infty} \frac{\xi}{d_n} = \operatorname*{plim}_{n \to \infty} \left[\begin{pmatrix} \hat{\alpha} \\ \hat{\lambda} \end{pmatrix} - \begin{pmatrix} \alpha \\ \lambda \end{pmatrix} \right] \tag{10.199}$$

which shows consistency.

The inference problem with respect to this model is thus completely solved and we have proved

THEOREM 10.1.   Consider a sample of size n, on the model

$$y_t = \alpha \sum_{\tau=0}^{\infty} \lambda^{\tau} x_{t-\tau} + u_t, \quad t = 1, 2, \dots, n \tag{10.200}$$

where

$$u_t = \sum_{j=0}^{\infty} \alpha_j \varepsilon_{t-j}, \quad \sum_{j=0}^{\infty} j \, |\alpha_j| < \infty \tag{10.201}$$

the ε process being one of *i.i.d.* random variables with mean zero, variance one and finite third (absolute) moment. Suppose further that the explanatory variable, x, is independent of the error process and obeys

$$d_n^2 = \sum_{t=1}^{n} x_t^2, \quad \lim d_n^2 = \infty$$

$$\lim_{n \to \infty} \frac{\max_{t \le n} x_t^2}{d_n^2} = 0, \quad \lim_{n \to \infty} \frac{\sum_{t=1}^{n} x_{t+\tau} x_t}{d_n} = \rho(\tau)$$

$$\rho(\tau) = \rho(-\tau) \tag{10.202}$$

Then:

(i) Minimizing

$$S = (y - r)' K_u^{-1} (y - r) \tag{10.203}$$

with respect to α and λ is (asymptotically) equivalent to minimizing

$$S = \sum_{j=-m+1}^{m} \left[\frac{\hat{f}_{yy}(\theta_j) - 2\alpha(1 - \lambda e^{-i\theta_j})^{-1} \hat{f}_{xy}(\theta_j) + \alpha^2 |1 - \lambda e^{i\theta_j}|^{-2} \hat{f}_{xx}(\theta_j)}{f_{uu}(\theta_j)} \right] \tag{10.204}$$

where

$$K_u = \begin{bmatrix} K_u(0) & K_u(1) & . & K_u(n-1) \\ K_u(1) & K_u(0) & . & K_u(n-2) \\ . & . & & . \\ K_u(n-1) & K_u(n-2) & . & K_u(0) \end{bmatrix}, \quad K_u(\tau) = E(u_{t+\tau}u_t)$$

(10.205)

$$r_t = \alpha \sum_{\tau=0}^{\infty} \lambda^{\tau} x_{t-\tau}, \quad r = (r_1, r_2, \ldots, r_n)', \quad y = (y_1, y_2, \ldots, y_n)'$$

(10.206)

and $\hat{f}_{yy}(\cdot), \hat{f}_{xx}(\cdot), \hat{f}_{xy}(\cdot)$ are the (consistently) estimated spectral and cross-spectral densities of the y and x processes[55];

(ii) The estimator

$$\begin{pmatrix} \hat{\alpha} \\ \hat{\lambda} \end{pmatrix} = P^{-1}q^*$$

(10.207)

where P and q^* are as defined in (10.151), is consistent; the elements of P and q^* are completely determined from the data, provided initial consistent estimators, say $\tilde{\alpha}, \tilde{\lambda}$, are available. From the residuals $\tilde{u}_t^* = y_t - \tilde{\alpha}x_t - \tilde{\lambda}y_{t-1}$, we can obtain $\hat{f}_{**}(\cdot)$, which is a consistent estimator of $f_{**}(\cdot)$, the latter being the spectral density of the process $u_t^* = u_t - \lambda u_{t-1}$.

(iii) Asymptotically,

$$d_n \left[\begin{pmatrix} \hat{\alpha} \\ \hat{\lambda} \end{pmatrix} - \begin{pmatrix} \alpha \\ \lambda \end{pmatrix} \right] \sim N(0, C^{-1})$$

where C is as defined in (10.193);

(iv) A consistent estimator of C is given by

$$\hat{C} = \hat{A}P$$

where P and $\hat{A}$ are defined, respectively, in (10.151) and (10.197);

(v) Let $\hat{c}^{11}, \hat{c}^{22}$ be the diagonal elements of $\hat{C}^{-1}$; then, asymptotically, $(d_n(\hat{\alpha} - \alpha)/\sqrt{\hat{c}^{11}}) \sim N(0, 1), (d_n(\hat{\lambda} - \lambda)/\sqrt{\hat{c}^{22}}) \sim N(0, 1)$. Hence, tests

---

[55] If the x process is not covariance stationary, the quantity $\hat{f}_{xx}(\theta) = (1/2\pi)\sum_{\tau=-n}^{n} \cdot a(\tau/m) \hat{K}_{xx}(\tau)e^{-i\tau\theta}$ is still well-defined, although it could not be interpreted as an estimated spectral density. Moreover, if the process is purely deterministic, say a time trend, certain other difficulties will arise as $n \to \infty$. Thus, one ought to use, instead, $nd_n^{-2}\hat{f}_{xx}(\theta)$.

on the significance of individual coefficients may be based, asymptotically, on the standard normal distribution; the test statistic of the hypothesis, say $\alpha = 0$, is the usual t-ratio $(d_n\hat{\alpha}/\sqrt{\hat{c}^{11}})$.

REMARK 10.9.   In their interesting paper, Amemiya and Fuller [3] have given a time domain interpretation of the estimator proposed by Hannan in connection with the model of Theorem 10.1. In the particular case where normality was assumed for the error process, it was asserted that the ML estimator (in the time domain) and the Hannan estimator (in the frequency domain) have the same asymptotic distribution. This, of course, ought to occasion no surprise since the two estimators minimize essentially the same objective functions but treat the variables of the problem in different forms. In one instance, we deal with variances and covariances, in the other with spectral and cross-spectral densities.

More interestingly, however, Amemiya and Fuller make the observation that the estimator proposed by Hannan is equivalent to the following two-step IV estimator

$$\begin{pmatrix} \hat{\alpha} \\ \hat{\lambda} \end{pmatrix} = [(x, \bar{y}_{-1})'\hat{\Phi}^{-1}(x, y_{-1})]^{-1}(x, \bar{y}_{-1})'\hat{\Phi}^{-1}y \qquad (10.208)$$

This is arrived at as follows. Consider the model of Theorem 10.1, but now take the error term as a first order Markov process with autocorrelation parameter ρ. Reduce the model to obtain

$$y_t = \alpha x_t + \lambda y_{t-1} + w_{t'}, \quad w_t = u_t - \lambda u_{t-1} \qquad (10.209)$$

If initial IV estimators, say $\tilde{\alpha}$, $\tilde{\lambda}$ are available, we can compute

$$\bar{y}_t = \tilde{\alpha} \sum_{\tau=0}^{t-1} \tilde{\lambda}^i x_{t-i'}, \quad \bar{u}_t = y_t - \bar{y}_t, \quad (\bar{y}_{-1} = \bar{y}_1, \bar{y}_2, \ldots, \bar{y}_{T-1})' \quad (10.210)$$

From the residuals in (10.210), we can estimate ρ. If $\sigma^2\Phi$ is the covariance matrix of the errors in the reduced model, then Φ depends only on λ and ρ and can thus be consistently estimated. Now, if in the context of (10.209) we use the instrumental matrix $\hat{\Phi}^{-1}(x, \bar{y}_{-1})$, we obtain the estimator in (10.208). Hence the term "two-step IV estimator."

In the context of (10.209), the feasible Aitken estimator is given by

$$\begin{pmatrix} \hat{\alpha} \\ \hat{\lambda} \end{pmatrix} = [(x, y_{-1})'\hat{\Phi}^{-1}(x, y_{-1})]^{-1}(x, y_{-1})'\hat{\Phi}^{-1}y \qquad (10.211)$$

where $\hat{\Phi}$ is estimated in exactly the same way as above. The two estimators in (10.208) and (10.211) look quite similar, but we know from the discussion of Chapters 6 and 7 that their asymptotic distributions are different.

In connection with (10.211), and considering the special case where it is known that $\rho = 0$, *Amemiya and Fuller observe that the asymptotic properties of this estimator are not the same as those of the estimator resulting when the covariance matrix of the errors in* (10.209) *is assumed to be known.* This is, of course, a rather artificial situation. On the other hand, no attempt is made to explain the differences in the properties of the two estimators in (10.208) and (10.211). Maddala [98] makes the observation that these two estimators do not solve the same equations, hence it is not surprising that their asymptotic properties differ.

Still, however, an intuitively satisfying explanation of this phenomenon is lacking in the discussions alluded to above. Actually, the difference between these two estimators in the context of the model of Theorem 10.1, but with errors assumed to be *i.i.d.* random variables, was pointed out in Problem 9 (end of Chapter 8). Indeed, what Dhrymes, Klein and Steiglitz [33] call the "modified ML estimator" is none other than the estimator in (10.211):

To see the intuitive reason why (10.211) is an inefficient estimator relative to that in (10.208) is a comparatively simple matter. Thus, consider the minimand

$$S = \left(y - \frac{\alpha I}{I - \lambda L} x \right)' \left(y - \frac{\alpha I}{I - \lambda L} x \right) \tag{10.212}$$

The first order conditions are

$$\left(y - \frac{\alpha I}{I - \lambda L} x \right)' \frac{I}{I - \lambda L} \ x = 0$$

$$\left(y - \frac{\alpha I}{I - \lambda L} \right)' \frac{I}{(I - \lambda L)^2} \ x_{-1} = 0 \tag{10.213}$$

If a prior consistent estimator of λ is available, say $\tilde{\lambda}$, we may define

$$\tilde{y}_t^* = \frac{I}{I - \tilde{\lambda} L} y_t, \quad \tilde{x}_t^{**} = \frac{I}{I - \tilde{\lambda} L} \tilde{x}_t^*, \quad \tilde{x}_t^* = \frac{I}{I - \tilde{\lambda} L} x_t$$

it being understood, e.g., that

$$\tilde{x}_t^* = \sum_{i=0}^{t-1} \tilde{\lambda}^i x_{t-i}, \text{ etc.}$$

Since we may write

$$y_t = \frac{I - \lambda L}{I - \lambda L} \, y_t \approx (I - \lambda L)\tilde{y}_t^*$$

we see that the estimator in (10.208) is the first iterate of the prefiltering procedure already discussed in Chapter 5, and which under normality would be a ML procedure. Hannan's results then suggest that *asymptotically*, we gain nothing by iterating the prefiltering procedure until convergence is obtained.

The estimator in (10.211), however, writes the minimand in (10.212) as

$$S^* = (y^* - \alpha x^* - \lambda y_{-1}^*)' \; (y^* - \alpha x - \lambda y_{-1}^*)$$

and proceeds to obtain the first order conditions by differentiating with respect to α and λ, *ignoring the fact that the starred quantities depend on λ.* The first order conditions are

$$(y^* - \alpha x^* - \lambda y_{-1}^*)'x^* = 0$$
$$(y^* - \alpha x^* - \lambda y_{-1}^*)'y_{-1}^* = 0 \qquad (10.214)$$

If we now compute the starred quantities using an initial consistent estimator of λ, say $\tilde{\lambda}$, and solve (10.214), we shall obtain the estimator in (10.211). This makes intuitive the difference between the two estimators by pointing out the "error" committed by the feasible Aitken estimator. This line of argument should also make clear that no matter how many times the feasible Aitken estimator is iterated, it remains, asymptotically, inefficient relative to that given in (10.208).

10.7 The General Rational Lag Structure

Here we shall extend the results of the last two sections to the model

$$y_t = \frac{A(L)}{B(L)} \, x_t + u_t \qquad (10.215)$$

where

$$A(L) = \sum_{s=0}^{k_1} a_s L^s, \quad B(L) = \sum_{s'=0}^{k_2} b_{s'} L^{s'}, \quad b_0 = 1 \qquad (10.216)$$

and the roots of the polynomial $B(\cdot)$ have modulus greater than unity. The explanatory variable and the error process obey the same conditions as in the previous two sections.

Define

$$r_t = \frac{A(L)}{B(L)} x_t = \sum_{\tau=0}^{\infty} w_\tau x_{t-\tau} \tag{10.217}$$

As in Section 10.5, we define

$$\Phi(\theta) = \sum_{t=0}^{\infty} w_t e^{-it\theta} = \frac{\sum_{s=0}^{k_1} a_s e^{-is\theta}}{\sum_{s'=0}^{k_2} b_{s'} e^{-is'\theta}} = \frac{A(\theta)}{B(\theta)} \tag{10.218}$$

Suppose we have n observations on the model in (10.215) and denote

$$u = (u_1, u, \ldots, u_n)'$$

$$\text{Cov}(u) = \begin{bmatrix} K_u(0) & K_u(1) & . & K_u(n-1) \\ K_u(1) & K_u(0) & . & K_u(n-2) \\ . & & & \\ K_u(n-1) & K_u(n-2) & . & K_u(0) \end{bmatrix} = K_u \tag{10.219}$$

We may obtain Aitken estimators of the parameters of the polynomials $A(\cdot)$, $B(\cdot)$ by minimizing

$$S = (y - r)' K_u^{-1} (y - r) \tag{10.220}$$

where

$$y = (y_1, y_2, \ldots, y_n)', \qquad r = (r_1, r_2, \ldots, r_n)'$$

Employing the same sequence of reasoning leading to Equation (10.117), we conclude that the minimand in (10.220) is well-approximated by

$$S = \frac{1}{2\pi} \sum_{j=-m+1}^{m} \left[\frac{\hat{f}_{yy}(\theta_j) - 2\Phi(\theta_j)\hat{f}_{xy}(\theta_j) + |\Phi(\theta_j)|^2 \hat{f}_{xx}(\theta_j)}{f_{uu}(\theta_j)} \right] \tag{10.221}$$

the symbols $\hat{f}_{yy}, \hat{f}_{xx}, \hat{f}_{xy}$ and f_{uu} having exactly the same meaning as before, with

$$\theta_j = \frac{\pi j}{m}, \quad j = -m+1, -m+2, \ldots, m \tag{10.222}$$

and m being the maximal lag utilized by the spectral window.

Minimizing (10.221) with respect to a_α, b_β, we have

$$\frac{\partial S}{\partial a_\alpha} = -\frac{2}{2\pi} \sum_{j=-m+1}^{m} \left[\frac{\hat{f}_{xy}(\theta_j) e^{-i\alpha\theta_j}}{B(\theta_j) f_u(\theta_j)} \right]$$

$$+ \frac{1}{2\pi} \sum_{j=-m+1}^{m} \left[\frac{(\bar{A}(\theta_j) e^{-i\alpha\theta_j} + A(\theta) e^{i\alpha\theta_j}) \hat{f}_{xx}(\theta_j)}{|B(\theta_j)|^2 f_{uu}(\theta_j)} \right] = 0$$

$$\alpha = 0, 1, \ldots, k_1 \tag{10.223}$$

$$\frac{\partial S}{\partial b_\beta} = \frac{2}{2\pi} \sum_{j=-m+1}^{m} \left[\frac{|A(\theta_j)|^2 \hat{f}_{xy}(\theta_j) e^{-i\beta\theta_j}}{B^2(\theta_j) f_{uu}(\theta_j)} \right]$$

$$- \frac{1}{2\pi} \sum_{j=-m+1}^{m} \left[\frac{(\bar{B}(\theta_j) e^{-i\beta\theta_j} + B(\theta_j) e^{i\beta\theta_j}) |A(\theta_j)|^2 \hat{f}_{xx}(\theta_j)}{|B(\theta_j)|^4 f_{uu}(\theta_j)} \right] = 0$$

$$\beta = 1, 2, \ldots, k_2 \qquad (10.224)$$

Since

$$A(\theta_{-j}) = \bar{A}(\theta_j), \quad B(\theta_{-j}) = \bar{B}(\theta_j), \quad |B(\theta_{-j})|^2 = |B(\theta_j)|^2$$
$$\hat{f}_{xx}(\theta_{-j}) = \hat{f}_{xx}(\theta_j), \quad f_{uu}(\theta_{-j}) = f_{uu}(\theta_j) \qquad (10.225)$$

we see that (10.223) and (10.224) can be rewritten more conveniently as

$$\sum_{j=-m+1}^{m} \left[\frac{\bar{A}(\theta_j) \hat{f}_{xx}(\theta_j) e^{-i\alpha\theta_j}}{|B(\theta_j)|^2 f_{uu}(\theta_j)} \right] - \sum_{j=-m+1}^{m} \left[\frac{\bar{B}(\theta_j) \hat{f}_{xy}(\theta_j) e^{-i\alpha\theta_j}}{|B(\theta_j)|^2 f_{uu}(\theta_j)} \right] = 0$$

$$\alpha = 0, 1, 2, \ldots, k_1 \qquad (10.226)$$

$$\sum_{j=-m+1}^{m} \left[\frac{\Phi(\theta_j) \bar{A}(\theta_j) \hat{f}_{xx}(\theta_j) e^{-i\beta\theta_j}}{|B(\theta_j)|^2 f_{uu}(\theta_j)} \right] \sum_{j=-m+1}^{m} \left[\frac{\Phi(\theta_j) \bar{B}(\theta_j) \hat{f}_{xy}(\theta_j) e^{-i\beta\theta_j}}{|B(\theta_j)|^2 f_{uu}(\theta_j)} \right] = 0$$

$$\beta = 1, 2, \ldots, k_2 \qquad (10.227)$$

Defining

$$u_t^* = B(L)u_t \qquad (10.228)$$

we observe that the spectral density of the u^* process—which is also covariance stationary—is simply

$$f_{**}(\theta) = |B(\theta)|^2 f_{uu}(\theta) \qquad (10.229)$$

But this is the denominator of the fractions in (10.226) and (10.227). If we could find a consistent estimator for it and use it in lieu of $f_{**}(\cdot)$ we could simplify these equations considerably; however, we would still have to contend with the term $\Phi(\cdot)$ in (10.227) which renders the equations nonlinear in the parameters a_α, b_β.

REMARK 10.10. The reader should observe the analogy between equations (10.119), (10.120) and the problems encounted just above. The expressions $|1 - \lambda e^{i\theta}|^2 f_{uu}(\theta)$, $(1 - \lambda e^{-i\theta})^{-1}$ in the latter equations correspond to the quantities $|B(\theta)|^2 f_{uu}(\theta)$ and $\Phi(\theta)$ in Equations (10.226) and (10.227) above. The first analogy is of course quite obvious; the expression corresponding to $\Phi(\theta)$ in the previous set would have been

$\alpha/(1 - \lambda e^{-i\theta})$; however, α cancels from both sides, thereby leaving $1/(1 - \lambda e^{-i\theta})$. No such cancellation is possible in the present case.

Let us now return to the problem of suitably linearizing Equations (10.226) and (10.227), so that estimators would be readily obtained. Thus, apply the operator $B(L)$ to both sides of (10.215) to obtain

$$y_t = \sum_{s=0}^{k_1} a_s x_{t-s} - \sum_{s'=1}^{k_2} b_{s'} y_{t-s'} + \sum_{j=0}^{k_2} b_j u_{t-j} \qquad (10.230)$$

From this relation we can obtain IV estimators for the parameters, say, $\tilde{a}_s, \tilde{b}_{s'}$ according to the procedure indicated in Remark 9.5 (Section 9.2).

Thus we can compute the residuals

$$\tilde{u}_t = y_t - \sum_{s=0}^{k_1} \tilde{a}_s x_{t-s} + \sum_{s'=1}^{k_2} \tilde{b}_{s'} y_{v-s'} \qquad (10.231)$$

and from these we can obtain a consistent estimator of the spectral ordinates, say $\hat{f}_{**}(\theta_j)$.

Moreover, we can compute the quantities

$$\varphi_j = \tilde{\Phi}(\theta_j) = \frac{\sum_{s=0}^{k_1} \tilde{a}_s e^{-is\theta_j}}{1 + \sum_{s'=1}^{k_2} \tilde{b}_{s'} e^{-is'\theta_j}}, \quad j = -m+1, -m+2, \ldots, m$$

$$(10.232)$$

Thus we can operate with the system

$$\sum_{s=0}^{k_1} a_s \left[\frac{1}{2m} \sum_{j=-m+1}^{m} \left(\frac{\hat{f}_{xx}(\theta_j) e^{i(s-\alpha)\theta_j}}{\hat{f}_{**}(\theta_j)} \right) \right]$$

$$- \sum_{s'=1}^{k_2} b_{s'} \left[\frac{1}{2m} \sum_{j=-m+1}^{m} \left(\frac{\hat{f}_{xy}(\theta_j) e^{i(s'-\alpha)\theta_j}}{\hat{f}_{**}(\theta_j)} \right) \right] = \frac{1}{2m} \sum_{j=-m+1}^{m} \left(\frac{\hat{f}_{xy}(\theta_j) e^{-i\alpha\theta_j}}{\hat{f}_{**}(\theta_j)} \right)$$

$$\alpha = 0, 1, 2, \ldots, k_1 \qquad (10.233)$$

$$\sum_{s=0}^{k_1} a_s \left[\frac{1}{2m} \sum_{j=-m+1}^{m} \left(\frac{\hat{f}_{xx}(\theta_j) \varphi_j e^{i(s-\beta)\theta_j}}{\hat{f}_{**}(\theta_j)} \right) \right]$$

$$- \sum_{s'=1}^{k_2} b_{s'} \left[\frac{1}{2m} \sum_{j=-m+1}^{m} \left(\frac{\hat{f}_{xy}(\theta_j) \varphi_j e^{i(s'-\beta)\theta_j}}{\hat{f}_{**}(\theta_j)} \right) \right] = \frac{1}{2m} \sum_{j=-m+1}^{m} \left(\frac{\hat{f}_{xy}(\theta_j) \varphi_j e^{-i\beta\theta_j}}{\hat{f}_{**}(\theta_j)} \right)$$

$$\beta = 1, 2, \ldots, k_2 \qquad (10.234)$$

Define

$$P = \begin{bmatrix} P_{11} & P_{12} \\ P_{21} & P_{22} \end{bmatrix}, \quad q^* = \begin{pmatrix} q_1^* \\ q_2^* \end{pmatrix}, \quad \gamma = \begin{pmatrix} a \\ -b \end{pmatrix},$$

$$a = (a_0, a_1, \ldots, a_{k_1})', \quad b = (b_1, b_2, \ldots, b_{k_2})' \qquad (10.235)$$

such that P_{11} is $(k_1 + 1) \times (k_1 + 1)$ and its (α, s) element is

$$\frac{1}{2m} \sum_{j=-m+1}^{m} \left(\frac{\hat{f}_{xx}(\theta_j) e^{i(s-\alpha)\theta_j}}{\hat{f}_{**}(\theta_j)} \right)$$

P_{12} is $(k_1 + 1) \times k_2$ and its (α, s') element is

$$\frac{1}{2m} \sum_{j=-m+1}^{m} \left(\frac{\hat{f}_{xy}(\theta_j) e^{i(s'-\alpha)\theta_j}}{\hat{f}_{**}(\theta_j)} \right)$$

P_{21} is $k_2 \times (k_1 + 1)$ and its (β, s) element is

$$\frac{1}{2m} \sum_{j=-m+1}^{m} \left(\frac{\hat{f}_{xx}(\theta_j) \varphi_j e^{i(s-\beta)\theta_j}}{\hat{f}_{**}(\theta_j)} \right)$$

P_{22} is $k_2 \times k_2$ and its (β, s') element is

$$\frac{1}{2m} \sum_{j=-m+1}^{m} \left(\frac{\hat{f}_{xy}(\theta_j) \varphi_j e^{i(s'-\beta)\theta_j}}{\hat{f}_{**}(\theta_j)} \right)$$

Finally, q_1^* is $(k_1 + 1) \times 1$ and its αth element is

$$\frac{1}{2m} \sum_{j=-m+1}^{m} \left(\frac{\hat{f}_{xy}(\theta_j) e^{-i\alpha\theta_j}}{\hat{f}_{**}(\theta_j)} \right)$$

q_2^* is $k_2 \times 1$ and its βth element is

$$\frac{1}{2m} \sum_{j=-m+1}^{m} \left(\frac{\hat{f}_{xy}(\theta_j) \varphi_j e^{-i\beta\theta_j}}{\hat{f}_{**}(\theta_j)} \right)$$

The system may then be written in the compact from

$$P\gamma = q^* \qquad (10.236)$$

The proposed estimator is

$$\hat{\gamma} = P^{-1}q^* \qquad (10.237)$$

Before we proceed with the determination of the properties of this estimator, we remark that since $1/f_{uu}(\theta)$ has a convergent Fourier expansion, then, by the Wiener-Lèvy theorem noted in the previous section, so does $1/f_{**}(\theta)$. This is so since $f_{**}(\theta) = |B)\theta)|^2 f_{uu}(\theta)$ and the roots of the polynomial

$$B(\chi) = \sum_{i=0}^{k_2} b_i \chi^i = 0 \tag{10.238}$$

are greater than unity in modulus. Thus we can write

$$B(\theta) = \prod_{j=1}^{k_2} (1 - \lambda_j e^{-i\theta}) \tag{10.239}$$

the λ_i being the reciprocals of the roots of (10.238). Since $1/(1 - \lambda_j e^{-i\theta})$ has the (absolutely) convergent Fourier series $\sum_{\tau=0}^{\infty} \lambda_j^\tau e^{-i\tau\theta}$, the assertion follows immediately. Thus we may write

$$\sum_{\tau=-\infty}^{\infty} c_\tau e^{i\tau\theta} = \frac{1}{f_{**}(\theta)}, \quad \sum_{\tau=-\infty}^{\infty} g_\tau e^{i\tau\theta} = \frac{\Phi(\theta)}{f_{**}(\theta)} \tag{10.240}$$

the series converging absolutely.

Now observe that

$$\hat{f}_{xy}(\theta) \approx \sum_{s=0}^{k_1} a_s \hat{f}_{xx}(\theta) e^{is\theta} - \sum_{s'=1}^{k_2} b_{s'} \hat{f}_{xy}(\theta) e^{is'\theta} + \hat{f}_{xu*}(\theta) \tag{10.241}$$

and verify immediately that

$$q^* = P\gamma + q \tag{10.242}$$

where

$$q = \begin{pmatrix} q_1 \\ q_2 \end{pmatrix} \tag{10.243}$$

q_1 being $(k_1 + 1) \times 1$ with αth element

$$\frac{1}{2m} \sum_{j=-m+1}^{m} \left(\frac{\hat{f}_{xu*}(\theta_j) e^{-i\alpha\theta_j}}{\hat{f}_{**}(\theta_j)} \right)$$

q_2 being $(k_2 \times 1)$ with βth element

$$\frac{1}{2m} \sum_{j=-m+1}^{m} \left(\frac{\varphi_j \hat{f}_{xu*}(\theta_j) e^{-i\beta\theta_j}}{\hat{f}_{**}(\theta_j)} \right)$$

Hence, substituting in (10.237), we have

$$\hat{\gamma} - \gamma = P^{-1} q \tag{10.244}$$

We shall now establish the probability limit of $(nd_n^{-2}P)$ and the asymptotic distribution of $nd_n^{-1}q$; in this manner we completely determine the asymptotic distribution of $d_n(\hat{\gamma} - \gamma)$, and thus establish the consistency of $\hat{\gamma}$ as an estimator γ.

Let us first obtain the probability limit of the (α, s) element of P_{11}; we have

$$\plim_{n\to\infty} \frac{nd_n^{-2}}{2m} \sum_{j=-m+1}^{m} \frac{\hat{f}_{xx}(\theta_j)e^{-i(\alpha-s)\theta_j}}{\hat{f}_{**}(\theta_j)} = \plim_{n\to\infty} \frac{nd_n^{-2}}{2m} \sum_{j=-m+1}^{m} \frac{\hat{f}_{xx}(\theta_j)e^{-i(\alpha-s)\theta_j}}{f_{**}(\theta_j)}$$

(10.245)

In view of the condition on the u process and the roots of the polynomial $B(\cdot)$, we can write

$$\frac{1}{f_{**}(\theta)} = \sum_{\tau=-\infty}^{\infty} c_\tau e^{i\tau\theta}$$

(10.246)

Hence,

$$\frac{nd_n^{-2}}{2m} \frac{\hat{f}_{xx}(\theta_j)e^{-i(\alpha-s)\theta_j}}{f_{**}(\theta_j)}$$

$$= \frac{1}{2\pi} \frac{1}{2m} \sum_{\tau=-\infty}^{\infty} c_\tau \sum_{\tau'=-n}^{n} a\left(\frac{\tau'}{m}\right) \frac{n\hat{K}_{xx}(\tau')}{d_n^2} e^{-i(\tau'-\tau-\alpha-s)\theta_j}$$

$$\approx \frac{1}{2\pi} \frac{1}{2m} \sum_{\tau=-\infty}^{\infty} c_\tau \sum_{\tau'=-n}^{n} a\left(\frac{\tau'}{m}\right) \frac{n\hat{K}_{x-\alpha x_{-s}}(\tau')}{d_n^2} e^{-i(\tau'-\tau)\theta}$$

(10.247)

where

$$\hat{K}_{x-\alpha x_{-s}}(\tau') = \frac{1}{n} \sum_t x_{t-\alpha+\tau'}x_{t-s}$$

(10.248)

By the same argument employed in connection with Equation (10.162), we conclude

$$\plim_{n\to\infty} \frac{nd_n^{-2}}{2} \sum_{j=-m+1}^{m} \frac{\hat{f}_{xx}(\theta_j)e^{-i(\alpha-s)\theta_j}}{\hat{f}_{**}(\theta_j)} = \frac{1}{2\pi} \sum_{\tau=-\infty}^{\infty} c_\tau \rho(\tau - \alpha + s)$$

$$= \frac{1}{2\pi} \int_{-\pi}^{\pi} \frac{e^{-i(\alpha-s)\theta}dF(\theta)}{f_{**}(\theta)}$$ (10.249)

The probability limit of the (α, s') element of P_{12} is obtained by an argument entirely similar to that employed above, bearing in mind that

$$f_{xy}(\theta) = \frac{1}{2\pi} \sum_{\tau=-n}^{n} a\left(\frac{\tau}{m}\right) \hat{K}_{xy}(\tau) e^{-i\tau\theta} \qquad (10.250)$$

But for $\tau \geq 0$,

$$\hat{K}_{xy}(\tau) = \frac{1}{n} \sum_{t=1}^{n-\tau} x_{t+\tau} y_t = \frac{1}{n} \sum_{j=0}^{\infty} w_j \sum_{t=1}^{n} x_{t+\tau} x_{t-j} + \frac{1}{n} \sum_{t=1}^{n} x_{t+\tau} u_t \qquad (10.251)$$

Hence,

$$\operatorname*{plim}_{n\to\infty} nd_n^{-2} \hat{K}_{xy}(\tau) = \sum_{j=0}^{\infty} w_j \rho(\tau + j) = \int_{-\pi}^{\pi} \bar{\Phi}(\theta) e^{i\tau\theta} dF(\theta) \qquad (10.252)$$

This follows, since $\rho(\tau + j) = \int_{-\pi}^{\pi} e^{i(\tau+j)\theta} dF(\theta)$, $\sum_{j=0}^{\infty} w_j e^{ij\theta} = \bar{A}(\theta)/\bar{B}(\theta)$ $= \bar{\Phi}(\theta)$, and the explanatory variable is independent of the error term. Consequently,

$$\operatorname*{plim}_{n\to\infty} \frac{nd_n^{-2}}{2m} \sum_{j=-m+1}^{m} \left(\frac{\hat{f}_{xy}(\theta_j) e^{-i(\alpha-s')\theta_j}}{\hat{f}_{**}(\theta_j)}\right) = \frac{1}{2\pi} \int_{-\pi}^{\pi} \frac{\bar{\Phi}(\theta) e^{-i(\alpha-s')\theta}}{f_{**}(\theta)} dF(\theta) \qquad (10.253)$$

Now,

$$\operatorname*{plim}_{n\to\infty} \frac{nd_n^{-2}}{2m} \sum_{j=-m+1}^{m} \left[\frac{\varphi_j \hat{f}_{xx}(\theta_j) e^{-i(\beta-s)\beta_j}}{\hat{f}_{**}(\theta_j)}\right]$$
$$= \operatorname*{plim}_{n\to\infty} \frac{nd_n^{-2}}{2m} \sum_{j=-m+1}^{m} \left[\frac{\Phi(\theta_j) \hat{f}_{xx}(\theta_j) e^{-i(\beta-s)\theta_j}}{\hat{f}_{**}(\theta_j)}\right] \qquad (10.254)$$

But we have the absolutely convergent Fourier expansion,

$$\frac{\Phi(\theta)}{f_{**}(\theta)} = \sum_{\tau=-\infty}^{\infty} g_\tau e^{i\tau\theta} \qquad (10.255)$$

Hence, the sum in the right member of (10.254) involves, approximately,

$$\frac{nd_n^{-2}}{2m} \frac{1}{2\pi} \sum_{\tau=-\infty}^{\infty} g_\tau \sum_{\tau'=-n}^{n} a\left(\frac{\tau'}{m}\right) \hat{K}_{x-\beta x-s}(\tau') \sum_{j=-m+1}^{m} e^{-i(\tau'-\tau)\theta_j}$$
$$\approx \frac{nd_n^{-2}}{2\pi} \sum_{\tau=-n}^{n} g_\tau a\left(\frac{\tau}{m}\right) \hat{K}_{x-\beta x-s}(\tau) \qquad (10.256)$$

This is so since, as we pointed out in the preceding section,

$$\sum_{j=-m+1}^{m} e^{-i(\tau'-\tau)\theta_j} = \delta_{\tau'\tau} 2m \qquad (10.257)$$

Hence we conclude

$$\operatorname*{plim}_{n\to\infty} \frac{nd_n^{-2}}{2m} \sum_{j=-m+1}^{m} \left[\frac{\varphi_j \hat{f}_{xx}(\theta_j) e^{-(\beta-s)\theta_j}}{\hat{f}_{**}(\theta_j)} \right] = \frac{1}{2\pi} \sum_{\tau=-\infty}^{m} g_\tau \rho(\tau + s - \beta)$$

$$= \frac{1}{2\pi} \int_{-\pi}^{\pi} \frac{\Phi(\theta) e^{-i(\beta-s)\theta}}{f_{**}(\theta)} dF(\theta)$$

$$(10.258)$$

Finally, combining the argument leading to (10.258) and that leading to (10.253) we conclude

$$\operatorname*{plim}_{n\to\infty} \frac{nd_n^{-2}}{2\pi} \sum_{j=-m+1}^{m} \left[\frac{\hat{f}_{xy}(\theta_j)\varphi_j e^{-i(\beta-s')\theta_j}}{\hat{f}_{**}(\theta_j)} \right]$$

$$= \frac{1}{2\pi} \int_{-\pi}^{\pi} \frac{|\Phi(\theta)|^2 e^{-i(\beta-s')\theta}}{f_{**}(\theta)} \right] dF(\theta) \qquad (10.259)$$

To state the preceding results compactly, define

$$\Psi(\theta) = \begin{bmatrix} e^{-i(\alpha-s)\theta} & e^{-i(\alpha-s')\theta} \\ e^{-i(\beta-s)\theta} & e^{-i(\beta-s')\theta} \end{bmatrix}, \quad \begin{array}{l} s, \alpha = 0, 1, 2, \ldots, k_1 \\ s', \beta = 1, 2, \ldots, k_2 \end{array} \qquad (10.260)$$

$$R(\theta) = \operatorname{diag}[1, 1, \ldots, 1, \Phi(\theta), \Phi(\theta), \ldots, \Phi(\theta)] \qquad (10.261)$$

so that $\Psi(\theta)$ is $(k_1 + k_2 + 1) \times (k_1 + k_2 + 1)$ and $R(\theta)$ is a diagonal matrix, the first $k_1 + 1$ elements on the diagonal being ones and the last k_2 being $\Phi(\theta)$.

The preceding discussion has established that

$$\operatorname*{plim}_{n\to\infty} nd_n^{-2} P = \frac{1}{2\pi} \int_{-\pi}^{\pi} \frac{R(\theta)\Psi(\theta)\bar{R}(\theta)}{f_{**}(\theta)} dF(\theta) \qquad (10.262)$$

REMARK 10.11. The reader should notice that the matrix corresponding to that in (10.262) in the context of the geometric lag model, and exhibited in (10.168) of the preceding section, is not Hermitian—actually symmetric—since it *only appears* to have complex elements. On the other hand, the matrix in (10.262) is indeed Hermitian. One would think that (10.168) is a special case of (10.262). Why the discrepancy? The answer to that is quite simple. The reader should observe that in the second equation in (10.123)—defining the estimator in the case of the geometric lag model—we have canceled from both sides the parameter α; in the case of the rational lag model, α corresponds to $A(\theta_j)$, which cannot be canceled, since we are to sum over j. Hence the discrepancy. It should also be pointed out that if we reintroduce α in the second equation of (10.123) and then take the probability limit of the matrix P of (10.151) (appropriately modified), then we shall obtain exactly the special case of (10.262) corresponding to $k_1 = 0$, $k_2 = 1$, $\Phi(\theta) = \alpha/1 - \lambda e^{-i\theta}$.

Let us now consider the problem of the asymptotic distribution of $nd_n^{-1}q$. If we denote by $q(f_{**}, \Phi)$, the vector resulting when, for $\hat{f}_{**}(\theta_j)$, φ_j, we substitute the true parameters $f_{**}(\theta_j)$, $\Phi(\theta_j)$, then it is obvious that, asymptotically,

$$nd_n^{-1}q(\hat{f}_{**}, \Phi) \sim nd_n^{-1}q(f_{**}, \Phi) \tag{10.263}$$

Hence, we shall operate with the quantity in the right member of (10.263), although for notational simplicity we shall continue to use the same symbols. Now the αth element of $nd_n^{-1}q_1$ is given by

$$\frac{nd_n^{-1}}{2m} \sum_{j=-m+1}^{m} \left[\frac{\hat{f}_{xu}*(\theta_j)e^{-i\alpha\theta_j}}{f_{**}(\theta_j)} \right]$$

$$= \frac{1}{2\pi} \frac{1}{2m} \sum_{j=-m+1}^{m} \sum_{\tau=-\infty}^{\infty} c_\tau \sum_{\tau'=-n}^{n} a\left(\frac{\tau'}{m}\right) nd_n^{-1}\hat{K}_{xu}*(\tau')e^{i(\tau-\tau')\theta_j}e^{-i\alpha\theta_j}$$

$$\approx \frac{1}{2\pi} \frac{1}{2m} \sum_{\tau=-\infty}^{\infty} c_\tau \sum_{\tau'=-n}^{n} a\left(\frac{\tau'}{m}\right) nd_n^{-1}\hat{K}_{x_\alpha u}*(\tau') \sum_{j=-m+1}^{m} e^{i(\tau-\tau')\theta_j}$$

$$\sim \frac{1}{2\pi} \sum_{\tau=-n}^{n} c_\tau a\left(\frac{\tau}{m}\right) nd_n^{-1}\hat{K}_{x_{-\alpha}u}*(\tau) \tag{10.264}$$

Similarly, the βth element of $nd_n^{-1}q_2$ is given by

$$\frac{nd_n^{-1}}{2m} \sum_{j=-m+1}^{m} \left[\frac{\Phi(\theta_j)\hat{f}_{xu}*(\theta_j)e^{-i\beta\theta_j}}{f_{**}(\theta^j)} \right]$$

$$= \frac{1}{2\pi} \frac{1}{2m} \sum_{j=-m+1}^{m} \sum_{\tau=-\infty}^{\infty} g_\tau \sum_{\tau'=-n}^{n} a\left(\frac{\tau'}{m}\right) nd_n^{-1}\hat{K}_{xu*}(\tau')e^{i(\tau-\tau')\theta_j}e^{-i\beta\theta_j}$$

$$\approx \frac{1}{2\pi} \frac{1}{2m} \sum_{\tau=-\infty}^{\infty} g_\tau \sum_{\tau'=-n}^{n} a\left(\frac{\tau'}{m}\right) nd_n^{-1}\hat{K}_{x_{-\beta}u*}(\tau') \sum_{j=-m+1}^{m} e^{i(\tau-\tau')\theta_j}$$

$$\sim \frac{1}{2\pi} \sum_{\tau=-n}^{n} g_\tau a\left(\frac{\tau}{m}\right) nd_n^{-1}\hat{K}_{x_{-\beta}u*}(\tau) \tag{10.265}$$

Define the $(k_1 + k_2 + 1)$-element vector

$$
\zeta_{t+\tau} = \begin{bmatrix} x_{t+\tau} \\ x_{t-1+\tau} \\ \vdots \\ x_{t-k_1+\tau} \\ x_{t-1+\tau} \\ x_{t-2+\tau} \\ \vdots \\ x_{t-k_2+\tau} \end{bmatrix} \tag{10.266}
$$

and observe that asymptotically,

$$
nd_n^{-1}q \sim \frac{1}{2\pi} \sum_{\tau=-n}^{n} \begin{pmatrix} c_\tau I & 0 \\ 0 & g_\tau I \end{pmatrix} \sum_t \left(\frac{\zeta_{t+\tau} u_t^*}{d_n} \right) \tag{10.267}
$$

This is so since $a(\tau/m)$ converges to unity as $n \to \infty$, and hence $m \to \infty$. In (10.267), the identity matrix multiplying c_τ is of order $(k_1 + 1)$, while that multiplying g_τ is of order k_2.

Since

$$
u_t = \sum_{j=0}^{\infty} \alpha_j \varepsilon_{t-j}, \quad u_t^* = B(L)u_t \tag{10.268}
$$

we conclude that

$$
u_t^* = \sum_{j=0}^{\infty} \alpha_j^* \varepsilon_{t-j}, \quad \alpha_j^* = \sum_{s=0}^{k_2} \alpha_{j-s} b_s \tag{10.269}
$$

In view of the conditions on the coefficients α_j and b_s, for any given $\delta_1, \delta_2 > 0$, there certainly exists an integer N such that

$$
Pr\left\{ \left| \sum_{j=N}^{\infty} \alpha_j^* \varepsilon_{t-j} \right| > \delta_1 \right\} < \delta_2 \tag{10.270}
$$

Hence, essentially,

$$
nd_n^{-1}q \sim \sum_\tau \begin{bmatrix} c_\tau I & 0 \\ 0 & g_\tau I \end{bmatrix} \sum_t \left(\frac{\zeta_{t+\tau} u_t^{*N}}{d_n} \right), \quad u_t^{*N} = \sum_{j=0}^{N-1} \alpha_j^* \varepsilon_{t-j} \tag{10.271}
$$

The variables u_t^{*N} are seen to be N-dependent. Since the same arguments employed in the previous section apply here as well, we shall be brief.

Instead of merely repeating the same argument, we shall derive the asymptotic distribution of

$$\frac{1}{d_n} \sum_t \binom{\zeta_{t+\tau}}{\zeta_{t+\tau'}} u_t^{*N}$$

thus obtaining the asymptotic covariance matrix of the binary products in the sum defining (asymptotically) $nd_n^{-1}q$.

Now consider

$$\varphi(t, \tau, \tau', n) = \frac{\alpha'_1\zeta_{t+\tau} + \alpha'_2\zeta_{t+\tau'}}{d_n} u_t^{*N}$$

$$= \varphi_1(t, \tau, n) + \varphi_2(t, \tau', n) \tag{10.272}$$

where α_1, α_2 are arbitrary vectors of constants, each with $k_1 + k_2 + 1$ elements. We wish to find the asymptotic distribution of $\sum_t \varphi(t, \tau, \tau', n)$. We easily verify that the summands are N-dependent variables, having third (absolute) moment that vanishes asymptotically, and finite second moment. Moreover, they have mean zero; hence Theorems 4.2 and 4.3 apply, and we conclude that the sum is asymptotically distributed with mean zero and a certain covariance matrix.

To determine the latter, we define

$$R_t = \sum_{j=0}^{N-1} \text{Cov} \left[\varphi(t + j, \tau, \tau', n)u_{t+j'}^{*N}, \varphi(t + N, \tau, \tau', n)u_{t+N}^{*N} \right.$$

$$+ \sum_{j=0}^{N-1} \text{Cov} \left[\varphi(t + N, \tau, \tau', n)u_{t+N}^{*N}, \varphi(t + j, \tau, \tau', n)u_{t+j}^{*N} \right]$$

$$+ \text{Var} \left[\varphi(t + N, \tau, \tau', n)u_{t+N}^{*N} \right] \tag{10.273}$$

Then the covariance matrix we seek is simply $\sum_{t=1}^{\infty} R_{t+r}$, provided the sum converges independently of r, which is the case here. Now,

$$\text{Cov} \left[\varphi(t + j, \tau, \tau', n)u_{t+j}^{*N}, \varphi(t + N, \tau, \tau', nu_{t+N}^{*N} \right]$$

$$= \varphi(t + j, \tau, \tau'n)\varphi(t + N, \tau, \tau', n)K_{**}(j - N) \tag{10.274}$$

where

$$K_{**}(j - N) = E[u_{t+j}^* u_{t+N}^*] \tag{10.275}$$

Moreover

$$\varphi(t + j, \tau, \tau', n)\varphi(t + N, \tau, \tau', n) = \alpha'_1\left[\frac{\zeta_{t+j+\tau}\zeta'_{t+N+\tau}}{d_n^2}\right]\alpha_1$$

$$+ \alpha'_1\left[\frac{\zeta_{t+j+\tau}\zeta'_{t+N+\tau'}}{d_n^2}\right]\alpha_2 + \alpha'_2\left[\frac{\zeta_{t+j+\tau'}\zeta'_{t+N+\tau}}{d_n^2}\right]\alpha_1$$

$$+ \alpha'_2\left[\frac{\zeta_{t+j+\tau'}\zeta'_{t+N+\tau'}}{d_n^2}\right]\alpha_2 \tag{10.276}$$

Similarly,

$$\text{Cov}\left[\varphi(t + N, \tau, \tau', n)u_{t+N}^{*N}, \varphi(t + j, \tau, \tau', n)u_{t+j}^{*N}\right]$$
$$= \varphi(t + N, \tau, \tau', n)\varphi(t + j, \tau, \tau', n)K_{**}(N - j) \tag{10.277}$$

and

$$\varphi(t + N, \tau, \tau', n)\varphi(t + j, \tau, \tau', n) = \alpha'_1\left[\frac{\zeta_{t+N+\tau}\zeta'_{t+j+\tau}}{d_n^2}\right]\alpha_1$$

$$+ \alpha'_1\left[\frac{\zeta_{t+N+\tau}\zeta'_{t+j+\tau'}}{d_n^2}\right]\alpha_2 + \alpha'_2\left[\frac{\zeta_{t+N+\tau'}\zeta'_{t+j+\tau}}{d_n^2}\right]\alpha_1$$

$$+ \alpha'_2\left[\frac{\zeta_{t+N+\tau'}\zeta'_{t+j+\tau'}}{d_n^2}\right]\alpha_2 \tag{10.278}$$

The asymptotic covariance matrix of $(1/d_n)\sum_t \zeta_{t+\tau}u_t^*$ and $(1/d_n)$ $\times \sum_t \zeta_{t+\tau'}u_t^*$ is given by the sum over j of the limit with respect to n, of the second terms in the right members of (10.276) and (10.278) plus a similar term contributed by the last term in (10.273). Thus we have

$$\sum_{j=0}^{N-1}\left\{\lim_{n\to\infty}\left[\sum_t\left(\frac{\zeta_{t+j+\tau}\zeta'_{t+N+\tau'}}{d_n^2}\right)\right]K_{**}(j - N)\right.$$

$$\left. + \sum_t\left(\frac{\zeta_{t+N+\tau}\zeta'_{t+j+\tau'}}{d_n^2}\right)K_{**}(N - j)\right]\right\}$$

$$+ \lim_{n\to\infty}\sum_t\left(\frac{\zeta_{t+N+\tau}\zeta'_{t+N+\tau'}}{d_n^2}\right)K_{**}(0)$$

$$= \sum_{j=-N}^{N}\mathscr{R}(j + \tau - \tau')K_{**}(j) \tag{10.279}$$

where

$$\mathscr{R}(j + \tau - \tau') = \begin{bmatrix}\mathscr{R}_{11}(j + \tau - \tau') & \mathscr{R}_{12}(j + \tau - \tau') \\ \mathscr{R}_{21}(j + \tau + \tau') & \mathscr{R}_{22}(j + \tau - \tau')\end{bmatrix} \tag{10.280}$$

$\mathscr{R}_{11}$ is $(k_1 + 1) \times (k_1 + 1)$ with (α, s) element $\rho(j + s - \alpha + \tau - \tau')$ and $\alpha, s = 0, 1, 2, \ldots, k_1$; $\mathscr{R}_{12}$ is $(k_1 + 1) \times k_2$ with (α, s') element $\rho(j + 1 + s' - \alpha + \tau - \tau')$, $\alpha = 0, 1, 2, \ldots, k_1$, $s' = 1, 2, \ldots, k_2$; $\mathscr{R}_{21}$ is $k_2 \times (k_1 + 1)$ with (β, s) element $\rho(j - 1 + s - \beta + \tau - \tau')$, $\beta = 1, 2, \ldots, k_2$, $s = 0, 1, 2, \ldots, k_1$; finally, $\mathscr{R}_{22}$ is $k_2 \times k_2$ with (β, s) elements $\rho(j + s - \beta + \tau - \tau')$, $\beta = 1, 2, \ldots, k_2$, $s = 1, 2, \ldots, k_2$.

The reader should verify directly that, asymptotically, the covariance matrix of $(1/d_n) \sum_t \zeta_{t+\tau} u_t^*$ is obtained from (10.279) by setting $\tau = \tau'$. Thus we conclude that

$$nd_n^{-1}q \sim N(0, C) \tag{10.281}$$

where

$$
\begin{aligned}
C &= \left(\frac{1}{2\pi}\right)^2 \sum_{j=-N}^{N} \sum_{\tau'=-\infty}^{\infty} \sum_{\tau=-\infty}^{\infty} \\
&\quad \times \begin{bmatrix} c_\tau \bar{c}_{\tau'} \, \mathscr{R}_{11}(j + \tau - \tau') & c_\tau \bar{g}_{\tau'} \, \mathscr{R}_{12}(j + \tau - \tau') \\ g_\tau \bar{c}_{\tau'} \, \mathscr{R}_{21}(j + \tau - \tau') & g_\tau \bar{g}_{\tau'} \, \mathscr{R}_{22}(j + \tau - \tau') \end{bmatrix} K_{**}(j) \\
&= \frac{1}{2\pi} \int_{-\pi}^{\pi} \left(\frac{R(\theta)\Psi(\theta)\bar{R}(\theta)}{f_{**}(\theta)} \right) dF(\theta) \tag{10.282}
\end{aligned}
$$

—the matrices $\Psi(\theta)$, $R(\theta)$ being defined as in (10.260) and (10.261) respectively. Hence,

$$d_n(\hat{\gamma} - \gamma) \sim N(0, C^{-1}) \tag{10.283}$$

To make the conclusions above, and particularly (10.281), perfectly transparent, we revert to Equation (10.267), truncate the sum in the right member at $n^* < n$, and thus deal with[56]

$$\frac{1}{2\pi} \sum_{\tau=-n^*}^{n^*} \begin{bmatrix} c_\tau I & 0 \\ 0 & g_\tau I \end{bmatrix} \sum_{t=1}^{n} \left(\frac{\zeta_{t+\tau} u_t^*}{d_n} \right)$$

What we have shown above is that as $n \to \infty$, the vector

$$\sum_{t=1}^{n} \left(\frac{\zeta_{t+\tau} u_t^{*N}}{d_n} \right)$$

---

[56] The upper limit of the sum over t was put at n, for notational simplicity only; depending on the element of the vector we consider, it should be $n - \tau$, $n - \tau + , \ldots, n - \tau + k_2, \ldots, n - \tau + k_1$, provided $\tau > k_1, k_2$. If the last condition holds, then the lower limit is appropriate; if not, however, it will have to be modified. To avoid such cumbersome but utterly inessential notational problems, we use the uniform limits $(1, n)$.

converges in distribution to a vector, say,

$$\xi_\tau = \begin{pmatrix} \xi_{1\tau} \\ \xi_{2\tau} \end{pmatrix} \tag{10.284}$$

such that

$$\xi_\tau \sim N\left[0, \sum_{j=-N}^{N} \mathscr{R}(j)K_{**}(j)\right] \tag{10.285}$$

Notice that $\xi_{1\tau}$ is $(k_1 + 1) \times 1$, while $\xi_{2\tau}$ is $k_2 \times 1$; $\xi_{1\tau}$ has covariance matrix

$$\sum_{j=-N}^{N} \mathscr{R}_{11}(j)K_{**}(j)$$

$\xi_{2\tau}$ has covariance matrix

$$\sum_{j=-N}^{N} \mathscr{R}_{22}(j)K_{**}(j)$$

and the cross-covariance matrix of $\xi_{1\tau}$ and $\xi_{2\tau}$ is

$$\sum_{j=-N}^{N} \mathscr{R}_{12}(j)K_{**}(j)$$

We have also shown above that the cross-covariance between the vectors ξ_τ, $\xi_{\tau'}$ is given by

$$\sum_{j=-N}^{N} \mathscr{R}(j + \tau - \tau')K_{**}(j)$$

In subsequent developments the limits of the summation over j will be taken to be $-\infty, \infty$.

Therefore, for fixed n^*, the right member of (10.267) has the asymptotic distribution $N[0, C^{(n^*)}]$, where

$$C^{(n^*)} = \frac{1}{(2\pi)^2} \sum_{\tau=-n^*}^{n^*} \sum_{\tau'=-n^*}^{n^*} \sum_{j=-\infty}^{\infty}$$

$$\times \begin{bmatrix} c_\tau \bar{c}_{\tau'} \mathscr{R}_{11}(j + \tau - \tau') & c_\tau \bar{g}_{\tau'} \mathscr{R}_{12}(j + \tau - \tau') \\ g_\tau \bar{c}_{\tau'} \mathscr{R}_{21}(j + \tau - \tau') & g_\tau \bar{g}_{\tau'} \mathscr{R}_{22}(j + \tau - \tau') \end{bmatrix} K_{**}(j)$$

$$\tag{10.286}$$

Now, the (α, s) element of the upper left block element in (10.286) is given by

$$
\frac{1}{(2\pi)^2} \sum_{\tau=-n^*}^{n^*} \sum_{\tau'=-n^*}^{n^*} \sum_{j=-\infty}^{\infty} c_\tau \bar{c}_{\tau'} \rho(j + s - \alpha + \tau - \tau') K_{**}(j)
$$

$$
= \frac{1}{2\pi} \int_{-\pi}^{\pi} \left(\sum_{\tau=-n^*}^{n^*} c_\tau e^{i\tau\theta} \right) \left(\sum_{\tau'=-n^*}^{n^*} \bar{c}_{\tau'} e^{-i\tau'\theta} \right)
$$

$$
\times \left(\frac{1}{2\pi} \sum_{j=-\infty}^{\infty} K_{**}(j) e^{ij\theta} \right) e^{-i(\alpha-s)\theta} \, dF(\theta)
$$

$$
= \frac{1}{2\pi} \int_{-\pi}^{\pi} \left(\sum_{\tau=-n^*}^{n^*} c_\tau e^{i\tau\theta} \right) \left(\sum_{\tau'=-n^*}^{n^*} \bar{c}_{\tau'} e^{-i\tau'\theta} \right) f_{**}(\theta) e^{-i(\alpha-s)\theta} \, dF(\theta)
$$

$$(10.287)$$

Letting $n^* \to \infty$ the terms in parentheses in the last member of (10.287) converge to $[1/f_{**}(\theta)]^2$; hence we conclude that

$$
\lim_{n^* \to \infty} \left(\frac{1}{2\pi} \right)^2 \sum_{\tau=-n^*}^{n^*} \sum_{\tau'=-n^*}^{n^*} \sum_{j=-\infty}^{\infty} c_\tau \bar{c}_{\tau'} \rho(j + s - \alpha + \tau - \tau') K_{**}(j)
$$

$$
= \frac{1}{2\pi} \int_{-\pi}^{\pi} \frac{e^{-i(\alpha-s)\theta}}{f_{**}(\theta)} \, dF(\theta) \tag{10.288}
$$

The (α, s') element of the upper right block element of (10.286) is

$$
\left(\frac{1}{2\pi} \right)^2 \sum_{\tau=-n^*}^{n^*} \sum_{\tau'=-n^*}^{n^*} \sum_{j=-\infty}^{\infty} c_\tau \bar{g}_{\tau'} \rho(j + s' - \alpha + \tau - \tau') K_{**}(j)
$$

$$
= \frac{1}{2\pi} \int_{-\pi}^{\pi} \left(\sum_{\tau=-n^*}^{n^*} c_\tau e^{i\tau\theta} \right) \left(\sum_{\tau'=-n^*}^{n^*} \bar{g}_{\tau'} e^{-i\tau'\theta} \right)
$$

$$
\times \left(\frac{1}{2\pi} \sum_{j=-\infty}^{\infty} e^{ij\theta} K_{**}(j) \right) e^{-i(\alpha-s')\theta} \, dF(\theta)
$$

$$
= \frac{1}{2\pi} \int_{-\pi}^{\pi} \left(\sum_{\tau=\infty}^{n^*} c_\tau e^{i\tau\theta} \right) \left(\sum_{\tau'=-n^*}^{n^*} \bar{g}_{\tau'} e^{-i\tau'\theta} \right) f_{**}(\theta) e^{-i(\alpha-s')\theta} \, dF(\theta)
$$

$$(10.289)$$

Letting $n^* \to \infty$, the expressions in parentheses in the last member of (10.289) converge respectively to $1/f_{**}(\theta)$ and $\bar{\Phi}(\theta)/f_{**}(\theta)$. There is no difficulty about taking limits under the summation sign, since the series there converge absolutely. There is no need to repeat these arguments for the lower left and right block elements of (10.286); the reader however, may wish to do so as an exercise. The development above makes it obvious that

$$\lim_{n^* \to \infty} C^{(n^*)} = C = \frac{1}{2\pi} \int_{-\pi}^{\pi} \frac{R(\theta)\Psi(\theta)\bar{R}(\theta)}{f_{**}(\theta)} dF(\theta) \qquad (10.290)$$

Since $d_n(\hat{\gamma} - \gamma)$ converges to a vector having a well-defined normal distribution, it is clear that

$$\plim_{n \to \infty} \hat{\gamma} = \gamma \qquad (10.291)$$

which establishes consistency.

We have therefore proved

THEOREM 10.2. Consider the model

$$y_t = \frac{A(L)}{B(L)} x_t + u_t, \quad t = 1, 2, \ldots, n \qquad (10.292)$$

where

$$A(L) = \sum_{i=0}^{k_1} a_i L^i, \quad B(L) = \sum_{j=0}^{k_2} b_j L^j, \quad b_0 = 1 \qquad (10.293)$$

and the roots of the polynomial

$$B(\chi) = \sum_{j=0}^{k_2} b_j \chi^j = 0 \qquad (10.294)$$

lie outside the unit circle.

Let the assumptions of Theorem 10.1, with respect to the explanatory variable and the error process, be valid. Then

(i) For the purpose of obtaining estimators of the parameters of the rational lag structure, minimizing

$$S = (y - r)' K_u^{-1} (y - r) \qquad (10.295)$$

is asymptotically equivalent to minimizing

$$S = \frac{1}{2\pi} \sum_{j=-m+1}^{m} \left[\frac{\hat{f}_{yy}(\theta_j) - 2\Phi(\theta_j)\hat{f}_{xy}(\theta_j) + |\Phi(\theta_j)|^2 \hat{f}_{xx}(\theta_j)}{f_{uu}(\theta_j)} \right] \qquad (10.296)$$

where $y = (y_1, y_2, \ldots, y_n)'$, $r = (r_1, r_2, \ldots, r_n)'$, $r_t = (A(L)/B(L)) x_t$, and $\hat{f}_{yy}(\cdot)$, $\hat{f}_{xx}(\cdot)$, $\hat{f}_{uu}(\cdot)$, $\hat{f}_{xy}(\cdot)$ are the spectral and cross-spectral densities of the variables of the problem—the carets indicating consistent estimators.

(ii)   The estimator $\hat{\gamma}$, of $\gamma = \begin{pmatrix} a \\ -b \end{pmatrix}$, $a = (a_0, a_1, \ldots, a_{k_1})'$, $b = (b_1, b_2, \ldots, b_{k_2})'$, defined by Equation (10.237), is consistent, i.e.,

$$\text{plim}_{n \to \infty} \hat{\gamma} = \gamma \tag{10.297}$$

(iii)   Asymptotically,

$$d_n(\hat{\gamma} - \gamma) \sim N(0, C^{-1}) \tag{10.298}$$

where $d_n^2 = \sum_{t=1}^{n} x_t^2$ and C is as defined in Equation (10.282).

(iv)   A consistent estimator of C is given by

$$\hat{C} = P \tag{10.299}$$

P being as defined in (10.235) and the subsequent discussion.

(v)   Tests of significance for individual elements of the vector γ can be based, asymptotically, on the $N(0, 1)$ distribution. The test statistic is the ratio $d_n\hat{\gamma}_i / \sqrt{p^{ii}}$, $\hat{\gamma}_i$ being the ith element of γ and p^{ii} being the corresponding element of P^{-1}.

REMARK 10.12.   The reader should note that, aside from the greater generality in the assumptions regarding the error term, the development above is essentially identical to that in Section 9.3. Using the same arguments as those following Equation (10.134) we conclude that if K_u is as defined in (10.219), then there exists a nonsingular matrix H such that

$$K_u = H^{-1}H'^{-1} \tag{10.300}$$

and furthermore,

$$\left| \sum_j h_{tj} e^{ij\theta} \right|^2 = \frac{I}{2\pi f_{uu}(\theta)} \tag{10.301}$$

independently of t.

Defining further,

$$\bar{x} = Hx, \quad \bar{x}_t^* = \frac{I}{B(L)} \bar{x}_t, \quad \bar{x}_t^{**} = \frac{A(L)}{B(L)} \bar{x}_t^* \tag{10.302}$$

we see that Equations (10.233) and (10.234) are approximately rendered as

$$\sum_{s=0}^{k_1} \hat{K}_{\bar{x}^* - \alpha \bar{x}^* - s}(0) a_s - \sum_{s=1}^{k_2} \hat{K}_{\bar{x}^* - \alpha \bar{y}^* - s}(0) b_{s'} = \hat{K}_{\bar{x}^* - \alpha \bar{y}^*}(0)$$

$$\alpha = 0, 1, 2, \ldots, k_1$$

$$\sum_{s=0}^{k_1} \hat{K}_{\tilde{x}^{**}-\beta\tilde{y}^*-s}(0)a_s + \sum_{s'=1}^{k_2} \hat{K}_{\tilde{x}^{**}-\beta\tilde{y}^*-s'}{}'(0)b_{s'} = \hat{K}_{\tilde{x}^{**}-\beta\tilde{y}^*}(0)$$

$$\beta = 1, 2, \ldots, k_2 \qquad\qquad (10.303)$$

This, however, is essentially the first equation in (9.103) if the matrix V there is interpreted as K_u.

Of course, it would be exceedingly cumbersome—in the time domain—to carry out the estimation scheme entailed by (10.303), since it would involve the estimation and inversion of the matrix K_u which would be of large order (n) if the number of observations is large.

In the frequency domain, we are not required to obtain the inverse of K_u; instead, we have to compute the spectrum of the u^* process, as well as $\hat{f}_{xx}(\cdot)$ and $\hat{f}_{xy}(\cdot)$.

REMARK 10.13. Although by now there are a number of computer programs performing complex arithmetic, still it may be useful to express the elements of P and q^* in real form. Thus, return to Equation (10.235) and consider the (α, s) element of P_{11}; we observe that $\hat{f}_{xx}(\cdot)$ and $\hat{f}_{**}(\cdot)$ are real quantities which assume the same value for θ_j and θ_{-j}.

Since

$$e^{-i(\alpha-s)\theta_j} + e^{-i(\alpha-s)\theta_{-j}} = 2\cos(\alpha - s)\theta_j \qquad\qquad (10.304)$$

we see that

$$\sum_{j=-m+1}^{m} \frac{\hat{f}_{xx}(\theta_j)e^{-i(\alpha-s)\theta_j}}{\hat{f}_{**}(\theta_j)} = 2\sum_{j=1}^{m-1} \frac{\hat{f}_{xx}(\theta_j)\cos(\alpha-s)\theta_j}{\hat{f}_{**}(\theta_j)} + \frac{\hat{f}_{xx}(0)}{\hat{f}_{**}(0)}$$

$$+ \frac{\hat{f}_{xx}(\pi)}{\hat{f}_{**}(\pi)}\cos(\alpha-s)\pi \qquad\qquad (10.305)$$

Similarly, we observe that the (α, s') element of P_{12} is

$$\sum_{j=-m+1}^{m} \frac{\hat{f}_{xy}(\theta_j)e^{-i(\alpha-s')\theta_j}}{\hat{f}_{**}(\theta_j)}$$

$$= 2\sum_{j=1}^{m-1} \left[\frac{\hat{c}_{xy}^*(\theta_j)\cos(\alpha-s')\theta_j + \hat{q}_{xy}^*(\theta_j)\sin(\alpha-s')\theta_j}{\hat{f}_{**}(\theta_j)}\right]$$

$$+ \frac{\hat{c}_{xy}^*(0)}{\hat{f}_{**}(0)} + \frac{\hat{c}_{xy}^*(\pi)}{\hat{f}_{**}(\pi)}\cos(\alpha-s')\pi \qquad\qquad (10.306)$$

The (β, s) element of P_{21} is

$$\sum_{j=-m+1}^{m} \left[\frac{\hat{f}_{xx}(\theta_j)\varphi_j e^{-i(\beta-s)\theta_j}}{\hat{f}_{**}(\theta_j)} \right]$$

$$= 2 \sum_{j=1}^{m-1} \left[\frac{\hat{f}_{xx}(\theta_j)(\varphi_{1j} \cos(\beta-s)\theta_j + \varphi_{2j} \sin(\beta-s)\theta_j)}{\hat{f}_{**}(\theta_j)} \right]$$

$$+ \frac{\hat{f}_{xx}(0)\varphi_{10}}{\hat{f}_{**}(0)} + \frac{\hat{f}_{xx}(\pi)\varphi_{1m} \cos(\beta-s)\pi}{\hat{f}_{**}(\pi)} \qquad (10.307)$$

The (β, s') element of P_{22} is

$$\sum_{j=-m+1}^{m} \left[\frac{\hat{f}_{xy}(\theta_j)\varphi_j e^{-i(\beta-s')\theta_j}}{\hat{f}_{**}(\theta_j)} \right]$$

$$= 2 \sum_{j=1}^{m-1} \{\hat{c}_{xy}^*(\theta_j)[\varphi_{1j} \cos(\beta-s')\theta_j + \varphi_{2j} \sin(\beta-s')\theta_j]$$

$$+ \hat{q}_{xy}^*(\theta_j)[\varphi_{1j} \sin(\beta-s_j)\theta_j - \theta_{2j} \cos(\beta-s')\theta_j]\}/\hat{f}_{**}(\theta_j)$$

$$+ \frac{\hat{c}_{xy}^*(0)\varphi_{1j}}{\hat{f}_{**}(0)} + \frac{(\hat{c}_{xy}^*(\pi)\varphi_{1j} - \hat{q}_{xy}^*(\pi)\varphi_{2j}) \cos(\beta-s')\pi}{\hat{f}_{**}(\pi)} \qquad (10.308)$$

In the above, we have put

$$\hat{f}_{xy}(\theta) = \hat{c}_{xy}^*(\theta) + i\hat{q}_{xy}^*(\theta), \quad \varphi_j = \varphi_{1j} + i\varphi_{2j} \qquad (10.309)$$

so that $\hat{q}_{xy}^*(\cdot)$—which has no relation with the vectors q_1^*, q_2^*—is the quadrature spectrum of the x and y processes, and $c_{xy}^*(\cdot)$ is the cospectrum. In this connection, recall the discussion in Section 10.3. Also, φ_{1j} is the real part of $\hat{\Phi}(\theta_j)$ and φ_{2j} is its imaginary part. Notice that $\varphi_{2j} = -\varphi_{2(-j)}$, and also

$$\varphi_{10} = \frac{\sum \bar{a}_s}{\sum \bar{b}_{s'}}, \quad \varphi_{1m} = \frac{\sum (-1)^s \bar{a}_s}{\sum (-1^{s'}) \bar{b}_{s'}}; \quad \text{of course,} \quad \varphi_{20} = \varphi_{2m} = 0$$

Obviously, the αth element of q_1^* is

$$\sum_{j=-m+1}^{m} \frac{\hat{f}_{xy}(\theta_j)e^{-i\alpha\theta_j}}{\hat{f}_{**}(\theta_j)} = 2 \sum_{j=1}^{m-1} \left[\frac{\hat{c}_{xy}^*(\theta_j) \cos \alpha\theta_j + \hat{q}_{xy}^*(\theta_j) \sin \alpha\theta_j}{\hat{f}_{**}(\theta_j)} \right]$$

$$+ \frac{\hat{c}_{xy}^*(0)}{\hat{f}_{**}(0)} + \frac{\hat{c}_{xy}^*(\pi) \cos \alpha\pi}{\hat{f}_{**}(\pi)} \qquad (10.310)$$

Finally, the βth element of q_2^* is

$$\sum_{j=-m+1}^{m} \frac{\hat{f}_{xy}(\theta_j)\varphi_j e^{-i\beta\theta_j}}{\hat{f}_{**}(\theta_j)}$$

$$= 2\sum_{j=1}^{m-1} \{\hat{c}_{xy}^*(\theta_j)[\varphi_{1j}\cos\beta\theta_j + \varphi_{2j}\sin\beta\theta_j]$$

$$+ \hat{q}_{yx}^*(\theta_j)[\varphi_{1j}\sin\beta\theta_j - \varphi_{2j}\cos\beta\theta_j]\}/\hat{f}_{**}(\theta_j)$$

$$+ \frac{\hat{c}_{xy}^*(0)\varphi_{1j}}{\hat{f}_{**}(0)} \left[\frac{\hat{c}_{xy}^*(\pi)\varphi_{1j} - \hat{q}_{xy}^*(\pi)\varphi_{2j}}{\hat{f}_{**}(\pi)}\right]\cos\beta\theta_j \qquad (10.311)$$

Chapter 11

DISCRIMINATION AMONG ALTERNATIVE LAG STRUCTURES; MISCELLANEOUS TOPICS

In this chapter we shall deal with a number of loosely connected topics, thus delineating several outstanding research problems. We shall not aim at providing definitive solutions to these problems, but rather at suggesting possible approaches to their analysis and ultimate solution. For this reason, the discussion will be relatively informal.

11.1 Tests of Hypotheses on the Parameters of the Rational Lag

In studying the problem of estimating the parameters of the general rational lag, we have observed that the finite and geometric lags—which have been extensively employed in empirical work—are special cases. In addition, we have established the asymptotic distribution of the estimators of the parameters of the two polynomials defining the rational lag structure. Thus, if we write the model as

$$y_t = \frac{A(L)}{B(L)} x_t + u_t \tag{11.1}$$

where

$$A(L) = \sum_{i=0}^{m} a_i L^i, \quad B(L) = \sum_{j=0}^{n} b_j L^j, \quad b_0 = 1 \tag{11.2}$$

we have obtained the asymptotic distribution of

$$\hat{\gamma} = \begin{pmatrix} \hat{a} \\ -\hat{b} \end{pmatrix}, \quad a = (a_0, a_1, \ldots, a_m)', \quad b = (b_1, b_2, \ldots, b_n)'$$

under a variety of assumptions on the properties of the error term. Hence, tests on the significance of individual coefficients are readily available. For example, to test the hypothesis

$$H_0: m = k_1, \quad n = k_2 - 1$$

as against the alternative,

$$H_1: m = k_1, \quad n = k_2$$

all we have to do is apply the estimation procedures of Chapters 9 or 10 and then test for the significance of the coefficient b_{k_2} by the usual normal (asymptotic) test. Of course, exactly the same procedure will apply to the case where *any* individual coefficient is tested for significance.

Now if it is desired to test, for fixed r,

$$H_0: m = k_1, \quad n = k_2 - r, \quad r \leq k_2$$

as against

$$H_1: m = k_1, \quad n = k_2$$

it is obvious that a chi square test is appropriate. This is so since if $d_T(\hat{\gamma} - \gamma) \sim N(0, W^{-1})$, where $d_T^2 = \sum_{t=1}^{T} x_t^2$ and W is the matrix $(1/\sigma^2)\Sigma$ of Section 9.2 or $(1/\sigma^2)\Phi$ of Section 9.3 or the matrix C of Section 10.7, then partition W by

$$W = \begin{bmatrix} W_{11} & W_{12} \\ W_{21} & W_{22} \end{bmatrix} \tag{11.3}$$

where W_{22} is $r \times r$ and corresponds to the parameter subvector $b^* = (b_{k_2-r+1}, b_{k_2-r+2}, \ldots, b_{k_2})'$. Thus, asymptotically,

$$d_T(\hat{b}^* - b^*) \sim N[0, (W_{22} - W_{21}W_{11}^{-1}W_{12})^{-1}] \tag{11.4}$$

and consequently, under H_0,

$$d_T^2 \hat{b}^{*\prime} [\hat{W}_{22} - \hat{W}_{21}\hat{W}_{11}^{-1}\hat{W}_{12}]\hat{b}^* \sim \chi_r^2 \tag{11.5}$$

The carets ($\wedge$) in (11.5) indicate the estimators of the corresponding parameters.

In particular, such a test would be appropriate for discriminating between a *geometric* and a *specific* rational lag. The appropriate formulation in this case would be to test

$$H_0: m = 0, \quad n = 1$$

as against

$$H_1: m = k_1, \quad n = k_2$$

where k_1 and k_2 are specified.

In such a case we would proceed as above, except that now W_{11} would be a 2×2 matrix corresponding to a_0 and b_1, while W_{22} would be $(k_1 + k_2 - 1)(k_1 + k_2 - 1)$, corresponding to $a_1, a_2, \ldots, a_{k_1}$ and $b_2, b_3, \ldots, b_{k_2}$.

There are two difficulties in such a scheme. First, the hypothesis is somewhat artificial, in that, intuitively, we would wish to test the geometric lag as against *some* rational lag alternative. In the preceding we artificially imposed the particular alternative $m = k_1$, $n = k_2$ where k_1 and k_2 were specified integers. It would be more desirable to formulate the alternative as $m > 0, n > 1$. This is the difference between a *simple* and a *composite* alternative hypothesis. Second, implicitly embedded in the preceding is the assertion, that if $b_{k_2} \neq 0$, then $b_j \neq 0$, $j = 1, 2, \ldots, k_2 - 1$. Of course, there is no reason why this should be so. While we are often reasonably certain of the order of the numerator polynomial, we would be rather uncertain of the order of the denominator polynomial. In such a case, we would wish to test a hypothesis of the form

$$H_0: m = k_1, \quad n = k_2 - r$$

as against the alternative,

$$H_1: m = k_1, \quad n = k_2 - r + s, \quad 0 < s \leq r$$

This implies that we are certain that the order of $B(\cdot)$ is *at most* k_2 and *at least* $k_2 - r$, and the problem is to decide on an order k_2^* such that $k_2 - r \leq k_2^* \leq k_2$. In this context, one might wish to employ a sequential test such as the one given by Anderson [5, ch. 3] in connection with the problem of fitting a polynomial time trend.

In this scheme, the problem is to decide which of the following hypotheses, if any, is true

$$H_r: m = k_1, \quad b_{k_2} \neq 0$$
$$H_{r-1}: m = k_1, \quad b_{k_2} = 0, \quad b_{k_2-1} \neq 0$$
$$\vdots$$
$$H_1: m = k_1, \quad b_{k_2} = b_{k_2-1} = \cdots = b_{k_2-r+2} = 0, \quad b_{k_2-r+1} \neq 0$$
$$H_0: m = k_1, \quad b_{k_2} = b_{k_2-1} = \cdots = b_{k_2-r+1} = 0$$

If any hypothesis above is true, then all preceding hypotheses are also true; conversely, if any hypothesis is false, then all succeeding hypotheses are also false.

We shall not give the details of this procedure since, in the present case, it would require excessive computations; for this reason it is not likely to find extensive use in empirical applications. Such a test, however, has certain optimal properties, and the interested reader is referred to Anderson [5] for a more comprehensive discussion.

From an intuitive point of view, the problem of discriminating between different lag structures is somewhat ticklish. Thus, suppose one specification yields the lag coefficient $\{\hat{w}_{\tau}^{(1)}: \tau = 0, 1, 2, \ldots\}$, while another yields $\{\hat{w}_{\tau}^{(2)}: \tau = 0, 1, 2, \ldots\}$, and each is generated by the quotient $A(L)/B(L)$—the two polynomials being of different orders in each of the two cases. It is quite possible for the two sequences to be substantially similar, while the two sets of polynomials are appreciably different.

In testing hypotheses on lag structures, it would appear to be intuitively more appealing if we could operate with the *sequence of lag coefficients*. Frequently, two entirely dissimilar specifications would yield very close mean lags or lag variabilities. This was pointed out by Griliches [56].

At any rate, the formulation of tests analogous to that given in Section 8.2 would be of considerable interest. The null hypothesis would still be the rational one, while the alternative would be that the lag coefficients $w_{\tau}: \tau = 0, 1, 2, \ldots, N$ are arbitrary (non-specified) constants. One would employ the likelihood ratio principle and obtain the asymptotic distribution of the likelihood ratio test statistic.

It would be highly desirable that such tests be clearly and precisely formulated and that empirical investigators report them routinely whenever rational lags are employed.

11.2 Separation of Parameters

By this somewhat mysterious title, we refer to the following problems: In many empirical investigations, notably those of Jorgenson [81], one encounters the formulation

$$y_t = \frac{A(L)}{B(L)} x_t + u_t \qquad (11.6)$$

together with the assertion that, at least, consistent estimators are obtained by applying ordinary least squares (OLS) to the reduced model

$$y_t = \sum_{i=0}^{k_1} a_i x_{t-i} - \sum_{j=1}^{k_2} b_j y_{t-j} + \text{error} \qquad (11.7)$$

Of course, for this to be so the error term in (11.7) must be independent of (or minimally uncorrelated with) the explanatory variables. Moreover, in order to compute the standard error of the estimator in the usual way, one would require that the errors in (11.7) be *i.i.d.* random variables with mean zero and variance, say, σ^2. *But this implies that the errors in* (11.6) *obey:*

$$u_t = \frac{I}{B(L)} \varepsilon_t \tag{11.8}$$

the ε_t being *i.i.d.* random variables. Furthermore, we observe that the estimation scheme of (11.7) could very well have materialized from

$$y_t = A^*(L)x_t + \frac{I}{B(L)} \varepsilon_t \tag{11.9}$$

under the interpretation that the a_i of (11.7) are determined by

$$A(L) = A^*(L)B(L) \tag{11.10}$$

Thus, estimating the model in (11.7) by ordinary least squares does not necessarily imply the existence of an infinite (rational) distributed lag; moreover, *if the interpretation in* (11.8) *is given in conjunction with* (11.6), *we are implying that we cannot separate the parameters of the lag structure from those of the probability structure of the error term.* However, there is no fundamental identification problem in the model under consideration, and *this difficulty arises solely because we insist on estimating the parameters by ordinary least squares.* There is certainly no reason why we should so restrict ourselves; indeed, in previous chapters we have derived several estimators designed to cope with a variety of assumptions on the error term structure.

Let us illustrate the nature of the considerations above with a simple example. Suppose,

$$y_t = \frac{\alpha I}{I - \lambda L} x_t + u_t \tag{11.11}$$

In conformity with the scheme in (11.6) and (11.8), suppose also that

$$u_t = \frac{I}{I - \rho L} \varepsilon_t \tag{11.12}$$

although there is certainly no reason why the explanatory variable and error term should exhibit the same type of lag structure.

In Chapter 6 we investigated just such a model; in particular, we obtained the asymptotic distribution of the maximum likelihood or minimum chi square estimator of the parameters α, λ, ρ. From that, we can easily obtain the (asymptotic) *marginal* (*joint*) *distribution* of $\hat{\lambda}$, $\hat{\rho}$— the estimators of λ and ρ, respectively. This distribution is also normal.

Instead of assuming *ab initio* that $\lambda = \rho$ and modifying the estimation scheme accordingly, we ought to test this very convenient, but rather implausible, assertion. We may do so as follows: From the joint distribution of $\hat{\lambda}$, $\hat{\rho}$, obtain the distribution of $\hat{\lambda} - \hat{\rho}$; this is also normal with mean $\lambda - \rho$ and variance equal to $\text{Var}(\hat{\lambda}) - 2\,\text{Cov}(\hat{\lambda}, \hat{\rho}) + \text{Var}(\hat{\rho}) = \sigma^{*2}$. Let $\hat{\sigma}^{*2}$ be the estimator of this quantity. Thus, under the null hypothesis,

$$H_0: \lambda = \rho$$

we have that asymptotically,

$$\frac{\sqrt{T}(\hat{\lambda} - \hat{\rho})}{\sigma^{*2}} \sim N(0, 1) \tag{11.13}$$

and the test of this complicated hypothesis reduces to determining whether the mean of a normal distribution is zero. But this is a very elementary test.

Given the rather restrictive assumptions in (11.11) and (11.12), it is certainly indicated that the test above should be carried out, especially since it is so simple to execute.

If the order of the denominator polynomial in (11.6) is small, then instead of assuming (11.8), one ought to test it. In such a case, one could easily employ the obvious extension of the linearized estimator we derived in Section 9.3, with suitable modifications to take into account the added complexity of the error term. Indeed, it would be an interesting exercise to carry out such tests on the many empirical studies employing the assumption of (11.8) in conjunction with the model in (11.6).

A more satisfactory way of approaching the problem is available when the sample is reasonably large, say $T = 100$ or more. In such a case, we can employ spectral techniques, and the following procedure becomes quite feasible.

Suppose the denominator polynomial in (11.6) is known to be of degree k_2. Let the error term be a covariance stationary process, and let it be desired to test the validity of (11.8). In such a case, we can proceed as in Section 10.7—thus obtaining estimators for the elements of the vector γ. Denote such estimators by $\hat{a}_i$, $i = 0, 1, 2, \ldots, k_1$, $\hat{b}_j$, $j = 1, 2, \ldots, k_2$. Then consider the residuals,

$$\hat{u}_t^* = y_t - \sum_{i=0}^{k_1} \hat{a}_i x_{t-i} + \sum_{j=1}^{k_2} \hat{b}_j y_{t-j} \tag{11.14}$$

These residuals correspond to the process,

$$u_t^* = B(L)u_t \tag{11.15}$$

If the hypothesis in (11.8) is correct, then the spectral density of the u^* process is given by

$$f_{**}(\theta) = \frac{\sigma^2}{2\pi} \tag{11.16}$$

where σ^2 is the common variance of the ε_t; notice that because we have imposed the normalization $b_0 = 1$, we cannot assert that the ε process has variance one, under the null hypothesis.

From the residuals in (11.14), we can certainly compute the spectral estimator $\hat{f}_{**}(\theta_j)$, where the points θ_j are sufficiently spaced so as to insure that the ordinates $\hat{f}_{**}(\theta_j)$, $j = 1, 2, \ldots, p$ are (asymptotically) mutually independent. The number p, which for convenience is taken to be even, is what is commonly called *equivalent number of independent estimates* (*ENIE*). For a discussion of this, see [32, ch. 11]. It can then be shown that asymptotically,

$$\ln \hat{f}_{**}(\theta_j) \sim N\left[f_{**}(\theta_j), \frac{M_T G(a)}{T} \right] \tag{11.17}$$

where T is the sample size, M_T is the number of lags employed by the spectral window generator $a(\cdot)$, and

$$G(a) = \int_{-\infty}^{\infty} a^2(u)du \tag{11.18}$$

In the case of the Parzen window, $G(a) = 0.54$. Now, consider the statistic

$$J = \frac{[\sum_{j=1}^{p/2} \ln \hat{f}_{**}(\theta_j) - \sum_{j=1}^{p/2} \ln \hat{f}_{**}(\theta_{p/2+j})]}{\sqrt{\frac{pM_T G(a)}{T}}} \tag{11.19}$$

Under the null hypothesis in (11.16), J—for large T—is approximately $N(0, 1)$, and hence a test of the validity of the assertion in (11.8) can be easily carried out. Other more powerful tests are also available.

11.3 Tests for Stability

In dealing with the model

$$y_t = \frac{A(L)}{B(L)} x_t + u_t \tag{11.20}$$

it is necessary to assert that the roots of the polynomial

$$\sum_{j=0}^{n} b_j \varphi^j = 0, \quad b_0 = 1 \tag{11.21}$$

are greater than unity in absolute value. This requirement was stressed repeatedly in Chapters 9 and 10. Indeed, when we examined the geometric lag model, this restriction was explicitly incorporated in the estimation procedure. Unfortunately, however, it is not simple to do so in the case of the general rational lag model. Such an undertaking would *require us to translate the restrictions on the roots to restrictions on the coefficients of the polynomial* $B(\cdot)$ *and to obtain estimators for the parameters of the model subject to these restrictions.* Thus, once *unrestricted* estimators have been obtained, it is important to test the validity of the stability assertion. Notice that if (any of) the roots of (11.21) are less than unity in absolute value, the meaning of (11.20) is not clear at all. In such a case, the behavior of the dependent variable, y_t, may be increasingly dominated by initial conditions; hence the representation in (11.20) would be invalid.

To develop tests for stability, we need to establish the (asymptotic) distribution of the relevant statistics. First, we observe that $\varphi = 0$ is not a root of the polynomial in (11.21); this is so since $b_0 = 1$. If the polynomial is indeed of degree n, $b_n \neq 0$, and it is obvious that if $\{\varphi_j : j = 1, 2, \ldots, n\}$ are the roots of (11.21), then they are also the roots of

$$\sum_{j=0}^{n} b_j^* \varphi^j = 0, \quad b_j^* = \frac{b_j}{b_n}, \quad j = 1, 2, \ldots, n \tag{11.22}$$

Since the polynomial in (11.22) is monic—i.e. the coefficient of its largest power is unity—it has the representation

$$\sum_{j=0}^{n} b_j^* \varphi^j = \prod_{j=1}^{n} (\varphi - \varphi_j) = (-1)^n \prod_{j=1}^{n} \varphi_j \prod_{j=1}^{n} \left(1 - \frac{\varphi}{\varphi_j}\right) \tag{11.23}$$

But,

$$(-1)^n \prod_{j=1}^{n} \varphi_j = b_0^* = \frac{1}{b_n} \tag{11.24}$$

Hence,

$$\sum_{j=1}^{n} b_j \varphi^j = \prod_{j=1}^{n} (1 - \lambda_j \varphi), \quad \lambda_j = \frac{1}{\varphi_j}, \quad j = 1, 2, \ldots, n \tag{11.25}$$

We therefore have the identification

$$b_1 = -\sum_{j=1}^{n} \lambda_j, \quad b_2 = \sum \lambda_{j_1}\lambda_{j_2}, \dots, \quad b_n = (-1)^n \prod_{j=1}^{n} \lambda_j \quad (11.26)$$

In general, b_k is the sum of all possible products of the roots taken k at a time and signed by $(-1)^k$. We further observe that the λ_j are the roots of

$$\sum_{j=0}^{n} b_j \varphi^{n-j} = 0 \qquad (11.27)$$

To show this, we shall establish that if φ_s is a root of (11.21) or of (11.22), then $1/\varphi_s$ is a root of (11.27). Thus,

$$\sum_{j=0}^{n} b_j \varphi_s^{-(n-j)} = \varphi_s^{-n} \sum_{j=0}^{n} b_j \varphi_s^{j} \qquad (11.28)$$

Since $\varphi_s \neq 0$ and φ_s is a root of (11.21), the right member of (11.28) is zero, whence we conclude

$$\sum_{j=0}^{n} b_j \varphi_s^{-(n-j)} = 0 \qquad (11.29)$$

which shows that $1/\varphi_s$ is a root of (11.27). But since $\lambda_j = 1/\varphi_j$, we see that the coefficients of the denominator polynomial are most conveniently expressed as functions of the roots of the polynomial in (11.29). We shall take this as a point of departure for the following discussion. In (11.26) we have established a relation between the roots of the polynomial in (11.27) and the coefficients of $B(\cdot)$. Moreover, in Chapters 9 and 10 we established the (marginal) asymptotic distribution of $d_T(\hat{b} - b^0)$, where $d_T^2 = \sum_{t=1}^{T} x_t^2$, $\hat{b}$ is the appropriate estimator and b^0 is the true parameter vector corresponding to the coefficients of $B(\cdot)$. In particular, we have

$$d_T(\hat{b} - b^0) \sim N(0, W) \qquad (11.30)$$

where W is the appropriate submatrix of $\sigma^2 \sum^{-1}$ of Section 9.2, or of $\sigma^2 \Phi^{-1}$ of Section 9.3, or of C^{-1} in Section 10.7.

The functional relation in (11.26) is continuously differentiable, and we shall assume that if λ^0 is the true vector of roots corresponding to the true coefficient vector b^0, then the Jacobian of this relation is nonsingular in a neighborhood of λ^0. Let (11.26) be expressed more conveniently as

$$b = h(\lambda) \qquad (11.31)$$

and let the Jacobian matrix be denoted by[57]

$$J(\lambda) = \left[\frac{\partial b_i}{\partial \lambda_j} \right], \quad i, j = 1, 2, \ldots, n \qquad (11.32)$$

The assumption above states that

$$|J(\lambda^0)| \neq 0 \qquad (11.33)$$

Thus, by the inverse function theorem, the relation is invertible in a neighborhood of (λ^0, b^0), so that

$$\lambda = g(b), \quad g(b) = h^{-1}(b) \qquad (11.34)$$

Moreover,

$$J^*(b^0) = [J(\lambda^0)]^{-1} \qquad (11.35)$$

where $J^*(b)$ is the Jacobian matrix of the transformation in (11.34). In view of the consistency of $\hat{b}$ as an estimator of b^0, it follows that if $\hat{\lambda}_j$, $j = 1, 2, \ldots, n$ are the roots of

$$\sum_{j=0}^{n} \hat{b}_j \varphi^{n-j} = 0 \qquad (11.36)$$

then

$$\plim_{T \to \infty} \hat{\lambda}_j = \lambda_j \qquad (11.37)$$

If the sample is sufficiently large and we number the roots of (11.36) according to decreasing absolute value—thus $|\hat{\lambda}_1| \geq |\hat{\lambda}_2| \geq |\hat{\lambda}_3| \cdots \geq |\hat{\lambda}_n|$ —then this ranking, with probability arbitrarily close to one, corresponds to the ranking of the true roots. Having made the ranking above, there is then no difficulty in pairing estimated and true parameters.

From (11.34), we have that

$$\hat{\lambda} = g(\hat{b}) \qquad (11.38)$$

Expand by Taylor series about the true parameter vector b^0 to obtain

$$\hat{\lambda} = g(b^0) + \frac{\partial g}{\partial b}(b^0)(\hat{b} - b^0) + \text{second order terms} \quad (11.39)$$

In view of the fact that $d_T(\hat{b} - b^0)$ possesses a well-defined asymptotic distribution, the second order terms, normalized by d_T, can be shown to

---

[57] We implicitly assume that the roots are *distinct*; if they are not, then considerable analytical complications are introduced. However, this restriction is minimal, since it is unlikely that repeated roots will arise extensively in practice.

vanish in probability. Consequently, we can operate with

$$d_T(\hat{\lambda} - \lambda^0) = J^*(b^0) d_T(\hat{b} - b^0) \qquad (11.40)$$

noting that $J^*(b^0) = (\partial g/\partial b)(b^0)$. But then it is obvious that asymptotically,

$$d_T(\hat{\lambda} - \lambda^0) \sim N[0, J^*(b^0) W J^*(b^0)'] \qquad (11.41)$$

To complete the inference problem, we need to give a consistent estimator of the covariance matrix in (11.41). In previous chapters we have, in fact, given a consistent estimator of W, so that we needed only be concerned about the estimator of $J^*(b^0)$. Now it is difficult to obtain $J^*(b)$ directly, since there is generally no "formula" for the roots of an nth order polynomial in terms of its coefficients. On the other hand, the relation in (11.35) renders the problem tractable. We observe that the first row of $J(\lambda)$ consists of the vector $(-1, -1, \ldots, -1)$; the second row has for its ith element, $\sum_{j \neq i} \lambda_j$; the third row has for its ith element the (negative of the) sum of all possible products of roots taken two at a time but *not* containing λ_i. In general, the kth row has for its ith element $(-1)^k$ times the sum of all possible products of roots taken k at a time, *but not containing* λ_i. Since consistent estimators of the roots are available, it follows that

$$\widehat{J^*(b^0)} = [J(\hat{\lambda})]^{-1} \qquad (11.42)$$

is a consistent estimator of $J^*(b^0)$, and that

$$\hat{W}^* = [J(\hat{\lambda})]^{-1} \hat{W} [J(\hat{\lambda})']^{-1} \qquad (11.43)$$

is a consistent estimator of the covariance matrix in (11.41); it is to be understood that $\hat{W}$ is a consistent estimator of the corresponding submatrix of $\sigma^2 \Sigma^{-1}$ or $\sigma^2 \Phi^{-1}$ or C^{-1}, as given in Chapters 9 and 10, depending on the assumptions made on the errors of the model.

From the preceding discussion, it is possible to deduce a test of the stability assertion. The test we shall propose is probably not an optimal one, and further research on this topic is indicated. However, it will certainly provide us with a means of verifying or rejecting the stability hypothesis. We first observe that, in view of the large sample properties investigated here, if the sample is sufficiently large and $\hat{\lambda}_1 > 0$, the hypothesis may be formulated as

$$H_0: \lambda_1 = 0.99$$

as against

$$H_1: \lambda_1 > 1$$

If $\hat{\lambda}_1 < 0$, then we can test

$$H_0: \lambda_1 = -0.99$$

as against

$$H_1: \lambda_1 < -1$$

The null hypothesis is somewhat artificial, but setting $\lambda_1 = 1$ or $\lambda_1 = -1$ is not an admissible procedure since, if true, the meaning of the model is in doubt, and then the distributional properties developed above are invalid. We shall formulate the test in terms of the first alternative; the reader may modify it if the second alternative is appropriate.

Let $\hat{w}_{11}^*$ be the $(1, 1)$ element of $\hat{W}^*$ in (11.43). Under the null hypothesis, asymptotically,

$$\frac{d_T(\hat{\lambda}_1 - 0.99)}{\sqrt{\hat{w}_{11}^*}} \sim N(0, 1) \qquad (11.44)$$

Let t_α be a number such that if $x \sim N(0, 1)$, then

$$\Pr\{x > t_\alpha\} = \alpha \qquad (11.45)$$

α being suitably small. From (11.45) we see that

$$\Pr\left\{ \frac{d_T(\hat{\lambda}_1 - 0.99)}{\sqrt{\hat{w}_{11}^*}} > t_\alpha \right\} = \alpha \qquad (11.46)$$

defines the rejection region of the null hypothesis at the α level of significance. Hence the test may be formulated as

$$\text{Reject} \quad H_0: \lambda_1 = 0.99$$

if

$$\hat{\lambda}_1 > \frac{t_\alpha \sqrt{\hat{w}_{11}^*}}{d_T} + 0.99 \qquad (11.47)$$

and otherwise accept it.

Notice that if the largest root in absolute value is less than one, then *all* roots are less than one. Hence, the stability assertion will be fully validated.

REMARK 11.1. The argument in this section, and in particular the test of the stability hypothesis, implicitly assumes that all roots are *real*. Of course, there is no reason why all roots should be real. Complex roots, however, do not present a problem insofar as distributional aspects are concerned. Suppose there are $2s$ complex roots and $r = n - 2s$ real roots. Since the complex roots appear in conjugate pairs, the $2s$ roots contain exactly $2s$ real parameters—their real and imaginary parts. Hence, the development leading to (11.41) is fully valid, provided the λ_j are reinterpreted as the real and imaginary parts of the roots. This reinterpretation affects only the computation of the Jacobian matrix $J(\lambda)$ and the reader may supply the details needed in order to make this discussion fully operational. If the largest root in absolute value is real, the test given in (11.47) is fully valid. If, however, it is imaginary and λ_1, λ_2 correspond to its real and imaginary parts, then in order to employ a test of stability, we have to develop the distribution of $d_T^2[\hat{\lambda}_1^2 + \hat{\lambda}_2^2]$, a task which lies beyond the scope of this book. Of course, if $\hat{W}_{22}^*$ is the submatrix of $\hat{W}^*$, consisting of its first two rows and columns, then asymptotically,

$$d_T^2(\hat{\lambda}_1 - \lambda_1, \hat{\lambda}_2 - \lambda_2)\,\hat{W}_{22}^{*-1}\begin{pmatrix}\hat{\lambda}_1 - \lambda_1\\ \hat{\lambda}_2 - \lambda_2\end{pmatrix} \sim \chi_2^2 \qquad (11.48)$$

Unfortunately, the condition $\lambda_1^2 + \lambda_2^2 = (0.99)^2$ is not uniquely translatable to conditions on λ_1 and λ_2 individually. On the other hand, it is rather unlikely that situations will frequently arise in practice that require this test apparatus.

11.4 Goodness of Fit Criteria and Related Topics

In the general linear model

$$y = X\beta + u \qquad (11.49)$$

where y is $T \times 1$, X is $T \times k$, β is $k \times 1$, u is $T \times 1$ and

$$\text{rank}(X) = k, \quad u \sim N(0, \sigma^2 I) \qquad (11.50)$$

the (unadjusted) coefficient of determination of multiple regression, R^2, is given by

$$R^2 = 1 - \frac{\hat{u}'\hat{u}}{(y - e\bar{y})'(y - e\bar{y})} \qquad (11.51)$$

where

$$\bar{y} = \frac{1}{T}\sum_{t=1}^{T} y_t, \quad e = (1, 1, 1, \ldots, 1)', \quad \hat{u} = y - X\hat{\beta} \qquad (11.52)$$

Thus it has the intuitive interpretation of denoting the fraction of the variability of the dependent variable explained by the regression. In addition, R^2 has an interpretation as the square of the simple correlation between predicted and actual values of the dependent variable within the sample. The square of the simple correlation between actual and predicted values is

$$r^2 = \frac{[(y - e\bar{y})'(\hat{y} - e\bar{y})]^2}{(\hat{y} - e\bar{y})'(\hat{y} - e\bar{y})(y - e\bar{y})'(y - e\bar{y})} \qquad (11.53)$$

since

$$\frac{1}{T} \sum_{t=1}^{T} \hat{y}_t = \frac{1}{T} \sum_{t=1}^{T} y_t = \bar{y} \qquad (11.54)$$

Now

$$(y - e\bar{y})'(\hat{y} - e\bar{y}) = (\hat{y} - e\bar{y})'(\hat{y} - e\bar{y}) = \hat{\beta}'X'X\hat{\beta} - T\bar{y}^2 \quad (11.55)$$

in view of the orthogonality of $\hat{u}$ and $\hat{y}$. Thus,

$$r^2 = \frac{(y - e\bar{y})'(\hat{y} - e\bar{y})}{(y - e\bar{y})'(y - e\bar{y})} = 1 - \frac{\hat{u}'\hat{u}}{(y - e\bar{y})'(y - e\bar{y})} = R^2 \quad (11.56)$$

Finally, it may be shown that $M(R^2/(1 - R^2))$, M being an appropriate constant, is the test statistic for testing the null hypothesis that the coefficients of all explanatory variables, excepting the constant term, are zero; under this null hypothesis, $M(R^2/(1 - R^2))$ is F-distributed.

Thus, the coefficient of determination of multiple regression possesses a number of desirable properties, both intuitive and rigorous. The reader should observe that in the preceding discussion *the orthogonality* between $\hat{u}$ and $X\hat{\beta}$ is of fundamental importance. Notice that y is partitioned into two orthogonal components, one contributed by the explanatory variables and one contributed by the error terms.

In the case of distributed lag models, such relationships are unfortunately lost. Thus, for example, consider the simple geometric lag model with *i.i.d.* errors and observations centered about respective sample means,

$$y_t = \frac{\alpha I}{I - \lambda L} x_t + u_t \qquad (11.57)$$

Let $\hat{\alpha}$, $\hat{\lambda}$ be the minimum chi square or ML estimators of the parameters, as the case may be. We can certainly compute

$$\hat{y}_t = \hat{\alpha} \sum_{i=0}^{t-1} \hat{\lambda}^i x_{t-i} \qquad (11.58)$$

and thus the residuals

$$\hat{u}_t = y_t - \hat{y}_t \qquad (11.59)$$

It is not true in this model that

$$\hat{y}'\hat{u} = 0 \tag{11.60}$$

Hence, although we can write

$$y = \hat{y} + \hat{u}, \quad \hat{y} = (\hat{y}_1, \hat{y}_2, \ldots, \hat{y}_T)', \quad \hat{u} = (\hat{u}_1, \hat{u}_2, \ldots, \hat{u}_T)' \tag{11.61}$$

and compute

$$R^2 = 1 - \frac{\hat{u}'\hat{u}}{y'y} \tag{11.62}$$

this is no longer the (relative) error remaining after regression. Notice, from (11.61), that

$$y'y = \hat{\alpha}^2 \bar{x}^{*\prime} \bar{x}^* + 2\hat{\alpha}\bar{x}^{*\prime}\hat{u} + \hat{u}'\hat{u} \tag{11.63}$$

where

$$\bar{x}_t^* = \sum_{i=0}^{t-1} \hat{\lambda}^i x_{t-i}, \quad \bar{x}^* = (\bar{x}_1^*, \bar{x}_2^*, \ldots, \bar{x}_T^*)',$$

and hence

$$R^2 = \frac{y'y - \hat{u}'\hat{u}}{y'y} = \frac{\hat{\alpha}^2 \bar{x}^{*\prime} \bar{x}^* + 2\hat{\alpha}\bar{x}^{*\prime}\hat{u}}{y'y} \tag{11.64}$$

Consequently, the first intuitive interpretation given to R^2 in the case of the general linear model becomes rather nebulous; it is quite apparent that the numerator of the quantity in (11.64) is *not* the "sum of squares due to the regression," because of the term $2\alpha\bar{x}^{*\prime}\hat{u}$. Of course, this term will vanish asymptotically, so that

$$\plim_{T \to \infty} R^2 = \frac{\alpha^2 \sigma_0}{\alpha^2 \sigma_0 + \sigma^2} \tag{11.65}$$

where

$$\sigma_0 = \lim_{T \to \infty} \frac{x^{*\prime} x^*}{T}, \quad x_t^* = \sum_{i=0}^{\infty} \lambda^i x_{t-i}, \quad x^* = (x_1^*, x_2^*, \ldots, x_T^*)' \tag{11.66}$$

Thus if the model is correctly specified, the quantity in (11.64) is a consistent estimator of the fraction of the variability of the dependent variable contributed by the explanatory variable. Similarly, the function $R^2/(1 - R^2)$ is not of any use in rigorous tests of significance on the parameters of the model. In earlier chapters, however, we have derived the asymptotic distribution of the estimators $\hat{\alpha}$, $\hat{\lambda}$, and thus we are perfectly capable of carrying out tests of significance which are asymptotically exact.

Thus we are left only with the interpretation of the coefficient of determination as the square of the simple correlation between predicted and actual values of the dependent variable within the sample period. This quantity is suitable as the basis for *judgmental determinations regarding the goodness of fit of the model,* and should be computed routinely in empirical studies employing rational lag structures.

Let us now obtain some of the properties of this quantity. We suppose that the data are centered about sample means, so that $e'y = 0$ $e'x = 0$, e being the vector of ones given in (11.52), y, x being the vectors of observation on the dependent and explanatory variables, respectively.

The vector of predicted values is given by

$$\hat{y} = \hat{\alpha}\hat{D}x \tag{11.67}$$

where

$$\hat{D} = \begin{bmatrix} 1 & 0 & 0 & . & 0 \\ \hat{\lambda} & 1 & 0 & . & 0 \\ \hat{\lambda}^2 & \hat{\lambda} & 1 & . & 0 \\ . & & & & \\ \hat{\lambda}^{T-1} & \hat{\lambda}^{T-2} & \hat{\lambda}^{T-3} & . & 1 \end{bmatrix} \tag{11.68}$$

and

$$e'\hat{y} = \frac{\hat{\alpha}}{1 - \hat{\lambda}}(1 - \hat{\lambda}^T, 1 - \hat{\lambda}^{T-1}, \ldots, 1 - \hat{\lambda})x = \frac{-\hat{\alpha}}{1 - \hat{\lambda}}\sum_{i=1}^{T}\hat{\lambda}^{T+1-i}x_i \tag{11.69}$$

Thus, even if the x_i are centered so that $e'x = 0$, $\sum_{i=1}^{T}\hat{\lambda}^{T+1-i}x_i \neq 0$ whence we conclude

$$\bar{y} = \frac{1}{T}e'\hat{y} \neq 0 \tag{11.70}$$

Now, the square of the simple correlation between predicted and actual values is given by

$$r^2 = \frac{[y'(\hat{y} - e\bar{y})]^2}{y'y(\hat{y} - e\bar{y})'(\hat{y} - e\bar{y})} \tag{11.71}$$

In the numerator of (11.71), we observe that

$$y'(\hat{y} - e\bar{\hat{y}}) = y'\hat{y} - y'e\bar{\hat{y}} = y'\hat{y} \tag{11.72}$$

The last equality is valid since $e'y = y'e = 0$. Furthermore,

$$(\hat{y} - e\bar{\hat{y}})'(\hat{y} - e\bar{\hat{y}}) = \hat{y}'\hat{y} - T\bar{\hat{y}}^2 \tag{11.73}$$

and the expression in (11.71) can be simplified to

$$r^2 = \frac{(y'\hat{y})^2}{y'y(\hat{y}'\hat{y} - T\bar{\hat{y}}^2)} \tag{11.74}$$

It is quite obvious from (11.69) that if the explanatory variable is, for example, a covariance stationary process or otherwise obeys the conditions imposed in Chapter 10, then

$$\plim_{T \to \infty} \bar{\hat{y}} = 0 \tag{11.75}$$

Hence,

$$\plim_{T \to \infty} r^2 = \frac{(\alpha^2\sigma_0)^2}{(\alpha^2\sigma_0 + \sigma^2)\alpha^2\sigma_0} = \frac{\alpha^2\sigma_0}{\alpha^2\sigma_0 + \sigma^2} \tag{11.76}$$

which is the same as the probability limit of the quantity R^2 as defined in (11.64). It is interesting, then, to ask how the two quantities differ for finite samples. We observe that

$$y'y - \hat{u}'\hat{u} = y'\hat{y} + \hat{y}'\hat{u} \tag{11.77}$$

and consequently,

$$R^2 = r^2\left(\frac{\hat{y}'\hat{y} - T\bar{\hat{y}}^2}{y'\hat{y}}\right) + \frac{\hat{y}'\hat{u}}{y'y} \tag{11.78}$$

The identity of the probability limits of the two quantities becomes quite transparent, since $\plim_{T \to \infty} \hat{y}'\hat{u}/y'y = 0$, $\plim_{T \to \infty} T\bar{\hat{y}}^2 = 0$ and $\plim_{T \to \infty} y'\hat{y}/T = \plim_{T \to \infty} \hat{y}'\hat{y}/T$.

From (11.78), we also see that r^2 is a more useful judgmental statistic for appraising the goodness of fit of the model, since R^2 introduces the irrelevant quantity $\hat{y}'\hat{u}$ in its numerator.

Finally, although the argument was carried out in terms of the geometric lag structure, the reader should observe that exactly the same argument can be made regarding the general rational lag model, irrespective of the assumptions made regarding the error process.

To recapitulate, in the context of distributed lag models the usual coefficient of determination computed as in (11.62) has no useful meaning, since it cannot form the basis of a rigorous test of significance on the parameters of the model, nor can it be interpreted as the (square of the) simple correlation coefficient between predicted and actual values of the dependent variables within the sample period.

Regarding rigorous tests of significance, we have, in earlier chapters, given the asymptotic distribution of parameters for a number of models under a wide variety of assumptions regarding the error structure. Thus, tests of significance can be based on these asymptotic distributions for moderately large samples.

If one wishes to form a judgment regarding the extent to which the model "explains" the data, then it seems preferable to do so in terms of the statistic r^2 given in (11.74). The small sample distribution of r^2 is quite intractable, and thus no rigorous judgment can be based on it.

In empirical investigations, one is often prone to write the model as

$$y_t = \sum_{i=1}^{k_1} a_i x_{t-i} - \sum_{j=0}^{k_2} b_j y_{t-j} + \text{error} \qquad (11.79)$$

and estimate the parameters by OLS, giving the usual R^2 as evidence of goodness of fit. This is an exceedingly risky procedure since, if it does not so happen that the error term in the original form is given by $[I/B(L)]\varepsilon_t$, and the ε_t are *i.i.d.* random variables, application of OLS to (11.79) will yield *inconsistent estimators*. In such a case, it is not clear what R^2 would mean and what judgmental determinations can be based on it. This problem is related to the point raised by Nerlove and Wallis [121] in the context of the model

$$y_t = \beta y_{t-1} + u_t \qquad (11.80)$$

These authors correctly indicate that *if one estimates β by ordinary least squares and subsequently computes the Durbin-Watson statistic*

$$\text{D.W.} = \frac{\sum_{t=2}^{T}(\hat{u}_t - \hat{u}_{t-1})^2}{\sum_{t=2}^{T} \hat{u}_{t-1}^2} \qquad (11.81)$$

where

$$\hat{u}_t = y_t - \hat{\beta} y_{t-1}, \quad \hat{\beta} = \frac{\sum_{t=2}^{T} y_t y_{t-1}}{\sum_{t=2}^{T} y_{t-1}^2} \qquad (11.82)$$

then if the error term is a sequence of i.i.d. random variables, the probability limit of D.W. is 2. On the other hand, if the alternative hypothesis is true, namely,

$$u_t = \rho u_{t-1} + \varepsilon_t, \quad |\rho| < 1 \qquad (11.83)$$

the ε_t being *i.i.d.* random variables, *then the probability limit is given by*

$$\operatorname*{plim}_{T \to \infty} \text{D.W.} = 2\left[1 - \frac{\rho\beta(\beta + \rho)}{1 + \beta\rho}\right] \neq 2[1 - \rho] \qquad (11.84)$$

The last member of (11.84) is the probability limit of the statistic one usually has in mind in such applications.

We should point out, however, that this particular problem arises *not because of the inapplicability of the distributional aspects of the usual Durbin-Watson test but rather, because, under the alternative hypothesis in* (11.83), *the OLS estimator of* β *is inconsistent.* If a consistent estimator for β is available, the point raised by Nerlove and Wallis will be obviated, although the problem of the proper (asymptotic) distribution of the Durbin-Watson statistic will still remain.

We illustrate these considerations with respect to the model

$$y_t = \frac{\alpha I}{I - \lambda L} x_t + u_t \qquad (11.85)$$

In analogy with the procedure in (11.79) we might consider the reduced model

$$y_t = \alpha x_t + \lambda y_{t-1} + u_t - \lambda u_{t-1} \qquad (11.86)$$

If

$$u_t - \lambda u_{t-1} = \varepsilon_t \qquad (11.87)$$

and the ε_t are *i.i.d.* random variables, then OLS will yield consistent estimators for α and λ and hence, the D.W. statistic will have the appropriate probability limit. On the other hand, if the presumed alternative is true, i.e.[58]

$$u_t - \lambda u_{t-1} = \frac{I}{I - \rho L}\varepsilon_t \qquad (11.88)$$

then the case examined by Nerlove and Wallis will prevail. In contrast to the model they considered, here we have meaningful instrumental variables (IV) estimators.

If the truth of (11.87) is not asserted with certainty, it seems inappropriate to use OLS in view of the inconsistency of the resulting estimators if the alternative hypothesis in (11.88) is true. Thus, let x_t and x_{t-1} be the instruments and consider the IV estimators

---

[58] Notice that (11.88) implies that the error term in (11.85) is a second order autoregressive process, i.e. $u_t = [I/(I - \lambda L)(I - \rho L)]) \, \varepsilon_t$, the ε_t being a sequence of *i.i.d.* random variables.

$$\begin{pmatrix} \tilde{\alpha} \\ \tilde{\lambda} \end{pmatrix} = (P'S)^{-1}P'y \tag{11.89}$$

where

$$x = (x_2, x_3, \ldots, x_T)', \quad y = (y_2, y_3, \ldots, y_T)',$$
$$x_{-1} = (x_1, x_2, \ldots, x_{T-1})', \quad y_{-1} = (y_1, y_2, \ldots, y_{T-1})', \tag{11.90}$$
$$P = (x, x_{-1}), \quad S = (x, y_{-1})$$

Making the appropriate substitutions, we find that

$$\begin{pmatrix} \tilde{\alpha} \\ \tilde{\lambda} \end{pmatrix} = \begin{pmatrix} \alpha \\ \lambda \end{pmatrix} + (P'S)^{-1}P'u^* \tag{11.91}$$

where

$$u_t^* = u_t - \lambda u_{t-1}, \quad u^* = (u_2^*, u_3^*, \ldots, u_T^*)' \tag{11.92}$$

Thus the residuals obey

$$\tilde{u}_t^* = y_t - (x_t, y_{t-1})\begin{pmatrix} \tilde{\alpha} \\ \tilde{\lambda} \end{pmatrix} = u_t^* - (x_t, y_{t-1})(P'S)^{-1}P'u^* \tag{11.93}$$

The Durbin-Watson statistic is given by

$$\text{D.W.} = \frac{\sum_{t=3}^{T}(\tilde{u}_t^* - \tilde{u}_{t-1}^*)^2}{\tilde{u}_{-1}^{*\prime}\tilde{u}_{-1}^*}, \quad \tilde{u}_{-1} = (\tilde{u}_2^*, \tilde{u}_3^*, \ldots, \tilde{u}_{T-1}^*)' \tag{11.94}$$

But it is clear that

$$\plim_{T \to \infty} \frac{\tilde{u}_{-1}^{*\prime}\tilde{u}_{-1}^*}{T} = \plim_{T \to \infty} \frac{1}{T} \sum_{t=2}^{T-1} u_t^{*2}$$
$$= (1 + \lambda^2)\,\text{Var}\,(u_t) - 2\lambda\,\text{Cov}\,(u_t, u_{t-1}) \tag{11.95}$$

Similarly,

$$\plim_{T \to \infty} \frac{1}{T} \sum_{t=3}^{T} (\tilde{u}_t^* - \tilde{u}_{t-1}^*)^2$$
$$= \plim_{T \to \infty} \frac{1}{T}\left[\sum_{t=3}^{T} \tilde{u}_t^{*2} - 2\sum_{t=3}^{T} \tilde{u}_t^*\tilde{u}_{t-1}^* + \sum_{t=2}^{T} \tilde{u}_{t-1}^{*2}\right]$$
$$= 2(1 + \lambda^2)\,\text{Var}\,(u_t) - 4\lambda\,\text{Cov}\,(u_t, u_{t-1}) - 2\,\text{Cov}\,(u_t, u_{t-1})$$
$$+ 2\lambda\,\text{Var}\,(u_t) + 2\lambda\,\text{Cov}\,(u_t, u_{t-2}) - 2\lambda^2\,\text{Cov}\,(u_t, u_{t-1}) \tag{11.96}$$

Under the null hypothesis in (11.87), we have

$$\text{Var}\,(u_t) = \frac{\sigma^2}{1 - \lambda^2}, \quad \text{Cov}\,(u_t, u_{t-\tau}) = \frac{\sigma^2\lambda^{|\tau|}}{1 - \lambda^2} \tag{11.97}$$

Hence,

$$\operatorname*{plim}_{T \to \infty} \text{D.W.} = \frac{2(1 + \lambda^2) - 4\lambda^2 - 2\lambda + 2\lambda + 2\lambda^3 - 2\lambda^3}{(1 + \lambda^2) - 2\lambda^2} = 2 \quad (11.98)$$

Under the alternative hypothesis in (11.88),

$$\operatorname*{plim}_{T \to \infty} \frac{\tilde{u}_{-1}^{*\prime} \tilde{u}_{-1}^{*}}{T} = \operatorname*{plim}_{T \to \infty} \frac{1}{T} \sum_{t=2}^{T-1} u_t^{*2} = \frac{\sigma^2}{1 - \rho^2} \quad (11.99)$$

$$\operatorname*{plim}_{T \to \infty} \frac{1}{T} \sum_{t=3}^{T} (\tilde{u}_t^* - \tilde{u}_{t-1}^*)^2 = \frac{2\sigma^2}{1 - \rho^2} - \frac{2\rho\sigma^2}{1 - \rho^2}$$

Consequently, in this case we have[59]

$$\operatorname*{plim}_{T \to \infty} \text{D.W.} = 2(1 - \rho) \quad (11.100)$$

We see, therefore, that the Durbin-Watson statistic has the proper probability limit under both the null and alternative hypothesis *if the parameters α, λ are consistently estimated.*

REMARK 11.2. Although the small sample distribution of the Durbin-Watson statistic in (11.94) is difficult to establish, we observe that neglecting end point effects,[60]

$$\text{D.W.} = 2(1 - \tilde{\rho}) \quad (11.101)$$

where

$$\tilde{\rho} = \frac{\sum_{t=3}^{T} \tilde{u}_t^* \tilde{u}_{t-1}^*}{\sum_{t=3}^{T} \tilde{u}_{t-1}^{*2}} \quad (11.102)$$

Hence, a test based on the D.W. statistic is equivalent to one based on $\tilde{\rho}$, if the sample is sufficiently large. But the asymptotic distribution of the quantity in (11.102), when (11.88) is valid, was established in Chapter 7; to this effect, see Equation (7.105).

In the present context we would have that, asymptotically,

$$\sqrt{T}(\tilde{\rho} - \rho) \sim \frac{1 - \rho^2}{\sigma^2} \frac{1}{\sqrt{T}} u_{-1}^{*\prime} \varepsilon - \frac{1 - \rho^2}{(1 - \lambda\rho)} \sqrt{T}(\tilde{\lambda} - \lambda) \quad (11.103)$$

---

[59] Alternatively, the reader may compute Cov $(u_t, u_{t-\tau})$, $\tau = 0, 1, 2$, given that under the alternative hypothesis, $u_t = [I/(I - \lambda L)(I - \rho L)]\varepsilon_t$, and thus Cov $(u_t, u_{t-\tau})$ $= \sum_i \sum_{i'} \sum_j \sum_{j'} \rho^i \rho^{i'} \lambda^j \lambda^{j'} E[\varepsilon_{t-i-j} \varepsilon_{t-\tau-i'-j'}]$.

[60] More precisely, the quantity in the right member of (11.101) should be

$$2(1 - \tilde{\rho}) - \frac{\tilde{u}_2^* - \tilde{u}_T^*}{\sum_{t=3}^{T} \tilde{u}_{t-1}^{*2}}$$

Now,

$$\sqrt{T}(\tilde{\lambda} - \lambda) = p_2. \frac{P'u^*}{T} \qquad (11.104)$$

where $p_2.$ is the last row of $P'S/T$. Let $\sigma^2 V$ be the covariance matrix of the error u_t^* when (11.88) is true, let M be a decomposition of V^{-1}, i.e. $M'M = V^{-1}$, and

$$\bar{p}_2. = \plim_{T \to \infty} p_2. \qquad (11.105)$$

It is obvious, then, that asymptotically,

$$\sqrt{T} \, (\tilde{\rho} - \rho) \sim \frac{1 - \rho^2}{\sigma^2} \frac{1}{\sqrt{T}} \, u_{-1}^{*\prime} \varepsilon - \left(\frac{1 - \rho^2}{1 - \lambda\rho} \right) \bar{p}_2. \frac{P'M^{-1}\varepsilon}{\sqrt{T}} \qquad (11.106)$$

This is so since, except for the first element,

$$Mu^* = \varepsilon \qquad (11.107)$$

By defining

$$u_t^{*N} = \sum_{i=0}^{N-1} \rho^i \varepsilon_{t-i} \qquad (11.108)$$

we see that the right member of (11.106) is essentially the sum of N-dependent variables. Determining the asymptotic distribution of the left member of (11.106) involves an argument that was presented many times in previous chapters and, thus, need not be repeated here. Consequently, in view of Theorem 4.3, the asymptotic distribution of the autocorrelation coefficient of the residuals is given by

$$\sqrt{T}(\tilde{\rho} - \rho) \sim N\left[0, (1 - \rho^2) + \left(\frac{1 - \rho^2}{1 - \lambda\rho} \right)^2 s^{nn} \right] \qquad (11.109)$$

s^{nn} being the asymptotic variance of the IV estimator of the coefficient of the lagged dependent variable. In the present case, this is simply the (2,2) element of

$$\sigma^2 \plim_{T \to \infty} \left[\left(\frac{P'S}{T} \right)^{-1} \frac{P'VP}{T} \left(\frac{S'P}{T} \right)^{-1} \right]$$

In Chapter 4 we examined the general linear model with autocorrelated errors. In that case, where no lagged endogenous variables appear as explanatory ones, the asymptotic distribution of the autocorrelation coefficient of residuals is $N(0, 1 - \rho^2)$. Thus, the introduction of lagged endogenous variables increases the variance of the asymptotic distribution of that quantity by the term $((1 - \rho^2)/(1 - \lambda\rho))^2 s^{nn}$. Observe, however, that in the former case we employ OLS while in the present we employ IV methods.

Finally, we see that a test for autocorrelation may be easily carried out from the results of the IV stage. If the hypothesis to be tested is

$$H_0: \rho = 0 \quad \text{as against}$$
$$H_1: \rho \neq 0 \tag{11.110}$$

then under the null hypothesis,

$$\sqrt{T}\tilde{\rho} \sim N[0, 1 + s^{nn}] \tag{11.111}$$

Consequently,

$$\frac{T\tilde{\rho}^2}{1 + s^{nn}} \sim \chi_1^2 \tag{11.112}$$

i.e., it is chi square with one degree of freedom. Alternatively, the square root is $N(0, 1)$. Since consistent estimators of s^{nn}, λ, ρ are simple byproducts of the IV stage, this test can be routinely carried out.

REMARK 11.3. As pointed out above, there is a loss of power in applying the Durbin-Watson test in a situation where some of the explanatory variables are lagged endogenous. In this connection, Durbin [37] has recently proposed an alternative test for autocorrelation. Before we explain the nature of the test, let us observe the schematic structure of the usual Durbin-Watson test.

Consider some model with parameters α, β, and suppose we have a sample of size T. Corresponding to the model and the sample, we have the likelihood function, say, $L(\alpha, \beta; y, X)$, y, X being the data. In the usual way of operating with the Durbin-Watson statistic, we assume $\alpha = \alpha_0$, α_0 being a fixed known value.[61] Subject to this we estimate β. Having done so we have its estimator, say, b. Now, subject to $\beta = b$ we go back and estimate α say by a.

The problem with the original formulation of the Durbin-Watson test when it is applied to models like the one in Equation (11.86), lies in the distributional properties ascribed to it. This aspect will be made perfectly transparent as the discussion unfolds.

In his recent work [37], Durbin derives the joint asymptotic distribu-

---

[61] For the particular context of this discussion, α is the autocorrelation coefficient ρ, and we assume that $\rho = 0$ in the initial stage of estimation.

tion of a and b as indicated above, and gives a test based on the asymptotic distribution of a. Again in the context of the autocorrelated errors model—where a would correspond to the estimator of ρ, which is obtained from residuals based on coefficient estimates $(\hat{\beta})$ that ignore the autocorrelated nature of the errors—this entails the asymptotic distribution of an inconsistent estimator of ρ, should it be the case that $\rho \neq 0$. There is, of course, no difficulty in obtaining the asymptotic distribution of inconsistent estimators provided they are properly centered.

To see the precise nature of Durbin's proposal and why the customary Durbin-Watson test is incorrect in the present case, we revert to the model

$$y_t = \sum_{i=1}^{n-1} \beta_i x_{ti} + \beta_n y_{t-1} + u_t, \quad t = 1, 2, \ldots, T \quad (11.113)$$

or more compactly,

$$y = X\beta + u, \quad X = (X^*, y_{-1}), \quad X^* = (x_{.1}, x_{.2}, \ldots, x_{.n-1}) \quad (11.114)$$

Suppose now that the error is specified as

$$u_t = \rho u_{t-1} + \varepsilon_t, \quad |\rho| < 1 \quad (11.115)$$

where $\{\varepsilon_t : t = 0, \pm 1, \pm 2, \ldots\}$ is a sequence of *i.i.d.* random variables with mean zero and variance σ^2.

The asymptotic distribution of the ML (or minimum chi square) estimator of the vector $\gamma = (\beta', \rho)'$, $\beta = (\beta_1, \beta_2, \cdots, \beta_{n-1})'$ was given in Equation (7.74). Partition the matrix Ω of that equation as

$$\Omega = \begin{bmatrix} \bar{\Omega} & r \\ r' & \omega \end{bmatrix} \quad (11.116)$$

where $\bar{\Omega}$ is $n \times n$, and ω is a scalar. Also observe that the *marginal asymptotic distribution* of ρ is given by

$$\sqrt{T}(\hat{\rho} - \rho) \sim N\left[0, \left(\frac{1}{1 - \rho^2} - \frac{\sigma^2 \bar{\omega}^{nn}}{(1 - \beta_n \rho)^2}\right)^{-1}\right] \quad (11.117)$$

where $\bar{\omega}^{nn}$ is the nth diagonal element of $\bar{\Omega}^{-1}$. If follows that, under H_0,

$$\sqrt{T}\hat{\rho} \sim N\left(0, \frac{1}{1 - \sigma^2 \bar{\omega}^{nn}}\right) \quad (11.118)$$

and consequently,

$$T\hat{\rho}^2(1 - \sigma^2\bar{\omega}^{nn}) \sim \chi_1^2 \qquad (11.119)$$

Under the null hypothesis,

$$\bar{\Omega} = \plim_{T\to\infty} \frac{1}{T} X'X \qquad (11.120)$$

Now, if parameters are estimated as in Chapter 7, the asymptotic variance of $\hat{\rho}$ is consistently estimated by the methods given in that chapter. Consequently, *the statistic*

$$T\hat{\rho}^2(1 - \hat{\sigma}^2\hat{\bar{\omega}}^{nn})$$

is asymptotically χ_1^2, the carets indicating consistent estimators as derived in the discussion of Chapter 7. Thus, we have at our disposal a correct asymptotic test for the autocorrelation hypothesis. The only drawback is that the estimation procedure leading to it is rather elaborate. With the availability of appropriate computer programs, however, this difficulty is a minor one, Nonetheless, one may wish to base a test on a somewhat simpler scheme, such as OLS.[62]

In such a case we obtain

$$\tilde{\beta} = (X'X)^{-1}X'y, \quad \tilde{u} = y - X\tilde{\beta} = u - X(\tilde{\beta} - \beta) \qquad (11.121)$$

The estimator of the autocorrelation coefficient is thus

$$\tilde{\rho} = \frac{\tilde{u}'\tilde{u}_{-1}}{\tilde{u}_{-1}'\tilde{u}_{-1}} \qquad (11.122)$$

and its *consistency, as an estimator of ρ, is easily verified under the null hypothesis in* (11.110). *It is important to realize, however, that although consistency is preserved, the asymptotic distribution of $\tilde{\rho}$ when the model contains lagged endogenous variables is not the same as in the case when such variables do not enter the model. It is precisely this fact that makes the customary Durbin-Watson test inapplicable in the present context.* We illustrate this by observing that under H_0 of (11.110),

$$\plim_{T\to\infty} \frac{1}{T}\tilde{u}_{-1}'\tilde{u}_{-1} = \sigma^2 \qquad (11.123)$$

---

[62] Simplicity was, indeed, Durbin's objective. Our discussion, however, does not follow the line of argument given in his paper [37], for two reasons. First, because of the more abstract context in which Durbin operates, the procedure and its asymptotic justification might appear more difficult than they actually are. Second, the derivation we employ is quite similar to that used in obtaining the conclusion in (11.109) and, thus, preserves the conceptual unity of this discussion.

Moreover,

$$\tilde{u}'\tilde{u}_{-1} = u'u_{-1} - u'X_{-1}(\tilde{\beta} - \beta) - (\tilde{\beta} - \beta)'X'u_{-1}$$
$$+ (\tilde{\beta} - \beta)'X'X_{-1}(\tilde{\beta} - \beta) \tag{11.124}$$

Since $\sqrt{T}(\tilde{\beta} - \beta)$ has a well-defined asymptotic distribution and $\text{plim}_{T\to\infty}(X'X/T)^{-1}$ may be assumed to be a matrix with finite elements, it follows that asymptotically,

$$\sqrt{T}\,\tilde{\rho} \sim \frac{1}{\sigma^2}\frac{u'u_{-1}}{\sqrt{T}} - \bar{p}'\frac{X'u}{\sqrt{T}} \tag{11.125}$$

where $\bar{p}'$ is the last row of the probability limit of the matrix $(X'X/T)^{-1}$.

Two things may be noted about the right member of (11.125). It is, *mutatis mutandis*, identical with (11.106) when the latter is stated under the conditions of the null hypothesis in (11.110). Moreover, *the second term in the right member of* (11.125) *would not have been present if the model did not contain lagged endogenous variables. It is this latter aspect that makes the usual Durbin-Watson test inapplicable in the present case, since it is based only on the distribution of the first term of the right member* (11.125). It is easily deduced, since under H_0 $\{u_t : t = 1, 2, \ldots\}$ is a sequence of *i.i.d.* random variables with mean zero and variance σ^2, that asymptotically,

$$\sqrt{T}\,\tilde{\rho} \sim N(0, 1 - \sigma^2\bar{\omega}^{nn}) \tag{11.126}$$

where $\bar{\omega}^{nn}$ is the nth diagonal element of the inverse of the matrix in (11.120). In effect, Durbin's proposed test is[63]

$$\frac{T\tilde{\rho}^2}{1 - \sigma^2\bar{\omega}^{nn}} \sim \chi_1^2 \tag{11.127}$$

Notice the difference between this test and the one obtained when the ML estimator of Chapter 7 is used.

It would be interesting to investigate by Monte Carlo methods the power of the three tests, i.e. those in Equations (11.112), (11.119) and (11.127). Briefly, the first is arrived at by estimating the parameters (β) of the model by IV methods and then obtaining the autocorrelation coefficient of the residuals. The second estimates the parameters (β) and the autocorrelation coefficient (ρ) simultaneously. The last estimates the parameters (β) by OLS and then obtains the autocorrelation co-

---

[63] In this and all other such tests in this discussion the square root of the test statistic is distributed as a N(0, 1) variable.

efficient of the residuals. Under H_0 the last would appear to be the most efficient estimates.

REMARK 11.4. Recall from Section 11.2 that in the context of the model

$$y_t = \frac{A(L)}{B(L)} x_t + u_t \qquad (11.128)$$

we provided a statistic for testing the hypothesis

$$B(L)u_t = \varepsilon_t \qquad (11.129)$$

the ε_t being *i.i.d.* random variables, as against the alternative that the u_t and hence $B(L)u_t$ constitute a general linear (covariance stationary) process.

Recall also, that when dealing with the general rational lag structure, we always required an initial consistent estimator for the parameters of the polynomials $A(\cdot)$ and $B(\cdot)$. Thus, we have a particularly simple means of testing the hypothesis in (11.129) as against the specific alternative,

$$B(L)u_t = \frac{I}{I - \rho L}\varepsilon_t \qquad (11.130)$$

the ε_t having the same properties as above. If we have consistent, IV estimators of the parameters of the reduced model

$$y_t = \sum_{i=0}^{k_1} a_i x_{t-i} - \sum_{j=1}^{k_2} b_j y_{t-j} + u_t^*, \quad u_t^* = B(L)u_t, \quad t = 1, 2, \ldots, T \qquad (11.131)$$

we may compute the residuals

$$\tilde{u}^* = y - X\tilde{\gamma} \qquad (11.132)$$

where

$$\gamma = \begin{pmatrix} a \\ -b \end{pmatrix}, \quad a = (a_0, a_1, \ldots a_{k_1})', \quad b = (b_0, b_1, \ldots, b_{k_2})' \qquad (11.133)$$

X is the matrix of the observations on the explanatory variables in (11.131) and $\tilde{\gamma}$ is the initial consistent estimator of γ. Using the autocorrelation coefficient of the residuals in (11.132), say $\tilde{\rho}$, we may in fact carry out a test of the hypothesis in (11.129), as against the alternative in (11.130), by the method leading to (11.112). The derivation of the asymptotic distribution of the estimator of $\tilde{\rho}$ is a rather simple extension of the results leading to (11.106) and (11.109). Thus it is left as an exercise for the reader.

Tests of the type described above would provide a useful guide to the appropriate approach in estimating the parameters of the model in (11.128). Clearly, if, after the initial stage, the hypothesis in (11.129) is accepted, then the parameters of (11.128) can be estimated efficiently by the procedure given in Durbin [35] or by the prefiltering procedure given in earlier chapters. If, on the other hand, (11.130) is accepted, then we may use the search procedure of Chapter 7 or other procedures which are equivalent to it. In such matters, to confine ourselves to OLS procedures is to be resigned to the acceptance of inconsistent estimators. The discussion in Remark 11.2 pertaining to the three types of tests of the autocorrelation hypothesis applies here as well. In view of the potentially fruitful empirical applications of the general rational model, such preliminary testing ought to become a standard component of econometric research.

REMARK 11.5.   The fact that we have additional lagged endogenous variables in the model of Remark 11.3, as compared with that of Remark 11.2, does not introduce complications. Thus, the asymptotic behavior of the residual autocorrelation coefficient in the case of the model in the preceding remark would, under the hypothesis in (11.129) be similar to that in (11.103)—the role of λ now being played by the coefficient of y_{t-1}. This is quite apparent, *mutatis mutandis*, from the discussion in Chapter 7.

REMARK 11.6.   There is a problem somewhat related to the preceding discussion that deserves further study. It has been alluded to in connection with Equations (11.9) and (11.10), and in earlier chapters, but was not specifically dealt with. The problem relates to a test of the hypothesis that the model is of the form

$$y_t = \alpha x_t + \frac{I}{I - \rho L}\varepsilon_t \qquad (11.134)$$

as against the alternative

$$y_t = \frac{\alpha I}{I - \lambda L}x_t + \varepsilon_t \qquad (11.135)$$

the ε-sequence being one of *i.i.d.* random variables and the explanatory variable being a suitably bounded sequence independent of the error process. Notice that the space of admissible parameters of one hypothesis does not constitute a subspace of that specified by the other. A promising line of attack would be the application of likelihood ratio tests.

Appendix

SOME MONTE CARLO EXPERIMENTS

In Chapter 5 we discussed, inter alia, the problem of estimating the parameters of models of the following form

$$y_t = \frac{\alpha_1 I}{I - \lambda L} x_{t1} + \alpha_2 x_t + \frac{I}{I - \rho L} \varepsilon_t \qquad (A.1)$$

$\{\varepsilon_t : t = 0, \pm 1, \pm 2, \ldots\}$ being a sequence of *i.i.d.* $N(0, \sigma^2)$ variables. In dealing with problems of inference, it was noted that tests of significance on individual (or groups of) coefficients could be based on the asymptotic distribution of the estimators, which was also derived in the discussion.

Due to the highly nonlinear character of the search estimator, the question naturally arises as to whether asymptotic properties could be expected to hold reasonably closely with sample sizes of 50 or so; quarterly data samples of that order are now commonplace. In order to answer that question in a reasonably satisfactory, if partial fashion, we may carry out a Monte Carlo experiment. For a brief discussion of the nature of such experiments the reader may refer to Dhrymes [32, ch. 8]. The design of the present experiment is as follows[1]: Three series of size 150 were obtained using standard computer random number generator programs. This particular program yields mutually independent $N(0, 1)$ variables. Denote the three series so generated by

$$\{(x_{t1}, z_{t2}, \varepsilon_t) : t = 1, 2, \ldots, 150\}$$

For a given value of λ and ρ, one may compute recursively

$$x_{t1}^* = \lambda x_{t-1,1}^* + x_{t1}, \quad u_t = \rho u_{t-1} + \varepsilon_t, \quad t = 1, 2, \ldots, 150 \quad (A.2)$$

using the initial conditions $x_{01}^* = u_0 = 0$.

---

[1] All computations were programmed and carried out by Eiji Nezu and Koji Shinjo. It is my pleasure to acknowledge their very able research assistance.

355

In order to make the explanatory variables correspond more closely to real world data we have defined

$$x_{t2} = 0.6x_{t1} + z_{t2}, \quad t = 1, 2, \ldots, 150 \qquad (A.3)$$

We observe, then, that by construction

$$\text{Var}(x_1) = 1, \quad \text{Var}(x_2) = 1.36, \quad \text{Cov}(x_1, x_2) = 0.6 \qquad (A.4)$$

the correlation between x_1 and x_2 being approximately 0.52.

The parameters α_1 and α_2 were specified by

$$\alpha_1 = 2.00, \quad \alpha_2 = 5.00 \qquad (A.5)$$

These parameters were held fixed for all experiments. On the other hand, λ, ρ were varied over their admissible range. For any given parameter vector $(\alpha_1, \alpha_2, \lambda, \rho)$, one may compute

$$y_t = \alpha_1 x_{t1}^* + \alpha_2 x_{t2} + u_t, \quad t = 1, 2, \ldots, 150 \qquad (A.6)$$

In order to minimize the impact of initial conditions, the first 50 observations are discarded. Thus, we are left with the series $\{(y_t, x_{t1}, x_{t2}): t = 51, 52, \ldots, 150\}$. These series are then split up into three samples $\{(y_t, x_{t1}, x_{t2}): t = 51, 52, \ldots, 70\}$, $\{(y_t, x_{t1}, x_{t2}): t = 51, 52, \ldots, 100\}$, $\{(y_t, x_{t1}, x_{t2}): t = 51, 52, \ldots, 150\}$.

From each such sample we obtained parameter estimates. For each parameter combination this procedure is replicated 100 times. Using other parametric combinations we follow the same procedure until the admissible space of λ and ρ has been adequately explored. Details will be given in Tables A.1 through A.6. One may raise two objections to the design above: First, it may be argued that it might have been better to generate the samples size 20, 50, 100 independently, instead of the nested samples we have actually used. In the present design, and for a given parameter combination, the results for sample size 20 are not independent of those of sample size 50, and so on. While this is true, the procedure we have followed mimics rather closely the limiting process in obtaining the asymptotic distribution. This, coupled with the substantial computational cost of Monte Carlo experiments, is an adequate response to the point raised above.

Second, it might have been better to use autocorrelated (as well as intercorrelated) explanatory variables. Certainly, economic data tend to be autocorrelated. This is, of course, partially valid. A number of experiments, however, led to the conclusion that it made little difference in terms of the qualitative conclusions whether or not the data were autocorrelated. Thus, in the interest of computational economy, the present framework was used.

We can answer by these Monte Carlo experiments the following:

(i) How quickly, i.e., for what sample size, does the small sample distribution become sufficiently close to the asymptotic distribution?

(ii) Does the "speed of convergence" depend on the parameters of the model?

(iii) How good are the estimators for "small" samples?

We must remark that (i) cannot be argued satisfactorily unless we undertake an enormous number of replications and actually plot the resulting empirical distribution. What we shall do is to discuss the speed at which the first two moments of the estimators converge to the asymptotic ones. The answer to question (ii) is to be understood in light of the comments just made. Finally, under (iii) we shall confine ourselves to the bias and mean square errors of the resulting estimators.

Let us now explain the nature of the tables below. A *replication* is one out of N samples of size T which has been generated with a fixed parameter vector and explanatory variables so that the variation from replication to replication occurs *only* with respect to the error process $\{\varepsilon_t\}$, and hence $\{u_t\}$.

In our experiment N is fixed at 100. Now, let the parameter point be denoted by θ. In our case

$$\theta = (\alpha_1, \alpha_2, \lambda, \rho)' \tag{A.7}$$

From each replication of sample size T we can obtain an estimate,[2] say, $\hat{\theta}^j$.

We define, respectively, the mean and bias vectors of sample size T estimators by

$$\bar{\theta}_T = \frac{1}{N} \sum_{j=1}^{N} \hat{\theta}^j, \quad b_T(\hat{\theta}) = \bar{\theta}_T - \theta^\circ \tag{A.8}$$

---

[2] The estimation procedure employed in these experiments is as follows: The range $[-0.99, 0.99]$ for ρ and $[0.01, 0.99]$ for λ is divided by 20 and 10 equidistant points, respectively, and the minimum is located, by the methods suggested in Chapter 5, *using the truncation remainder term.* When the apparent minimum is located, say at $(\rho_{i_0}, \lambda_{j_0})$ then *the same procedure is applied* over the range

$$[\rho_{i_0-1}, \rho_{i_0+1}], \quad [\lambda_{j_0-1}, \lambda_{j_0+1}]$$

and the estimators resulting from the global minimum so determined are the estimators obtained by the search procedure.

θ° being the relevant *true* parameter point. We define the matrix of mean squared errors by

$$\mathrm{MSE}_T(\hat{\theta}) = \frac{1}{N} \sum_{j=1}^{N} (\hat{\theta}^j - \theta^\circ)(\hat{\theta}^j - \theta^\circ)' = \mathrm{Cov}_T(\hat{\theta}) + [b_T(\hat{\theta})][b_T(\hat{\theta})]'$$

$$(A.9)$$

We observe that, *confining our attention to the diagonal elements of the MSE_T matrix, these multiplied by T correspond to the diagonal elements of the covariance matrix of the asymptotic distribution of $\sqrt{T}\,(\hat{\theta} - \theta^\circ)$.* Similarly, $\sqrt{T}\,b_T(\hat{\theta})$ corresponds to the mean vector of the asymptotic distribution of $\sqrt{T}\,(\hat{\theta} - \theta^\circ)$, θ° being the true parameter vector.

We may actually compare corresponding elements in the MSE_T and asymptotic covariance matrices, since in the case of Monte Carlo studies the last matrix is known exactly. For the particular model examined in this appendix, the covariance matrix of the estimators for $\alpha_1, \alpha_2, \lambda$ is given by

$$\begin{bmatrix} 1 + \dfrac{(\lambda - \rho)^2}{1 - \lambda^2} & 0.6(1 + \rho^2 - \rho\lambda) & \dfrac{\alpha_1(\lambda - \rho)(1 - \lambda\rho)}{(1 - \lambda^2)^2} \\[2.5ex] 0.6(1 + \rho^2 - \rho\lambda) & 1.36(1 + \rho^2) & -0.6\rho\alpha_1 \\[2.5ex] \dfrac{\alpha_1(\lambda - \rho)(1 - \lambda\rho)}{(1 - \lambda^2)^2} & -0.6\rho\alpha_1 & \alpha_1{}^2\dfrac{(\lambda - \rho)^2 + (1 - \lambda\rho)^2}{(1 - \lambda^2)^3} \end{bmatrix}^{-1}$$

The results of these experiments are set forth in the tables below. Tables A.1, A.2, and A.3 contain information regarding the bias while Tables A.4, A.5, and A.6 contain information regarding the mean squared error of the estimators.

Considering the bias aspects of the estimator, note that Table A.1 contains information for the cases where λ is held at the value 0.1, ρ being varied from -0.9 to 0.9. For sample size 100 the bias of the estimator of α_1 is rather small, never exceeding 0.5% of the magnitude of the parameter and typically much smaller. The bias of the estimator of α_2 is even smaller, it being of the order of 0.05% of the magnitude of the parameter. The bias of the estimator of λ never exceeds 7% of the magnitude of the parameter. The bias of the estimator for ρ is never larger than approximately 2.8% of the magnitude of the parameter and typically considerably smaller.

The results for sample size 50 are roughly comparable to those noted above; generally, biases for sample size 100 are smaller than for samples size 50, but the differences are not such as to constitute substantial

Table A.1

Bias Properties of Estimators

Case 6 $(\lambda = 0.5, \; \rho = -0.9)$

T	100	50	20
α_1	-0.0084	-0.0121	-0.0010
α_2	-0.0056	-0.0094	-0.0170
λ	0.0077	0.0105	0.0280
ρ	-0.0123	-0.0423	-0.0286

Case 7 $(\lambda = 0.5, \; \rho = -0.5)$

T	100	50	20
α_1	-0.0098	-0.0083	-0.0028
α_2	-0.0036	-0.0072	-0.0144
λ	0.0070	0.0077	0.0416
ρ	-0.0137	-0.0428	-0.0382

Case 3 $(\lambda = 0.1, \; \rho = 0.0)$

T	100	50	20
α_1	-0.0011	-0.0016	0.0285
α_2	0.0015	-0.0017	-0.0270
λ	0.0043	0.0076	0.0477
ρ	0.0006	-0.0157	-0.0022

Case 4 $(\lambda = 0.1, \; \rho = 0.5)$

T	100	50	20
α_1	-0.0115	0.0052	0.0487
α_2	0.0056	0.0050	-0.0196
λ	-0.0006	0.0080	0.0613
ρ	0.0028	-0.0293	-0.0479

Case 5 $(\lambda = 0.1, \; \rho = 0.9)$

T	100	50	20
α_1	-0.0013	0.0039	0.0548
α_2	0.0063	0.0087	-0.0149
λ	-0.0045	0.0035	0.0478
ρ	-0.0275	-0.0507	-0.0918

Table A.2
Bias Properties of Estimators

Case 6 ($\lambda = 0.5$, $\rho = -0.9$)

T	100	50	20
α_1	-0.0028	-0.0023	0.0286
α_2	-0.0065	-0.0040	-0.0316
λ	0.0035	0.0001	-0.0052
ρ	-0.0132	-0.0405	-0.0439

Case 7 ($\lambda = 0.5$, $\rho = -0.5$)

T	100	50	20
α_1	-0.0070	-0.0041	0.0353
α_2	-0.0041	-0.0024	-0.0287
λ	0.0048	0.0001	-0.0065
ρ	-0.0185	-0.0605	-0.0885

Case 8 ($\lambda = 0.5$, $\rho = 0.0$)

T	100	50	20
α_1	-0.0011	-0.0049	0.0499
α_2	0.0006	0.0047	-0.0146
λ	0.0051	-0.0038	-0.0131
ρ	-0.0127	-0.0418	-0.0794

Case 9 ($\lambda = 0.5$, $\rho = 0.5$)

T	100	50	20
α_1	-0.0014	-0.0036	0.0598
α_2	0.0057	0.0082	0.0031
λ	0.0036	-0.0057	0.0036
ρ	-0.0093	-0.0507	-0.1094

Case 10 ($\lambda = 0.5$, $\rho = 0.9$)

T	100	50	20
α_1	-0.0025	-0.0029	0.0357
α_2	0.0076	0.0093	0.0056
λ	-0.0004	-0.0043	0.0112
ρ	-0.0292	-0.0528	-0.1123

Table A.3

Bias Properties of Estimators

Case 11 $(\lambda = 0.9, \ \rho = -0.9)$

T	100	50	20
α_1	0.0333	0.0091	0.0069
α_2	−0.0342	−0.0250	−0.0171
λ	−0.0028	−0.0030	−0.0015
ρ	−0.0108	−0.0425	−0.0447

Case 12 $(\lambda = 0.9, \ \rho = -0.5)$

T	100	50	20
α_1	0.0349	0.0012	0.0100
α_2	−0.0348	−0.0149	−0.0234
λ	−0.0030	−0.0021	−0.0039
ρ	−0.0118	−0.0649	−0.1270

Case 13 $(\lambda = 0.9, \ \rho = 0.0)$

T	100	50	20
α_1	0.0336	−0.0016	0.0099
α_2	−0.0256	−0.0068	−0.0397
λ	−0.0030	−0.0030	−0.0243
ρ	−0.0154	−0.0610	−0.1402

Case 14 $(\lambda = 0.9, \ \rho = 0.5)$

T	100	50	20
α_1	0.0065	−0.0079	0.0054
α_2	−0.0031	0.0072	−0.0190
λ	−0.0009	−0.0069	−0.0436
ρ	−0.0275	−0.0882	−0.1845

Case 15 $(\lambda = 0.9, \ \rho = 0.9)$

T	100	50	20
α_1	−0.0014	−0.0056	0.0319
α_2	0.0056	0.0100	−0.0029
λ	0.0001	−0.0071	−0.0220
ρ	−0.0472	−0.0938	−0.2415

Table A.4
Mean Square Error Characteristics of Estimators

Case 1 ($\lambda = 0.1$, $\rho = -0.9$)

	DEACM	100	50	20
α_1	0.8816	0.520	0.666	1.225
α_2	0.5525	0.436	0.469	1.618
λ	0.1529	0.112	0.131	0.161
ρ	0.19	0.279	0.448	0.270

Case 2 ($\lambda = 0.1$, $\rho = -0.5$)

	DEACM	100	50	20
α_1	1.2044	0.719	0.796	1.884
α_2	0.79998	0.646	0.643	1.973
λ	0.20823	0.162	0.161	0.251
ρ	0.75	0.828	1.209	1.321

Case 3 ($\lambda = 0.1$, $\rho = 0.0$)

	DEACM	100	50	20
α_1	1.3598	0.953	1.031	2.372
α_2	0.99996	0.922	0.960	1.634
λ	0.2434	0.191	0.192	0.301
ρ	1.0	1.078	1.319	1.597

Case 4 ($\lambda = 0.1$, $\rho = 0.5$)

	DEACM	100	50	20
α_1	1.2635	1.00	1.011	2.110
α_2	0.79998	0.797	0.951	1.106
λ	0.2597	0.153	0.198	0.433
ρ	0.75	0.761	0.757	1.141

Case 5 ($\lambda = 0.1$, $\rho = 0.9$)

	DEACM	100	50	20
α_1	0.9779	0.823	0.852	1.546
α_2	0.5525	0.588	0.717	0.806
λ	0.2128	0.122	0.150	0.246
ρ	0.19	0.265	0.408	0.572

Table A.5

Mean Square Error Characteristics of Estimators

Case 6 $(\lambda = 0.5, \; \rho = -0.9)$

	DEACM	100	50	20
α_1	0.5836	0.444	0.523	0.853
α_2	0.5427	0.441	0.527	1.671
λ	0.04397	0.042	0.058	0.131
ρ	0.19	0.295	0.430	0.211

Case 7 $(\lambda = 0.5, \; \rho = -0.5)$

	DEACM	100	50	20
α_1	0.8698	0.638	0.686	1.334
α_2	0.7847	0.666	0.753	2.117
λ	0.0671	0.061	0.089	0.205
ρ	0.75	0.831	1.226	1.186

Case 8 $(\lambda = 0.5, \; \rho = 0.0)$

	DEACM	100	50	20
α_1	1.247	0.876	0.979	2.251
α_2	0.9780	0.967	1.058	1.924
λ	0.1124	0.106	0.161	0.425
ρ	1.0	1.103	1.338	1.881

Case 9 $(\lambda = 0.5, \; \rho = 0.5)$

	DEACM	100	50	20
α_1	1.2829	0.971	1.163	2.393
α_2	0.7859	0.856	0.956	1.154
λ	0.1975	0.173	0.329	0.707
ρ	0.75	0.913	0.946	1.642

Case 10 $(\lambda = 0.5, \; \rho = 0.9)$

	DEACM	100	50	20
α_1	1.1115	0.931	1.035	1.969
α_2	0.5453	0.598	0.718	0.787
λ	0.2688	0.229	0.339	0.562
ρ	0.19	0.329	0.428	0.867

Table A.6
Mean Square Error Characteristics of Estimators

Case 11 ($\lambda = 0.9$, $\rho = -0.9$)

	DEACM	100	50	20
α_1	0.1171	0.158	0.363	0.766
α_2	0.4510	0.420	0.855	1.160
λ	0.0005	0.001	0.006	0.044
ρ	0.19	0.27	0.389	0.216

Case 12 ($\lambda = 0.9$, $\rho = -0.5$)

	DEACM	100	50	20
α_1	0.1852	0.202	0.523	1.172
α_2	0.6513	0.591	1.098	1.518
λ	0.0008	0.001	0.009	0.068
ρ	0.75	0.851	1.202	1.152

Case 13 ($\lambda = 0.9$, $\rho = 0.0$)

	DEACM	100	50	20
α_1	0.3783	0.384	0.823	2.114
α_2	0.8089	0.791	1.330	1.611
λ	0.0018	0.003	0.016	0.179
ρ	1.0	1.021	1.286	2.038

Case 14 ($\lambda = 0.9$, $\rho = 0.5$)

	DEACM	100	50	20
α_1	0.5291	0.950	1.152	3.222
α_2	0.6359	0.850	0.992	1.113
λ	0.0048	0.010	0.060	0.474
ρ	0.75	0.904	1.309	2.300

Case 15 ($\lambda = 0.9$, $\rho = 0.9$)

	DEACM	100	50	20
α_1	1.1759	0.887	1.305	2.470
α_2	0.4887	0.546	0.735	0.784
λ	0.0487	0.047	0.209	0.384
ρ	0.19	0.591	1.015	2.583

qualitative distinctions. Notice, however, some interesting reversals in the expected pattern, particularly for α_1, in cases 3 and 4.

For sample size 20 the bias characteristics for all estimators are quite encouraging. Although the absolute differences between the biases for sample size 20 and 100 are very small, still it is typically the case that biases for sample size 100 are only a small fraction of the biases for sample size 20. In Table A.2, λ is held fixed at 0.5 while ρ is varied between -0.9 and 0.9; similarly, in Table A.3, λ is fixed at 0.9 while ρ is varied between -0.9 and 0.9.

Qualitatively, the results remain the same, i.e., biases are generally rather small and tend to decline with sample size, with an occasional exception for the estimators of α_1 and α_2. The magnitude of such departures from the expected pattern, however, is rather miniscule. In nearly all cases the biases of the estimators for λ and ρ decline with increasing sample size. The only interesting deviation from the pattern established in Table A.1 is that *the bias of the estimator of λ tends to decline and that of the estimator of ρ to increase as the magnitude of the (true) parameter λ increases.*

Finally, there are two observations to be made with respect to all sample size and parameter combinations. The bias of the estimator of ρ is always negative, i.e., the estimator *underestimates the autocorrelation parameter.* One can find no compelling argument why this should be so. The second observation is that λ is estimated with a smaller bias than is ρ.

The first observation has a consequence worth pointing out. When the true parameter (ρ) is -0.9, the minimum is often located on the boundary of the interval used for the search. For example, when $\rho = -0.9$, $\lambda = 0.1$ and sample size is 20, 75 of the 100 replications yield an estimate of -0.99 for ρ; when the sample size is 50, the number of replications yielding a boundary estimate (-0.99) is 66; when the sample size is 100 the number of such replications is only 24.

For the case $\rho = -0.9$, $\lambda = 0.5$, the corresponding results are as follows: sample size 20, 79 replications; sample size 50, 65 replications; sample size 100, 24 replications.

For the case $\rho = -0.9$, $\lambda = 0.9$ we have: sample size 20, 80 replications; sample size 50, 65 replications; sample size 100, 23 replications.

It is rather remarkable that the incidence of such boundary estimates is nearly unaffected as the value of λ is varied from 0.1 to 0.9. However, this phenomenon has an important consequence: If as the value of ρ is varied, in a search procedure, the sum of squared residuals (or the likelihood function) continues to increase (decline) then one can only conclude that the minimum (maximum) occurs at the left boundary point —in the present case this was set at -0.99, the right boundary point being set at 0.99.

Of course, another investigator might have chosen 0.999, etc. This is really of little import. But the reader should note that the procedure is valid when we *know* that the true parameter point lies in the interval $[-0.99, 0.99]$. When dealing with a real world sample, however, we cannot be so certain of the error specification. Thus, when a boundary estimate is encountered, i.e., when the criterion function either continuously rises or falls within the admissible range of the relevant parameter, it is a proper procedure to reject the first order specification and substitute a second order one. The Monte Carlo results above show that for small samples this will occur as a rule, even if the first order specification is correct, provided that $\rho = -0.9$ or at any rate close to -1.0. Boundary estimates in such schemes occur with lessening frequency as the sample size increases.

Using a second order specification on the errors, when in truth a first order is valid, will increase the computational costs but will not affect the asymptotic properties of the resulting estimators, as the reader may easily verify analytically. An indication of this is provided by Tables A.1 through A.3 in the cases where $\rho = 0$ but in estimating we assume a first order process and search over ρ as well. Incidentally, *the fact that, in so many cases, the minimum occurs at a boundary point shows the vulnerability of iterative techniques of estimation which seek to locate an extremum of a function by various gradient methods. In such a case they will either break down or else locate an interior local extremum which is not what we are after.* There is only one consolation regarding the disturbing phenomenon of boundary estimates and negative bias for the estimator of ρ. The consequences will be considerable only if the true parameter ρ is located near the left boundary, i.e., near -1.0. Fortunately, most experience with United States aggregate data indicates positive autocorrelation in the residuals and, superficially at least, would seem to indicate that the problem is not likely to be encountered widely in empirical practice.

The second moment characteristics of the estimators are given in Tables A.4, A.5, and A.6. The first column labelled DEACM denotes the diagonal elements of the asymptotic covariance matrix. The remaining columns give T times the mean squared error (MSE). Thus, e.g., the (first) entry 0.520 in the second column of Table A.4, case $\lambda = 0.1$, $\rho = -0.9$, means that the mean squared error of the sample size 100 estimator of α_1 is 0.0052.

The first comment with regard to all entries in these three tables is that the MSE of all estimators for all sample sizes and parameter combinations is remarkably small. For example, even for sample size 20, the mean squared error of the estimator of λ (case $\lambda = 0.1$, $\rho = -0.9$) is 0.008 which is only 8% of the true magnitude of the parameter, and it never exceeds approximately 20%. Relatively, the worst estimated parameter is ρ.

Thus, the impression one has from the two sets of tables is that *maximum likelihood estimation, when properly executed through the search technique, is a very powerful procedure even for relatively small samples.*

Again, it bears emphasizing that various gradient techniques for finding extrema of nonlinear functions can only locate *local extrema* while search techniques give us *global extrema*. Against this advantage one must set the substantial computation costs. In particular, when dealing with a search over three or more parameters, the computational aspects become hopelessly expensive. For one or two parameters, however, this scheme is entirely feasible and appears to yield extremely good results.

Concerning the first two questions raised at the beginning of this discussion, viz., how quickly do we approach second moment asymptotic results, and does the "speed of convergence" depend on the parameters of the model, the tables point quite clearly to some answers. By and large, when $\lambda = 0.1$ or $\lambda = 0.5$, a sample of size 50 is sufficiently large so that the asymptotic variances of the estimators of α_1, α_2, and λ are approximated quite well by their respective mean squared errors (multiplied by T). This is not quite so for the estimator of ρ. Notice that this qualitative result is not altered as (the true) ρ is varied between -0.9 and 0.9. Thus, from the point of view of second moments, a sample size between 20 and 50 (probably around 35 or so) could be considered "large." One peculiar feature of Tables A.4 and A.5 is that for sample size 100, T times MSE is uniformly lower than the corresponding asymptotic variance for the estimators of α_1, α_2, and λ. This is never so for the estimator of ρ, which is the relatively worst estimated parameter in terms of a MSE criterion as well.

Generally, with a few exceptions, T times MSE for $\hat{\rho}$ declines as sample size increases and appears to approximate rather well the asymptotic variance of this estimator (which is, incidentally, $1 - \rho^2$) for sample size 100. One other peculiar feature of Tables A.4 and A.5 which deserves to be brought to the attention of the reader is the systematic and appreciable difference between the asymptotic variance and T times MSE for $\hat{\alpha}_1$ in the case of sample size 100 and to a lesser degree for sample size 50. The former is always larger. There appears no good reason why this should be so. This phenomenon, by and large, disappears when $\lambda = 0.9$ (see Table A.6). Instead, for $\lambda = 0.9$ and, as ρ is varied between -0.9 and 0.9, we observe a monotone decline of T times MSE until, when sample size is 100, the asymptotic variances of corresponding estimators are well approximated.

Another important difference in Table A.6 is that, for this parametric combination, a sample of size 35 or so is no longer "large." Rather, one would suspect that close second moment approximation to asymptotic results is attained for samples of size 75 or 80.

Thus, to recapitulate the results of this aspect of the Monte Carlo experiments, we have found the following:

(i) Maximum likelihood estimation, properly executed by the search procedure, is a very powerful estimation method, yielding small biases and mean squared errors, even for relatively small samples.

(ii) Although all parameters are estimated with remarkable precision, α_1, α_2 are relatively best estimated, λ next best, and ρ relatively worst. In addition, the bias of the estimator of λ seems to decline as λ_0 (the true parameter) increases, while that of the estimator of ρ, by and large, tends to increase as ρ_0 increases. The cogency of this finding is impaired by the fact that α_1, α_2 have not been varied, but were held fixed at 2.00 and 5.00, respectively.

(iii) For $\lambda = 0.1$, $\lambda = 0.5$, and all values of ρ, a sample of size about 35 appears to be "large" in terms of close correspondence between asymptotic first and second moments, and the quantities $\sqrt{T}$ times bias, T times mean squared error as obtained from these experiments. On the other hand, for $\lambda = 0.9$ and all values of ρ, a sample of size 75 or 80 appears to be required to obtain as close a correspondence as indicated above.

(iv) Although in some preliminary experiments the qualitative properties of the results did not appear to be affected whether the explanatory variables were autocorrelated or not, still the reader is cautioned on one of the inescapable weaknesses of Monte Carlo experiments. Unless all possible variations have been thoroughly investigated, we cannot cogently assert more than the fact that *in circumstances holding with respect to the experiments actually conducted certain results have been obtained.* To argue beyond that framework is not strictly warranted. It is merely a conjecture that bears further investigation.

In the remainder of this appendix we report the results of a less exhaustive Monte Carlo experiment[3] designed to investigate the small sample performance of some estimators in the context of the model

$$y_t = \lambda y_{t-1} + \alpha x_t + u_t \tag{A.10}$$

where

$$u_t = \rho u_{t-1} + \varepsilon_t$$

the ε-sequence being one of mutually independent identically distributed (*i.i.d.*) random variables.

Data in this experiment were generated as follows: The u-sequence was generated exactly as before, so we need not give a description of the method. It should be noted, however, that for the results given in Tables A.7 through A.22 the variance of the u-process was held constant at 0.1; thus, as ρ was varied the ε-process was obtained as a sequence of *i.i.d.* normal variables with mean zero and variance

$$\sigma^2 = 0.1(1 - \rho^2) \tag{A.11}$$

The x-sequence was generated from a random number generator program yielding $N(0, 1)$ variables, with the exception of one experiment in which the x-sequence is generated by

$$x_t = 0.8 x_{t-1} + z_t \tag{A.12}$$

the z-sequence being one of *i.i.d.* random variables with mean zero and variance 0.36. Thus, the x-process has variance one, in all experiments. Given the x- and u-sequences, the y-sequence is obtained by putting, recursively,

$$y_t = \lambda y_{t-1} + \alpha x_t + u_t, \quad t = 1, 2, \ldots, T + 50 \tag{A.13}$$

and utilizing the initial condition

$$y_0 = 0 \tag{A.14}$$

As before, the first 50 observations so generated are discarded in order to minimize the import of the initial condition in (A.14). Thus, we are left with the data $\{(y_t, x_t) : t = 51, 52, \ldots, T + 50\}$. In these experiments T is taken as 10, 20, 40, and 80. The number of replications is $N = 50$.

---

[3] This experiment was programmed and computations were carried out by Bridger Mitchell and A. Basu.

In contrast to the previous set of experiments here we do not use nested samples. Rather, for every parameter combination and sample size, each replication is generated *de novo*. Thus, there is independence among the results obtained for every sample size. As the reader will readily verify below, the qualitative conclusions do not depart from the pattern established with respect to the preceding set of experiments.

The parameters were set as follows

$$\alpha = 0.5$$
$$\lambda = 0.1, \qquad \lambda = 0.5, \qquad \lambda = 0.9 \tag{A.15}$$

$$\rho = 0.9, \qquad \rho = 0.6, \qquad \rho = 0.3, \qquad \rho = 0.0$$
$$\rho = -0.3, \qquad \rho = -0.6, \qquad \rho = -0.9 \tag{A.16}$$

Although we are primarily interested in the comparative performance of the minimum chi square (search) and two-step (2S) estimators described in Chapter 7, we have included for comparison results on the ordinary least squares (OLS) and maximum likelihood (ML) estimators.

As in the previous group of experiments, the asymptotic distribution of these estimators has been derived and is, thus, exactly known under the conditions of the experiments whose results are reported below. Thus, the covariance matrix of the asymptotic distribution of the minimum chi square (MCS) estimator is given—in the case of a non-auto-correlated x-sequence—by

$$\sigma^2 \Omega^{*-1} = \sigma^2 \begin{bmatrix} 1 + \rho^2 & -\alpha\rho \\ -\alpha\rho & \alpha^2 + \alpha^2 \dfrac{(\lambda - \rho)^2}{1 - \lambda^2} + \dfrac{\sigma^2(\lambda - \rho)^2}{(1 - \lambda^2)(1 - \lambda\rho)^2} \end{bmatrix}^{-1} \tag{A.17}$$

where the first diagonal element refers to the parameter α, while the second refers to the parameter λ.

When the x-sequence is given by (A.12), then we have

$$\sigma^2 \Omega^{*-1} = \sigma^2 \begin{bmatrix} 1 + \rho^2 - 1.6\rho \\ \dfrac{\alpha}{1 - 0.8\lambda}(0.8 + 0.8\rho^2 - \rho - 0.64\rho) \\ \end{bmatrix}$$

$$
\left[\begin{array}{l} \dfrac{\alpha}{1 - 0.8\lambda}(0.8 + 0.8\rho^2 - \rho - 0.64\rho) \\[3mm] \dfrac{\alpha^2}{(1 - \lambda^2)(1 - 0.8\lambda)}[(1 + \rho^2)(1 + 0.8\lambda) - 2\rho(\lambda + 0.8)] \\[3mm] + \dfrac{\sigma^2(\lambda - \rho)^2}{(1 - \lambda^2)(1 - \lambda\rho)^2} \end{array} \right]^{-1} \quad \text{(A.18)}
$$

The MCS estimator was obtained by a crude search over the interval $(-0.99, 0.99)$; thus, the estimators were selected as those corresponding to the minimum of the residual variance when ρ was varied over the set $-0.99, -0.9, -0.8, -0.7, \ldots, 0.7, 0.8, 0.9, 0.99$. *No second search was performed over the region of apparent (first stage) minimum.* Consequently, the reported results for this estimator understate its properties; in particular, such a crude search would tend to increase the mean squared error of the resulting estimators over what it could be if a second stage (finer) search were carried out. The two-step estimator uses an initial instrumental variables estimator of α and λ to obtain the residuals, say $\bar{u}_t$. From these it calculates an estimate of ρ, say $\tilde{\rho}$, and then obtains the final estimate of α and λ using a feasible Aitken technique. This is possible since ρ is the only unknown parameter in the covariance matrix of the errors which is required in the process of Aitken estimation. The covariance matrix of the asymptotic distribution of this estimator (of α and λ) is given by

$$
\sigma^2 \Sigma^{-1} \Omega_0 \Sigma^{-1}
$$

where

$$
\Sigma = \Omega^* + \begin{bmatrix} 0 & 0 \\ 0 & \mu \end{bmatrix}, \quad \mu = \sigma^2 \frac{1 - \rho^2}{(1 - \lambda\rho)^2} \quad \text{(A.19)}
$$

$$
\Omega_0 = \Omega^* + \begin{bmatrix} 0 & 0 \\ 0 & \phi \end{bmatrix}, \quad \phi = \frac{2\sigma^2(1 - \rho^2)}{(1 - \lambda\rho)^2} + \frac{\sigma^2(1 - \rho^2)^2}{(1 - \lambda\rho)^2} s^{nn} \quad \text{(A.20)}
$$

In (A.20) s^{nn} is the asymptotic variance of the instrumental variables (first stage) estimator of λ.

The matrix Ω^* is implicitly defined by (A.17) in the case of non-autocorrelated x-sequence, and by (A.18) in the case of autocorrelated x-sequence. Thus, (A.19) and (A.20) completely describe the asymptotic covariance matrix of the two-step estimator for both types of x-sequence, with the exception of the quantity s^{nn}. The latter is given by

$$s^{nn} = \frac{\sigma^2}{(1 - \rho^2)\alpha^2} \tag{A.21}$$

when the x-sequence is non-autocorrelated and by the second diagonal element of

$$\sigma^2 \begin{bmatrix} 1 & \dfrac{0.8\alpha}{1 - 0.8\lambda} \\ 0.8 & \dfrac{\alpha}{1 - 0.8\lambda} \end{bmatrix}^{-1} \begin{bmatrix} \dfrac{1 + 0.8\rho}{(1 - 0.8\rho)(1 - \rho^2)} & \dfrac{0.8 + \rho}{(1 - 0.8\rho)(1 - \rho^2)} \\ \dfrac{0.8 + \rho}{(1 - 0.8\rho)(1 - \rho^2)} & \dfrac{1 + 0.8\rho}{(1 - 0.8\rho)(1 - \rho^2)} \end{bmatrix}$$

$$\times \begin{bmatrix} 1 & 0.8 \\ \dfrac{0.8\alpha}{1 - 0.8\lambda} & \dfrac{\alpha}{1 - 0.8\lambda} \end{bmatrix}^{-1}$$

when the x-sequence is given by (A.12).

It should be apparent from the preceding that the instruments used in the first stage were x_t and x_{t-1}.[4]

The OLS estimator is an inconsistent one. Its inconsistency is easily calculated as

$$c = \begin{pmatrix} c_1 \\ c_2 \end{pmatrix} = \plim_{T \to \infty} \left\{ \frac{1}{T} \begin{bmatrix} x'x & x'y_{-1} \\ y'_{-1}x & y'_{-1}y_{-1} \end{bmatrix} \right\}^{-1} \plim_{T \to \infty} \frac{1}{T} \begin{pmatrix} x'u \\ y'_{-1}u \end{pmatrix} \tag{A.22}$$

But, by construction of the data sets,

$$\plim_{T \to \infty} \frac{1}{T} x'u = 0, \quad \plim_{T \to \infty} \frac{1}{T} y'_{-1}u = \frac{\sigma^2 \rho}{(1 - \rho^2)(1 - \lambda\rho)} \tag{A.23}$$

$$\plim_{T \to \infty} \frac{1}{T} x'x = 1, \quad \plim_{T \to \infty} \frac{1}{T} x'y_{-1} = \frac{\alpha r}{1 - \lambda r}$$

$$\tag{A.24}$$

$$\plim_{T \to \infty} \frac{1}{T} y'_{-1}y_{-1} = \frac{\alpha^2(1 + \lambda r)}{(1 - \lambda^2)(1 - \lambda r)} + \frac{\sigma^2(1 + \lambda\rho)}{(1 - \lambda^2)(1 - \lambda\rho)(1 - \rho^2)}$$

---

[4] In the matrix just presented the reader may substitute a parameter r whenever 0.8 appears. Then, he will obtain the covariance matrix of the asymptotic distribution of the instrumental variables estimator when the x-sequence is characterized by the autocorrelation parameter r. Consequently, by varying r he may study the sensitivity of such estimators to the autocorrelation properties of the x-sequence. In this context notice that the sequence is standardized to have variance one.

Consequently,

$$
c = \left[
\begin{array}{cc}
1 & \dfrac{\alpha r}{1 - \lambda r} \\[2ex]
\dfrac{\alpha r}{1 - \lambda r} & \dfrac{\alpha^2(1 + \lambda r)}{(1 - \lambda^2)(1 - \lambda r)} + \dfrac{\sigma^2(1 + \lambda \rho)}{(1 - \lambda^2)(1 - \lambda \rho)(1 - \rho^2)}
\end{array}
\right]^{-1}
$$

$$
\times \left[
\begin{array}{c}
0 \\[2ex]
\dfrac{\sigma^2 \rho}{(1 - \rho^2)(1 - \lambda \rho)}
\end{array}
\right]
\tag{A.25}
$$

and we see that if the x-sequence is a *non-autocorrelated* one, i.e., if $r = 0$, then $c_1 = 0$ *so that α is consistently estimated by OLS.* In this case the inconsistency of the OLS estimator of λ is given by

$$
c_2 = \frac{\sigma^2 \rho / (1 - \rho^2)}{a_1 + a_2}
\tag{A.26}
$$

where

$$
a_1 = \frac{\alpha^2(1 - \lambda \rho)}{(1 - \lambda^2)}, \qquad a_2 = \frac{\sigma^2}{1 - \rho^2}\left[\frac{1 + \lambda \rho}{1 - \lambda^2}\right]
\tag{A.27}
$$

Since a_1, a_2 are both positive, the inconsistency of this estimator will be positive or negative according as $\rho \gtrless 0$. In certain ranges of λ the quantities a_1 and a_2 are increasing functions of λ and, thus, the inconsistency of this estimator may be expected to decline (absolutely) as λ increases. We shall return to this consideration when we review the results of the experiments. We have not troubled to deduce the asymptotic distribution of this estimator; the reader may do so quite easily using the methods employed repeatedly in the discussion of the foregoing chapters. He must remember, however, that in view of the inconsistency of this estimator he must consider the sequence

$$
\sqrt{T}\left[\binom{\tilde{\alpha}}{\tilde{\lambda}} - \binom{\alpha}{\lambda} - \binom{c_1}{c_2}\right]
$$

In terms of the experimental results reported the quantity that comes closest to a measure of the inconsistency of OLS estimator is its bias. Conceptually, "inconsistency" and "bias" refer to distinct attributes, although in some instances they may coincide.

In terms of asymptotic theory we know that MCS dominates 2S by the criterion of relative asymptotic efficiency, and, presumably, both dominate OLS once its inconsistency is taken into account. When $\rho = 0$, OLS is consistent; indeed, one would conjecture that it is also (asymptotically) efficient relative to the other two estimators. However, in order to rigorously demonstrate this fact one would have to derive the asymptotic distribution of the OLS estimator. Thus, beyond the questions raised in connection with the previous set of experiments, we may now ask if, by and large, the ranking is preserved, or whether, in small samples, there arise systematic deviations from the expected pattern.

Finally we should perhaps explain the entries labelled ML (maximum likelihood). As pointed out in the discussion of Chapter 7, the difference between MCS and ML estimators is that the former minimizes $\hat{\sigma}^2(\rho)$ while the latter minimizes $\hat{\sigma}^2(\rho)/(1 - \rho^2)^{1/T}$, where $\hat{\sigma}^2(\rho)$ is given, for the model under consideration, by

$$\hat{\sigma}^2(\rho) = \frac{1}{T} y'[V^{-1} - V^{-1}X(X'V^{-1}X)^{-1}X'V^{-1}]y \qquad (A.28)$$

where

$$X = (x, y_{-1}), \quad \text{Cov}(u) = \frac{\sigma^2}{1 - \rho^2} \begin{bmatrix} 1 & \rho & \cdot & \cdot & \cdot & \rho^{T-1} \\ \rho & 1 & \rho & \cdot & \cdot & \cdot \\ \cdot & \cdot & \cdot & \cdot & \cdot & \cdot \\ \cdot & \cdot & \cdot & \cdot & \cdot & \rho \\ \rho^{T-1} & \cdot & \cdot & \rho & \cdot & 1 \end{bmatrix} \qquad (A.29)$$

u being the error vector of the model in (A.10) and (A.11). Strictly speaking, the criterion function $\sigma^2(\rho)/(1 - \rho^2)^{1/T}$ is not correct for the ML estimator when the sample size is finite (small). It ignores the fact that a system such as the one exhibited in (A.13) depends, in its stochastic properties, on the initial condition y_0. Thus, the likelihood function, as one would customarily write it, is merely a conditional one.

If it is asserted that it is known that $y_0 = 0$ then, strictly speaking, one cannot write the covariance matrix of the errors as in (A.29). On the other hand, as the sample size increases, this discrepancy disappears and, asymptotically, MCS and ML estimators have the same distributions.

Because of the comparative nature of this Monte Carlo experiment we shall discuss *separately* the properties of various estimators of a given parameter.

Table A.7

Bias Properties of Various Estimators of α

$\alpha = 0.5, \quad \lambda = 0.1, \quad \sigma_u^2 = 0.1, \quad N = 50$

T \ ρ	0.9	0.6	0.3	0	−0.3	−0.6	−0.9
$T = 10$							
OLS	0.0043	−0.0077	−0.0122	0.0052	0.0099	−0.0378	−0.0095
2S	0.0077	0.0012	−0.0049	0.0136	0.0228	0.0091	0.0132
MCS	0.0179	0.0011	−0.0018	0.0046	0.0209	0.0089	0.0130
ML	0.0176	0.0016	0.0007	0.0071	0.0226	0.0125	0.0144
$T = 20$							
OLS	−0.0183	−0.0109	−0.0081	−0.0006	−0.0018	0.0158	0.0245
2S	−0.0013	0.0064	0.0073	−0.0025	−0.0018	0.0037	0.0031
MCS	−0.0031	0.0066	0.0060	−0.0050	−0.0037	−0.0004	0.0002
ML	−0.0027	0.0060	0.0061	−0.0046	−0.0035	0.0007	0.0004
$T = 40$							
OLS	−0.0099	0.0040	−0.0111	−0.0016	0.0029	−0.0029	0.0087
2S	−0.0014	0.0117	−0.0090	−0.0001	0.0042	−0.0046	0.0010
MCS	−0.0024	0.0085	−0.0101	−0.0010	0.0025	0.0064	−0.0015
ML	−0.0021	0.0091	−0.0098	−0.0010	0.0028	−0.0057	−0.0011
$T = 80$							
OLS	−0.0073	0.0024	−0.0022	0.0038	0.0076	−0.0061	0.0053
2S	0.0021	0.0072	−0.0005	0.0048	0.0070	−0.0034	0.0020
MCS	0.0015	0.0061	−0.0005	0.0043	0.0067	−0.0043	0.0017
ML	0.0018	0.0066	−0.0001	0.0043	0.0067	−0.0041	0.0018

Table A.8

Bias Properties of Various Estimators of α

$\alpha = 0.5, \quad \lambda = 0.5, \quad \sigma_u^2 = 0.1, \quad N = 50$

T \ ρ	0.9	0.6	0.3	0	−0.3	−0.6	−0.9
$T = 10$							
OLS	0.0089	0.0097	0.0248	−0.0041	−0.0125	−0.0086	−0.0528
2S	0.0118	0.0084	0.0336	0.0065	0.0134	0.0269	0.0051
MCS	0.0114	0.0043	0.0258	0.0109	0.0254	0.0249	0.0068
ML	0.0133	0.0054	0.0286	0.0098	0.0246	0.0246	0.0069

Table A.8 (Continued)

T \ ρ	0.9	0.6	0.3	0	−0.3	−0.6	−0.9
$T = 20$							
OLS	−0.0069	0.0073	−0.0001	0.0163	0.0083	0.0036	0.0148
2S	0.0030	0.0126	0.0015	0.0179	0.0095	0.0025	0.0010
MCS	−0.0001	0.0112	0.0008	0.0159	0.0111	0.0014	−0.0020
ML	0.0012	0.0116	0.0014	0.0165	0.0109	0.0017	−0.0019
$T = 40$							
OLS	−0.0049	−0.0129	0.0008	−0.0048	0.0122	−0.0022	0.0122
2S	0.0066	−0.0020	0.0044	−0.0047	0.0104	−0.0051	0.0008
MCS	0.0040	−0.0042	0.0029	−0.0058	0.0079	−0.0075	−0.0008
ML	0.0051	−0.0032	0.0037	−0.0058	0.0080	−0.0075	−0.0007
$T = 80$							
OLS	−0.0026	−0.0026	−0.0030	0 0057	0.0018	−0.0071	0.0056
2S	0.0029	−0.0011	−0.0019	0.0058	0.0037	−0.0038	−0.0001
MCS	0.0014	−0.0025	−0.0022	0.0051	0.0021	−0.0048	−0.0005
ML	0.0022	−0.0019	−0.0022	0.0051	0.0021	−0.0046	−0.0004

Table A.9

Bias Properties of Various Estimators of α

$\alpha = 0.5,\ \lambda = 0.9,\ \sigma_u^2 = 0.1,\ N = 50$

T \ ρ	0.9	0.6	0.3	0	−0.3	−0.6	−0.9
$T = 10$							
OLS	0.0076	−0.0060	−0.0030	−0.0020	−0.0066	−0.0170	−0.0022
2S	0.0036	−0.0121	0.0085	0 0043	−0.0027	0.0070	0.0094
MCS	0.0036	−0.0187	−0.0108	0.0111	−0.0098	0.0093	0.0123
ML	0.0036	−0.0121	−0.0099	0.0105	−0.0083	0.0103	0.0117
$T = 20$							
OLS	0.0069	0.0041	0.0234	−0.0041	0.0036	0.0021	−0.0071
2S	−0.0020	0.0016	0.0108	−0.0047	0.0059	0.0034	0.0005
MCS	−0.0034	0.0008	0.0125	−0.0013	0.0085	0.0025	0.0055
ML	−0.0025	0.0016	0.0140	−0.0014	0.0081	0.0024	0.0050

Table A.9 (Continued)

ρ T	0.9	0.6	0.3	0	−0.3	−0.6	−0.9
$T = 40$							
OLS	0.0041	0.0145	0.0023	0.0028	−0.0146	0.0014	0.0049
2S	−0.0018	0.0033	−0.0053	−0.0025	−0.0136	0.0047	0.0035
MCS	−0.0039	0.0007	−0.0040	0.0019	−0.0105	0.0060	0.0001
ML	−0.0023	0.0033	−0.0038	0.0019	−0.0106	0.0061	0.0001
$T = 80$							
OLS	−0.0009	0.0022	0.0007	0.0056	−0.0019	−0.0011	−0.0040
2S	−0.0013	−0.0019	−0.0011	0.0066	−0.0001	0.0005	0.0026
MCS	−0.0026	−0.0033	−0.0012	0.0066	0.0013	−0.0001	0.0025
ML	−0.0018	−0.0019	−0.0012	0.0065	0.0013	−0.0001	0.0025
$T = 160$							
OLS	0.0007						
2S	−0.0007						
MCS	−0.0016						
ML	−0.0016						
$T = 320$							
OLS	−0.0087						
2S	0.0007						
MCS	0.0007						
ML	0.0011						
$T = 640$							
OLS	−0.0062						
2S	0.0006						
MCS	−0.0007						
ML	−0.0005						
$T = 1280$							
OLS	−0.0019						
2S	0.0002						
MCS	−0.0004						
ML	−0.0002						

Table A.10*
Bias Properties of Various Estimators of λ
$\alpha = 0.5, \quad \lambda = 0.1, \quad \sigma_u^2 = 0.1, \quad N = 50$

T \ ρ	0.9	0.6	0.3	0	−0.3	−0.6	−0.9
$T = 10$							
OLS	0.0460	0.0657	0.0272	−0.0431	−0.1365	−0.2128	−0.1888
2S	0.0365	0.0364	0.0176	−0.0205	−0.0708	−0.1092	−0.0492
MCS	0.0507	0.0245	0.0475	−0.0316	−0.0404	−0.0909	−0.0285
ML	0.0510	0.0291	0.0422	−0.0339	−0.0508	−0.1089	−0.0362
$T = 20$							
OLS	0.1028	0.0952	0.0579	−0.0184	−0.0783	−0.1256	−0.1789
2S	0.0238	0.0238	0.0290	0.0050	−0.0355	−0.0071	−0.0114
MCS	0.0102	0.0116	0.0208	0.0143	−0.0273	0.0043	−0.0024
ML	0.0140	0.0141	0.0240	0.0091	−0.0298	0.0009	−0.0039
$T = 40$							
OLS	0.1302	0.1173	0.0845	−0.0184	−0.0766	−0.1583	−0.1862
2S	0.0094	0.0082	0.0329	−0.0097	−0.0063	−0.0243	−0.0037
MCS	0.0050	−0.0037	0.0292	−0.0085	−0.0003	−0.0183	0.0043
ML	0.0060	−0.0009	−0.0089	−0.0008	−0.0032	−0.0211	0.0029
$T = 80$							
OLS	0.1973	0.1624	0.0739	−0.0054	−0.0901	−0.1664	−0.2493
2S	0.0016	0.0246	−0.0049	0.0006	−0.0141	−0.0043	−0.0058
MCS	−0.0005	0.0198	−0.0095	0.0005	−0.0139	−0.0009	−0.0046
ML	0.0009	0.0232	−0.0159	0.0005	−0.0152	−0.0019	−0.0048
$T = \infty$							
OLS	0.2648	0.1742	0.0859	0.0000	−0.0835	−0.1655	−0.2451

* The entry for $T = \infty$ records the inconsistency of the OLS estimator, as appropriately calculated from Equation (A.25).

Table A.11*
Bias Properties of Various Estimators of λ
$\alpha = 0.5, \quad \lambda = 0.5, \quad \sigma_u^2 = 0.1, \quad N = 50$

T \ ρ	0.9	0.6	0.3	0	−0.3	−0.6	−0.9
$T = 10$							
OLS	0.0301	0.0394	0.0344	−0.0802	−0.1229	−0.1642	−0.1748
2S	0.0204	0.0080	0.0182	−0.0564	−0.0748	−0.0700	−0.0141
MCS	0.0053	−0.0051	0.0413	−0.0584	−0.0640	−0.0311	−0.0008
ML	0.0168	0.0019	0.0472	−0.0578	−0.0698	−0.0382	−0.0041

Table A.11 (Continued)

ρ / T	0.9	0.6	0.3	0	−0.3	−0.6	−0.9
$T = 20$							
OLS	0.0732	0.0309	−0.0104	−0.0224	−0.0621	−0.0772	−0.0845
2S	0.0223	0.0014	−0.0262	−0.0207	−0.0278	−0.0072	−0.0074
MCS	0.0076	−0.0034	−0.0312	−0.0170	−0.0234	−0.0023	−0.0015
ML	0.0142	−0.0009	−0.0304	−0.0159	−0.0248	−0.0029	−0.0019
$T = 40$							
OLS	0.1304	0.0884	0.0332	−0.0254	−0.0493	−0.0882	−0.1389
2S	0.0177	−0.0121	−0.0245	−0.0228	−0.0067	−0.0007	−0.0030
MCS	0.0071	−0.0219	−0.0183	−0.0137	0.0020	0.0067	0.0039
ML	0.0119	−0.0159	−0.0128	−0.0141	0.0022	0.0059	0.0038
$T = 80$							
OLS	0.1724	0.1228	0.0577	−0.0124	−0.0734	−0.1044	−0.1883
2S	0.0075	−0.0032	0.0001	−0.0155	−0.0119	0.0033	−0.0080
MCS	0.0013	−0.0087	0.0056	−0.0125	−0.0056	0.0056	−0.0069
ML	0.0048	−0.0049	0.0068	−0.0125	−0.0058	0.0049	−0.0068
$T = \infty$							
OLS	0.2389	0.1475	0.0671	0.0000	−0.0604	−0.1139	−0.1616

* See explanation in Table A.10.

Table A.12*

Bias Properties of Various Estimators of λ

$\alpha = 0.5, \quad \lambda = 0.9, \quad \sigma_u^2 = 0.1, \quad N = 50$

ρ / T	0.9	0.6	0.3	0	−0.3	−0.6	−0.9
$T = 10$							
OLS	0.0104	−0.0494	−0.0538	−0.1142	−0.1014	−0.0942	−0.1244
2S	0.0018	−0.0720	−0.0586	−0.1113	−0.0674	−0.0280	−0.0123
MCS	0.0105	−0.0873	−0.0801	−0.1212	−0.0814	−0.0210	−0.0128
ML	0.0108	−0.0692	−0.0708	−0.1152	−0.0776	−0.0246	−0.0131
$T = 20$							
OLS	0.0164	−0.0124	−0.0089	−0.0413	−0.0378	−0.0474	−0.0518
2S	−0.0081	−0.0458	−0.0221	−0.0517	−0.0315	−0.0243	−0.0267
MCS	−0.0144	−0.0443	−0.0189	−0.0343	−0.0170	−0.0122	0.0083
ML	−0.0101	−0.0396	−0.0168	−0.0336	−0.0171	−0.0137	0.0081

Table A.12 (Continued)

ρ \ T	0.9	0.6	0.3	0	−0.3	−0.6	−0.9
T = 40							
OLS	0.0264	0.0071	−0.0024	−0.0183	−0.0309	−0.0288	−0.0383
2S	−0.0173	−0.0230	−0.0280	−0.0219	−0.0245	−0.0102	−0.0064
MCS	−0.0248	−0.0312	−0.0219	−0.0157	−0.0160	−0.0055	0.0006
ML	−0.0178	−0.0249	−0.0213	0.0058	−0.0159	−0.0062	0.0007
T = 80							
OLS	0.0454	0.0182	−0.0053	−0.0114	−0.0208	−0.0301	−0.0328
2S	−0.0082	−0.0211	−0.0200	−0.0177	−0.0104	−0.0091	−0.0057
MCS	−0.0135	−0.0253	−0.0145	−0.0121	−0.0077	−0.0093	−0.0054
ML	−0.0096	−0.0187	−0.0142	−0.0119	−0.0078	−0.0088	−0.0049
T = 160							
OLS	0.0660						
2S	0.0016						
MCS	−0.0017						
ML	0.0023						
T = 320							
OLS	0.0620						
2S	0.0010						
MCS	0.0010						
ML	0.0027						
T = 640							
OLS	0.0650						
2S	0.0037						
MCS	−0.0012						
ML	−0.0006						
T = 1280							
OLS	0.0700						
2S	0.0012						
MCS	−0.0011						
ML	−0.0005						
T = ∞							
OLS	0.0748	0.0423	0.0184	0.0000	−0.0145	−0.0264	−0.0362

* See explanation in Table A.10.

Table A.13*

Mean Square Properties of Various Estimators of α

$\alpha = 0.5, \; \lambda = 0.1, \; \sigma_u^2 = 0.1, \; N = 50$

$\diagdown \; \rho$ $T \diagdown$	0.9	0.6	0.3	0	−0.3	−0.6	−0.9
$T = 10$							
OLS	0.0452	0.0974	0.1148	0.1169	0.0793	0.1555	0.0752
2S	0.0384	0.0791	0.1047	0.1266	0.0902	0.0858	0.0250
MCS	0.0262	0.1124	0.1182	0.1258	0.1143	0.0909	0.0201
ML	0.0250	0.1041	0.1018	0.1213	0.1115	0.0877	0.0210
$T = 20$							
OLS	0.0420	0.0984	0.0785	0.0502	0.0501	0.0528	0.0782
2S	0.0142	0.0603	0.0726	0.0526	0.0465	0.0323	0.0125
MCS	0.0123	0.0621	0.0718	0.0522	0.0439	0.0301	0.0079
ML	0.0121	0.0622	0.0701	0.0529	0.0458	0.0300	0.0080
$T = 40$							
OLS	0.0400	0.1118	0.0689	0.0790	0.1243	0.0762	0.0879
2S	0.0162	0.0718	0.0659	0.0809	0.1042	0.0479	0.0119
MCS	0.0161	0.0640	0.0689	0.0828	0.1001	0.0523	0.0118
ML	0.0160	0.0682	0.0679	0.0829	0.1000	0.0524	0.0117
$T = 80$							
OLS	0.0561	0.0801	0.0872	0.0753	0.1442	0.0958	0.0476
2S	0.0159	0.0643	0.0859	0.0732	0.1278	0.0643	0.0079
MCS	0.0159	0.0643	0.0880	0.0731	0.1203	0.0718	0.0079
ML	0.0158	0.0644	0.0869	0.0729	0.1280	0.0721	0.0078
$T = \infty$							
2S	0.0141	0.0601	0.0909	0.1001	0.0900	0.0558	0.0130
MCS and ML	0.0140	0.0590	0.0909	0.1000	0.0900	0.0557	0.0129

* For $T = \infty$ entries represent appropriate diagonal elements in the covariance matrix of the corresponding asymptotic distribution; for $T < \infty$, they represent TMSE.

Table A.14*

Mean Square Properties of Various Estimators of α

$\alpha = 0.5, \; \lambda = 0.5, \; \sigma_u^2 = 0.1, \; N = 50$

$\diagdown \; \rho$ $T \diagdown$	0.9	0.6	0.3	0	−0.3	−0.6	−0.9
$T = 10$							
OLS	0.0510	0.1090	0.1082	0.1764	0.1496	0.1905	0.1940
2S	0.0353	0.0961	0.1008	0.1746	0.1417	0.1203	0.0351
MCS	0.0351	0.1362	0.1172	0.1859	0.1658	0.1101	0.0284
ML	0.0323	0.1250	0.1068	0.1830	0.1640	0.1105	0.0282

Table A.14 (Continued)

T \ ρ	0.9	0.6	0.3	0	-0.3	-0.6	-0.9
$T = 20$							
OLS	0.0390	0.0862	0.0480	0.0902	0.0761	0.0619	0.0381
2S	0.0160	0.0631	0.0441	0.0961	0.0678	0.0342	0.0079
MCS	0.0141	0.0630	0.0469	0.0960	0.0698	0.0340	0.0021
ML	0.0140	0.0314	0.0454	0.0960	0.0696	0.0340	0.0079
$T = 40$							
OLS	0.0370	0.0741	0.1321	0.0796	0.0961	0.0843	0.1364
2S	0.0152	0.0442	0.1038	0.0839	0.0841	0.0479	0.0118
MCS	0.0132	0.0431	0.1082	0.0878	0.0758	0.0481	0.0120
ML	0.0138	0.0429	0.1081	0.0879	0.0757	0.0480	0.0121
$T = 80$							
OLS	0.0371	0.1152	0.0959	0.1174	0.1125	0.1118	0.0721
2S	0.0189	0.0882	0.0881	0.1153	0.0962	0.0718	0.0076
MCS	0.0201	0.0868	0.0958	0.1152	0.0961	0.0642	0.0079
ML	0.0209	0.0878	0.0959	0.1151	0.0958	0.0718	0.0078
$T = \infty$							
2S	0.0162	0.0640	0.0904	0.1004	0.0870	0.0521	0.0122
MCS and ML	0.0160	0.0638	0.0902	0.1003	0.0868	0.0520	0.0121

* See explanation in Table A.13.

Table A.15*

Mean Square Properties of Various Estimators of α

$\alpha = 0.5$, $\lambda = 0.9$, $\sigma_u{}^2 = 0.1$, $N = 50$

T \ ρ	0.9	0.6	0.3	0	-0.3	-0.6	-0.9
$T = 10$							
OLS	0.0772	0.1249	0.1539	0.1421	0.1056	0.2314	0.2201
2S	0.0416	0.1236	0.1388	0.1401	0.1090	0.1389	0.0276
MCS	0.0428	0.1681	0.1387	0.2060	0.1254	0.1459	0.0208
ML	0.0429	0.1568	0.1369	0.1901	0.1161	0.1398	0.0207
$T = 20$							
OLS	0.0401	0.1245	0.0876	0.0758	0.0739	0.0444	0.0443
2S	0.0152	0.0758	0.0749	0.0781	0.0962	0.0239	0.0202
MCS	0.0139	0.0918	0.0802	0.0759	0.0738	0.0224	0.0578
ML	0.0138	0.0931	0.0778	0.0758	0.0729	0.0198	0.0577

Table A.15 (Continued)

T \ ρ	0.9	0.6	0.3	0	−0.3	−0.6	−0.9
$T = 40$							
OLS	0.0581	0.0878	0.0879	0.1010	0.1182	0.0679	0.1405
2S	0.0141	0.0492	0.0829	0.1152	0.1279	0.0478	0.0559
MCS	0.0140	0.0562	0.0938	0.1052	0.0867	0.0320	0.0120
ML	0.0149	0.0528	0.0940	0.1049	0.0859	0.0321	0.0119
$T = 80$							
OLS	0.0510	0.1032	0.1308	0.1131	0.0852	0.0719	0.0879
2S	0.0140	0.0641	0.1164	0.1282	0.0881	0.0479	0.0082
MCS	0.0179	0.0708	0.1188	0.1228	0.0812	0.0482	0.0081
ML	0.0168	0.0629	0.1187	0.1228	0.0811	0.0483	0.0079
$T = 160$							
OLS	0.0610						
2S	0.0165						
MCS	0.0164						
ML	0.0178						
$T = 320$							
OLS	0.0963						
2S	0.0204						
MCS	0.0209						
ML	0.0208						
$T = 640$							
OLS	0.1159						
2S	0.0202						
MCS	0.0178						
ML	0.0189						
$T = 1280$							
OLS	0.0468						
2S	0.0214						
MCS	0.0151						
ML	0.0176						
$T = \infty$							
2S	0.0221	0.0554	0.0852	0.1002	0.0837	0.0480	0.0112
MCS and ML	0.0191	0.0538	0.0850	0.1001	0.0836	0.0480	0.0111

* See explanation in Table A.13.

Table A.16*

Mean Square Properties of Various Estimators of λ

$\alpha = 0.5, \quad \lambda = 0.1, \quad \sigma_u^2 = 0.1, \quad N = 50$

T \ ρ	0.9	0.6	0.3	0	−0.3	−0.6	−0.9
$T = 10$							
OLS	0.2462	0.4384	0.3329	0.4101	0.5472	0.7370	0.7218
2S	0.2320	0.2859	0.4789	0.4582	0.4358	0.4128	0.1477
MCS	0.1795	0.2231	0.4788	0.5018	0.4930	0.3773	0.0837
ML	0.1781	0.2309	0.4528	0.5239	0.4778	0.4019	0.1001
$T = 20$							
OLS	0.4261	0.3882	0.2881	0.2488	0.3440	0.5478	1.0320
2S	0.0738	0.1978	0.2641	0.2629	0.2764	0.1443	0.0319
MCS	0.0640	0.1920	0.3160	0.2779	0.2740	0.1600	0.0242
ML	0.0657	0.1938	0.3019	0.2768	0.2718	0.1598	0.0219
$T = 40$							
OLS	0.9760	0.8842	0.5162	0.2250	0.4443	1.3761	1.9442
2S	0.0598	0.2321	0.3154	0.2792	0.1918	0.2320	0.0322
MCS	0.0522	0.2361	0.3301	0.3065	0.1840	0.2200	0.0241
ML	0.0559	0.2242	0.3348	0.3048	0.1838	0.2238	0.0239
$T = 80$							
OLS	3.5842	2.3841	0.7120	0.3461	0.8960	2.5201	5.6480
2S	0.0562	0.2718	0.2931	0.5034	0.2558	0.2318	0.0480
MCS	0.0480	0.2240	0.3349	0.4952	0.2640	0.2240	0.0480
ML	0.0478	0.2318	0.3319	0.4948	0.2638	0.2316	0.0479
$T = \infty$							
2S	0.0601	0.2448	0.3762	0.3954	0.3248	0.1934	0.0473
MCS and ML	0.0600	0.2410	0.3738	0.3941	0.3209	0.1908	0.0468

* See explanation in Table A.13.

Table A.17*

Mean Square Properties of Various Estimators of λ

$\alpha = 0.5, \quad \lambda = 0.5, \quad \sigma_u^2 = 0.1, \quad N = 50$

T \ ρ	0.9	0.6	0.3	0	−0.3	−0.6	−0.9
$T = 10$							
OLS	0.2030	0.7089	0.3741	0.5810	0.5132	0.6978	0.7922
2S	0.1972	0.5882	0.3442	0.5302	0.4134	0.4770	0.1120
MCS	0.1951	0.4962	0.5363	0.5761	0.3789	0.3517	0.0797
ML	0.1949	0.4976	0.4828	0.5502	0.3668	0.3627	0.0828

Table A.17 (Continued)

ρ / T	0.9	0.6	0.3	0	−0.3	−0.6	−0.9
T = 20							
OLS	0.2532	0.1732	0.2501	0.1700	0.1908	0.2182	0.2820
2S	0.0828	0.1650	0.2902	0.1861	0.1398	0.0878	0.0141
MCS	0.0761	0.1630	0.3150	0.2020	0.1320	0.0920	0.0120
ML	0.0759	0.1598	0.3089	0.1938	0.1337	0.0918	0.0118
T = 40							
OLS	0.9932	0.5453	0.2560	0.2079	0.2081	0.5162	1.1121
2S	0.1222	0.1818	0.3802	0.2278	0.1042	0.0680	0.0161
MCS	0.0958	0.2037	0.4640	0.2440	0.1040	0.0680	0.0160
ML	0.1027	0.1897	0.4201	0.2437	0.1038	0.0678	0.0159
T = 80							
OLS	2.7641	1.4882	0.4721	0.3101	0.6324	1.0321	3.4241
2S	0.1039	0.3558	0.2480	0.4302	0.1923	0.1124	0.0241
MCS	0.1002	0.3577	0.3120	0.4285	0.1680	0.1040	0.0240
ML	0.0968	0.3789	0.3038	0.4318	0.1679	0.1037	0.0239
T = ∞							
2S	0.0941	0.3452	0.3679	0.2787	0.1841	0.0990	0.0231
MCS and ML	0.0930	0.3390	0.3647	0.2731	0.1806	0.0990	0.0230

* See explanation in Table A.13.

Table A.18*

Mean Square Properties of Various Estimators of λ

$\alpha = 0.5, \quad \lambda = 0.9, \quad \sigma_u^2 = 0.1, \quad N = 50$

ρ / T	0.9	0.6	0.3	0	−0.3	−0.6	−0.9
T = 10							
OLS	0.2881	0.3128	0.3400	0.6191	0.3901	0.3150	0.3369
2S	0.1964	0.3301	0.3509	0.5902	0.3452	0.2014	0.0480
MCS	0.2066	0.3636	0.3303	0.5936	0.4113	0.1743	0.0421
ML	0.2087	0.3238	0.3279	0.5786	0.3789	0.1708	0.0409
T = 20							
OLS	0.1290	0.1750	0.1052	0.1449	0.0990	0.0901	0.0862
2S	0.0639	0.1871	0.1001	0.2580	0.1061	0.0402	0.0204
MCS	0.0767	0.2398	0.1180	0.1610	0.0720	0.0760	0.3240
ML	0.0766	0.2198	0.1117	0.1508	0.0708	0.0658	0.3238

Table A.18 (Continued)

T \ ρ	0.9	0.6	0.3	0	−0.9	−0.6	−0.3
$T = 40$							
OLS	0.1853	0.0890	0.0884	0.0852	0.1020	0.0600	0.0880
2S	0.1022	0.1425	0.1712	0.0983	0.0852	0.0202	0.0124
MCS	0.1148	0.2149	0.1403	0.0894	0.0618	0.0160	0.0040
ML	0.0949	0.1729	0.1348	0.0887	0.0619	0.0158	0.0038
$T = 80$							
OLS	0.2512	0.1012	0.0612	0.0681	0.1050	0.1204	0.1205
2S	0.0992	0.2538	0.1443	0.1092	0.0558	0.0318	0.0081
MCS	0.1447	0.3511	0.0997	0.0724	0.0555	0.0320	0.0080
ML	0.1246	0.2198	0.0996	0.0709	0.0556	0.0317	0.0079
$T = 160$							
OLS	0.7331						
2S	0.1312						
MCS	0.1335						
ML	0.1387						
$T = 320$							
OLS	1.2720						
2S	0.1062						
MCS	0.0953						
ML	0.1077						
$T = 640$							
OLS	2.7531						
2S	0.1401						
MCS	0.0924						
ML	0.1032						
$T = 1280$							
OLS	6.3500						
2S	0.1452						
MCS	0.0808						
ML	0.1270						
$T = \infty$							
2S	0.1842	0.1671	0.0940	0.0581	0.0364	0.0182	0.0040
MCS and ML	0.1381	0.1440	0.0891	0.0570	0.0362	0.0181	0.0040

* See explanation in Table A.13.

Table A.19*

Bias Properties of Various Estimators of α

$\alpha = 0.5$, $\sigma_u^2 = 0.1$, $r_x = 0.8$, $T = 80$, $N = 50$

ρ \ λ	0.9	0.6	0.3	0	-0.3	-0.6	-0.9
$\lambda = 0.1$							
$T = \infty$ (OLS)	-0.1883	-0.1253	-0.0626	0.0000	0.0593	0.1249	0.1872
OLS	-0.1516	-0.1132	-0.0444	0.0094	0.0730	0.1357	0.1751
2S	0.0010	-0.0045	0.0112	0.0106	0.0159	0.0106	0.0070
MCS	-0.0004	-0.0029	0.0124	0.0093	0.0165	0.0094	0.0057
ML	-0.0003	-0.0041	0.0109	0.0093	0.0168	0.0104	0.0062
$\lambda = 0.5$							
$T = \infty$ (OLS)	-0.1592	-0.0983	-0.0458	0.0000	0.0402	0.0759	0.1077
OLS	-0.1180	-0.0710	-0.0420	0.0005	0.0559	0.0817	0.1157
2S	-0.0010	0.0077	-0.0076	0.0015	0.0108	0.0068	0.0014
MCS	-0.0012	0.0095	-0.0077	0.0011	0.0075	0.0060	0.0009
ML	-0.0009	0.0088	-0.0079	0.0011	0.0082	0.0064	0.0011
$\lambda = 0.9$							
$T = \infty$ (OLS)	-0.0610	-0.0238	-0.0084	0.0000	0.0053	0.0090	0.0182
OLS	-0.0309	-0.0043	0.0081	0.0112	0.0116	0.0081	0.0132
2S	0.0032	-0.0025	0.0145	0.0113	0.0066	0.0012	0.0013
MCS	0.0033	0.0023	0.0129	0.0109	0.0065	0.0007	0.0011
ML	0.0032	0.0013	0.0126	0.0105	0.0065	0.0008	0.0012

* The entry for $T = \infty$ records the inconsistency of the OLS estimator as appropriately calculated from Equation (A.25).

Table A.20*

Bias Properties of Various Estimators of λ

$\alpha = 0.5$, $\sigma_u^2 = 0.1$, $r_x = 0.8$, $T = 80$, $N = 50$

ρ \ λ	0.9	0.6	0.3	0	-0.3	-0.6	-0.9
$\lambda = 0.1$							
$T = \infty$	0.4331	0.2902	0.1439	0.0000	-0.1368	-0.2873	-0.4307
OLS	0.3317	0.2609	0.1224	-0.0140	-0.1538	-0.2952	-0.3851
2S	0.0046	0.0339	0.0045	-0.0159	-0.0248	-0.0174	-0.0126
MCS	-0.0071	0.0213	0.0003	-0.0131	-0.0264	-0.0152	-0.0099
ML	-0.0041	-0.0251	0.0042	-0.0131	-0.0292	-0.0173	-0.0109

Table A.20 (Continued)

λ \ ρ	0.9	0.6	0.3	0	-0.3	-0.6	-0.9
$\lambda = 0.5$							
$T = \infty$	0.2389	0.1474	0.0686	0.0000	-0.0581	-0.1139	-0.1616
OLS	0.1693	0.0985	0.0630	-0.0044	-0.0722	-0.1059	-0.1614
2S	0.0147	-0.0162	-0.0100	-0.0058	-0.0098	-0.0003	0.0001
MCS	0.0085	-0.0196	0.0089	-0.0053	-0.0057	0.0007	0.0007
ML	0.0114	-0.0173	0.0094	-0.0053	-0.0067	0.0002	0.0004
$\lambda = 0.9$							
$T = \infty$	0.0428	0.0166	0.0058	0.0000	-0.0037	-0.0063	-0.0081
OLS	0.0155	0.0016	0.0002	-0.0032	-0.0061	-0.0072	-0.0083
2S	-0.0083	-0.0122	-0.0055	-0.0031	-0.0029	-0.0015	-0.0002
MCS	-0.0103	-0.0123	-0.0044	-0.0026	-0.0025	-0.0012	-0.0001
ML	-0.0083	-0.0110	-0.0042	-0.0026	-0.0025	-0.0012	-0.0001

* See explanation in Table A.19.

**Table A.21*

Mean Square Properties of Various Estimators of α

$\alpha = 0.5, \quad \sigma_u^2 = 0.1, \quad r_x = 0.8, \quad T = 80, \quad N = 50$

λ \ ρ	0.9	0.6	0.3	0	-0.3	-0.6	-0.9
$\lambda = 0.1$							
OLS	2.1473	1.3021	0.3454	0.2030	0.6251	1.6882	2.7980
2S	0.0481	0.3160	0.2541	0.2132	0.2863	0.1266	0.0310
MCS	0.0482	0.3351	0.2495	0.2296	0.2957	0.1195	0.0281
ML	0.0467	0.3280	0.2568	0.2287	0.3021	0.1210	0.0278
DEACM							
2S	0.0521	0.1724	0.2468	0.2750	0.2161	0.1152	0.0260
MCS and ML	0.0520	0.1711	0.2467	0.2740	0.2080	0.1108	0.0260
$\lambda = 0.5$							
OLS	1.4801	0.6642	0.3840	0.1621	0.4364	0.7150	1.3577
2S	0.0698	0.1071	0.2626	0.1767	0.1809	0.0905	0.0145
MCS	0.0687	0.1092	0.2792	0.1731	0.1649	0.0873	0.0141
ML	0.0690	0.1103	0.2767	0.1731	0.1660	0.0860	0.0145
DEACM							
2S	0.0520	0.1774	0.2461	0.2242	0.1520	0.0786	0.0180
MCS and ML	0.0520	0.1772	0.2450	0.2213	0.1501	0.0784	0.0179

Table A.21 (Continued)

λ \ ρ	0.9	0.6	0.3	0	−0.3	−0.6	−0.9
$\lambda = 0.9$							
OLS	0.4740	0.4438	0.2027	0.1051	0.1105	0.0413	0.0381
2S	0.0752	0.2040	0.2111	0.1071	0.0908	0.0328	0.0099
MCS	0.0746	0.2162	0.2058	0.1068	0.0917	0.0344	0.0096
ML	0.0746	0.2160	0.2041	0.1067	0.0917	0.0343	0.0096
DEACM							
2S	0.0530	0.1701	0.1814	0.1324	0.0792	0.0381	0.0081
MCS and ML	0.0530	0.1690	0.1812	0.1321	0.0791	0.0381	0.0081

* Entries represent TMSE, except that those labeled DEACM represent diagonal elements of asymptotic covariance matrices.

Table A.22*

Mean Square Properties of Various Estimators of λ

$\alpha = 0.5, \quad \sigma_u^2 = 0.1, \quad r_x = 0.8, \quad T = 80, \quad N = 50$

λ \ ρ	0.9	0.6	0.3	0	−0.3	−0.6	−0.9
$\lambda = 0.1$							
OLS	10.0350	5.9510	1.5510	0.6508	2.3251	7.6178	13.4372
2S	0.1184	0.6432	0.5916	0.7241	0.9016	0.3132	0.1174
MCS	0.1225	0.7247	0.5917	0.7425	0.9518	0.2914	0.1064
ML	0.1240	0.7261	0.6201	0.7425	0.9747	0.2861	0.1081
DEACM							
2S	0.1801	0.5792	0.8570	0.9269	0.7092	0.3703	0.0861
MCS and ML	0.1790	0.5470	0.8358	0.9216	0.6728	0.3530	0.0860
$\lambda = 0.5$							
OLS	2.8167	1.1699	0.5310	0.1821	0.6661	1.0847	2.5927
2S	0.2481	0.4963	0.3074	0.2313	0.2467	0.0734	0.0188
MCS	0.2276	0.5144	0.3583	0.2258	0.2241	0.0718	0.0184
ML	0.2387	0.5234	0.3554	0.2258	0.2261	0.0687	0.0180
DEACM							
2S	0.1613	0.3714	0.3590	0.2791	0.1794	0.0921	0.0210
MCS and ML	0.1587	0.3678	0.3538	0.2732	0.1760	0.0920	0.0208
$\lambda = 0.9$							
OLS	0.0996	0.0403	0.0269	0.0191	0.0180	0.0102	0.0082
2S	0.0561	0.0762	0.0361	0.0197	0.0132	0.0054	0.0009
MCS	0.0645	0.0769	0.0331	0.0198	0.0135	0.0054	0.0010
ML	0.0567	0.0694	0.0326	0.0191	0.0132	0.0050	0.0010
DEACM							
2S	0.0792	0.0443	0.0254	0.0153	0.0090	0.0041	0.0010
MCS and ML	0.0780	0.0441	0.0251	0.0152	0.0090	0.0040	0.0010

* See explanation in Table A.21.

Table A.23*

Bias and Mean Square Properties of Various Estimators of α

$\alpha = 0.5, \quad \lambda = 0.9, \quad r_x = 0, \quad \sigma_u^2 = 1, \quad N = 50$

ρ	0.9		0.6		0.3	
T	Bias	TMSE	Bias	TMSE	Bias	TMSE
$T = 80$						
OLS	0.0062	0.3858	−0.0090	0.8286	0.0027	0.7884
2S	0.0010	0.1179	−0.0449	0.7622	−0.0218	0.8771
MCS	0.0013	0.1380	−0.0396	0.6865	−0.0127	0.7729
ML	0.0017	0.1292	−0.0348	0.6694	−0.0078	0.7286
$T = 320$						
OLS	−0.0184	0.6139	−0.0113	0.7695		
2S	−0.0018	0.1695	−0.0067	0.4573		
MCS	0.0004	0.1437	−0.0104	0.5656		
ML	0.0005	0.1475	−0.0076	0.4905		
$T = 1280$						
OLS	−0.0100	0.5963	−0.0036	0.7253		
2S	0.0025	0.2824	−0.0003	0.4212		
MCS	0.0040	0.1458	0.0007	0.3926		
ML	0.0030	0.1469	0.0010	0.3873		
$T = \infty$						
OLS	0.0000		0.0000		0.0000	
2S		0.3152		0.5104		0.8449
MCS and ML		0.1900		0.4851		0.8392

* Entries under $T = \infty$ have the following meaning: Entry in bias column records the inconsistency of the OLS estimator as appropriately calculated from Equation (A.25). Entries in TMSE column record the appropriate diagonal elements in the covariance matrix of the corresponding asymptotic distribution.

Table A.24*

Bias and Mean Square Properties of Various Estimators of λ

$\alpha = 0.5, \quad \lambda = 0.9, \quad r_x = 0, \quad \sigma_u^2 = 1, \quad N = 50$

ρ	0.9		0.6		0.3	
T	Bias	TMSE	Bias	TMSE	Bias	TMSE
$T = 80$						
OLS	0.0948	0.7535	0.0502	0.2510	0.0129	0.1901
2S	−0.0056	0.3800	−0.1040	2.0111	−0.1278	3.2826
MCS	−0.0052	0.3385	−0.0832	1.4256	−0.1015	2.7302
ML	0.0131	0.2618	−0.0612	0.8725	−0.0760	1.6415

Table A.24 (Continued)

ρ / T	0.9		0.6		0.3	
	Bias	TMSE	Bias	TMSE	Bias	TMSE
$T = 320$						
OLS	0.0880	2.4880	0.0627	1.2948		
2S	0.0054	0.4838	−0.0224	1.3700		
MCS	0.0039	0.4453	−0.0370	2.6170		
ML	0.0042	0.4620	−0.0240	1.3105		
$T = 1280$						
OLS	0.0915	10.7302	0.0664	5.6678		
2S	0.0057	2.2195	−0.0134	1.9203		
MCS	0.0006	0.4260	−0.0075	0.6220		
ML	0.0030	0.5894	−0.0063	0.4655		
$T = \infty$						
OLS	0.0920		0.0689		0.0392	
2S		3.4014		1.3787		0.5327
MCS and ML		1.3756		0.3688		0.2310

* See explanation in Table A.23.

The bias properties of the four estimators (OLS, 2S, MCS, ML) of α are found in Tables A.7, A.8, A.9, A.19 and A.23. In the first three tables we have a non-autocorrelated x-sequence and $\sigma_u^2 = 0.1$. For extremely small samples, $T = 10$, OLS does as well as any other estimator. The 2S estimator performs worse than MCS and ML for small λ but relatively better for $\lambda = 0.9$. As the sample size increases, the relative standing of OLS worsens, except for the case $\rho = 0$, when it performs as well as, or slightly better than, any other estimator.

The bias of all estimators is relatively small and, on considerations of bias of the estimator of α alone, there is no compelling reason to prefer any one of the four estimators considered. This is, of course, in part a reflection of a fact noted earlier, viz., when the x-sequence is not autocorrelated, the OLS estimator of α is consistent. What the experiments indicate, except for the case $\rho = 0$, is that as sample size increases the estimators other than OLS converge slightly faster to the parameter they seek to estimate.

In Table A.19 we deal with an *autocorrelated* x-sequence and a single sample size $T = 80$. In this context OLS is inconsistent and its inconsistency is recorded in the table. It is rather remarkable that its bias for this sample size is very close to its inconsistency. *Both the recorded bias and inconsistency of the estimator appear to decline (absolutely) with increasing λ.* Thus, contrary to intuition, the OLS estimator of α is better, in terms of bias, the higher the value of the parameter λ. If no asymptotic analysis had been performed, the casual reader of this table may have concluded that this is perhaps an accidental small sample result due to sampling variability—especially so in view of the small number of replications employed. However, what we observe is that both the *sign* and *magnitude* of the recorded bias agree fairly closely (the sign always agrees) with the inconsistency of the estimator. Consequently, what the table shows is that asymptotic theory is quite useful and (reasonably) accurately applicable in the small sample context we examine here. As before, OLS does as well as other estimators when $\rho = 0$.

Generally, 2S is inferior to MCS and ML estimators, but the difference in the magnitude of their respective biases is not very large. MCS and ML perform equally well. There does not appear to be any particular pattern in the bias of the other three estimators as a function of the magnitude of λ; generally it is quite small, in most instances being of the order of magnitude 10^{-2}. In Table A.23 we consider again a non-autocorrelated x-sequence and a single parameter value $\lambda = 0.9$. The objective here is to observe the behavior of estimators when we are dealing with large σ_u^2. In the table are given the results of experiments with $\sigma_u^2 = 1$ and $T = 80$, $T = 320$ and $T = 1280$. The objective of considering such large samples is to determine whether, as the sample size becomes quite large, the improvement of MSE continues at the same rate as in the range $T = 10$ to $T = 80$. Thus, it has little bearing on the bias properties we are dealing with in this discussion, except in the case of OLS where we would possibly expect bias for large samples to approach the inconsistency of the estimator. The point of considering a "large" σ_u^2 will become evident from the following considerations: If we obtain the final form of the model we find

$$y_t = \frac{\alpha I}{I - \lambda L} x_t + \frac{I}{I - \lambda L} u_t \qquad (A.30)$$

The systematic part, $[\alpha I/(I - \lambda L)]x_t$, is often called the *signal*, while the random component, $[I/(I - \lambda L)]u_t$ is called the *noise*. In the context of the model under consideration, the two components are independent; the extent to which variations in the dependent variable y can be explained by variations in the x-sequence may be indexed by the signal to noise ratio which may be defined as the ratio of the variances of the systematic and random components. We thus obtain (S/N being the signal to noise ratio)

$$\frac{S}{N} = \frac{\alpha^2/(1 - \lambda^2)}{\sigma^2(1 + \lambda\rho)/(1 - \rho^2)(1 - \lambda^2)(1 - \lambda\rho)} = \frac{\alpha^2(1 - \lambda\rho)}{\sigma_u^2(1 + \lambda\rho)} \quad \text{(A.31)}$$

In most of the preceding experiments we held the parameters α and σ_u^2 at $\alpha = 0.5$, $\sigma_u^2 = 0.1$; as λ and ρ vary, respectively, in the intervals $[0.1, 0.9]$, $[-0.9, 0.9]$ the signal to noise ratio varies between 0.2624 and 23.3157. Thus,[5] we have already covered a very wide variety of circumstances. In Table A.23 we examine a circumstance in which the signal to noise ratio is particularly small. One does not expect such circumstances to arise frequently in empirical situations of interest; nonetheless, we examine it in order to shed some light on the robustness of the various estimators when the dependent variable is dominated by its noise component.

Table A.23 conveys, essentially, results very similar to those obtained earlier, viz., OLS compares rather favorably to the rest of the estimators; its bias appears to converge to zero at approximately the same rate as that of the others. Overall, in terms of the bias properties for the estimators of α, there is little to choose from among the four procedures under consideration, although OLS does slightly worse than the others.

The mean squared error of the various estimators of α is given in Tables A.13, A.14, A.15, A.21, and A.23. In the first three we are dealing with a non-autocorrelated x-sequence.

The first obvious impression conveyed by these tables is that OLS is distinctly inferior to the other three estimators. This, coupled with the slightly more pronounced bias properties exhibited in Tables A.7, A.8, A.9, A.19, and A.23, should lead to rejection of OLS as a useful estimator in the context of models involving lagged endogenous variables. It is interesting to note that, even when error autocorrelation is absent, i.e., when $\rho = 0$, OLS does not, on the whole, perform better than other estimators. It has a very slight advantage for very small samples, $T = 10$

---

[5] The preceding implies that the asymptotic correlation coefficient for such an equation varies between 0.2 and 0.96. The asymptotic correlation coefficient is interpreted as $S/(S + N)$. When $\sigma_u^2 = 1$ the corresponding variation is 0.024 to 0.7. This interpretation may be based on the (square of the) sample correlation between y_t and $\tilde{y}_t$, the latter defined by

$$\tilde{y}_t = \tilde{\alpha} \sum_{i=0}^{t-1} \tilde{\lambda} x^i_{t-i}$$

$\tilde{\alpha}$ and $\tilde{\lambda}$ being consistent estimators of the corresponding parameters.

and possibly $T = 20$, but for larger samples, neither its bias nor its MSE properties appreciably deviate from those of the other estimators for $T = 40$ or $T = 80$. Contrary to what one might be led to expect intuitively, the MSE of the OLS estimator does not deteriorate appreciably as the magnitude of the parameter λ increases. It is clear, of course, that the smaller λ is, the more the model approaches the simple general linear model, and the higher λ is, the less similar it is to the general linear model. If we fix λ, MSE seems to increase with ρ, although this is not a universal phenomenon. The exceptions appear to occur when λ and ρ are of opposite sign and $\lambda + \rho$ is small. Thus, when $\lambda = 0.1$, in Table A.13, TMSE seems to decline about $\rho = 0$. When $\lambda = 0.5$, Table A.14, this phenomenon tends to occur at $\rho = -0.3$ and $\rho = -0.6$. While such results are suggestive, they do not, unfortunately, convey reliable generalizations.[6]

When dealing with the bias properties of the OLS estimator of α we observed that bias is increased substantially when the x-sequence is autoregressive. The same is true when we consider its MSE properties. Care should be exercised in interpreting such findings. The first impression is that the faults of this estimator are exacerbated when the x-sequence is autoregressive. While this may well be true, it *need not be so*. It is possible that the asymptotic variance of this estimator, appropriately centered, is an increasing function of r_x, the autocorrelation parameter of the x-sequence. Thus, what is relevant for such an inference is the change in magnitude of the reported TMSE statistics compared with the change in the asymptotic variances attributable to the autoregressive character of the x-sequence. We shall return to this topic below when we deal with the other estimators. Finally, the OLS estimator of α is sensitive to changes in the magnitude of σ_u^2. A relevant comparison is that of Tables A.15 and A.23. As we vary σ_u^2 from 0.1 to 1, TMSE (for $T = 80$, $\rho = 0.9$, $\lambda = 0.9$) moves from 0.0510 to 0.3858. The corresponding variation for $T = 1280$ and the same parameter value is 0.0468 to 0.5963. In both cases the variation is roughly proportional to the change in magnitude of the parameter σ_u^2.

---

[6] If one wishes to determine how various moments of the OLS estimator depend on λ and ρ, one ought to determine the (exact) small sample distribution of this estimator. The problem is similar, but not necessarily identical, to that of determining the small sample distribution of *certain simultaneous equations estimators*, e.g., the OLS one. If successful, one can investigate the nature of this dependence analytically. Failing that, one could obtain the asymptotic distribution of the estimator, taking into account its inconsistency, as given in Equation (A.22). If the estimator is appropriately centered, there is no difficulty in obtaining its asymptotic distribution.

Turning now to the other three estimators, we note that MCS and ML estimators are almost indistinguishable in their small sample properties as they pertain to the TMSE statistics of the estimators of α. Overall, the ML estimator has a slight advantage. Another question of interest in this connection is the closeness of the TMSE statistics for these estimators relative to their asymptotic variance. For $\lambda = 0.1$ we see that even for $T = 20$ we have results very closely approximating the asymptotic variance. This is so particularly for $\rho = 0.9$ and $\rho = 0.6$. We also find that, typically, there is a very substantial reduction in MSE in the transition from $T = 10$ to $T = 20$, but a smaller reduction in the transition from $T = 20$ to $T = 40$ and $T = 80$. Similar results are obtained for $\lambda = 0.5$ and $\lambda = 0.9$, although for $\lambda = 0.9$ the correspondence between TMSE and asymptotic variance is less striking. In all such situations convergence of the TMSE statistics to the corresponding asymptotic variances is not monotone. In general, there appears a tendency for TMSE to lie below the corresponding asymptotic variance for $T = 20$ and to approach it in an oscillatory fashion as T increases.

Over the signal noise ratio range, implied by holding $\sigma_u^2 = 0.1$, a sample size $T = 40$ is already "large" if our criterion is proximity of the first two (sample) moments to the corresponding moments of the asymptotic distribution. This, however, does not hold if $\sigma_u^2 = 1$ (see Table A.23). It is interesting, however, that in Table A.23 the TMSE statistics lie almost invariably *below* the corresponding variances of the asymptotic distributions.

Finally, we note that MCS and ML are obtained by a very crude search procedure. Doubtless, better results would be obtained in terms of smaller bias and MSE characteristics if the search were repeated over the region of apparent minimum using a finer grid.

Considering now the 2S (two-step) estimator in comparison with MCS and ML estimators, we note the following: In Tables A.13, A.14, A.15, and A.21, where the x-sequence employed is non-autocorrelated, the asymptotic variance of the estimator of α does not differ very much between 2S and MCS or ML. This is a reflection of the fact that $\sigma_u^2 = 0.1$ for all such situations, and hence that the variance of ε-sequence is given by $0.1(1 - \rho^2)$. As we noted in Chapter 7, the (asymptotic) efficiency of the MCS (or ML) relative to the 2S estimator hinges on the magnitude of

$$\left(\frac{\sigma^2}{1 - \rho^2} \right)^2 \frac{(1 - \rho^2)^4}{(1 - \lambda\rho)^4} \left(s^{22} - \sigma^2 \omega^{*22} \right)$$

where s^{22} and $\sigma^2\omega^{*22}$ are, respectively, the asymptotic variance of the IV and MCS estimator of λ, and σ^2 is the variance of the ε-sequence. By holding $\sigma_u^2 [= \sigma^2/(1 - \rho^2)]$ fixed at 0.1 the factor multiplying[7] $s^{22} - \sigma^2 \omega^{*22}$ is kept quite small; so, when $\rho = 0$ or $\lambda = \rho = 0.9$, it assumes its minimum which is 0.001. Consequently, the inefficiency of the initial IV estimators which could be quite considerable is appreciably reduced in passing to the 2S estimator. The latter is, of course, particularly vulnerable to change in σ_u^2. In addition to the signal to noise ratio argument given earlier, this is rather obvious from the preceding discussion. Consequently, in Tables A.23 and A.24 we report the outcome of experiments designed to determine the vulnerability of 2S and other estimators to variations in σ_u^2. The tables convey the impression that 2S and MCS (or ML) estimators are more likely to have similar properties when the signal to noise ratio is high, i.e., when λ and ρ are of opposite sign. This is true whether the comparison is in terms of TMSE statistics or in terms of corresponding asymptotic variances. For the experiments in which $\sigma_u^2 = 0.1$, the 2S does, on the whole, worse than the MCS or ML estimators. It has, however, a slight edge over the others for very small samples, e.g., $T = 10$ or $T = 20$. On the other hand, this advantage disappears as sample size increases, and for larger samples it is perceptibly inferior to the others.

When the x-sequence is autocorrelated (Table A.21) the performance of 2S and ML estimators is indistinguishable; this, however, is merely a reflection of the fact that their asymptotic variances are almost identical. The vulnerability of 2S to variations in σ_u^2 is brought out quite clearly in Table A.23; in the cases reported there, 2S performs distinctly worse than the other estimators except OLS. One interesting fact, however, appears to be that MSE for 2S is reduced rapidly with increasing sample size up to $T = 80$; thereafter it decreases more slowly than is the case with the ML estimator. Thus, e.g., for $\sigma_u^2 = 1$, $\rho = 0.9$, in Table A.23, 2S and ML TMSE statistics are comparable for $T = 80$, while for $T = 1280$, TMSE for 2S is about twice that for ML. Roughly similar phenomena occur for $\rho = 0.6$. To summarize the results this far, if we have to base our judgment on the bias and mean squared error characteristics of the four methods as they apply to the estimator of α *only*, we would conclude the following:

(i) For extremely small samples, $T = 10$, all methods do equally well or badly. If one is pressed to choose among them, one probably

---

[7] The magnitude of the difference $(s^{22} - \sigma^2 \omega^{*22})$ is affected by the presence or absence of autocorrelation in the x-sequence, as well as the magnitude of the other parameters; see Equation (A.21) and the ensuing discussion.

will choose first OLS, then 2S, and then MCS or ML.

(ii) As the sample size increases, MCS and ML become indistinguishable and maintain a slight edge over 2S, which ranks second; OLS does decidedly worse for moderate or large samples except for $\rho = 0$, when it does generally better than the other estimators. The difference in performance, however, is not appreciable.

(iii) A sample size between 20 and 40 may be considered large when we keep $\sigma_u^2 = 0.1$. The criterion employed is that there be a close correspondence between the first two moments of the finite sample distribution as measured here by bias and mean squared error and the corresponding moments of the asymptotic distributions of the appropriately centered estimators.

(iv) Variation in σ_u^2 has two effects. For $\sigma_u^2 = 1$ it is no longer true that a sample of size 20 to 40 is "large." This cannot be a direct conclusion since such sample sizes have not been experimented with. But in the context of the limited experiments carried out, a sample size $T = 80$ does not lead to close correspondence of the criteria set forth under (iii). What is observed, however, is that for sample size $T = 80$, the TMSE statistics for 2S, MCS, and ML are generally lower than the corresponding asymptotic variances.

(v) The presence of autocorrelation in the x-sequence does not affect the ranking of estimators as given under (ii). Here we have only one sample size, $T = 80$, and in terms of the criteria under (iii), this is already "large." It is possible that a sample of size $T = 40$ might not be so regarded, but we have no experiments on this case.

Thus, we should deduce from the preceding discussion that if the sample size is $T = 35$, or so, the use of the MCS or ML estimators is to be preferred to the alternatives considered. *Even a crude version appears to give a slightly superior performance to the 2S estimator. A more refined version would definitely be expected to do better. This preference will be strengthened when the signal to noise ratio is small and weakened when the signal to noise ratio is large.* If the sample size is extremely small, there is no point in employing anything but OLS, which is simpler and far less expensive to execute than the alternatives we considered above.

Turning now to the comparative performance of the various estimators of λ, we note that their bias characteristics are given in Tables A.10, A.11, A.12, A.20 and A.24. In the first three tables we deal with a non-autocorrelated x-sequence. Contrary to the case of the estimator of α, the OLS estimator of λ is now *inconsistent*. Generally, the bias of the OLS estimator increases with sample size (note that we do *not* record

$\sqrt{T}$ (bias), but rather bias in the tables). For given λ, bias seems to increase (absolutely) as ρ varies from 0.9 to -0.9. This result is far more pronounced in the case of small samples, say, $T = 10$. As the sample size increases to $T = 40$ or $T = 80$, this phenomenon disappears. Of course, the preceding statements do not apply to the case $\rho = 0$; rather, what is meant is that for given distance of ρ from zero, the OLS estimator of λ tends to be more biased (absolutely) if $\rho < 0$ relative to the case $\rho > 0$.

Another remarkable phenomenon is that both the relative and absolute bias of the OLS estimator of λ declines as the true parameter increases, other parameters held fixed. This is quite clearly evident from Tables A.10, A.11, and A.12. At sample size $T = 80$, the bias of OLS accords very closely with its inconsistency, possible exceptions being the parameter combination $\rho = 0.9$, all λ, and $\lambda = 0.9$, all ρ. In the latter case we note that for $\lambda = 0.9$ and $\rho = 0.9$, the bias of OLS for $T = 1280$ is 0.0700, while its inconsistency is 0.0748. Since the inconsistency of the OLS estimator of λ declines as the true parameter λ increases, it is not surprising that the bias statistics behave similarly.[8] The results for 2S and MCS (or ML) are a bit more mixed; on the whole, 2S does worse than MCS or ML for almost all sample sizes and all parameter combinations, but the difference in their bias performance is not very pronounced. All three estimators do better than OLS, except for the case $\rho = 0$ when no clear distinction is possible.

When an autocorrelated x-sequence is employed (Table A.20), the bias characteristics of OLS are considerably worsened. This is a consequence of the fact that its inconsistency is thereby increased. As before, both recorded bias and the inconsistency of the OLS estimator decline as λ increases. The fact that the x-sequence is autocorrelated does not seem to affect the bias of the other estimators in any discernible pattern. It would appear that for large λ ($\lambda = 0.9$) the biases of all estimators are reduced by the introduction of autocorrelation in the x-sequence. This, however, is not true for $\lambda = 0.5$. The ML estimator does relatively best, but again the differences are not appreciable.

Variation of σ_u^2 does not produce any significant pattern in its effects on the bias characteristics of the four estimators. As is evident from Table A.24, the rankings are unaltered and the bias of OLS appears to be converging rather closely to its inconsistency. A brief comment is

---

[8] In this connection recall that for the OLS estimator of α, no such pattern was discernible; also note that for a non-autocorrelated x-sequence, $\tilde{\alpha}_{\text{OLS}}$ is a consistent estimator of α.

perhaps appropriate regarding MCS and ML estimators; while the two differ somewhat for very small samples, say $T = 10$ or $T = 20$, they tend to be substantially similar for $T=40$ or larger sample size. For such samples, ML tends to exhibit somewhat smaller bias; thus, in Table A.24, for $\rho = 0.9$, the bias of ML is about half that of MCS, although in both cases bias is extremely small. When $T = 640$, MCS and ML have bias -0.012 and -0.0006, respectively; when $T = 1280$ the corresponding quantities are -0.0011 and -0.0005. In these cases the true value of λ is 0.9.

Let us turn finally to the mean squared error characteristics of the estimator of λ. The latter is a most important parameter since it determines the stability and other long run characteristics of the economic model typified by Equation (A.10). The mean squared error performance of the various estimators is given in Tables A.16, A.17, A.18, A.22, and A.24. In the first three, we fix $\sigma_u^2 = 0.1$ and the x-sequence is non-autocorrelated; in Table A.22 $\sigma_u^2 = 0.1$ but the x-sequence is autocorrelated; in Table A.24 the x-sequence is non-autocorrelated but $\sigma_u^2 = 1$.

From Tables A.16, A.17, and A.18 it is quite clear that OLS is dominated by the other estimators, except for the case $\rho = 0$, when it clearly dominates. This, of course, is the expected result. Among the remaining three estimators, ML typically dominates 2S, although this is not a universal phenomenon. For $\lambda = 0.1$ this is typically so for all sample sizes and for values of ρ *other than* $\rho = 0.3$ and $\rho = 0$. For $\rho = 0.3$, ML dominates 2S only for $T = 10$; for $\rho = 0$, ML dominates 2S only for $T = 80$. In all cases, however, the dominance is not appreciable. This is in accord with the asymptotic variances of the two estimators—given in the tables under the heading $T = \infty$. For $\lambda = 0.5$ the findings are roughly similar to those for $\lambda = 0.1$; for $\lambda = 0.9$ the differences in the mean squared error of the estimators are more pronounced but the pattern is more erratic. Notice, for instance, that OLS dominates all other estimators for $\rho = 0.6$, $\rho = 0.3$, $\rho = 0$, when $T = 40$ and $T = 80$. The differences in the performance of these estimators are brought out more clearly as the sample size becomes very large. The inferiority of 2S to MCS or ML is then quite evident for $T = 640$ or $T = 1280$. By and large, MCS and ML behave similarly,[9] and overall have a slight edge over 2S, much as the asymptotic results would indicate.

One aspect that ought to be brought out in connection with Tables

---

[9] There is a systematic departure from this pattern in Table A.18, for $T > 160$; there, MCS does better than ML. There is no explanation for this phenomenon.

A.16, A.17, and A.18 is that the TMSE statistics are not as close to the corresponding asymptotic variances as was noted in previous discussions. Thus, although for $\lambda = 0.1$ a sample size between $T = 20$ and $T = 40$ would be considered "large," this is not so for $\lambda = 0.5$ or $\lambda = 0.9$. A "large" sample for these cases would be something between $T = 40$ and $T = 80$, probably close to 80.

In Table A.22 we deal with an autoregressive x-process. It is instructive to note several important consequences of this, in comparison with the case where we deal with a non-autoregressive x-sequence. First, for $\lambda = 0.1$, the asymptotic variances of 2S and ML (or MCS) are invariably increased substantially. Second, for $\lambda = 0.5$, these quantities are appreciably increased only for $\rho = 0.9$. For other values of ρ such quantities are substantially unaffected, and in some instances they even decline slightly. *Third, for $\lambda = 0.9$, the introduction of (positive) autocorrelation in the x-sequence brings about a substantial and uniform reduction in the asymptotic variances of all estimators, i.e., 2S, ML, and MCS.*

These tendencies are faithfully reflected in the TMSE characteristics of the various estimators given in Table A.22. For $\lambda = 0.1$ and $\lambda = 0.5$ OLS is very substantially inferior to the other estimators except for $\rho = 0$. For these parameter values 2S has a very slight edge over ML (or MCS), although rankings are not consistent; thus, e.g., 2S seems to do better than ML for $\rho > 0$ and worse than ML for $\rho > 0$. For $\lambda = 0.9$, however, ML dominates 2S most uniformly, but the difference in their respective TMSE is rather small.

The great surprise for $\lambda = 0.9$ lies in the performance of OLS; generally, this estimator is dominated by the others except for $\rho = 0.6$, $\rho = 0.3$, $\rho = 0$; even though it is dominated, however, its mean squared error is rather small. This corroborates other results noted earlier which point to the conclusion that OLS is a rather good estimator for the model under consideration when λ is "large" and the x-sequence is positively autocorrelated. This is an aspect that deserves further analytical consideration—for the combination noted above represents a rather common occurrence in empirical work—if one is to judge from published results. Whatever the conclusions of such investigations, the results pointed up by this Monte Carlo experiment are rather counterintuitive. One would normally have expected that when ρ is "large," λ is "large," r_x is "large," then OLS would yield very poor results. Thus, it is quite important that this matter be elucidated. One approach would be to obtain the asymptotic distribution of the OLS estimator (centered about its probability limit) and examine whether the elements of its covariance matrix are reduced as λ, ρ, and r_x increase. Such an investigation would help resolve this apparent paradox. If one verifies the conjecture just stated, then what we observe in Table A.22 is merely a reflection of the asymptotic properties of the estimator—a phenomenon which is devoid of any particular significance.

Finally, in Table A.24 we deal with a non-autocorrelated x-sequence and $\sigma_u^2 = 1$. The important feature of this table is the appreciable inferiority of 2S relative to the ML (or MCS) estimator, a result also suggested by asymptotic theory.

To recapitulate, the major results of the Monte Carlo study regarding various estimators in the context of the model in (A.10) and (A.11), are as follows:

(i) Overall, ML dominates all other estimators.

(ii) ML and MCS behave rather similarly.

(iii) 2S, although dominated by MCS or ML, is a very good estimator, except when the signal to noise ratio is small.

(iv) When λ is small, a sample of size between 20 and 40 is "large" in terms of the criterion that the first two moments of the small sample distribution, as measured by the bias and TMSE statistics, agree with the first two moments of the corresponding (centered) asymptotic distribution. When λ is large, however, a larger sample size is required in order to produce a similar degree of correspondence.

(v) Introduction of an autocorrelated x-sequence does not disturb the findings above, which are in general accord with what one would deduce from the corresponding asymptotic distributions.

(vi) The inconsistency of the OLS estimator is well measured by its bias.

(vii) The OLS estimator is a remarkably good estimator for large values of λ, say, $\lambda = 0.9$. Particularly so when the x-sequence exhibits large positive autocorrelation. It is, of course, dominated by ML but the difference in the two estimators is not very large.

(viii) Asymptotic theory is an excellent qualitative guide to small sample properties even when samples are of the order of 40 or so. This is to be distinguished from the point made under (iv), since now we are making no claim regarding the proximity of small sample to asymptotic distribution moments.

BIBLIOGRAPHY

[1] Almon, S., "The Distributed Lag between Capital Appropriations and Expenditures," *Econometrica*, **33**, 1965, pp. 178-196.

[2] Alt, F. L., "Distributed Lags," *Econometrica*, **10**, 1942, pp. 113-128.

[3] Amemiya, T. and W. Fuller, "A Comparative Study of Alternative Estimators in a Distributed-Lag Model," *Econometrica*, **35**, 1967, pp. 509-529.

[4] Anderson, R. L., "Distribution of the Serial Correlation Coefficient," *Annals of Mathematical Statistics*, **13**, 1942, pp. 1-13.

[5] Anderson, T. W., *Time Series Analysis*, John Wiley & Sons, Inc., New York, 1971.

[6] Apostol, T. M., *Mathematical Analysis*, Addison-Wesley Publishing Company, Inc., Reading, Massachusetts, 1957.

[7] Bailey, M. J., *National Income and the Price Level*, McGraw-Hill Book Company, Inc., New York, 1962, pp. 223-268.

[8] ———, "Prediction of an Autoregressive Variable Subject both to Disturbances and to Errors of Observation," *Journal of the American Statistical Association*, **60**, 1965, pp. 164-181.

[9] Bartlett, M. S., "Periodogram Analysis and Continuous Spectrum," *Biometrika*, **37**, 1950, pp. 1-16.

[10] Bellman, R., *Stability Theory of Differential Equations*, McGraw-Hill Book Company, Inc., New York, 1953.

[11] ———, *Introduction to Matrix Analysis*, McGraw-Hill Book Company, Inc., New York, 1960.

[12] Bernstein, S., "Sur l'Extension du Theoreme Limite du Calcul des Probabilités aux Sommes de Quantités Dependantes," *Mathematische Annalen*, **97**, 1927, pp. 1-59.

[13] Bischoff, C. W., *The Lag Between Orders and Production of Machinery and Equipment: A Reexamination of the Kareken-Solow Results*, Working Paper 138, Department of Economics, University of California, Berkeley, 1968.

[14] Box, G. P. E. and G. M. Jenkins, "Some Statistical Aspects of Adaptive Optimization and Control," *Journal of the Royal Statistical Society*, Series 8, **24**, 1962, pp. 297-343.

[15] ———, "Further Contributions to Adaptive Quality Control: Simultaneous Estimation of Dynamics: Nonzero Costs," *Bulletin of the International Statistical Institute*, Bk: II, **40**, 34th Session, Ottawa, 1963, pp. 943-974.

[16] Breiman, L., *Probability*, Addison-Wesley, Reading, Mass., 1968.

[17] Brown, E.C., et al., *Stabilization Policies* (prepared for the Commission of Money and Credit), Prentice-Hall, Inc., Englewood Cliffs, N. J., 1963.

[18] Cagan, P., "The Monetary Dynamics of Hyper Inflations," in *Studies in the Quantity Theory of Money*, M. Friedman (ed.), University of Chicago Press, Chicago, 1946.

[19] Chenery, H., "Over Capacity and the Acceleration Principle," *Econometrica*, **20**, 1952, pp. 1–28.

[20] Chiang, C. L., "On Regular Best Asymptotically Normal Estimates," *Annals of Mathematical Statistics*, **27**, 1956, pp. 336–351.

[21] Cochrane, D. and G. Orcutt, "Application of Least Squares Regression to Relationships Containing Auto-correlated Error Terms," *Journal of the American Statistical Association*, **44**, 1949, p. 32.

[22] Courant, R. and D. Hilbert, *Methods of Mathematical Physics*, **1**, Interscience Publishers, New York, 1953.

[23] Cox, D. R., "Prediction by Exponentially Weighted Moving Averages and Related Methods," *Journal of the Royal Statistical Society*, Series B, **23**, 1961, pp. 414–422.

[24] Cramer, H., *Mathematical Methods of Statistics*, Princeton University Press, Princeton, N. J., 1946.

[25] ———, *Random Variables and Probability Distributions*, (Second Edition), Cambridge University Press, Cambridge, 1962.

[26] De Leeuw, F., "The Demand for Capital Goods by Manufacturers: A Study of Quarterly Time Series," *Econometrica*, **30**, 1962, pp. 407–423.

[27] Dhrymes, P. J., "On the Treatment of Certain Recurrent Non-Linearities in Regression Analysis," *Southern Economic Journal*, **33**, 1966, pp. 187–196.

[28] ———, "Adjustment Dynamics and the Estimation of the CES Class of Production Functions," *International Economic Review*, **8**, 1967, pp. 209–217.

[29] ———, "A Note on 3 Pass Least Squares and an Alternative Estimation Method," *Discussion Paper No. 71*, University of Pennsylvania, September, 1967.

[30] ———, "Efficient Estimation of Distributed Lags with Autocorrelated Errors," *International Economic Review*, **10**, 1969, pp. 47–67.

[31] ———, "A Model of Short-Run Labor Adjustment," in *The Brookings Model: Some Further Results*, J. S. Duesenberry, G. Fromm, L. R. Klein, E. Kuh (eds.), Rand McNally & Company, Chicago, 1969.

[32] ———, "*Econometrics: Statistical Foundations and Applications*, Harper & Row, New York, 1970.

[33] ———, L. R. Klein, and K. Steiglitz, "Estimation of Distributed Lags." *International Economic Review*, **11**, 1970, pp. 235–250.

[34] Dobb, J. L., *Stochastic Processes*, John Wiley & Sons, Inc., New York 1953.

[35] Durbin, J., "Estimation of Parameters in Time Series Regression Models," *Journal of the Royal Statistical Society*, Series B, **22**, 1960, pp. 139–153.

[36] ———, and G. S. Watson, "Testing for Serial Correlation in Least Squares Regression," I. *Biometrika*, **37**, 1950, pp. 409–428; II. *Bio-*

metrika, **38**, 1951, pp. 159–177.

[37] Durbin, J., "Testing for Serial Correlation in Least Squares Regression when Some of the Regressors are Lagged Dependent Variables," *Econometrica*, **38**, 1970, pp. 410–421.

[38] Eisner, R., "Investment Plans and Realizations," *American Economic Review*, **52**, 1962, pp. 190–203.

[39] ————, "Realization of Investment Anticipations," in *The Brookings SSRC Quarterly Econometric Model of the U. S.*, J. S. Duesenberry, G. Fromm, L. R. Klein, E. Kuh (eds.), Rand McNally & Company, Chicago, 1965.

[40] ————, and R. Strotz, "Determinants of Business Investment," in CMC, *Impacts of Monetary Policy*, Prentice-Hall, Inc., Englewood Cliffs, New Jersey, 1963, pp. 59–337.

[41] Ferguson, T., "A Method of Generating Best Asymptotically Normal Estimates with Application to the Estimation of Bacterial Densities," *Annals of Mathematical Statistics*, **29**, 1958, pp. 1046–1062.

[42] Fisher, I., "Note on a Short-Cut Method for Calculating Distributed Lags," *Bulletin de L'Institut International de Statistique*, **29**, 1957, pp. 323–328.

[43] Fishman, G. S., *Spectral Methods in Econometrics*, Harvard University Press, Cambridge, 1969.

[44] Friedman, M., *A Theory of the Consumption Function*, Princeton University Press, Princeton, 1957.

[45] Fuller, W. A., "Estimating the Reliability of Quantities Derived from Empirical Production Functions," *Journal of Farm Economics*, **44**, 1962, pp. 82–99.

[46] ———— and J. E. Martin, "The Effects of Autocorrelated Errors on the Statistical Estimation of Distributed Lag Models," *Journal of Farm Economics*, **43**, 1961, pp. 71–82.

[47] Gikhman, I. I. and A. V. Skorokhod, *Introduction to the Theory of Random Processes*, N. B. Saunders, Philadelphia, 1969.

[48] Goldberger, A. S., *Econometric Theory*, John Wiley & Sons, Inc., New York, 1964.

[49] Granger, C. W. J., in association with M. Hatanaka, *Spectral Analysis of Economic Time Series*, Princeton University Press, Princeton, 1964.

[50] Graybill, F. A., *An Introduction to Linear Statistical Models*, **1**, McGraw-Hill Book Company, Inc., New York, 1961.

[51] Greenberg, E., "A Stock-Adjustment Investment Model," *Econometrica*, **32**, 1964, pp. 339–357.

[52] Grenander, U. and M. Rosenblatt, *Statistical Analysis of Stationary Time Series*, John Wiley & Sons, Inc., New York, 1957.

[53] Grenander, U. and G. Szego, *Toeplitz Forms and Their Applications*, University of California Press, Berkeley and Los Angeles, 1958.

[54] Griliches, Z., "The Demand for a Durable Input: Farm Tractors in the United States, 1921–1957," in *The Demand for Durable Goods*, A. C. Harberger (ed.), University of Chicago Press, Chicago, 1960, pp. 181–207.

[55] ————, "A Note on Serial Correlation Bias in Estimates of Dis-

tributed Lags," *Econometrica*, **29**, 1961, pp. 65–73.

[56] ———, "Distributed Lags: A Survey," *Econometrica*, **35**, 1967, pp. 16–49.

[57] ——— and N. Wallace, "The Determinants of Investment Revisited," *International Economic Review*, **6**, 1965, pp. 311–329.

[58] Griliches, Z., G. S. Maddala, R. Lucas and N. Wallace, "Notes on Estimated Aggregate Quarterly Consumption Functions," *Econometrica*, **30**, 1962, pp. 491–500.

[59] Gupta, Y. P., "Least Squares Variant of the Dhrymes Two-Step Estimation Procedure of the Distributed Lag Model," *International Economic Review*, **10**, 1969, pp. 112–113.

[60] Haavelmo, T., *A Study in Theory of Investment*, University of Chicago Press, Chicago, 1960.

[61] Hall, R. E. and D. W. Jorgenson, "The Quantitative Impact of Tax Policy on Investment Expenditures," presented at the Conference on the Effect of Tax Incentives on Investment, The Brookings Institution, November 3, 1967.

[62] Hamburger, M. J., "Household Demand for Financial Assets," *Econometrica*, **36**, 1968, pp. 97–118.

[63] Hannan, E. J., *Time Series Analysis*, Methuen, London, 1960.

[64] ———, "Regression for Time Series with Errors of Measurement," *Biometrika*, **50**, 1963, pp. 293–302.

[65] ———, "Regression for Time Series," in *Proceedings of the Symposium on Time Series Analysis*, M. Rosenblatt (ed.) John Wiley & Sons, Inc., New York, 1963, pp. 17–37.

[66] ———, "The Estimation of Relationships Involving Distributed Lags," *Econometrica*, **33**, 1965, pp. 206–224.

[67] ———, "The Estimation of a Lagged Regression Relation," *Biometrika*, **54**, 1967, pp. 409–418.

[68] Harberger, A. C. (ed.), *The Demand for Durable Goods*, University of Chicago Press, Chicago, 1960.

[69] Hartley, H. O. and A. Booker, "Nonlinear Least-Squares Estimation," *The Annals of Mathematical Statistics*, **36**, 1965, pp. 638–650.

[70] Hickman, B., *Investment Demand and U. S. Economic Growth*, The Brookings Institution, Washington, 1965.

[71] Hicks, J. R., *A Contribution to the Theory of the Trade Cycle*, Oxford University Press, Oxford, 1950.

[72] Hildreth, C. and J. Y. Lu, *Demand Relations with Auto-correlated Disturbances*, Michigan State University, Agricultural Experimental Station, Technical Bulletin 276, 1960.

[73] Hoeffding, W. and H. Robbins, "The Central Limit Theorem for Dependent Variables," *Duke Mathematical Journal*, **15**, 1948, pp. 773–780.

[74] Hoffman, K. M. and R. A. Kunze, *Linear Algebra*, Prentice-Hall, Inc., Englewood Cliffs, N. J., 1961.

[75] Holt, C. C., F. Modigliani, J. F. Muth and H. Simon, *Planning Production, Inventories, and Work Force*, Prentice-Hall, Inc., Englewood Cliffs, N. J., 1960.

[76] Houthakker, H. S. and L. D. Taylor, *Consumer Demand in the United*

States, 1929-1970, Harvard University Press, Cambridge, Mass., 1966.

[77] Huzurbazar, V. S., "The Likelihood Equation, Consistency and the Maxima of the Likelihood Function," *Annals of Eugenics*, **14**, 1948, pp. 185-200.

[78] Jenkins, G. M. and D. G. Watts, *Spectral Analysis and Its Applications*, Holden-Day, Inc., San Francisco, 1968.

[79] Jennrich, R. I., "Asymptotic Properties of Nonlinear Least Squares Estimators," *Annals of Mathematical Statistics*, **40**, 1969, pp. 633-643.

[80] Jorgenson, D. W., "Capital Theory and Investment Behavior," *American Economic Review*, **53**, 1963, pp. 247-259.

[81] ———, "Anticipations and Investment Behavior," in *The Brookings Quarterly Econometric Model of the United States*, J. S. Duesenberry, G. Fromm, L. R. Klein and E. Kuh (eds.),Rand McNally & Company, Chicago, 1965, pp. 35-94.

[82] ———, "Rational Distributed Lag Functions," *Econometrica*, **34**, 1966, pp. 135-149.

[83] ———, "The Theory of Investment Behavior," in *Determinants of Investment Behavior*, National Bureau of Economic Research, New York, 1967, pp. 129-156.

[84] ——— and J. A. Stephenson, "The Time Structure of Investment Behavior in United States Manufacturing, 1947-1960," *Review of Economics and Statistics*, **49**, 1967, pp. 16-27.

[85] ———, "Investment Behavior in U. S. Manufacturing, 1947-1960," *Econometrica*, **35**, 1967, pp. 169-220.

[86] Jury, E. J., *The Theory and Application of the z-Transform Method*, John Wiley & Sons, New York, 1964.

[87] Kendall, M. G. and A. Stuart, *The Advanced Theory of Statistics*, Volume 2, Hafner Publishing Co., New York, 1961.

[88] Klein, L. R., "The Estimation of Distributed Lags," *Econometrica*, **26**, 1958, pp. 553-56.

[89] ——— and A. S. Goldberger, *An Econometric Model of the U. S.*, 1929-1952, North-Holland Publishing Co., Amsterdam, 1955.

[90] Kolmogorov, A. N. and S. V. Fomin, *Elements of the Theory of Functions and Functional Analysis*, vol. 1, Graylock Press, Rochester, New York, 1957.

[91] Koopmans, T. C., H. Rubin, and R. B. Leipnik, "Measuring the Equation Systems of Dynamic Economics," in *Statistical Inference in Dynamic Economic Models*, John Wiley & Sons, Inc., New York, 1950, pp. 53-237.

[92] Koyck, L. M., *Distributed Lags and Investment Analysis*, North-Holland Publishing Company, Amsterdam, 1954.

[93] Kuh, E., *Capital Stock Growth: A Micro-Econometric Approach*, North-Holland Publishing Company, Amsterdam, 1963.

[94] ———, "Theory and Institutions in the Study of Investment Behavior," *American Economic Review*, **53**, 1963, pp. 260-268.

[95] ———, "Income Distribution and Employment over the Business Cycle," in *The Brookings Model: Some Further Results*, J. S. Duesenberry, G. Fromm, L. R. Klein, and E. Kuh (eds.), Rand McNally

& Company, Chicago, 1965.

[96] Liviatan, N., "Consistent Estimation of Distributed Lags," *International Economic Review*, 4, 1963, pp. 44-52.

[97] Lucas, R. E. Jr., "Optimal Investment Policy and the Flexible Accelerator," *International Economic Review*, 8, 1967, pp. 78-85.

[98] Maddala, G. S., "Generalized Least Squares with an Estimated Variance Covariance Matrix," *Econometrica*, 39, 1971, pp. 23-33.

[99] Malinvaud, E., "Estimation et Prevision dans les Modeles Economiques Autoregressifs," *Review of the International Statistical Institute*, 29, 1961, pp. 1-32.

[100] ————, The Estimation of Distributed Lags: A Comment," *Econometrica*, 29, 1961, pp. 430-433.

[101] ————, *Statistical Methods of Econometrics*, Rand McNally & Company, Chicago, 1966.

[102] Mann, H. B, and A. Wald, "On the Statistical Treatment of Linear Stochastic Difference Equations," *Econometrica*, 11, 1943, pp. 173-220.

[103] ————, "On Stochastic Limit and Order Relationships," *Annals of Mathematical Statistics*, 14, 1943, pp. 217-226.

[104] Martin, J. E., "Computer Progams for Estimating Certain Classes of Non-linear Distributed Lag Models," in *Maryland Agricultural Experiment Stations, Misc. Publication No. 546*, 1965.

[105] Meyer, J. R. and R. R. Glauber, *Investment Decisions, Economic Forecasting, and Public Policy*, Division of Research, Graduate School of Business Administration, Boston, Harvard University, 1964.

[106] Meyer, J. and E. Kuh, *The Investment Decision*, Harvard University Press, Cambridge, Mass., 1957.

[107] Modigliani, F. and K. J. Cohen, *The Role of Anticipations and Plans in Economic Behavior and their Use in Economic Analysis and Forecasting*, University of Illinois Press, Urbana, 1961.

[108] Modigliani, F. and H. M. Weingartner, "Forecasting Uses of Anticipatory Data on Investment and Sales," *Quarterly Journal of Economics*, 72, 1958, pp. 23-54.

[109] ————, "Forecasting Uses of Anticipatory Data: Reply," *Quarterly Journal of Economics*, 73, 1959, pp. 171-172.

[110] Morrison, J. L., "Small Sample Properties of Selected Distributed Lag Estimators: A Monte Carlo Experiment," *International Economic Review*, 11, 1970, pp. 13-23.

[111] Mundlak, Y., "Aggregation over Time in Distributed Lag Models," *International Economic Review*, 2, 1961, pp. 154-163.

[112] ————, "On the Microeconomic Theory of Distributed Lags," *Review of Economics and Statistics*, 48, 1966, pp. 51-60.

[113] ————, "Long-Run Coefficients and Distributed Lag Analysis: A Reformulation," *Econometrica*, 35, 1967, pp. 278-293.

[114] Muth, J. F., "Optimal Properties of Exponentially Weighted Forecasts of Time Series with Permanent and Transitory Components," *Journal of the American Statistical Association*, 55, 1960, pp. 299-306.

[115] Nagar, A. L. and Y. P. Gupta, "The Bias of Liviatan's Consistent Esti-

mator in a Distributed Lag Model," *Econometrica*, **36**, 1968, pp. 337–342.

[116] Nerlove, M., "Estimates of the Elasticities of Supply of Selected Agricultural Commodities," *Journal of Farm Economics*, **38**, 1956, pp. 496–509.

[117] Nerlove, M., *Distributed Lags and Demand Analysis for Agricultural and Other Commodities*, U. S. Department of Agriculture, Agricultural Marketing Service, Agricultural Handbook No. 141, Washington, 1958.

[118] ———, *The Dynamics of Supply: Estimation of Farmers' Response to Price*, The Johns Hopkins Press, Baltimore, 1958.

[119] ———, "Distributed Lags and Unobserved Components in Economic Time Series," in W. Fellner (ed.), *Ten Studies in the Tradition of Irving Fisher*, John Wiley & Sons, Inc., New York, 1968.

[120] ——— and S. Wage, "On the Optimality of Adaptive Forecasting," *Management Science*, **10**, 1964.

[121] ——— and K. F. Wallis, "Use of the Durbin-Watson Statistic in Inappropriate Situations," *Econometrica*, **34**, 1966, pp. 235–238.

[122] Padé, H., "Sur la Représentation Aprochée d'une Fonction par des Fractions Rationelles," *Annales Scientifiques de l'Ecole Normale Superieure*, 3rd Series, (Supplement), **9**, 1892, pp. 3–93.

[123] Parzen, E., *Modern Probability Theory and its Applications*, John Wiley & Sons, Inc., New York, 1960.

[124] ———, "Mathematical Considerations in the Estimation of Spectra," *Technometrics*, **3**, 1961, pp. 167–190.

[125] ———, *Stochastic Processes*, Holden-Day, Inc., San Francisco, 1962.

[126] ———, *Time Series Analysis Papers*, Holden-Day, Inc., San Francisco, 1967.

[127] Phillips, A. W., "Some Notes on the Estimation of Time-Forms of Reactions in Interdependent Dynamic Systems," *Econometrica*, **23**, 1956, pp. 99–113.

[128] ———, "Analysis Estimation and Control of Linear Systems," (Mimeographed, undated ca. 1963).

[129] Quenouille, M. H., *The Analysis of Multiple Time Series*, Griffin, London, 1957.

[130] Rao, C. R., *Advanced Statistical Methods in Biometric Research*, John Wiley & Sons, Inc., New York, 1962.

[131] ———, *Linear Statistical Inference and Its Applications*, John Wiley & Sons, Inc., New York, 1965.

[132] Sargan, J. D., "Wages and Prices in the United Kindgom: A Study in Econometric Methodology," in *Econometric Analysis for National Economic Planning*, P. E. Hart et al. (eds.), Butterworth, 1964.

[133] Sims, C., "Discrete Approximations to Continuous Time Distributed Lags in Econometrics," (Forthcoming in *Econometrica*).

[134] ———, "The Role of Prior Restrictions in Distributed Lag Estimation," (Mimeographed) 1970.

[135] Smith, V, L., *Investment and Prediction: A Study in the Theory of the Capital-using Enterprise*, Harvard University Press, Cambridge, Mass., 1961.

[136] Solow, R. M., "A Note on Dynamic Multipliers," *Econometrica*, **19**, 1951, pp. 306–316.

[137] ———, "On a Family of Lag Distributions," *Econometrica*, **28**, 1960, pp. 393–406.

[138] Steiglitz, K. and L. E. McBride, "A Technique for the Identification of Linear Systems," *IEEE Transactions on Automatic Control*, **AC-10**, 1965, pp. 461–464.

[139] ———, "Iterative Methods for Systems Identification," Technical Report No. 15, Department of Electrical Engineering, Princeton University, Princeton, N. J., June, 1966.

[140] Suits, D. B. *et al.* (eds.), Commission on Money and Credit, *Impacts of Monetary Policy*, Prentice-Hall, Inc., Englewood Cliffs, N. J., 1963.

[141] Taylor, L. D. and T. A. Wilson, "Three-pass Least Squares: A Method for Estimating Models with a Lagged Dependent Variable," *Review of Economics and Statistics*, **46**, 1964, pp. 329–346.

[142] Theil, H. and R. M. Stern, "A Simple Unimodal Lag Distribution," *Metroeconomica*, **12**, 1960, pp. 111–119.

[143] Thornber, H., "Finite Sample Monte Carlo Studies: An Autoregressive Illustration," *Journal of the American Statistical Association*, **62**, 1967, pp. 801–818.

[144] Tobin, J. and H. S. Houthakker, "The Effects of Rationing on Demand Elasticities," *Review of Economic Studies*, **18**, 1951, pp. 140–153.

[145] Uspensky, J. V., *Theory of Equations*, McGraw-Hill Book Company, New York, 1948.

[146] Wahba, G., "On the Distribution of Some Statistics Useful in the Analysis of Jointly Stationary Time Series," *Annals of Mathematical Statistics*, **39**, 1968, pp. 1849–1862.

[147] Wald, A., "Tests of Statistical Hypotheses Concerning Several Parameters when the Number of Observations is Large," *Transactions of the American Mathematical Society*, **54**, 1943, pp. 462–482.

[148] ———, "Note on the Consistency of the Maximum Likelihood Estimate," *Annals of Mathematical Statistics*, **20**, 1949, pp. 595–601.

[149] Walker, A. M., "On Durbin's Formula for the Limiting Generalized Variance of a Sample of Consecutive Observations from a Moving-average Process," *Biometrika*, **48**, 1961, pp. 197–199.

[150] ———, "Large-sample Estimation of Parameters for Moving-average Models," *Biometrika*, **48**, 1961, pp. 343–357.

[151] Wallis, K. F., "Distributed Lag Relationships between Retail Sales and Inventories," unpublished Technical Report No. 14, Institute for Mathematical Studies in the Social Sciences, Stanford University, Stanford, Calif., 1965.

[152] ———, " Lagged Dependent Variables and Serially Correlated Errors: A Reappraisal of Three-Pass Least Squares," *The Review of Economics and Statistics*, **69**, 1967, pp. 555–567.

[153] Watson, G. S., "Serial Correlation in Regression Analysis," *Biometrika*, **42**, 1955, pp. 327–341.

[154] Whittle, P., *Prediction and Regulation by Linear Least Squares Methods*, Van Nostrand, Princeton, N. J., 1963.

410 BIBLIOGRAPHY

[155] ———, "On the Fitting of Multivariate Autoregressions, and the Approximate Canonical Factorization of a Spectral Density Matrix," *Biometrika*, **50**, 1963, pp. 129–134.

[156] Widder, D. V., *Advanced Calculus*, Prentice-Hall, Inc., New York, 1947.

[157] Wise, J., "Regression Analysis of Relationships between Autocorrelated Time Series," *Journal of the Royal Statistical Society*, Series B, **18**, 1956, pp. 240–256.

[158] Wolfowitz, J., "On Wald's Proof of the Consistency of the Maximum Likelihood Estimate," *Annals of Mathematical Statistics*, **20**, 1949, pp. 601–602.

[159] Wynne, P., "The Rational Approximation of Functions which are Formally Defined by a Power Series Expansion," *Mathematics of Computation*, **14**, 1960, pp. 147–186.

[160] Zellner, A. and C. J. Park, "Bayesian Analysis of a Class of Distributed Lag Models," *The Econometric Annual of the Indian Economic Journal*, **13**, 1965, pp. 432–444.

[161] ——— and G. C. Tiao, "Bayesian Analysis of the Regression Model with Autocorrelated Errors," *Journal of the American Statistical Association*, **59**, 1964, pp. 763–778.

[162] ———, D. S. Huang and L. C. Chen, "Further Analysis of the Short-Run Consumption Function with Emphasis on the Role of Liquid Assets," *Econometrica*, **33**, 1965, pp. 571–581.

[163] Zygmund, A., *Trigonometric Series*, vol. 1, Cambridge University Press, Cambridge, 1959.

INDEX